Richard Harwood and Ian Lodge

Cambridge IGCSE®

Chemistry

Coursebook

Third edition

CAMBRIDGE
UNIVERSITY PRESS

CAMBRIDGE UNIVERSITY PRESS
Cambridge, New York, Melbourne, Madrid, Cape Town,
Singapore, São Paulo, Delhi, Mexico City

Cambridge University Press
The Edinburgh Building, Cambridge CB2 8RU, UK

www.cambridge.org
Information on this title: www.cambridge.org/9780521153331

First published 1998
Second edition 2002
Third edition 2010
8th printing 2013

Printed in Italy by L.E.G.O. S.p.A.

A catalogue record for this publication is available from the British Library

ISBN 978-0-521-15333-1 Paperback with CD-ROM for Windows® and Mac®

Contents

Introduction

Chemistry is a laboratory science: its subject material and theories are based on experimental observation. However, its scope reaches out beyond the laboratory into every aspect of our lives – to our understanding of the nature of our planet, the environment we live in, the resources available to us and the factors that affect our health.

This book thoroughly covers the Cambridge International Examinations (CIE) Chemistry syllabus and includes features which are aimed at helping you grasp the concepts and detail involved. The areas that cover the **Core** and **Supplement** material of the syllabus are clearly marked (the **Supplement** material having a purple dotted line like the one here in the margin) so that you can see which topics will be tested on each exam paper that you will take. The topic summaries, 'quick-check' questions and 'exam-style' questions are also clearly marked so that you can pick out, study and revise the material relevant to the 'core' and 'extended' papers.

The first chapter of the book serves to set chemistry in its broader context and as such contains material that 'sets the scene' as well as syllabus material. At various points in this and other chapters there is material that provides and develops some of the context in which chemical ideas are important. These are areas such as:

- the importance of chemistry to life, and the nature of the universe (Chapter **1**)
- health issues (Chapter **10**)
- our need to develop alternative energy sources (Chapter **11**).

This additional material is included to provide context. It also links together the ideas covered by the syllabus in a way that will help you gain an overall picture of the relevance of chemistry and aid your understanding of the subject. The additional material is clearly marked by being set in a green-bordered box with an E icon.

Features of the book and the Student CD-ROM

The book is divided into broad **chapters** covering important areas of the syllabus. These chapters are then divided into different **sections** to help you manage your understanding of the ideas involved. At the end of each section there is a list of **key ideas** and short **quick-check questions** to help you check that you have followed the ideas covered. The answers to these short questions are provided at the end of the book to help you with this.

Each chapter finishes with a **summary** of Core and Supplement material to help you particularly with your revision. This is followed by selection of **exam-style questions** which are there to help you become familiar with the style of question set in each examination.

Answering questions is a great way to get to grips with each of the topics. However, it is not the only way! The **Student CD-ROM** provides information on revision skills and resources available on the internet to help with your study of chemistry. A copy of the syllabus is provided on the CD-ROM, which shows where the different topics are covered in the book – and you can use this interactively as a checklist during revision. 'Mind-mapping' ideas and other revision strategies are discussed on the CD-ROM, and we hope that you can find ideas that will help you study in the most personally effective way.

An important feature which appears both in the book and on the Student CD-ROM is the **glossary**. The terms included in the glossary are highlighted in the text in **dark red bold**. Do use this resource in addition to the text in order to help you understand the meaning of chemical terms. But more than that, it is important that you can express your ideas clearly in an exam – that is why we have included so many practice questions in the book and in the **practice tests** that appear on the CD-ROM. It is also why we have tried to cover the ideas in each chapter thoroughly in our wording. Chemistry, and science in general, can often use certain words in a very precise way, so it is important to read carefully and get used to writing down your answers clearly.

Practical work

We began by saying that chemistry was a practical science and we have aimed to help your preparation for the practical element of the exam in various ways:

- Chapter **12** of the book gives a summary of the different ways that practical work is assessed and some exemplar questions.
- There is a practice 'alternative to practical' paper (Paper 6) on the Student CD-ROM.
- The separate **Student Workbook** contains exercises involving practice at the key skills of writing up your observations and making deductions from your results. Included there are methods that you can use to assess (by yourself, and with your teacher) how well you are developing your data handling and presentation skills.

Chemistry is an important, exciting and challenging subject that impacts on every aspect of our lives. As we face the challenges of the future, the chemical 'angle' on things will figure in our thinking, whatever future course we personally take in our careers. We hope that this book will help you enjoy chemistry, give you some understanding of the ideas involved and help you be successful in the IGCSE course.

Richard Harwood
Ian Lodge

1 Planet Earth

E

A brief history of the Earth

Figure 1.1 A satellite image over Africa: one view of the 'blue marble'.

The Earth is a ball of rock orbiting a star along with a group of other planets (Figure **1.1**). The star is one of many billions of stars in a galaxy which, in turn, is one of many billion galaxies in a constantly expanding Universe. As such the Earth is unremarkable. However, a view of the Earth from space shows it to be a very beautiful ball of rock, and it is also the ball of rock upon which we are totally dependent for our existence. It is the chemicals which make up the Earth and the ways in which they interact with each other that make life in general, and human life in particular, possible.

- At the start, the Earth was a ball of molten rock.
- The surface solidified to a solid crust as it cooled and contracted; cracks appeared.
- Volcanoes shot molten rock and gases from this surface.
- The first atmosphere (mainly carbon dioxide and water vapour) was formed in this way (Figure **1.2**, overleaf).
- The water vapour condensed and fell back to the surface, forming the first seas.
- Over many millions of years, plant life developed in these warm shallow seas. These used carbon dioxide and, crucially, put oxygen into the atmosphere. The atmosphere of the Earth is different from that of its neighbours because 'life' happened on this planet.
- Plants gradually used the carbon dioxide in **photosynthesis** and produced oxygen.
- Once sufficient oxygen was present, animal life developed.
- Nitrogen entered the atmosphere from bacteria. It is unreactive and so was not removed. It has built up to a large percentage of the atmosphere.
- Plant and animal life continued to develop over millions of years until the Earth reached its present balance of chemicals.
- The activity of humans is now altering this chemical balance.

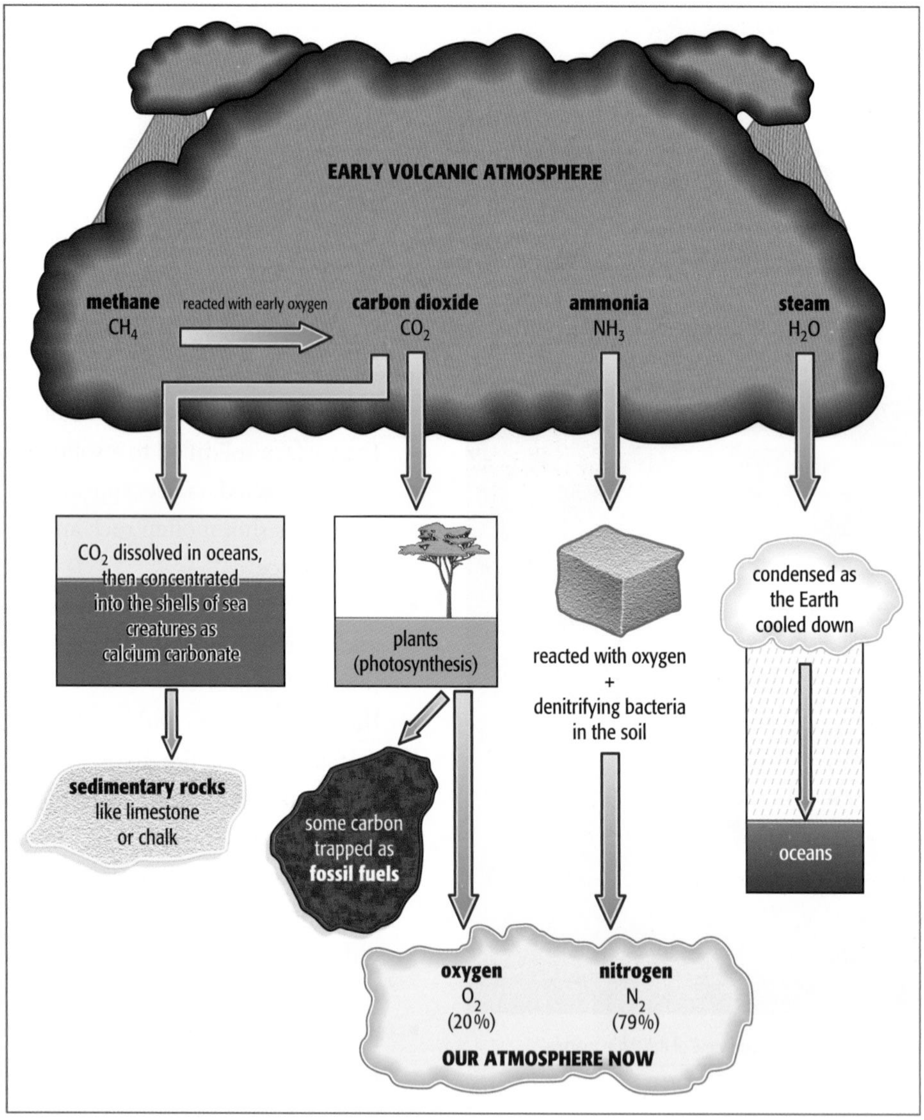

Figure 1.2 The development of the Earth's atmosphere.

This chapter covers the following ideas:

- the water cycle
- (S) the carbon cycle
- the nitrogen cycle
- the composition and uses of the gases in the air
- (S) the separation of air into its components
- the sources of air pollution
- the problems of air pollution, and their solution
- 'greenhouse gases' and climate change
- water treatment and sewage treatment
- the pollution of water
- metal ores and limestone
- fossil fuels and the problems they cause
- alternative sources of energy
- hydrogen as a fuel
- (S) the hydrogen fuel cell

Exam tip

This chapter is aimed at providing a context for the chemistry that you study. As such, it makes some general comments about the origins of the Earth and the nature of the natural resource cycles that occur. The list at the start of this chapter is similar to those given at the beginning of each chapter. It gives you an idea of the material in this chapter that is contained in the syllabus, and can therefore be examined.

1.1 Natural cycles and resources

E

The rock cycle

As the Earth's crust moves, rock is constantly being taken down into the molten rock beneath the surface (Figure **1.3**):

- This rock is changed and sometimes decomposed before it rises back to the surface and cools.
- These processes give rise to the different types of rock as shown in the diagram. The decomposition also produces gases, mainly carbon dioxide and water vapour. These, together with molten rock, escape from the Earth's **crust** in volcanoes.
- This is a very slow process. The plates of the Earth's crust are moving only a few centimetres each year. This **rock cycle** is powered by energy produced by radioactive decay and heat from the Earth's **core**. We use the rocks that are near the surface by mining and quarrying.

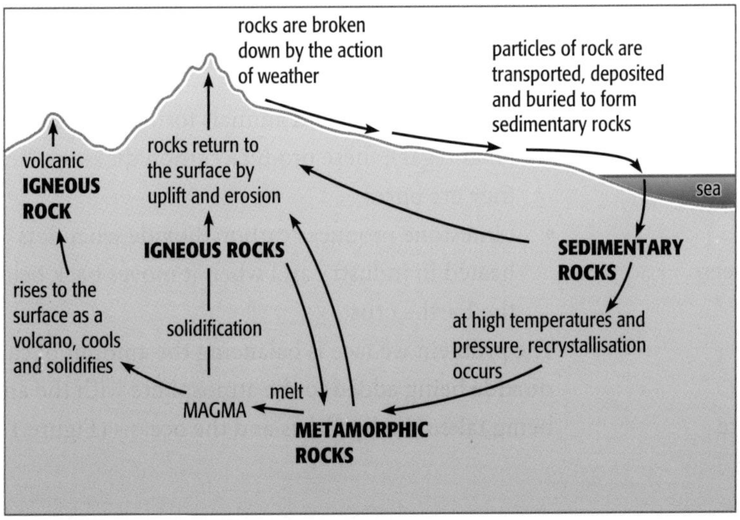

Figure 1.3 The rock cycle.

The water cycle

The Earth is sometimes referred to as the 'blue marble' because of the predominance of water on the surface and the swirling cloud formations seen in satellite images. The Earth is distinctive in the solar system in that its surface temperature is such that all three states of water exist on the surface. There is a distinct '**water cycle**' taking place on the Earth's surface (Figure **1.4**, overleaf).

- The energy to drive this cycle comes from the Sun.
- Water evaporates from the sea and from other areas of water, such as lakes, and enters the atmosphere.
- As it cools, it changes back into liquid water and forms clouds (tiny water droplets).
- As the water droplets stick together, rain clouds are formed and the water falls back to the surface as rain, snow or hail.
- Water then either flows back to the sea or is taken in by plants, which put it back into the atmosphere through their leaves.
- We use the water by trapping it on its way back to the sea.

S

The carbon cycle

Carbon is only the twelfth most common element in the Earth, making up less than 1% of the crust. It is,

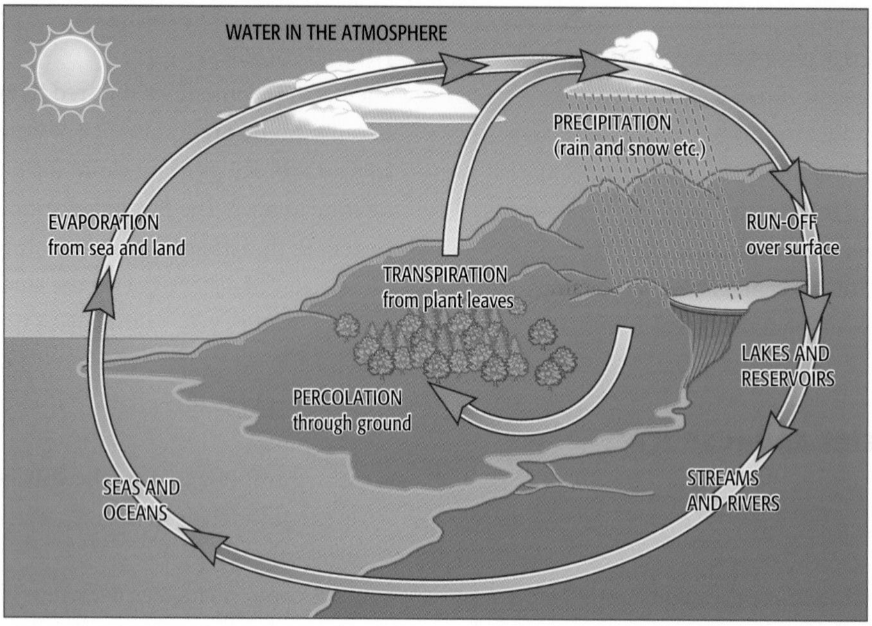

Figure 1.4 The water cycle.

however, very important to us. Without carbon, life would not exist. The way in which carbon moves around in the **carbon cycle** is vital to all life (Figure 1.5). The source of the carbon in the cycle is carbon dioxide in the atmosphere. Only about 0.04% of the atmosphere is carbon dioxide.

Carbon dioxide leaves the atmosphere in the following ways:

- Green plants take carbon dioxide and water, combining them together to form glucose and oxygen. This process uses energy from the Sun and is called **photosynthesis**. The word equation for the reaction is:

  carbon dioxide + water → glucose + oxygen

- Carbon dioxide dissolves in water (mainly seawater), where it is used by animals and plants. Plants use it in photosynthesis; animals use it to make their shells.

This is what happens to the carbon once it has been captured from the atmosphere:

- The plants are eaten by animals.
- Animals and plants die and rot away, or are buried, and slowly (over millions of years) are fossilised.
- Tiny sea creatures die and their bodies fall to the bottom of the sea, where they slowly (over millions of years) change to limestone.

These are the ways in which carbon dioxide is put back into the atmosphere:

- Animals and plants 'breathe out' carbon dioxide when they respire food. The process of **respiration** uses oxygen from the air, and releases carbon dioxide:

  glucose + oxygen → carbon dioxide + water

- When plants and animals decay after death, carbon dioxide is produced.
- Wood can be burnt. This **combustion** produces carbon dioxide:

  carbon + oxygen → carbon dioxide

- Fossilised plants and animals form **fossil fuels** (coal, oil and gas); these produce carbon dioxide when they are burnt.
- Limestone produces carbon dioxide when it is heated in industry and when it moves back below the Earth's crust.

The problem we face is balancing the amount of carbon dioxide being added to the atmosphere with the amount being taken out by plants and the oceans (Figure 1.6).

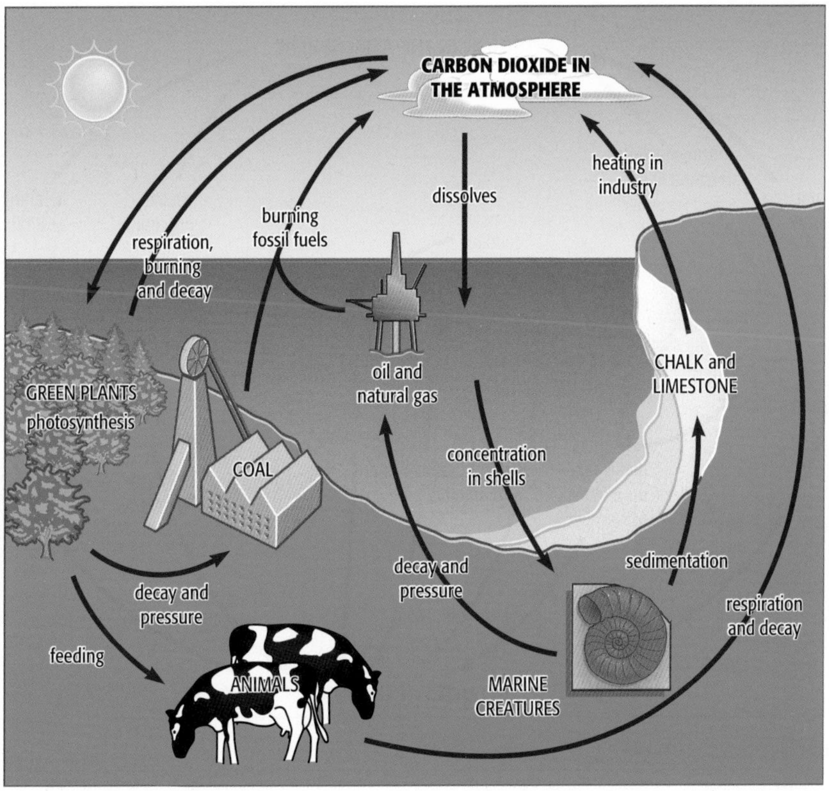

Figure 1.5 The carbon cycle.

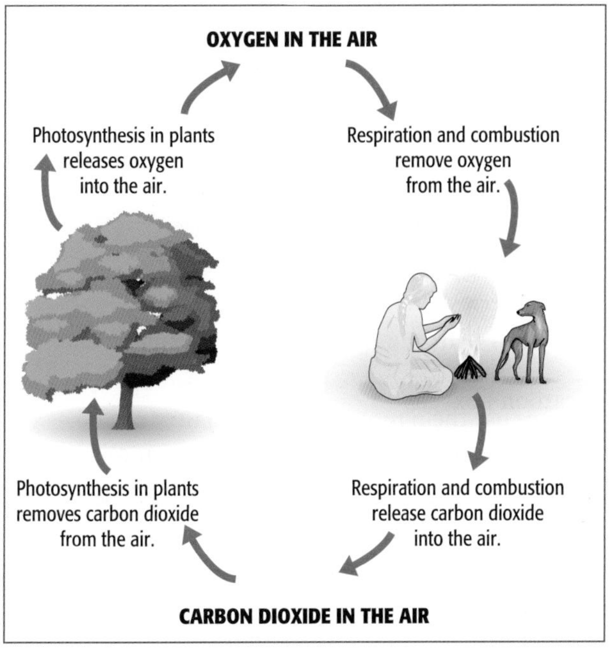

Figure 1.6 Maintaining the levels of oxygen and carbon dioxide in the air.

The nitrogen cycle

Nitrogen is essential for plant growth and, therefore, for the life of animals (Figure 1.7, overleaf). There is plenty (78%) of nitrogen in the atmosphere but it is unreactive and so it is difficult to get it into the soil for plants to use.

Plants get their nitrogen from nitrates in the soil and animals get theirs from plants.

When plants and animals die and decay, their nitrogen returns to the soil as bacteria help their bodies to decay.

There are also bacteria that live in the roots of some plants (e.g. beans and clover) which can 'fix' nitrogen from the atmosphere which the plants can then use.

During thunderstorms, the very high temperature of the lightning provides enough energy to cause nitrogen and oxygen in the atmosphere to react. This reacts with water in the atmosphere to form nitric acid. When this falls with rain, it forms nitrates in the soil. Nitrogen is also taken from the air by the chemical industry when fertiliser is made by the Haber process.

Taken together these processes form the **nitrogen cycle** (Figure 1.7).

These four major cycles – of water, carbon, nitrogen and rocks – interlink and, between them, provide us with the resources we need.

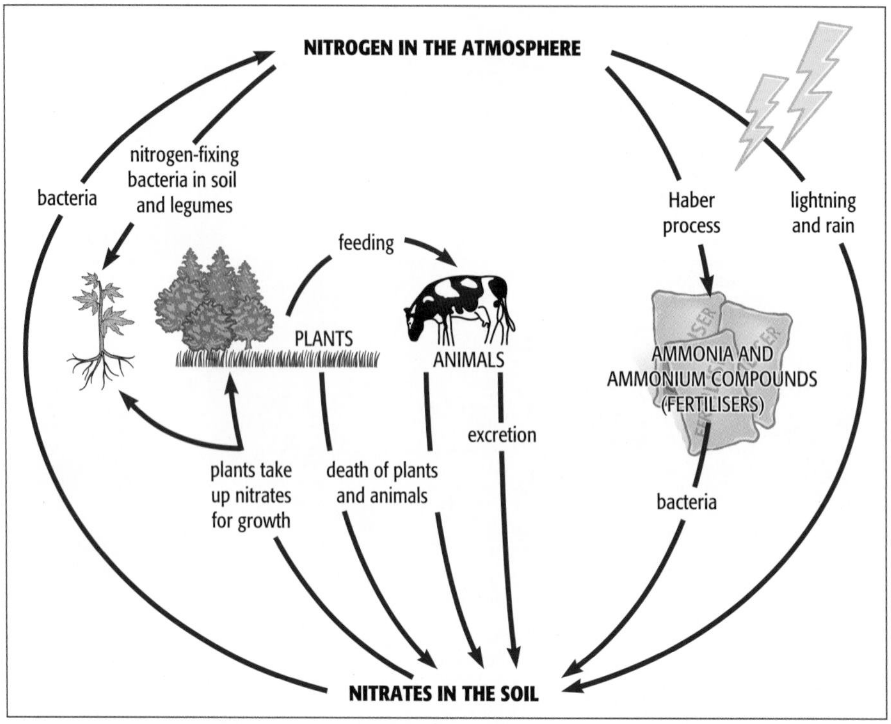

Figure 1.7 The nitrogen cycle.

E

The Earth's resources

In human terms, **resources** are materials we get from the environment to meet our needs. Some are the basic material resources we and other organisms need to keep alive. Others are materials from which we obtain energy, or substances useful for our civilised way of life. Chemistry helps us to understand how the basic resources sustain our life. It also provides the methods of extraction and use of other resources. Figure **1.8** summarises the major types of material resources. It subdivides them into **renewable**, potentially renewable and **non-renewable** resources, based on our short human timescale.

The biggest concern is the depletion of non-renewable resources. Once they are used up, then we will have to manage without them. Metal ores, especially those of iron, aluminium and copper, are becoming more scarce. The ores that still exist are often of lower quality, making the process of extraction more costly. Fossil fuels are another concern. New deposits of oil are being discovered but the speed at which we are using the oil we have is increasing. There will be a time when all the oil, and eventually all the coal, will run out.

- **Non-renewable resources** are those which exist in a fixed quantity in the Earth's crust. They were formed over geological periods of time (millions of years) and, over a shorter timescale, are being used up faster than they are formed.
- **Renewable resources** are those which essentially will never run out (are inexhaustible).
- **Potentially renewable resources** can be renewed, but they can become used up if we use them more quickly than they can be renewed.

Phosphate minerals, essential for the manufacture of fertilisers, are also beginning to become scarcer.

Some of these problems can be helped by recycling some of the substances we use. Recycling metals helps conserve metal ores. Recycling plastics helps conserve the petroleum from which they are made. All recycling helps save energy, which is mainly produced from fossil fuels.

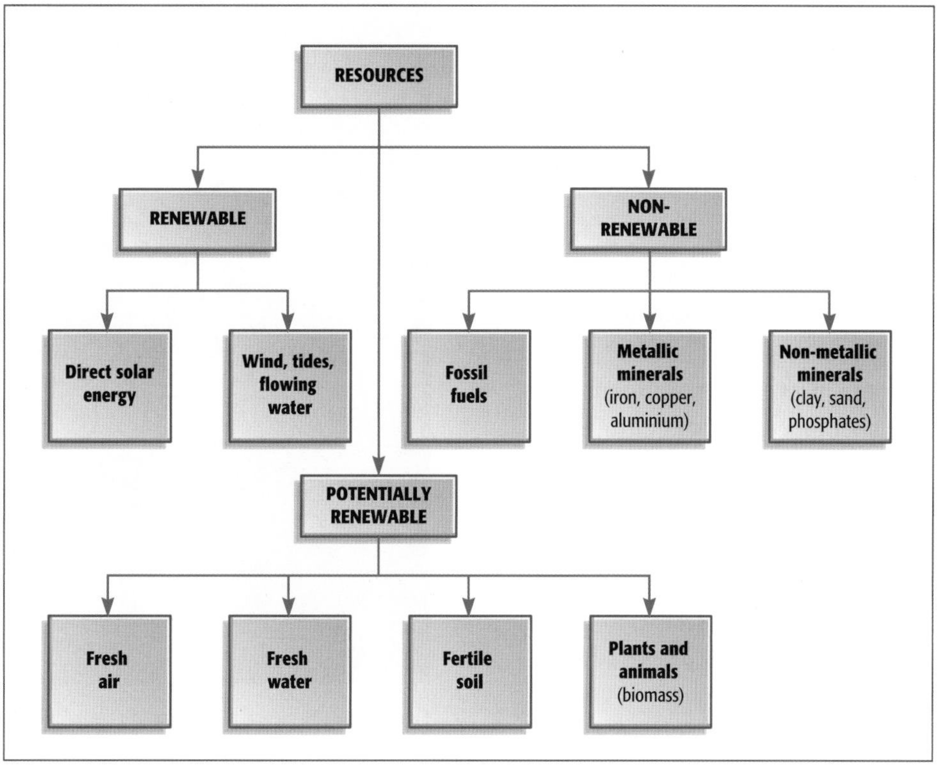

Figure 1.8 Renewable and non-renewable resources.

Fossil fuels are a bigger problem. We will always need energy. A partial solution is to make more use of our renewable resources. Wind power, solar power and water power from rivers, tides and waves can all be used to generate electricity.

An increasing problem is the way in which our 'potentially renewable resources' are being affected by over-use and pollution. More detail on these problems will appear in the next three sections.

Key ideas so far

- The Earth is our only source of the chemical and other resources which we need.
- The balance of chemicals in our environment is maintained by a number of natural cycles.
- Some of the Earth's resources are finite and non-renewable.
- Renewable sources of energy can be used to generate electricity.
- S The carbon cycle moves carbon in and out of the atmosphere by the processes of respiration, combustion and photosynthesis.

Quick-check questions

1. How does the Sun keep the water cycle working?
2. How does the Sun keep the carbon cycle working?
3. How could the Sun be the source of our energy in the future?
4. Write the word equations for: S
   - **a** photosynthesis
   - **b** the complete combustion of carbon in air
   - **c** respiration.

1.2 The atmosphere

Uses of the gases of the air

Clean air has, approximately, the following composition: nitrogen 79%, oxygen 20%, argon 0.9%, and 'other gases' (including carbon dioxide, water vapour, neon and other noble gases) 0.1%.

Carbon dioxide is an important part of the air but makes up only about 0.04% of it. The carbon dioxide which is used by humans is not usually obtained from the air.

Nitrogen is used in the manufacture of ammonia and fertilisers in the Haber process. Liquid nitrogen is used in cryogenics (the storing of embryos and other types of living tissue at very low temperatures). Nitrogen is also sometimes used where an unreactive gas is needed to keep air away from certain products; for example, it is used to fill bags of crisps (chips) to ensure that the crisps neither get crushed nor go rancid by contact with oxygen in the air.

The biggest single use of oxygen is in the production of steel from cast iron. Oxygen is also used to make the high-temperature flames needed to cut and weld metals (oxy-acetylene torches). In cylinders it is also used in hospitals to aid the breathing of sick people.

Exam tip

If you are asked for a use of oxygen, 'breathing' is not considered to be a correct answer. A use of pure oxygen is needed, and we breathe air.

Argon and other noble gases are used in different types of light. Argon is used to 'fill' light bulbs to prevent the tungsten filament burning away (Figure **1.9**). It does not react with tungsten even at very high temperatures. The other noble gases are used in advertising signs, as they glow with different colours when electricity flows through them.

S Before any of the gases in the air can be used separately they have to be separated from the air in the atmosphere. The method used is fractional distillation, which works because the gases have different boiling points (Table **1.1**).

Figure 1.9 Filament light bulbs contain argon, as it does not react with the hot tungsten filament.

S

Gas	Boiling point / °C	Proportion in mixture / %
carbon dioxide (sublimes)	−32	0.04
xenon	−108	—[a]
krypton	−153	—[a]
oxygen	−183	20
argon	−186	0.9
nitrogen	−196	79
neon	−246	—[a]
helium	−249	—[a]

[a] *All the other gases in the air make up 0.06% of the total.*

Table 1.1 The boiling points of the gases in air.

Exam tip

Remember to be careful with temperatures below 0 °C (with a negative sign). The boiling point of nitrogen (−196 °C) is a lower temperature than −183 °C (the boiling point of oxygen).

S

The process of **fractional distillation** involves two stages.

- First the air must be cooled until it turns into a liquid.
- Then the liquid air is allowed to warm up again. The various gases boil off one at a time at different temperatures.

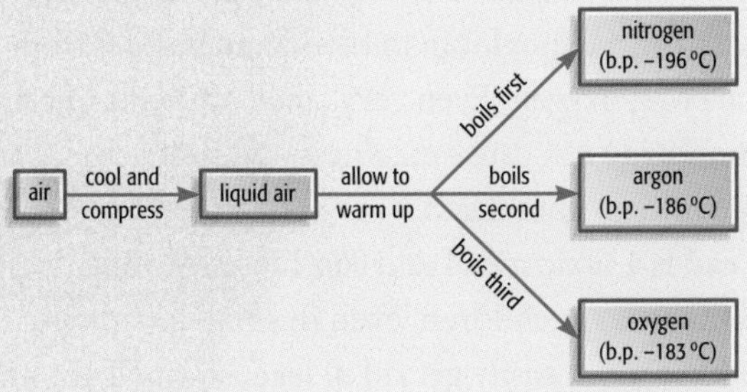

Pollution of the air

Many gases are accidentally or deliberately released into the air. Some are harmless but many create problems for the environment. The main source of 'problem' gases is the burning of fossil fuels.

Most countries produce electricity by burning coal or oil. Both these fuels are contaminated with sulfur, which produces sulfur dioxide when it burns:

sulfur + oxygen → sulfur dioxide

$$S + O_2 \rightarrow SO_2$$

Oxides of nitrogen (NO_x) (for example nitrogen dioxide, NO_2) are also produced when air is heated in furnaces. These gases dissolve in rain water to produce 'acid rain' (Figure **1.10**).

There are numerous effects of **acid rain**.

- Limestone buildings, statues, etc., are worn away.
- Lakes are acidified, and metal ions (for example Al^{3+} ions) that are leached (washed) out of the soil damage the gills of fish, which may die.
- Nutrients are leached out of the soil and from leaves. Trees are deprived of these nutrients. Aluminium ions are freed from clays as aluminium sulfate, and damage tree roots. The tree is unable to draw up enough water through the damaged roots, and it dies.

The wind can carry acid rain clouds away from the industrialised areas, causing the **pollution** to fall on other countries.

There are some remedies for the effects of acid rain:

- Lime can be added to lakes and the surrounding land, to decrease the acidity.

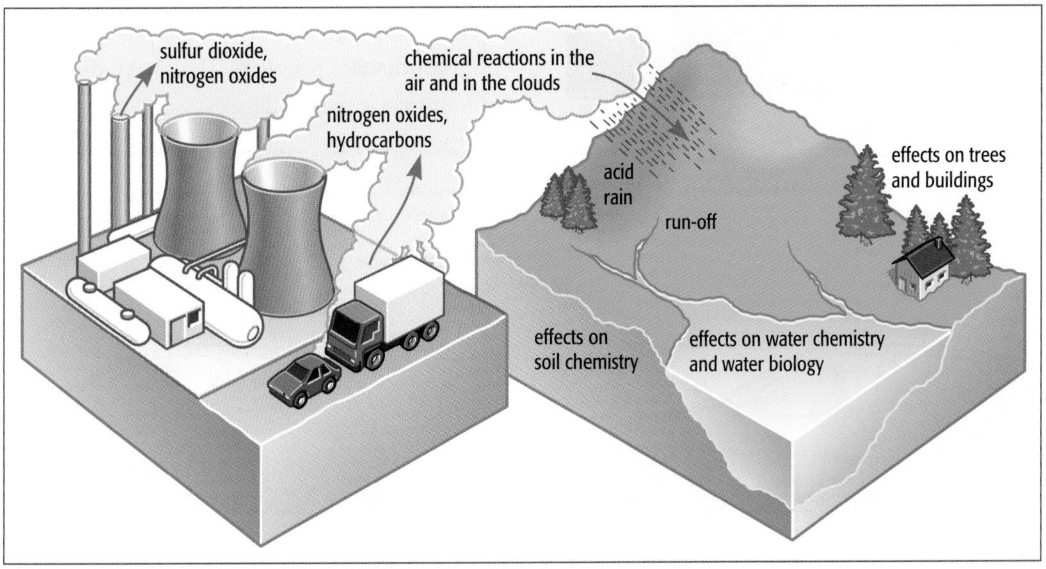

Figure 1.10 The formation of acid rain.

- The best solution is to prevent the acidic gases from being released in the first place. 'Scrubbers' are fitted to power station furnaces. In these devices, the acidic gases are passed through an alkaline substance such as lime. This removes the acids, making the escaping gases much less harmful. In many countries, however, acidic gases from power stations are still a serious problem.

Petrol (gasoline) and diesel for use in road transport has most of its sulfur removed when it is refined. Sulfur dioxide is not a serious problem with motor vehicles. However, the other contents of vehicle exhaust fumes (Figure **1.11**) can cause problems. Nitrogen dioxide is still produced though. The high temperature inside the engine's cylinders causes the nitrogen and oxygen in the air to react together:

$$\text{nitrogen} + \text{oxygen} \rightarrow \text{nitrogen dioxide}$$
$$N_2 + 2O_2 \rightarrow 2NO_2$$

In the enclosed space of an engine the fuel does not usually burn completely, owing to lack of oxygen, and carbon monoxide, CO, is formed.

Another pollution problem arising from motor vehicles is due to the use of tetraethyl lead in petrol (leaded petrol). Burning this type of petrol releases the toxic metal lead into the environment (Figure **1.11**). The use of lead in petrol has decreased significantly, over the last 20 years, with over 50 countries now banning its use. In 2009 over 80% of petrol sold was unleaded.

The dangers of these pollutants are as follows.

- **Nitrogen dioxide** causes acid rain and can combine with other gases in very hot weather to cause **photochemical smog**. This contains low-level ozone and is likely to cause breathing problems, especially for people with asthma.
- **Carbon monoxide** is a very toxic gas. It combines with the haemoglobin in blood and stops it from carrying oxygen. Even very small amounts of carbon monoxide can cause dizziness and headaches. Larger quantities cause death.
- **Lead** is a toxic metal and can cause learning difficulties in children, even in small quantities. The body cannot easily get rid of lead, so small amounts can build up to dangerous levels over time.

There are solutions to some of these problems. **Catalytic converters** can be attached to the exhaust systems of cars (Figure **1.12**). These convert carbon monoxide and nitrogen dioxide into carbon dioxide and nitrogen. Unfortunately, if there is lead in the petrol being used, the **catalyst** becomes poisoned and will no longer work. This means that in countries where leaded petrol is still being used, catalytic converters cannot be used either.

Figure 1.11 Fumes from a car exhaust.

Exam tip

Try to keep these different atmospheric pollution problems clear and distinct in your mind rather than letting them merge together into one (confused?) problem. They have distinctive causes and clear consequences.

Figure 1.12 A catalytic converter changes harmful exhaust gases into safer gases.

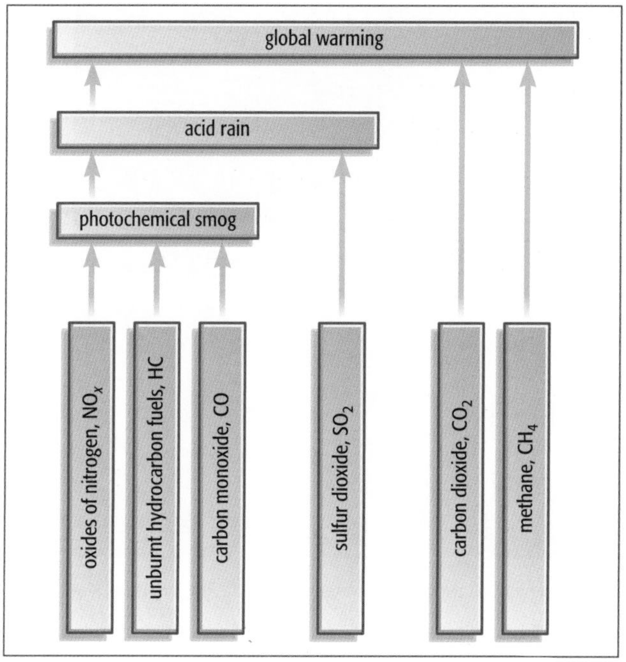

Figure 1.13 A summary of various atmospheric pollution problems caused by human activity.

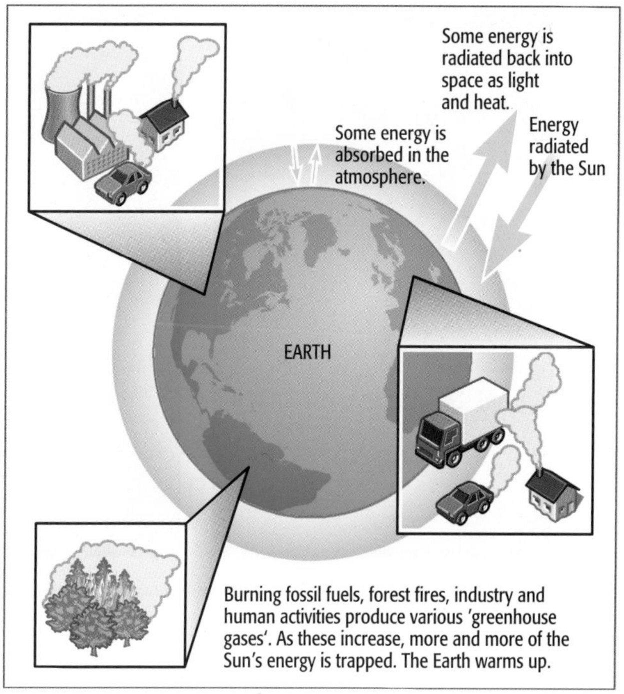

Figure 1.14 The greenhouse effect.

Figure **1.13** summarises the effects of the main pollutants of the air.

Global warming and the 'greenhouse effect'

There are two gases in Figure **1.13**, carbon dioxide and methane, which are not in the list of pollutants given so far. These, together with water vapour and oxides of nitrogen, are causing **global warming** due to the '**greenhouse effect**'. The Earth is warmed by the Sun but this heat would quickly escape if it were not for our atmosphere. It is always colder on a clear night because there are no clouds to keep the heat in. Some gases are better at keeping heat in than others, and if there is too much of these gases in the atmosphere the Earth gets warmer and this causes problems (Figure **1.14**).

Some of the problems global warming will cause are listed below.

- Glaciers and polar ice will melt. This will cause a rise in sea level, and low-lying land will be flooded.
- The surface temperature will increase. Deserts will spread and millions of people will have less water.
- Severe weather events will increase in frequency, and hurricanes and flooding will become more common.
- In some areas it may become easier to grow food crops but in others it will certainly become more difficult.

Carbon dioxide and methane are the two main problem gases; methane is around 20 times more effective at stopping heat escaping than carbon dioxide is.

Carbon dioxide enters the air through respiration and burning and is removed by plants in photosynthesis. Burning more fuel and cutting down the forests increase the problem. Burning less fossil fuel and planting more trees would help to solve it.

Methane is produced by animals such as cows: it is a by-product of digesting their food. It emerges from both ends of the cow (but mostly from the mouth). Intriguingly, termites are also significant contributors to the methane in the atmosphere (Figure **1.15a,** overleaf). It is also produced by the decay of food and other dead organic matter. It is produced in large quantities by rice paddy fields (Figure **1.15b**) and landfill sites. Treating organic waste so that the methane could be collected and burned as fuel would help solve the problem.

Figure 1.15 **a** A termite mound in Northern Territory, Australia – termites produce methane from digestion in their guts. **b** Terraced rice fields in Bali, Indonesia. Rice is the staple diet of about half the world's population.

Key ideas so far

- Air is predominantly made up of nitrogen (79%) and oxygen (20%). The main noble gas in the air is argon (0.9%).
- Carbon dioxide is an important part of the air but makes up only about 0.04% of it.
- Sulfur dioxide is a pollutant gas causing acid rain. It comes mainly from the burning of coal.
- Nitrogen dioxide causes breathing problems and comes from car exhausts.
- Carbon monoxide, from car exhausts, is toxic because it stops the blood carrying oxygen.
- Lead is present in petrol in some countries. It can cause learning difficulties in children.
- Oxygen is used in steel extraction, welding torches and breathing apparatus.
- Nitrogen is used in the manufacture of fertilisers.
- Argon and other noble gases are used in lighting.
- Air can be separated into its parts by fractional distillation.
- Pollutants in car exhausts can be controlled by using catalytic converters.
- Global warming is caused by gases in the air, chiefly carbon dioxide and methane.
- Global warming can cause a rise in sea level, droughts and severe weather.

Quick-check questions

1. Which gases contribute most significantly to acid rain?
2. How do the gases responsible for acid rain get into the atmosphere?
3. What are the problems caused by acid rain?
4. What is photochemical smog and why is it a problem?
5. Why does carbon monoxide stop the blood from carrying oxygen?
6. Why are light bulbs filled with argon?
7. How does methane get into the air?
8. What is the 'greenhouse effect'?
9. What does a catalytic converter do to the exhaust gases from a car?
10. Why is it possible to separate the gases in the air by fractional distillation?

1.3 Seas and rivers

There is plenty of water on the Earth but most of it is in seas and oceans, where the salts dissolved in it make it unsuitable for most uses. The amount of fresh water (less than 3% of the total) is still sufficient but it is not always in the places where it is needed. Figure **1.16** shows how the Earth's water is distributed.

You will see from the diagram that only a teaspoon of water out of every 100 litres is easily available for human use. This would still be sufficient but it is not equally distributed around the world. Rain forests can have over 11 metres of rainfall a year and desert areas less than one centimetre. There are places on Earth where it hasn't rained for more than ten years.

Water is essential to life but it can also carry disease. Polluted water kills many millions of people every year. It is important that the water we drink is treated to make it safe, and even more important that sewage (human and animal waste) is treated before being allowed back into rivers used for drinking water.

Water treatment

Water from rivers and lakes, and from underground, can contain dissolved salts, solid particles and bacteria. The water purification process is designed to remove the last two of these. At its simplest, water treatment involves filtering the water to remove solid particles and adding chlorine to kill any bacteria which could cause disease.

Figure **1.17** (overleaf) shows a modern water treatment process. The main difference from the simple treatment is in the use of ozone to remove pesticides and some other dissolved substances which can cause health problems. The water is still not totally pure as it contains some dissolved solids. Some of these, such as calcium salts, can aid health, whereas others, such as nitrate fertilisers, can be harmful.

In some parts of the world, seawater is made drinkable by **desalination** (taking the salt out). This can be done by distillation or by forcing the water through special membranes using high pressures (reverse osmosis). Desalination is particularly important in countries such as Saudi Arabia.

Our water supply is very important. Not only is it used in the home, as shown in Figure **1.18** (overleaf), but it is also used in large quantities by industry. Most of the water used by industry is used as a solvent for other substances, to cool down reactions or to transfer heat from one part of a factory to another.

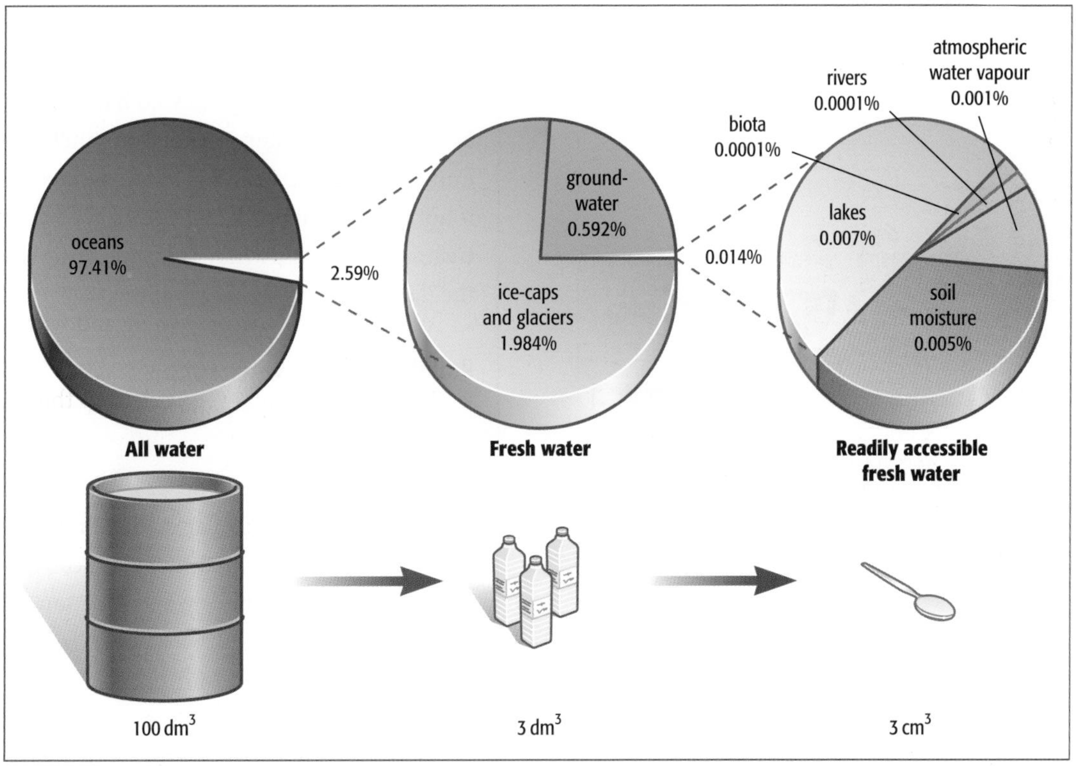

Figure 1.16 The availability of water on Earth.

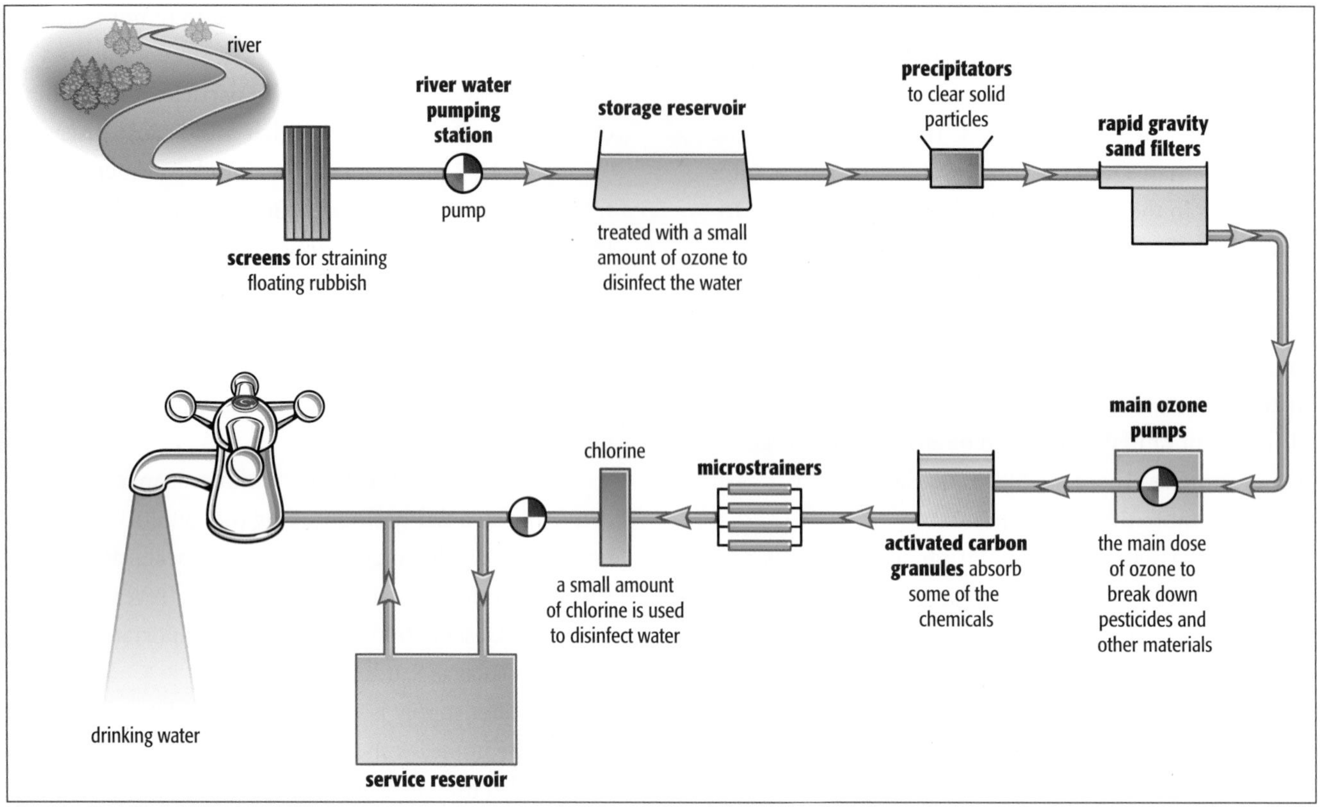

Figure 1.17 Purifying water for the domestic and industrial supply.

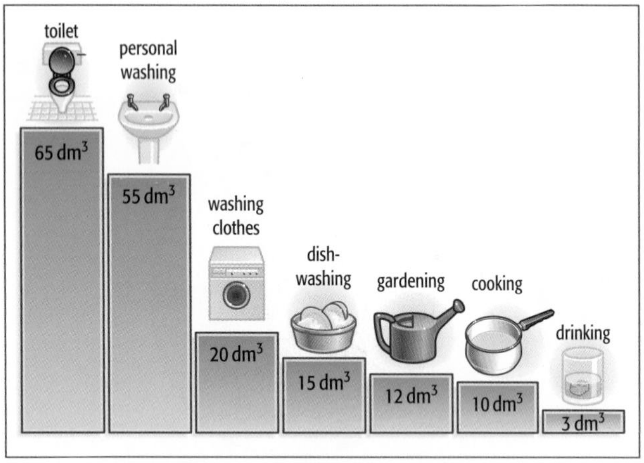

Figure 1.18 The main uses of water in a UK home. The numbers show how much water is used on average per person for each activity every day.

Sewage treatment

In Western Europe each person uses about 180 dm^3 of water per day. Figure **1.18** shows how this is used. After use, the water becomes **sewage**. It contains a wide variety of materials: soap, detergent, grease, food, body waste and factory waste. Waste water from drains needs to be treated before being allowed back into rivers or the sea. This water can contain much larger numbers of bacteria and is likely to cause disease if not treated. Figure **1.19** shows a typical sewage treatment process, where solid waste and most of the dangerous bacteria are removed.

Pollution of the water supply

Issues concerning the pollution of water include the following.

- Nitrate fertilisers can be washed into streams and rivers from farmland. These nitrates are not removed by water treatment and can cause health problems for old people and for young children.
- Industry sometimes discharges toxic and harmful substances into rivers.
- Untreated sewage and other animal waste can be released into rivers, especially in areas where there are no sewers.

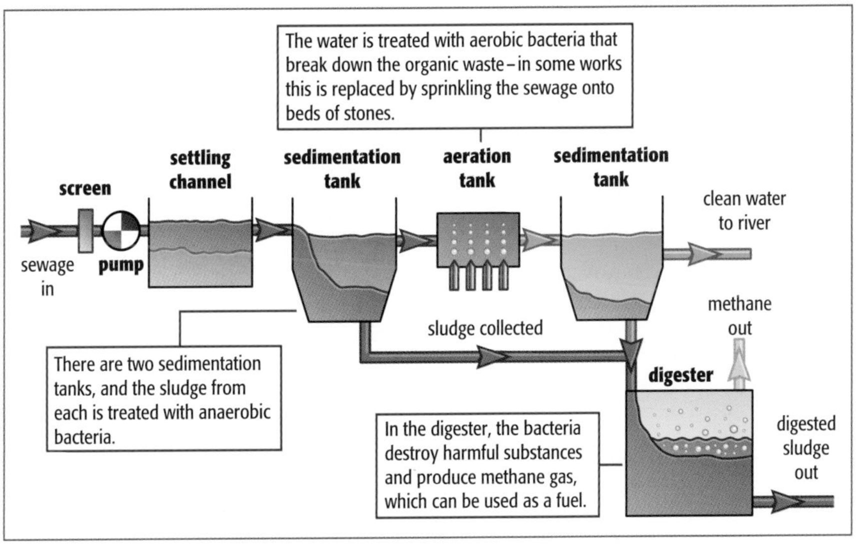

Figure 1.19 An outline of sewage treatment.

- The use of water for cooling by industry can result in warm water being discharged into rivers. Warm water can dissolve less oxygen than cold water, so animals living in the water may be left with insufficient oxygen.

All of these, and others, lead to problems in rivers but the problem is greater in lakes where there isn't a constant flow of water to remove the pollutants.

Figure 1.20 shows some of these problems as they affect a lake environment. A lake ecosystem can become overloaded by nutrients. The growth of plants and algae increases. They die and are decomposed by aerobic bacteria. Oxygen levels in the lake drop, and plants and animals in the water die as a result.

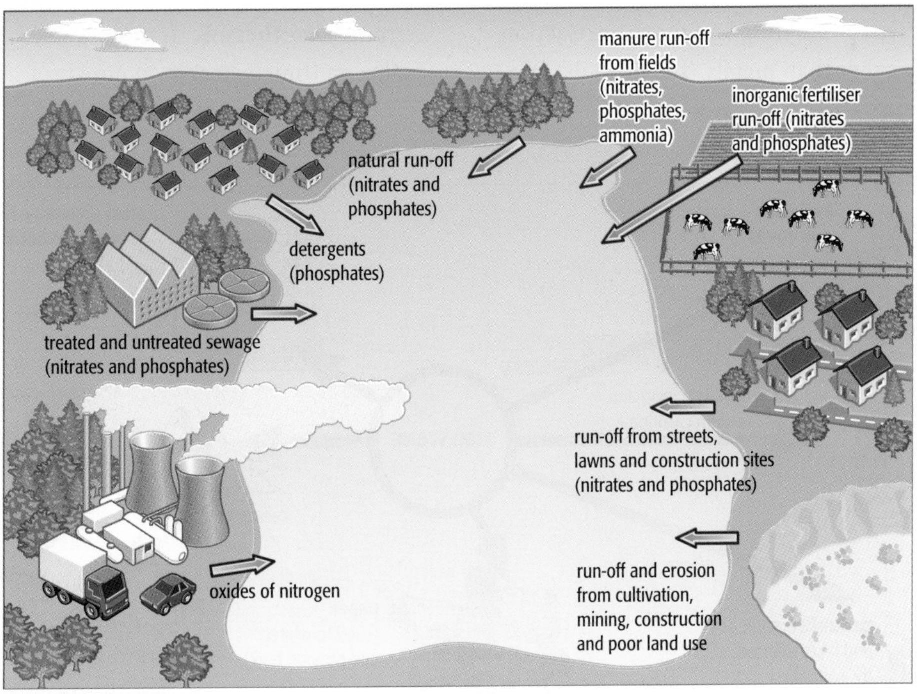

Figure 1.20 A lake ecosystem can become overloaded by nutrients. The overall result is a drop in oxygen levels in the lake. Plants and animals in the water die as a result.

Key ideas so far

- Most of the water on the Earth is not suitable for drinking or for many other uses.
- Water needs to be treated before it is safe to drink.
- Waste water (sewage) also needs treating before going back into rivers.
- Some pollutants can be removed from water by these treatments, but others cannot.

Quick-check questions

1 Why is water filtered before other treatments?
2 Why is chlorine added to water?
3 Why is distillation of sea water an expensive way of making drinking water?
4 What is the main danger of letting untreated sewage into rivers?
5 Why are nitrates from fertilisers dangerous in the water supply?

1.4 The Earth's crust

The Earth's **crust** is the top layer of solid rock of the planet. The crust varies in thickness from 5 km below some parts of the ocean to around 50 km in some parts of the landmass. Since the distance from the Earth's surface to its **core** is over 6000 km, the crust is a very thin surface layer. The crust is where the majority of the chemicals which we use come from.

Metal **ores** are rocks which have a relatively high concentration of a mineral containing a certain metal. For more details of ores and methods of obtaining metals from them, see Chapters **8** and **9**.

Rocks can be used for building and for the extraction of useful chemicals other than metals. The most useful of these is **limestone**.

The limestone cycle

Limestone is an important resource from which a useful range of compounds can be made. Figure **1.21** shows some of the important uses of limestone and the related compounds quicklime and slaked lime. The reactions involved in producing these compounds can be imitated in the laboratory (Figure **1.22**).

A piece of calcium carbonate can be heated strongly for some time to produce **lime** (quicklime, calcium oxide). The piece of lime is allowed to cool and then a few drops of water are added. The solid flakes and expands, crumbling into 'slaked lime'. This reaction is strongly **exothermic**. If more water is added, an alkaline solution (limewater) is obtained.

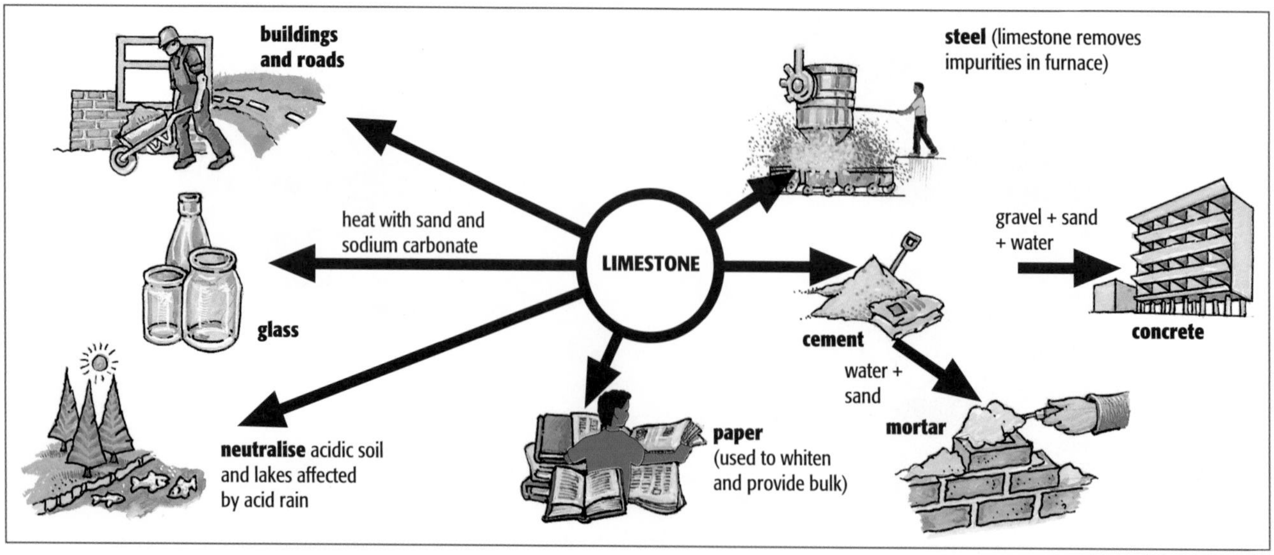

Figure 1.21 Some of the uses of limestone (calcium carbonate).

The cycle can be completed by bubbling carbon dioxide into the solution. A white precipitate of calcium carbonate is formed. We can complete what is sometimes referred to as the **limestone cycle** (Figure **1.23**).

More detail on the importance of limestone and the chemicals derived from it can be found in Section **9.6**. This includes the method of making lime industrially.

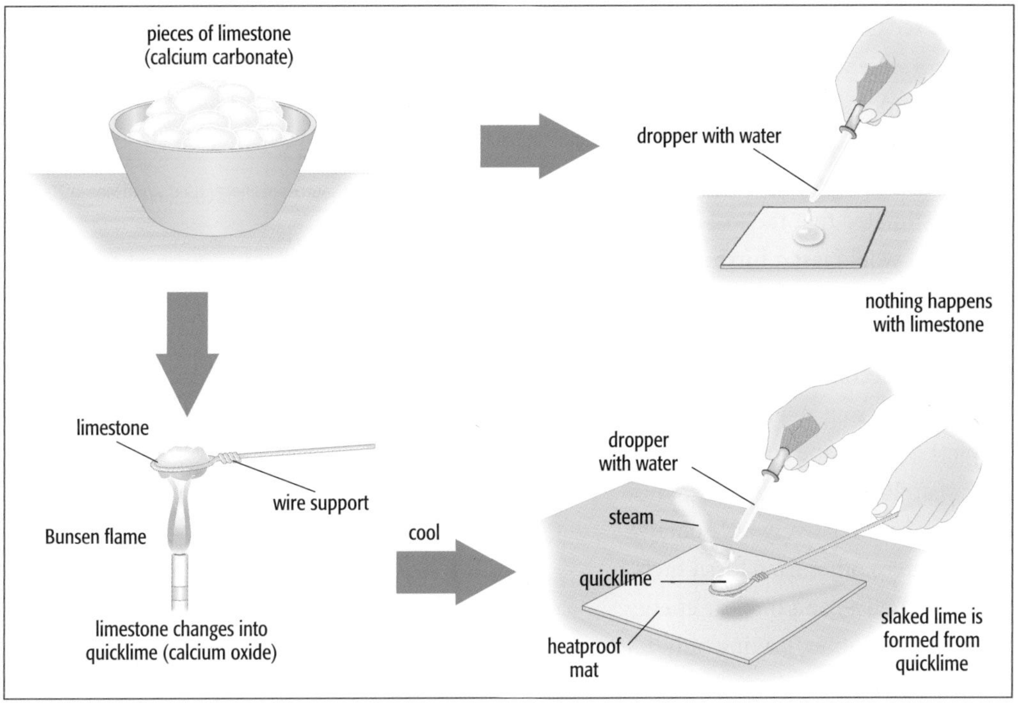

Figure 1.22 The formation of quicklime and slaked lime in the laboratory.

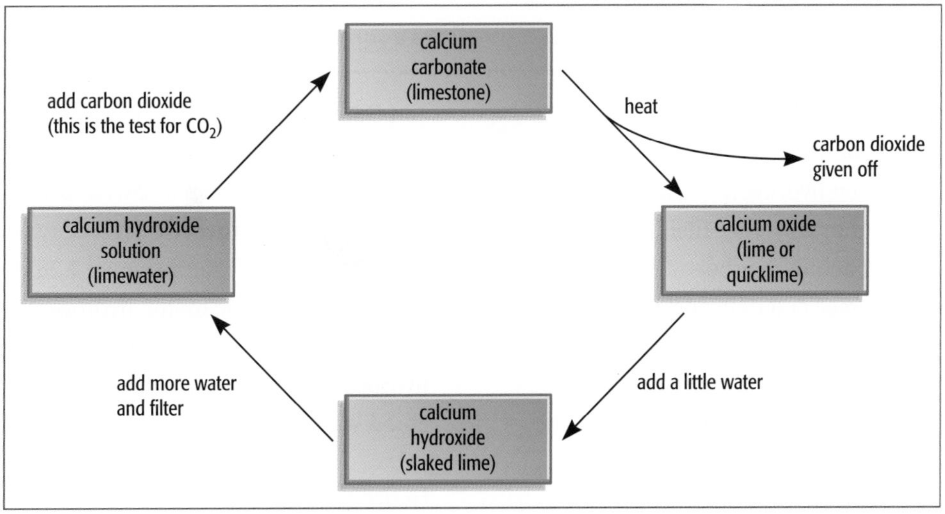

Figure 1.23 The limestone cycle.

E

The problem of fossil fuels

The major **fossil fuels** are **coal**, **petroleum** (or **crude oil**) and **natural gas**. These are important sources of energy but are also very important as sources of raw materials for making plastics, drugs, detergents and many other useful substances. For more detail of fossil fuels and their uses see Chapter **11**.

If these resources were used not as fuels, but only as a source of the chemicals we need, there wouldn't be a problem. They are, however, mostly used as fuels and they are a limited, non-renewable resource.

In 2007 it was estimated that the fossil fuel supplies we currently know of would last a further 43 years in the case of petroleum, 167 years for natural gas and 417 years for coal.

As more countries become industrialised, energy use in the world is increasing at a faster rate than the population. Table **1.2** shows the sources of energy drawn on in the year 2006.

Energy source	Percentage of energy from this source (%)
petroleum	36.8
coal	26.6
natural gas	22.9
hydroelectric power	6.3
nuclear energy	6.0
other sources (solar, wind etc.)	1.4

Table 1.2 The sources of energy used worldwide in 2006.

The figures show how relatively little energy is obtained from sources other than fossil fuels. Hydroelectric power (6.3%) and nuclear energy (6.0%) do make a contribution, leaving only 1.4% of energy from solar power, wind power and wave power combined.

Clearly change is necessary (Figure **1.24**). The Sun is the greatest provider of energy to the Earth. The solar energy falling on one square kilometere of desert is equivalent to the amount that could be obtained from 300 000 tonnes of coal or 1.5 million barrels of oil.

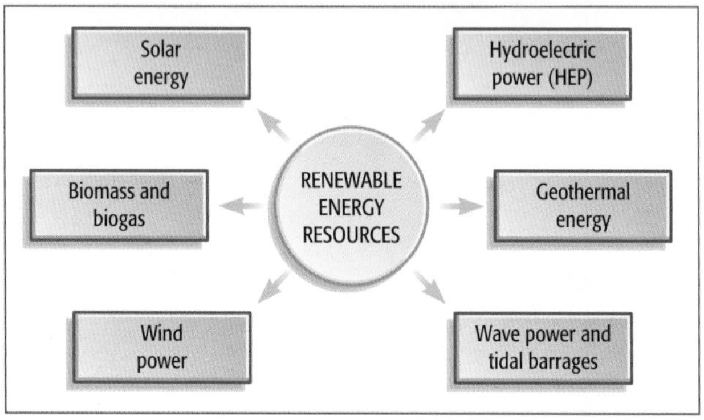

Figure 1.24 Renewable energy resources suitable for development to reduce our dependence on fossil fuels.

Hydrogen is one possible fuel for the future, either as a substance to burn or for use in fuel cells.

Hydrogen as a fuel

Hydrogen gas has attractions as a **fuel**. All it produces on burning is water. When hydrogen burns, it produces more energy per gram than any other fuel (Figure **1.25**).

A future 'hydrogen economy' has been talked of, but there are problems of storage and transport. The gas itself is difficult to store and transport because of its low density. The first vehicles to run on hydrogen were the rockets of the US space programme. Hydrogen is not cheap. The main method of obtaining it on a large scale is by the electrolysis of water. However, this is not very economic. It is possible that cheap surplus electricity from nuclear power may make electrolysis more economic. Others have suggested the use of electricity from solar power.

Despite these difficulties, prototype hydrogen-powered cars have been tried. Nissan and Mazda in Japan, and Daimler–Benz in Germany, have built and tested cars. The Japanese prototype burns the hydrogen in the engine, while the German–Swiss–British venture uses the hydrogen in a **fuel cell**. Electricity from this cell then powers an electric motor (Figure **1.26**). Using a fuel cell operating an electric motor, hydrogen has an efficiency of 60% compared with 35% for a petrol engine. The 'hydrogen economy' may have life in it yet! The advantages and disadvantages are summarised in Table **1.3**.

Hydrogen fuel cells

S

Research has found a much more efficient way of changing chemical energy into electrical energy by using a fuel cell. A hydrogen fuel cell can be used to power a car. Such a cell operates continuously, with no need for recharging. The cell supplies energy as long as

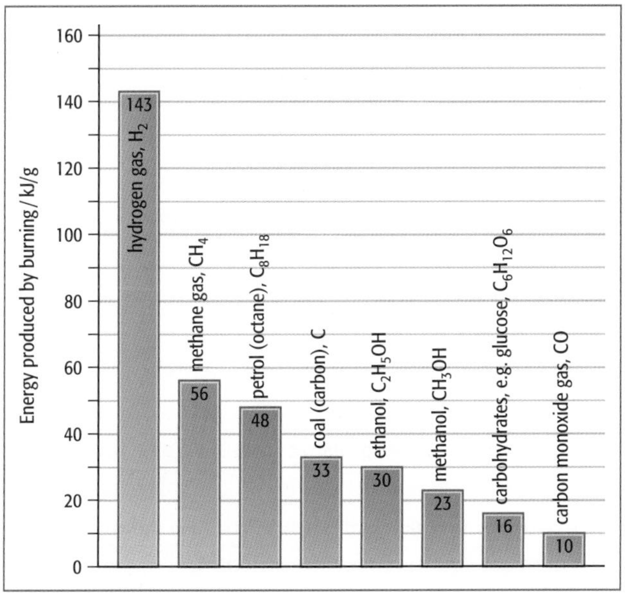

Figure 1.25 The energy produced on burning one gram of various fuels, to produce water and carbon dioxide. Hydrogen produces more energy per gram than any other fuel.

Advantages	Disadvantages
• renewable if produced using solar energy • lower flammability than gasoline (petrol) • virtually emission-free • zero emissions of CO_2 • non-toxic	• non-renewable if generated using nuclear energy or energy from fossil fuels • large fuel tank required • there are no 'filling stations', where a car could be topped up with hydrogen, at present • engine redesign needed or a fuel cell system • currently expensive

Table 1.3 The advantages and disadvantages of hydrogen as a fuel for motor vehicles.

S the reactants are fed in to the electrodes. The overall reaction of the hydrogen–oxygen fuel cell is:

$$\text{hydrogen} + \text{oxygen} \rightarrow \text{water}$$
$$2H_2(g) + O_2(g) \rightarrow 2H_2O(g)$$

Land pollution

Cities throughout the world are covered in litter. Some make an effort to control it but it is always there. Most of our waste material is buried and this can lead to problems. Toxic and radioactive waste can make the land unusable and many countries strictly control what can be buried and where. Companies are required, by law, to treat their waste products to make them as harmless as possible.

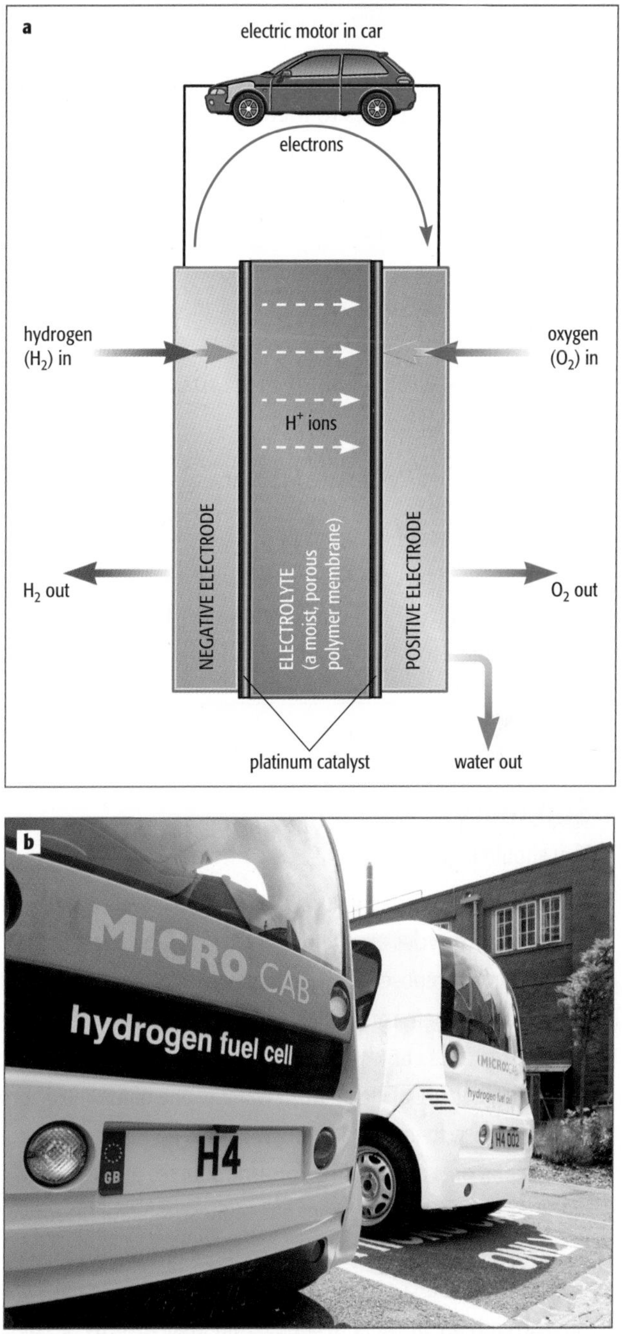

Figure 1.26 **a** How a car runs on a hydrogen fuel cell. The car is powered by electrons released at the negative electrode. Inside the fuel cell, hydrogen ions move to the positive electrode, where they react with oxygen to (form water). **b** These hydrogen-powered mini-cabs are part of a development project at the University of Birmingham in the UK.

Domestic waste should be recycled whenever possible. Waste which cannot be treated in this way should be burned to create energy. If left in landfill sites it decays, producing methane gas (by a process known as **anaerobic decay**). Methane is much more harmful to the environment than the carbon dioxide produced by burning it, as it is a more powerful greenhouse gas.

Key ideas so far

- Some rocks in the Earth's crust are very useful. This particularly applies to metal ores and limestone.
- Fossil fuels (coal, oil and gas) are a non-renewable resource.
- Fossil fuels are also a useful source of many chemicals.
- Reserves of fossil fuels can be conserved by using alternative energy sources.
- Burying waste in landfill sites can release methane, a 'greenhouse gas'.
- Hydrogen has the potential to be a very useful fuel in the future.
- Hydrogen fuel cells are being used to power prototype cars.
- Hydrogen fuel cells use the combustion reaction of hydrogen to produce electrical energy.

? Quick-check questions

1. What makes an ore different from any other type of rock?
2. What is the difference between lime and slaked lime?
3. What useful chemicals can be made from petroleum?
4. Name **four** types of 'alternative energy'.
5. What makes a gas a 'greenhouse gas'?
6. Give an advantage of using hydrogen as a fuel.
7. What is the essential reaction taking place in a hydrogen fuel cell? Give the word and balanced chemical equations for the reaction.

Summary

You should know that:

- there are important natural cycles that involve the movement of resources within the Earth's ecology
- three such cycles are the water cycle, carbon and nitrogen cycles
- the air is composed predominantly of nitrogen and oxygen, but other gases have major roles to play too
- the atmosphere can be polluted by human activities. There are several major atmospheric pollution problems that are changing the nature of our world: acid rain and photochemical smog in our cities are among these
- the availability of clean, fresh water is one of the major problems in the world
- we have systems for cleaning water for domestic and industrial use, and for treatment of water after its use in order to recycle it
- mineral ores and crude oil provide sources of metals and chemicals for industrial use
- limestone is an example of one of these mineral resources that has a range of uses, from the making of cement and concrete to the extraction of iron in the blast furnace
- natural resources can be classed as renewable or non-renewable
- currently we are very dependent on fossil fuels as the source of our energy supply
- there are various alternative energy sources that are available for development – they include solar power, wind power, hydroelectric and nuclear power
- one energy source currently under development is the use of hydrogen
- hydrogen is seen as being an environmentally clean source as the only product of its combustion is water
- the gases of the air can be separated by the fractional distillation of liquid air, and the separated gases have their own uses
- global warming is a further atmospheric problem facing the world; the climate changes resulting from this are a major area of concern. Global warming is caused by an increase in the atmosphere of certain 'greenhouse gases' such as carbon dioxide and methane
- the most advanced area of development for hydrogen as an energy source is as an alternative to petrol (gasoline) in cars
- the hydrogen fuel cell can be used to power cars
- the hydrogen fuel cell is based on the production of electrical power using the combustion reaction for hydrogen.

Exam-style questions

1 The diagram shows a water treatment works.

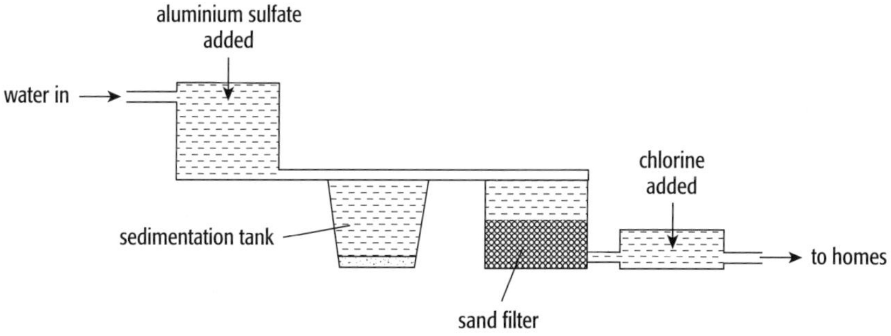

a State **one** use of water in industry. [1]

b Explain how the sand filter helps purify the water. [2]

c The aluminium ions in aluminium sulfate cause clay particles to clump together. Describe a test for aluminium ions. [3]

d Why is chlorine added to the water? [1]

CIE IGCSE, June 2008, paper 2, q.4 part

2 The diagram shows a statue in a park in an industrial town. The statue is made from limestone.

a State the name of the chemical present in limestone. [1]

b Use ideas about the chemistry of atmospheric pollutants to suggest how and why the statue changes over 20 years. [4]

c Parts of the statue are joined together with iron pins. After 30 years, the arm falls off the statue. Suggest why the arm falls off. [1]

CIE IGCSE, June 2008, paper 2, q.2 part

3 Copy the diagram and match up the atmospheric pollutants on the left with their main source on the right. The first one has been done for you.

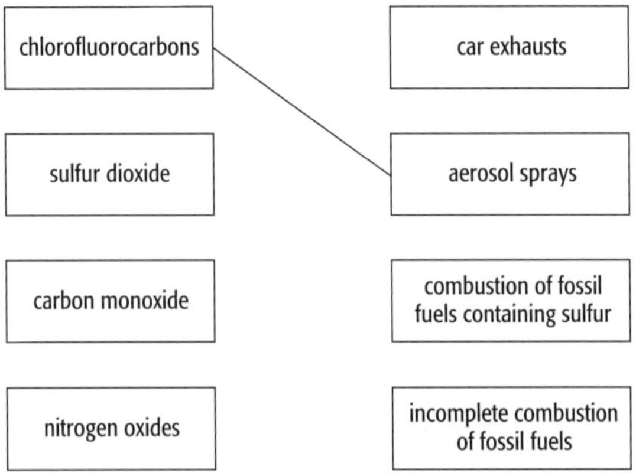

[3]

CIE IGCSE, November 2008, paper 2, q.2 part

4

A

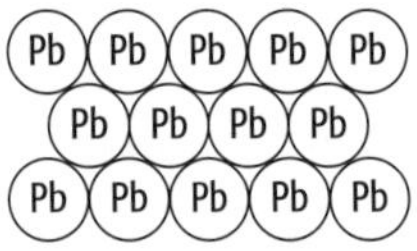

B

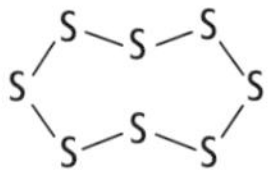

a Structure **A** is lead.

i What is the source of the small amount of lead present in the air? [1]

ii State an adverse effect of lead on health. [1]

b Structure **B** is sulfur.

Explain why burning fossil fuels containing sulfur is harmful to the environment. [2]

CIE IGCSE, June 2007, paper 2, q.1 part

5 A student collected some water from a polluted river.

The water contained soluble solids and insoluble clay and had a pH of 5.

a How can the student separate the clay from the rest of the river water? [1]

b The student uses litmus paper to show that the river water is acidic.

What will be the result of this test? [1]

c The student then boiled the river water to obtain the soluble solids. The diagram shows how she heated the water.

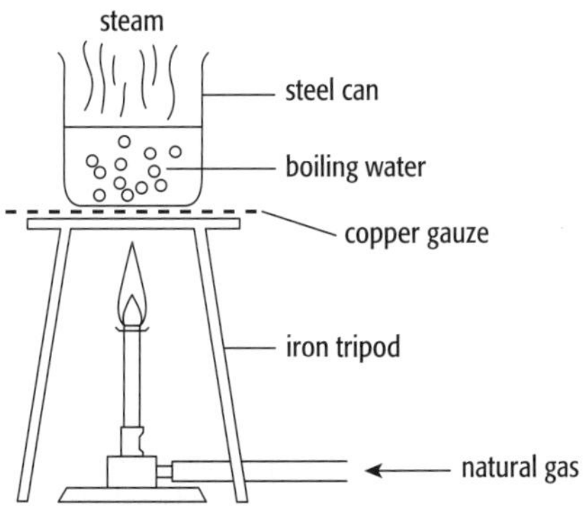

Which of the substances named in the diagram is

i an alloy [1]

ii a compound which is liquid at room temperature [1]

iii an element [1]

iv a fuel? [1]

d Name the main substance in natural gas. [1]

e What is the temperature of boiling water? [1]

f After the student boiled off the water, she analysed the white powder on the inside of the steel can. The table shows her results.

Name of ion	Formula of ion	Mass of ion present / milligrams
calcium	Ca^{2+}	16
carbonate	CO_3^{2-}	35
chloride	Cl^-	8
nitrate	NO_3^-	4
sodium	Na^+	8
sulfate	SO_4^{2-}	6

i Which positive ion had the greatest concentration in the sample of river water? [1]

ii Copy and complete the following equation to show how a sodium ion is formed from a sodium atom.

$Na \rightarrow Na^+ +$ .... [1]

g Instead of using natural gas, the student could have used butane to heat the water. The formula of butane is C_4H_{10}.

i What products are formed when butane burns in excess air? [1]

ii Name the poisonous gas formed when butane undergoes incomplete combustion. [1]

CIE IGCSE, June 2005, paper 2, q.2

6 Two of the stages in water purification are filtration and chlorination. The diagram below shows a filter tank.

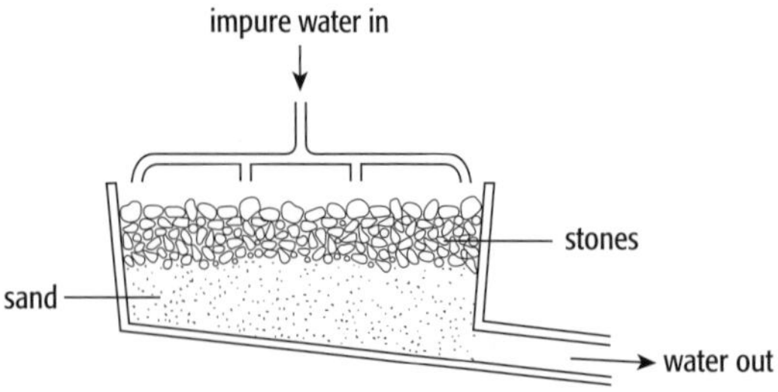

a Explain how this filter helps purify the water. [2]

b **i** Why is chlorine added during water purification?

ii After chlorination, the water is acidic. A small amount of slaked lime is added to the acidic water. Explain why slaked lime is added.

iii What is the chemical name for slaked lime?

iv State **one** other use of slaked lime. [4]

c **i** State the boiling point of pure water. [1]

ii Describe a chemical test for water. [2]

iii State **one** use of water in the home. [1]

d The diagram shows the arrangement of particles in the three different states of water.

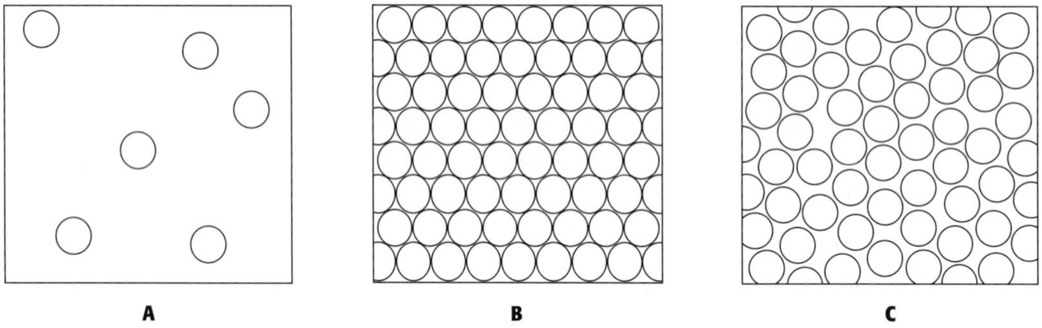

Which of these diagrams, **A**, **B** or **C**, shows water in a solid state? [1]

CIE IGCSE, June 2004, paper 2, q.2 part

7 Clean air contains a number of different gases.

a State the names of the **two** gases which make up most of the air. [2]

b A sample of air is drawn through the apparatus shown below.

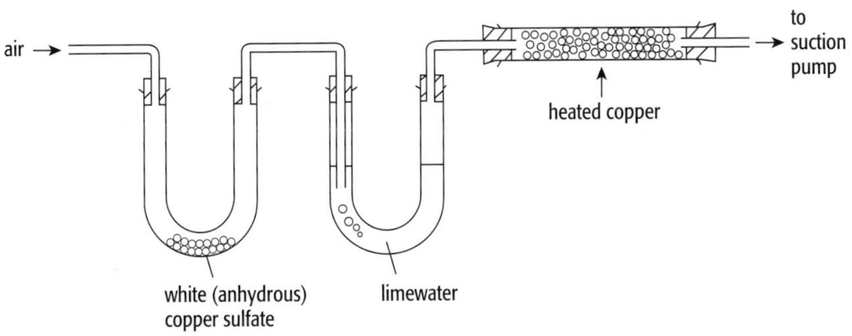

i When the air is drawn through the apparatus, the limewater turns milky. Which gas turns limewater milky? [1]

ii The white (anhydrous) copper sulfate turns blue. State the name of the substance which turns white copper sulfate blue. [1]

iii Oxygen is removed from the air by passing it over heated copper. Complete the equation for this reaction.

$2Cu + \ldots\ldots \rightarrow \ldots\ldots CuO$ [2]

c Pure air contains about 1% argon.

i In which Period of the Periodic Table is argon? [1]

ii State the **name** of the Group of elements to which argon belongs. [1]

iii Draw the electronic structure of argon. [1]

iv Why is argon used in lamps? [1]

v An isotope of argon has a mass number of 40. Calculate the number of neutrons in this isotope of argon. [1]

CIE IGCSE, June 2007, paper 2, q.2 part

8 When fuels are burnt, carbon dioxide and water are formed.

a Copy and complete the equation for the burning of propane.

$C_3H_8 + \ldots\ldots O_2 \rightarrow 3CO_2 + 4H_2O$ [1]

b Describe a chemical test for water. [2]

c In which **two** of the following is carbon dioxide produced?

- a car driven by a petrol engine
- magnesium carbonate reacting with an acid
- sodium reacting with water
- zinc reacting with hydrochloric acid [2]

d The diagram shows a water heater.

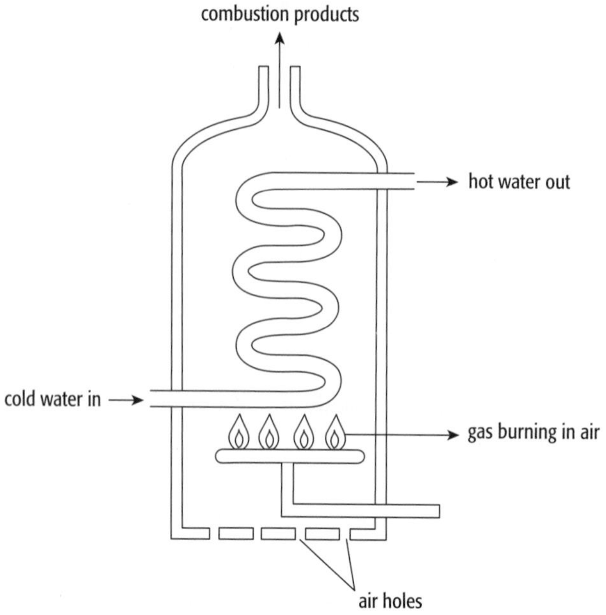

If some of the air holes become blocked, a poisonous gas is produced.

i State the name of this poisonous gas.

ii Explain how this poisonous gas has been formed. [2]

e The table below compares the amounts of carbon dioxide and sulfur dioxide formed when 1 kilogram of different fuels are burnt.

Fuel	Mass of carbon dioxide produced / g	Mass of sulfur dioxide produced / g
oil	2900	5.0
gas	2500	0.1
coal	2500	11.0

i Which fuel is **least** polluting?

ii Which fuel, when burnt, contributes most to the formation of acid rain?

iii State **two** harmful effects of acid rain.

iv When acid rain falls on the ground, it can react with insoluble aluminium compounds in the soil. A solution of aluminium ions is formed.
Describe what you would observe when aqueous sodium hydroxide is added to a solution containing aluminium ions. [6]

CIE IGCSE, November 2003, paper 2, q.5

S **9** Minimising air pollution is essential for health and for the environment.

a Natural gas is methane.

i Write the equation for the complete combustion of methane. [2]

ii Explain why it is dangerous to use a gas fire in a poorly ventilated room. [2]

b Low-sulfur fuels are being introduced. Ordinary diesel contains 500 ppm of sulfur but low-sulfur diesel contains less than 50 ppm. Why is this an advantage to the environment? [2]

c Catalytic converters reduce pollution from motor vehicles, as shown in the following diagram.

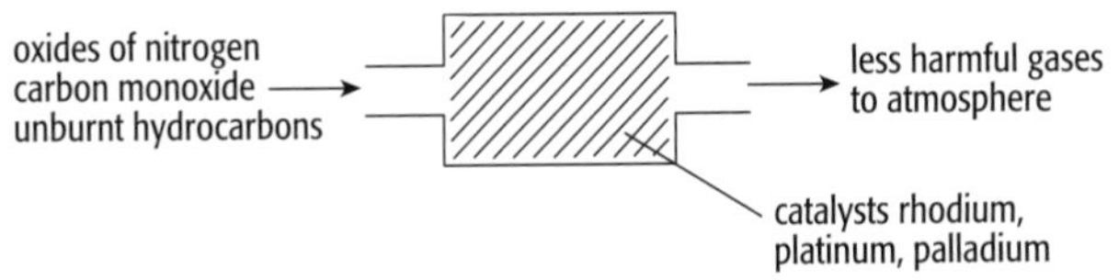

i What type of elements are the metals rhodium, platinum and palladium? [1]

ii Rhodium catalyses the decomposition of the oxides of nitrogen:

$2NO \rightarrow N_2 + O_2$

Two other pollutants are carbon monoxide and unburnt hydrocarbons. How are they made into less harmful substances? [2]

CIE IGCSE, November 2006, paper 3, q.4

10 a Two of the gases in air are nitrogen and oxygen. Name **two** other gases present in unpolluted air. [2]

b Two common pollutants present in air are sulfur dioxide and lead compounds. State the source and harmful effect of each.

i sulfur dioxide [3]

ii lead compounds [2]

c Respiration and photosynthesis are two of the processes that determine the percentage of oxygen and of carbon dioxide in the air.

i Name another process that changes the percentages of these two gases in air. [1]

ii The equation for photosynthesis is given below.

$6CO_2 + 6H_2O \rightarrow C_6H_{12}O_6 + 6O_2$

This is an endothermic reaction.
Complete the reaction for respiration.

$C_6H_{12}O_6 + 6O_2 \rightarrow$ .... + ...

This is an .... reaction. [2]

CIE IGCSE, November 2004, paper 3, q.1 part

11 '*Hydrogen – A Fuel for the Future*'

It has been suggested that hydrogen could be used as a fuel instead of the fossil fuels that are used at present. The equation below shows how hydrogen burns in air:

$2H_2 + O_2 \rightarrow 2H_2O$ strongly exothermic

The hydrogen would be made by the electrolysis of water using energy obtained from renewable sources such as wind or solar power. The water-splitting reaction requires a lot of energy. (The following bond energies will be useful for part of the question: H—H = 436 kJ/mol, O—H = 464 kJ/mol, O=O = 497 kJ/mol)

a Hydrogen was successfully used as a fuel for a Russian airliner in 1988. Why would hydrogen be a good fuel for use in an aeroplane? [2]

b The water-splitting reaction is shown in the equation below:

$2H_2O \rightarrow 2H_2 + O_2$

i Calculate the energy needed to split the water molecules in the equation into H and O atoms:

$2H_2O \rightarrow 4H + 2O$ [3]

ii Calculate the energy change when the H and O atoms join to form H_2 and O_2 molecules:

$4H + 2O \rightarrow 2H_2 + O_2$ [2]

iii Is the overall reaction:

$2H_2O \rightarrow 2H_2 + O_2$

exothermic or endothermic? Use your answers to parts **i** and **ii** to explain your choice. [4]

c In the Periodic Table, hydrogen is placed on its own at the top and in the middle. It is difficult to position because it has properties of metals and non-metals.

i Where would you expect hydrogen to be placed in the Periodic Table on the basis of the arrangement of electrons in hydrogen atoms? Explain your answer. [2]

ii Give **one** way in which hydrogen behaves like a metal. [1]

iii Give **one** way in which hydrogen behaves like a non-metal. [1]

2 The nature of matter

This chapter covers the following ideas:

- the three states of matter, and changes of state
- separating and purifying substances
- filtration
- use of separating funnel
- evaporation and crystallisation
- distillation
- paper chromatography
- criteria of purity
- elements and compounds
- atomic theory
- the kinetic theory and changes of state
- diffusion
- atomic structure and subatomic particles
- proton (atomic) number and nucleon (mass) number
- isotopes
- relative atomic mass
- uses of radioactivity
- the arrangement of electrons in atoms

2.1 Different types of substance

Saturn is perhaps the most beautiful of the planets of the Solar System. It has fascinated astronomers because of its mysterious rings (Figure 2.1). The Pioneer and Voyager space-probes sent back a great deal of information on the nature of the rings and the mass of Saturn itself.

Each ring is made up of a stream of icy particles, following each other nose-to-tail around the planet. The particles can be of widely varying sizes. The rings resemble a snowstorm, in which tiny snowflakes are mixed with snowballs up to the size of a house. The ice that surrounds one of the most spectacular planets of our solar system is made of water – the same substance (with the same formula) that covers so much of the Earth's surface.

Figure 2.1 Saturn and its rings silhouetted against the Sun: a photograph taken by the Cassini probe. The rings are made of ice and dust.

The planet of Saturn is made of gases, mainly hydrogen and helium. Deep in the centre of these lightweight gases is a small rocky core, surrounded by a liquid layer of the gases. The inner parts of the planet, nearest to the core, are squashed together (compressed) so much that they become solid. Study of Saturn's physical structure emphasises how substances that we know on Earth can exist in different physical states in different environments.

How do changing conditions affect the appearance, properties and behaviour of different substances?

The states of matter

There are many different kinds of **matter**. The word is used to cover all the substances and materials of which the Universe is composed. Samples of all of these materials have two properties in common: they each occupy space (they have volume) and they have mass.

Physical state	Volume	Density	Shape	Fluidity
solid	has a fixed volume	high	has a definite shape	does not flow
liquid	has a fixed volume	moderate to high	no definite shape – takes the shape of the container	generally flows easily[a]
gas	no fixed volume – expands to fill the container	low	no definite shape – takes the shape of the container	flows easily[a]

[a]*Liquids and gases are called* ***fluids****.*

Table 2.1 Differences in the properties of the three states of matter.

Chemistry is the study of how matter behaves, and of how one kind of substance can be changed into another. Whichever chemical substance we study, we find it can exist in three different forms (or physical states) depending on the conditions. These three different **states of matter** are known as **solid**, **liquid** and **gas**. Changing temperature and/or pressure can change the state in which a substance exists.

The different physical states have certain general characteristics that are true whatever chemical substance is being considered. These are summarised in Table **2.1**.

> Matter is defined as anything that has mass and takes up space. There are three physical states:
> - solid
> - liquid
> - gas.

The three physical states show differences in the way they respond to changes in temperature and pressure. All three show an increase in volume (an expansion) when the temperature is increased, and a decrease in volume (a contraction) when the temperature is lowered. The effect is much bigger for a gas than for either a solid or a liquid.

The volume of a gas at a fixed temperature can easily be reduced by increasing the pressure on the gas. Gases are easy to 'squash' – they are easily compressible. Liquids, on the other hand, are only slightly compressible, and the volume of a solid is unaffected by changing the pressure.

Changes in physical state

Large changes in temperature and pressure can cause changes that are more dramatic than expansion or contraction. They can cause a substance to change its physical state. The changes between the three states of matter are shown in Figure **2.2**. At atmospheric pressure, these changes can be brought about by raising or lowering the temperature of the substance.

Melting and freezing

The temperature at which a pure substance turns to a liquid is called the **melting point** (m.p.). This always happens at one particular temperature for each pure substance (Figure **2.3**). The process is reversed at precisely the same temperature if a liquid is cooled down. It is then called the **freezing point** (f.p.). The melting point and freezing point of any given substance are both the same temperature. For example, the melting and freezing of pure water take place at 0 °C.

Gallium is a metal that has a melting point just above room temperature. Because of this it will melt in a person's hand (Figure **2.4**).

Sublimation

A few solids, such as carbon dioxide ('dry ice'), do not melt when they are heated. Instead they turn directly into gas. This change of state is called **sublimation**: the solid **sublimes**. Like melting, this also happens at one particular temperature for each pure solid. Iodine is another solid that sublimes. It produces a purple vapour, but then condenses again on a cold surface (Figure **2.5**, overleaf).

Evaporation, boiling and condensation

If a liquid is left with its surface exposed to the air, it evaporates. Splashes of water evaporate at room temperature. After rain, puddles dry up! When liquids

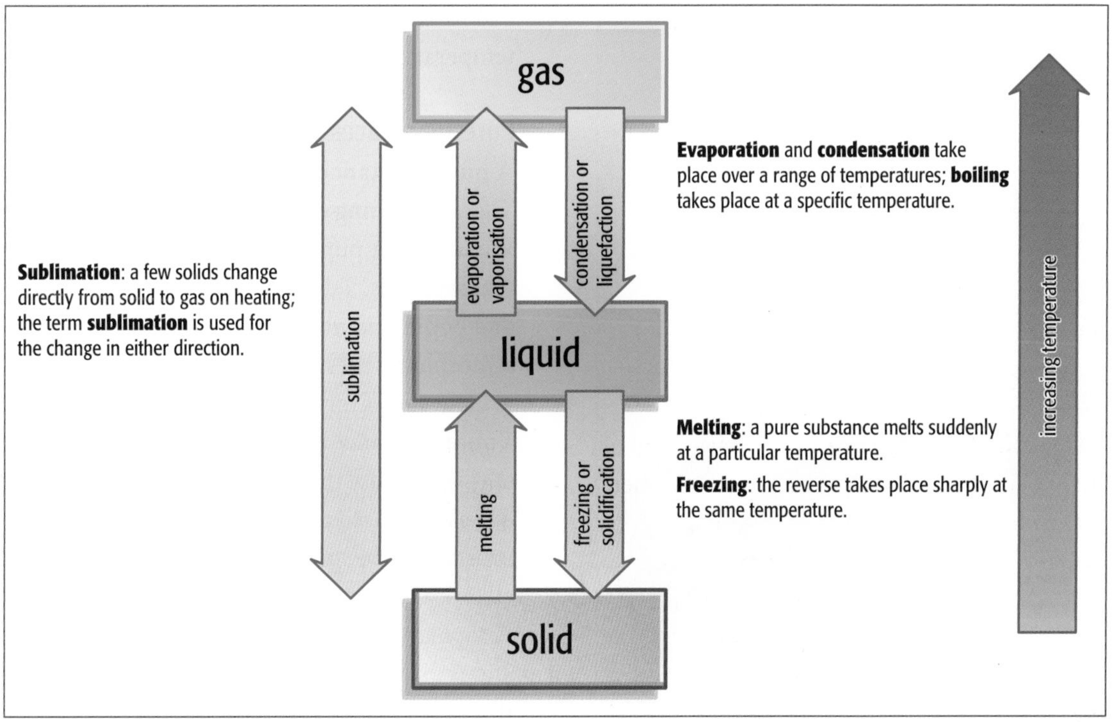

Figure 2.2 Changes of physical state and the effect of increasing temperature.

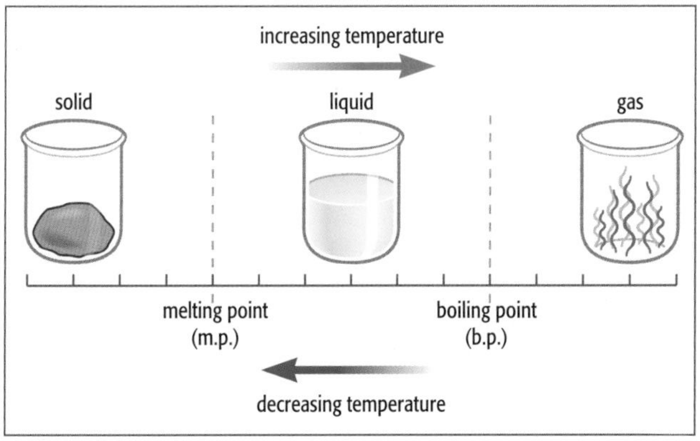

Figure 2.3 The relationship between the melting and boiling point of a substance.

change into gases in this way, the process is called **evaporation**. Evaporation takes place from the surface of the liquid. The larger the surface area, the faster the liquid evaporates.

The warmer the liquid is, the faster it evaporates. Eventually, at a certain temperature, it becomes hot enough for gas to form within the liquid and not just at the surface. Bubbles of gas appear inside the liquid. This process is known as **boiling**. It takes place at a specific temperature, known as the **boiling point** (b.p.) for each

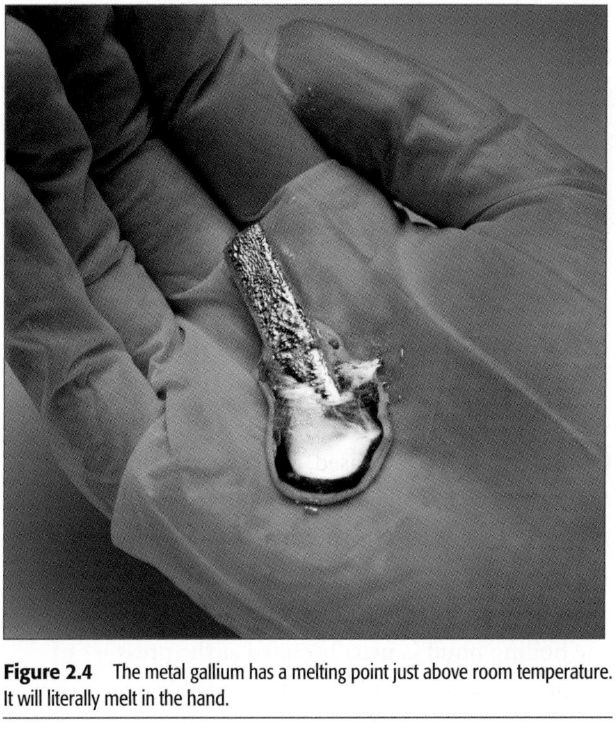

Figure 2.4 The metal gallium has a melting point just above room temperature. It will literally melt in the hand.

pure liquid (Figure 2.3). Water evaporates fairly easily and has a relatively low boiling point – it is quite a **volatile** liquid. Ethanol, with a boiling point of 78 °C, is more volatile than water. It has a higher **volatility** than water.

Figure 2.5 Iodine sublimes. On warming, it produces a purple vapour which then condenses again on the cool part of the tube.

- A volatile liquid is one which evaporates easily and has a relatively low boiling point.
- Ethanol (b.p. 78 °C) is a more volatile liquid than water (b.p. 100 °C).

The reverse of evaporation is **condensation**. This is usually brought about by cooling. However, we saw earlier that the gas state is the one most affected by changes in pressure. It is possible, at normal temperatures, to condense a gas into a liquid by increasing the pressure, without cooling.

The boiling point of a liquid can change if the surrounding pressure changes. The value given for the boiling point is usually stated at the pressure of the atmosphere at sea level (**atmospheric pressure** or **standard pressure**). If the surrounding pressure falls, the boiling point falls. The boiling point of water at standard pressure is 100 °C. On a high mountain it is lower than 100 °C. If the surrounding pressure is increased, the boiling point rises. In a pressure cooker, the boiling point of water is raised to around 120 °C and food cooks more quickly at this higher temperature.

Pure substances

A **pure substance** consists of only one substance. There is nothing else in it: it has no contaminating impurities. A pure substance melts and boils at definite temperatures. Table **2.2** shows the melting points and boiling points of some common substances at atmospheric pressure.

The values for the melting point and boiling point of a pure substance are precise and predictable. This means that we can use them to test the purity of a sample. They can also be used to check the identity of an unknown substance. The melting point can be measured using an electrically heated melting-point apparatus (Figure **2.6**). A capillary tube is filled with a small amount of the solid and is placed in the heating block. The melting is viewed through a magnifying lens.

A substance's melting and boiling points in relation to room temperature (taken as 20 °C) determine whether it is usually seen as a solid, a liquid or a gas. For example, if the m.p. is below 20 °C and the b.p. is above 20 °C, the substance will be a liquid at room temperature.

Substance	Physical state at room temperature (20 °C)	Melting point/°C	Boiling point/°C
oxygen	gas	−219	−183
nitrogen	gas	−210	−196
ethanol (alcohol)	liquid	−117	78
water	liquid	0	100
sulfur	solid	115	444
common salt (sodium chloride)	solid	801	1465
copper	solid	1083	2600
carbon dioxide	gas	−78[(a)]	

[(a)] *Sublimes.*

Table 2.2 The melting and boiling points of some common chemical substances.

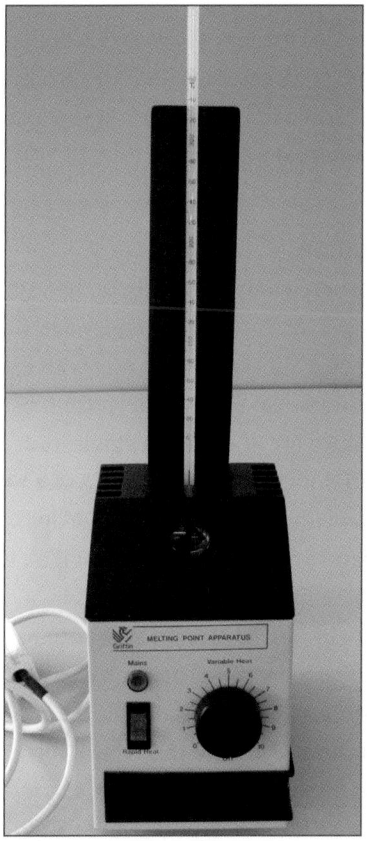

Figure 2.6 An electrical melting-point apparatus.

The presence of an impurity in a substance:

- **lowers** the melting point, and
- **raises** the boiling point of the substance.

Exam tip

Remember that pure substances have definite, sharp melting and boiling points. The presence of an impurity means that these changes will be spread over a range of temperatures in each case.

Exam tip

Remember to practise using melting and boiling point data to decide whether a particular substance is a solid, liquid or gas at room temperature. These are quite common questions.

Be careful with temperatures below 0 °C; −100 °C is a higher temperature than −150 °C.

The effect of impurities

Seawater is impure water. You can show this if you put some seawater in an evaporating dish and boil away the water, because a solid residue of salt is left behind in the dish. Seawater freezes at a temperature well below the freezing point of pure water (0 °C) and boils at a temperature above the boiling point of pure water (100 °C). Other impure substances show similar differences.

In addition, the impurity can also reduce the 'sharpness' of the melting or boiling point. An impure substance sometimes melts or boils over a range of temperatures, not at a particular point.

Heating and cooling curves

The melting point of a solid can be measured using the apparatus shown in Figure 2.7. A powdered solid is put in a narrow melting-point tube so that it can be heated easily. An oil bath is used so that melting points above 100 °C can be measured. We can follow the temperature of the sample before and after melting. These results can then be used to produce a heating curve (Figure **2.8**, overleaf).

Figure **2.8** shows how the temperature changes when a sample of solid naphthalene (a single pure substance) is heated steadily. The solid melts at precisely 80 °C. Notice that, while the solid is melting, the temperature stops rising. It will only begin to rise again when all the naphthalene has melted. Generally, the heating curve for a pure solid stops rising at its melting point. The heating curve for wax, which is a mixture of

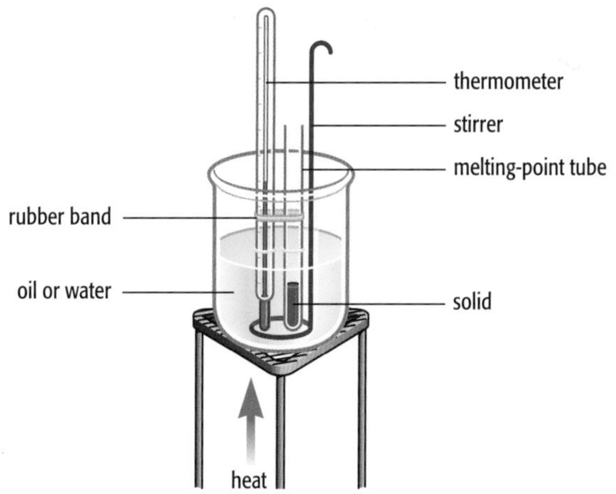

Figure 2.7 Apparatus for measuring the melting point or following the heating curve of a solid. A water bath can be used for melting points below 100 °C and an oil bath for those above 100 °C.

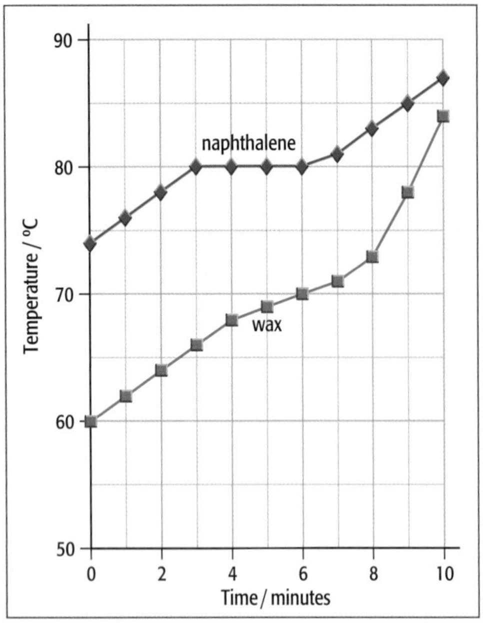

Figure 2.8 The heating curves for naphthalene (a pure substance) and wax (a mixture of substances).

substances, shows the solid wax melting over a **range** of temperatures.

It is possible to heat a liquid in the same apparatus as shown in Figure **2.7** until its boiling point is reached. Again, the temperature stays the same until all the liquid has boiled. The reverse processes can be shown if a sample of gas is allowed to cool. This produces a cooling curve (Figure **2.9**). The level portions of the curve occur where the gas condenses to a liquid, and when the liquid freezes.

These experiments show that heat energy is needed to change a solid into a liquid, or a liquid into a gas. During the reverse processes, heat energy is given out.

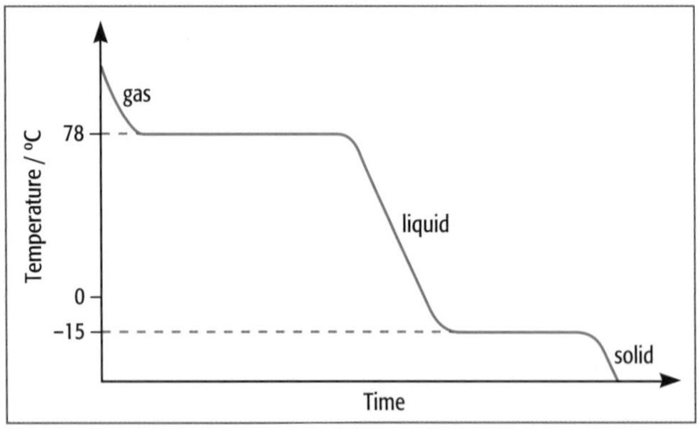

Figure 2.9 The cooling curve for a substance. The temperature stays constant while the gas condenses, and while the liquid freezes. A cooling mixture of ice and salt could be used to lower the temperature below 0 °C.

When a solid is melted, or a liquid is boiled, the temperature stays constant until the process is complete. The same is true in reverse when a gas condenses or a liquid freezes.

Types of mixture

Our world is very complex, owing to the vast range of pure substances available, and to the variety of ways in which these pure substances can mix with each other. In everyday life we do not 'handle' **pure** substances very often. The air we breathe is not a single, pure substance – and we could not live in it if it were! Water would be rather tasteless if we drank it pure (distilled).

Each **mixture** must be made from at least two parts, which may be solid, liquid or gas. There are a number of different ways in which the three states can be combined. In some, the states are completely mixed to become one single state or phase – 'you cannot see the join'. Technically, the term **solution** is used for this type of mixture.

Solid salt dissolves in liquid water to produce a liquid mixture – a salt solution (Figure **2.10**). In general terms, the solid that dissolves in the liquid is called the **solute**. The liquid in which the solid dissolves is called the **solvent**. In other types of mixture, the states remain separate. One phase is broken up into small particles, droplets, or bubbles, within the main phase. Perhaps the most obvious example of this type of mixture is a **suspension** of fine particles of a solid in a liquid, such as we often get after a precipitation reaction.

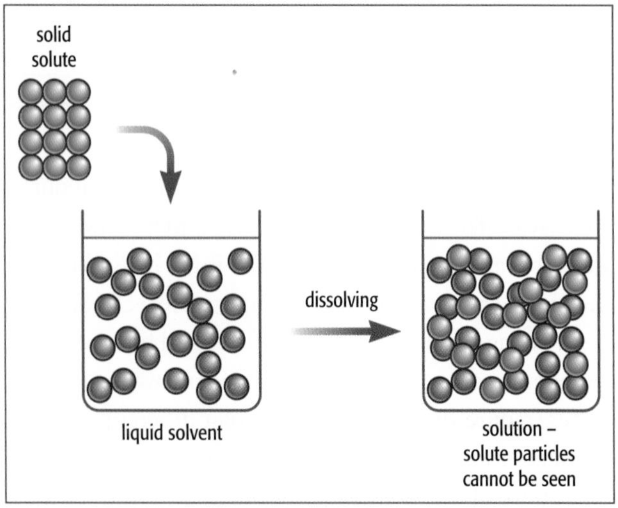

Figure 2.10 When a solute dissolves in a solvent, the solute particles are completely dispersed in the liquid.

Solutions

There are various ways in which substances in different states can combine. Perhaps the most important idea here is that of one substance dissolving in another – the idea of a **solution**. We most often think of a solution as being made of a solid dissolved in a liquid. Two-thirds of the Earth's surface is covered by a solution of various salts in water. The salts are totally dispersed in the water and cannot be seen. However, other substances that are not normally solid are dissolved in seawater. For example, the dissolved gases, oxygen and carbon dioxide, are important for life to exist in the oceans.

Less obvious perhaps, but quite common, are solutions of one liquid in another. Alcohol mixes (dissolves) completely with water. Beer, wine and whisky do not separate out into layers of alcohol and water (even when the alcohol content is quite high). Alcohol and water are completely **miscible**: they make a solution.

Alloys are similar mixtures of metals, though we do not usually call them solutions. They are made by mixing the liquid metals together (dissolving one metal in the other) before solidifying the alloy.

Key ideas so far

- There are three states of matter – solid, liquid and gas.
- There are specifically named processes involved in moving from one physical state to another.
- Energy is required to move from the solid state to a liquid, and then to a gas.
- Changes in physical state can be brought about by a change in temperature and/or pressure.
- The melting and/or boiling point of a substance can be used to assess its purity.
- A pure substance will melt or boil precisely at a particular temperature.
- The presence of an impurity raises the boiling point and lowers the melting point.
- Soluble solids can be dissolved in a liquid solvent. The commonest solvent is water.
- Insoluble solids do not dissolve but they can form suspensions in a liquid.

? Quick-check questions

1 Give the names for the following physical changes:
  a liquid to solid
  b liquid to gas at a precise temperature
  c gas to liquid
  d solid to gas directly
2 What effect does the presence of an impurity have on the freezing point of a liquid?
3 Sketch a cooling curve for water from 80 °C to −20 °C, noting what is taking place in the different regions of the graph.
4 What do you understand by the word **volatile** when used in chemistry?
5 Put these three liquids in order of **volatility**, with the most volatile first: water (b.p. 100 °C), ethanoic acid (b.p. 128 °C), ethanol (b.p. 78 °C).

2.2 Separating and purifying substances

To make sense of the material world around us, we need methods for physically separating the many and varied mixtures that we come across. Being able to purify and identify the many substances present in these mixtures not only satisfies our curiosity but is crucial to our well-being and health. A range of physical techniques are available to make the necessary separations (Table **2.3**, overleaf). They all depend in some way on a difference in the physical properties of the substances in the mixture.

The most useful separation method for a particular mixture depends on:

- the type of mixture, and
- which substance in the mixture we are most interested in.

Separating insoluble solids from liquids

In some ways these are the easiest mixtures to separate. Quite often, just leaving a suspension of a solid in a liquid to stand achieves a separation – especially if the particles of solid are large enough. Once the solid has

Mixture	Method of separation
solid + solid (powdered mixture)	use some difference in properties, e.g. density, solubility, sublimation, magnetism
suspension of solid in liquid	filtration or centrifugation
liquid + liquid (immiscible)	use a separating funnel or decantation
solution of solid in liquid	to obtain solid: use evaporation (crystallisation) to obtain liquid: use distillation
two (or more) liquids mixed together (miscible)	fractional distillation
solution of two (or more) solids in a liquid	chromatography

Table 2.3 Separating different types of mixture.

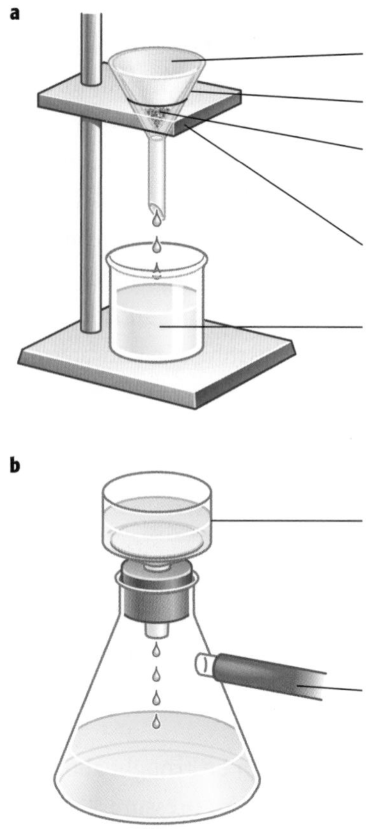

Figure 2.11 Filtration separates an insoluble solid from a liquid.

settled to the bottom, the liquid can be carefully poured off (this is called **decanting**).

A more generally useful method for separating solids from liquids is **filtration** (Figure **2.11a**). Here the insoluble material is collected as a **residue** on filter paper. Filtration is useful because both phases can be obtained in one process. The liquid phase is collected as the **filtrate**. The process can be speeded up by using a vacuum pump to 'suck' the liquid through the filter paper in a Buchner funnel and flask (Figure **2.11b**). Various large-scale filtration methods are used in industry. Perhaps the most useful of these are the filter beds used to treat water for household use.

Another method of separating an insoluble solid from a liquid is **centrifugation** where the mixture is spun at high speed in a centrifuge. This causes the solid to be deposited at the bottom of the centrifuge tube. The liquid can be carefully decanted off.

Separating immiscible liquids

Mixtures of two **immiscible** liquids can be separated if the mixture is placed in a separating funnel and allowed to stand. The liquids separate into different layers. The lower, denser layer is then 'tapped' off at the bottom (Figure **2.12**). This type of separation is useful in industry. For example, at the base of the blast furnace the molten slag forms a separate layer on top of the liquid iron. The two can then be 'tapped' off separately.

Separating mixtures of solids

The separation of a solid from a mixture of solids depends largely on the particular substance being purified. Some suitable difference in physical properties needs to be found. Usually it helps if the mixture is ground to a powder before any separation is attempted.

Separations based on differences in density

'Panning' for gold is still carried out in the search for new deposits. In Amazonia, river-beds are mechanically sifted ('vacuum-cleaned') to collect gold dust. These methods depend on the gold dust being denser than the other substances in the river sediment. This type of method is also used in purifying the ores of zinc and copper, although in these cases the metals are less dense than the ores and so float on the surface.

Separations based on magnetic properties

Magnetic iron ore can be separated from other material in the crushed ore by using an electromagnet. In the Amazonian gold diggings, magnets are used to clean away iron-containing, red-brown dust from

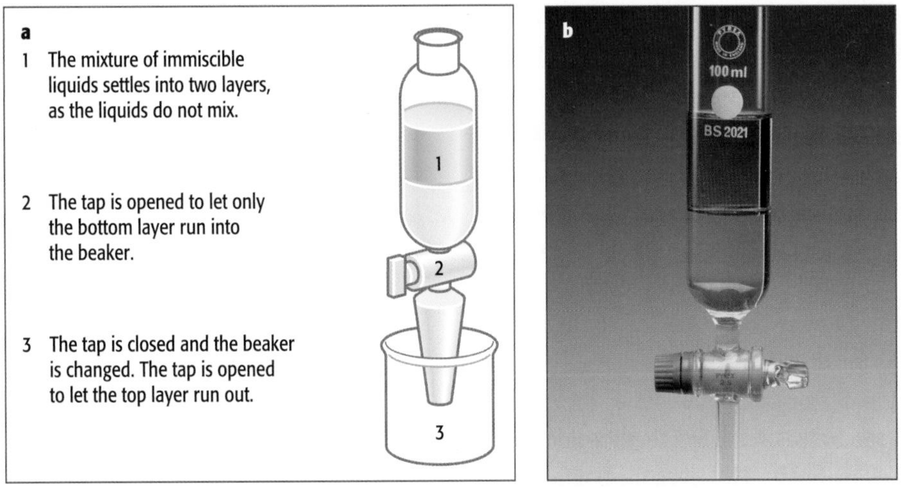

Figure 2.12 **a** A separating funnel can be used to separate two immiscible liquids. **b** Oil and water in a separating funnel.

the powdered gold. In the environmentally and economically important processes of recycling metals, iron objects can be picked out from other scrap metal using electromagnets.

Separations based on differences in solubility

One very useful way of separating a soluble substance from a solid mixture is as follows. The mixture is first ground to a powder. A suitable liquid solvent is added. The solvent must dissolve one of the solid substances present, but not the others. The solvent is often water, but other liquids can be useful. The mixture in the solvent is then warmed and stirred. Care must be taken at the warming stage when using solvents other than water. The warm mixture is then filtered (Figure **2.11**). This gives the insoluble substances as a residue on the filter paper, which can be dried. The soluble substance is in the liquid filtrate. Dry crystals can be obtained by evaporation and **crystallisation** (Figure 2.13).

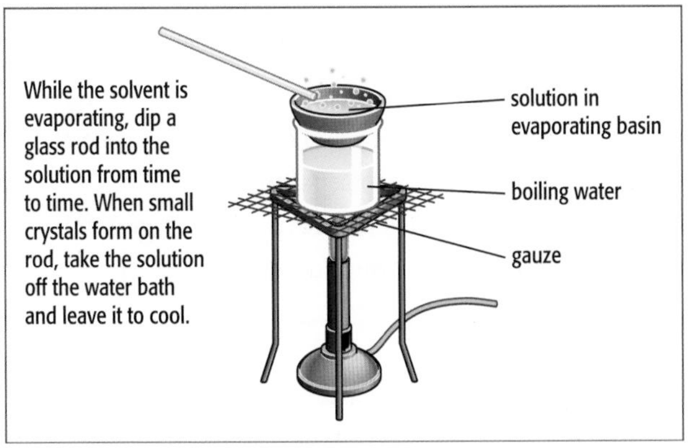

Figure 2.13 An evaporation method. This method should not be used if the solvent is flammable. Instead, use an electrical heating element and an oil or water bath.

Separations based on sublimation

A solid that sublimes can be separated from others using this property (Figure **2.14**).

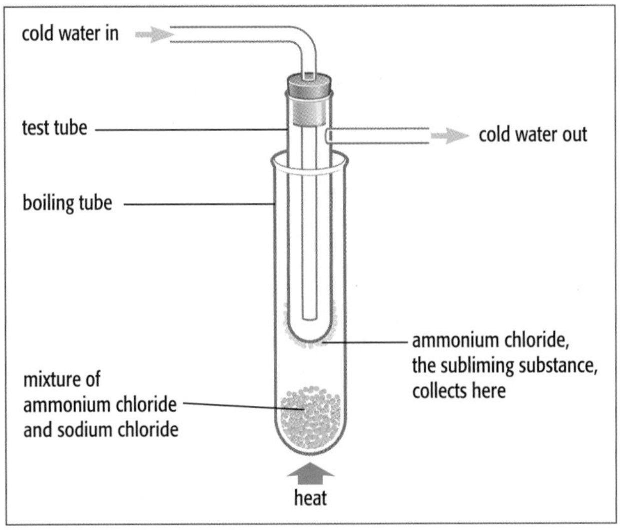

Figure 2.14 Ammonium chloride can be separated from a mixture because it sublimes. The crystals condense on the cooled surface.

Separating solutions

The separation of this type of mixture is often slightly more complicated because there is no physical separation of the phases in the original mixture. The methods of separation usually depend on solubility properties or on differences in boiling point (or volatility).

Separating a solid from solution in a liquid can be carried out by evaporation or crystallisation. Evaporation gives only a powder, but crystallisation can result in proper crystals. Both processes begin by evaporating away the liquid but, when crystals are needed, evaporation is stopped when the solution has been concentrated enough.

Figure 2.13 shows how this can be judged and done safely. The concentrated solution is allowed to cool slowly. The crystals formed can then be filtered off and dried.

Separating a liquid from a solution is usually carried out by **distillation** (Figure **2.15**). The boiling point of the liquid is usually very much lower than that of the dissolved solid. The liquid is more volatile than the dissolved solid and can easily be evaporated off in a distillation flask. It is condensed by passing it down a water-cooled condenser, and then collected as the **distillate**.

Separating the liquids from a mixture of two (or more) miscible liquids is again based on the fact that the liquids will have different boiling points. However, the boiling points are closer together than for a solid-in-liquid solution and **fractional distillation** must be used (Figure **2.16**). In fractional distillation the most volatile liquid in the mixture distils over first, the least volatile liquid boils over last.

For example, ethanol boils at 78 °C whereas water boils at 100 °C. When the mixture is heated, ethanol and water vapours enter the **fractionating column**. Glass beads in the column provide a large surface area for condensation (Figure **2.16b**). Evaporation and condensation take place many times as the vapours rise up the column. Ethanol passes through the condenser first as the temperature of the column is raised above its boiling point. Water condenses in the column and flows back into the flask because the temperature of the column is below its boiling point of 100 °C.

The temperature on the thermometer stays at 78 °C until all the ethanol has distilled over. Only then does the temperature on the thermometer rise to 100 °C and the water distil over. By watching the temperature carefully, the two liquids (**fractions**) can be collected separately.

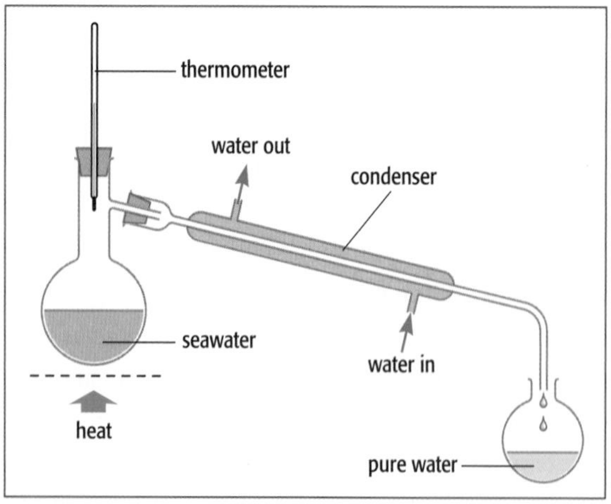

Figure 2.15 The distillation of seawater.

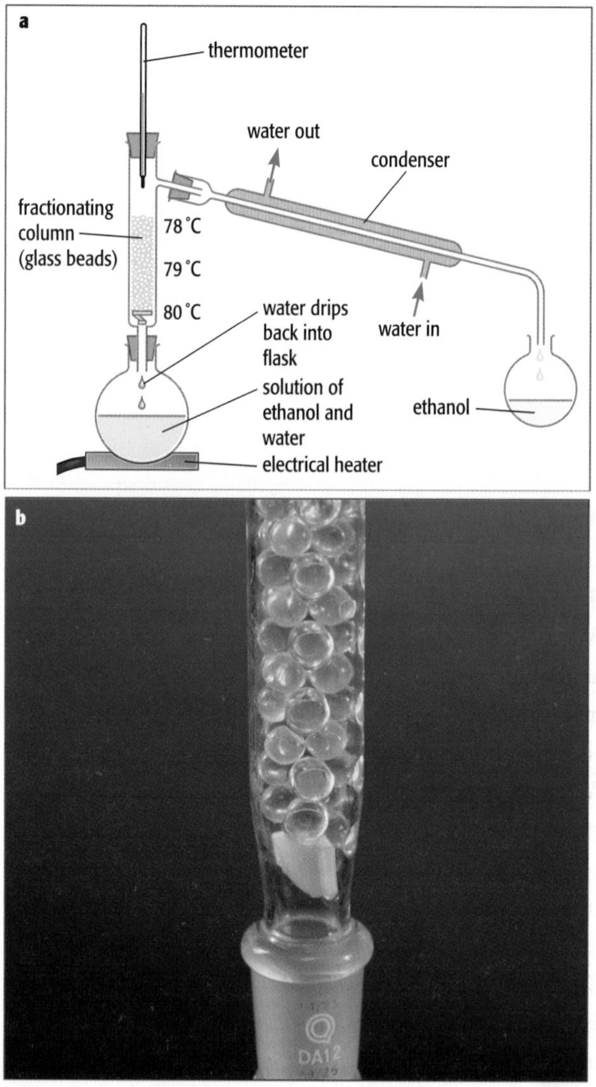

Figure 2.16 **a** Separating a mixture of ethanol (alcohol) and water by fractional distillation. **b** A close up of the glass beads in the column.

Fractional distillation is used to separate any solution containing liquids with different boiling points. The liquid in the mixture with the lowest boiling point (the most volatile) distils over first. The final liquid to distil over is the one with the highest boiling point (the least volatile). Fractional distillation can be adapted as a continuous process and is used industrially to separate:

- the various fractions from crude oil (page **318**),
- the different gases from liquid air (page **8**).

Exam tip

In fractional distillation remember that it is the liquid with the lowest boiling point that distils over first.

Separating two or more dissolved solids in solution can be carried out by **chromatography**. There are several types of chromatography, but they all follow the same basic principles. Paper chromatography is probably the simplest form to set up and is very useful if we want to analyse the substances present in a solution. For example, it can tell us whether a solution has become contaminated. This can be very important, because contamination of food or drinking water, for instance, may be dangerous to our health.

A drop of concentrated solution is usually placed on a **pencil** line near the bottom edge of a strip of chromatography paper. The paper is then dipped in the solvent. The level of the solvent must start below the sample. Figure **2.17** shows the process in action.

Many different solvents are used in chromatography. Water and organic solvents (carbon-containing solvents) such as ethanol, ethanoic acid solution and propanone are common. Organic solvents are useful because they dissolve many substances which are insoluble in water. When an organic solvent is used, the process is carried out in a tank with a lid to stop the solvent evaporating.

S

The substances separate according to their solubility in the solvent. As the solvent moves up the paper, the substances are carried with it and begin to separate. The substance that is most soluble moves fastest up the paper. An insoluble substance would remain at the origin. The run is stopped just before the **solvent front** reaches the top of the paper.

The distance moved by a particular spot is measured and related to the position of the solvent front. The ratio of these distances is called the ***R***R_f **value**. This value is used to identify the substance:

$$R_f = \frac{\text{distance moved by the substance}}{\text{distance moved by the solvent front}}$$

Originally, paper chromatography was used to separate solutions of coloured substances (dyes and pigments) since they could be seen as they moved up the paper. However, the usefulness of chromatography has been greatly increased by the use of **locating agents** (Figure **2.18**, overleaf). These mean that the method can also be used for separating substances that are **not** coloured. The paper is treated with locating agent after the chromatography run. The agent reacts with the samples to produce coloured spots.

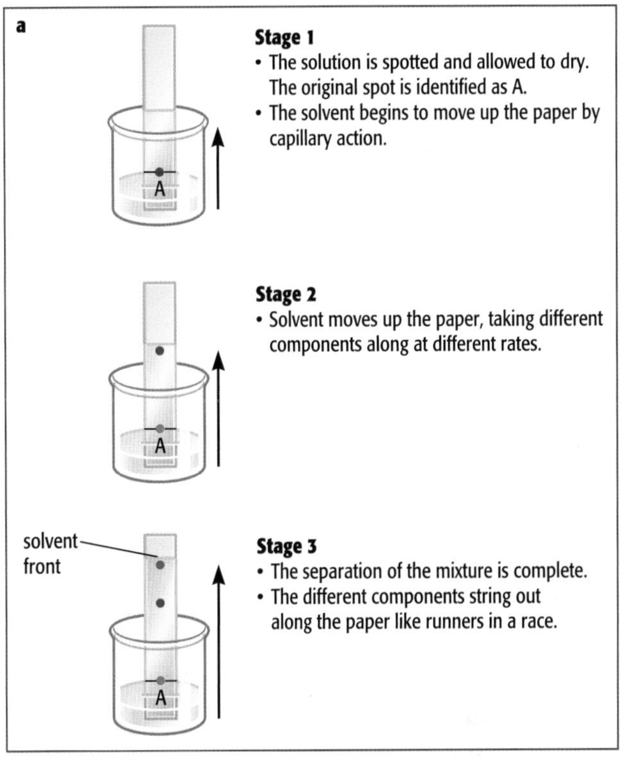

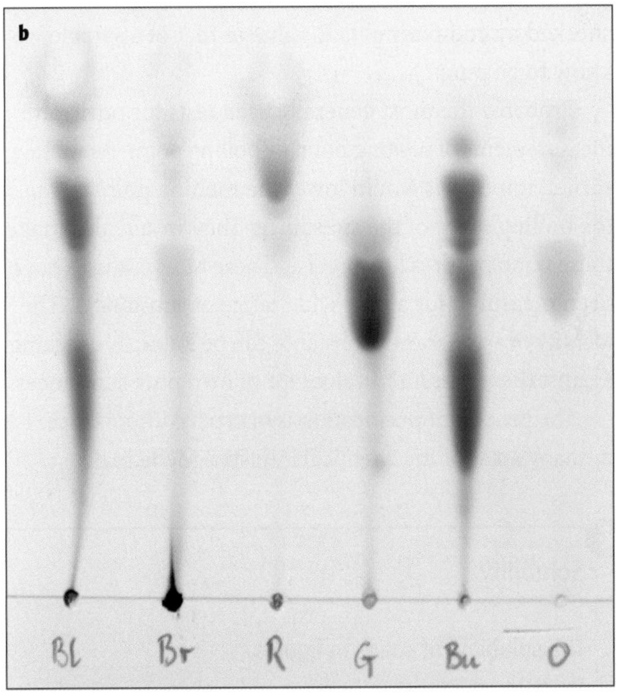

Figure 2.17 **a** Various stages during paper chromatography. The sample is separated as it moves up the paper. **b** A paper chromatogram.

S

Chromatography has proved very useful in the analysis of biologically important molecules such as sugars, amino acids and nucleotide bases. In fact, molecules such as amino acids can be 'seen' if the paper **chromatogram** is viewed under ultraviolet light.

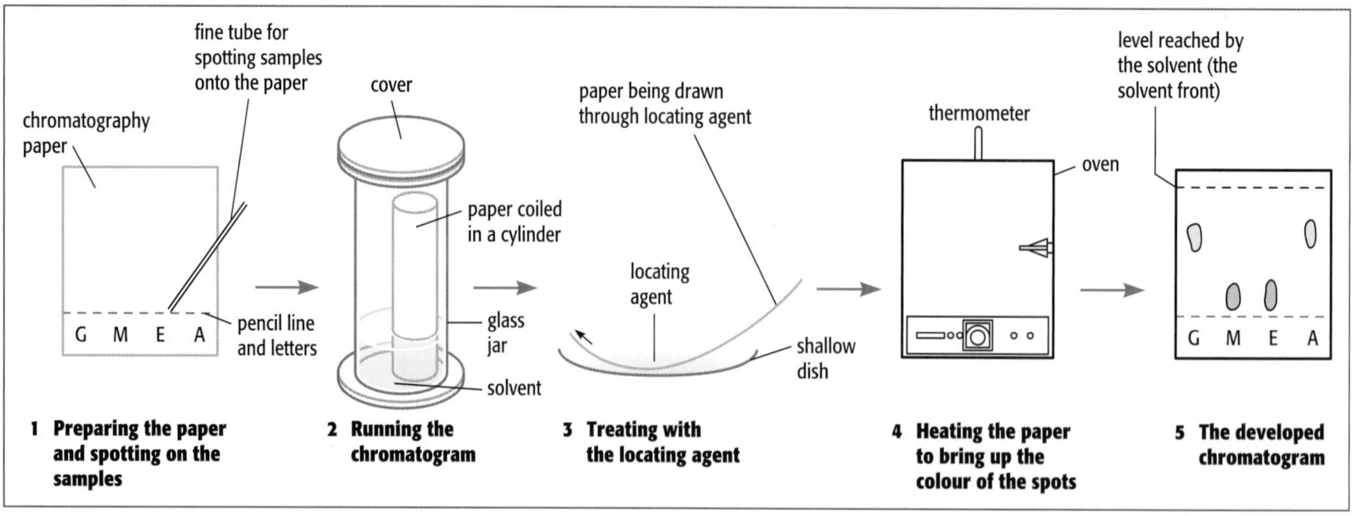

Figure 2.18 Chromatography using a locating agent to detect the spots on the paper. Alternatively, the locating agent can be sprayed on the paper.

The purity and identity of substances

Paper chromatography is one test that can be used to check for the **purity** of a substance. If the sample is pure, it should only give **one** spot when run in several different solvents. The **identity** of the sample can also be checked by comparing its R_f value to that of a sample we know to be pure.

Probably the most generally used tests for purity are measurements of melting point or boiling point. As we saw earlier, impurities would lower the melting point or raise the boiling point of the substance. They would also make these temperatures less precise. These temperatures have been measured for a very wide range of substances. The identity of an unknown substance can be found by checking against these measured values for known pure substances.

The process of purification is of crucial importance in many areas of the chemical industry. Medicinal **drugs** (pharmaceuticals) must be of the highest possible purity. Any contaminating substances, even in very small amounts, may have harmful side-effects. Coloured dyes (food colourings) are added to food and drinks to improve their appearance. The colourings added need to be carefully controlled. In Europe the permitted colourings are listed as E100 to E180. Many dyes that were once added are now banned. Even those which are permitted may still cause problems for some people. The yellow colouring tartrazine (E102) is found in many drinks, sauces, sweets and snacks. To most people it is harmless, but in some children it appears to cause hyperactivity and allergic reactions, for example asthma. Even where there is overall government regulation, individuals need to be aware of how particular foods affect them.

E

Solubility

The solubility of solids in liquids

Probably the most important and common examples of mixtures are solutions of solids in liquids.

> A **solution** is made up of two parts:
> - the solid that dissolves is known as the **solute**
> - the liquid in which it dissolves is called the **solvent**.

Water is the commonest solvent in use, but other liquids are also important. These other solvents are generally organic liquids such as ethanol, propanone and trichloroethane. These organic solvents are important because they will often dissolve substances that do not dissolve in water. If a substance dissolves in a solvent, it is said to be **soluble**: if it does not dissolve, it is **insoluble**.

If we try to dissolve a substance such as copper(II) sulfate in a fixed volume of water, the solution becomes more concentrated as we add more solid. A **concentrated** solution contains a high proportion of solute; a **dilute** solution contains a small proportion of solute. The **concentration** of a solution is the mass of solute dissolved in a particular volume of solvent, usually 1 dm^3 (1 litre). Suppose we wanted a solution of copper(II) sulfate in water with a known concentration of 10 g/dm^3, this is what we would do:

1 Take a graduated flask and approximately half-fill it with distilled water, the solvent.
2 Weigh out 10.00 g of copper(II) sulfate, the solute.
3 Carefully add the solute to the solvent in the flask.
4 Gently shake the flask to dissolve all the solute.
5 Add more distilled water to make up the volume of the solution to exactly the 1.00 dm^3 mark on the neck of the graduated flask.

If we keep adding more solid, a point is reached where no more will dissolve at that temperature. This is a **saturated solution**. To get more solid to dissolve, the temperature must be increased. The concentration of solute in a saturated solution is the **solubility** of the solute at that temperature. Solubility is measured as the mass of solute that will saturate 100 g of water at a particular temperature.

Solubility curves

Curves showing how the solubility of a solid changes with temperature are known as **solubility curves**. The curves in Figure **2.19** show how the solubilities of several salts change with temperature. You can see that the solubility of most solids increases with temperature. The increase for sodium chloride is very small. The process of crystallisation depends on these observations. When a saturated solution is cooled, it can hold less solute at the lower temperature, and some solute crystallises out.

The solubility of gases in liquids

Unlike most solids, gases become less soluble in water as the temperature rises (Figure **2.20**). The solubility of gases from the air in water is quite small, but the amount of dissolved oxygen is enough to support fish and other aquatic life. Interestingly, oxygen is more soluble in water than nitrogen is. So when air is dissolved in water, the proportions of the two gases become 61% nitrogen and 37% oxygen. There is an enrichment in life-supporting oxygen compared to air (79% nitrogen and 20% oxygen).

The solubility of gases increases with pressure. Sparkling drinks contain carbon dioxide dissolved under pressure. They 'fizz' when the pressure is

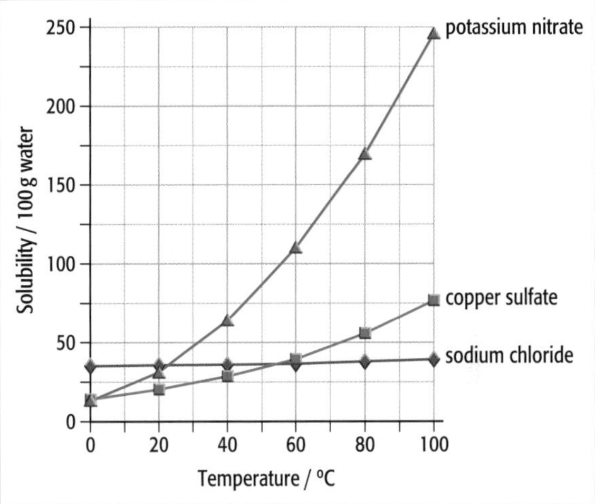

Figure 2.19 Solubility curves for three solids in water.

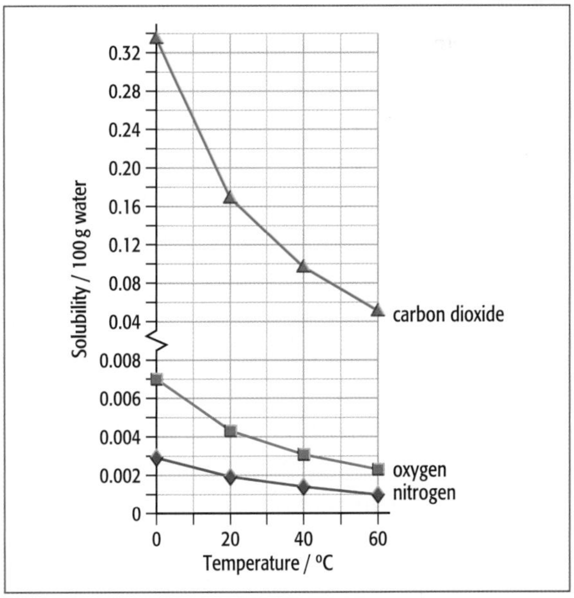

Figure 2.20 The solubility of three gases from the air in water (solubility measured in grams of gas per 100 g of water).

released by opening the container. They go 'flat' if left to stand open, even more so if left to stand in a warm place.

A deep-sea diver (Figure **2.21**) may suffer the consequences of these properties of gases. A diver coming up too rapidly may suffer from the 'bends'. The pressure increases as you go deeper, and at the bottom it is several times greater than at the surface. If the diver is breathing a mixture of nitrogen and oxygen, more nitrogen dissolves in the diver's blood than at the surface. If the diver rises too quickly, the pressure falls rapidly. The nitrogen 'boils' out of the blood. The bubbles of gas collect, particularly in the joints of the legs and arms, causing pain. They can also interfere with blood flow and damage nerves. To reduce the problem, scuba tanks are often filled with helium–oxygen mixtures. Helium has a much lower solubility in blood than nitrogen does.

You will notice in Figure **2.20** that carbon dioxide is more soluble than either nitrogen or oxygen. This is because it reacts with water to produce carbonic acid. The world is not chemically static. Substances are not only **mixing** with each other, but also chemically **reacting**. This produces a world that is continuously changing. To gain a better understanding of this, we need to look more deeply into the 'make-up' of chemical substances.

Figure 2.21 Deep-sea divers can suffer from the 'bends' if they surface too quickly.

Key ideas so far

- Substances can be purified using certain practical techniques such as filtration, evaporation and crystallisation, distillation and chromatography.
- These separation techniques depend on differences in physical properties between substances; properties such as boiling point, solubility, density and ability to undergo sublimation can be the basis of a separation.
- For most solids the solubility in water increases with temperature.
- Chromatography can be used to separate colourless substances if a locating agent is used once the chromatography is finished.

Quick-check questions

1 How would you separate the following?
   - **a** water from seawater
   - **b** ethanol from an ethanol/water mixture
   - **c** sugar crystals from a sugar solution

2 What do you understand by the term **sublimation**?

3 What type of substance was chromatography originally designed to separate?

4 How can we now expand the use of chromatography to separate colourless substances?

5 Define the term $\boldsymbol{R_f}$ **value** in connection with chromatography.

2.3 Atoms and molecules

Elements and compounds

Earlier in this chapter you were introduced to pure substances, and to ways of purifying and identifying them. But what are 'pure substances'?

> There are two types of pure substance: elements and compounds.
> - **Elements** are substances that cannot be chemically broken down into simpler substances.
> - **Compounds** are pure substances made from two, or more, elements chemically combined together.

Figure **2.22** summarises what we now know about matter in simple terms. Elements are the 'building blocks' from which the Universe is constructed. There are over a hundred known elements, but the vast majority of the Universe consists of just two. Hydrogen (92%) and helium (7%) make up most of the mass of the Universe, with all the other elements contributing only 1% to the total. The concentration, or 'coming together', of certain of these elements to make the Earth is of great interest and significance. There are 94 elements found naturally on Earth altogether, but eight account for more than 98% of the mass of the Earth's crust. Two elements, silicon and oxygen, which are bound together in silicate rocks, make up almost three-quarters of the crust. Only certain of the elements are able to form the complex compounds that are found in living things. For example, the human body contains 65% oxygen, 18% carbon, 10% hydrogen, 3% nitrogen, 2% calcium and 2% of other elements.

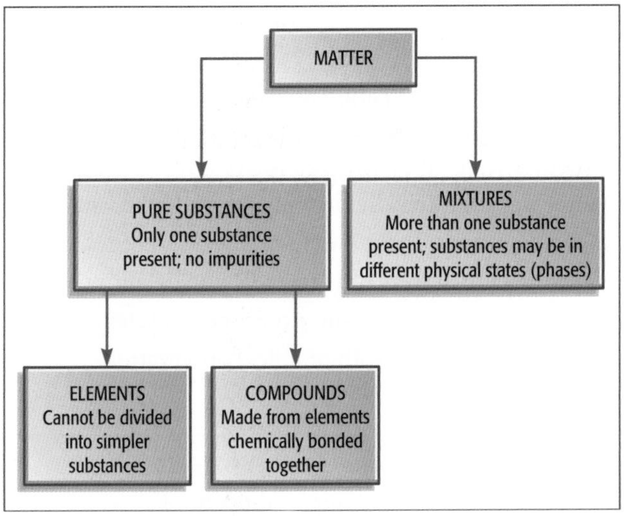

Figure 2.22 Schematic representation of the different types of matter, including elements and compounds.

Chemical reactions and physical changes

Substances can mix in a variety of ways, and they can also react chemically with each other. In a reaction, one substance can be transformed (changed) into another. Copper(II) carbonate is a green solid, but on heating it is changed into a black powder (Figure **2.23**). Closer investigation shows that the gas carbon dioxide is also produced. This type of chemical reaction, where a compound breaks down to form two or more substances, is known as **decomposition**.

Decomposition can also be brought about by electricity. Some substances, although they do not conduct electricity when solid, **do** conduct when they are melted or in solution. In the process of conduction, they are broken down into simpler substances. Thus, lead(II) bromide, which is a white powder, can be melted. When a current is passed through molten lead(II) bromide, a silver-grey metal (lead) and a brown vapour (bromine) are formed. Neither of these products can be split into any simpler substances.

The opposite type of reaction, where the substance is formed by the combination of two or more other substances, is known as **synthesis**. For example, if a piece of burning magnesium is plunged into a gas jar of oxygen, the intensity (brightness) of the brilliant white flame increases.

Figure 2.23 Heating copper carbonate.

Figure 2.24 Burning magnesium produces a brilliant white flame.

When a mixture forms ...	When a compound forms ...
the substances are simply mixed together; no reaction takes place	the substances chemically react together to form a new compound
the composition of the mixture can be varied	the composition of the new compound is always the same
the properties of the substances present remain the same	the properties of the new compound are very different from those of the elements in it
the substances in the mixture can be separated by physical methods such as filtration, distillation or magnetic attraction	the compound cannot easily be separated into its elements

Table 2.4 The differences between mixtures and pure compounds.

When the reaction has burnt out, a white ash remains (Figure **2.24**). The ash has totally different properties from the original silver-grey metal strip and colourless gas we started with. A new compound, magnesium oxide, has been formed from magnesium and oxygen.

Although many other reactions are not as spectacular as this, the burning of magnesium shows the general features of chemical reactions.

In a **chemical reaction**:

- new chemical substance(s) are formed
- usually the process is not easily reversed
- energy is often given out.

These characteristics of a chemical reaction contrast with those of a simple physical change such as melting or dissolving. In a **physical change** the substances involved do not change identity. They can be easily returned to their original form by some physical process such as cooling or evaporation. Sugar dissolves in water, but we can get the solid sugar back by evaporating off the water.

Another synthesis reaction takes place between powdered iron and sulfur. The two solids are finely ground and well mixed. The mixture is heated with a Bunsen burner. The reaction mixture continues to glow after the Bunsen burner is removed. Heat energy is given out. There has been a reaction and we are left with a black non-magnetic solid, iron(II) sulfide, which cannot easily be changed back to iron and sulfur. This example also illustrates some important differences between a mixture (in this case the powders of iron and sulfur) and a compound (in this case the final product of the reaction). The general differences between making a mixture of substances and forming a new compound are shown in Table **2.4**.

Atomic theory

Elements and compounds mix and react to produce the world around us. They produce massive objects such as the 'gas giants' (the planets Jupiter and Saturn), and tiny highly structured crystals of solid sugar. How do the elements organise themselves to give this variety? How can any one element exist in the three different states of matter simply through a change in temperature?

Our modern understanding is based on the atomic theory put forward by John Dalton in 1807. His theory re-introduced the ideas of Democritus (460–370 BCE) and other Greek philosophers who suggested that all matter was infinitely divided into very small particles known as **atoms**. These ideas were not widely accepted at the time. They were only revived when Dalton developed them further and experimental science was able to back them up with practical observation.

Dalton suggested that:

- a pure element is composed of atoms
- the atoms of each element are different in size and mass

- atoms are the smallest particles that take part in a chemical reaction
- atoms of different elements can combine to make **molecules** of a compound.

Certain parts of the theory may need changing as a result of what we have discovered since Dalton's time. However, Dalton's theory was one of the great leaps of understanding in chemistry. It meant that we could explain many natural processes. Whereas Dalton only had theories for the existence of atoms, modern techniques (such as scanning tunnelling microscopy) can now directly reveal the presence of individual atoms. It has even been possible to create an 'atomic logo' (Figure **2.25**) by using individual atoms, and it may soon be possible to 'see' a reaction between individual atoms.

Figure 2.25 An 'atomic logo' produced by xenon atoms on a nickel surface 'seen' using scanning tunnelling microscopy.

A chemical language

Dalton suggested that each element should have its own **symbol** – a form of chemical shorthand. He could then write the formulae of compounds without writing out the name every time. Our modern system uses letters taken from the name of the element. This is an international code. Some elements have been known for a long time and their symbol is taken from their Latin name.

The symbol for an element consists of one or two letters. Where the names of several elements begin with the same letter, the second letter of the name is usually included in lower case (Table **2.5**). As more elements were discovered, they were named after a wider range of people, cities, countries and even particular universities. We shall see in Chapter **3** how useful it is to be able to use symbols, and how they can be combined to show the formulae of complex chemical compounds. A full list of the elements and their symbols is found in the Periodic Table (see the Appendix).

Element	Latin name	Symbol
hydrogen		H
helium		He
carbon		C
calcium		Ca
copper	cuprum	Cu
chlorine		Cl
nitrogen		N
sodium	natrium	Na
phosphorus		P
potassium	kalium	K
iron	ferrum	Fe
lead	plumbum	Pb
silver	argentum	Ag
gold	aurum	Au

Table 2.5 The symbols of some chemical elements.

The kinetic theory of matter

The idea that all substances consist of very small particles begins to explain the structure of the three different states of matter. The kinetic theory of matter describes these states, and the changes between them, in terms of the movement of particles.

The main points of the **kinetic theory** are:

- all matter is made up of very small particles (different substances contain different types of particles – such as atoms or molecules)
- the particles are moving all the time (the higher the temperature, the higher the average energy of the particles)
- the freedom of movement and the arrangement of the particles is different for the three states of matter (Figure **2.26**, overleaf).

Figure **2.26** is a summary of the organisation of the particles in the three states of matter, and helps to explain their different overall physical properties.

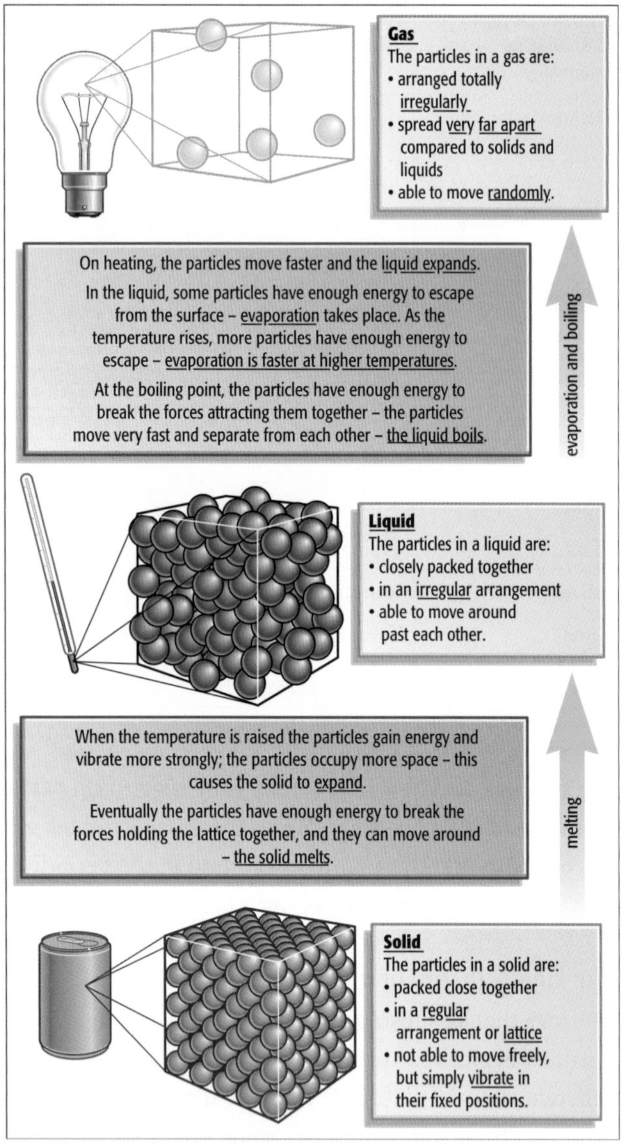

Figure 2.26 Applying the kinetic theory to changes in physical state.

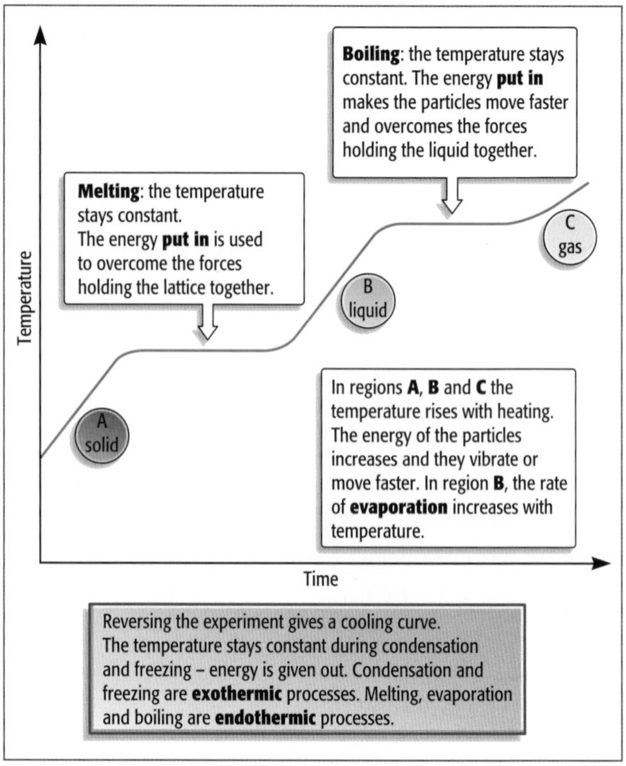

Figure 2.27 The energy changes taking place during heating and cooling.

The highly structured, ordered microscopic arrangements (**lattices**) in solids can produce the regular crystal structures seen in this state. The ability of the particles to move in the liquid and gas phases produces their fluid properties. The particles are very widely separated in a gas, but are close together in a liquid or solid. The space between the particles can be called the **intermolecular space** (IMS). In a gas, the intermolecular space is large and can be reduced by increasing the external pressure – gases are compressible. In liquids, this space is very much smaller – liquids are not very compressible.

The way the particles in the three states are arranged also helps to explain the temperature changes when a substance is heated or cooled. Figure **2.27** summarises the energy changes taking place at the different stages of a heating-curve or cooling-curve experiment.

Exam tip

It's important to realise that even in a liquid the particles are still close together, although they can move around and past each other.

E

We are aware of energy changes in our everyday life. Sweating helps to cool the body. Sweat is a liquid and energy is needed before it can evaporate. The energy comes from the heat of the body, and so the body cools down. Another example is refrigeration. The invention of efficient ice-making and refrigeration was a major breakthrough in the transportation and storage of food. Refrigerators use the energy changes involved in changing state to provide a cold environment (see Figures **2.27** and **2.28**).

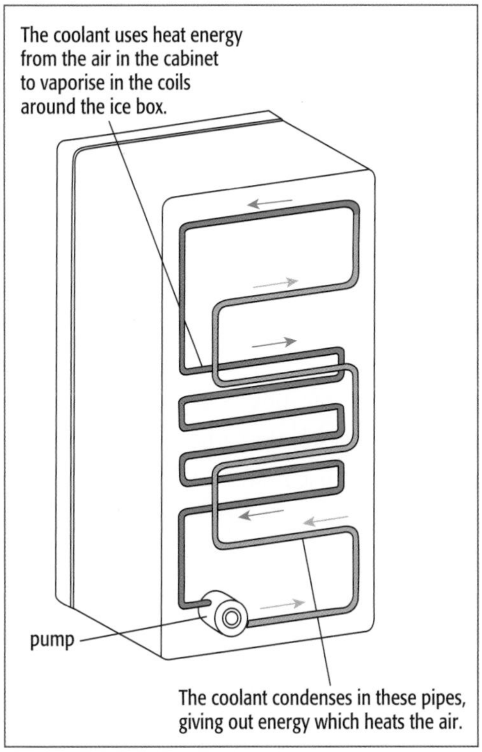

Figure 2.28 The cooling system of a refrigerator.

1. The refrigerator is controlled by a thermostat. When it warms up inside, the pump is switched on.
2. The pump compresses the coolant, which is a gas, so that it condenses to a liquid. This gives out energy, so the liquid gets hot.
3. The liquid is cooled down by the air outside as it passes through fins at the back of the refrigerator.
4. The liquid passes through the refrigerator, where it warms up and becomes a gas again. This takes in energy, so the inside of the refrigerator cools down.

Diffusion in fluids

The idea that fluids are made up of moving particles helps us to explain processes involving **diffusion**.

Dissolving

A potassium manganate(VII) crystal is placed at the bottom of a dish of water. It is then left to stand. At first the water around the crystal becomes purple as the solid dissolves (Figure **2.29**). Particles move off the surface of the crystal into the water. Eventually the crystal dissolves completely and the whole solution becomes purple. The particles from the solid become evenly spread through the water.

Figure 2.29 The diffusion of potassium manganate(VII) in water as it dissolves.

Whether a solid begins to break up like this in a liquid depends on the particular solid and liquid involved. But the spreading of the solute particles throughout the liquid is an example of diffusion. Diffusion in solution is also important when the solute is a gas. This is especially important in breathing! Diffusion contributes to the movement of oxygen from the lungs to the blood, and of carbon dioxide from the blood to the lungs.

- Diffusion involves the movement of particles from a region of higher concentration towards a region of lower concentration. Eventually the particles are evenly spread – their concentration is the same throughout.
- Diffusion does not take place in solids.
- Diffusion in liquids is much slower than in gases.

The diffusion of gases

A few drops of liquid bromine are put into a gas jar and the lid is replaced. After a short time the jar becomes full of brown gas. Bromine vaporises easily and its gas will completely fill the container (Figure **2.30**, overleaf). Gases diffuse to fill all the space available to them. Diffusion is important for our 'sensing' of the world around us. It is the way smells reach us, whether they are pleasant or harmful.

Exam tip

The key idea about diffusion is the idea of particles spreading to fill the space available to the molecules.

Figure 2.30 Bromine vapour diffuses (spreads) throughout the container to fill all the space.

Not all gases diffuse at the same rate. This is shown by the experiment in Figure 2.31. The ammonia and hydrochloric acid fumes react when they meet, producing a white 'smoke-ring' of ammonium chloride. The fact that the ring is not formed half-way along the tube shows that ammonia, the lighter molecule of the two, diffuses faster.

The speeds of gas atoms or molecules are high. We are being bombarded constantly by nitrogen and oxygen molecules in the air which are travelling at about 500 m/s (1800 km/h). However, these particles collide very frequently with other particles in the air (many millions of collisions per second), so their path is not particularly direct! These very frequent collisions slow down the overall rate of diffusion from one place to another.

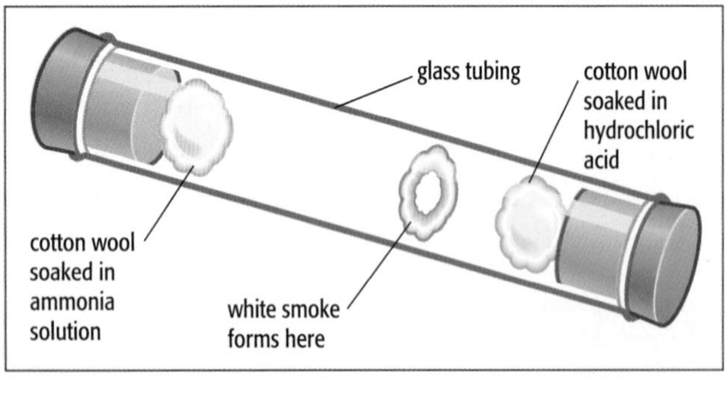

Figure 2.31 Ammonia and hydrochloric acid fumes diffuse at different rates.

Three important points derived from kinetic theory are relevant here:

- Heavier particles move more slowly than lighter particles at the same temperature; larger molecules diffuse more slowly than smaller ones.
- The pressure of a gas is the result of collisions of the fast-moving particles with the walls of the container.
- The average speed of the particles increases with an increase in temperature.

The absolute scale of temperature

The behaviour of gases as explained by kinetic theory led Lord Kelvin to define a new temperature scale in 1850.

If the temperature of a gas in a container of fixed volume is raised, the speed and momentum of the particles will increase. This means that the particles will collide with the walls more frequently and with more force, so the pressure of the gas will increase. If a similar experiment is done in which the pressure of the gas is kept constant, then the gas expands as its temperature is increased. This is because the increasing temperature gives the gas particles more energy so they move faster and collide more frequently and generally occupy more space. Hot-air balloons work on this principle. When the burner is on, the air in the balloon expands and so is less dense than the surrounding air; the balloon rises. When the burner is stopped, the air contracts and the density increases; the balloon falls. The balloon rises and falls as the temperature of the gas in the balloon rises and falls.

If you plot a graph of volume against temperature for a particular gas, you will get a straight line. This shows that the volume is proportional to the temperature. However, the volume of the gas is not zero at 0 °C. In fact, the volume of the gas reaches zero at −273 °C.

A graph of pressure against temperature for a gas shows a similar straight line, as the pressure of a gas is proportional to the temperature and is zero at −273 °C. Since gas pressure is produced by the particles colliding with the container walls, we can conclude that at −273 °C the particles are not moving. At this temperature, the particles have no energy. This temperature is known as **absolute zero**. It is impossible to get colder than absolute zero. The **absolute temperature** scale (or Kelvin scale – named after Lord Kelvin) starts at 0 K (zero kelvin). On this new scale, the freezing point of water is 273 K, and its boiling point is 373 K (both at atmospheric pressure). Note that the unit of temperature on the Kelvin scale is just 'kelvin'. It is **not** 'degrees kelvin'.

Atoms and molecules

The behaviour of some gaseous elements (their diffusion and pressure) shows that they are made up of molecules, not separate atoms. This is true of hydrogen (H_2), nitrogen (N_2), oxygen (O_2) and others. But, as we discussed on page 45, Dalton had originally introduced the idea of molecules to explain the particles making up **compounds** such as water, carbon dioxide and methane. Molecules of these compounds consist of atoms of **different elements** chemically bonded together. Water is made up of two atoms of hydrogen bonded to one atom of oxygen, giving the formula H_2O. Methane (CH_4) has one atom of carbon bonded to four atoms of hydrogen, and hydrogen chloride (HCl) has one atom of hydrogen and one atom of chlorine bonded together. Models of these are shown in Figure **2.32**.

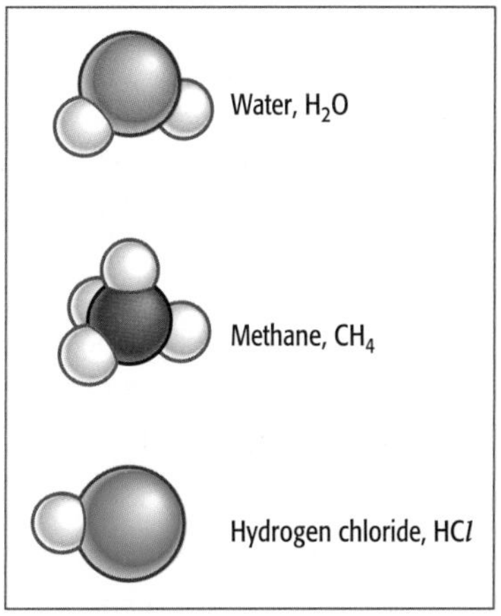

Figure 2.32 Simple compounds consisting of molecules made up of atoms of two different elements.

Key ideas so far

- In a chemical reaction new substances are made.
- Elements can chemically combine to make compounds.
- The atoms or molecules are arranged differently in the three states of matter.
- Diffusion can take place in the fluid states – the liquid or gaseous states.
- Heavier atoms or molecules diffuse more slowly than lighter ones.

Quick-check questions

1. Define an element.
2. Define a compound.
3. Summarise the differences between the three states of matter in terms of the arrangement of the particles and their movement.
4. Which gas diffuses faster, ammonia or hydrogen chloride? Briefly describe an experiment which demonstrates this difference.
5. Which gas will diffuse fastest of all?

2.4 The structure of the atom

Atomic structure

How can atoms join together to make molecules? What makes certain atoms more ready to do this? Why do hydrogen atoms pair up, but helium atoms remain single? To find answers to questions like these, we need first to consider the structure of atoms in general. Dalton thought they were solid, indivisible particles. But research since then has shown that atoms are made up of various subatomic particles. By 1932, it was clear that atoms consisted of three **subatomic particles – protons, neutrons** and **electrons**. These particles are universal – all atoms are made from them. The atom remains the smallest particle that shows the characteristics of a particular element.

Measuring the size of atoms

Modern methods such as scanning tunnelling microscopy have allowed us to 'see' individual atoms in a structure. However, atoms are amazingly small! A magnification of 100 million times is necessary to show the stacking pattern of the atoms that make up a gold bar.

A single atom is so small that it cannot be weighed on a balance. However, the mass of one atom can be compared with that of another using a **mass spectrometer**. The element carbon is chosen as the standard. The masses of atoms of all other elements are compared to the mass of a carbon atom. This gives a series of values of **relative atomic mass** for the elements. Carbon is given a relative atomic mass of exactly 12, which can be written as carbon-12. Table **2.6** gives some examples of the values obtained for other elements. It shows that carbon atoms are 12 times as heavy as hydrogen atoms, which are the lightest atoms of all. Calcium atoms are 40 times as heavy as hydrogen atoms.

Element	Atomic symbol	Relative atomic mass
carbon	C	12
hydrogen	H	1
oxygen	O	16
calcium	Ca	40
copper	Cu	64
gold	Au	197

Table 2.6 The relative atomic masses of some elements.

Subatomic particles

E

Evidence for the structure of the atom came from studying:

- the nature of rays produced in discharge tubes (for example cathode-ray tubes)
- the light given out by excited gases
- the nature of radioactivity.

J. J. Thomson (in 1897) found that cathode ray tubes (the early ancestors of television tubes) produced beams of small particles that could be deflected (bent) by an electric field (Figure **2.33**). He found that these rays were beams of negatively charged particles, which were named electrons. Using a different type of discharge tube filled with a small amount of hydrogen, Thomson also discovered a positively charged particle, the proton. Then, in 1932, Chadwick discovered a neutral particle, the neutron, by bombarding metal targets with radiation from radioactive material.

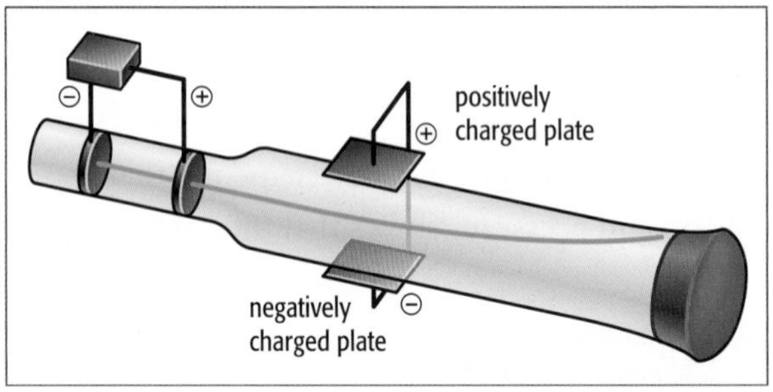

Figure 2.33 A cathode-ray tube produces a beam of particles that are deflected towards a positive plate. The beam is made up of electrons.

Dalton had suggested that atoms were solid particles. But crucial experiments carried out in Rutherford's laboratory in Manchester in 1909 showed that an atom is largely empty space. Rutherford calculated that an atom is mostly space occupied by the negatively charged electrons, surrounding a very small, positively charged **nucleus**. The nucleus is at the centre of the atom and contains almost all the mass of the atom. It is made up of the protons and neutrons.

Subatomic particle	Relative mass	Relative charge	Location in atom
proton	1	+1	in nucleus
neutron	1	0	in nucleus
electron	$\frac{1}{1840}$ (negligible)	−1	outside nucleus

Table 2.7 Properties of the subatomic particles.

To get some idea of **how** small the nucleus is in comparison to the rest of the atom, here is a simple comparison. If the atom were the size of a football stadium, the nucleus (at the centre-spot) would be the size of a pea!

Protons and neutrons have almost the same mass. Electrons have virtually no mass at all ($\frac{1}{1840}$ of the mass of a proton). The other important feature of these particles is their electric charge. Protons and electrons have equal and opposite charges, while neutrons are electrically neutral (have no charge). The characteristics of these three subatomic particles are listed in Table **2.7**.

A single atom is electrically neutral (it has no overall electric charge). This means that in any atom there must be equal numbers of protons and electrons. In this way the total positive charge on the nucleus (due to the protons) is balanced by the total negative charge of the orbiting electrons. The simplest atom of all has one proton in its nucleus. This is the hydrogen atom. It is the only atom that has no neutrons; it consists of one proton and one electron. Atoms of different elements are increasingly complex.

The next simplest atom is that of helium. This has two protons and two neutrons in the nucleus, and two orbiting electrons (Figure **2.34**).

The next, lithium, has three protons, four neutrons and three electrons. The arrangements in the following atoms get more complicated with the addition of more protons and electrons. The number of neutrons required to hold the nucleus together increases as the atomic size increases. Thus an atom of gold consists of 79 protons (p^+), 118 neutrons (n^0) and 79 electrons (e^-).

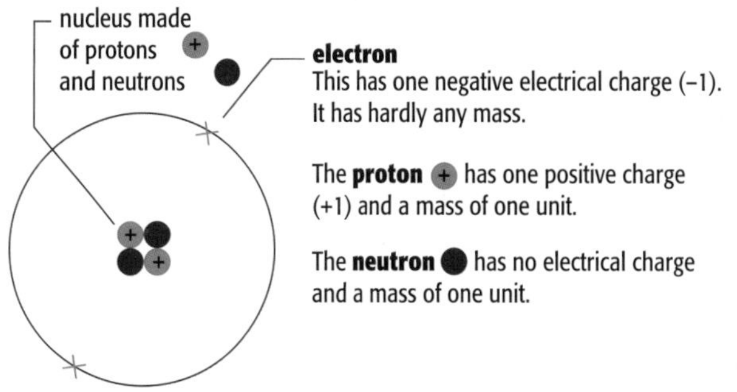

A helium atom has these charged particles in it:

2 protons — charge +2
2 electrons — charge −2
these charges cancel out

We say the charges **balance**. The atom has no overall electrical charge.

A helium atom has:

2 protons — mass 2 units
2 neutrons — mass 2 units
2 electrons — with hardly any mass

So a helium atom has a total mass of:

2 + 2 = 4 units

Figure 2.34 The structure of a helium atom.

Proton (atomic) number and nucleon number

Only hydrogen atoms have one proton in their nuclei. Only helium atoms have two protons. Indeed, only gold atoms have 79 protons. This shows that the number of protons in the nucleus of an atom decides which element it is. This very important number is known as the **proton number** (or **atomic number**, given the symbol Z) of an atom.

Protons alone do not make up all the mass of an atom. The neutrons in the nucleus also contribute to the total mass. The mass of the electrons can be regarded as so small that it can be ignored. As a proton and a neutron have the same mass, the mass of a particular atom depends on the total number of protons and neutrons present. This number is called the **nucleon number** (or **mass number**, given the symbol A) of an atom.

The atomic number Z and mass number A of an atom of an element can be written alongside the symbol for that element, in the general way as $^{A}_{Z}X$. So the symbol for an atom of lithium is $^{7}_{3}Li$. The symbols for carbon, oxygen and uranium atoms are $^{12}_{6}C$, $^{16}_{8}O$ and $^{238}_{92}U$.

If these two important numbers for any atom are known, then its subatomic composition can be worked out.

For proton number and nucleon number we have:

- proton (atomic) number (Z)
  = number of protons in the nucleus
- nucleon (mass) number (A)
  = number of protons + number of neutrons.

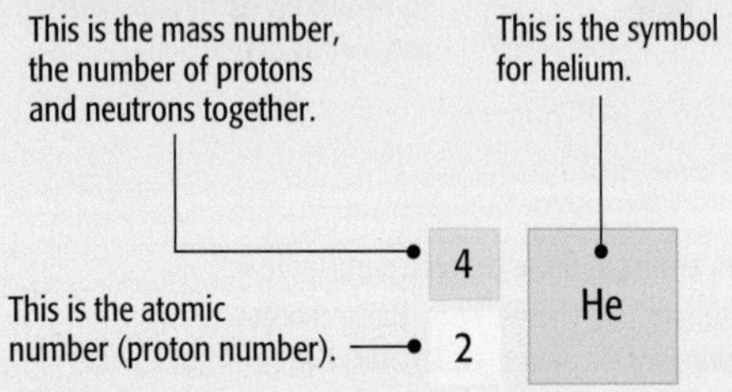

These two relationships are useful:

- number of electrons = number of protons
  = atomic (proton) number
- number of neutrons
  = nucleon number – proton number
  = $A - Z$

Table **2.8** shows the numbers of protons, neutrons and electrons in some different atoms. Note that the rules apply even to the largest, most complicated atom found naturally in substantial amounts.

Exam tip

Remember that you can use the Periodic Table you have in the exam for information on these numbers for any atom. Magnesium is the twelfth atom in the table, so it must have 12 protons and 12 electrons in its atoms.

Isotopes

Measurements of the atomic masses of some elements using the mass spectrometer were puzzling. Pure samples of elements such as carbon, chlorine and many others were found to contain atoms with different masses even though they contained the same numbers of protons and electrons. The different masses were caused by different numbers of neutrons in their nuclei. Such atoms are called **isotopes**.

- Isotopes are atoms of the same element with different mass numbers.
- They have the **same** number of protons and electrons in each atom, but **different** numbers of neutrons in the nucleus.

Atom	Symbol	Atomic number, Z	Mass number, A	Inside the nucleus:		Outside the nucleus:
				Protons (Z)	Neutrons ($A - Z$)	Electrons (Z)
hydrogen	H	1	1	1	0	1
helium	He	2	4	2	2	2
lithium	Li	3	7	3	4	3
beryllium	Be	4	9	4	5	4
carbon	C	6	12	6	6	6
oxygen	O	8	16	8	8	8
sodium	Na	11	23	11	12	11
calcium	Ca	20	40	20	20	20
gold	Au	79	197	79	118	79
uranium	U	92	238	92	146	92

Table 2.8 The subatomic composition and structure of certain atoms.

Exam tip

Remember that it is just the number of neutrons in the atoms that is the difference between isotopes. They have the same number of protons and electrons.

The isotopes of an element have the same chemical properties because they contain the same number of electrons. It is the number of electrons in an atom that decides the way in which it forms bonds and reacts with other atoms. However, some physical properties of the isotopes **are** different. The masses of the atoms differ, and therefore other properties, such as density and rate of diffusion, also vary. The modern mass spectrometer shows that most elements have several different isotopes that occur naturally. Others, such as tritium – an isotope of hydrogen (Table **2.9**) – can be made artificially.

Tritium and carbon-14 illustrate another difference in physical properties that can occur between isotopes, as they are **radioactive**. The extra neutrons in their nuclei cause them to be unstable so the nuclei break up spontaneously (that is, without any external energy being supplied), emitting certain types of radiation. They are known as radio-isotopes.

- Isotopes of an element have the same chemical properties. They differ in a few physical properties such as density.
- Some isotopes have unstable nuclei; they are radio-isotopes and emit various forms of radiation.

Element	Isotopes		
Hydrogen	hydrogen (99.99%)	deuterium (0.01%)	tritium[a]
	$^{1}_{1}H$	$^{2}_{1}H$	$^{3}_{1}H$
	1 proton	1 proton	1 proton
	0 neutrons	1 neutron	2 neutrons
	1 electron	1 electron	1 electron
Carbon	carbon-12 (98.9%)	carbon-13 (1.1%)	carbon-14[a] (trace)
	$^{12}_{6}C$	$^{13}_{6}C$	$^{14}_{6}C$
	6 protons	6 protons	6 protons
	6 neutrons	7 neutrons	8 neutrons
	6 electrons	6 electrons	6 electrons
Neon	neon-20 (90.5%)	neon-21 (0.3%)	neon-22 (9.2%)
	$^{20}_{10}Ne$	$^{21}_{10}Ne$	$^{22}_{10}Ne$
	10 protons	10 protons	10 protons
	10 neutrons	11 neutrons	12 neutrons
	10 electrons	10 electrons	10 electrons
Chlorine	chlorine-35 (75%)	chlorine-37 (25%)	
	$^{35}_{17}Cl$	$^{37}_{17}Cl$	
	17 protons	17 protons	
	18 neutrons	20 neutrons	
	17 electrons	17 electrons	

[a] *Tritium and carbon-14 atoms are radioactive isotopes because their nuclei are unstable.*

Table 2.9 Several elements that exist as mixtures of isotopes.

Relative atomic masses

Most elements exist naturally as a mixture of isotopes. Therefore, the value we use for the atomic mass of an element is an average mass. This takes into account the proportions (abundance) of all the naturally occurring isotopes. If a particular isotope is present in high proportion, it will make a large contribution to the average. This average value for the mass of an atom of an element is known as the relative atomic mass (A_r).

> The **relative atomic mass (A_r)** is the average mass of an atom of an element, taking account of its natural isotopes and their percentage abundance.

Because there are several isotopes of carbon, the standard against which all atomic masses are measured has to be defined precisely. The isotope carbon-12 is used as the standard. One atom of carbon-12 is given the mass of 12 precisely. From this we get that 1 atomic mass unit (a.m.u.) = $\frac{1}{12}$ × mass of one atom of carbon-12.

The existence of isotopes also explains why most relative atomic masses are not whole numbers. But, to make calculation easier, in this book they are rounded to the nearest whole number. There is one exception, chlorine, where this would be misleading. Chlorine contains two isotopes, chlorine-35 and chlorine-37, in a ratio of 3:1 (or 75%:25%). If the mixture were 50%:50%, then the relative atomic mass of chlorine would be 36. The fact that there is more of the lighter isotope moves the value lower than 36. The actual value is 35.5. The relative atomic mass of chlorine can be calculated by finding the total mass of 100 atoms:

$$\text{mass of 100 atoms} = (35 \times 75) + (37 \times 25) = 3550$$

Then,

$$\text{average mass of 1 atom} = \frac{3550}{100} = 35.5$$

Thus, for chlorine:

$$A_r(\text{Cl}) = 35.5$$

E

Radioactivity

Some elements have unstable isotopes, such as tritium and carbon-14. The extra neutrons in their nuclei cause them to disintegrate or decay spontaneously. This is **radioactivity** and takes place through nuclear fission. The result of these disintegrations is the release of heat energy and various forms of radioactive radiation. The heat produced by the decay of radioactive material deep in the Earth keeps the outer core molten. It provides the energy for all volcanic activity and produces the convection currents in the mantle that power continental drift. Uranium-235 is a radioactive isotope which is used as a controlled source of energy in nuclear power stations.

Each radioactive isotope decays at its own rate. The decay is a completely random process and is unaffected by temperature or whether the isotope is part of a compound or present as the free element. Radioactive decay is a nuclear process and not a chemical reaction.

The uses of radioactivity

E

Radioactive dating

Each radioactive isotope decays at its own rate. However, the time taken for the radioactivity in a sample to halve is constant for a particular radio-isotope. This time is called the **half-life**. Some isotopes have very short half-lives of only seconds: for example oxygen-14 has a half-life of 71 s. Other half-lives are quite long: for example carbon-14 has a half-life of 5730 years.

One important use of half-life values is in radioactive dating. Radiocarbon dating (which uses carbon-14) can be used to date wooden and organic objects. The decay of other elements can be tracked to give estimates of the age of rocks. The oldest rock so far dated was found in northern Canada and is 3.96 billion years old. Radioactive dating of meteorites and of rocks from the Moon suggests that all the solar system was formed at the same time – about 4.6 billion years ago.

Industrial uses of radio-isotopes

Despite the need to handle them with strict safety precautions, radioactive isotopes are widely used in industry and medicine. Most important is the use of an isotope of uranium, ^{235}U, in nuclear power stations. Here, as the isotope splits into smaller parts, as a result of being bombarded with neutrons, huge amounts of energy are produced. This nuclear fission reaction is the same as that used in the atomic bomb. The difference is that in a nuclear power station, the reaction is controlled.

E

Other industrial uses of radio-isotopes include monitoring the level of filling in containers, checking the thickness of sheets of plastic, paper or metal foil (for example aluminium baking foil) during continuous production, and detecting leaks in gas or oil pipes (Figure **2.35**).

Medical and food-safety uses of radio-isotopes

The ease of detection of radio-isotopes gives rise to several of their other uses, and in medicine some of their most dangerous properties can be turned to advantage. Several medical uses of radiation depend on the fact that biological cells are sensitive to radioactive emissions. Cells that are growing and dividing are particularly likely to be damaged. Cancer cells are cells that are growing out of control in a tissue of the body. Because of this they are more easily killed by radiation than are healthy cells. Penetrating γ-radiation from the radio-isotope cobalt-60 is used to treat internal cancer tumours. Skin cancer tumours can be treated with less-penetrating radiation. This is done by strapping sheets containing phosphorus-32 or strontium-90 to the affected area of the skin.

Bacterial cells grow and divide rapidly. They are particularly sensitive to radiation. Medical instruments, dressings and syringes can be sterilised by sealing them in polythene bags and exposing them to intense doses of γ-radiation. This has proved a very effective method of killing any bacteria on them.

Exam tip

For the examination you simply need to know a medical and an industrial use for radioactivity. Do be clear about the difference between radiotherapy and chemotherapy in the treatment of cancer. It is radiotherapy that involves the use of radioactivity to kill the tumour cells.

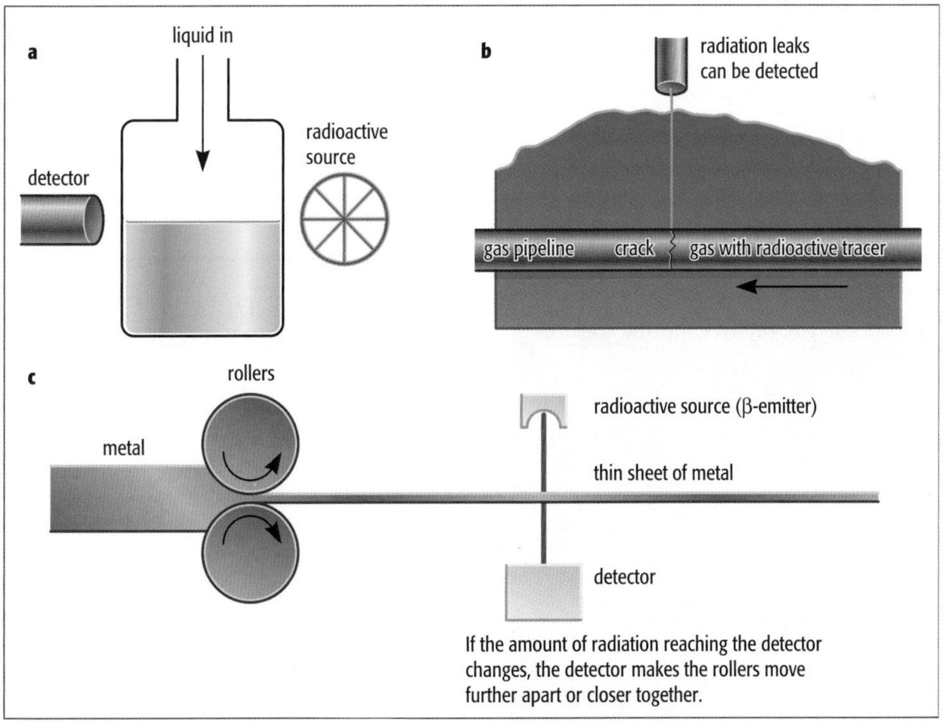

Figure 2.35 Uses of radioactivity: **a** detecting the level of liquid in a container, **b** detecting leaks in underground pipes, and **c** controlling the thickness of metal sheets.

Key ideas so far

- Atoms are made up of three subatomic particles: protons, neutrons and electrons.
- The protons and neutrons of an atom form the nucleus at the centre of the atom.
- The proton number of an atom defines which element it is and is the number of protons in the atom.
- Atoms are electrically neutral so they have the same number of electrons orbiting the nucleus as they have protons.
- The nucleon number of an atom is the number of protons plus the number of neutrons in the nucleus of the atom.
- Atoms of the same element can have different numbers of neutrons in their nuclei. These atoms are different isotopes of the element.
- Some isotopes have unstable nuclei: they are radioactive.

Quick-check questions

1. What are the relative masses of a proton, neutron and electron given that a proton has a mass of 1?
2. How many protons, neutrons and electrons are there in an atom of phosphorus which has a proton number of 15 and a nucleon number of 31?
3. What is the difference in terms of subatomic particles between an atom of chlorine-35 and an atom of chlorine-37?
4. Give **one** medical and **one** industrial use of radioactivity.

2.5 Electron arrangements in atoms

The aurora borealis (Figure **2.36**) is a spectacular display seen in the sky in the far north (a similar phenomenon – the aurora australis – occurs in the night sky of the far south). It is caused by radiation from the Sun moving the electrons in atoms of the gases of the atmosphere.

Similar colour effects can be created in a simpler way in the laboratory by heating the compounds of some metals in a Bunsen flame (see page **233**). These colours are also seen in fireworks. The colours produced are due to electrons in the atom moving between two different **energy levels**.

Figure 2.36 The aurora borealis or northern lights as seen from Finland.

In 1913 Niels Bohr, working with Rutherford in Manchester, developed a theory to explain how electrons were arranged in atoms. This theory helps to explain how the colours referred to above come about.

A simplified version of **Bohr's theory** of the arrangement of electrons in an atom can be summarised as follows (see also Figure **2.37**).

- Electrons are in orbit around the central nucleus of the atom.
- The electron orbits are called **shells** (or **energy levels**) and have different energies.

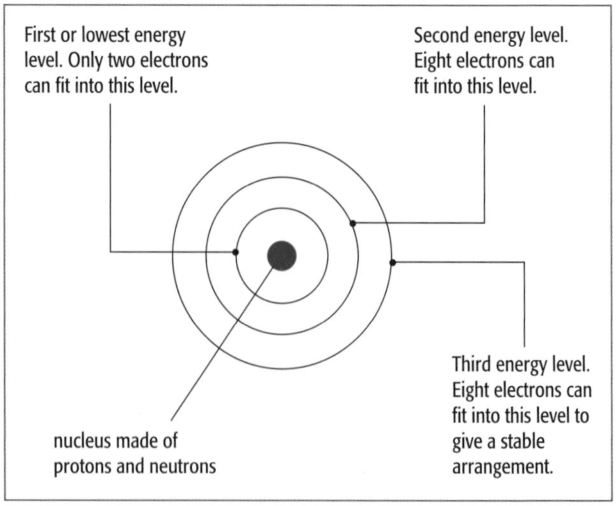

Figure 2.37 Bohr's theory of the arrangement of electrons in an atom.

- Shells which are further from the nucleus have higher energies.
- The shells are filled starting with the one with lowest energy (closest to the nucleus).
- The first shell can hold only 2 electrons.
- The second and subsequent shells can hold 8 electrons to give a stable (noble gas) arrangement of electrons.

Other evidence was found which supported these ideas of how the electrons are arranged in atoms. The number and arrangement of the electrons in the atoms of the first 20 elements in the Periodic Table (see the Appendix) are shown in Table **2.10**.

When the two essential numbers describing a particular atom are known, the numbers of protons and neutrons, a subatomic picture can be drawn. Figure **2.38** shows such a picture for perhaps the most versatile atom in the Universe, an atom of carbon-12. Studying the organisation of the electrons of an atom is valuable. It begins to explain the patterns in properties of the elements that are the basis of the Periodic Table. This will be discussed in the next chapter.

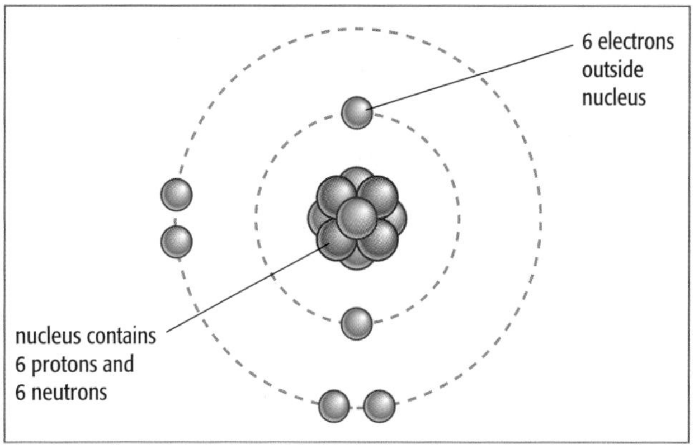

Figure 2.38 Possibly the most versatile atom in the Universe – the carbon-12 atom.

Element	Symbol	Atomic number, *Z*	First shell	Second shell	Third shell	Fourth shell	Electron configuration
hydrogen	H	1	●				1
helium	He	2	●●				2
lithium	Li	3	●●	●			2,1
beryllium	Be	4	●●	●●			2,2
boron	B	5	●●	●●●			2,3
carbon	C	6	●●	●●●●			2,4
nitrogen	N	7	●●	●●●●●			2,5
oxygen	O	8	●●	●●●●●●			2,6
fluorine	F	9	●●	●●●●●●●			2,7
neon	Ne	10	●●	●●●●●●●●			2,8
sodium	Na	11	●●	●●●●●●●●	●		2,8,1
magnesium	Mg	12	●●	●●●●●●●●	●●		2,8,2
aluminium	Al	13	●●	●●●●●●●●	●●●		2,8,3
silicon	Si	14	●●	●●●●●●●●	●●●●		2,8,4
phosphorus	P	15	●●	●●●●●●●●	●●●●●		2,8,5
sulfur	S	16	●●	●●●●●●●●	●●●●●●		2,8,6
chlorine	Cl	17	●●	●●●●●●●●	●●●●●●●		2,8,7
argon	Ar	18	●●	●●●●●●●●	●●●●●●●●		2,8,8
potassium	K	19	●●	●●●●●●●●	●●●●●●●●	●	2,8,8,1
calcium	Ca	20	●●	●●●●●●●●	●●●●●●●●	●●	2,8,8,2

Table 2.10 The electron arrangements of the first 20 elements.

Exam tip

Make sure that you remember how to work out the electron arrangements of the first 20 elements and can draw them in rings (shells) as in Figure **2.39**. Also remember that you can give the electron arrangement simply in terms of numbers: 2,8,4 for silicon, for example.

You can see from these elements that the number of outer electrons in an atom is the same as the number of the group in the Periodic Table that the element is in. The number of shells of electrons in an atom tells you the period (row) of the element in the table. We will look at this further in the next chapter.

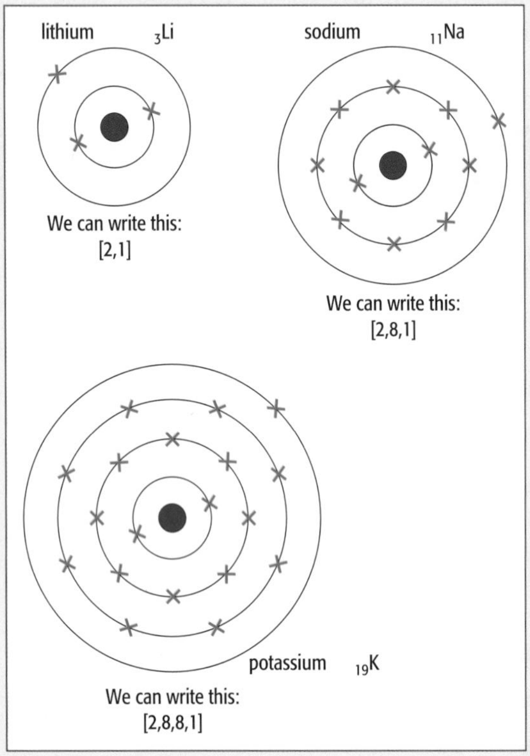

Figure 2.39 Different ways of showing electron structure.

Key ideas so far

- Electrons are arranged in orbit around the central nucleus of the atom. They are arranged in shells or 'energy levels'.
- Shells are filled in order, lowest energy first.
- The first shell holds up to 2 electrons, others can hold 8.

Quick-check questions

1 What are the maximum numbers of electrons that can fill the first and the second shells (energy levels) of an atom?

2 What is the electron arrangement of a calcium atom, which has an atomic number of 20?

3 How many electrons are there in the outer shells of the atoms of the noble gases, argon and neon?

4 Carbon-12 and carbon-14 are different isotopes of carbon. How many electrons are there in an atom of each isotope?

Summary

You should know that:

- there are three different physical states in which a substance can exist
- changes in state can be made by changing the temperature and/or the pressure
- sublimation is a change of state in which the liquid phase is bypassed
- pure substances have precise melting and boiling points – their sharpness can be taken as an indication of the degree of purity of the substance
- the processes of melting and boiling require energy – when heating a substance, the temperature stays constant during these processes
- the solubility of most solids increases with rising temperature, whereas gases are less soluble at higher temperatures
- a range of separation methods exist to purify one substance from a mixture, for example
  - filtration separates an insoluble substance from suspension in a liquid
  - distillation separates a liquid from the solutes dissolved in it
  - fractional distillation separates liquids that mix but have different boiling points
  - chromatography separates substances, particularly coloured dyes, by differences in their solubility in a solvent
- elements are the basic building units of the material world – they cannot be chemically broken down into anything simpler
- compounds are made from two or more elements chemically combined together
- the properties of a compound are very different from those of the elements it is made from
- chemical reactions produce new substances and involve energy changes
- each element is made from atoms
- the atoms of each element can be represented by a chemical symbol
- atoms can join together to make the molecules either of an element or of a compound
- the particles (atoms, molecules or ions) of a substance are in constant motion – the kinetic theory
- the nature and amount of motion of these particles differs in a solid, liquid or gas
- the kinetic theory explains the processes involved in changing state and diffusion
- the atoms of the elements are made up of different combinations of the subatomic particles – protons, neutrons and electrons
- each element is made from atoms that contain a characteristic number of protons and electrons
- the number of protons and electrons in any atom is always the same, and defined by the proton (atomic) number (Z) of the element
- in any atom the protons and neutrons are bound together in a central nucleus, and the electrons 'orbit' the nucleus
- the mass of an electron is negligible compared to that of a proton or neutron, which have approximately equal mass
- the nucleon (mass) number (A) defines the total number of protons and neutrons in any atom
- isotopes of the same element can exist that differ only in the number of neutrons in their nuclei
- some isotopes of many elements have unstable nuclei and this makes them radioactive
- the different forms of radiation from radio-isotopes have scientific, industrial, medical and food-safety uses
- the electrons in atoms are arranged in an organised way in different shells (or energy levels)
- these electron shells have different energies and are at different distances from the nucleus of the atom
- electrons are placed in the shells closest to the nucleus first, and each shell has a maximum number of electrons that it can contain
- paper chromatography can be extended to colourless substances by the use of locating agents
- chromatography can help identify unknown substances, particularly using the measurement of R_f values
- the rate of diffusion of gaseous atoms and molecules is inversely proportional to the mass of the particles – the lighter the particles, the faster they diffuse.

S

Exam-style questions

1 The electronic structures of various atoms are shown below.

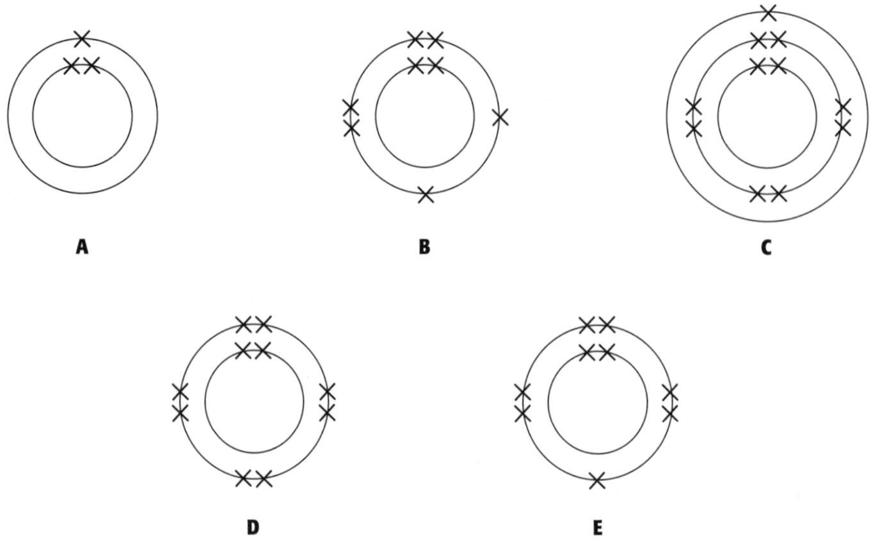

a i Which **one** of these structures A to E represents a noble gas? [1]

ii Which **two** of these structures represent atoms from the same Group of the Periodic Table? [1]

iii Which **one** of these structures represents an atom with an atomic number of 8? [1]

iv Which **one** of these structures is in Period 3 of the Periodic Table (refer to Table **2.10** and the Appendix)? [1]

CIE IGCSE, June 2006, paper 2, q.3 part

2 The states of matter are solid, liquid and gas.
The diagram below shows how the molecules are arranged in these three states.

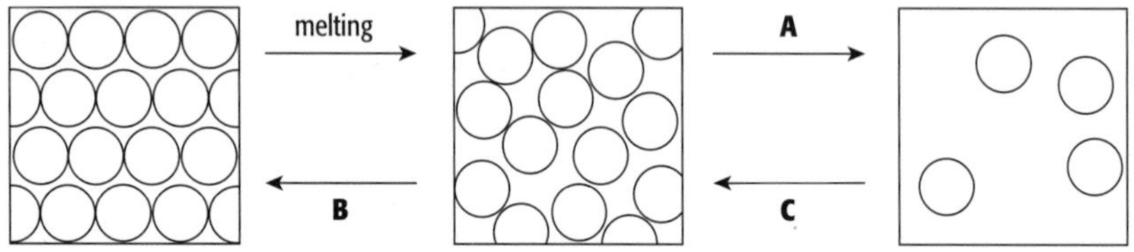

a State the name given to the change of state labelled

i A

ii B

iii C [3]

b Which **one** of the following best describes the movement of molecules in the liquid state?

- The molecules are not moving from place to place.
- The molecules are sliding over each other.
- The molecules are moving freely. [1]

c Which of the changes A, B or C, is endothermic? Explain your answer. [2]

d Choose from the following list of substances to answer the questions below.

bromine chlorine iron mercury sodium chloride sulfur

Name a substance which is

i a gas at room temperature

ii a non-metallic liquid at room temperature

iii a compound which is a solid at room temperature. [3]

e A student set up the apparatus shown in the diagram below.

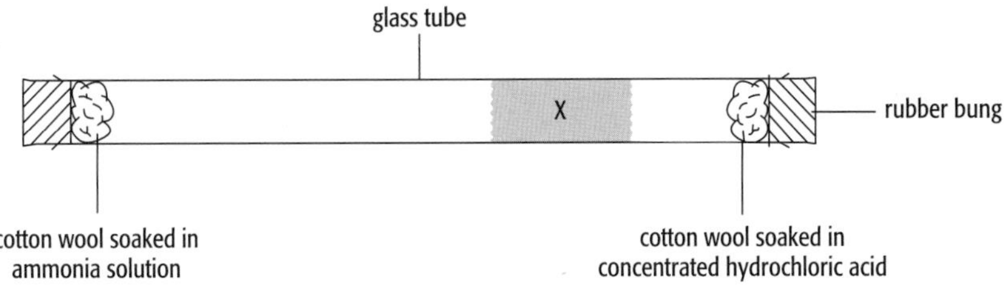

The white solid is formed because the molecules of hydrogen chloride gas and ammonia gas move at random throughout the tube and eventually react with each other.

i State the name given to this random movement of molecules.

ii State the name of the white solid formed at X.

iii Suggest why the white solid is formed towards one end of the tube and not in the middle. [3]

f What type of chemical reaction takes place when ammonia reacts with hydrochloric acid? [1]

g The diagram below shows a simple apparatus that can be used for measuring the melting point of a solid.

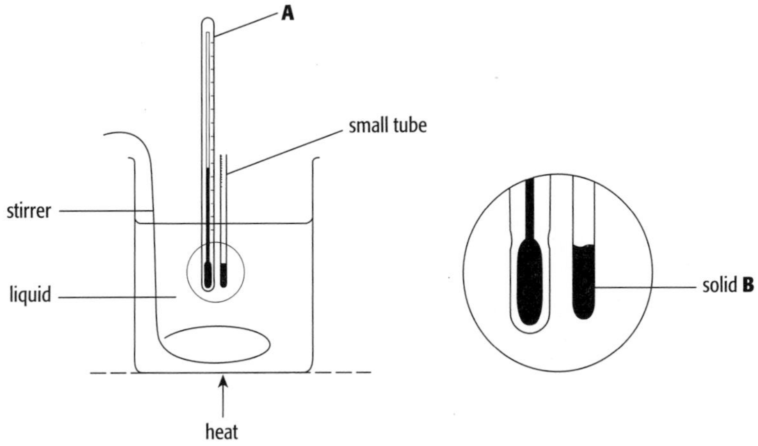

The liquid in the beaker is heated slowly and the temperature at which the solid B melts is recorded.

i State the name of the piece of apparatus labelled A.

ii Solid B melted at 155 °C.

Why would water **not** be a suitable liquid to put in the beaker when using this apparatus to find the melting point of solid B?

iii Suggest why the liquid needs to be kept stirred. [3]

CIE IGCSE, June 2003, paper 2, q.3

3 A student took a sample of seawater and heated it using the apparatus shown below.

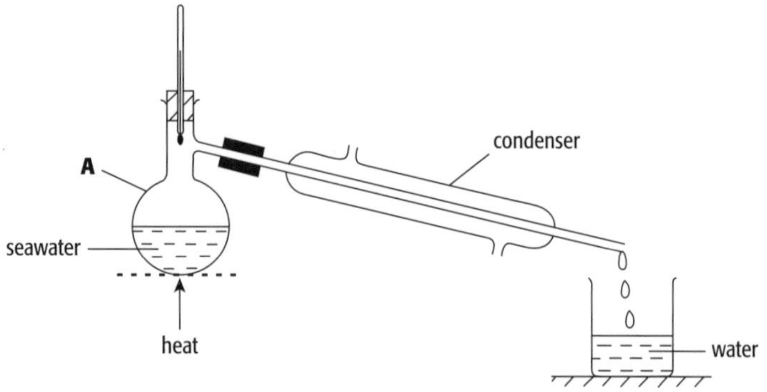

a What is the name given to the process shown in the diagram? [1]

b State the name of the piece of apparatus labelled A. [1]

c Explain the function of the condenser. [2]

d Pure water collects in the beaker. State the boiling point of pure water. [1]

CIE IGCSE, November 2002, paper 2, q.6, part

S

4 Nitrogen dioxide, NO_2, is a dark brown gas.
When nitrogen dioxide is cooled, it forms a yellow liquid and then pale yellow crystals. These crystals are heated and the temperature is measured every minute. The following graph can be drawn.

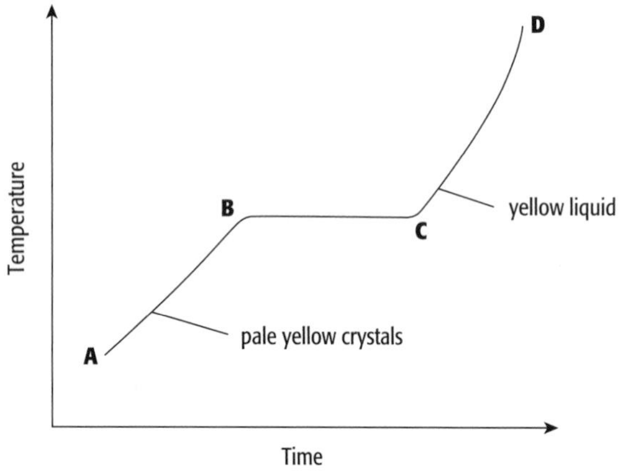

a Describe the arrangement and movement of the molecules in the region A–B. [3]

b Name the change that occurs in the region B–C [1]

CIE IGCSE, June 2003, paper 3, q.4 part

5 **a** Copy and complete the table, which gives the names, symbols, relative masses and relative charges of the three subatomic particles.

Name	Symbol	Relative mass	Relative charge
electron	e^-		
proton		1	
	n		0

[3]

b Use the information in the table to explain the following.

i Atoms contain charged particles but they are electrically neutral because they have no overall charge. [2]

ii Atoms of the same element can have different masses. [2]

iii Scientists are certain that there are no undiscovered elements missing from the Periodic Table from hydrogen to lawrencium. [1]

CIE IGCSE, June 2008, paper 3, q.2 part

3 Elements and compounds

This chapter covers the following ideas:

- the structure of the Periodic Table
- metals and non-metals in the Periodic Table
- electron arrangement in the Periodic Table
- trends in Group I – the alkali metals
- trends in Group VII – the halogens
- the noble gases
- trends across a period
- the transition elements
- bonding in metals
- bonding in covalent compounds
- bonding in ionic compounds
- formulae and names of ionic compounds
- formulae and names of covalent compounds
- the nature of metal crystals and alloys
- the nature of ionic crystals
- the nature of giant covalent structures

3.1 The Periodic Table – classifying the elements

E

Building up the modern **Periodic Table** has been a major scientific achievement! The first steps towards working out this table were taken long before anyone had any ideas about the structure of atoms. The number of elements discovered increased steadily during the nineteenth century. Chemists began to find patterns in their properties. Döbereiner, Newlands and Meyer all described groupings of elements with similar chemical and physical characteristics. But, although they were partly successful, these groupings were limited or flawed. The breakthrough came in 1869 when Mendeleev put forward his ideas of a periodic table. In his first attempt he used 32 of the 61 elements known at that time (Figure **3.1**).

He drew up his table based on atomic masses, as others had done before him. But his success was mainly due to his leaving **gaps** for possible elements still to be discovered. He did not try to force the elements into patterns for which there was no evidence.

Mendeleev's great success lay in **predicting** the properties of elements that had not yet been discovered. He predicted the discovery of ten elements. He then put forward detailed ideas on the particular properties of four of these elements. Remarkably, when the elements gallium and germanium were discovered, their properties were very similar to his predictions. Table **3.1** shows the predicted and actual properties of gallium – the metal that melts in your hand! In Mendeleev's periodic table, there was a space for this element below aluminium. He called the missing, unknown, element 'eka-aluminium'.

This success convinced chemists that there were repetitive patterns to the characteristics of the elements. All modern versions of the Periodic Table are based on the one put forward by Mendeleev. An example is given in Figure **3.2** (overleaf).

Figure 3.1 Mendeleev's early periodic table carved on the wall of a university building in St. Petersburg, with a statue of Mendeleev in front.

Property	Eka-aluminium (predicted)	Gallium (actual)
atomic mass	about 68	70
density/g/cm^3	5.9	5.94
melting point/°C	low	30.2
formula of chloride	$EaCl_3$	$GaCl_3$
formula of oxide	Ea_2O_3	Ga_2O_3
	oxide would be amphoteric[(a)]	oxide is amphoteric[(a)]

[(a)] *This term is explained in Section* 5.3.

Table 3.1 The predicted and actual properties of gallium.

In the **Periodic Table**:

- the elements are arranged in order of increasing proton number (atomic number)
- the vertical columns of elements with similar properties are called **groups**
- the horizontal rows are called **periods**.

The main distinction in the table is between **metals** and **non-metals**. Metals are clearly separated from non-metals. The non-metals are grouped into the top right-hand region of the table, above the thick stepped line in Figure **3.2**. One of the first uses of the Periodic Table now becomes clear. Although we may never have seen a sample of the element hafnium (Hf), we know from a glance at the table that it is a metal. We may also be able to predict some of its properties.

Metals and non-metals

There are 94 naturally occurring elements. Some are very rare. Francium, for instance, has never been seen. The radioactive metals neptunium and plutonium, which we make artifically in quite large amounts, occur only in very small (trace) quantities naturally. Most of the elements (70) can be classified as metals. Together they form a group of elements whose structures are held together by a particular type of bonding between the atoms. The metals have a number of physical properties that are broadly the same for all of them (Table **3.2**, overleaf).

The chemical properties of metals and non-metals are also very different, as is the type of bonding present in their compounds. The distinction is therefore a very important one.

The Periodic Table does not list substances such as steel, bronze and brass, which in everyday terms we call metals and which share the properties listed for metals. They are **not** elements! They are in fact **alloys**, mixtures of elements (usually metals) designed to have properties that are useful for a particular purpose.

Non-metals are a less uniform group of elements. They show a much wider range of properties. This reflects the wider differences in the types of structure shown by non-metals.

Key: a = relative atomic mass; X = symbol; b = atomic number (box shows a / X / Name / b)

	Group I	Group II											Group III	Group IV	Group V	Group VI	Group VII	Group 0
Period 1								1 H Hydrogen 1										4 He Helium 2
Period 2	7 Li Lithium 3	9 Be Beryllium 4											11 B Boron 5	12 C Carbon 6	14 N Nitrogen 7	16 O Oxygen 8	19 F Fluorine 9	20 Ne Neon 10
Period 3	23 Na Sodium 11	24 Mg Magnesium 12											27 Al Aluminium 13	28 Si Silicon 14	31 P Phosphorus 15	32 S Sulfur 16	35.5 Cl Chlorine 17	40 Ar Argon 18
Period 4	39 K Potassium 19	40 Ca Calcium 20	45 Sc Scandium 21	48 Ti Titanium 22	51 V Vanadium 23	52 Cr Chromium 24	55 Mn Manganese 25	56 Fe Iron 26	59 Co Cobalt 27	59 Ni Nickel 28	64 Cu Copper 29	65 Zn Zinc 30	70 Ga Gallium 31	73 Ge Germanium 32	75 As Arsenic 33	79 Se Selenium 34	80 Br Bromine 35	84 Kr Krypton 36
Period 5	86 Rb Rubidium 37	88 Sr Strontium 38	89 Y Yttrium 39	91 Zr Zirconium 40	93 Nb Niobium 41	96 Mo Molybdenum 42	– Tc Technetium 43	101 Ru Ruthenium 44	103 Rh Rhodium 45	106 Pd Palladium 46	108 Ag Silver 47	112 Cd Cadmium 48	115 In Indium 49	119 Sn Tin 50	122 Sb Antimony 51	128 Te Tellurium 52	127 I Iodine 53	131 Xe Xenon 54
Period 6	133 Cs Caesium 55	137 Ba Barium 56	La to Lu	178 Hf Hafnium 72	181 Ta Tantalum 73	184 W Tungsten 74	186 Re Rhenium 75	190 Os Osmium 76	192 Ir Iridium 77	195 Pt Platinum 78	197 Au Gold 79	201 Hg Mercury 80	204 Tl Thallium 81	207 Pb Lead 82	209 Bi Bismuth 83	– Po Polonium 84	– At Astatine 85	– Rn Radon 86
Period 7	– Fr Francium 87	– Ra Radium 88	Ac to Lr															

139 La Lanthanum 57	140 Ce Cerium 58	141 Pr Praseodymium 59	144 Nd Neodymium 60	– Pm Promethium 61	150 Sm Samarium 62	152 Eu Europium 63	157 Gd Gadolinium 64	159 Tb Terbium 65	163 Dy Dysprosium 66	165 Ho Holmium 67	167 Er Erbium 68	169 Tm Thulium 69	173 Yb Ytterbium 70	175 Lu Lutetium 71
– Ac Actinium 89	– Th Thorium 90	– Pa Protactinium 91	– U Uranium 92	– Np Neptunium 93	– Pu Plutonium 94	– Am Americium 95	– Cm Curium 96	– Bk Berkelium 97	– Cf Californium 98	– Es Einsteinium 99	– Fm Fermium 100	– Md Mendelevium 101	– No Nobelium 102	– Lr Lawrencium 103

Elements in Groups I to 0 are sometimes known as the **main-group elements.**

- The **reactive metals**: Group I – the alkali metals; Group II – the alkaline earth metals
- The **'poor' metals**
- The **non-metals**: includes Group VII – the halogens
- The **transition elements**: hard, strong and dense metals
- The **metalloids**: includes semiconductors, e.g. silicon and germanium
- The **noble gases**: very unreactive

Figure 3.2 The Periodic Table, showing the major regions. (Except for chlorine, the relative atomic masses are given to the nearest whole number.)

Metals	Non-metals
They are usually **solids** (except for mercury, which is a liquid) at room temperature. Their melting and boiling points are usually high.	They are **solids** or **gases** (except for bromine, which is a liquid) at room temperature. Their melting and boiling points are often low.
They are usually hard and dense.	Most non-metals are softer than metals (but diamond is very hard). Their densities are often low.
All metals are good conductors of electricity[a].	They are poor conductors of electricity (except graphite, a form of carbon). They tend to be insulators.
They are good conductors of heat.	They are poor thermal conductors.
Their shape can be changed by hammering (they are **malleable**). They can also be pulled out into wires (they are **ductile**).	Most non-metals are brittle when solid.
They are grey in colour (except gold and copper). They can be polished.	They vary in colour. They often have a dull surface when solid.
They usually make a ringing sound when struck (they are **sonorous**).	They are not sonorous.

[a]*Electrical conductivity is usually taken as the simplest test of whether a substance is metallic or not.*

Table 3.2 Comparison of the physical properties of metals and non-metals.

- A metal is an element that conducts electricity and is malleable and ductile.
- A non-metal is an element that does not conduct electricity well and is neither malleable nor ductile.

Exam tip

If asked to say how you would test to see whether an element was a metal or a non-metal, the key test is electrical conductivity. Describe the setting up of a simple circuit using a battery and a light bulb, and then connect in a sample of the element and see if the bulb lights up (Figure 3.3).

The other properties which are most clearly those of a metal are malleability and ductility. These, and electrical conductivity, are the properties where there are fewest exceptions.

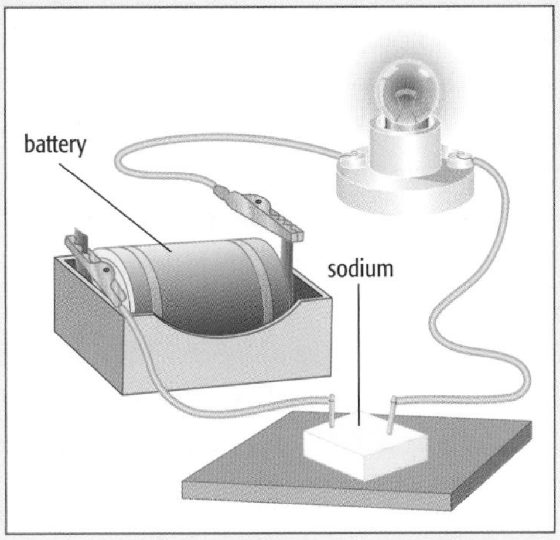

Figure 3.3 Testing the electrical conductivity of a possible metal.

The change from metallic to non-metallic properties in the elements is not as clear-cut as suggested by drawing the line between the two regions of the Periodic Table. The elements close to the line show properties that lie between these extremes. These elements are now often referred to as **metalloids** (or semi-metals). Such elements have some of the properties of metals and others that are more characteristic of non-metals. There are eight elements which are called metalloids. They often look like metals, but are brittle like non-metals. They are neither conductors nor insulators, but make excellent semiconductors. The prime example of this type of element is silicon (Figure 3.4)

Figure 3.4 A sample of the element silicon, the basis of the semiconductor industry.

Groups and Periods in the Periodic Table

The Periodic Table allows us to make even more useful subdivisions of elements than simply deciding which are metals and which are non-metals. The elements present in Groups I to 0 of the table are sometimes known as the **main-group elements**. These vertical groups show most clearly how elements within the same group have similar chemical and physical properties. Some of these groups have particular names as well as numbers. These are given in Figure 3.2. Between Groups II and III of these main groups of elements is a block of metals known as the **transition elements** (or **transition metals**). The first row of these elements occurs in Period 4. This row includes such important metals as iron, copper and zinc.

The noble gases, in Group 0 on the right-hand side of the table, are the least reactive elements in the table. However, the group next to them, Group VII which are also known as the halogens, and the group on the left-hand side of the table, Group I or the alkali metals, are the most reactive elements. The more unreactive elements, whether metals or non-metals, are in the centre of the table.

Exam tip

If you are asked a question about an element in the Periodic Table, use the table at the back of the examination paper to help you answer it.

Electron arrangement and the Periodic Table

When the first attempts were made to construct a periodic table, nobody knew about the structure of the atom. We can now directly link the properties of an element with its position in the table and its electron arrangement (Figure **3.5**). The number of outer electrons in the atoms of each element has been found. Elements in the same group have the same number of outer electrons. We also know that, as you move across a period in the table, a shell of electrons is being filled.

There is a clear relationship between electron arrangement and position in the Periodic Table for the main-group elements. The elements in Group II have two outer electrons. The elements in Period 3 have three shells of electrons. A magnesium atom has two electrons in its third, outer, shell, and is in Group II. An argon atom has an outer shell containing eight electrons – a very stable arrangement – and is in Group 0. A potassium atom has one electron in its outer shell, and is in Group I and Period 4.

It is the outer electrons of an atom that are mainly responsible for the chemical properties of any element. Therefore, elements in the same group will have similar properties.

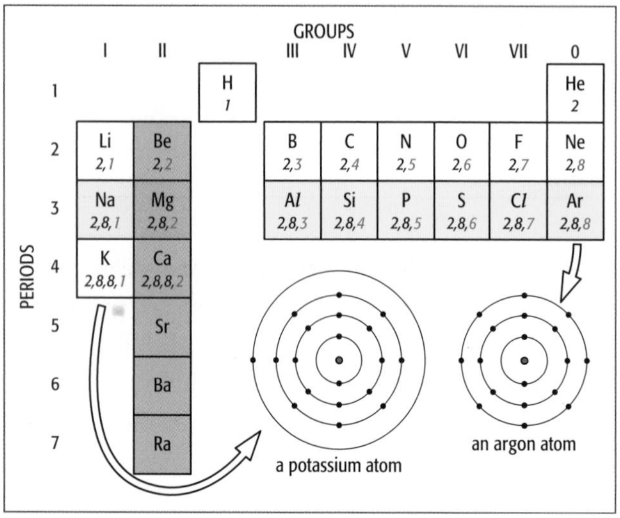

Figure 3.5 The relationship between an element's position in the Periodic Table and the electron arrangement of its atoms.

The **electron arrangements** of atoms are linked to position in the Periodic Table.

- Elements in the same group have the same number of electrons in their outer shell.
- For the main-group elements, the number of the group is the number of electrons in the outer shell.
- The periods also have numbers. This number shows us how many shells of electrons the atom has.

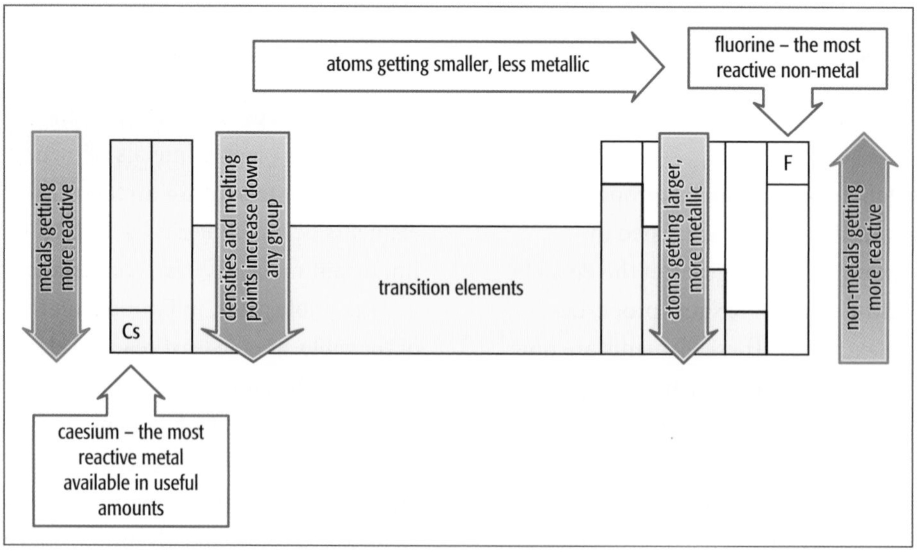

Figure 3.6 General trends in the Periodic Table, leaving aside the noble gases in Group 0.

Certain electron arrangements are found to be more stable than others. This makes them more difficult to break up. The most stable arrangements are those of the **noble gases**, and this fits in with the fact that they are so unreactive.

There are links between the organisation of particles in the atom and the regular variation in properties of the elements in the Periodic Table. This means that we can see certain broad trends in the table (Figure 3.6). These trends become most obvious if we leave aside the noble gases in Group 0. Individual groups show certain 'group characteristics'. These properties follow a trend in particular groups.

Key ideas so far

- Atomic size increases going down a group but decreases across a period.
- Elements become more metallic as we go down a group and to the left of a period.
- Metals are good conductors of electricity and heat. They are malleable and ductile.
- Non-metals are poor conductors of heat and electricity. They are brittle when solid.
- In the metallic groups, reactivity increases down a group. The most reactive metal is at the bottom of Group I.
- In a group of non-metals, the most reactive element is at the top of the group. The most reactive element is at the top of Group VII.
- The link between an element's position in the Periodic Table and the electron arrangement in its atoms helps to explain the trends we see.

Quick-check questions

1 What is the name of the most reactive non-metal?
2 What is the similarity in the electron arrangement in the noble gases?
3 How many elements are there in Period 1?
4 Where, in the Periodic Table, will the largest atom be found?
5 Sort the following properties into those characteristic of a metal, and those typical of a non-metal.

is an insulator | **can be beaten into sheets**
gives a ringing sound when hit | **conducts heat**
has a dull surface | **conducts electricity**

3.2 Trends in groups

Group I – the alkali metals

The metals in Group I are often called the **alkali metals**. They are soft solids with relatively low melting points and low densities (Figure 3.7). They are highly reactive and are stored in oil to prevent them reacting with the oxygen and water vapour in the air. When freshly cut with a knife, all these metals have a light-grey, silvery surface, which quickly tarnishes (becomes dull). Reactivity increases as we go down the group. All Group I metals react with water to form hydrogen and an alkaline solution of the metal hydroxide. The reactions range from vigorous in the case of lithium to explosive in the case of caesium. You might predict that francium, at the bottom of Group I, would be the most reactive of all the metals. However, it is highly radioactive and very rare because it decays with a half-life of 5 minutes. It has been estimated that there are only 17 atoms of francium in existence on Earth at any one moment in time.

Figure 3.7 The alkali metals are all soft and can be cut with a knife. This is a sample of lithium.

The physical properties of the alkali metals also change as we go down the group. The melting points become lower while the density of the metals increases.

The alkali metals (Group I) are the most reactive metals that occur. They are known as the alkali metals because they react vigorously with water to produce hydrogen and an alkali solution.

Group VII – the halogens

The most reactive non-metals are the **halogens** in Group VII of the table (Figure **3.8**). In contrast with Group I, here reactivity decreases **down** the group. For example, fluorine is a dangerously reactive, pale yellow gas at room temperature. There is a steady increase in melting points and boiling points as we go down the group, and the elements change from gases to solids as the atomic number increases. Interestingly, the lowest element in this group is also a highly radioactive and rare element, astatine. The actual properties of astatine remain a mystery to us, but we could make a good guess at some of them.

The halogen family found in Group VII of the Periodic Table shows clearly the similarities of elements in the group.

> The halogens have the following common properties:
>
> - They are all poisonous and have a similar strong smell.
> - They are all non-metals.
> - They all form diatomic molecules (for example Cl_2, Br_2, I_2).
> - They all have a **valency** (combining power) of 1 and form compounds with similar formulae, for example hydrogen chloride (HCl), hydrogen bromide (HBr), hydrogen iodide (HI).
> - Their compounds with hydrogen are usually strong acids when dissolved in water, for example hydrochloric acid (HCl), hydrobromic acid (HBr), hydriodic acid (HI).
> - They each produce a series of compounds with other elements: chlorides, bromides and iodides. Together these are known as **halides**.
> - The halogens themselves can react directly with metals to form metal halides (or **salts**).
> - They all form negative ions carrying a single charge, for example chloride ions (Cl^-), bromide ions (Br^-), iodide ions (I^-).

There are gradual changes in properties between the halogens (see Figure **3.8**). As you go down the group, the boiling points increase. Also there is a change from gas to liquid to solid. The intensity of the colour

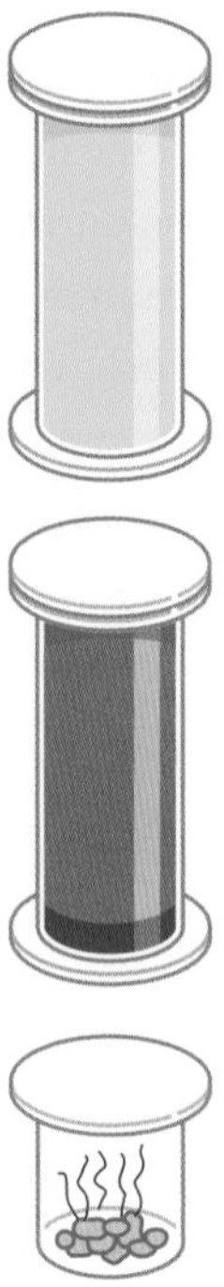

Chlorine (Cl_2)

- dense pale-green gas
- smelly and poisonous
- occurs as chlorides, especially sodium chloride in the sea
- relative atomic mass 35.5

Bromine (Br_2)

- deep-red liquid with red-brown vapour
- smelly and poisonous
- occurs as bromides, especially magnesium bromide in the sea
- relative atomic mass 80

Iodine (I_2)

- grey solid with purple vapour
- smelly and poisonous
- occurs as iodides and iodates in some rocks and in seaweed
- relative atomic mass 127

Figure 3.8 The general properties of the halogens (Group VII).

of the element also increases, from pale to dark. Following these trends, it should not surprise you to know that fluorine is a pale yellow gas at room temperature.

The chemical reactivity of the halogens

Fluorine and chlorine are very reactive. They combine strongly with both metals and non-metals. A piece of Dutch metal foil – an alloy of copper and zinc – will burst into flames when placed in a gas jar of chlorine. When chlorine is passed over heated aluminium, the metal glows white and forms aluminium chloride:

$$2Al + 3Cl_2 \xrightarrow{\text{heat}} 2AlCl_3$$

Aluminium also reacts strongly with bromine and iodine. The reaction between a dry mixture of powdered aluminium and iodine can be triggered by adding just a few drops of water. The reaction is highly exothermic and some of the iodine is given off as purple fumes before it has a chance to react.

Hydrogen will burn in chlorine to form hydrogen chloride. Carried out a different way, the reaction can be explosive:

$$H_2 + Cl_2 \rightarrow 2HCl$$

Chlorine dissolves in water to give an acidic solution. This mixture is called **chlorine water** and contains two acids:

$$\underset{}{Cl_2 + H_2O} \rightarrow \underset{\text{hydrochloric acid}}{HCl} + \underset{\text{hypochlorous acid}}{HClO}$$

Chlorine water acts as an oxidising agent – hypochlorous acid can give up its oxygen to other substances. It also acts as a bleach because some coloured substances lose their colour when they are oxidised. This reaction is used as the chemical test for chlorine gas. Damp litmus or Universal Indicator paper is bleached when held in the gas. The halogens become steadily less reactive as you go down the group. Table **3.3** gives some examples of the reactivity of the halogens.

The displacement reactions shown in the lower part of Table **3.3** demonstrate the order of reactivity of the three major halogens. For example, if you add chlorine to a solution of potassium bromide, the chlorine displaces bromine (Figure **3.9**). Chlorine is more reactive than bromine, so it replaces it and potassium chloride is formed. Potassium bromide solution is colourless. It turns orange when chlorine is bubbled through it:

$$Cl_2 + \underset{\text{colourless}}{2KBr} \rightarrow 2KCl + \underset{\text{orange}}{Br_2}$$

Figure 3.9 Bromine is displaced by chlorine from a colourless solution of potassium bromide.

Chlorine will also displace iodine from potassium iodide:

$$Cl_2 + \underset{\text{colourless}}{2KI} \rightarrow 2KCl + \underset{\text{yellow-brown}}{I_2}$$

You will find more information about the halogens and their uses on page **268**.

Exam tip

When asked to put elements from a group in order of reactivity you must be very careful when reading the question to see whether the answer should be in order of increasing or decreasing reactivity.

Reaction with	Chlorine	Bromine	Iodine
Coloured dyes	bleaches easily	bleaches slowly	bleaches very slowly
Iron wool	iron wool reacts strongly to form iron(III) chloride; needs heat to start	iron reacts steadily to form iron(III) bromide; needs continuous heating	iron reacts slowly, even with continuous heating, to form iron(III) iodide
Chlorides	—	no reaction	no reaction
Bromides	displaces bromine, e.g. $Cl_2 + 2KBr \rightarrow 2KCl + Br_2$	—	no reaction
Iodides	displaces iodine, e.g. $Cl_2 + 2KI \rightarrow 2KCl + I_2$	displaces iodine, e.g. $Br_2 + 2KI \rightarrow 2KBr + I_2$	—

Table 3.3 Some reactions of the halogens.

Group 0 – the noble gases

When Mendeleev first constructed his table, part of his triumph was to predict the existence and properties of some undiscovered elements. However, there was no indication that a whole **group** of elements (Group 0) remained to be discovered! Because of their lack of reactivity, there was no clear sign of their existence. However, analysis of the gases in air led to the discovery of argon. There was no suitable place in the table for an individual element with argon's properties. This pointed to the existence of an entirely new group! In the 1890s, helium, which had first been detected by spectroscopy of light from the Sun during an eclipse, and the other noble gases in the group (Group 0) were isolated. The radioactive gas, radon, was the last to be purified, in 1908. One man, William Ramsay, was involved in the isolation of all the elements in the group. He was awarded the Nobel Prize for this major contribution.

All the noble gases are present in the Earth's atmosphere. Together they make up about 1% of the total, though argon is the most common. These gases are particularly unreactive. They were sometimes referred to as the **inert gases**, meaning they did not react at all. However, since the 1960s some compounds of xenon and krypton have been made and their name was changed to the **noble gases**. The uses of the noble gases depend on this unreacivity. Helium is used in airships and balloons because it is both light and unreactive. Argon is used to fill light bulbs because it will not react with the filament even at high temperatures. The best known use of the noble gases is, perhaps, its use in 'neon' lights (Figure **3.10**). The brightly coloured advertising lights work when an electric discharge takes place in a tube containg a little of a noble gas. Different gases give different colours.

The atoms of the noble gases do not combine with each other to form molecules or any other form of structure. Their melting points and boiling points are extremely low (Figure **3.11**). Helium has the lowest melting point of any element, and cannot be solidified by cooling alone (pressure is needed also). All these properties point to the atoms of the noble gases being particularly stable.

Put more precisely:

- the electron arrangements of the atoms of the noble gases are very stable,
- this means that they do not react readily with other atoms,
- in many situations where atoms of other elements bond or react chemically, they are trying to achieve that stable arrangement of electrons found in the noble gases.

The elements of Group 0 are between the two most reactive groups of elements (Groups I and VII). Indeed, it is their closeness to this group with stable electron arrangements that makes the alkali metals and the halogens so reactive. They can fairly easily achieve a noble-gas electron structure. The Group VII elements **gain** or **share** electrons and the Group I elements **lose** electrons to reach a noble-gas electron arrangement.

Figure 3.10 'Neon' lights give colour to our city centres by their use in advertising displays. The different colours are caused by different gases.

Figure 3.11 A small piece of rapidly melting 'argon ice' the melting point is −189 °C.

Key ideas so far

- The alkali metals are a group of soft, reactive metals which react with cold water to form hydrogen and an alkaline solution.
- The reactivity of the metals increases down the group.
- The melting points of the alkali metals decrease as the group is descended.
- The halogens are a group of reactive non-metals – Group VII in the Periodic Table.
- They all exist as diatomic molecules (Cl_2, for example).
- Their physical properties change as you go down the group – their melting points and boiling points increase, and the intensity of their colour deepens.
- Their chemical reactivity decreases down the group – the more reactive halogens will displace the lower halogens from halides.
- The noble gases are chemically unreactive and their uses depend on this.
- Their unreactivity is linked to their electron structure.

Quick-check questions

1 What is the name of the alkali formed when potassium reacts with water?
2 Write a word equation for the reaction between lithium and water.
3 Which halogen(s) will displace bromine from a solution of potassium bromide?
4 Give a use and a test for chlorine.

3.3 Trends across a period

The vertical groups of elements show similar properties, but following a period across the table highlights the trend from metallic to non-metallic properties. This can be explored by looking across a period. The first period of the table contains just two elements, hydrogen and helium, both of which are distinctive in different ways. The final period in the table is as yet incomplete. Each of the five remaining periods of elements starts with a reactive alkali metal and finishes with an unreactive, non-metallic, noble gas. In Period 3, for example, from sodium to argon, there appears to be a gradual change in physical properties across the period. The change in properties seems to centre around silicon; elements before this behave as metals and those after it as non-metals (Figure **3.12**).

The changeover in properties is emphasised if we look at Group IV as well. As we go down this group, the change is from non-metal to metal. The metalloids, silicon and germanium, are in the centre of the group (Figure **3.12**).

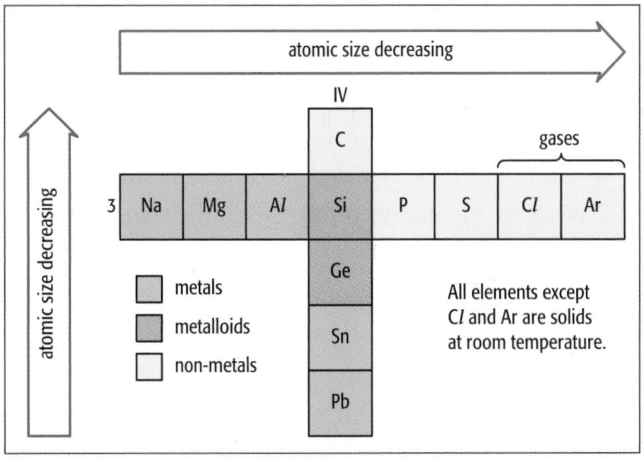

Figure 3.12 The changes in properties of the elements in Period 3 and in Group IV of the Periodic Table.

The transition elements

If we look at Period 4 in the table we see that there is a whole 'block' of elements in the centre of the table. This block of elements falls outside the main groups of elements that we have talked of so far. They are best considered not as a vertical group of elements but as a row or block. They are usually referred to as the **transition elements** (or **transition metals**). Their properties make them amongst the most useful metallic elements available to us (Figure **3.13**, overleaf). They are much less reactive than the metals in Groups I and II. Many have excellent corrosion resistance, for example chromium. The very high melting point of tungsten (3410 °C) has led to its use in the filaments of light bulbs.

Many familiar objects are made from transition metals. Figure **3.13** shows a range of these: steel nails, chrome bottle stopper, copper pipe joints, iron horseshoe magnet, cupro-nickel coins (a mix of 75% copper, 25% nickel) and copper-plated steel coins.

These **general** properties mean that the transition elements are useful in a number of different ways. In

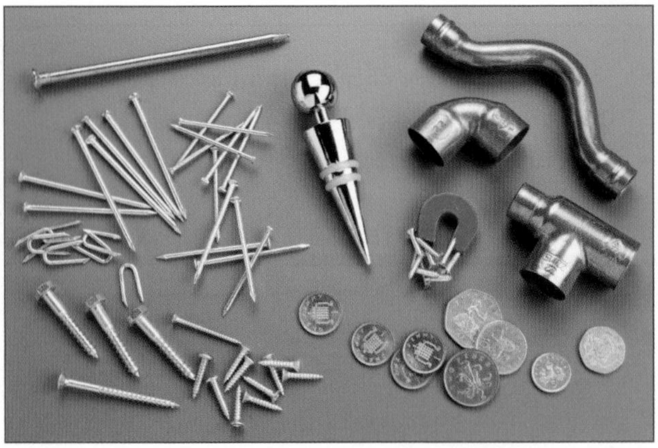

Figure 3.13 Some everyday objects made from transition metals.

addition there are **particular** properties that make these metals distinctive and useful for more specific purposes. One important feature of transition metals is that their compounds are often coloured (Figure 3.14).

> The transition metals have the following general features:
> - they are hard and strong
> - they have high density
> - they have high melting and boiling points.
>
> Two of the distinctive properties of the transition elements are:
> - many of their compounds are coloured,
> - these metals often show more than one valency – they form more than one type of ion. For example, iron can form compounds containing iron(II) ions, Fe^{2+}, or iron(III) ions, Fe^{3+}.

The position of hydrogen in the Periodic Table

Hydrogen is difficult to place in the Periodic Table. Different versions place it above Group I or Group VII. More often, in modern tables, it is left by itself (Figure **3.15**). This is because, as the smallest atom of all, its properties are distinctive and unique. It does not fit easily into the trends shown in any one group (Table **3.4**).

$_1$H hydrogen — hydrogen doesn't belong to any group

Group I	II	III	IV	V	VI	VII	
							$_2$He helium
$_3$Li lithium	$_4$Be beryllium	$_5$B boron	$_6$C carbon	$_7$N nitrogen	$_8$O oxygen	$_9$F fluorine	$_{10}$Ne neon
$_{11}$Na sodium	$_{12}$Mg magnesium	$_{13}$Al aluminium	$_{14}$Si slicon	$_{15}$P phosphorus	$_{16}$S sulfur	$_{17}$Cl chlorine	$_{18}$Ar argon
$_{19}$K potassium	$_{20}$Ca calcium						

Figure 3.15 The position of hydrogen in the Periodic Table.

Lithium	Hydrogen	Fluorine
solid at room temperature	gas	gas
metal	non-metal; forms diatomic molecules (H_2)	non-metal; forms diatomic molecules (F_2)
has one electron in outer shell	has one electron in outer shell	has seven electrons in outer shell
can lose one electron to achieve a noble-gas arrangement (forms a positive ion)	can form **either** a positive **or** a negative ion; can gain one electron to achieve a noble-gas arrangement, or lose its only electron	can gain one electron to achieve a noble-gas arrangement (forms a negative ion)

Table 3.4 A comparison of hydrogen atoms with those of lithium (Group I) and fluorine (Group VII).

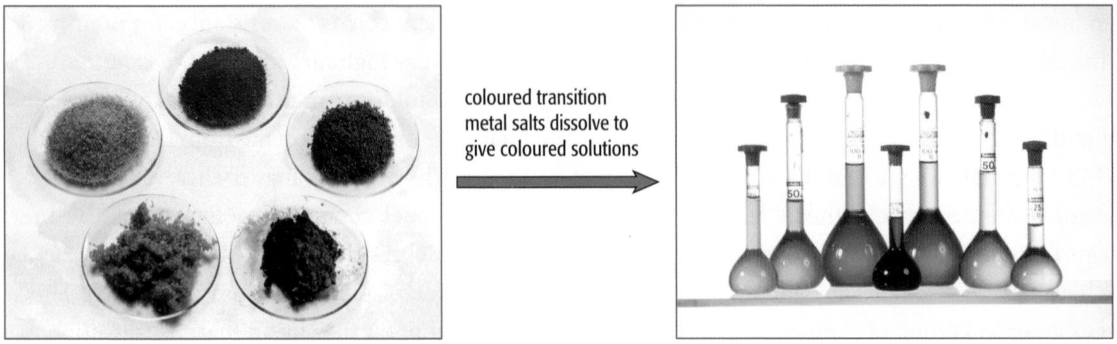

Figure 3.14 Many of the compounds of transition metals are coloured, and when they dissolve they give coloured solutions.

Key ideas so far

- The Periodic Table lists the elements of the Universe in order of increasing proton number (atomic number).
- The Periodic Table has a structure that provides useful information, and the elements are grouped so that certain patterns of properties repeat themselves.
- The elements are broadly divided into metals and non-metals.
- The metals have certain characteristic properties, the most important being that they conduct electricity and are malleable and ductile.
- The Periodic Table is divided into vertical groups and horizontal periods.
- There is a close relationship between the electron arrangement of an element and its position in the Periodic Table.
- Certain groups of elements have specific names, for example the alkali metals, and show 'family' properties.
- There is a block of elements in the centre of the table known as the transition metals.
- The transition metals have certain distinctive properties: they have high densities, high melting points, form coloured compounds and the metals (or their compounds) are often good catalysts.

Quick-check questions

1 In which direction does the change in element type run, when going across a period from left to right?

2 Which metal has the highest melting point in Period 3?

3 Which metal is the softest and least dense in Period 3?

4 What is the formula of chlorine?

5 Which of the elements in Period 3 has the highest melting point?

6 Why is copper(II) sulfate blue?

3.4 Chemical bonding in elements and compounds

E

We live on the 'water planet'. The surface of the Earth is distinctive because so much of it is covered with water. From space, it is the blue colours of water in seas and oceans and the white of the moisture-laden clouds that distinguish the Earth from other planets. The Earth is unique in being the only planet in our solar system where conditions allow water to exist in all three states of matter.

Simple compounds such as water, ammonia and methane begin to show the variety that can be achieved when the atoms of elements combine together. Water is formed from hydrogen and oxygen. Each water molecule contains two hydrogen atoms bonded to an oxygen atom. In fact, the formula of water (H_2O) is perhaps the best known chemical formula.

Chemical bonding involves the outer electrons of each atom. As we examine a range of substances, we shall see that, whatever type of bonding holds the structure together, it is the outer electrons that are used. The diversity of the material world is produced by the different ways in which atoms can join together.

Bonding in the elements

Earlier we saw that some elements are not simply made up of separate atoms individually arranged. Elements such as oxygen (O_2) and hydrogen (H_2) consist of **diatomic molecules**. Indeed, the only elements that are made up of individual atoms moving almost independently of each other are the noble gases (Group 0). These are the elements whose electron arrangements are most stable and so their atoms do not combine with each other.

Most of the elements **do** form structures. Their atoms are linked by some type of bonding. Most elements are metals. The structures in this case are held together by **metallic bonding**. The non-metallic elements to the right of the Periodic Table are held together by **covalent bonding**. Both these types of bonding use the outer electrons in some way.

> **Bonding in the elements:**
> - Metallic elements are held together by **metallic bonding**, which results in **metallic lattices.**
> - Non-metallic elements are held together by **covalent bonding** or exist as **separate atoms** (the noble gases). Covalent bonding results in **simple molecules** or **giant molecular lattices.**

Bonding in metals

Metal atoms have relatively few electrons in their outer shells. When they are packed together, each metal atom loses its outer electrons into a 'sea' of free electrons (or mobile electrons). Having lost electrons, the atoms are no longer electrically neutral. They become positive **ions** because they have lost electrons but the number of protons in the nucleus has remained unchanged.

Therefore the structure of a metal is made up of positive ions packed together. These ions are surrounded by electrons, which can move freely between the ions. These free electrons are **delocalised** (not restricted to orbiting one positive ion) and form a kind of electrostatic 'glue' holding the structure together (Figure **3.16**). In an electrical circuit, metals can conduct electricity because the mobile electrons can move through the structure, carrying the current. This type of bonding (called **metallic bonding**) is present in alloys as well. Alloys such as solder and brass, for example, will conduct electricity.

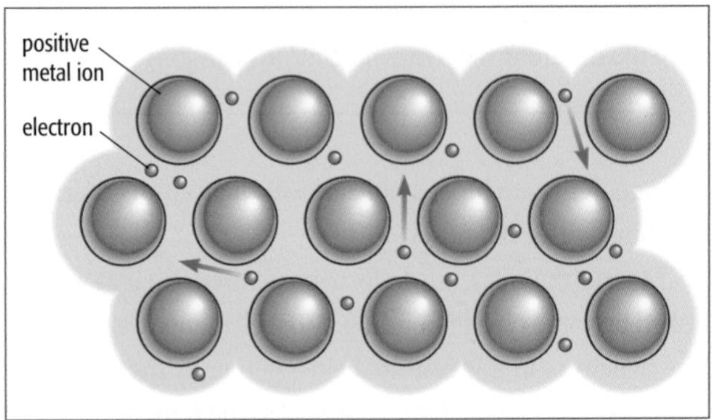

Figure 3.16 Metallic bonding – the metal ions are surrounded by a 'sea' of mobile electrons.

> - An **ion** is a charged particle made from an atom by the loss or gain of electrons.
> - Metal atoms most easily lose electrons, so they become **positive ions**. In doing so they achieve a more stable electron arrangement, usually that of the nearest noble gas.

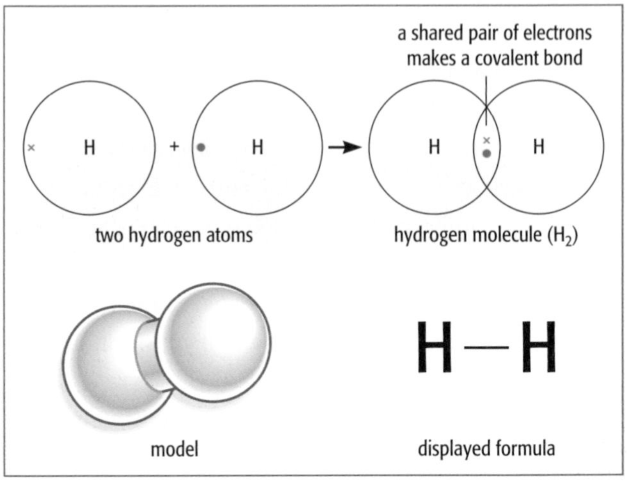

Figure 3.17 The hydrogen molecule is formed by **sharing** the electrons from the atoms. A space-filling model can be used to show the atoms overlapping.

Bonding in non-metals

Hydrogen normally exists in the form of diatomic molecules (H_2). Two atoms bond together by sharing their electrons. The orbits overlap and a molecule is formed (Figure **3.17**).

Through this sharing, each atom gains a share in two electrons. This is the number of electrons in the outer shell of helium, the nearest noble gas to hydrogen. (Remember that the electron arrangement of helium is very stable; helium atoms do **not** form He_2 molecules.) Sharing electrons like this is known as **covalent bonding**. It has been shown that in a hydrogen molecule the electrons are more likely to be found between the two nuclei. The forces of attraction between the shared electrons and the nuclei are greater than any repulsive forces. The molecule is held together by the bond.

> The features of covalent bonding are:
> - the bond is formed by the sharing of a pair of electrons between two atoms
> - each atom contributes one electron to each bond
> - molecules are formed from atoms linked together by covalent bonds.

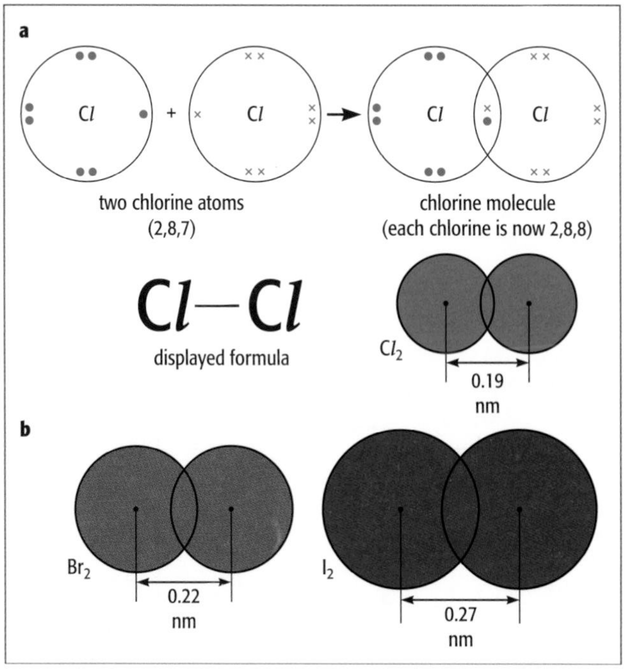

Figure 3.18 **a** The formation of the covalent bond in chlorine molecules (Cl_2). Each atom gains a share in eight electrons in its outer shell. The diagram can be drawn showing the outer electrons only, because the inner electrons are not involved in the bonding. **b** Molecules of Br_2 and I_2 are formed in the same way. They are larger because the original atoms are bigger.

Many non-metallic elements form diatomic molecules. However, elements other than hydrogen bond in order to gain a share of **eight** electrons in their outer shells. This is the number of electrons in the outer shell of all the noble gases apart from helium. Thus the halogens (Group VII) form covalent molecules (Figure **3.18**).

Molecules of hydrogen and the halogens are each held together by a single covalent bond. Such a single bond uses two electrons, one from each atom. The bond can be drawn as a single line between the two atoms.

Note that when drawing diagrams showing the overlap of the outer shells, we can show the outer electrons only, because the inner electrons are not involved in the bonding. Each atom gains a share in eight electrons in its outer shell.

Phosphorus (P_4) and sulfur (S_8) form the most complicated simple molecules. These are held together by single covalent bonds. In the case of P_4, the atoms are arranged in a tetrahedron and there are six single covalent bonds linking the atoms. For S_8, the atoms form a 'crown-shaped' ring with eight single covalent bonds between the atoms.

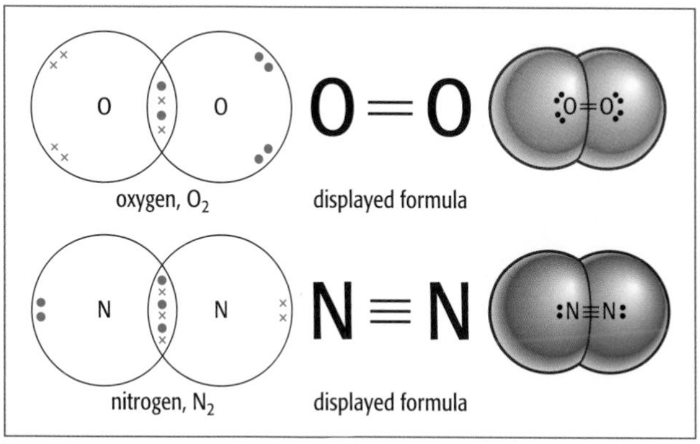

Figure 3.19 The structures of oxygen (O_2) and nitrogen (N_2) molecules involve multiple covalent bonding. An oxygen molecule contains a double bond, while nitrogen contains a triple bond.

When molecules of oxygen (O_2) or nitrogen (N_2) are formed, more electrons have to be used in bonding if the atoms are to gain a share of eight electrons. These molecules are held together by a double bond (O_2) or a triple bond (N_2) (Figure **3.19**).

The non-metals in the middle of the main-group elements, for example carbon and silicon, do not form simple molecules. They exist as **giant molecular structures** held together by single covalent bonds. In these structures, the atoms are joined to each other in an extensive network or **lattice** (see Figure **3.42**, page **92**). Such structures are very strong because all the atoms are interlinked by strong covalent bonds. The structure of the carbon atoms in diamond is a three-dimensional lattice structure in which each carbon atom is joined to four others by strong covalent bonds. A similar structure exists in silicon, which is an important element in the electronics industry.

Chemical bonding in compounds

Different elements combine together to form the vast range of compounds that make up our world. They vary from inert and heat-resistant ceramic materials to high explosives, and from lethal poisons to the molecules of life. All depend on the means of chemical bonding. Two major types of bond hold compounds together. The first is covalent bonding, which, as we have seen, involves **sharing** electrons between atoms. However, the behaviour of metal plus non-metal compounds arises from a different type of bonding. Here electrons are **transferred** from one atom to another. These compounds are held together by **electrostatic forces** between separate ions: **ionic bonding**.

Bonding in compounds:

- Non-metal plus non-metal compounds are held together by **covalent bonding**, which results in **simple molecules** or **giant molecular lattices.**
- Metal plus non-metal compounds are held together by **ionic bonding**, which results in **giant ionic lattices.**

Covalent compounds

In covalent compounds, bonds are again made by sharing electrons between atoms. In simple molecules, the atoms combine to achieve a more stable arrangement of electrons, most often that of a noble gas. The formation of hydrogen chloride (HCl) involves the two atoms sharing a pair of electrons (Figure **3.20**).

The examples shown in Figure **3.21** illustrate different ways of representing this sharing. They also show how the formula of the compound corresponds to the numbers of each atom in a molecule.

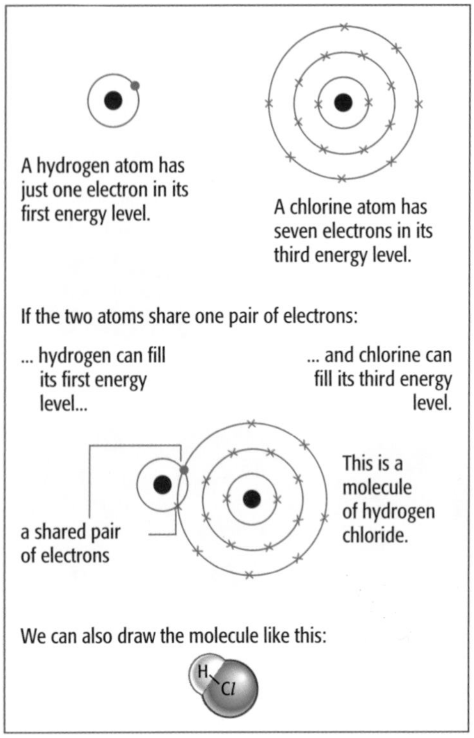

Figure 3.20 Hydrogen and chlorine atoms share a pair of electrons to form a molecule of hydrogen chloride.

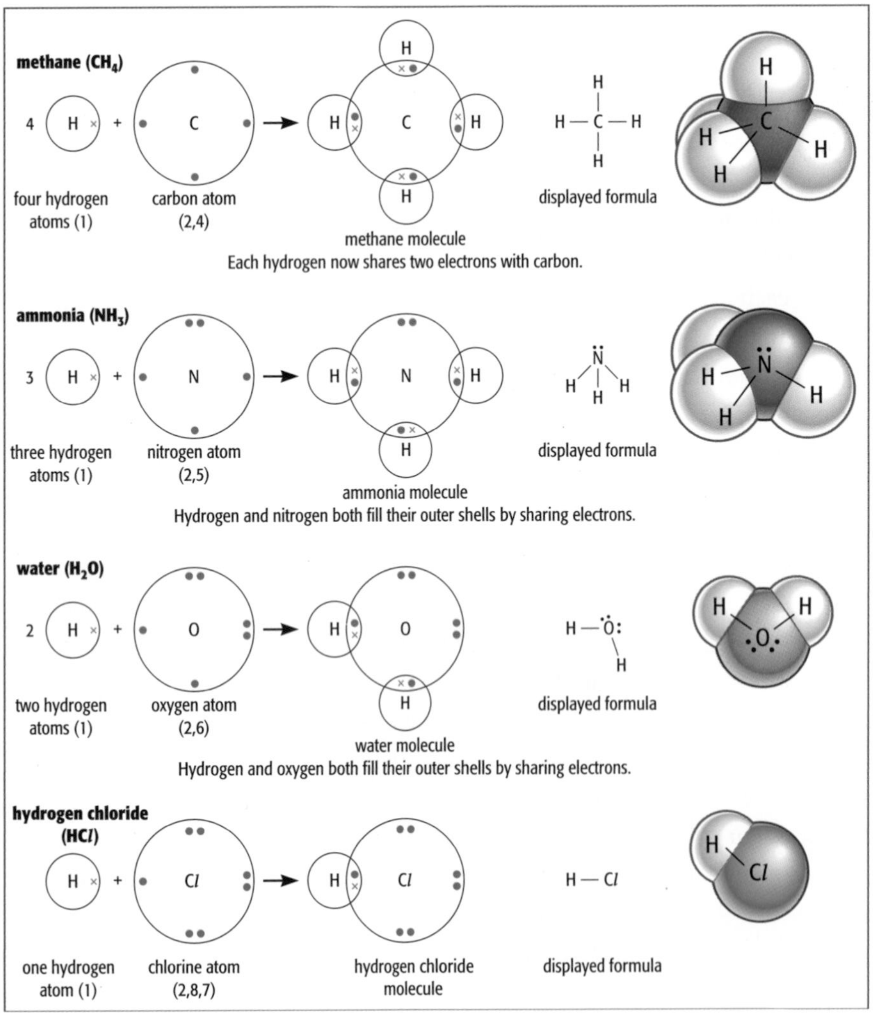

Figure 3.21 Examples of the formation of simple covalent molecules. Again, only the outer electrons of the atoms are shown. More complex examples are shown opposite.

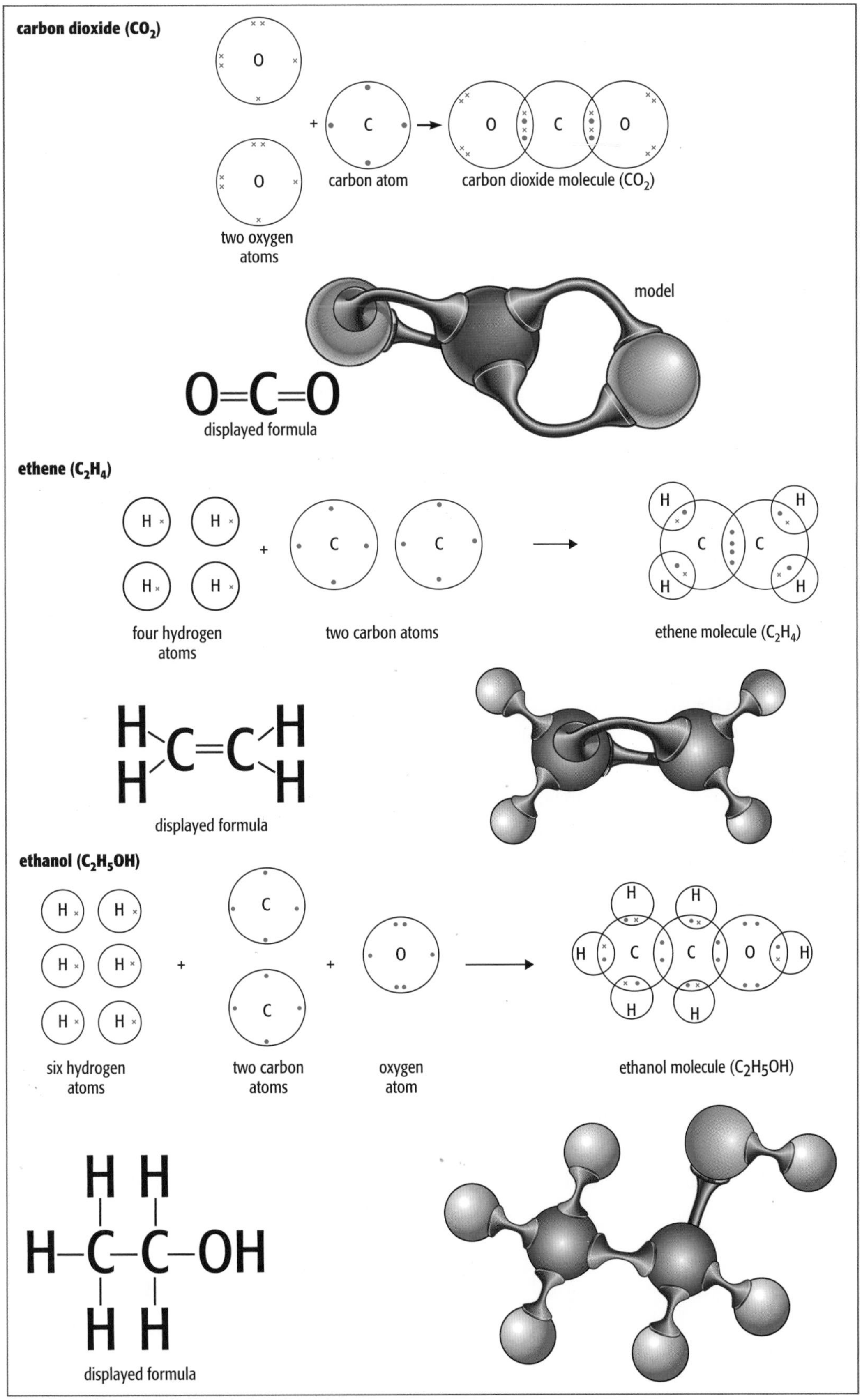

Figure 3.22 The formation of the carbon dioxide, ethene and ethanol molecules, showing the outer electrons only. Ball-and-stick models can be used to show the structure.

In each case, the atoms achieve a share in the same number of electrons as the noble gas nearest to that element in the Periodic Table. In all but the case of hydrogen, this means a share of eight electrons in their outer shell.

Earlier we saw that multiple covalent bonds can exist in molecules of the elements oxygen and nitrogen. They can exist in compounds too. The carbon dioxide molecule is held together by double bonds between the atoms (Figure **3.22**, on page **79**). This figure also shows some other examples of bonding in compounds that you will meet again in Chapter **10**.

Ionic compounds

Compounds of a metal plus a non-metal generally adopt a third type of bonding. This involves the **transfer** of electrons from one atom to another. This transfer of electrons results in the formation of positive and negative ions. The oppositely charged ions are then attracted to each other by **electrostatic forces**.

- Ions are charged particles formed from atoms by the loss or gain of electrons.
- The electrons involved in the formation of ions are those in the outer shell of the atoms.
- Metal atoms lose their outer electrons to become positive ions. In doing so they achieve the more stable electron arrangement of the nearest noble gas.
- Generally, atoms of non-metals gain electrons to become negative ions. Again, in doing so they achieve the stable electron arrangement of the nearest noble gas to them in the Periodic Table.

A common example of a compound that involves ionic bonding is sodium chloride (Figure **3.23**). The sodium atoms, which have an electron arrangement of 2,8,1,

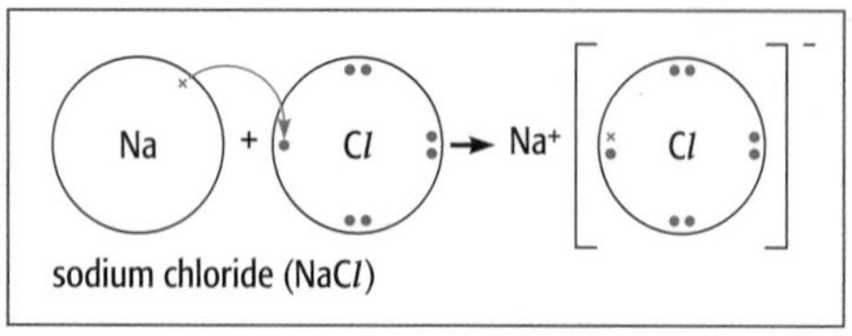

Figure 3.23 The transfer of electrons from a sodium atom to a chlorine atom to form ions.

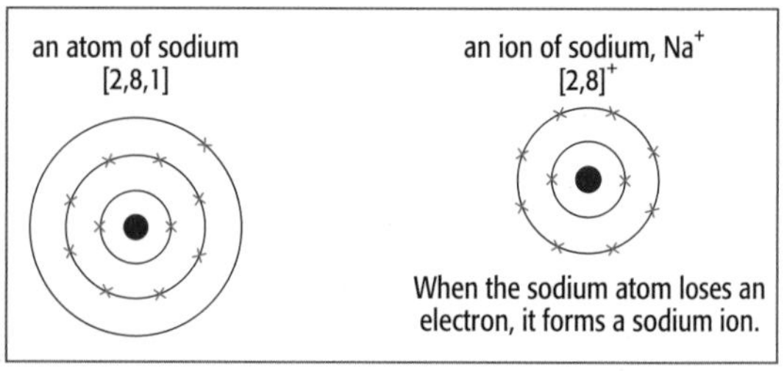

Figure 3.24 A sodium atom loses an electron to become a sodium ion.

each lose their one outer electron to form sodium ions (Na^+) (Figure **3.24**).

The sodium ion then has the stable electron arrangement (2,8) of a neon atom – the element just before it in the Periodic Table. The electron released is transferred to a chlorine atom. The sodium ion has a single positive charge because it now has just 10 electrons in total, but there are still 11 protons in the nucleus of the atom.

The chlorine atoms, electron arrangement 2,8,7, each gain an electron released from the sodium atoms and they become chloride ions (Cl^-) (Figure **3.25**). The chloride ion (electron arrangement 2,8,8) has the electron arrangement of an argon atom. The chloride ion has a negative charge because it has one more electron (18) than there are protons in the nucleus.

The positive and negative ions in sodium chloride are held together by the electrostatic attraction between opposite charges.

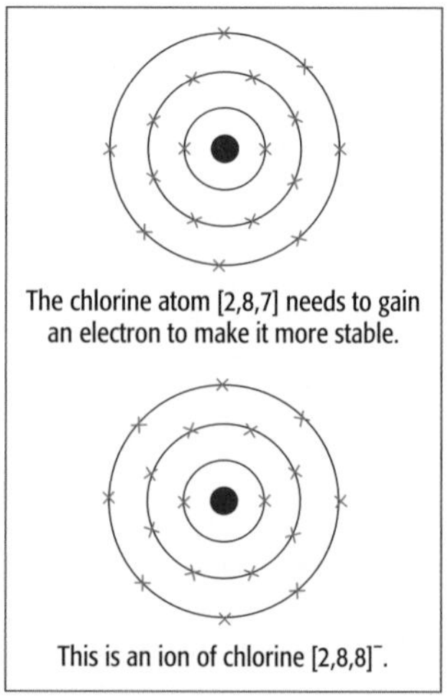

Figure 3.25 A chlorine atom gains an electron to become a chloride ion.

Exam tip

For the Core paper, the examples of ionic bonding you need to be familiar with are those between Group I metals and Group VII non-metals – the alkali metals and the halogens. Try drawing diagrams such as Figure **3.23** for compounds such as lithium fluoride or potassium bromide. You will see that there is a great similarity in the diagrams.

S More complex ionic compounds than those formed between the alkali metals and the halogens require care in working out the transfer of a greater number of electrons. Figure **3.26** shows two examples of such compounds.

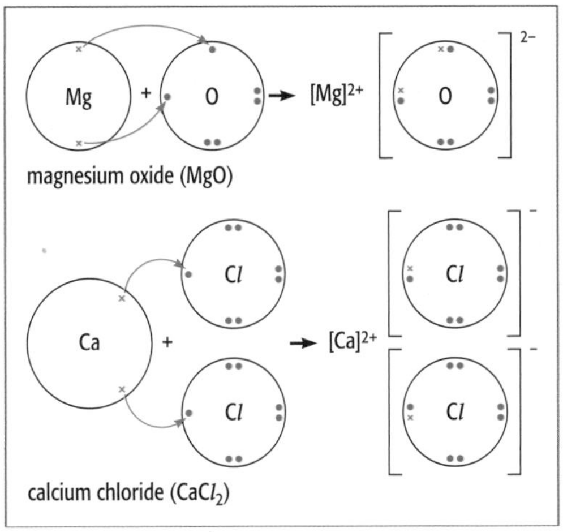

Figure 3.26 Diagrams showing the formation of ionic bonds in magnesium oxide and calcium chloride. Again, only the outer electrons are shown.

There are certain features common to **ionic bonding**:

- metal atoms always lose their outer electrons to form positive ions
- the number of positive charges on a metal ion is equal to the number of electrons lost
- non-metal atoms, with the exception of hydrogen, always gain electrons to become negative ions
- the number of negative charges on a non-metal ion is equal to the number of electrons gained
- in both cases the ions formed have a more stable electron arrangement, usually that of the noble gas nearest to the element concerned
- ionic (electrovalent) bonds result from the attraction between oppositely charged ions.

Exam tip

Do practise drawing the diagrams for both covalent and ionic bonding so that you can draw them accurately in the exam.

When drawing the diagrams of ionic bonding, make sure you remember to put in the charges outside the brackets on each ion.

S Ionic compounds (such as sodium chloride) are solids at room temperature. The ions arrange themselves into a regular lattice (Figure **3.27**). In the lattice each ion is surrounded by ions of the opposite charge. The whole **giant ionic structure** is held together by the electrostatic forces of attraction that occur between particles of opposite charge (see Section **3.6**).

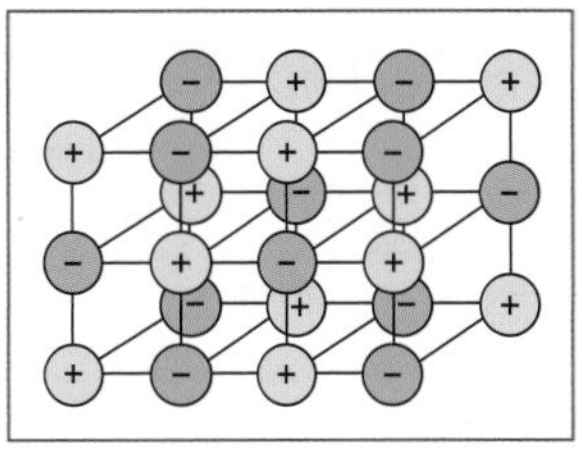

Figure 3.27 A giant ionic lattice where each ion is surrounded by ions of opposite charge.

E

Polyatomic (compound) ions

The ionic compounds mentioned so far have been made from simple ions, for example Na^+, K^+, Mg^{2+}, Cl^-, O^{2-}. However, in many important ionic compounds the metal ion is combined with a negative ion containing a **group** of atoms (for example SO_4^{2-}, NO_3^-, CO_3^{2-}). These **polyatomic ions** (or **compound ions** or **groups**) are made up of atoms covalently bonded together. These groups have a negative charge because they have gained electrons to make a stable structure. Examples of such ions are shown in Figure **3.28** (overleaf). In addition to these negative compound ions, there is one important polyatomic ion that is positively charged, the ammonium ion, NH_4^+ (Figure **3.28**). Table **3.5** (overleaf) gives a summary of some simple and polyatomic ions.

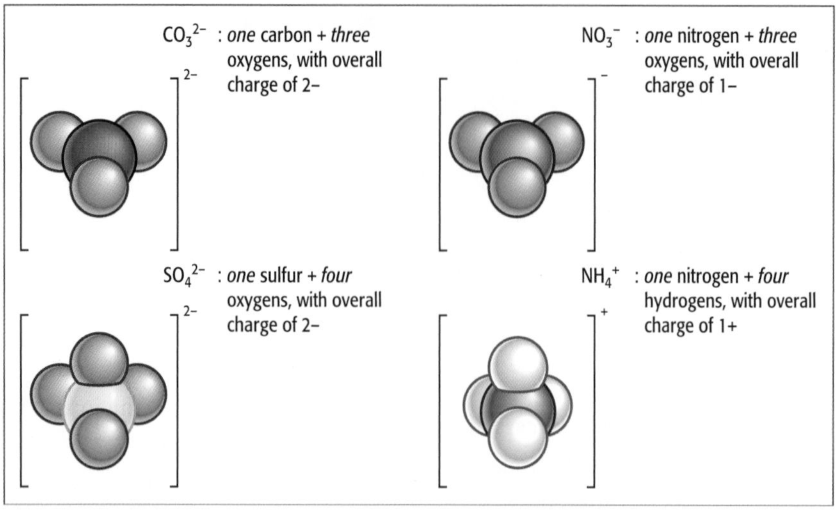

Figure 3.28 Three examples of negatively charged polyatomic ions and a positively charged polyatomic ion. The numbers of atoms and the overall charge carried by each group of atoms are shown.

Valency	Simple metal ions	Simple non-metallic ions		Polyatomic (or compound) ions	
	(+ve)	(+ve)	(–ve)	(+ve)	(–ve)
1	sodium, Na^+	hydrogen, H^+	hydride, H^-	ammonium, NH_4^+	hydroxide, OH^-
	potassium, K^+		chloride, Cl^-		nitrate, NO_3^-
	silver, Ag^+		bromide, Br^-		hydrogencarbonate, HCO_3^-
	copper(I), Cu^+		iodide, I^-		
2	magnesium, Mg^{2+}		oxide, O^{2-}		sulfate, SO_4^{2-}
	calcium, Ca^{2+}		sulfide, S^{2-}		carbonate, CO_3^{2-}
	zinc, Zn^{2+}				
	iron(II), Fe^{2+}				
	copper(II), Cu^{2+}				
3	aluminium, Al^{3+}		nitride, N^{3-}		phosphate, PO_4^{3-}
	iron(III), Fe^{3+}				

Table 3.5 Some common simple and polyatomic ions.

Through our discussion of elements and compounds we have seen that there are three major types of **chemical bonding**:

- metallic bonding
- covalent bonding
- ionic bonding.

The types of structure based on these methods of bonding are summarised in Figure **3.29**.

The physical properties of ionic and covalent compounds

Knowledge of how atoms combine to make different types of structure helps us begin to understand why substances have different physical properties. Table **3.6** shows the broad differences in properties of ionic and simple covalent compounds.

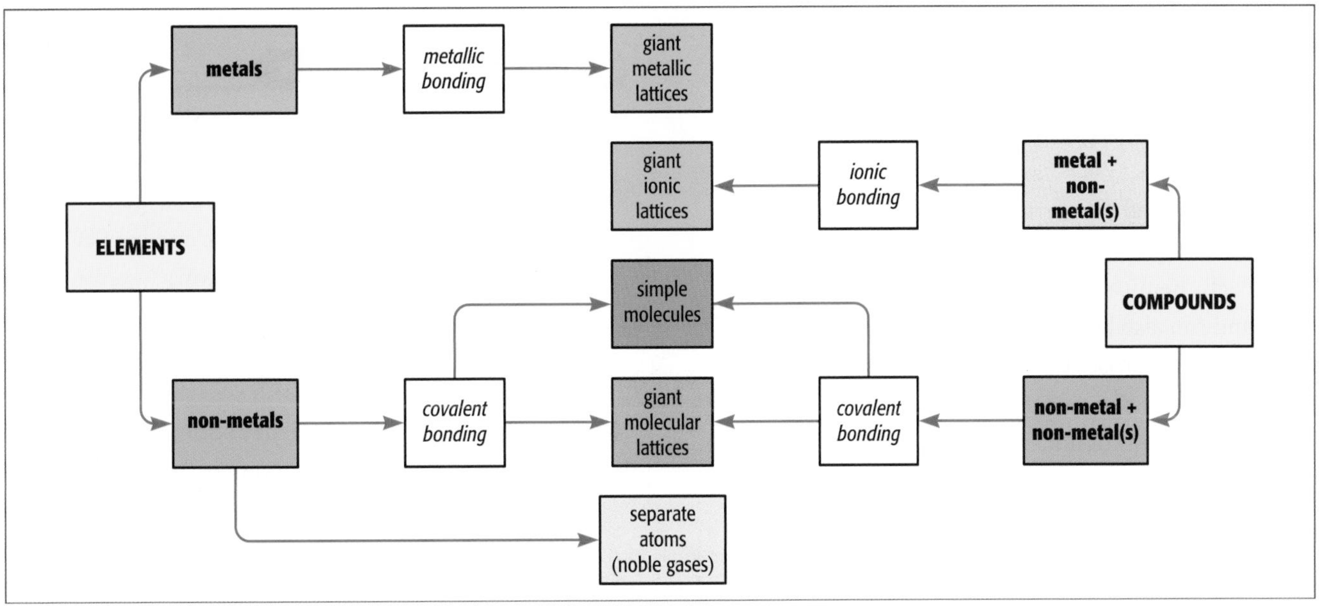

Figure 3.29 An overall summary of the bonding in elements and compounds.

Properties of typical ionic compounds	Reason for these properties
They are crystalline solids at room temperature.	There is a regular arrangement of the ions in a lattice. Ions with opposite charge are next to each other.
They have high melting and boiling points.	Ions are attracted to each other by strong electrostatic forces. Large amounts of energy are needed to separate them.
They are often soluble in water (not usually soluble in organic solvents, e.g. ethanol, methylbenzene).	Water is attracted to charged ions and so many ionic solids dissolve.
They conduct electricity when molten or dissolved in water (not when solid).	In the liquid or solution, the ions are free to move about. They can move towards the electrodes when a voltage is applied.
Properties of simple covalent compounds	**Reason for these properties**
They are often liquids or gases at room temperature.	These substances are made of simple molecules. The atoms are joined together by covalent bonds.
They have low melting and boiling points.	The forces between the molecules (intermolecular forces) are only very weak. Not much energy is needed to move the molecules further apart.
They are soluble in organic solvents such as ethanol or methylbenzene (very few are soluble in water).	Covalent molecular substances dissolve in covalent solvents.
They do not conduct electricity.	There are no ions present to carry the current.

Table 3.6 The properties of ionic and simple covalent compounds.

Key ideas so far

- The structures of all substances are made up of either atoms, ions or molecules.
- There are three main types of chemical bonding that hold these structures together – metallic, ionic and covalent bonding.
- Covalent bonding occurs in some elements and non-metallic compounds, and involves the 'sharing' of electrons between atoms to form stable molecules.

- Compounds of a metal plus a non-metal involve ionic bonding, in which positive and negative ions are held together by strong electrostatic forces.
- The physical properties of a substance are related to the type of bonding present.
- Each chemical compound has a particular name and can also be represented by a chemical formula that summarises the atoms or ions present.
- Two types of covalent structure can be formed by the atoms of non-metals – simple molecule and giant molecular (macromolecular) structures.
- Diamond and graphite have giant molecular structures made up of carbon atoms.
- Metallic bonding involves the closely packed atoms losing their outer electrons into a 'sea' of mobile electrons.
- Covalent compounds can have **simple molecular structures** – carbon dioxide and water, for example – or giant molecular (macromolecular) structures, silicon(IV) oxide, for instance.

? Quick-check questions

1 What type of bond would be found between the following pairs of elements?
a sulfur and chlorine **b** carbon and oxygen
c magnesium and nitrogen **d** zinc and copper

2 Why is the formula of hydrogen always written as H_2?

3 What force holds the sodium and chlorine together in sodium chloride?

4 Draw diagrams of the covalent bonding in the following elements and compounds (show the outer electrons only in your diagrams):
a hydrogen **b** water **c** ammonia **d** methane

5 Draw diagrams of the ionic bonding in the following compounds:
a sodium chloride **b** lithium fluoride

6 Why is it true to say that calcium carbonate has both ionic and covalent bonds?

7 Draw diagrams of the ionic bonding in the following compounds:
a magnesium oxide **b** calcium chloride

3.5 The chemical formulae of elements and compounds

The chemical 'shorthand' of representing an element by its symbol can be taken further. It is even more useful to be able quickly to sum up the basic structure of an element or compound using its **chemical formula**.

The formulae of elements

Those elements which are made up of individual atoms or small molecules (up to three atoms covalently bonded together) are represented by the formula of the particle present (Figure 3.30). Where elements exist as giant structures, whether held together by metallic or covalent bonding, the formula is simply the symbol of the element (for example Cu, Mg, Fe, Na, K, etc., and C, Si, Ge). For convenience, the same applies to elements such as phosphorus (P) or sulfur (S). In these cases, the molecules contain more than three atoms.

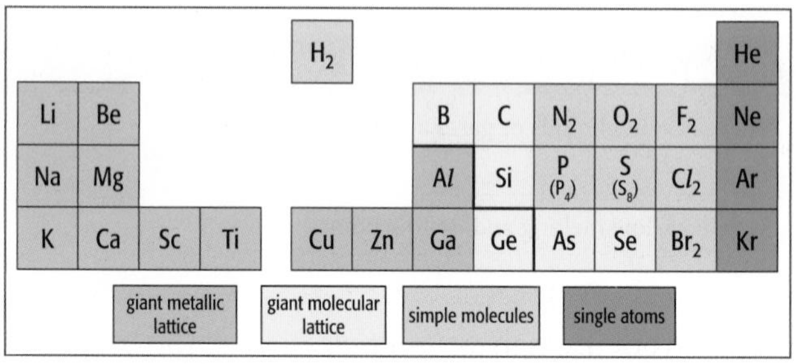

Figure 3.30 The formulae of the elements are linked to their structure and their position in the Periodic Table.

The formulae of ionic compounds

Ionic compounds are solids at room temperature, and their formulae are simply the whole-number ratio of the positive to negative ions in the structure. Thus, in magnesium chloride, there are two chloride ions (Cl^-) for each magnesium ion (Mg^{2+}).

ions present	Mg^{2+}	Cl^-
		Cl^-
total charge	2+	2−

The formula is $MgCl_2$. The overall structure must be neutral. The positive and negative charges must balance each other.

The size of the charge on an ion is a measure of its valency, see Table **3.5** on page **82**, or combining power. Mg^{2+} ions can combine with Cl^- ions in a ratio of 1 : 2, but Na^+ ions can only bond in a 1 : 1 ratio with Cl^- ions. This idea of valency can be used to ensure that you always use the correct formula for an ionic compound. Follow the examples of aluminium oxide and calcium oxide (below), and make sure you understand how this works.

Formula for aluminium oxide

Write down the correct symbols

Write down the charges on the ions

Formula $\mathbf{Al_2O_3}$

Formula for calcium oxide

Write down the correct symbols

Write down the charges on the ions

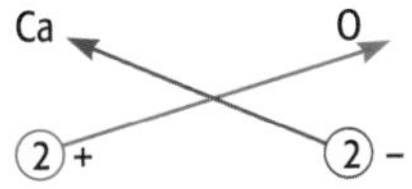

Ca_2O_2
Simplify the ratio:
Formula **CaO**

The same rules apply when writing the formulae of compounds containing polyatomic ions because each of them has an overall charge (see Table **3.5** on page **82**). It is useful to put the formula of the polyatomic ion in brackets. This emphasises that it cannot be changed. For example the formula of the carbonate ion is always CO_3^{2-}. Work through the examples for sodium carbonate and ammonium sulfate below.

Formula of sodium carbonate

Write down the correct 'symbols'

Write down the charges on the ions

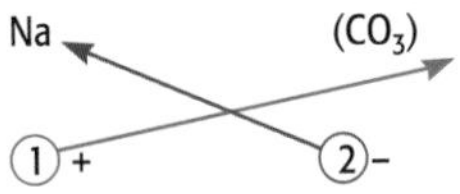

Formula $\mathbf{Na_2CO_3}$
The brackets are not needed if there is only one ion present.

Formula of ammonium sulfate

Write down the correct 'symbols'

Write down the charges on the ions

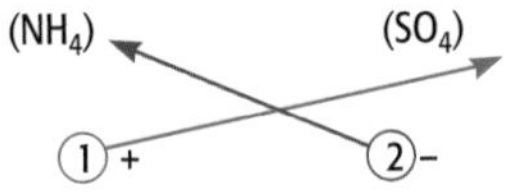

Formula $\mathbf{(NH_4)_2SO_4}$

Name	Formula	Ions present		Ratio
sodium chloride	NaCl	Na^+	Cl^-	1 : 1
ammonium nitrate	NH_4NO_3	NH_4^+	NO_3^-	1 : 1
potassium sulfate	K_2SO_4	K^+	SO_4^{2-}	2 : 1
calcium hydrogen-carbonate	$Ca(HCO_3)_2$	Ca^{2+}	HCO_3^-	1 : 2
copper(II) sulfate	$CuSO_4$	Cu^{2+}	SO_4^{2-}	1 : 1
magnesium nitrate	$Mg(NO_3)_2$	Mg^{2+}	NO_3^-	1 : 2
aluminium chloride	$AlCl_3$	Al^{3+}	Cl^-	1 : 3

Table 3.7 The formulae of some ionic compounds.

Table **3.7** summarises the formulae of some important ionic compounds.

Exam tip

Be very careful when writing chemical formulae to get the symbols of the elements correct. Remember the unusual symbols: that sodium is Na and not So, for example.

Remember that the second letter in any symbol is lower case: Na not NA, Cl not CL and Co not CO, for instance.

The formulae of covalent compounds

The idea of an atom having a valency, or combining power, can also be applied to working out the formulae of **covalent** compounds. Here the valency of an atom is the number of covalent bonds it can form. The 'cross-over' method for working out chemical formulae can be applied to covalent compounds in two situations:

- simple molecules with a central atom, for example water, methane, carbon dioxide and ammonia:

Formula of ammonia

Write down the symbols

Write down the valencies

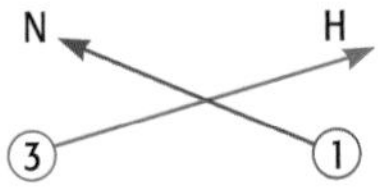

Formula $\mathbf{NH_3}$

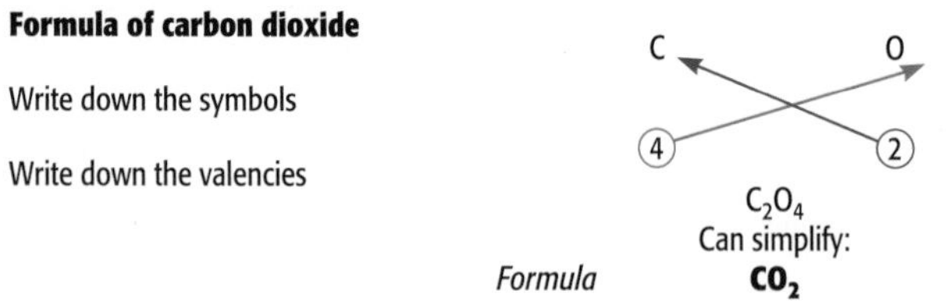

- giant covalent molecules, where the formula is simply the whole-number ratio of the atoms present in the giant lattice, for example silica.

The valency of an element in the main groups of the Periodic Table can be worked out from the group number of the element. The relationship is as follows.

For elements in Groups I–IV,

valency = group number

For elements in Groups V–VII,

valency = 8 – group number

Elements in Group 0 have a valency of 0.

This trend in valency with the group number can be seen by looking at typical compounds of the elements of Period 3. You can see that the valency rises to a value of 4 and then decreases to zero as we cross the period.

Group	I	II	III	IV	V	VI	VII	0
Valency	1	2	3	4	3	2	1	0
Typical compound	$NaCl$	$MgCl_2$	$AlCl_3$	$SiCl_4$	PH_3	H_2S	HCl	–

For example, carbon is in Group IV, so its valency is 4, and oxygen is in Group VI, so its valency is 8 – 6 = 2.

Examples of writing formulae

The method for working out formulae above does **not** work for the many covalent molecules that do not have a single central atom, for example H_2O_2, C_2H_6, C_3H_6, etc. The formulae of these compounds still obey the valency rules. However, the numbers in the formula represent the actual number of atoms of each element present in a molecule of the compound (Figure 3.31).

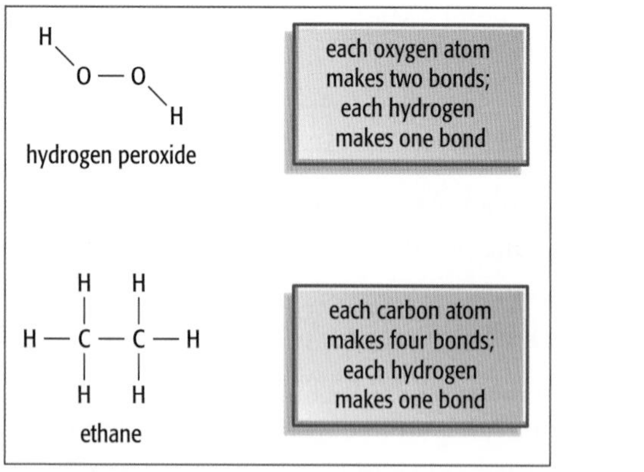

Figure 3.31 The structures of hydrogen peroxide (H_2O_2) and ethane (C_2H_6), showing the bonds made.

'What's in a name?' – naming chemical compounds

Giving a name to a compound is a way of classifying it. Not all names are as informative as others, but modern systems do aim to be consistent. Some common and important compounds have historical names that do not seem to fit into a system, for example water (H_2O), ammonia (NH_3) and methane (CH_4). These apart, there are some basic generalisations that are useful.

- If there is a metal in the compound, it is named first.
- Where the metal can form more than one ion, then the name indicates which ion is present; for example, iron(II) chloride contains the Fe^{2+} ion, while iron(III) chloride contains the Fe^{3+} ion.
- Compounds containing only two elements have names ending in…**ide**; for example sodium chloride ($NaCl$), calcium bromide ($CaBr_2$), magnesium nitride (Mg_3N_2). The important exception to this is the hydroxides, which contain the hydroxide (OH^-) ion.
- Compounds containing a polyatomic ion (usually containing oxygen) have names that end with…**ate**; for example calcium carbonate ($CaCO_3$), potassium nitrate (KNO_3), magnesium sulfate ($MgSO_4$), sodium ethanoate (CH_3COONa).
- The names of some compounds use prefixes to tell you the number of that particular atom in the molecule. This is useful if two elements form more than one compound; for example carbon **mono**xide (CO) and carbon **di**oxide (CO_2), nitrogen **di**oxide (NO_2) and **di**nitrogen **tetra**oxide (N_2O_4), sulfur **di**oxide (SO_2) and sulfur **tri**oxide (SO_3).

The names commonly used for the important mineral acids are **not** systematic and must be learnt; for example, sulfuric acid (H_2SO_4).

Two important oxidising agents contain polyatomic negative ions involving metal and oxygen atoms. Their modern names (potassium manganate(VII) ($KMnO_4$) and potassium dichromate(VI) ($K_2Cr_2O_7$) include the oxidation state of the metal. At this stage you will not need to write equations using these compounds, but you will need to recognise their names and formulae.

Key ideas so far

- The chemical formula of an element or compound shows how the atoms are combined in a particular substance.
- Certain elements – hydrogen, oxygen, nitrogen and the halogens – normally exist as diatomic molecules.
- The valencies, or combining powers, of the atoms involved are important in working out the formula of a compound.
- For elements in the main groups (I to VIII) of the Periodic Table the valency of an atom can be worked out from the group number.
- Where an element in a compound can have more than one valency this is indicated in the name of the compound – copper(II) sulfate contains the Cu^{2+} ion, for example.

? Quick-check questions

1 What names would you give these compounds?
a NaI **b** MgS **c** K_2O **d** Li_3N **e** $Ca(OH)_2$
f NO **g** NO_2 **h** SO_3

2 Use your Periodic Table to help you give the formula of these compounds:
a silicon chloride **b** carbon sulfide
c phosphorus chloride **d** silicon oxide

3 a How many atoms of the different elements are there in the formulae of these compounds?
- **i** sodium hydroxide, NaOH
- **ii** ethane, C_2H_6
- **iii** sulfuric acid, H_2SO_4
- **iv** copper nitrate, $Cu(NO_3)_2$
- **v** sucrose (sugar), $C_{12}H_{22}O_{11}$

b What are the names of the compounds whose formulae are the following?

i	KBr	**vi**	HNO_3
ii	$Al(OH)_3$	**vii**	$SiCl_4$
iii	$CuCO_3$	**viii**	$FeSO_4$
iv	Mg_3N_2	**ix**	CH_4
v	PCl_3	**x**	H_2SO_4

c Give the formulae for the following compounds:
- **i** potassium sulfate
- **ii** aluminium fluoride
- **iii** iron(III) oxide
- **iv** calcium nitrate
- **v** zinc chloride
- **vi** ammonia
- **vii** hydrochloric acid
- **viii** copper(II) sulfate
- **ix** sulfur trioxide

4 The diagram shows the arrangement of the outer electrons only in a molecule of ethanoic acid.

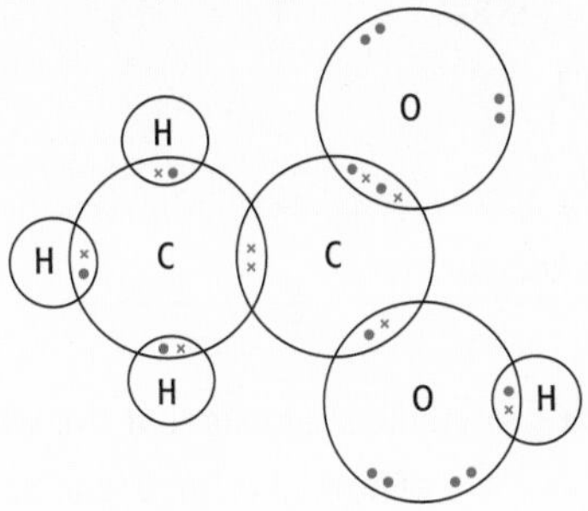

a Name the different elements found in this compound.
b What is the total number of atoms present in this molecule?
c Between which two atoms is there a double covalent bond?
d How many covalent bonds does each carbon atom make?
e Would you expect this compound to be a solid or a liquid at room temperature? Give a reason for your answer.
f Ethanoic acid will dissolve in methylbenzene. Would you expect the solution to conduct electricity? Give a reason for your answer.

3.6 Metals, alloys and crystals

The hexagonal shapes of snowflake crystals demonstrate how simple molecules can combine to produce complex and beautiful solid structures (Figure 3.32).

Figure 3.32 A snowflake crystal.

The regularity of a snowflake suggests that the water molecules it contains are arranged in an organised way. In general, there are three basic units from which solids are constructed – atoms, ions and molecules. These different particles produce a range of structures in the solid state, which can be classified into four broad types.

The four different types of solid physical structures are:

- **giant metallic lattice** – a lattice of positive ions in a 'sea' of electrons
- **giant ionic lattice** – a lattice of alternating positive and negative ions
- **giant molecular lattice** – a giant molecule (**macromolecule**) making the lattice
- **simple molecular lattice** – simple molecules in a lattice held together by weak forces (Figure 3.33).

Structures of these different types surround us in the real world. In some cases we use and adapt their physical properties to engineer materials to suit a particular purpose.

Substances that consist of simple molecules have relativity low melting points and boiling points.

This is because there are only weak forces between the molecules They don't conduct electricity.

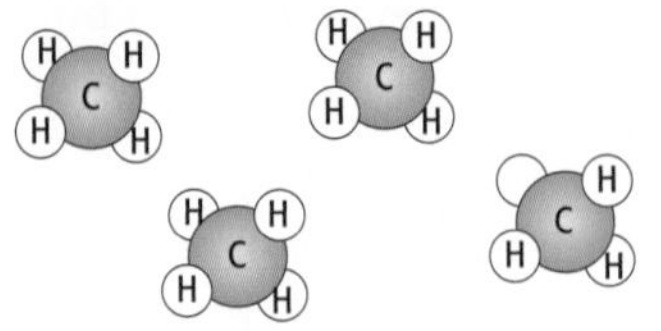

Figure 3.33 Simple molecular substances have low melting points.

Metal crystals

The idea of the regular packing of metal ions into a lattice surrounded by a 'sea' of mobile electrons helps to explain many of the physical properties of metals. In most metals the packing is as close as possible. This explains why metals usually have a high density. In some metals the ions are less closely packed. These metals, for example the alkali metals, have the lowest densities of all metals. So, lithium and sodium will float on water.

The layers of identical ions in a pure metal can be moved over one another without breaking the structure (Figure 3.34). This flexibility in the layered structure means that metals can be beaten or rolled into sheets (they are **malleable**). Metals are more malleable when hot, and steel, for instance, is rolled when hot. They can also be stretched into wires (they are **ductile**). The strength of the metallic bonds means that the metal does not easily break under these forces. The bonds are strong but not rigid. This means that metals generally have a high tensile strength.

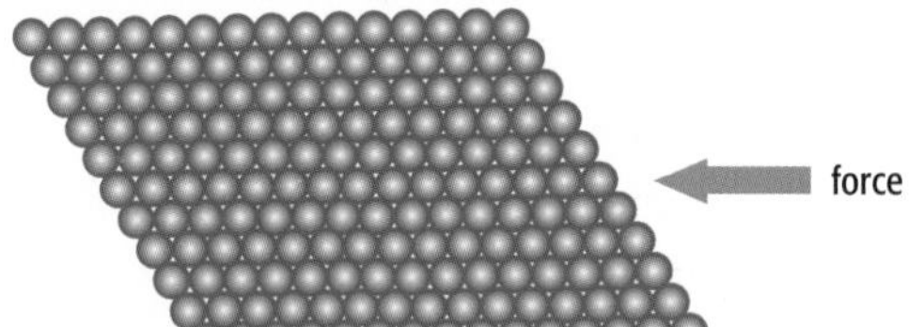

Figure 3.34 The layers in a metal lattice can slide over each other.

The mobility of the delocalised electrons in a metal means that metals conduct electricity very well. Copper is a particularly good conductor, and most electrical wires are made from it. For overhead power lines aluminium is used, as it is lighter. However, because aluminium is not strong, a steel core has to be used.

Metals have a crystalline structure. You can see this if you look at a metal surface under the microscope. Look, too, at the surface of a galvanised iron lamp-post, some railings or the inside of a dustbin or iron bucket (Figure 3.35). Irregular-shaped zinc crystals can be seen (zinc is coated on iron in the galvanisation process). These crystalline areas are called **grains**. The boundaries between them are the **grain boundaries**. Figure 3.36 describes their formation. In general, the smaller the grain size, the stronger and harder the metal is.

Figure 3.35 A photograph of zinc grains on a galvanised post.

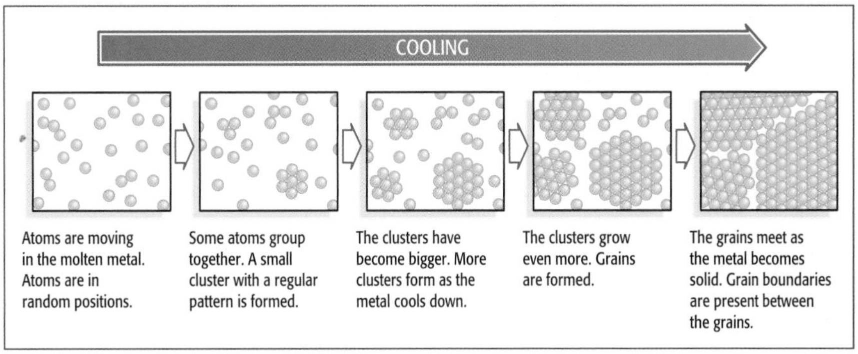

Figure 3.36 The process of formation of grains as a molten metal cools.

Alloys

Making alloys with other metals is one of the most common ways of changing the properties of metals. Alloys are formed by mixing the molten metals together thoroughly and then allowing them to cool and form a solid.

Alloying often results in a metal that is stronger than the original individual metals. 'Silver' coins are minted from cupro-nickel alloy, which is much harder than copper itself (Figure 3.37). Aluminium is a low-density metal that is not very strong. When mixed with 4% copper and smaller amounts of other elements, it gives a metal (duralumin) that combines strength and lightness and is ideal for aircraft building. Other examples of alloys and their properties are given in Table 3.8, overleaf.

Figure 3.37 Many different coins are made from cupro-nickel alloys.

Alloy	Typical composition		Particular properties
brass	copper	70%	harder than pure copper; 'gold' coloured
	zinc	30%	
bronze	copper	90%	harder than pure copper
	tin	10%	
mild steel	iron	99.7%	stronger and harder than pure iron
	carbon	0.3%	
stainless steel	iron	70%	harder than pure iron; does not rust
	chromium	20%	
	nickel	10%	
solder	tin	50%	lower melting point than either tin or lead
	lead	50%	

Table 3.8 Some important alloys

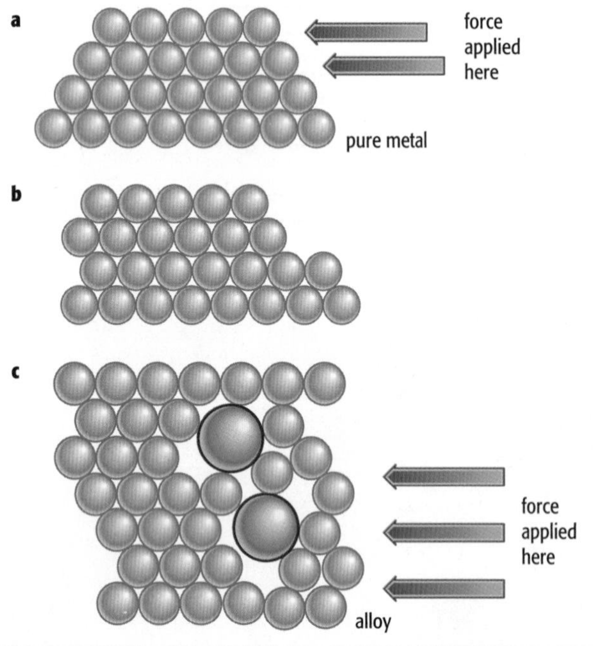

Figure 3.38 **a** The positions of atoms in a pure metal crystal before a force is applied. **b** After the force is applied, slippage has taken place. The layers in a pure metal can slide over each other. **c** In an alloy, slippage is prevented because the atoms of different size cannot slide over each other.

Figure **3.38** shows how the presence of the 'impurity' atoms makes it more difficult for the metal ions to slip over each other. This makes the alloy stronger but more brittle than the metals it is made from.

Strength is not the only property to think about when designing an alloy. For example, solder is an alloy of tin and lead. It is useful for making electrical connections because its melting point is lower than that of either of the two separate metals. Also, steel, which rusts when in contact with oxygen and water, can be prevented from doing so when alloyed with chromium and nickel. This forms stainless steel (see Table **3.8**).

Exam tip

Not only is it important that you learn which elements are present in certain alloys, such as brass, bronze, mild steel and stainless steel, but you should be familiar with certain key uses for each alloy. The syllabus gives uses for mild steel (car bodies and machinery) and stainless steel (chemical plant and cutlery) so do make sure you are aware of these.

Ionic crystals

S

Ionic compounds form lattices consisting of positive and negative ions. In an ionic lattice, the nearest neighbours of an ion are always of the opposite charge. Thus, in sodium chloride, each sodium (Na^+) ion is surrounded by six chloride (Cl^-) ions (Figure **3.39**), and each Cl^- ion is surrounded by six Na^+ ions. Overall there are equal numbers of Na^+ and Cl^- ions, so that the charges balance.

The actual arrangement of the ions in other compounds depends on the numbers of ions involved, and on their sizes. However, it is important to remember that all ionic compounds are electrically neutral.

E

Ionic crystals are hard but much more brittle than metallic crystals. This is a result of the structure of the layers. In a **metallic** crystal, the ions are identical and held together by the mobile electrons. This remains true if one layer is slid against the next. However, pushing one layer against another in an **ionic** crystal brings ions of the same charge next to each other. The repulsions force the layers apart (Figure **3.40**).

Disruption of an ionic lattice is also brought about by water. Many ionic compounds dissolve in water. Water molecules are able to interact with both positive and negative ions. When an ionic crystal dissolves, each ion becomes surrounded by water molecules. This breaks up the lattice and keeps the ions apart (Figure **3.41**). For those ionic compounds that do not dissolve in water, the forces between the ions must be very strong.

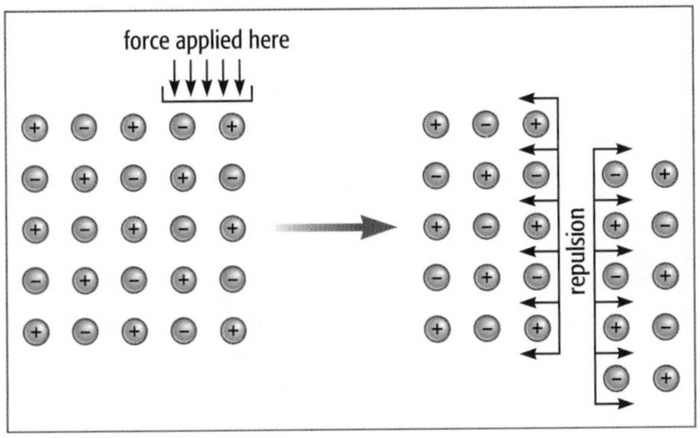

Figure 3.40 In ionic crystals, when one layer is forced to slide against another, repulsions cause the crystal to fracture.

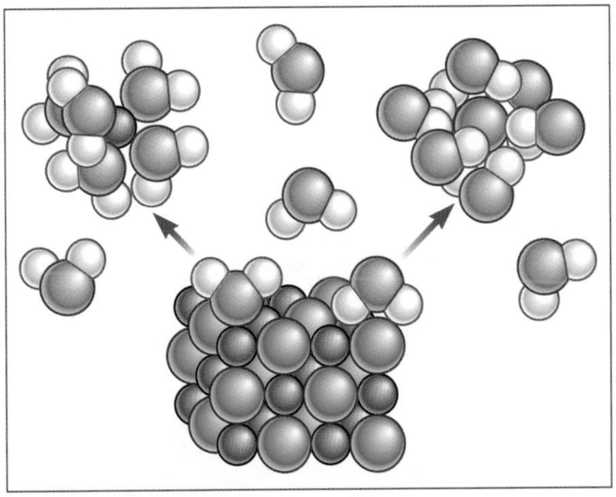

Figure 3.41 Water molecules form 'shells' around metal (grey) and non-metal (green) ions. This helps ionic substances (like sodium chloride, NaCl) to dissolve in water.

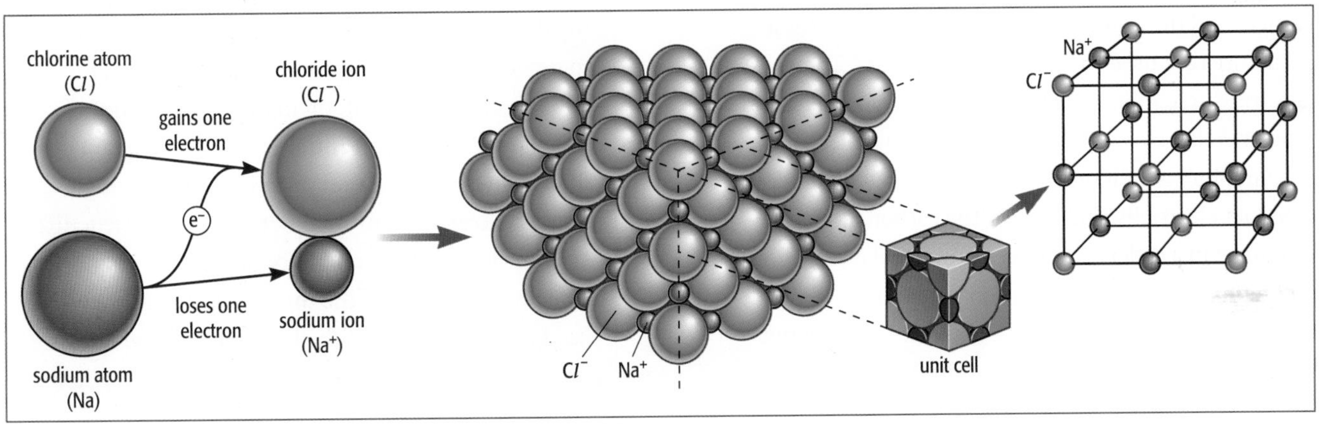

Figure 3.39 The arrangement of the positive and negative ions in a sodium chloride crystal.

Ions in solution are able to move, so the solution can carry an electric current. Ionic compounds can conduct electricity when dissolved in water. This is also true when they are melted because, here again, the ions are able to move through the liquid and carry the current.

Giant molecular crystals (macromolecules)

Giant molecular crystals are held together by strong covalent bonds. This type of structure is shown by some elements (for example carbon, in the form of diamond and graphite), and also by some compounds (for example silica, SiO_2).

The properties of diamond are due to the fact that the strong covalent bonds extend in all directions through the whole crystal. Each carbon atom is attached to four others – the atoms are arranged tetrahedrally (Figure **3.42a**, overleaf). Diamond has a very high melting point and, because the bonding extends throughout the whole structure, it is very hard and is used in cutting tools. The bonds are rigid, however, and

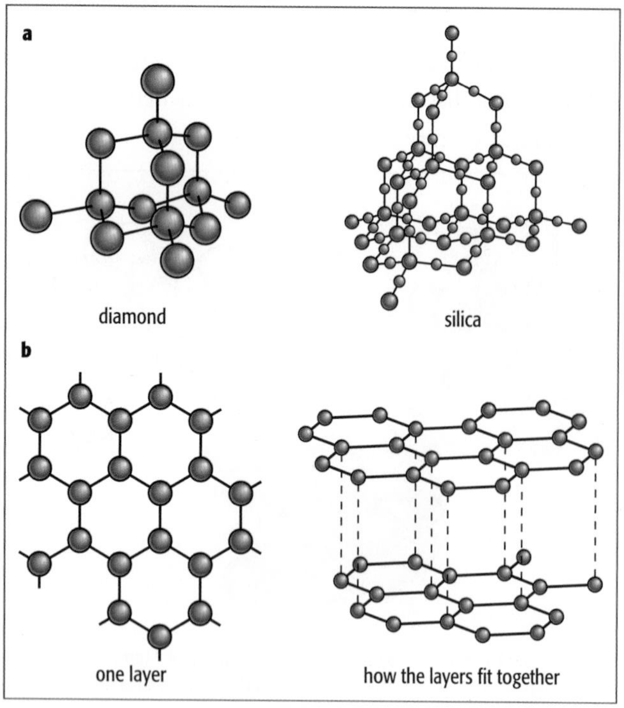

Figure 3.42 **a** The tetrahedral structure of diamond and silica (silicon(IV) oxide). **b** The layered structure of graphite.

these structures are much more brittle than giant metallic lattices. All the outer electrons of the atoms in these structures are used to form covalent bonds. There are no electrons free to move. Diamond is therefore a typical non-metallic element. It does not conduct electricity.

Graphite is a different form of carbon which does conduct electricity (Table **3.9**). The carbon atoms are arranged in a different way in the molecular structure of graphite. They are arranged in flat layers of linked hexagons (Figure **3.42b**). Each graphite layer is a two-dimensional giant molecule. Within these layers, each carbon atom is bonded to three others by strong covalent bonds. Between the layers there are weaker forces of attraction. The layers are able to slide over each other easily. This means that graphite feels slippery and can be used as a lubricant. Pencil 'lead' is, in fact, graphite. When we write with a pencil, thin layers of graphite are left stuck to the paper. The most distinctive property, however, arises from the free electrons not used by the layered atoms in covalent bonding. These electrons can move between the layers, carrying charge, so that graphite can conduct electricity in a similar way to metals.

The giant structures of diamond and silica are very similar (Figure **3.42a**). As a result, they show similar physical properties. They are both very hard and have high melting points. Sand and quartz are examples of silica (silicon(IV) oxide or silicon dioxide, SiO_2). The whole structure of silicon and oxygen atoms is held together throughout by strong covalent bonds.

Exam tip

It is important that you can recognise the structures of diamond and graphite if you are presented with the diagrams in an exam question. Do make sure that you can describe the essential features of the two structures and link them to the properties of the two forms. So you should be able to explain the hardness of diamond in terms of the strongly bonded three-dimensional network of the structure.

The electrical conductivity of graphite is explained in terms of the mobile electrons not used in the bonding of the layers. It is these 'free'

	Diamond		Graphite	
	Properties	**Uses**	**Properties**	**Uses**
appearance	colourless, transparent crystals that sparkle in light	in jewellery and ornamental objects	dark grey, shiny solid	
hardness	the hardest natural substance	in drill bits, diamond saws and glass-cutters	soft – the layers can slide over each other – and solid has a slippery feel	in pencils, and as a lubricant
density	more dense than graphite (3.51 g/cm³)		less dense than diamond (2.25 g/cm³)	
electrical conductivity	does not conduct electricity		conducts electricity	as electrodes and for the brushes in electric motors

Table 3.9 A comparison of the properties and uses of diamond and graphite.

electrons that are able to move and carry the current, not those involved in the covalent bonding of the layers.

The use of graphite as a solid lubricant is a result of the molecular layers in graphite being able to slide over each other.

Molecular crystals

Some non-metals (e.g. iodine and sulfur) and some covalently bonded compounds exist as solids with low melting points. In these crystals, molecules of these elements or compounds are held together by weak intermolecular forces to form a crystal which is easily broken down by heat. The molecules are then free to move but, unlike the particles in an ionic crystal, have no charge. Neither the liquid nor the solid forms of these substances conduct electricity.

A summary of the physical properties of the different types of structure

The properties of a substance can be related to the type of structure it has. The four different types of structure are summarised in Figure 3.43.

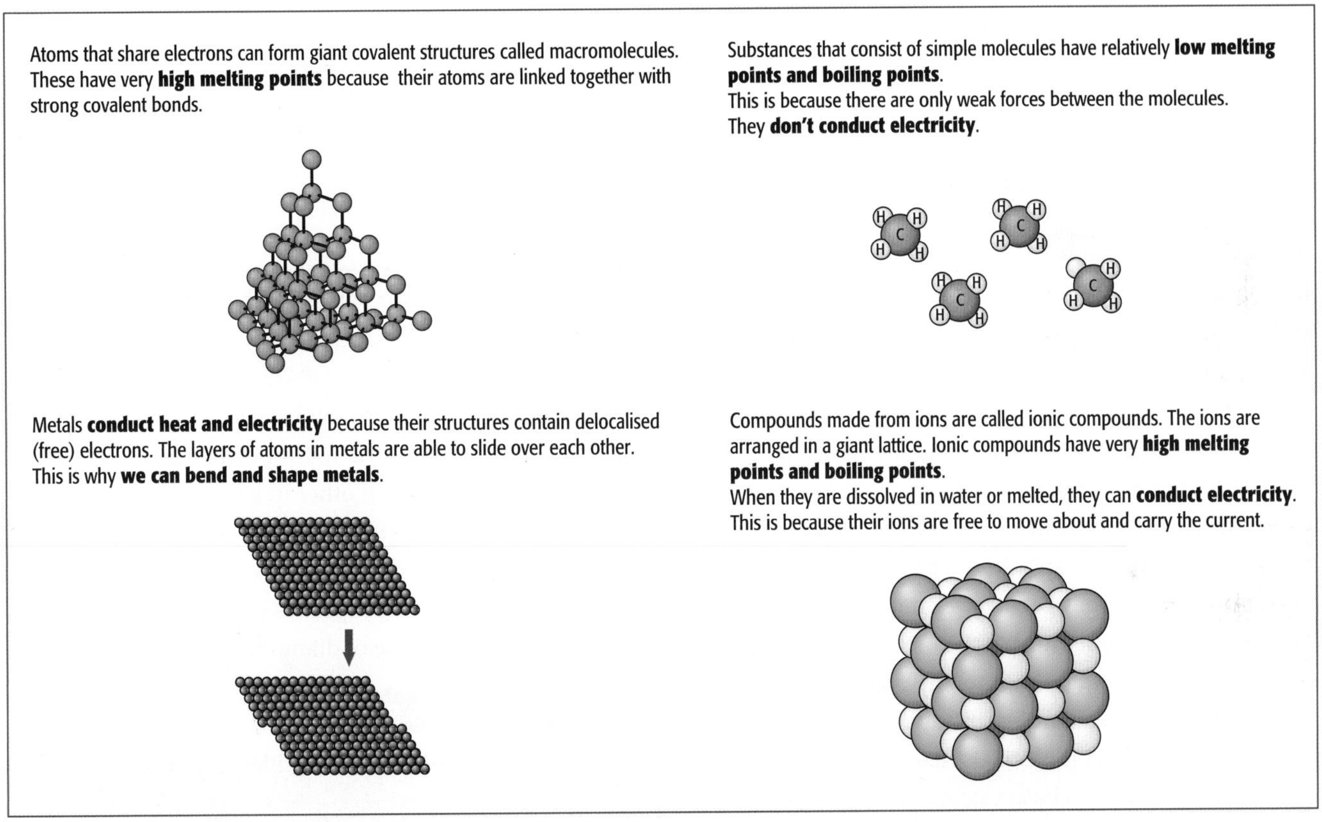

Figure 3.43 Summary of the different types of structure.

E

Changes in physical structure of Period 3 elements

We have seen earlier that there is a gradual shift in properties as we move across each horizontal row in the Periodic Table. For example, the general trend across Period 3 is from metal to metalloid and then to non-metal. Closer examination shows that this trend is linked to the type of structure adopted by each element.

The elements to the left of the period have few outer electrons. Atoms of these elements can readily lose these electrons and so they form metallic solids. The strength of the metallic bonding gets stronger as more electrons are released by the atoms to form ions. The three metals at the start of Period 3 show increasing melting points, boiling points and densities (Figure **3.44**). Of the non-metals, silicon has the highest value for each of these physical properties. This is a result of its giant molecular structure. The melting points and boiling points then decrease steadily to the end of the period. Chlorine and argon have low densities as they are gaseous simple molecular substances.

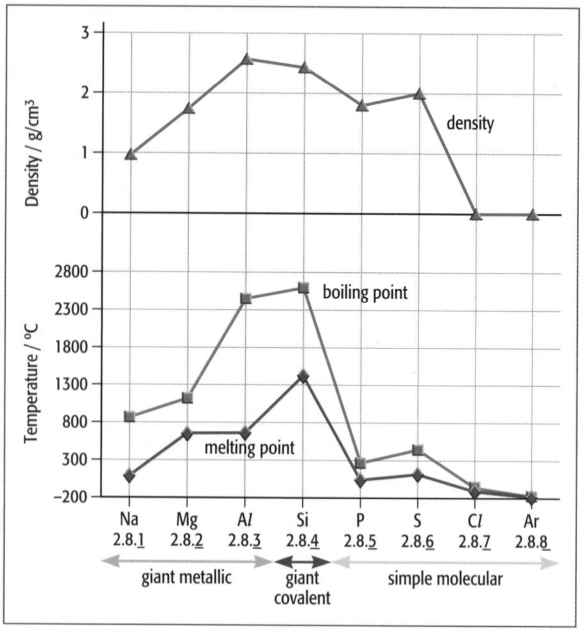

Figure 3.44 Trends in the structure and physical properties of the elements across Period 3.

Key ideas so far

- There is a link between the physical properties of a solid substance and the microscopic structure of its atoms, ions or molecules.
- There is a wide range of physical properties to be considered, from hardness and density to solubility and ability to conduct electricity.
- The characteristic properties of metals can be adapted to suit a specific purpose by alloying.
- Alloys can be designed, for example, for strength (steel and duralumin), resistance to corrosion (stainless steel), or low melting point (solder).
- Some non-metallic elements, particularly carbon, consist of giant molecular (macromolecular) structures linked by covalent bonds.
- Diamond and graphite are two different forms of carbon, with different structures and distinctly different physical properties.
- Other covalent substances are made up of small molecules held together by weak intermolecular forces.
- These substances have low melting points and do not conduct electricity.
- Understanding the closely packed structure of metals can explain the characteristic properties of metals and how one metal can strengthen another when the two form an alloy.
- Ionic substances are often soluble in water because water molecules can break down the structure of the ionic crystal.
- Ionic compounds are solid at room temperature and form crystals where the positive and negative ions are next to each other in a framework (lattice).
- Some covalent compounds, e.g. silicon(IV) oxide, form giant molecular structures.
- The structure and properties of silicon(IV) oxide are similar to those of diamond.

Quick-check questions

1 How does molten sodium chloride conduct electricity?
2 Why does sodium chloride not conduct when it is solid?
3 Why can graphite
  a conduct electricity, and
  b be used as a lubricant?
4 Why is diamond much harder than graphite?
5 Why do molecular crystals never conduct electricity?
6 Why can metals conduct electricity?
7 How is the structure of silicon(IV) oxide similar to that of diamond?

Summary

You should know that:

- the Periodic Table lists the elements of the Universe in order of increasing atomic number
- the Periodic Table has a structure that provides useful information, and the elements are grouped so that certain patterns of properties repeat themselves
- the elements are broadly divided into metals and non-metals
- the metals have certain characteristic properties, the most important being that they conduct electricity and are malleable and ductile
- the Periodic Table is divided into vertical groups and horizontal periods
- certain groups of elements have specific names, for example the alkali metals, and show 'family' properties
- there is a trend from metallic to non-metallic properties as you go across the Periodic Table
- the halogens are a group of reactive non-metals – Group VII in the Periodic Table
- the halogens all exist as diatomic molecules (Cl_2, for example)
- their physical properties change as you go down the group – their melting points and boiling points increase, and the intensity of their colour deepens
- their chemical reactivity decreases down the group – the more reactive halogens will displace the lower halogens from salts
- the structures of all substances are made up of either atoms, ions or molecules
- there are three main types of chemical bonding that hold these structures together – metallic, ionic and covalent bonding
- covalent bonding occurs in some elements and non-metallic compounds, and involves the 'sharing' of electrons between atoms to form stable molecules
- two types of covalent structure can be formed – simple molecules and giant molecular (macromolecular) structures
- compounds of a metal plus a non-metal involve ionic bonding, in which positive and negative ions are held together by strong electrostatic forces
- the physical properties of a substance are related to the type of bonding present
- each chemical compound has a particular name and can also be represented by a chemical formula that summarises the atoms or ions present
- there is a link between the physical properties of a solid substance and the microscopic structure of its atoms, ions or molecules
- the characteristic properties of metals can be adapted to suit a specific purpose by alloying
- alloys can be designed, for example, for strength (steel and duralumin), resistance to corrosion (stainless steel) or low melting point (solder)
- giant molecular structures linked by covalent bonds can be formed by some elements; carbon (diamond and graphite) and silicon, for example
- diamond and graphite are two different forms of carbon, with different structures and distinctly different physical properties

S

- there is a close relationship between the electron arrangement of an element and its position in the Periodic Table
- metallic bonding involves the closely packed atoms losing their outer electrons into a 'sea' of mobile electrons
- understanding the closely packed structure of metals can explain the characteristic properties of metals and how one metal can strengthen another when the two form an alloy
- ionic compounds are solid at room temperature and form crystals where the positive and negative ions are next to each other in a framework (lattice)
- ionic substances are often soluble in water because water molecules can break down the structure of the ionic crystal
- giant molecular structures linked by covalent bonds can be formed by some elements and compounds
- other covalent substances are simple molecular substances; these include elements such as oxygen and chlorine, and compounc such as water.

Exam-style questions

1 The table below shows an early form of the Periodic Table made by John Newlands in 1866.

H	F	Cl	Co, Ni	Br
Li	Na	K	Cu	Rb
Be	Mg	Ca	Zn	Sr
B	*Al*	Cr	Y	
C	Si	Ti	In	
N	P	Mn	As	
O	S	Fe	Sc	

a Newlands arranged the elements according to their relative atomic masses. What governs the order of the elements in the modern Periodic Table? [1]

b Use your modern Periodic Table to suggest why Newlands put cobalt and nickel in the same place. [1]

c Which group of elements is missing from Newlands' table? [1]

d Describe **three other** differences between Newlands' table and the modern Periodic Table. You must not give any of the answers you mentioned in parts **a**, **b** or **c**. [3]

e Carbon exists in two forms, graphite and diamond.

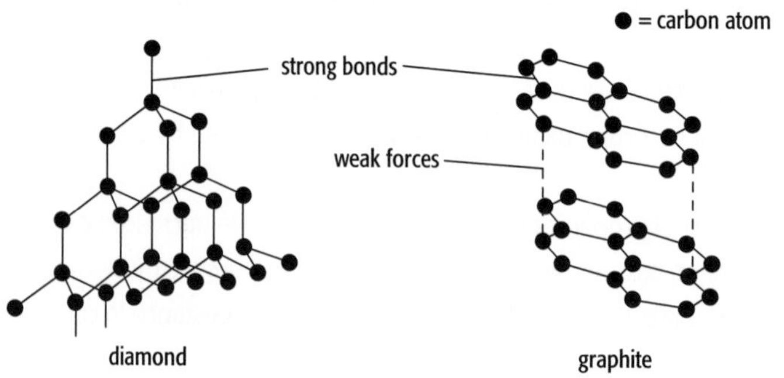

Use ideas about structure and bonding to suggest

i why graphite is used as a lubricant, [1]

ii why diamond is very hard. [1]

CIE IGCSE, November 2007, paper 2, q.6

2 The table shows the concentration of some ions present in seawater.

Name of ion	Formula of ion	Concentration of ion in g/dm³
bromide	Br^-	0.07
calcium	Ca^{2+}	0.4
chloride	Cl^-	19.1
magnesium	Mg^{2+}	1.2
potassium	K^+	0.3
sodium	Na^+	10.6
	SO_4^{2-}	0.8

a Which negative ion has the highest concentration in seawater? [1]

b State the name of the ion with the formula SO_4^{2-}. [1]

c Which **two** ions in the table are formed from Group I elements? [1]

d When seawater is evaporated, a number of different compounds are formed.
State the name of the compound which is present in the greatest quantity. [1]

e State the names of **two** ions in the table which move to the cathode when seawater is electrolysed. [2]

f When concentrated seawater is electrolysed, chlorine is formed at one of the electrodes.

i To which Period in the Periodic Table does chlorine belong? [1]

ii Draw the electronic structure of a chlorine molecule. Show only the outer electrons. [2]

g Drinking water can be obtained by purifying seawater. Explain why distillation rather than filtration is used to purify seawater for drinking. [2]

CIE IGCSE, June 2008, paper 2, q.3

3 **a** The table gives some information about five elements, **A**, **B**, **C**, **D** and **E**. Copy and complete the table by writing either 'metal' or 'non-metal' in the last column.

Element	Properties	Metal or non-metal?
A	shiny solid which conducts electricity	
B	reddish brown liquid with a low boiling point	
C	a form of carbon which is black in colour and conducts electricity	
D	white solid which is an insulator and has a high melting point	
E	dull yellow solid which does not conduct heat	

[5]

b Describe how metallic character changes across a Period. [1]

c Sodium is in Group I of the Periodic Table.

i Draw a diagram to show the full electronic structure of sodium. [1]

ii Copy and complete the equation to show what happens when a sodium atom forms a sodium ion.

$Na \rightarrow Na^+ + ...$ [1]

d Copy and complete these sentences about the properties of the Group I elements using words from the list.

acidic basic decrease hard increase lithium potassium soft

The Group I elements are relatively .... metals which .... in reactivity going down the Group. Sodium reacts more violently with water than .... The Group I metals all form .... oxides. [4]

CIE IGCSE, November 2008, paper 2, q.1

4 The diagram shows the structures of calcium chloride, calcium and chlorine.

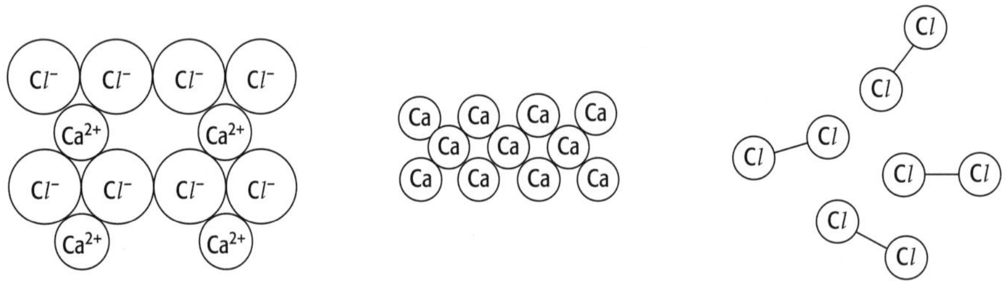

calcium chloride calcium chlorine

Use ideas about structure and bonding to explain the following:

a Calcium chloride conducts electricity when molten but not when solid. [2]

b At room temperature, calcium is a solid but chlorine is a gas. [2]

CIE IGCSE, November 2008, paper 2, q.7 part

5 The diagram shows part of the Periodic Table.

				He
C	N	O	F	Ne
		S	Cl	Ar
			Br	Kr

a Answer these questions using **only** the elements shown in the diagram.
Write down the symbol for an element which

i has five electrons in its outer shell [1]

ii has diatomic molecules [1]

iii reacts with sodium to form sodium bromide [1]

iv is a noble gas [1]

v has a giant covalent structure [1]

vi has a lower proton number than fluorine [1]

vii is the most abundant gas in the air. [1]

b Write down a use for each of the following elements.

i argon [1]

ii helium [1]

iii oxygen [1]

c i Draw a diagram to show the electronic structure of argon. [2]

ii Why is argon very unreactive? [1]

CIE IGCSE, November 2005, paper 2, q.1

6 The diagram shows part of the Periodic Table.

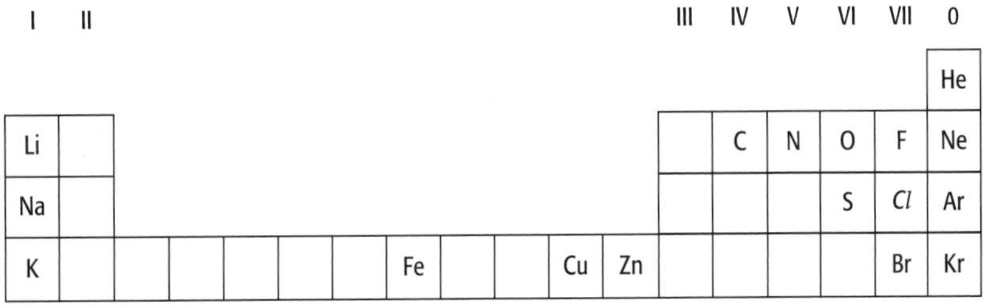

a Answer these questions using **only** the elements shown in the diagram.
Write down the symbol for an element which

i is a transition metal

ii forms an acidic oxide

iii has six electrons in its outer shell

iv has a giant covalent structure

v reacts rapidly with water

vi has a higher proton (atomic) number than iron. [6]

b Some uses of some non-metallic elements are shown below.
Copy and complete the diagram and draw lines between the boxes to link the elements to their correct uses. The first one has been done for you.

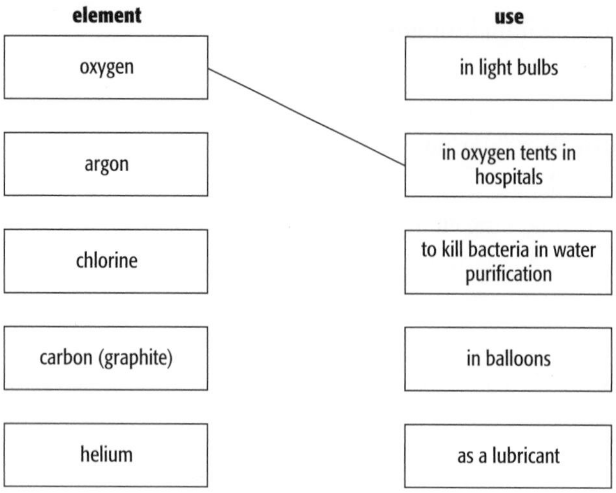

[4]

c The structures of some halogen compounds are shown below.

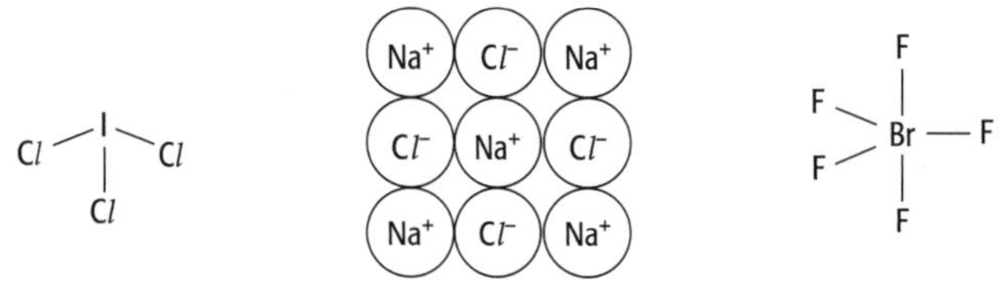

A **B** **C**

i Describe the type of bonding in compound **A**.
ii State the simplest formula for compound **C**.
iii Explain why compound **B** does not conduct electricity when solid but does conduct when molten. [4]

CIE IGCSE, June 2003, paper 2, q.1

7 Look at the list of five elements below.

argon **bromine** **chlorine** **iodine** **potassium**

a Put these five elements in order of increasing proton number. [1]
b Put these five elements in order of increasing relative atomic mass. [1]
c The orders of proton number and relative atomic mass for these five elements are different. Which **one** of the following is the most likely explanation for this?
i The proton number of a particular element may vary.
ii The presence of neutrons.
iii The atoms easily gain or lose electrons.
iv The number of protons must always equal the number of neutrons. [1]
d Which of the five elements in the list are in the same group of the Periodic Table? [1]

e **i** From the list, choose **one** element which has one electron in its outer shell. [1]

ii From the list, choose **one** element which has a full outer shell of electrons. [1]

f Which **two** of the following statements about argon are correct?

i Argon is a noble gas.

ii Argon reacts readily with potassium.

iii Argon is used to fill weather balloons.

iv Argon is used in light bulbs. [2]

g Potassium chloride can be made by reacting potassium with chlorine. The bonding in potassium chloride is ionic. What does this information tell you about

i the boiling point of potassium chloride,

ii the electrical conductivity of molten potassium chloride? [2]

h Describe the change in the electronic structure of potassium and chlorine atoms when they combine to make potassium chloride.

i change in potassium atom

ii change in chlorine atom [2]

CIE IGCSE, June 2004, paper 2, q.5

8 The halogens are a group of diatomic non-metals showing a trend in colour, state and reactivity.

a In this description, what is the meaning of

i diatomic

ii state? [2]

b The table gives some information about some of the halogens.

Element	Melting point/°C	Boiling point/°C	Colour	State at room temperature
chlorine	−101	−35	green	
bromine	−7	+59		
iodine	+114		grey–black	

i Complete the last column in the table to show the state of each of the halogens at room temperature. [2]

ii State the colour of bromine. [1]

iii Suggest a value for the boiling point of iodine. [1]

c Copy and complete the word equation for the reaction of chlorine with potassium iodide.

chlorine + potassium iodide → .... + ... [2]

CIE IGCSE, June 2005, paper 2, q.5 part

9 The diagram shows models of various elements.

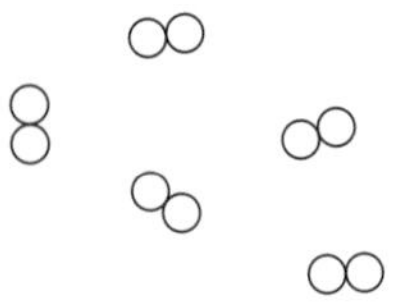

A

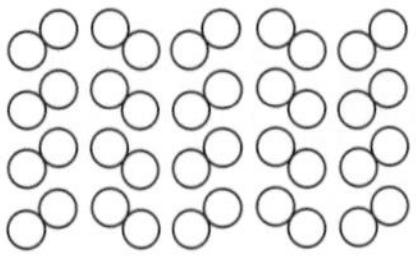

B

C

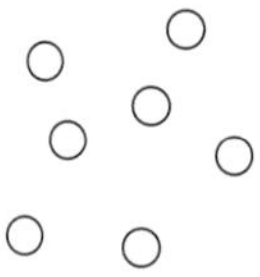

D

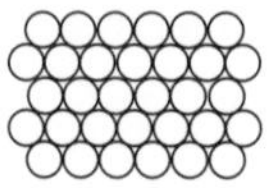

E

a Define the term **element**. [1]

b Which **one** of the models A to E represents a solid containing diatomic molecules? [1]

c Which **two** of the models A to E represent gases? [1]

d **i** Which **one** of the models A to E represents diamond? [1]

ii State the name of the element present in diamond. [1]

iii State a use of diamond other than in jewellery. [1]

e Structure E is a metal. State **three** physical properties which are characteristic of all metals. [3]

f Metals are sometimes mixed with other elements in order to change their properties.

i What is the name given to a mixture of metals with other elements? [1]

ii Match up the metals in the boxes on the left with their uses on the right. The first one has been done for you.

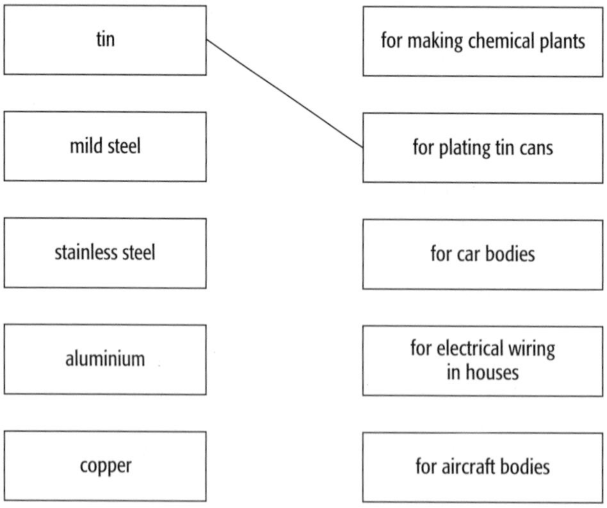

[4]

CIE IGCSE, June 2006, paper 2, q.1

10 a The structure of a typical ionic compound is a regular arrangement of positive and negative ions.

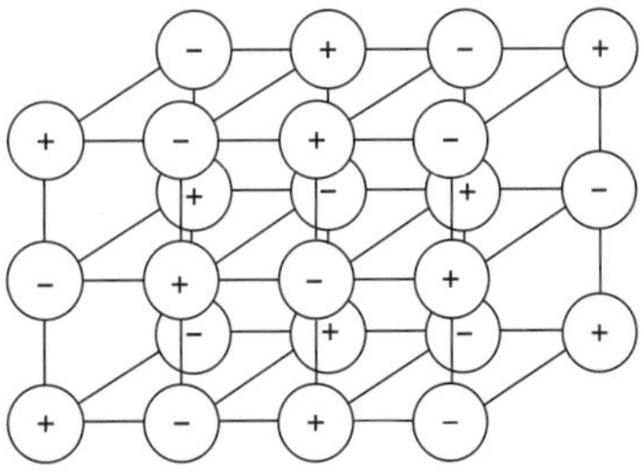

i What is the name of this regular arrangement of particles? [1]

ii Give **two** physical properties of ionic compounds. [2]

b Ions are formed by electron loss or gain. The electron distribution of a magnesium atom is 2 + 8 + 2 and of a nitrogen atom is 2 + 5.

i Give the formula of the magnesium ion. [1]

ii Give the formula of the nitride ion. [1]

iii What is the formula of the ionic compound, magnesium nitride? [1]

iv In this compound there is an ionic bond. Why are the two ions attracted to each other? [1]

CIE IGCSE, November 2005, paper 3, q.1

11 There are three types of giant structure – ionic, metallic and macromolecular.

a Sodium nitride is an ionic compound. Draw a diagram that shows the formula of the compound, the charges on the ions and the arrangement of the valency electrons around the negative ion.
Use × to represent an electron from a sodium atom.
Use o to represent an electron from a nitrogen atom. [3]

b i Describe metallic bonding. [3]

ii Use the above ideas to explain why

- metals are good conductors of electricity, [1]
- metals are malleable. [2]

c Silicon(IV) oxide has a macromolecular structure.

i **Describe** the structure of silicon(IV) oxide (a diagram is not acceptable). [3]

ii Diamond has a similar structure and consequently similar properties.
Give **two** physical properties common to both diamond and silicon(IV) oxide. [2]

CIE IGCSE, paper 3, November 2008, q.2

12 Use your copy of the Periodic Table to help you answer these questions.

a Predict the formula of each of the following compounds.

i barium oxide [1]

ii boron oxide [1]

b Give the formula of the following ions.

i sulfide [1]

ii gallium [1]

c Draw a diagram showing the arrangement of the valency electrons in one molecule of the covalent compound nitrogen trichloride.

Use × to represent an electron from a nitrogen atom.

Use o to represent an electron from a chlorine atom. [3]

d Potassium and vanadium are elements in Period 4.

i State **two** differences in their physical properties. [2]

ii Give **two** differences in their chemical properties. [2]

e Fluorine and astatine are halogens. Use your knowledge of the other halogens to predict the following:

i
- The physical state of fluorine at r.t.p.
- The physical state of astatine at r.t.p. [2]

ii **Two** similarities in their chemical properties [2]

CIE IGCSE, June 2007, paper 3, q.4

13 Copy and complete the following table.

Type of structure	**Particles present**	**Electrical conductivity of solid**	**Electrical conductivity of liquid**	**Example**
ionic	positive and negative ions	poor	....	....
macromolecular	atoms of two different elements in a giant covalent structure	poor	poor	....
metallic	.... and	good	....	copper

[6]

CIE IGCSE, June 2007, paper 3, q.2

14 Strontium and sulfur chlorides both have a formula of the type XCl_2 but they have different properties.

Property	Strontium chloride	Sulfur chloride
Appearance	white crystalline solid	red liquid
Melting point/°C	873	−80
Particles present	ions	molecules
Electrical conductivity of solid	poor	poor
Electrical conductivity of liquid	good	poor

a The formulae of the chlorides are similar because both elements have a valency of 2.
Explain why Group II and Group VI elements both have a valency of 2. [2]

b Draw a diagram showing the arrangement of the valency electrons in one covalent molecule of sulfur chloride.
Use × to represent an electron from a sulfur atom.
Use o to represent an electron from a chlorine atom. [3]

c Explain the difference in electrical conductivity between the following.

i solid and liquid strontium chloride [1]

ii liquid strontium chloride and liquid sulfur chloride [1]

CIE IGCSE, November 2004, paper 3, q.5

4 Chemical reactions

This chapter covers the following ideas:

- the differences between physical and chemical changes
- word equations and balanced chemical equations for reactions
- different types of chemical reaction, including oxidation and reduction
- (S) oxidation and reduction as the transfer of electrons
- (S) the use of state symbols in an equation
- (S) the writing of ionic equations
- electricity and chemistry – conductivity of metals
- the electrolysis of ionic compounds
- industrial applications of electrolysis
  - (S) – extraction of aluminium
  - (S) – the electrolysis of concentrated brine
  - – electroplating
  - (S) – the refining of copper

4.1 Chemical reactions and equations

The Chinese character for 'chemistry' literally means 'change study' (Figure **4.1**). Chemistry deals with how substances react with each other. Chemical reactions range from the very simple through to the interconnecting reactions that keep our bodies alive.

We need answers to questions like:

- What controls such reactions?
- How can we decide which changes are possible and which are not?
- What are the products of various changes? Under what circumstances do particular reactions happen?
- Can we predict chemical changes?

But first we must ask: What is a chemical reaction? How does it differ from a simple physical change?

变化

Figure 4.1 The Chinese symbols for 'change'.

Physical change

Ice, snow and water may look different, but they are all made of water molecules (H_2O). They are different **physical** forms of the same substance – water – existing under different conditions of temperature and pressure. One form can change into another if those conditions change. In such changes, no new **chemical** substances are formed. Dissolving sugar in ethanol or water is another example of a physical change. It produces a solution, but the substances can easily be separated again by distillation.

This is what we know about **physical changes:**

- In a physical change, the substances present remain chemically the same: no new substances are formed.
- Physical changes are often easy to reverse. Any mixtures produced are usually easy to separate.

Chemical change

When magnesium burns in oxygen (Figure **4.2**), the white ash produced is a new substance – the compound, magnesium oxide. Burning magnesium produces

Figure 4.2 Magnesium burns strongly in oxygen.

a brilliant white flame. Energy is **given out** in the form of heat and light. The reaction is **exothermic**. The combination of the two elements magnesium and oxygen to form the new compound is difficult to reverse. Some other chemical reactions, such as those in fluorescent 'light-sticks' (Figure 4.3), also give out energy in the form of light.

Figure 4.3 Glow-in-the-dark bracelets. Glow bracelets are single-use, see-through, plastic tubes containing isolated chemicals. When the tube is squeezed, a glass partition keeping the chemicals apart breaks, and a reaction takes place that produces chemiluminescence.

The reaction between nitrogen and oxygen to make nitrogen monoxide is an example of another type of reaction. During this reaction, heat energy is **taken in** from the surroundings. The reaction is **endothermic**. Such reactions are much less common than exothermic ones.

This is what we know about **chemical changes:**

- The major feature of a chemical change, or reaction, is that new substance(s) are made during the reaction.
- Many reactions, but not all of them, are difficult to reverse.
- During a chemical reaction energy can be given out or taken in:
  - when energy is given out, the reaction is exothermic
  - when energy is taken in, the reaction is endothermic.
- There are many more exothermic reactions than endothermic reactions.

Key ideas so far

- There are physical and chemical changes.
- In a physical change there is no change of substance.
- In a chemical change new chemical substances are made.
- Chemical and physical changes can be exothermic or endothermic.
- Exothermic changes involve energy, usually heat, being given out; endothermic changes take energy in.

Quick-check questions

1 State whether the following changes are physical or chemical.
  - **a** the melting of ice
  - **b** the burning of magnesium
  - **c** the sublimation of solid carbon dioxide
  - **d** the dissolving of sugar in water

2 State whether the following changes are exothermic or endothermic.

   a the condensation of steam to water
   b the burning of magnesium
   c the addition of concentrated sulfuric acid to water
   d the evaporation of a volatile liquid

3 What is the most important thing that shows us a chemical reaction has taken place?

4.2 Equations for chemical reactions

When some chemical reactions occur, it is obvious that 'something has happened'. But this is not the case for others. When a solid explosive reacts to produce large amounts of gas products, the rapid expansion may blast the surroundings apart. The 'volcano reaction', in which ammonium dichromate is decomposed, gives out a large amount of energy and produces nitrogen gas (Figure **4.4**). Other reactions produce gases much less violently. The neutralisation of an acid solution with an alkali produces no change that you can see. However, a reaction **has** happened. The temperature of the mixture increases, and new substances have formed which can be separated and purified.

Figure 4.4 The decomposition of ammonium dichromate – the 'volcano experiment' – produces heat, light and an apparently large amount of powder.

Word equations

We can write out descriptions of chemical reactions, but these would be quite long. To understand and group similar reactions together, it is useful to have a shorter way of describing them. The simplest way to do this is in the form of a **word equation**.

This type of equation links together the names of the substances that react (the **reactants**) with those of the new substances formed (the **products**). The word equation for burning magnesium in oxygen would be:

magnesium + oxygen → magnesium oxide

reactants — product

The reaction between hydrogen and oxygen is another highly exothermic reaction. The take-off of the Space Shuttle depends on the energy given out in this reaction. Large tanks beneath the Shuttle contain liquid hydrogen and liquid oxygen as fuel. The word equation for this reaction is:

hydrogen + oxygen → water

Note that, although a large amount of energy is produced in this reaction, it is **not** included in the equation. An equation includes only the chemical substances involved, and energy is not a chemical substance.

This type of equation gives us **some** information. But equations can be made even more useful if we write them using **chemical formulae**.

Balanced symbol equations

From investigations of a large number of different chemical reactions, a very important point about all reactions has been discovered. It is summed up in a law, known as the **law of the conservation of mass**.

The **law of the conservation of mass**:
The total mass of all the products of a chemical reaction is equal to the total mass of all the reactants.

No matter how spectacular the reaction, this statement is always true – though it is easier to collect all the products in some cases than in others!

This important law becomes clear if we consider what is happening to the atoms and molecules involved in a reaction. During a chemical reaction, the atoms of one element are not changed into those of another element. Nor do atoms disappear from the mixture, or appear from nowhere. A reaction involves the breaking of some bonds between atoms, and then the making of new bonds between atoms to give the new products. During a chemical reaction, some of the atoms present 'change partners', sometimes spectacularly (Figure **4.5**).

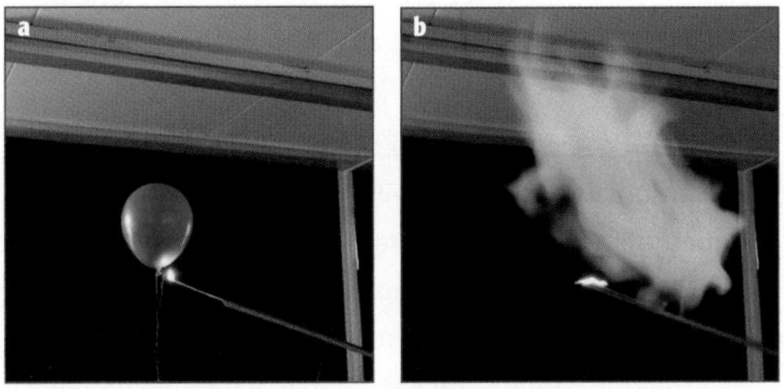

Figure 4.5 **a** A balloon filled with hydrogen and oxygen **b** is ignited spectacularly.

Look more closely at the reaction between hydrogen and oxygen molecules:

hydrogen + oxygen → water

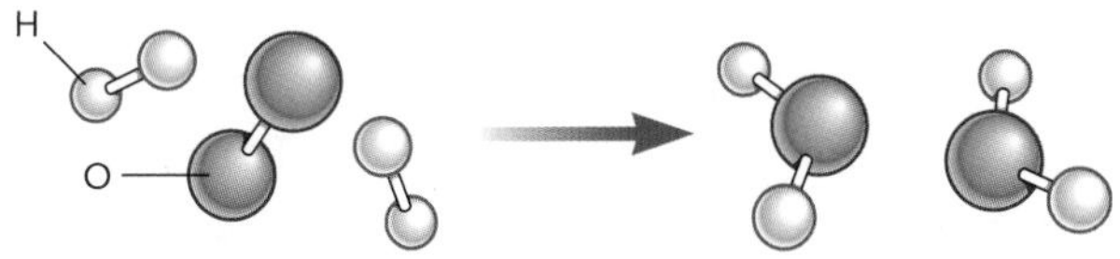

Each molecule of water (formula H_2O) contains only one oxygen atom (O). It follows that one molecule of oxygen (O_2) has enough oxygen atoms to produce two molecules of water (H_2O). Therefore, two molecules of hydrogen (H_2) will be needed to provide enough hydrogen atoms (H) to react with each oxygen molecule. The numbers of hydrogen and oxygen atoms are then the same on both sides of the equation.

The symbol equation for the reaction between hydrogen and oxygen is therefore written:

$$2H_2 + O_2 \rightarrow 2H_2O$$

This is a **balanced equation**. The numbers of each type of atom are the same on both the reactant side and the product side of the equation: four hydrogen atoms and two oxygen atoms on each side (Figure **4.6**).

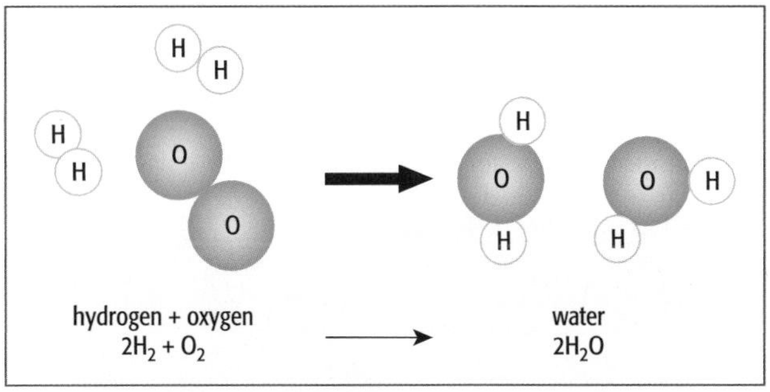

Figure 4.6 Summary of the reaction between hydrogen and oxygen.

Writing balanced equations

A balanced equation gives us more information about a reaction than we can get from a simple word equation. Below is a step-by-step approach to working out the balanced equation for a reaction.

- *Step 1:* Make sure you know what the reactants and products are. For example, magnesium burns in air (oxygen) to form magnesium oxide.
- *Step 2:* From this you can write out the word equation:

  magnesium + oxygen → magnesium oxide

- *Step 3:* Write out the equation using the formulae of the elements and compounds:

  $Mg + O_2 \rightarrow MgO$

Remember that oxygen exists as diatomic molecules. This equation is not balanced: there are two oxygen atoms on the left, but only one on the right.

- *Step 4:* Balance the equation:

  $2Mg + O_2 \rightarrow 2MgO$

Remember that we cannot alter the formulae of the substances involved in the reaction. These are fixed by the bonding in the substance itself. We can only put multiplying numbers in front of each formula where necessary.

Chemical reactions do not only involve **elements** reacting together. In most reactions, **compounds** are involved. For example, potassium metal is very reactive and gives hydrogen gas when it comes into contact with water. Potassium reacts with water to produce potassium hydroxide and hydrogen (Figure **4.7**). All the alkali metals do this. So, if you know one of these reactions, you know them all. In fact, you could learn the general equation:

alkali metal + water → metal hydroxide + hydrogen

Figure 4.7 Potassium reacts strongly with water to produce hydrogen.

Therefore

potassium + water → potassium hydroxide + hydrogen

Then

$$K + H_2O \rightarrow KOH + H_2$$

This symbolic equation needs to be balanced. An even number of H atoms is needed on the product side, because on the reactant side the hydrogen occurs as H_2O. Therefore, the amount of KOH must be doubled. Then the number of potassium atoms and water molecules must be doubled on the left:

$$2K + 2H_2O \rightarrow 2KOH + H_2$$

This equation is now balanced. Check for yourself that the numbers of the three types of atom are the same on both sides.

Exam tip

It is important to remember that when balancing equations you cannot change the formulae of the substances themselves. These are fixed by the nature of the atoms and their bonding.

The only things you can change when balancing are the numbers in front of the formulae.

Key ideas so far

- In a chemical reaction the reactants are changed into the products.
- It is possible to write a word equation for a chemical reaction indicating the new substances formed from the reactants.
- In a chemical reaction there is conservation of mass. Matter cannot be created or destroyed in a chemical reaction.
- It is possible to write a chemical equation using formulae for a reaction that has taken place.
- A chemical equation must be balanced so that there are the same number of atoms of each element involved on both sides of the equation.

? Quick-check questions

1 Write word equations for the reactions described below.

a iron rusts because it reacts with oxygen in the air to form a compound called iron(III) oxide

b sodium hydroxide neutralises sulfuric acid to form sodium sulfate and water

c sodium reacts strongly with water to give a solution of sodium hydroxide; hydrogen gas is also given off

2 Copy out and balance the following equations.

a $\ldots Cu + O_2 \rightarrow \ldots CuO$

b $N_2 + \ldots H_2 \rightleftharpoons \ldots NH_3$

c $\ldots Na + O_2 \rightarrow \ldots Na_2O$

d $\ldots NaOH + H_2SO_4 \rightarrow Na_2SO_4 + \ldots H_2O$

e $\ldots Al + \ldots Cl_2 \rightarrow \ldots AlCl_3$

f $\ldots Fe + \ldots H_2O \rightarrow \ldots Fe_3O_4 + \ldots H_2$

4.3 Types of chemical reaction

There are very many different chemical reactions. To make sense of them, it is useful to try to group certain types of reaction together (Figure **4.8**). These types do not cover all reactions; and some reactions, such as redox reactions, may fit into more than one category. Organic reactions such as polymerisation have been left until later chapters.

Synthesis and decomposition

It is possible to distinguish reactions in which complex compounds are built from simpler substances (synthesis), from those where the reverse happens (decomposition).

Synthesis (or direct combination) reactions occur where two or more substances react together to form just **one** product. The reaction between iron and sulfur is an example of this (Figure **4.9**):

iron + sulfur → iron(II) sulfide

$Fe + S \rightarrow FeS$

Heat is required to start the reaction but, once started, it continues exothermically.

Various salts can be prepared by this method, for example aluminium iodide. The reaction between aluminium and iodine powders is quite spectacular. If the two powders are mixed well, then the reaction can be started by a few drops of water.

Figure 4.9 The synthesis reaction between iron and sulfur.

No heating is needed:

aluminium + iodine → aluminium iodide

$2Al + 3I_2 \rightarrow 2AlI_3$

The synthesis reaction between aluminium foil and bromine liquid is similarly **spontaneous** (Figure **4.10**, overleaf).

Reactions such as the burning of magnesium and the explosive reaction of a hydrogen–oxygen mixture could also be included in this category. Synthesis reactions such as those above are usually **exothermic**, though they often require an input of heat energy to start them.

However, there is one very important synthesis reaction which is **endothermic**: namely **photosynthesis**. This reaction is essential for life on Earth. It takes place in the green leaves of plants and requires energy from sunlight. It is a **photochemical reaction**.

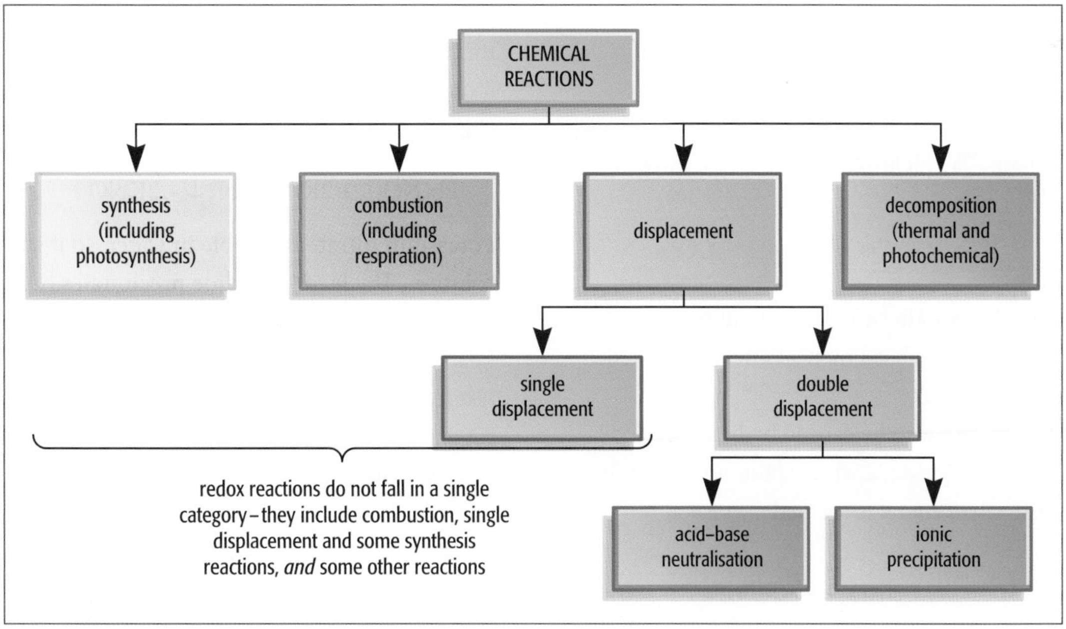

Figure 4.8 A summary of some of the different types of chemical reaction.

Figure 4.10 The reaction between aluminium and bromine is very vigorous, producing aluminium bromide. This experiment should not be attempted in the laboratory.

Small molecules of carbon dioxide and water are used to make glucose:

$$\text{carbon dioxide} + \text{water} \xrightarrow[\text{chlorophyll}]{\text{sunlight}} \text{glucose} + \text{oxygen}$$

$$6CO_2 + 6H_2O \longrightarrow C_6H_{12}O_6 + 6O_2$$

The green pigment **chlorophyll** is essential for this reaction because it traps energy from the Sun.

Decomposition reactions have just one reactant, which breaks down to give two or more simpler products. Joseph Priestley (in 1774) first made oxygen by heating mercury(II) oxide:

$$\text{mercury(II) oxide} \xrightarrow{\text{heat}} \text{mercury} + \text{oxygen}$$

$$2Hg_2O \xrightarrow{\text{heat}} 2Hg + O_2$$

Lime for agriculture and for making cement is manufactured industrially by the decomposition of limestone (calcium carbonate):

$$\underset{\text{limestone}}{\text{calcium carbonate}} \xrightarrow{\text{heat}} \underset{\text{lime}}{\text{calcium oxide}} + \text{carbon dioxide}$$

$$CaCO_3 \xrightarrow{\text{heat}} CaO + CO_2$$

These reactions are endothermic. They require heat energy. Decomposition caused by heat energy is called **thermal decomposition.**

Decomposition can also be caused by light energy. For example, silver chloride, a white solid, turns grey in sunlight because silver metal is formed:

$$\text{silver chloride} \xrightarrow{\text{light}} \text{silver} + \text{chlorine}$$

$$2AgCl \xrightarrow{\text{light}} 2Ag + Cl_2$$

Silver bromide and silver iodide behave in the same way. These photochemical reactions are the basis of photography.

Neutralisation and precipitation

Salts are a useful type of chemical compound that we will meet in detail in Chapter 5. A few salts, mainly chlorides, bromides and iodides, can be made by synthesis (direct combination) as mentioned above. The majority, though, have to be made either by neutralisation or by precipitation.

Neutralisation reactions involve acids. When acids react with bases or alkalis, their acidity is destroyed. They are neutralised and a **salt** is produced. Such reactions are known as neutralisation reactions. An example is

$$H_2SO_4 + CuO \rightarrow CuSO_4 + H_2O$$

$$\text{acid} + \text{base} \rightarrow \text{salt} + \text{water}$$

Precipitation reactions involve the formation of an insoluble product.

Precipitation is the sudden formation of a solid, either:

- when two solutions are mixed, or
- when a gas is bubbled into a solution.

This type of reaction can be used to prepare insoluble salts. For example, lead(II) iodide can be made by mixing solutions of lead(II) nitrate and potassium iodide. A yellow precipitate of lead(II) iodide is formed (Figure **4.11a**):

$$Pb(NO_3)_2 + 2KI \rightarrow PbI_2\downarrow + 2KNO_3$$

Potassium nitrate is soluble in water, so it stays in solution. The lead(II) iodide precipitates because it is insoluble; the downward arrow can be used to show this. Lead(II) nitrate solution can be used as an analytical test for iodides (although the scheme for this exam uses silver nitrate as the test for iodide – see page **341**).

The **limewater** test for carbon dioxide also depends on precipitation. Here the insoluble product is calcium carbonate (Figure **4.11b**). A milky suspension of insoluble calcium carbonate is formed:

$$CO_2 + Ca(OH)_2 \rightarrow CaCO_3\downarrow + H_2O$$

Figure 4.11 Precipitation reactions produce an insoluble product. **a** Yellow lead(II) iodide is precipitated from lead(II) nitrate solution by potassium iodide. **b** Calcium carbonate is precipitated from limewater by carbon dioxide.

Precipitation reactions are very useful in analysis and are also used in the paint industry for making insoluble pigments.

Displacement reactions

Displacement reactions are useful in working out the patterns of reactivity of elements of the same type. A **displacement reaction** occurs because a more reactive element will displace a less reactive one from a solution of one of its compounds.

Zinc is a more reactive metal than copper. If a piece of zinc is placed in a copper(II) sulfate solution, a red-brown deposit of copper forms on the zinc (Figure **4.12a**). The blue colour of the copper(II) sulfate solution fades. Zinc displaces copper from copper(II) sulfate solution:

$$Zn + CuSO_4 \rightarrow ZnSO_4 + Cu$$

A similar reaction takes place when reactive metals are placed in acids. Hydrogen is displaced from the acid solution by the metal. For example:

$$Mg + 2HCl \rightarrow MgCl_2 + H_2$$

Some metals are so reactive that they will displace hydrogen from water (see Figure **4.7** on page **110**). For example:

$$2K + 2H_2O \rightarrow 2KOH + H_2$$

The halogens can be placed in order of reactivity using displacement reactions. Thus, chlorine gas will

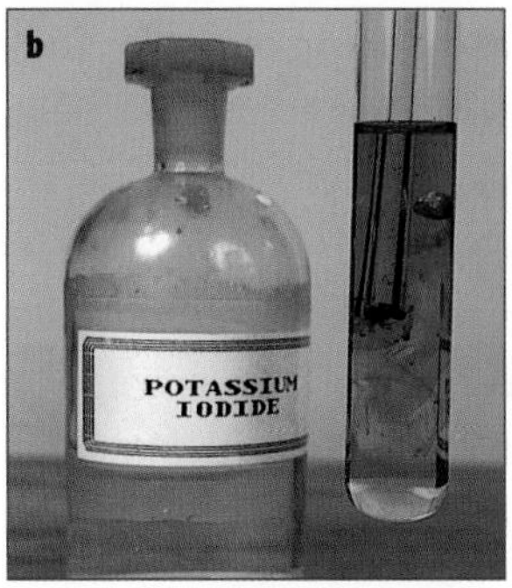

Figure 4.12 Displacement reactions. **a** Zinc will displace copper from copper(II) sulfate solution, and the colour of the solution fades as the copper forms on the zinc surface. **b** Chlorine displaces iodine from a potassium iodide solution. The colourless solution turns yellow–brown.

displace iodine from potassium iodide solution. The colourless solution turns yellow–brown as iodine appears (Figure **4.12b**):

$$Cl_2 + 2KI \rightarrow 2KCl + I_2$$

Combustion, oxidation and reduction

Combustion reactions are of great importance and can be very useful or destructive.

- **Combustion** of a substance involves its reaction with oxygen and the release of energy.
- These reactions are exothermic and often involve a flame.
- Combustion in which a flame is produced is described as **burning**.

The combustion of natural gas is an important source of energy for homes and industry. Natural gas is mainly methane. Its complete combustion produces carbon dioxide and water vapour:

methane + oxygen → carbon dioxide + water

$$CH_4 + 2O_2 \rightarrow CO_2 + 2H_2O$$

Substances such as methane, which undergo combustion readily and give out a large amount of energy, are known as **fuels**.

Our bodies need energy to make possible the reactions that take place in our cells. These reactions allow us to carry out our everyday activities. We need energy to stay alive. We get this energy from food. During **digestion**, food is broken down into simpler substances. For example, the carbohydrates in rice, potatoes and bread are broken down to form glucose. The combustion of glucose with oxygen in the cells of our body provides energy:

glucose + oxygen → carbon dioxide + water

$$C_6H_{12}O_6 + 6O_2 \rightarrow 6CO_2 + 6H_2O$$

This reaction is exothermic and is known by a special name: **respiration**.

In combustion reactions, the substance involved is **oxidised**. Oxygen is added and oxides are formed. Not all reactions with oxygen produce a great amount of energy. For example, when air is passed over heated copper, the surface becomes coated with black copper(II) oxide. There is no flame, nor is the reaction very exothermic. But it is still an **oxidation** reaction (Figure **4.13a**):

$$\text{copper} + \text{oxygen} \xrightarrow{\text{heat}} \text{copper(II) oxide}$$

$$2Cu + O_2 \xrightarrow{\text{heat}} 2CuO$$

This process can be reversed, and the copper surface regenerated, if hydrogen gas is passed over the heated material. The black coating on the surface turns pink as the reaction takes place (Figure **4.13b**):

$$\text{copper(II) oxide} + \text{hydrogen} \xrightarrow{\text{heat}} \text{copper} + \text{water}$$

During this reaction, the copper(II) oxide is losing oxygen. The copper(II) oxide is undergoing **reduction** – it is losing oxygen and being reduced. The hydrogen is gaining oxygen. It is being oxidised:

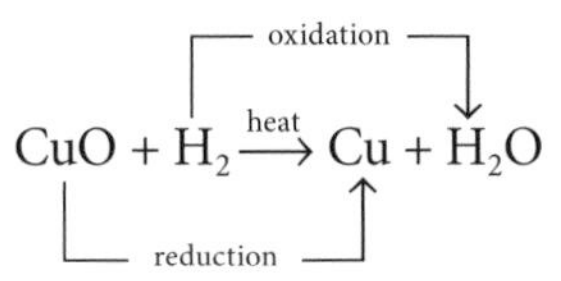

- If a substance **gains** oxygen during a reaction, it is oxidised.
- If a substance **loses** oxygen during a reaction, it is reduced.

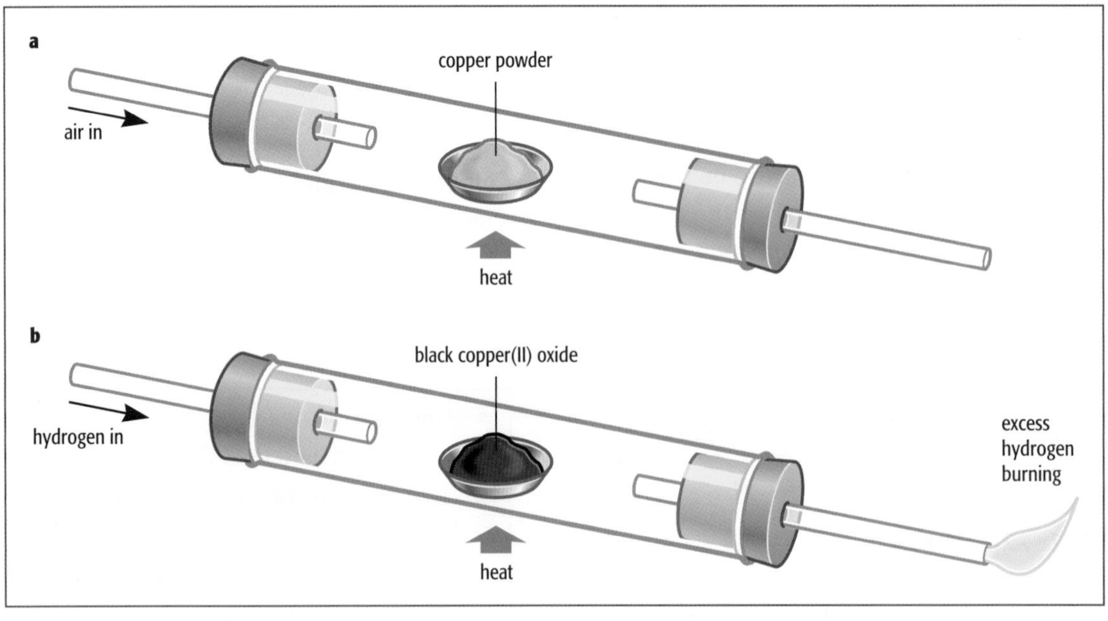

Figure 4.13 **a** The oxidation of copper to copper(II) oxide. **b** The reduction of copper(II) oxide back to copper using hydrogen.

Notice that the two processes of oxidation and reduction take place together during the same reaction. This is true for a whole range of similar reactions. Consider the following reaction:

zinc oxide + carbon → zinc + carbon monoxide

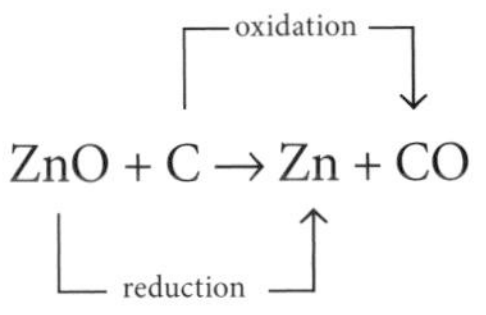

Again, in this reaction, the two processes occur together. Since oxidation never takes place without reduction, it is better to call these reactions oxidation–reduction reactions or **redox reactions**.

In this last example, carbon removes oxygen from zinc oxide. Carbon is an example of a reducing agent.

- A **reducing agent** is an element or compound that will **remove** oxygen from other substances.
- The commonest reducing agents are hydrogen, carbon and carbon monoxide.

Reduction is very important in industry as it provides a way of extracting metals from the metal oxide ores that occur in the Earth's crust. A good example is the blast furnace for extracting iron from hematite (Fe_2O_3) (Chapter **9**).

Some substances are capable of giving oxygen to others. These substances are known as oxidising agents.

- An **oxidising agent** is a substance that will **add** oxygen to another substance.
- The commonest oxidising agents are oxygen (or air), hydrogen peroxide, potassium manganate(VII) and potassium dichromate(VI).

Exam tip

Remember that, in the process of acting as a reducing agent, that substance will itself be oxidised. The reducing agent will gain the oxygen it is removing from the other compound.

The reverse is true for an oxidising agent.

There are two common examples of oxidation reactions that we might meet in our everyday lives.

- **Corrosion.** If a metal is reactive, its surface may be attacked by air, water, or other substances around it. The effect is called **corrosion**. When iron or steel slowly corrodes in damp air, the product is a brown, flaky substance we call **rust**. Rust is a form of iron(III) oxide. Rusting weakens structures such as car bodies, iron railings, ships' hulls and bridges. Rust prevention is a major economic cost.
- **Rancidity.** Oxidation also has damaging effects on food. When the fats and oils in butter and margarine are oxidised, they become **rancid**. Their taste and smell change and become very unpleasant. Manufacturers sometimes add anti-oxidants to fatty foods and oils to prevent oxidation. Keeping foods in a refrigerator can slow down the oxidation process. Storage in air-tight containers also helps. Crisps manufacturers fill crisps bags with nitrogen to prevent the crisps being oxidised.

Key ideas so far

- There is a range of different types of chemical reaction.
- Synthesis reactions involve the making of a more complex substance from simpler ones.
- Decomposition is the reverse of synthesis: a substance is split into simpler ones. This can be brought about by heat in thermal decomposition.
- Acids and alkalis take part in neutralisation reactions.
- Precipitation is the sudden formation of a solid during a reaction.
- Combustion reactions involve an exothermic reaction with oxygen.
- Oxidation is the gain of oxygen during a reaction.
- Reduction is the opposite of oxidation; a substance loses oxygen during reduction.

Quick-check questions

1 The halogens are a group of elements showing trends in colour, state and reaction with other halide ions.

  a Copy and complete the word equation for the reaction of chlorine with aqueous potassium bromide.

  chlorine + potassium bromide → ....

  b Explain why an aqueous solution of iodine does not react with potassium chloride.

2 Some types of chemical reaction are listed below.

decomposition **neutralisation**
combustion **oxidation–reduction (redox)**

Which reaction type best describes the following changes?

  a hexane + oxygen → carbon dioxide + water

  b calcium carbonate → calcium oxide + carbon dioxide

  c magnesium + copper oxide → magnesium oxide + copper

  d hydrochloric acid + sodium hydroxide → sodium chloride + water

3 Write word and balanced chemical equations for the reactions between:

  a sodium and water

  b magnesium and steam

  c calcium and oxygen

  d bromine and potassium iodide solution

  e zinc and copper sulfate solution.

4.4 A closer look at reactions, particularly redox reactions

State symbols

So far, our equations have told us nothing about the physical state of the reactants and products.

Chemical equations can be made more useful by including symbols that give us this information. These are called **state symbols**. They show clearly whether a gas is given off or a solid precipitate is formed during a reaction. The four symbols used are shown in Table **4.1**.

The following examples show how they can be used. They can show clearly when a gas or a precipitate is produced in a reaction (the points of particular interest are shown in **bold type**). Note that when water itself is produced in a reaction it has the symbol (l) for liquid, not (aq).

Symbol	Meaning
s	solid
l	liquid
g	gas
aq	aqueous solution, i.e. dissolved in water

Table 4.1 The state symbols used in chemical equations.

magnesium + nitric acid → magnesium nitrate + hydrogen

$Mg(s) + 2HNO_3(aq) \rightarrow Mg(NO_3)_2(aq) + \mathbf{H_2(g)}$

hydrochloric acid + sodium hydroxide → sodium chloride + water

$HCl(aq) + NaOH(aq) \rightarrow NaCl(aq) + \mathbf{H_2O(l)}$

copper(II) sulfate + sodium hydroxide → copper(II) hydroxide + sodium sulfate

$CuSO_4(aq) + 2NaOH(aq) \rightarrow \mathbf{Cu(OH)_2(s)} + Na_2SO_4(aq)$

Ionic equations

The last two examples above are useful for showing a further modification in writing equations. This modification identifies more clearly those particles which are actually taking part in a particular reaction. These two reactions involve mixing solutions that contain ions. Only some of the ions present actually change their status – by changing either their bonding or their physical state. The other ions present are simply **spectator ions** to the change; they do not take part in the reaction.

The equation given above for neutralising hydrochloric acid with sodium hydroxide solution is:

$HCl(aq) + NaOH(aq) \rightarrow NaCl(aq) + H_2O(l)$

Writing out all the ions present, we get

$$[H^+(aq) + \cancel{Cl^-(aq)}] + [\cancel{Na^+(aq)} + OH^-(aq)] \rightarrow [\cancel{Na^+(aq)} + \cancel{Cl^-(aq)}] + H_2O(l)$$

The use of state symbols clearly shows which ions have not changed during the reaction. They have been crossed out (~~like this~~) and can be left out of the equation. This leaves us with the essential **ionic equation** for all neutralisation reactions:

$$H^+(aq) + OH^-(aq) \rightarrow H_2O(l)$$

Applying the same principles to a precipitation reaction again gives us a clear picture of which ions are reacting (Figure **4.14**). The equation

$$CuSO_4(aq) + 2NaOH(aq) \rightarrow Cu(OH)_2(s) + Na_2SO_4(aq)$$

for the precipitation of copper(II) hydroxide, which was given above, becomes

$$Cu^{2+}(aq) + 2OH^-(aq) \rightarrow Cu(OH)_2(s)$$

This is the essential ionic equation for the precipitation of copper(II) hydroxide; the spectator ions (sulfate and sodium ions) have been left out.

Redox reactions

Chemists' ideas about oxidation and reduction have expanded as a wider range of reactions have been studied. Look again at the reaction between copper and oxygen:

$$\text{copper} + \text{oxygen} \xrightarrow{\text{heat}} \text{copper(II) oxide}$$

$$2CuO + O_2 \xrightarrow{\text{heat}} 2CuO$$

It is clear that copper has been oxidised; but what has been reduced? We can apply the ideas behind ionic equations to analyse the changes taking place during this reaction. It then becomes clear that:

- the copper atoms in the metal have become copper ions (Cu^{2+}) in copper(II) oxide
- the oxygen molecules in the gas have split and become oxide ions (O^{2-}) in the black solid copper(II) oxide.

The copper atoms, which clearly were oxidised during the reaction, have in the process **lost** electrons. The oxygen atoms have **gained** electrons in the process.

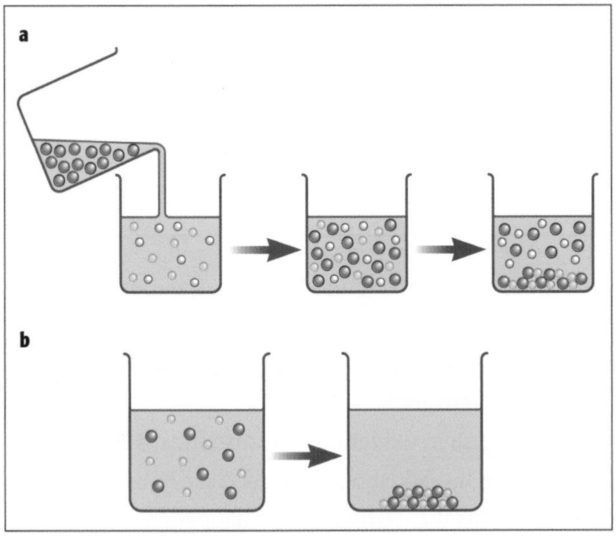

Figure 4.14 A precipitation reaction in which two solutions containing ions are mixed: **a** the overall reaction, **b** the net reaction with the spectator ions not shown.

A new, broader definition of oxidation and reduction can now be put forward.

- Oxidation is the **loss** of electrons.
- Reduction is the **gain** of electrons.

We can remember this by using the memory aid '**OIL-RIG**':

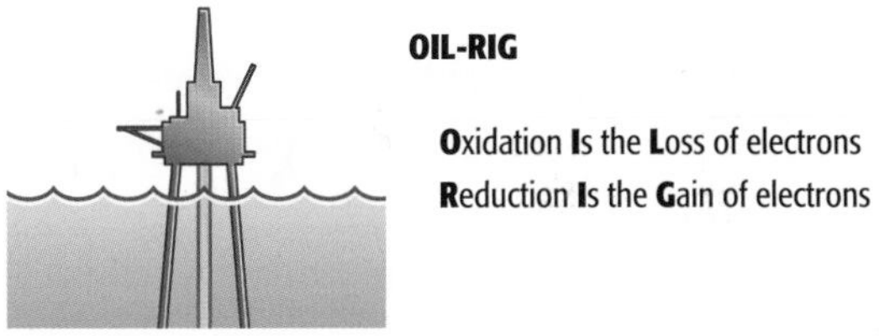

This new definition of redox changes increases the number of reactions that can be called redox reactions. For instance, displacement reactions where there is no transfer of oxygen are now included. This is best seen by looking at an ionic equation. For example:

$$Zn(s) + CuSO_4(aq) \rightarrow ZnSO_4(aq) + Cu(s)$$

As an ionic equation this becomes:

$$Zn(s) + Cu^{2+}(aq) \rightarrow Zn^{2+}(aq) + Cu(s)$$

(reduction: $Cu^{2+}(aq) \rightarrow Cu(s)$; oxidation: $Zn(s) \rightarrow Zn^{2+}(aq)$)

Zinc has lost two electrons and copper has gained them. This reaction is a redox reaction as there has been both loss and gain of electrons by different elements during the reaction.

It is on the basis of this definition that chlorine, for instance, is a good oxidising agent. It displaces iodine from potassium iodide solution (see Figure **4.12b** on page **113**). Is this reaction a redox reaction?

$$Cl_2(aq) + 2Br^-(aq) \rightarrow 2Cl^-(aq) + Br_2(aq)$$

From the ionic equation we can see that chlorine atoms have gained electrons to become chloride ions. They have been reduced. The bromide ions have lost electrons to form bromine. They have been oxidised.

If we look closely at these reactions we can see that a further definition of oxidation is possible. In the metal displacement reaction, each zinc atom has lost two electrons and the copper ions have gained them. The loss or gain of electrons in the reaction means that changes in **oxidation state** have taken place:

reduction

$$\underset{0}{Zn(s)} + \underset{+2}{Cu^{2+}(aq)} \rightarrow \underset{+2}{Zn^{2+}(aq)} + \underset{0}{Cu(s)}$$

oxidation state

oxidation

During the reaction, the oxidation state of zinc has increased by 2, from 0 to +2. Meanwhile the oxidation state of copper has decreased by 2, from +2 to 0.

> Thus the definitions of oxidation and reduction may be adapted still further to apply to particular atoms or ions during a reaction.
> - Oxidation is the **increase** in oxidation state of an atom or ion.
> - Reduction is the **decrease** in oxidation state of an atom or ion.

In the halogen displacement reaction, chlorine displaces iodine from potassium iodide solution. Consider the changes in oxidation state during the reaction:

reduction

$$\underset{0}{Cl_2(g)} + \underset{+1\ \ -1}{2KI(aq)} \rightarrow \underset{+1\ \ -1}{2KCl(aq)} + \underset{0}{I_2(aq)}$$

oxidation state

oxidation

- The oxidation state of iodine changes from −1 to 0. It has increased. Iodide ions are **oxidised** to iodine.
- The oxidation state of chlorine changes from 0 to −1. It has decreased. Chlorine is **reduced** to chloride ions.

Tests for oxidising and reducing agents

Reactions involving potassium iodide can be very useful as a test for any oxidising agent, because a colour change is produced. The iodide ion (I^-) is oxidised to iodine (I_2). The colour of the solution changes from colourless to yellow–brown. If starch indicator is added, then a dark blue colour is produced.

Reactions involving acidified potassium manganate(VII) are useful for detecting a reducing agent. The manganese is in a very high oxidation state (+7) in the manganate(VII) ion (MnO_4^-). A solution containing the manganate(VII) ion has a purple colour. When it is reduced, the manganate(VII) ion loses its purple colour and the solution becomes colourless.

Acidified potassium dichromate solution could also be used as a test. In this case the colour change seen is from orange to green.

Key ideas so far

- State symbols can be used in chemical reactions to give further information.
- Ionic equations can be written for many reactions. These equations help clarify which species (ions) are actually reacting; the 'spectator' ions are omitted from the equation.
- Oxidation and reduction can be defined in terms of the loss or gain of electrons during a reaction.
- Oxidation is the loss of electrons. Reduction is the gain of electrons.
- An increase in oxidation state also means that oxidation has taken place. A decrease in oxidation state means that reduction has happened.

Quick-check questions

1 **a** Explain the meaning of the symbols (s), (l), (aq) and (g) in the following equation, with reference to each reactant and product:

$$Na_2CO_3(s) + 2HCl(aq) \rightarrow 2NaCl(aq) + H_2O(l) + CO_2(g)$$

b Write an ionic equation, including state symbols, for each of the following reactions:

i silver nitrate solution + sodium chloride solution → silver chloride + silver nitrate solution

ii sodium sulfate solution + barium nitrate solution → sodium nitrate solution + barium sulfate

iii dilute hydrochloric acid + potassium hydroxide solution → potassium chloride solution + water

iv dilute hydrochloric acid + copper carbonate → copper chloride solution + water + carbon dioxide

2 Copy and complete the following statement: .... is the gain of electrons; .... is the loss of electrons. During a redox reaction the oxidising agent .... electrons; the oxidising agent is itself .... during the reaction.

4.5 Electrolysis

Electricity has had a great effect on our way of living. Large urban areas, such as Hong Kong, could not function without the electricity supply. The results of the large-scale supply of electricity can be seen in the pylons and power lines that mark our landscape. But electricity is also important on the very small scale. The silicon chip enables a vast range of products to work, and many people now have access to products containing electronic circuits – from MP3 players to washing machines.

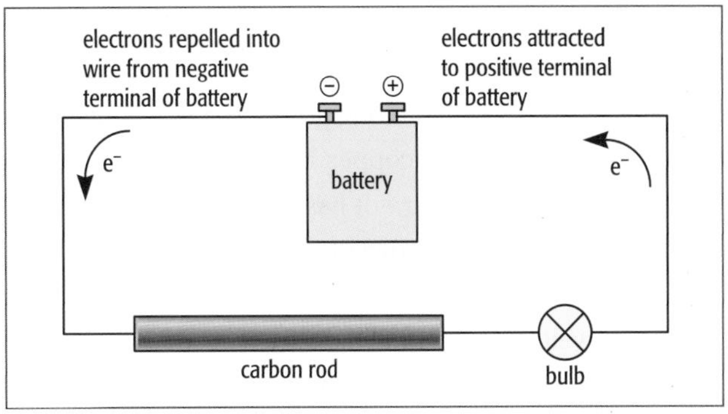

Figure 4.15 Testing a solid material to see if it conducts electricity, by whether it lights a bulb.

Conductivity in solids – conductors and insulators

The ability to conduct electricity is the major simple difference between elements that are metals and elements that are non-metals. All metals conduct electricity, but carbon in the form of graphite is the only non-metallic element that conducts electricity. A simple circuit can be used to test whether any solid conducts or not (Figure **4.15**). The circuit is made up of a battery (a source of direct current), some connecting copper wires fitted with clips and a light bulb to show when a current is flowing. The material to be tested is clipped into the circuit. If the bulb lights up, then the material is an **electrical conductor**.

For a solid to conduct, it must have a structure that contains 'free' electrons that are able to flow through it. There is a flow of electrons in the completed circuit. The battery acts as an 'electron pump'. Electrons are repelled (pushed) into the circuit from the negative terminal of the battery. They are attracted to the positive terminal. Metals (and graphite) conduct electricity because they have mobile free electrons in their structure. The battery 'pumps' all the free electrons in one direction. Metallic alloys are held together by the same type of bonding as the metal elements, so they also can conduct electricity. Solid covalent non-metals do not conduct electricity. Whether they are giant molecular or simple molecular structures, there are no electrons that are not involved in bonding – there are no free electrons. Such substances are called non-conductors or **insulators** (Table **4.2**, overleaf).

There is no chemical change when an electric current is passed through a metal or graphite. The copper wire is still copper when the current is switched off!

Conductors	Insulators (non-conductors)	
	Giant molecular	Simple molecular
copper	diamond	sulfur
silver	poly(ethene)	iodine
aluminium	poly(chloroethene), PVC	
steel	poly(tetrafluoroethene), PTFE	
brass		
graphite		

Table 4.2 Solid electrical conductors and insulators.

An **electrical conductor** is a substance that conducts electricity but is not chemically changed in the process.

Supplying electricity

Electricity is transmitted along power cables. Many of these cables are made of copper, because copper is a very good electrical conductor – it has a very high electrical conductivity. Overhead power cables are made from aluminium (Figure **4.16**), which not only conducts electricity well but has a low density, preventing sagging. Aluminium is also very resistant to corrosion. The cables then strengthened with a steel core.

Domestic cables are covered (sheathed) in plastic, which is a non-conductor. This cover (or insulation) is needed for safety reasons. Leakage of power from overhead cables is prevented by using **ceramic** materials between the cable and the pylons. These plastic and ceramic materials are examples of insulators.

Exam tip

The steel core in overhead power cables is present to strengthen the cable.

Conductivity in liquids – electrolytes and non-electrolytes

The conductivity of liquids can be tested in a similar way to solids, but the simple testing circuit is changed (Figure **4.17**). Instead of clipping the solid material to be tested into the circuit, graphite rods are dipped into the test liquid. Liquid compounds, solutions and molten

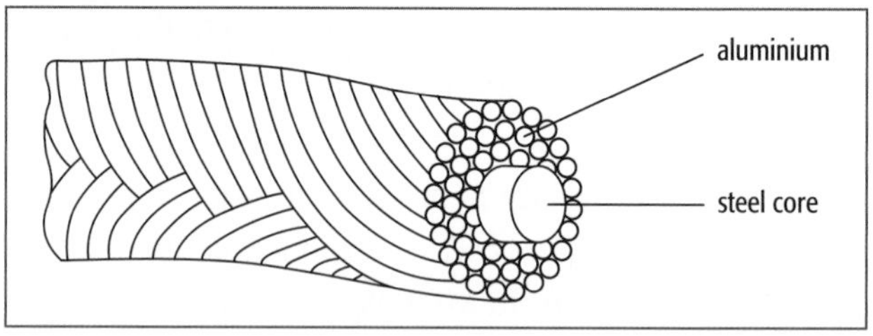

Figure 4.16 Overhead power lines are made of steel-cored aluminium cables. Note the ceramic plates that insulate the pylons from the cables.

materials can all be tested in this way. Molten metals, and mercury, which is liquid at room temperature, conduct electricity. Electrons are still able to move through the liquid metal to carry the charge. As in solid metals, no chemical change takes place when liquid metals conduct electricity.

If liquid compounds or solutions are tested using the apparatus in Figure **4.17**, then the result will depend on the type of bonding holding the compound together. If the compound is bonded covalently, then it will **not** conduct electricity as a liquid, or as a solution. Examples of such liquids are ethanol, petrol, pure water and sugar solution (Table **4.3**). Ionic compounds **will** conduct electricity if they are either molten or dissolved in water. Examples of this are molten lead bromide, sodium chloride solution and copper(II) sulfate solution.

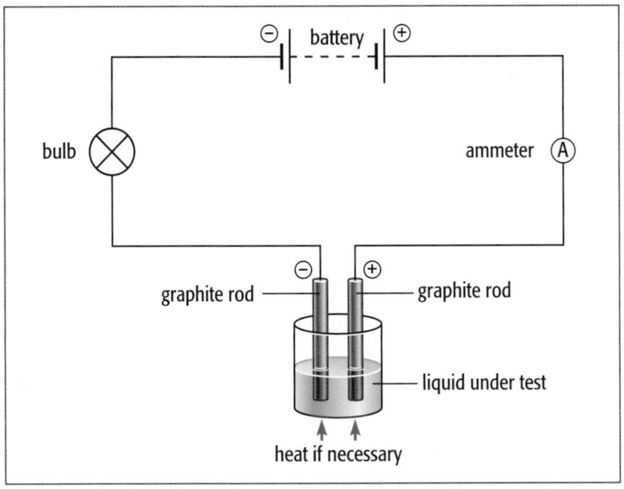

Figure 4.17 The apparatus for testing the conductivity of liquids.

Electrolytes	Non-electrolytes
molten zinc chloride	distilled water
molten lead bromide	ethanol
sodium chloride solution	petrol
hydrochloric acid	paraffin
copper(II) chloride solution	molten sulfur
ethanoic acid	sugar solution
sulfuric acid	
sodium hydroxide solution	

Table 4.3 Some electrolytes and non-electrolytes.

When these liquids conduct, they do so in a different way from metals. In this case they conduct because the ions present can move through the liquid; when metals conduct, electrons move through the metal.

Ionic compounds will not conduct electricity when solid because their ions are fixed in position and cannot move. Liquids which conduct electricity by movement of ions are called **electrolytes.** Liquids which do not conduct in this way are called **non-electrolytes.**

When electrolytes conduct electricity, chemical change takes place and the ionic compound is split up. For example, lead bromide is changed to lead and bromine:

$$PbBr_2(l) \rightarrow Pb(l) + Br_2(g)$$

This type of change is called **electrolysis** and is described in more detail below.

In summary, the following substances are electrolytes:

- molten salts
- solutions of salts in water
- solutions of acids
- solutions of alkalis.

The two distinct types of electrical conductivity are called metallic and electrolytic conductivity. They differ from each other in important ways.

Metallic conductivity:

- electrons flow
- a property of elements (metals and carbon, as graphite) and alloys
- takes place in solids and liquids
- no chemical change takes place.

Electrolytic conductivity:

- ions flow
- a property of ionic compounds
- takes place in liquids and solutions (not solids)
- chemical decomposition takes place.

The movement of ions

The conductivity of ionic compounds is explained by the fact that ions move in a particular direction in an electric field. This can be shown in experiments with coloured salts.

For example, copper(II) chromate(VI) ($CuCrO_4$) dissolves in water to give a green solution. This solution is placed in the lower part of a U-tube. A colourless solution of dilute hydrochloric acid is then layered on top of the salt solution in each arm, and graphite rods are fitted (Figure **4.18**, overleaf). These rods carry the current into and out of the solution. They are known as **electrodes**. In electrolysis, the negative electrode is called the **cathode**; the positive electrode is the **anode**.

After passing the current for a short time, the solution around the cathode becomes blue. Around the anode the solution becomes yellow. These colours are produced by the movement (migration) of the ions in the salt. The positive copper ions (Cu^{2+}) are blue in solution. They are attracted to the cathode (the negative electrode). The negative chromate ions (CrO_4^{2-}) are yellow in solution. They are attracted to the anode (the positive electrode). The use of coloured ions in solution

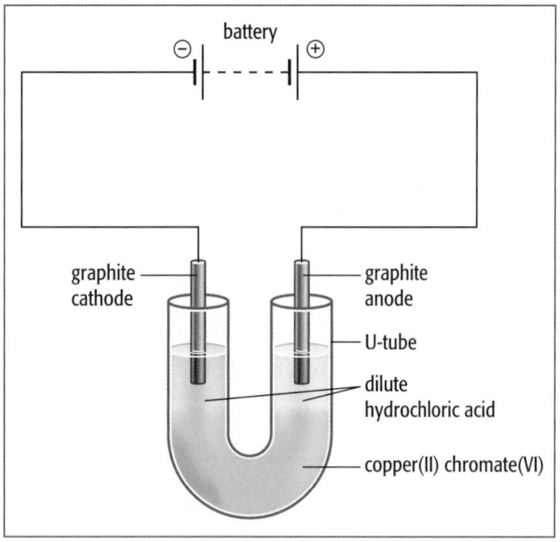

Figure 4.18 An experiment to show ionic movement by using a salt solution containing coloured ions. The acid solution was colourless at the start of the experiment.

has shown the direction that positive and negative ions move in an electric field.

> During electrolysis:
> - **positive ions** (metal ions or H^+ ions) move towards the **cathode**; they are known as **cations**
> - **negative ions** (non-metal ions) move towards the **anode**; they are known as **anions**.

Exam tip

It is important to remember that it is electrons that move through the wire when a metal conducts. However, when a salt solution conducts it is the ions in the solution that move to the electrodes. They are then discharged at the electrodes.

A solid ionic compound will not conduct electricity, because the ions are in fixed positions in a solid; they cannot move. The electrolyte must be melted or dissolved in water for it to conduct.

The electrolytic cell

The apparatus in which electrolysis is carried out is known as an **electrolytic cell**. The direct current is supplied by a battery or power pack. Graphite electrodes carry the current into and out of the liquid electrolyte. Graphite is chosen because it is quite unreactive (inert). It will not react with the electrolyte or with the products of electrolysis. Electrons flow from the negative terminal of the battery around the circuit and back to the positive terminal. In the electrolyte it is the **ions** that move to carry the current.

Electrolysis of molten compounds

An electrolytic cell can be used to electrolyse molten compounds. Heat must be supplied to keep the salt molten. Figure **4.19** shows the electrolysis of molten zinc chloride.

When the switch is closed, the current flows and chlorine gas (which is pale green) begins to bubble off at the anode. After a little time, a bead of molten zinc collects at the cathode. The electrical energy from the cell has caused a chemical change (decomposition). The cell decomposes the molten zinc chloride because the ions present move to opposite electrodes where they lose their charge (they are **discharged**). Figure **4.19** shows this movement. The chloride ions (Cl^-) move to the anode. Each chloride ion gives up (donates) one electron to become a chlorine atom:

at the anode $Cl^- \rightarrow Cl + e^-$

Then two chlorine atoms bond together to make a chlorine molecule:

$Cl + Cl \rightarrow Cl_2$

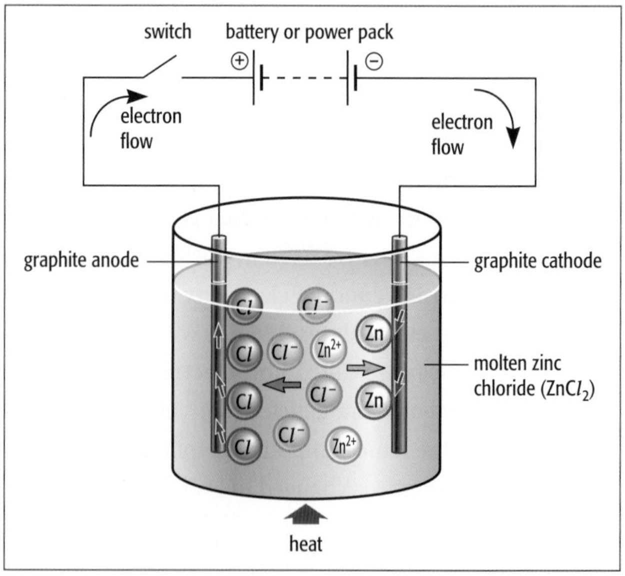

Figure 4.19 The movement of ions in the electrolysis of a molten salt, zinc chloride.

The zinc ions (Zn^{2+}) move to the cathode. There each zinc ion picks up (accepts) two electrons and becomes a zinc atom:

at the cathode $Zn^{2+} + 2e^- \rightarrow Zn$

During electrolysis, the flow of electrons continues through the circuit. For every two electrons taken from the cathode by a zinc ion, two electrons are set free at the anode by two chloride ions. So overall the electrons released at the anode flow through the circuit towards the cathode. During the electrolysis of molten salts, the metal ions, which are always positive (cations), move to the cathode and are discharged. Non-metal ions (except hydrogen), however, are always negative. They are anions and move to the anode to be discharged.

When a molten ionic compound is electrolysed:
- the metal is always formed at the cathode
- the non-metal is always formed at the anode.

Table **4.4** (overleaf) shows some further examples of this type of electrolysis, and the electrolysis of lead(II) bromide to form lead and bromine vapour is summarised diagrammatically in Figure **4.20**. Electrolysis of molten salts is easier if the melting point of the salt is not too high.

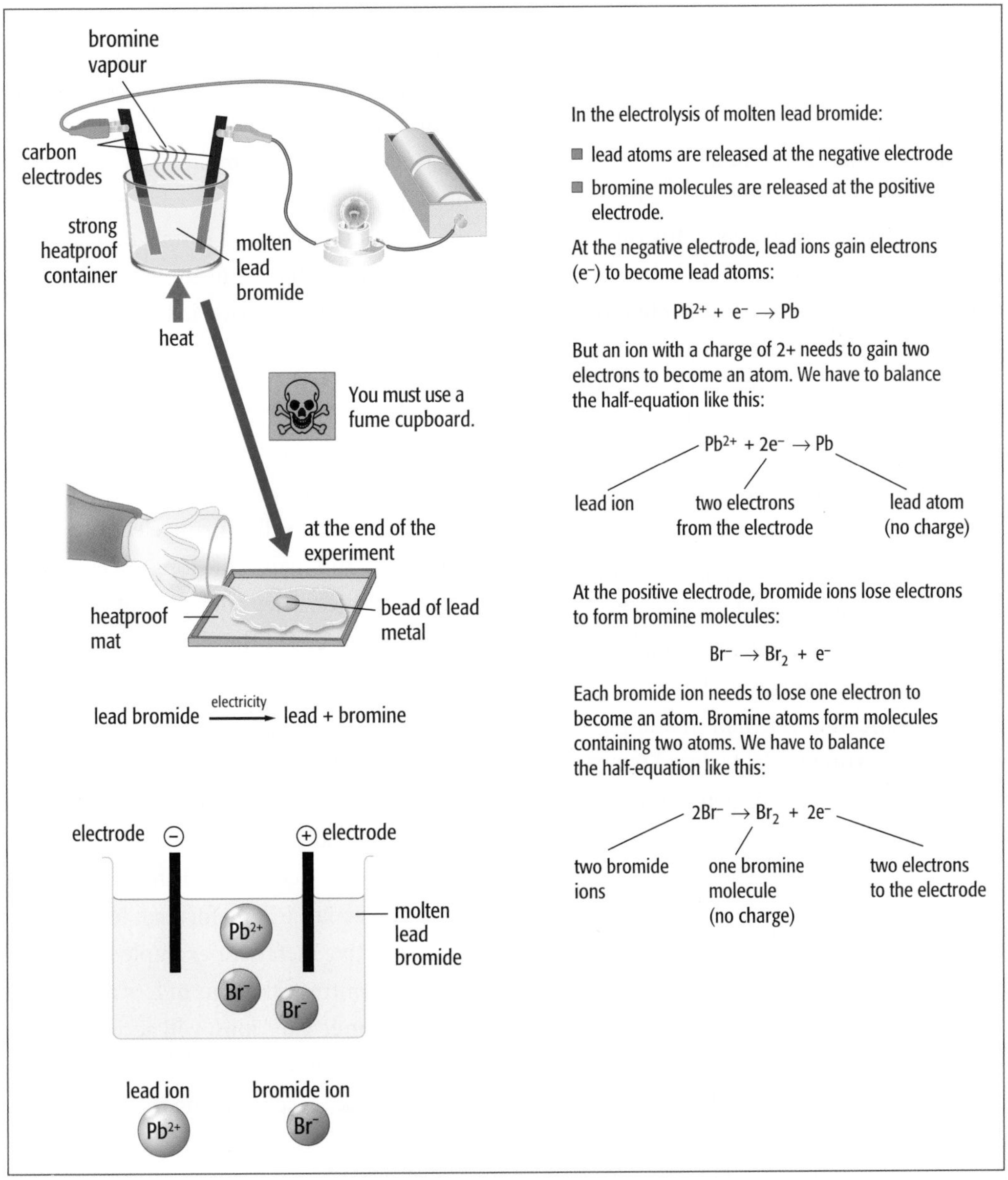

Figure 4.20 The electrolysis of lead(II) bromide.

Electrolyte	Decomposition products	Cathode reaction	Anode reaction[a]
lead bromide, $PbBr_2$	lead (Pb) and bromine (Br_2)	$Pb^{2+} + 2e^- \rightarrow Pb$	$2Br^- \rightarrow Br_2 + 2e^-$
sodium chloride, NaCl	sodium (Na) and chlorine (Cl_2)	$Na^+ + e^- \rightarrow Na$	$2Cl^- \rightarrow Cl_2 + 2e^-$
potassium iodide, KI	potassium (K) and iodine (I_2)	$K^+ + e^- \rightarrow K$	$2I^- \rightarrow I_2 + 2e^-$
copper(II) bromide, $CuBr_2$	copper (Cu) and bromine (Br_2)	$Cu^{2+} + 2e^- \rightarrow Cu$	$2Br^- \rightarrow Br_2 + 2e^-$

[a] *These anode reactions are the sum of the two stages written in the text. The loss of an electron from a negative ion like Cl^- can also be written $2Cl^- - 2e^- \rightarrow Cl_2$.*

Table 4.4 Some examples of the electrolysis of molten salts.

Industrial electrolysis of molten compounds

Electrolysis is important industrially because it is the only method of extraction available for the most reactive metals. Metals in Groups I and II, and aluminium, are too reactive to be extracted by chemical reduction using carbon like other metals. Metals such as sodium and magnesium are obtained by electrolysis of their molten chlorides. The metal is produced at the cathode.

One of the most important discoveries in industrial electrolysis was finding suitable conditions for extracting aluminium from its mineral ore, bauxite. The bauxite ore is first treated to produce pure aluminium oxide. This is then dissolved in molten cryolite (sodium aluminium fluoride). The melting point of the mixture is much lower than that of pure aluminium oxide. The mixture is electrolysed between graphite electrodes (Figure **4.21**). Molten aluminium is attracted to the cathode and collects at the bottom of the cell:

at the cathode $Al^{3+} + 3e^- \rightarrow Al$

Oxygen is released at the anodes:

at the anode $2O^{2-} \rightarrow O_2 + 4e^-$

At the operating temperature of about 1000 °C, the graphite anodes burn away in the oxygen to give carbon dioxide. So they have to be replaced regularly.

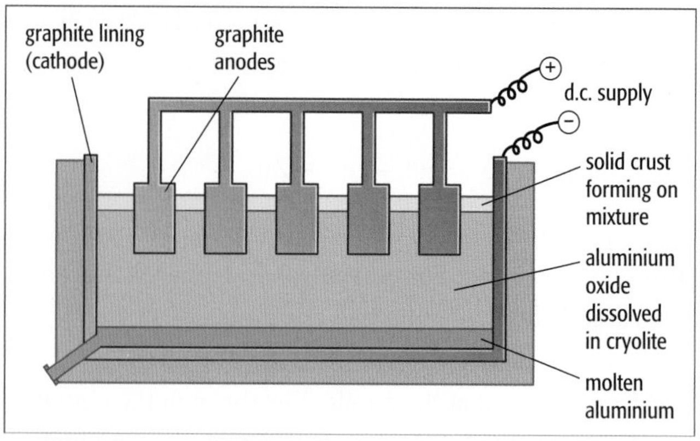

Figure 4.21 The industrial electrolysis of molten aluminium oxide to produce aluminium.

Electrolysis of solutions

The electrolysis of ionic solutions also produces chemical change. However, the products from electrolysis of a solution of a salt may be different from those obtained by electrolysis of the molten salt. This is because water itself produces ions.

Although water is a simple molecular substance, a very small fraction of its molecules split into hydrogen ions (H^+) and hydroxide ions (OH^-):

$$H_2O \rightleftharpoons H^+ + OH^-$$

most molecules intact — only a very few molecules split into ions

Not enough ions are produced for pure water to conduct electricity very well. During electrolysis, however, these hydrogen and hydroxide ions are also able to move to the electrodes. They compete with the ions from the salt to be discharged at the electrodes. But at each electrode just **one** type of ion gets discharged.

At the **cathode:**

- The more reactive a metal, the more it tends to stay as ions and not be discharged. The H^+ ions will accept electrons instead. Hydrogen molecules will be formed, leaving the ions of the reactive metal, for example Na^+ ions, in solution.
- In contrast, the ions of less reactive metals, for example Cu^{2+} ions, will accept electrons readily and form metal atoms. In this case, the metal will be discharged, leaving the H^+ ions in solution (Figure **4.22**).

Figure 4.22 Copper is quite unreactive so it can be seen deposited on the cathode when copper(II) sulfate solution is electrolysed.

At the **anode:**

- If the ions of a halogen (Cl^-, Br^- or I^-) are present in a high enough concentration, they will give up electrons more readily than OH^- ions will. Molecules of chlorine, bromine or iodine are formed. The OH^- ions remain in solution.
- If no halogen ions are present, the OH^- ions will give up electrons more easily than any other non-metal anion. Sulfate and nitrate ions are not discharged in preference to OH^- ions. When OH^- ions are discharged, oxygen is formed.

Electrolysis of sodium chloride solution

A concentrated solution of sodium chloride can be electrolysed in the laboratory (Figure **4.23**). There are four different ions present in the solution. The positive ions (cations), Na^+ and H^+, flow to the cathode, attracted by its negative charge. The negative ions (anions), Cl^- and OH^-, travel to the anode.

At the **cathode**, it is the H^+ ions that accept electrons, as sodium is more reactive than hydrogen:

$$H^+ + e^- \rightarrow H$$

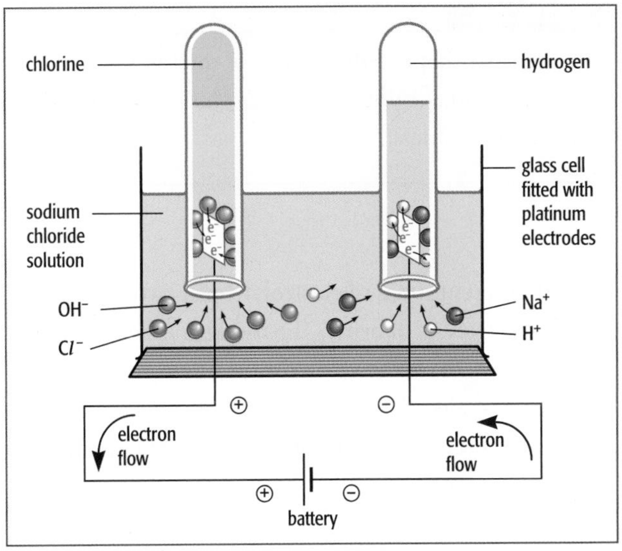

Figure 4.23 The movement and discharge of ions in the electrolysis of sodium chloride solution.

Then two hydrogen atoms combine to form a hydrogen molecule:

$$H + H \rightarrow H_2$$

So, overall, hydrogen gas bubbles off at the cathode:

$$2H^+ + 2e^- \rightarrow H_2$$

At the **anode**, the Cl^- ions are discharged more readily than the OH^- ions:

$$Cl^- \rightarrow Cl + e^-$$

Then two chlorine atoms combine to make a chlorine molecule:

$$Cl + Cl \rightarrow Cl_2$$

So, overall, pale green chlorine gas bubbles off at the anode:

$$2Cl^- \rightarrow Cl_2 + 2e^-$$

Left behind in solution are Na^+ and OH^- ions; this is sodium hydroxide solution. The solution therefore becomes alkaline. This can be shown by adding indicator to the solution. These products – hydrogen, chlorine and sodium hydroxide – are very important industrially as the basis for the chlor-alkali industry. So the electrolysis of concentrated brine (salt water) is a very important manufacturing process.

Exam tip

Remember that the electrolysis of molten sodium chloride and a sodium chloride solution will give different products.

Several different types of electrolytic cell have been used for the electrolysis of brine. The modern membrane cell (Figure **4.24**) is the safest for the environment and uses the least electricity. Other types of cell use either a flowing mercury cathode, or a diaphragm (partition) made from asbestos.

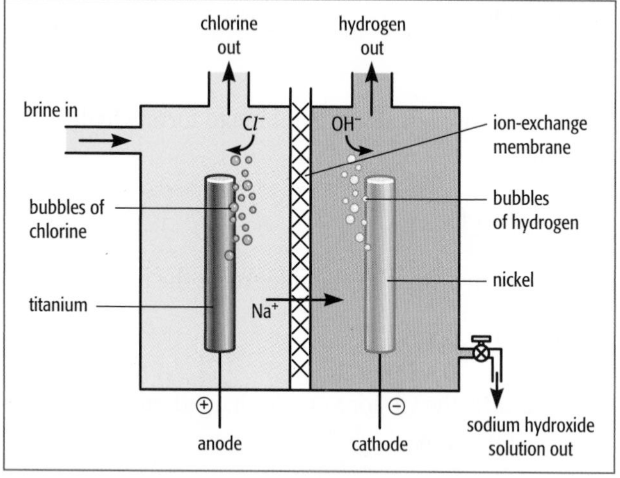

Figure 4.24 The membrane cell for the electrolysis of concentrated brine. The selective ion-exchange membrane allows only Na^+ ions to pass through it.

The **membrane cell** has a titanium anode and a nickel cathode. Titanium is chosen for the anode as it is not attacked by chlorine. The anode and cathode compartments are separated by an ion-exchange membrane. This membrane is selective; it allows Na^+ ions and water to flow through, but no other ions. This means that, while Na^+ ions can move freely to the cathode, the products are kept separate and cannot react with each other. The Na^+ and OH^- ions collect in the cathode compartment. The sodium hydroxide solution is removed and purified.

Exam tip

In these examples of industrial electrolysis you will not be expected to draw a diagram in an exam. You will need to be able to recognise and label a diagram and give the electrode half-equations.

You will also be expected to know the major reasons for the distinctive aspects of the process.

Electrolysis of copper(II) chloride

Copper is a metal that is less reactive than hydrogen. As a result, the electrolysis of solutions of copper salts using graphite electrodes produces red-brown deposits of copper on the **cathode** – hydrogen ions are not discharged:

$$Cu^{2+} + 2e^- \rightarrow Cu$$

As in the electrolysis of sodium chloride solution, when copper(II) chloride is electrolysed, pale green chlorine gas bubbles off from the **anode** (Figure **4.25**):

$$2Cl^- \rightarrow Cl_2 + 2e^-$$

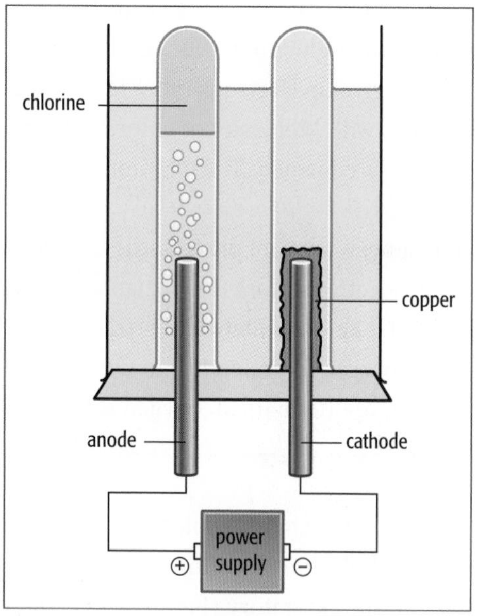

Figure 4.25 The electrolysis of copper(II) chloride solution.

Electroplating

The fact that an unreactive metal can be coated onto the surface of the cathode by electrolysis means that useful metal objects can be 'plated' with a chosen metal. **Electroplating** can be used to coat one metal with another.

For electroplating, the electrolysis cell is adapted from the type usually used. The cathode is the object to be plated and the anode is made from the metal being used to plate it. The electrolyte is a salt of the same metal. As the process proceeds the anode dissolves away into the solution, replacing the metal plated onto the object, and the concentration of the solution remains the same.

Exam tip

Usually the electrodes used in electrolysis are inert (graphite or platinum). However, in electroplating the anode is made of the metal to be plated. It is not inert, and it reacts. The anode decreases in size as it dissolves away.

The most commonly used metals for electroplating are copper, chromium, silver and tin. One purpose of electroplating is to give a protective coating to the metal underneath; an example is the tin-plating of steel cans to prevent them rusting. This is also the idea behind chromium-plating articles such as car bumpers, kettles, bath taps, etc. Chromium does not corrode; it is a hard metal that resists scratching and wear, and can also be polished to give an attractive finish.

Figure 4.26 The industrial electroplating of metal objects.

The attractive appearance of silver can be achieved by electroplating silver onto an article made from a cheaper metal such as nickel silver (Figure **4.26**). The 'EPNS' seen on cutlery and other objects stands for 'electroplated nickel silver'. 'Nickel silver' is an alloy of copper, zinc and nickel – it contains no silver at all! It is often used as the base metal for silver-plated articles.

The basic rules for electroplating an object with a metal M are as follows:

- the object must be made the cathode
- the electrolyte must be a solution of a salt of metal M
- the anode is made of a strip of metal M.

E

The electrolysis must be carried out under careful control to make sure that the metal layer sticks firmly to the article being plated. Steel objects often have to be coated first with layers of copper and nickel, before they can be chromium-plated. Chromium will not stick firmly to steel directly. Figure **4.27** shows in outline how an object is silver-plated. The object must be very clean and free of grease. It must also be rotated so that the layer forms evenly on all sides. The current, the temperature and the concentration of the electrolyte must be controlled so that the layer does not form too fast, otherwise it will flake off.

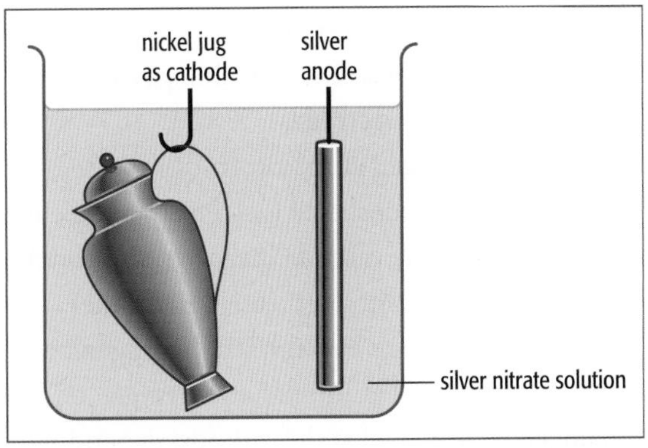

Figure 4.27 Electroplating – the basic requirements for silver-plating.

Electrolysis of acid solutions

Pure water is a very poor conductor of electricity. However, it can be made to decompose if some dilute sulfuric acid is added. A Hofmann voltameter (Figure **4.28**) can be used to keep the gases produced separate. After a short time the volume of gas in each arm can be measured and tested. The gas collected above the cathode is hydrogen. Oxygen collects at the anode. The ratio of the volumes is approximately 2 : 1. Effectively this experiment is the electrolysis of water:

at the cathode $2H^+ + 2e^- \rightarrow H_2$

at the anode $4OH^- \rightarrow 2H_2O + O_2 + 4e^-$

The electrolysis of concentrated hydrochloric acid can also be carried out in this apparatus. Again two gases are collected, this time hydrogen and chlorine:

at the cathode $2H^+ + 2e^- \rightarrow H_2$

at the anode $2Cl^- \rightarrow Cl_2 + 2e^-$

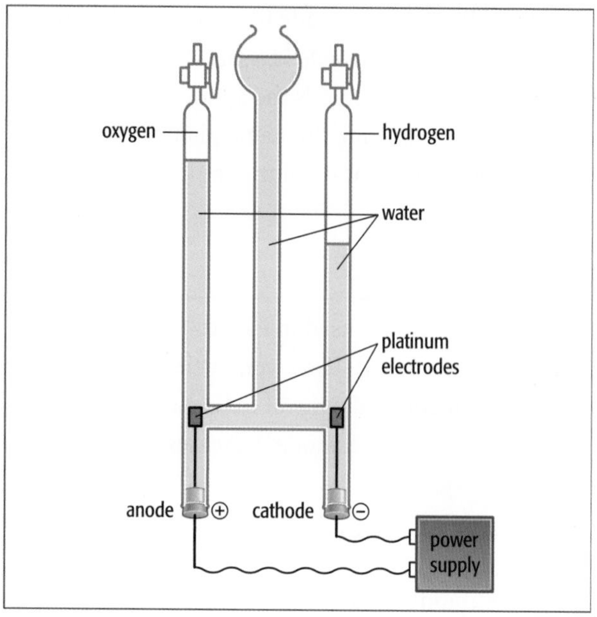

Figure 4.28 The Hofmann voltameter for the electrolysis of water.

Key ideas so far

- When metals conduct electricity, it is electrons that flow through the metal to produce the current.
- Graphite is the one non-metal that conducts electricity.
- Ionic substances can conduct electricity, but they must be molten or dissolved in water.
- In electrolysis, it is ions which move through the electrolyte to carry the current.
- Electrolysis involves chemical change as reactions take place at the electrodes.
- Ions are discharged at the electrodes.
- When a molten substance is electrolysed, the metal is produced at the cathode (negative electrode), the non-metal at the anode (positive electrode).
- When solutions are electrolysed, hydrogen or a metal is produced at the cathode. Oxygen or a halogen is produced at the cathode, depending on the electrolyte used.
- Electroplating is a useful technique to produce a decorative and/or protective coat of one metal on another.
- Electrolysis is used in the extraction of aluminium from molten aluminium oxide.
- The electrolysis of brine (concentrated sodium chloride solution) is used in the industrial manufacture of sodium hydroxide.

Quick-check questions

1 An experiment was carried out to investigate the effect of electricity on molten lead(II) bromide ($PbBr_2$).

a What happens to a compound during electrolysis?

b Why does solid lead(II) bromide not allow the passage of electricity?

c What colour is the vapour seen at the positive electrode?

d Give **one** reason why this electrolysis should be carried out in a fume cupboard.

e What is the alternative name for the negative electrode?

2 A metal object is to be copper plated.

a Which electrode should the object be made?

b Name a solution that could be used as the electrolyte.

3 In the electrolysis of molten lead(II) bromide, the reaction occurring at the negative electrode was:

$$Pb^{2+} + 2e^{-} \rightarrow Pb$$

a Write the equation for the reaction taking place at the positive electrode.

b Why is the reaction taking place at the negative electrode viewed as a reduction reaction?

4 The tables list the results of the electrolysis of a number of aqueous solutions using inert electrodes.

Use the information in the first table to complete the second table. The solutions were electrolysed under exactly the same conditions as the ones above.

Solution (electrolyte)	Gas given off at the anode	Gas given off or metal deposited at the cathode	Substance left in solution at the end of electrolysis
copper(II) sulfate	oxygen	copper	sulfuric acid
sodium sulfate	oxygen	hydrogen	sodium sulfate
silver nitrate	oxygen	silver	nitric acid
concentrated sodium chloride	chlorine	hydrogen	sodium hydroxide
copper(II) nitrate	oxygen	copper	nitric acid

Solution (electrolyte)	Gas given off at the anode	Gas given off or metal deposited at the cathode	Substance left in solution at the end of electrolysis
silver sulfate	oxygen		
sodium nitrate		hydrogen	sodium nitrate

4.6 A closer look at electrode reactions

The electrolysis of hydrochloric acid demonstrates one factor that is important in electrolysis: the **concentration** of the ions present.

When the concentration of the acid is lowered, the gas given off at the anode changes. As the solution becomes very dilute, chloride ions are not discharged. At these low concentrations, oxygen is produced from the discharge of hydroxide ions. The different products of the electrolysis of hydrochloric acid are shown in Table **4.5**.

There is a similar change in the product at the anode for very dilute solutions of sodium chloride. Again, oxygen is given off rather than chlorine. These results suggest that the discharge of Cl^- ions over OH^- ions (called preferential discharge) only applies if the concentration of Cl^- is sufficiently high.

Electrolyte	Product at anode	Product at cathode
concentrated hydrochloric acid	chlorine $2Cl^- \rightarrow Cl_2 + 2e^-$	hydrogen $2H^+ + 2e^- \rightarrow H_2$
very dilute hydrochloric acid	oxygen $4OH^- \rightarrow 2H_2O + O_2 + 4e^-$	hydrogen $2H^+ + 2e^- \rightarrow H_2$

Table 4.5 Electrolysis of dilute and concentrated hydrochloric acid.

Oxidation and reduction during electrolysis

The reactions that take place at the electrodes during electrolysis involve the loss and gain of electrons. Negative ions always travel to the anode, where they lose electrons. In contrast, positive ions always flow to the cathode, where they gain electrons. As we saw earlier (page 117), oxidation can be defined as the loss of electrons, and reduction as the gain of electrons. Therefore, electrolysis can be seen as a process in which oxidation and reduction are physically separated.

During **electrolysis**:
- the oxidation of non-metal ions always takes place at the anode
- the reduction of metal or hydrogen ions always takes place at the cathode.

Just as in redox reactions, where both oxidation and reduction occur at the same time, the two processes must take place together to produce electrolytic decomposition.

The refining (purification) of copper by electrolysis

Closer examination of an electroplating cell suggests an interesting method of purifying a metal. During electroplating, the oxidation process at the anode involves the metal anode actually dissolving. Metal atoms lose electrons and pass into solution as positive metal ions. In turn, metal ions are discharged at the cathode as the object becomes plated.

A cell can be set up to electrolyse copper(II) sulfate solution using **copper** electrodes (not graphite). As electrolysis takes place, the cathode gains mass as copper is deposited on it (Figure **4.29**):

at the cathode $Cu^{2+}(aq) + 2e^- \rightarrow Cu(s)$

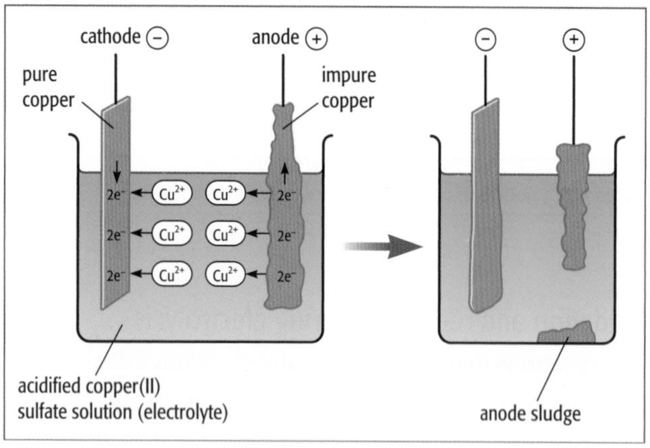

Figure 4.29 The purification of copper by electrolysis. The movement of ions effectively transfers copper from one electrode to another.

The anode, however, loses mass as copper dissolves from it:

at the anode $Cu(s) \rightarrow Cu^{2+}(aq) + 2e^-$

So, overall, there is a transfer of copper from the anode to the cathode. The colour of the copper(II) sulfate solution does not change because the concentration of the Cu^{2+} ions remains the same.

The copper used in electrical wiring must be very pure (99.99%). Copper made by roasting its sulfide ore in air is about 99.5% pure (so it has an impurity level of 0.5%). This level of impurity cuts down its electrical conductivity significantly. Blocks of this impure metal are used as the anodes in a cell containing acidified copper(II) sulfate solution (Figure **4.30**). The cathodes are made of thin sheets of pure copper. During the refining process, pure copper is removed from the impure anodes and deposited on the cathodes. Any impurities fall to the bottom of the cell. This material, or **anode sludge**, contains precious metals such as gold, silver and platinum. These can be purified from this sludge.

Although unusual, the anode reactions in copper refining and electroplating are still oxidation reactions. Electrons are being lost from the metal atoms as they pass into solution. These electrons are then 'pumped' round the circuit by the power source.

Figure 4.30 A copper refinery worker removes electrodes with extracted copper from an electrolytic bath in a Chilean copper refinery.

Exam tip

Remember the key observations during electroplating. The object thickens as it becomes plated. The anode dissolves away. The electrolyte solution maintains the same concentration (thus, if it is coloured, the intensity of the colour stays the same).

Key ideas so far

- The product of electrolysis at the anode can depend on the concentration of the solution used.
- The reactions taking place at the electrodes during electrolysis are redox reactions. Oxidation takes place at the anode; reduction takes place at the cathode.
- Electrolysis can be used to purify (refine) copper to produce the very pure metal needed for electrical circuits.

Quick-check questions

1 **a** The apparatus below was used to plate a strip of metal with copper. One electrode was made of copper and the other was the metal strip to be plated.

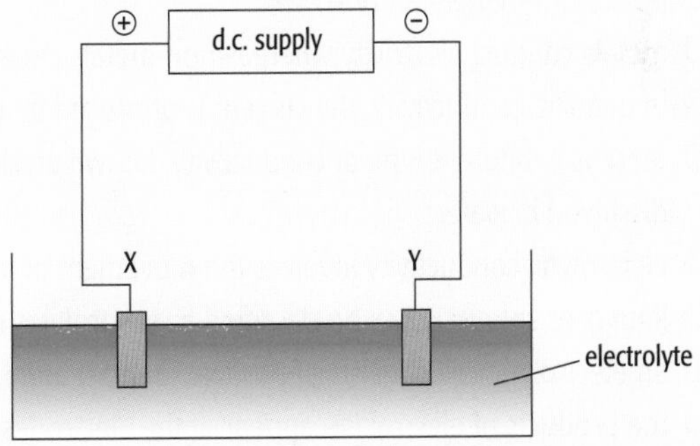

i Which electrode, X or Y, is the metal strip?
ii Is the metal strip an anode or a cathode?

b If graphite were used instead of the copper electrode in **a**, what change would you notice to the electrolyte during the experiment?

c In industry, some plastics are electroplated. Why must the plastic be coated with a thin film of graphite before plating?

2 An electrolysis cell is one method of physically separating the processes involved in a redox reaction.

At which electrode does **a** the oxidation process, and **b** the reduction process, take place?

c Why can we use these terms in connection with the electrode processes taking place?

Summary

You should know that:

- chemical reactions differ from physical changes such as melting or dissolving because new chemical substance(s) are produced
- there is no loss or gain in total mass during a chemical reaction (the law of conservation of mass)
- reactions can be represented by word equations and balanced chemical equations
- balancing an equation involves making sure that there are the same numbers of each type of atom involved on the reactants side and products side of the equation
- reactions involve an energy change – with most reactions being exothermic and only a few being endothermic
- there is a variety of different types of chemical reaction
- synthesis and decomposition represent opposite processes
- neutralisation reactions involve the reaction of an acid with a base to produce a salt and water only
- insoluble salts can be produced by precipitation reactions
- reactive elements can displace other, less reactive, elements from their compounds in displacement reactions
- combustion reactions involve reaction with oxygen and include the biologically important reaction known as respiration, while combustion reactions that produce a flame are known as burning
- redox reactions involve the loss or gain of oxygen by substances – oxidation being the gain of oxygen and reduction being the loss of oxygen
- some substances are reducing agents (for example hydrogen, carbon), while others are oxidising agents (for example oxygen, potassium manganate(VII))
- metals conduct electricity whereas non-metals (except graphite) do not
- in metallic conductivity, the current is produced by electrons moving through the solid or liquid metal
- there is a different type of conductivity, known as electrolytic conductivity, in which ionic compounds conduct when molten or dissolved in water
- electrolytic conductivity involves the movement of ions and results in a chemical change (electrolysis)
- liquids or solutions can be classified as electrolytes or non-electrolytes
- an electrolytic cell consists of positive (anode) and negative (cathode) electrodes and an electrolyte
- the products of electrolysis appear at the electrodes, where ions are discharged
- there are various rules that help us to predict the products of electrolysis, but generally metals or hydrogen are always produced at the negative electrode (the cathode)
- electroplating can be used to produce a protective and/or decorative layer of one metal on another
- equations can be made more informative by including state symbols
- for reactions involving ions (for example neutralisation and precipitation reactions), an equation can be simplified to include only those ions taking part in the reaction – the 'spectator ions' are omitted from the equation
- the definitions of oxidation and reduction can be extended to include reactions involving the transfer of electrons – oxidation is the loss of electrons and reduction is the gain of electrons
- the reactions taking place at the electrodes during electrolysis can be regarded as oxidation or reduction reactions because the ions either lose or gain electrons when they are discharged
- electrolysis is industrially important for the extraction of very reactive metals (for example aluminium) and the production of sodium hydroxide and chlorine
- oxidation takes place at the positive electrode (the anode), and reduction at the negative electrode (the cathode)
- the products of electrolysis can depend on the concentration of ions in the solution
- the method of electroplating can be adapted to provide a method of purifying (refining) copper – in these processes the electrodes are not inert and the anode actually dissolves.

Exam-style questions

1 A student electrolysed molten zinc chloride. State the name of the product formed at

a the anode [1]

b the cathode. [1]

2 The electroplating of iron with chromium involves four stages:

1. The iron object is cleaned with sulfuric acid, then washed with water.
2. The iron is plated with copper.
3. It is then plated with nickel to prevent corrosion.
4. It is then plated with chromium.

a The equation for stage 1 is

$Fe + H_2SO_4 \rightarrow FeSO_4 + H_2$

i Write a word equation for this reaction. [2]

ii Describe a test for the gas given off in this reaction. [2]

b The diagram shows how iron is electroplated with copper.

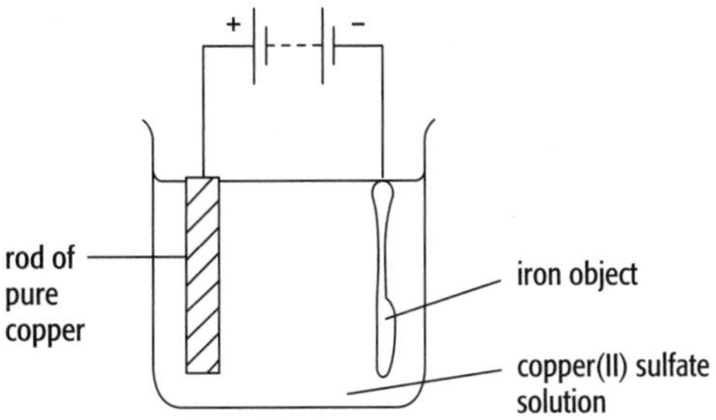

i Choose a word from the list below which describes the iron object.

anion **anode** **cathode** **cation** [1]

ii What is the purpose of the copper(II) sulfate solution? [1]

iii Describe what happens during the electroplating, to the iron object, and to the rod of pure copper respectively. [2]

c Suggest why chromium is used to electroplate articles. [1]

CIE IGCSE, June 2005, paper 2, q.6 part

3 Magnesium is a very reactive metal which will react vigorously with oxygen, and even with nitrogen and carbon dioxide.

a Magnesium burns strongly in oxygen.

i Write a word equation for the reaction. [2]

ii Copy out and balance the following equation for the reaction.

$\ldots Mg + O_2 \rightarrow \ldots MgO$ [2]

iii Describe what you see when the magnesium burns. [2]

b When burning magnesium is placed in a gas jar of carbon dioxide, it continues to burn and a black solid is produced.

i How could you show that the gas jar contains carbon dioxide? [2]

ii Suggest what the black solid is. [1]

iii Suggest the name of the other product of the reaction. [1]

c Copy out and complete the following balanced symbol equations for these reactions:

i $\ldots Mg + CO_2 \rightarrow \ldots\ldots\ldots + \ldots\ldots\ldots$ [3]

ii $\ldots Mg + N_2 \xrightarrow{+3H_2O} \ldots\ldots \quad \ldots\ldots + \ldots NH_3$ [2]

d The reaction between magnesium and carbon dioxide involves magnesium removing oxygen from carbon dioxide. What is the name given to this process? [1]

S

4 A student set up an experiment like this to look at the movement of ions. The filter paper is moist and a small crystal of the solid being studied is placed in the centre as shown.

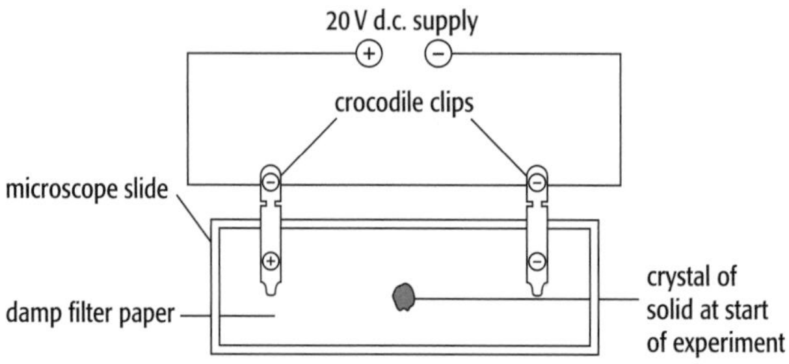

The results are shown in the table.

Substance	**Colour of crystals**	**Changes seen on the filter paper**
potassium chromate, K_2CrO_4	yellow	yellow colour moves towards positive
potassium sulfate, K_2SO_4	white	no colours seen
copper sulfate, $CuSO_4$	blue	blue colour moves towards negative

a Select which of these ions is yellow. [1]

chromate **copper** **potassium** **sulfate**

b Explain why the yellow colour moves towards the positive terminal in the potassium chromate experiment. [2]

c Suggest and explain what will happen if this experiment is repeated with copper chromate. [2]

5 The first three elements in Period 6 of the Periodic Table of the elements are caesium, barium and lanthanum.

a All three metals can be obtained by the electrolysis of a molten halide. The electrolysis of the aqueous halides does not produce the metal.

i Copy and complete the equation for the reduction of lanthanum ions at the negative electrode (cathode).

La^{3+} + …………… → …………… [3]

ii Name the **three** products formed by the electrolysis of aqueous caesium bromide. [4]

b All three metals react with cold water. Copy and complete the word equation for these reactions.

metal + water → …………… [2]

CIE IGCSE, June 2003, paper 3, q.5 part

5 Acids, bases and salts

This chapter covers the following ideas:

- common acids – where and how they occur
- organic acids and mineral acids
- the pH scale
- indicators – the colour changes of litmus and Universal Indicator
- the ions present in acid and alkali solutions
- the differences between acids and alkalis
- the acid–base properties of non-metal oxides and metal oxides
- (S) neutral and amphoteric oxides
- some common examples of the importance of acids and pH, including soil pH and plant growth
- alkalis and bases
- uses of common alkalis, bases and 'antacids', including indigestion treatments, the treatment of acid soils and waste water treatment
- characteristic reactions of acids
  - with metals
  - with alkalis and bases, called neutralisation
  - with metal carbonates
- acids and alkalis in the analysis of salts
- the importance of 'common salt' (sodium chloride)
- the solubility of salts in water
- the preparation of soluble salts by various methods, including titration
- (S) choosing a method of salt preparation
- (S) the preparation of insoluble salts by precipitation
- (S) strong acids and strong alkalis are completely ionised in water
- (S) weak acids and weak alkalis are partially dissociated into ions in water
- (S) the ionic reactions in acid–base neutralisation
- (S) acids as proton donors and bases as proton acceptors
- (S) the 'basicity' of acids

5.1 What is an acid?

The major acids

Originally the word **acid** was applied to substances with a 'sour' taste. Vinegar, lemon juice, grapefruit juice and spoilt milk are all sour tasting because of the presence of acids (Figure 5.1). These acids are present in animal and plant material and are known as **organic acids** (Table 5.1).

Carbonic acid from carbon dioxide dissolved in water is present in Coca Cola®, Pepsi® and other fizzy drinks. The acids present in these circumstances are weak and dilute. But taste is not a test that should be tried – some acids would be dangerous, even deadly, to taste!

A number of acids are also **corrosive**. They can eat their way through clothing, are dangerous on the skin,

Figure 5.1 Citrus fruits have a sour or sharp taste because they contain acids.

Type	Name	Formula	Strong or weak?	Where found or used
Organic acids	ethanoic acid	CH_3COOH	weak	in vinegar
	methanoic acid	$HCOOH$	weak	in ant and nettle stings; used in kettle descaler
	lactic acid	$CH_3CCH(OH)$ | $COOH$	weak	in sour milk
	citric acid	$C_6H_8O_7$	weak	in lemons, oranges and other citrus fruits
Mineral acids	carbonic acid	H_2CO_3	weak	in fizzy soft drinks
	hydrochloric acid	HCl	strong	used in cleaning metal surfaces; found as the dilute acid in the stomach
	nitric acid	HNO_3	strong	used in making fertilisers and explosives
	sulfuric acid	H_2SO_4	strong	in car batteries; used in making fertilisers, paints and detergents
	phosphoric acid	H_3PO_4	strong	in anti-rust paint; used in making fertilisers

Table 5.1 Some common acids.

and some are able to attack stonework and metals. These powerful acids are often called **mineral acids** (Table **5.1**). Table **5.1** also gives us some idea of how commonly acids occur.

The easiest way to detect whether a solution is acidic or not is to use an **indicator**. Indicators are substances that change colour if they are put into an acid or alkaline solution. The commonest indicator is **litmus**.

What is litmus?

Certain coloured substances (many extracted from plants) have been found to change colour if added to an acid solution. This colour change is reversed if the acid is 'cancelled out' or neutralised. Substances that do this are known as **indicators**. Coloured extracts can be made from red cabbage or blackberries, but probably the most used indicator is litmus. This is extracted from lichens.

Litmus is purple in neutral solution. When added to an acidic solution, it turns **red**. This colour change of litmus needs a chemical reaction. The molecules of the indicator are actually changed in the presence of the acid. Substances with the opposite chemical effect to acids are needed to reverse the change, and these are called **alkalis**. They turn litmus solution **blue**.

You can also use litmus **paper**. This is paper that has been soaked in litmus solution. It comes in blue and red forms. The blue form of litmus paper changes colour to red when dipped into acid solutions. Red litmus paper turns blue in alkali solutions. Note that litmus just gives a single colour change.

Exam tip

It may seem simple to remember the colour change that litmus shows in acid and alkali, but it is important. This simple visual memory aid may help you to remember:

r
e
acid/base
l
u
e

The presence of water is very important in the action of acids and alkalis. One practical consequence of this is that when we use litmus paper to test gases it **must always be damp**. The gas needs to dissolve in the moisture to bring about the colour change. This is important in your practical work.

Litmus is not the only single indicator that chemists find useful. Others that are frequently used are phenolphthalein and methyl orange. They give different colour changes from litmus (Table **5.2**, overleaf). These changes are sometimes easier to 'see' than that of litmus.

Indicator	Colour in acid	Neutral colour	Colour in alkali
litmus	red	purple	blue
phenolphthalein	colourless	colourless	pink
methyl orange	red	orange	yellow

Table 5.2 Some common indicator colour changes.

Universal Indicator

Another commonly used indicator, **Universal Indicator** (or full-range indicator), is a **mixture** of indicator dyes. The idea of a Universal Indicator mixture is to imitate the colours of the rainbow when measuring acidity. Such an indicator is useful because it gives a range of colours (a 'spectrum') depending on the strength of the acid or alkali added (Figure 5.2). When you use Universal Indicator, you see that solutions of different acids produce different colours. Indeed, solutions of the same acid with different concentrations will also give different colours.

The more acidic solutions (for example, battery acid) turn Universal Indicator bright red. A less acidic solution (for example, vinegar) will only turn it orange-yellow. There are also colour differences produced with different alkali solutions. The most alkaline solutions give a violet colour.

The pH scale

The most useful measure of the strength of an acid solution was worked out by the Danish biochemist Søren Sørensen. He worked in the laboratories of the Carlsberg breweries and was interested in checking the acidity of beer. The scale he introduced was the **pH scale**. The scale runs from 1 to 14, and the following general rules apply.

Rules for the pH scale:

- acids have a pH less than 7
- the more acidic a solution, the lower the pH
- neutral substances, such as pure water, have a pH of 7
- alkalis have a pH greater than 7.

The pH of a solution can be measured in several ways. Universal Indicator papers that are sensitive over the full range of values can be used. Alternatively, if the approximate pH value is known, then we can use a more accurate test paper that is sensitive over a narrow range. The most accurate method is to use a pH meter (Figure 5.3), which uses an electrode to measure pH electrically. The pH values of some common solutions are shown in Table 5.3.

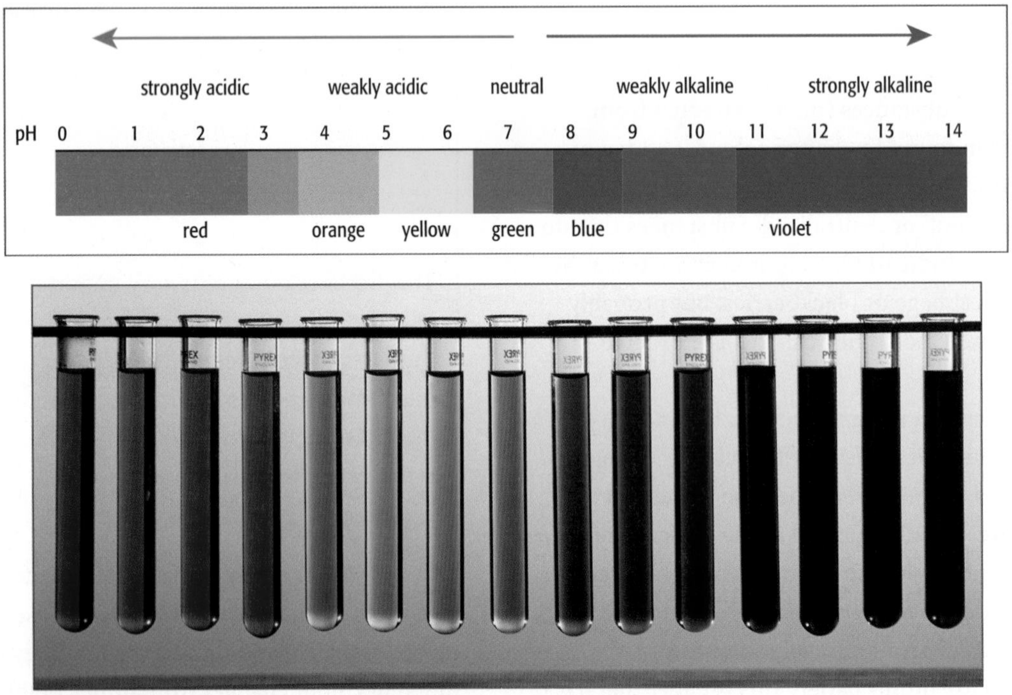

Figure 5.2 How the colour of Universal Indicator changes in solutions of different pH values.

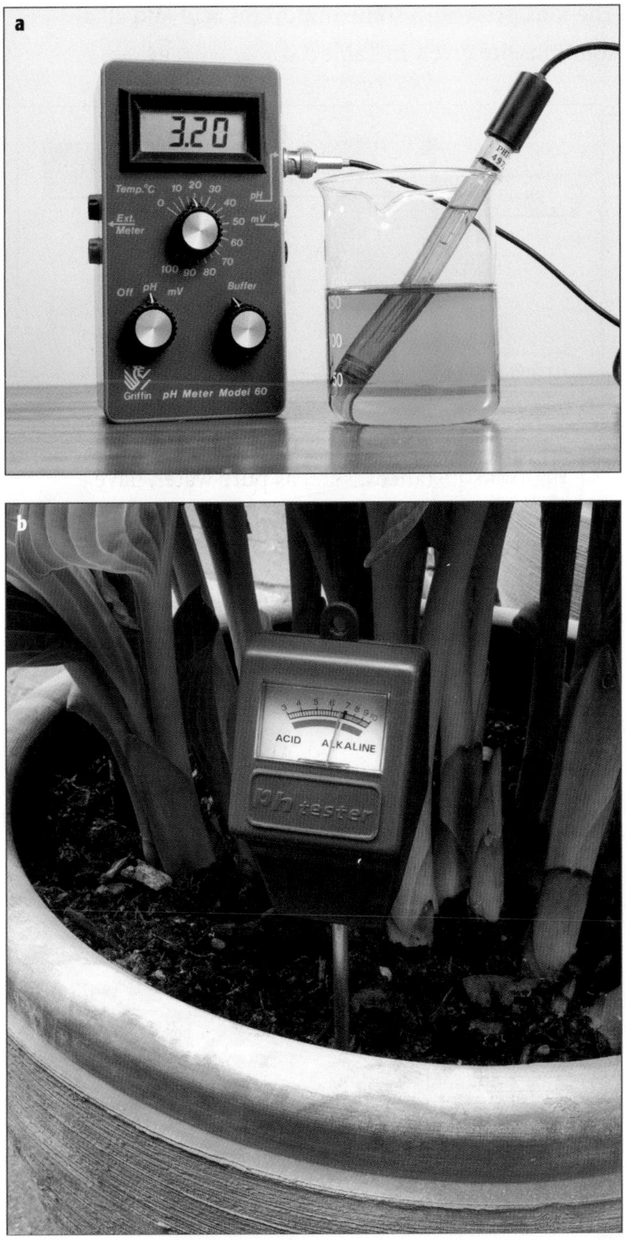

Figure 5.3 pH meters in use **a** in the laboratory and **b** for testing soil.

	Substance	pH
strongly acidic	hydrochloric acid (HCl)	0.0
↑	gastric juices	1.0
	lemon juice	2.5
	vinegar	3.0
	wine	3.5
	tomato juice	4.1
	black coffee	5.0
	acid rain	5.6
	urine	6.0
weakly acidic	rain water	6.5
	milk	6.5
NEUTRAL	pure water, sugar solution	7.0
weakly alkaline	blood	7.4
	baking soda solution	8.5
	toothpaste	9.0
	borax solution	9.2
	Milk of Magnesia	10.5
↓	limewater	11.0
strongly alkaline	household ammonia	12.0
	sodium hydroxide (NaOH)	14.0

Table 5.3 The pH values of some common solutions.

Exam tip

It's very important to remember that the 'reference point' when measuring pH is neutrality, pH 7 – the mid-point of the scale.

As we move **down** from 7, the solution is getting **more** acidic.

Moving **up** from pH 7, the solution is getting **more** alkaline.

Key ideas so far

- The original idea of an acid was of a sour-tasting substance found in natural situations such as citrus fruits, wine and vinegar, and sour milk. These are organic acids.
- More harmful acids are the mineral acids such as sulfuric and nitric acids. These acids are corrosive.
- Litmus is a natural indicator that changes colour depending on whether it is placed in an acid or alkaline solution.
- Universal Indicator is a mixture of indicator dyes that gives a spectrum of colours depending on how acidic or alkaline a solution is. The colours copy those of the colours of the rainbow.
- The pH scale gives a numerical value to how acidic or alkaline a solution is. The scale runs from 0 to 14, with water being neutral at pH 7.0.

Quick-check questions

1. What do you understand by the word **corrosive**?
2. Which acid is present in orange or lemon juice?
3. Is a solution acidic, alkaline or neutral if its pH is **a** 11 **b** 7 **c** 8 **d** 3?
4. Methyl orange is an **indicator**. What does this mean?
5. Which solution is more acidic: one with a pH of 4, or one with a pH of 1?
6. What colour is Universal Indicator in a sugar solution?
7. Which acid is present in vinegar?

5.2 Acid and alkali solutions

The importance of hydrogen ions

If we look again at the chemical formulae of some of the best known acids (Table **5.1**, page **137**), we see that one element is common to them all. They all contain **hydrogen**. If solutions of these acids are checked to see if they conduct electricity, we find that they all do. Also, they conduct electricity much better than distilled water does. This shows that the solutions contain **ions**. Water itself contains very few ions. In pure water, the concentrations of hydrogen ions (H^+) and hydroxide ions (OH^-) are equal. All acids dissolve in water to produce hydrogen ions (H^+ ions). Therefore, all acid solutions contain more H^+ ions than OH^- ions. The pH scale is designed around the fact that acid solutions have this excess of hydrogen ions. The term pH is taken from the German '**p**otenz **H**(ydrogen)', meaning the power of the hydrogen-ion concentration of a solution.

Alkali solutions also conduct electricity better than distilled water. All alkalis dissolve in water to produce hydroxide ions (OH^- ions). Therefore, all alkali solutions contain an excess of OH^- ions. An indicator, like litmus, is affected by the presence of H^+ or OH^- ions (Figure **5.4**).

- The hydrogen ions (H^+) in acid solutions make litmus go **red**.
- The hydroxide ions (OH^-) in alkali solutions make litmus go **blue**.

The ions present in some important acid and alkali solutions are given in Table **5.4**.

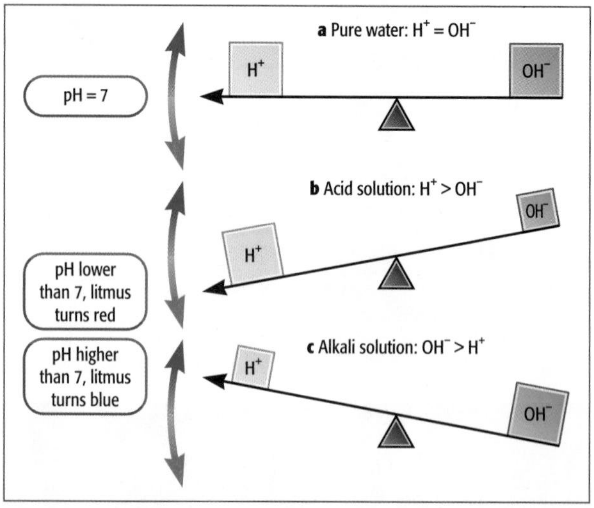

Figure 5.4 pH and the balance of hydrogen ions and hydroxide ions in solution.

	Name	Ions present
Acids	hydrochloric acid	H^+**(aq)** and Cl^-(aq)
	nitric acid	H^+**(aq)** and NO_3^-(aq)
	sulfuric acid	H^+**(aq)**, HSO_4^-(aq) and SO_4^{2-}(aq)
Alkalis	sodium hydroxide	Na^+(aq) and OH^-**(aq)**
	potassium hydroxide	K^+(aq) and OH^-**(aq)**
	calcium hydroxide	Ca^{2+}(aq) and OH^-**(aq)**
	ammonia solution	NH_4^+(aq) and OH^-**(aq)**

Table 5.4 The ions present in solutions of some acids and alkalis.

The importance of water

E

When is an acid not an acid, but simply an 'acid-in-waiting'? Hydrochloric acid is a good example to illustrate this problem. The gas hydrogen chloride is made up of covalently bonded molecules. If the gas is dissolved in an organic solvent, such as methylbenzene, it does not show any of the properties of an acid. For example, it does not conduct electricity or turn a piece of blue litmus paper red. However, when the gas is dissolved in water, a strongly acidic solution **is** produced. The **acidic oxides** of sulfur, phosphorus and carbon listed in Table **5.5** (page **142**) are similar. They are covalent molecules when pure, but show acidic properties when dissolved in water.

An **acid** is a substance that dissolves in water to produce hydrogen ions (H^+). This solution:

- contains an excess of H^+ ions
- turns litmus red
- has a pH lower than 7.

An **alkali** is a substance that dissolves in water to produce hydroxide ions (OH^-). This solution:

- contains an excess of OH^- ions
- turns litmus blue
- has a pH higher than 7.

Thus, in our most useful definition of an acid, the characteristic properties of an acid are shown when dissolved in water. Alkalis are also normally used in aqueous solution. Both acids and alkalis can be used in dilute or concentrated solutions. If a large volume of water is added to a small amount of acid or alkali, then the solution is **dilute**; using less water gives a more **concentrated** solution.

Key ideas so far

- All acids contain the element hydrogen.
- All acid and alkali solutions conduct electricity.
- Acid solutions contain an excess of H^+ ions.
- Alkali solutions contain an excess of OH^- ions.
- A solution of an acid or an alkali can be dilute or concentrated depending on how much water is present.

Quick-check questions

1 Which element do all acids contain?

2 Which ion is in excess in an alkali solution?

3 Which ions are present in

a nitric acid solution

b calcium hydroxide solution

c ammonia solution?

4 What is the formula for

a sulfuric acid

b hydrochloric acid?

5 What statement can we make about the concentrations of hydrogen ions and hydroxide ions in water?

5.3 Metal oxides and non-metal oxides

Acidic and basic oxides

Venus, the Earth's nearest neighbour, is identical in size and density to the Earth. But Venus has yielded its secrets reluctantly, because it is veiled in clouds and has an atmosphere that destroys space probes. Magellan, the latest space probe to Venus, has looked from a distance. If it went into the atmosphere, it would meet with thick clouds of sulfuric acid and temperatures similar to those in a self-cleaning oven – acid rain with a vengeance! The probe would not last long!

The sulfuric acid clouds of Venus are the product of great volcanic activity (Figure 5.5). This has thrown out huge amounts of water vapour and the oxides of sulfur into the planet's atmosphere. Similar acidic clouds can be made in a gas jar by lowering burning sulfur into oxygen (Figure 5.6, overleaf):

$$S(s) + O_2(g) \rightarrow SO_2(g)$$

Figure 5.5 Image of the European Space Agency probe orbiting above the clouds of the Venus atmosphere. The Venus Express spacecraft was launched to study the thick atmosphere responsible for the intense greenhouse effect on the planet.

Other burning non-metals (carbon, for example) react in the same way to produce acidic gases:

$$C(s) + O_2(g) \rightarrow CO_2(g)$$

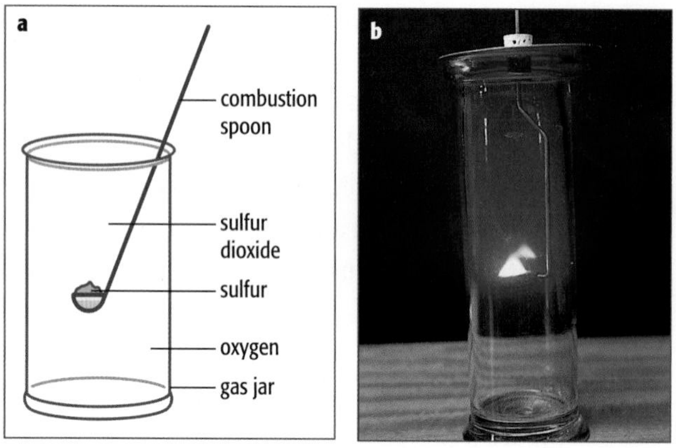

Figure 5.6 Burning sulfur in a gas jar of oxygen.

When water is added to the gas jars, it dissolves the gases and gives solutions that **turn blue litmus paper red**.

Metals burning in oxygen produce solid products. Some of these dissolve in water to give solutions that **turn red litmus paper blue**. You might be able to work out a pattern in the reactions of some elements with oxygen, as shown in Table 5.5.

Turning litmus paper red shows that some of these solutions contain acids. These solutions are the product of burning non-metals to produce **acidic oxides**. Burning metals produces oxides that, if they dissolve, give solutions that turn litmus paper blue. The metal oxides produced in these reactions react with acids to neutralise them – they are said to be **basic oxides**.

The characteristics of oxides:

- Non-metals generally form **acidic oxides** that dissolve in water to form **acidic** solutions.
- Metals form oxides that are solids. If they dissolve in water, these oxides give **alkaline** solutions. These metal oxides neutralise acids and are **basic oxides**.

Neutral and amphoteric oxides

Water can be thought of as hydrogen oxide. It has a pH of 7 and is therefore a **neutral oxide**. It is an exception to the broad 'rule' that the oxides of non-metals are acidic oxides. Neutral oxides do not react with either acids or alkalis. There are a few other exceptions to this 'rule' (see Figure 5.7). The most important is carbon monoxide (CO), noted for being poisonous. The 'rule' that most non-metal oxides are acidic remains useful and important, however.

Of more importance is the unusual behaviour of some metal oxides. These metal oxides react and neutralize acids, which would be expected. However, they also neutralise alkalis, which is unusual.

Element	How it reacts	Product	Effect of adding water and testing with litmus
Non-metals			
sulfur	burns with bright blue flame	colourless gas (sulfur dioxide, SO_2)	dissolves, turns litmus **red**
phosphorus	burns with yellow flame	white solid (phosphorus(V) oxide, P_2O_5)	dissolves, turns litmus **red**
carbon	glows red	colourless gas (carbon dioxide, CO_2)	dissolves slightly, slowly turns litmus **red**
Metals			
sodium	burns with yellow flame	white solid (sodium oxide, Na_2O)	dissolves, turns litmus **blue**
magnesium	burns with bright white flame	white solid (magnesium oxide, MgO)	dissolves slightly, turns litmus **blue**
calcium	burns with red flame	white solid (calcium oxide, CaO)	dissolves, turns litmus **blue**
iron	burns with yellow sparks	blue-black solid (iron oxide, FeO)	insoluble
copper	does not burn, turns black	black solid (copper oxide, CuO)	insoluble

Table 5.5 The reactions of certain elements with oxygen.

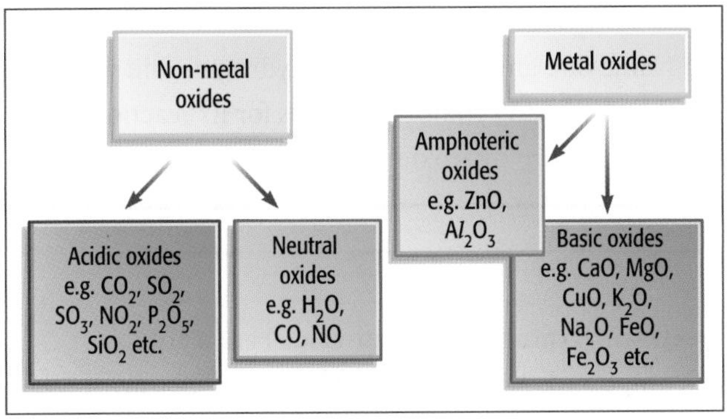

Figure 5.7 The classification of non-metal and metal oxides.

An **amphoteric** metal oxide or hydroxide is one that reacts with both an acid and an alkali to give a salt and water.

The most important examples of metals that have amphoteric compounds are zinc and aluminium. The fact that zinc hydroxide and aluminium hydroxide are amphoteric helps in the identification of salts of these metals using sodium hydroxide. If sodium hydroxide solution is added to a solution of a salt of either of these metals, a white precipitate of the metal hydroxide is formed. For example:

$$ZnCl_2(aq) + 2NaOH(aq) \rightarrow Zn(OH)_2(s) + 2NaCl(aq)$$

$$Zn^{2+}(aq) + 2OH^-(aq) \rightarrow Zn(OH)_2(s)$$

However, this precipitate will re-dissolve if excess sodium hydroxide is added, because zinc hydroxide is amphoteric:

zinc hydroxide + sodium hydroxide
→ sodium zincate + water

$$Zn(OH)_2(s) + 2NaOH(aq) \rightarrow Na_2ZnO_2(aq) + 2H_2O(l)$$

Aluminium salts will give a similar set of reactions. This test distinguishes zinc and aluminium salts from others, but not from each other (see Sections **5.7** and **12.1**).

We can tell zinc and aluminium salts apart by repeating the test using ammonia solution (a weak alkali). The precipitate of zinc hydroxide re-dissolves in ammonia solution, but the aluminium hydroxide does not.

Exam tip

In these last reactions, the zinc hydroxide and aluminium hydroxide precipitates re-dissolve in excess sodium hydroxide because they are **amphoteric.**

They are reacting as acids with the sodium hydroxide and producing a salt and water as the products.

acid + alkali → salt + water

zinc hydroxide + sodium hydroxide
→ **sodium zincate** + water
Na_2ZnO_2

aluminium hydroxide + sodium hydroxide
→ **sodium aluminate** + water
$NaAlO_2$

Do notice how these rather unusual salts are named.

Key ideas so far

- When non-metals burn in air or oxygen they generally produce acidic oxides.
- When metals burn in oxygen they produce solids. If these solid oxides dissolve in water they generally give alkaline solutions.
- Some non-metal oxides are neutral oxides. Neutral oxides do not react with either acids or alkalis.
- Some metal oxides are amphoteric. Amphoteric metal oxides react with both acids and alkalis to produce a salt and water.

? Quick-check questions

1 What colour is the flame when sulfur burns?
2 What colour flame is produced when magnesium burns?
3 Write the word equation for the reaction when sulfur burns in oxygen.
4 What is the chemical equation for the reaction in question **3**?

5 Write the word equation for magnesium burning in air.

6 Which oxide of carbon is neutral?

7 Name **one** amphoteric metal hydroxide and write the word and symbol equations for its reaction with sodium hydroxide solution.

5.4 Acid reactions in everyday life

Indigestion, headaches and neutralisation

The dilute hydrochloric acid in our stomach is there to help digest our food. However, excess acid causes indigestion, which can be painful and eventually give rise to ulcers. To ease this, we can take an antacid treatment. **Antacids** (or 'anti-acids') are a group of compounds with no toxic effects on the body. They are used to neutralise the effects of acid indigestion. Some of these antacids, such as 'Milk of Magnesia', contain insoluble material to counteract the acid. 'Milk of Magnesia' contains insoluble magnesium hydroxide.

Other effervescent or 'fizzy' antacids, such as Alka-Seltzer®, contain soluble material, including sodium hydrogencarbonate. These tablets also contain some citric acid – a solid acid. On adding water, the acid and some of the sodium hydrogencarbonate react, producing carbon dioxide gas – the 'fizz' in the glass (see Figure **5.8**). This helps to spread and dissolve the other less soluble material. When the mixture is drunk, more sodium hydrogencarbonate neutralises the excess hydrochloric acid in the stomach, thus easing the indigestion.

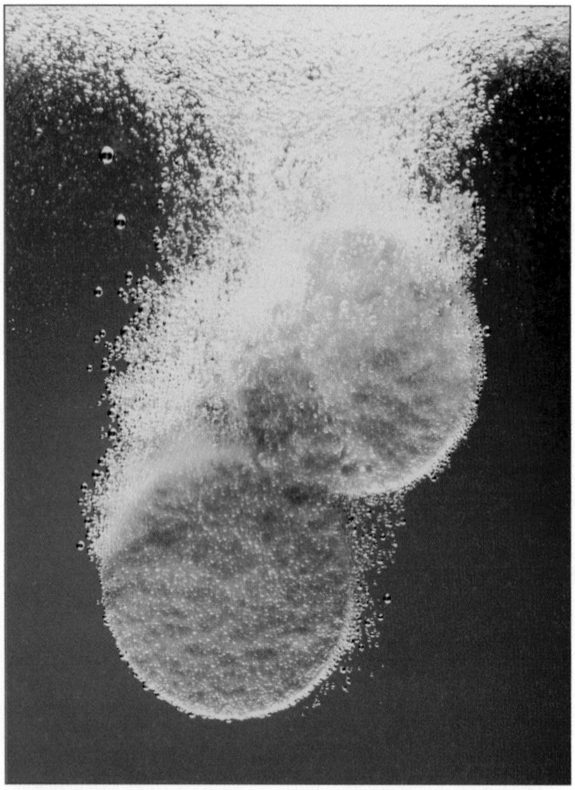

Figure 5.8 Soluble antacid tablets dissolving and giving off carbon dioxide.

Some antacid tablets also contain a painkiller to relieve headaches. Vitamin C (ascorbic acid – another soluble acid) can also be added to the tablet. Note the importance of adding water to start the action of the acid. The tablets do not react in the packet!

'Soluble aspirin' tablets dissolve in a similar way to Alka-Seltzer tablets.

Descaling kettles

Limescale collects inside kettles and water heaters in hard-water areas. Hard-water areas tend to be geographically located in limestone areas. Hard water contains more dissolved calcium ions than normal water. Calcium carbonate forms when the water is boiled (Figure **5.9**). This **limescale** can be removed by treatment with an acid that is strong enough to react with calcium carbonate, but not strong enough to damage the metal. Vinegar can be used to descale kettles. Commercial 'descalers' use other acid solutions such as methanoic acid.

Toothpaste and tooth decay

Acid forms in the mouth after sugary food has been eaten. The pH of a sugar solution is about 7. However, bacteria in your mouth break down the

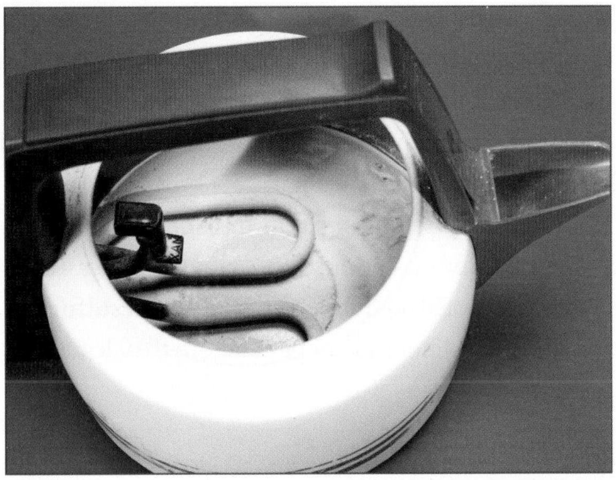

Figure 5.9 A build-up of white 'limescale' in a kettle.

sugar to form acids, for example lactic acid. These acids lower the pH. Tooth decay begins when the pH falls below 5.8. This happens about 2–3 minutes after eating sweet things. The tooth enamel can be attacked by the acid.

To help take away this acidity, many types of toothpaste contain substances to neutralise the acid (Figure **5.10**). Their pH is alkaline (higher than 7) (see Table **5.3** on page **139**). The pH of saliva is slightly alkaline (pH 7.4), so it can also help to counteract the acid, particularly after a meal. After eating a sweet, for example, it takes about 15 minutes for saliva to raise the pH above 5.8, and stop further decay.

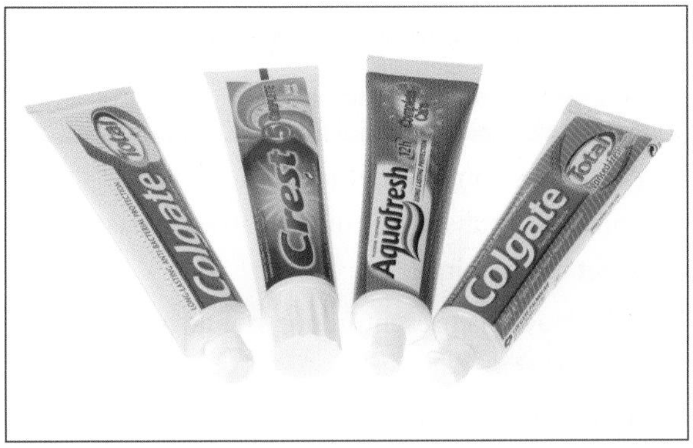

Figure 5.10 Toothpaste samples from the local supermarket.

Nature's defences - stings galore!

When an ant or a bee stings you, it injects an acid under your skin (Figure **5.11a**). In this case the acid is methanoic acid. You can neutralise the sting by rubbing on baking soda (sodium hydrogencarbonate) or calamine lotion (which contains zinc carbonate). Nettles also sting you with methanoic acid (Figure **5.11b**). This can be neutralised in the same way, or by rubbing with dock leaves. In contrast, a wasp sting is alkaline and can be neutralised using lemon juice.

Figure 5.11 **a** A scanning electron microscope picture of an ant sting. **b** The stinging hairs of a nettle.

Soil pH and plant growth

Plant growth is affected by the acidity or alkalinity of the soil. Soils with high peat content, or with minerals such as iron compounds, or with rotting vegetation and lack of oxygen, tend to be acidic. Their soil pH can reach as low as pH 4. Soils in limestone or chalky areas are alkaline – up to pH 8.3. The soil pH is also affected by the use of fertilisers and the acidity of rainfall. Different plants prefer different pH conditions (Table **5.6**). Farmers and gardeners can test the soil pH to see whether it suits the needs of particular plants.

If the soil is too **acidic**, it is usually treated by 'liming'. 'Lime' here is a loose term meaning either calcium oxide, calcium hydroxide, or powdered chalk or limestone (calcium carbonate). These compounds all have the effect of neutralising the acidity of the soil. If the soil is too **alkaline**, it helps to dig in some peat or decaying organic matter (compost or manure).

Vegetables	Preferred pH range
potatoes	4.5–6.0
chicory, parsley	5.0–6.5
carrot, sweet potato	5.5–6.5
cauliflower, garlic, tomato	5.5–7.5
broad bean, onion, cabbage and many others	6.0–7.5

Table 5.6 Preferred soil pH conditions for different vegetables.

E

Some flowering plants carry their own 'built-in' pH indicator. The flowers of a hydrangea bush are blue when grown on acid soil and pink when the soil pH is alkaline (Figure **5.12**).

Figure 5.12 The colour of the flowers of some types of hydrangea depend on soil pH. Here the flowers are showing signs of the colour change between pink and blue.

Effluent and waste water treatment

Liquid waste from factories is often acidic. If such waste gets into a river, the acid will kill fish and other river life. Slaked lime is often added to the waste to neutralise it. Slaked lime is similarly used to treat streams, rivers and lakes affected by acid rain (Figure **5.13**).

To reduce emissions of sulfur dioxide, many modern factories and power stations now spray acidic waste gases with jets of slaked lime in a **flue gas-desulfuriser** (or 'scrubber') to neutralise them before they leave the chimneys.

Figure 5.13 Controlled addition of lime to a stream in Sweden to neutralise the effects of acidity.

Key ideas so far

- Acids, bases and metal carbonates play a significant part in our everyday lives, playing a part in everything from indigestion and insect bites, to plant growth and waste treatment.

Quick-check questions

1. Ant stings contain methanoic acid. What household substance could be used to ease the effect of the sting?
2. Which acid is present in our stomachs, and why is it there?
3. Indigestion tablets contain a base or antacid. Name **two** compounds that we use in these tablets.

5.5 Alkalis and bases

What types of substance are alkalis and bases?

In Section **5.4** we saw that the effects of acids could be neutralised by alkalis. Alkalis are substances that dissolve in water to give solutions with a pH greater than 7 and turn litmus blue. The solutions contain an excess of hydroxide, OH^-, ions.

However, among the antacids we use to relieve indigestion is **insoluble** magnesium hydroxide, which also neutralises acids. As we investigate further, it is found that **all** metal oxides and hydroxides will neutralise acids, whether they dissolve in water or not. Therefore the soluble alkalis are just a small part of a group of substances – the oxides and hydroxides of metals – that neutralise acids. These substances are known as bases. These bases all react in the same way with acids.

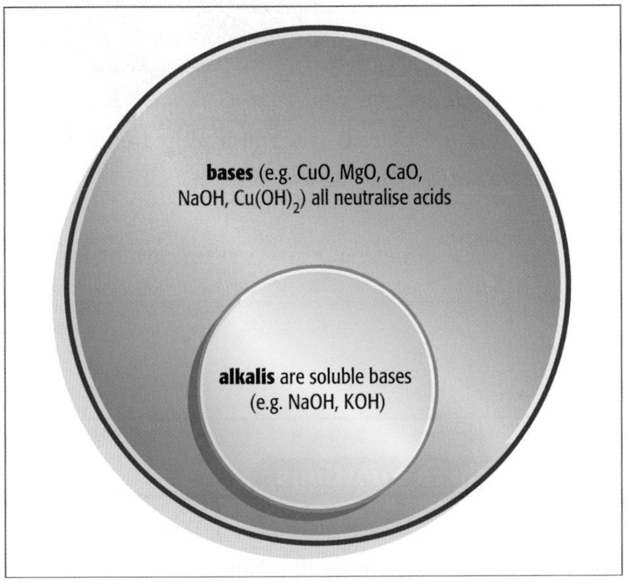

Figure 5.14 This Venn diagram shows the relationship between bases and alkalis. All alkalis are bases, but not all bases are alkalis.

The relationship of alkalis to bases can be summed up in a mathematical device known as a Venn diagram (Figure **5.14**). In more general terms it is something like the difference between our immediate family and our extended family. The bases are the extended family of compounds. The alkalis are a particular small group of that extended family.

A base will neutralise an acid, and in the process a **salt** is formed. This type of reaction is known as a **neutralisation reaction**. It can be summed up in a general equation:

> acid + base → salt + water

Therefore a base can be defined in the following way.

> A **base** is a substance that reacts with an acid to form a salt and water only.

Most bases are insoluble in water. This makes the few bases that **do** dissolve in water more significant. They are given a special name – **alkalis.**

> An **alkali** is a base that is soluble in water. They are usually used in the laboratory as aqueous solutions.

The common alkalis are:

- sodium hydroxide solution
- potassium hydroxide solution
- calcium hydroxide solution (often known as limewater)
- ammonia solution (also known as ammonium hydroxide).

These solutions contain OH^- ions, turn litmus blue and have a pH higher than 7. The first two are stronger alkalis than the others.

Exam tip

These four solutions are the alkalis you will need to know for your course. They are by far and away the commonest, and likely to be the only ones you refer to.

It is worth making sure you learn their names and formulae! Just as you should do the same for the four commonest acids you'll need to know: hydrochloric acid, sulfuric acid, nitric acid and ethanoic acid.

Type	Name	Formula	Strong or weak?	Where found or used
Alkalis	sodium hydroxide (caustic soda)	$NaOH$	strong	in oven cleaners (degreasing agent); in making soap and paper; other industrial uses
	calcium hydroxide (limewater)	$Ca(OH)_2$	strong	to neutralise soil acidity; to neutralise acid gases produced by power stations
	ammonia solution (ammonium hydroxide)	$NH_3(aq)$ or NH_4OH	weak	in cleaning fluids in the home (degreasing agent); making fertilisers
Bases	calcium oxide	CaO	strong	neutralising soil acidity and industrial waste; making cement and concrete
	magnesium oxide	MgO	strong	in antacid indigestion tablets

Table 5.7 Some common alkalis and bases.

Properties and uses of alkalis and bases

Alkalis feel soapy to the skin. They convert the oils in your skin into soap. They are used as degreasing agents because they convert oil and grease into soluble soaps, which can be washed away easily. The common uses of some alkalis and bases are shown in Table 5.7.

The properties of bases, alkalis and antacids can be summarised as follows.

Bases:
- neutralise acids to give a salt and water only
- are the oxides and hydroxides of metals
- are mainly insoluble in water.

Alkalis are bases that dissolve in water, and
- feel soapy to the skin
- turn litmus blue
- give solutions with a pH greater than 7
- give solutions that contain OH^- ions.

Antacids are compounds that are used to neutralise acid indigestion and include:
- magnesium oxide and magnesium hydroxide
- sodium carbonate and sodium hydrogencarbonate
- calcium carbonate and magnesium carbonate.

Key ideas so far

- Bases are substances that will neutralise acids to give a salt and water as the only products.
- Metal oxides and hydroxides are bases.
- Most bases are insoluble in water.
- The few bases that do dissolve in water are often referred to as alkalis.
- The main alkalis are sodium hydroxide, potassium hydroxide, calcium hydroxide (limewater) and ammonia solution.
- Alkali solutions have a pH greater than 7 and contain an excess of hydroxide (OH^-) ions.
- Antacids are compounds that we use to neutralise the excess acid in our stomachs when suffering from indigestion.

? Quick-check questions

1 Give the names of **two** examples of insoluble bases, and **two** examples of alkalis.

2 Write word and balanced symbol equations for the reaction between:

a sodium hydroxide and hydrochloric acid

b potassium hydroxide and sulfuric acid

c copper oxide and nitric acid.

3 Name the **four** main alkalis.

4 Which of the four alkalis in question **3** is only a weak alkali?

5.6 Characteristic reactions of acids

The reactions of acids

All acids can take part in neutralisation reactions. But are there any other reactions that are characteristic of all acids? The answer is 'Yes'. There are three major chemical reactions in which all acids will take part. These reactions are best seen using dilute acid solutions. In these reactions, the acid reacts with:

- a reactive metal (for example magnesium or zinc – Figure 5.15)
- a base (or alkali) – a neutralisation reaction
- a metal carbonate (or metal hydrogencarbonate).

Figure 5.15 **a** Magnesium ribbon and **b** zinc granules, reacting with hydrochloric acid – giving off hydrogen.

One type of product is common to all these reactions. They all produce a metal compound called a **salt**. In all of them, the hydrogen present in the acid is replaced by a metal to give the salt. The acid from which the salt is made is often called the parent acid of the salt.

Normally we use the word 'salt' to mean 'common salt', which is sodium chloride. This is the salt we put on our food, the main salt found in seawater, and the salt used over centuries to preserve food. However, in chemistry, the word has a more general meaning.

A **salt** is a compound made from an acid when a metal takes the place of the hydrogen in the acid.

The reaction of acids with metals

Metals that are **quite** reactive (not the **very** reactive ones, see page **241**) can be used to displace the hydrogen from an acid safely. Hydrogen gas is given off. The salt made depends on the combination of metal and acid used:

metal + acid → salt + hydrogen

It is unsafe to try this reaction with **very** reactive metals such as sodium or calcium. The reaction is too violent. No reaction occurs with metals such as copper, which are less reactive than lead. Even with lead, it is difficult to see any reaction in a short time.

The salt made depends on the acid:

- hydrochloric acid always gives a chloride
- nitric acid always gives a nitrate
- sulfuric acid always gives a sulfate
- ethanoic acid always gives an ethanoate.

For example:

magnesium + nitric acid → magnesium nitrate + hydrogen

$$Mg(s) + 2HNO_3(aq) \rightarrow Mg(NO_3)_2(aq) + H_2(g)$$

zinc + hydrochloric acid → zinc chloride + hydrogen

$$Zn(s) + 2HCl(aq) \rightarrow ZnCl_2(aq) + H_2(g)$$

Exam tip

You may be asked a question where you have to suggest a metal that will react with an acid to give hydrogen. Do **not** give any of the very reactive metals, such as calcium, as an answer. You will not gain the mark as this reaction is unsafe!

The reaction of acids with bases and alkalis

This is the neutralisation reaction that we saw on page **147**:

acid + base → salt + water

The salt produced by this reaction will again depend on the combination of reactants used. To make a particular salt, you choose a suitable acid and base to give a solution of the salt you want. For example:

sodium hydroxide + hydrochloric acid
→ sodium chloride + water

$NaOH(aq) + HCl(aq) \rightarrow NaCl(aq) + H_2O(l)$

Other examples of salts made from different combinations of acid and base are shown in Table **5.8**.

Exam tip

It's useful to realise the origins of a salt as it helps you predict which salt you get from a particular combination of acid and base. The cubic crystals of sodium chloride come from the neutralisation of hydrochloric acid with sodium hydroxide solution.

For example:

SODIUM CHLORIDE

NaC*l*

the metal comes from the base or alkali

sodium hydroxide in this case

the non-metallic part comes from the acid

hydrochloric acid in this case

Base	Salt made with …		
	Hydrochloric acid (HCl)	Nitric acid (HNO_3)	Sulfuric acid (H_2SO_4)
sodium hydroxide (NaOH)	sodium chloride, NaCl	sodium nitrate, $NaNO_3$	sodium sulfate, Na_2SO_4
potassium hydroxide (KOH)	potassium chloride, KCl	potassium nitrate, KNO_3	potassium sulfate, K_2SO_4
magnesium oxide (MgO)	magnesium chloride, $MgCl_2$	magnesium nitrate, $Mg(NO_3)_2$	magnesium sulfate, $MgSO_4$
copper oxide (CuO)	copper chloride, $CuCl_2$	copper nitrate, $Cu(NO_3)_2$	copper sulfate, $CuSO_4$

Table 5.8 Some examples of making salts.

The reaction of acids with carbonates

All carbonates give off carbon dioxide when they react with acids (Figure **5.16**). We have seen that this reaction occurs with effervescent antacid tablets. The result is to neutralise the acid and produce a salt solution:

acid + metal carbonate
→ salt + water + carbon dioxide

The normal method of preparing carbon dioxide in the laboratory is based on this reaction. Dilute hydrochloric acid is reacted with marble chips (calcium carbonate):

hydrochloric acid + calcium carbonate
→ calcium chloride + water + carbon dioxide

$2HCl(aq) + CaCO_3(s)$
$\rightarrow CaCl_2(aq) + H_2O(l) + CO_2(g)$

Figure 5.16 Limestone (calcium carbonate) reacting with acid.

E

The practical thermochemistry of neutralisation

Neutralisation reactions are exothermic (they produce heat). Therefore, the end-point of such a reaction can be found by following the temperature change as the acid and alkali are mixed. The alkali is placed in an insulated container and acid is added in small volumes. The temperature rises with each addition of acid until neutralisation is complete. The volume of acid added when the temperature reaches a maximum is the amount just needed to neutralise the alkali.

Exam tip

Students taking the Core paper will need to be able to give word equations for the reactions in this section.

Students taking the extended paper will need to be able to give balanced chemical equations.

Key ideas so far

- Bases (metal oxides and hydroxides) neutralise acids to give a salt and water as the only products. Alkalis are simply the few bases that dissolve in water.
- The effects of acids can also be overcome using carbonates, but they give off the gas carbon dioxide as well as producing a salt.
- Acids react safely with moderately reactive metals to give off hydrogen gas.
- It is important to remember the three key reactions of acids:
  i with metals, **ii** with bases (including alkalis), and **iii** with metal carbonates.

Quick-check questions

1 What are the names and formulae of the **three** most important mineral acids?

2 Write word equations for the reaction of hydrochloric acid with
  a potassium hydroxide
  b copper oxide
  c zinc
  d sodium carbonate.

3 Write balanced chemical equations for the reactions listed in question **2**.

5.7 Acids and alkalis in chemical analysis

One important part of chemistry is the analysis of unknown substances to find out what they are. There is a series of tests which are important for this (see Section **12.1**). Acids and alkalis play an important part in some of these tests. The chemistry of these tests is discussed here.

Exam tip

These analytical tests are very important – particularly the tests for metal ions that give coloured precipitates. Also important is the way that we can identify zinc and aluminium salts using alkali.

These tests come up frequently as they are so distinctive, and you can be asked them on Paper 6 too, so it would be good to learn them. The ability to tell an iron(II) salt from an iron(III) salt is important.

The test for carbonates using acid

All carbonates will react with acids to give off carbon dioxide. We can use this as a test to find out if an unknown substance is a carbonate or not. A piece of rock that we think is limestone can be checked by dropping a few drops of vinegar on it. If it 'fizzes', then it could be limestone. A more usual test would be to add dilute hydrochloric acid to the powdered substance. Any gas given off would be passed into limewater (calcium hydroxide solution) to see if it went cloudy. If the limewater **does** turn cloudy, the gas is carbon dioxide, and the substance is a carbonate. Figure **5.17** shows how an antacid tablet can be tested to see if it contains a carbonate.

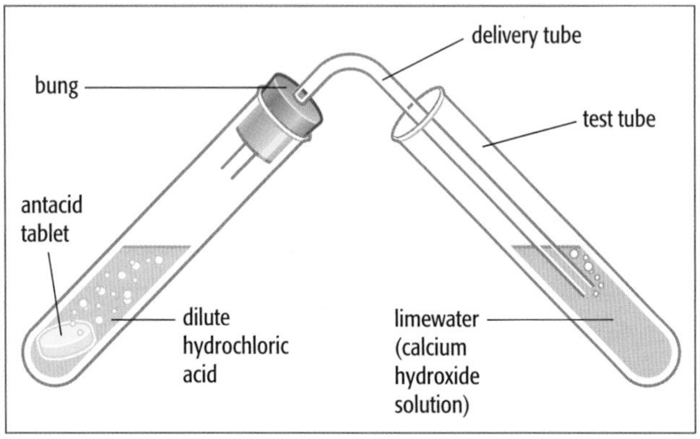

Figure 5.17 Testing an antacid tablet containing a carbonate as the active ingredient.

Tests for metal ions in salts using alkalis

All salts are ionic compounds. They are made up of a positive metal ion, combined with a negative non-metal ion. Thus common salt, sodium chloride, is made up of sodium metal ions (Na^+ ions) and chloride non-metal ions (Cl^- ions). Table **5.9** shows the ions that form certain important salts.

Salt	Positive ion	Negative ion
sodium chloride	Na^+	Cl^-
potassium nitrate	K^+	NO_3^-
copper(II) sulfate	Cu^{2+}	SO_4^{2-}
calcium carbonate	Ca^{2+}	CO_3^{2-}
sodium ethanoate	Na^+	CH_3COO^-

Table 5.9 The ions making up certain important salts.

In analysis it would be useful to have tests for the metal ions in salts. We have seen that most metal hydroxides are insoluble. By adding an alkali to a solution of the unknown salt we can begin to identify the salt.

Coloured hydroxide precipitates

Some of the hydroxide precipitates are coloured. As a result, a solution of a salt can be tested by adding an alkali to it and checking the colour of the precipitate (Figure **5.18**):

- Copper(II) salts give a light blue precipitate of copper(II) hydroxide.
- Iron(II) salts give a light green precipitate of iron(II) hydroxide.
- Iron(III) salts give a red-brown precipitate of iron(III) hydroxide.

For example:

iron(II) sulfate + sodium hydroxide
→ iron(II) hydroxide + sodium sulfate

$$FeSO_4(aq) + 2NaOH(aq) \rightarrow Fe(OH)_2(s) + Na_2SO_4(aq)$$

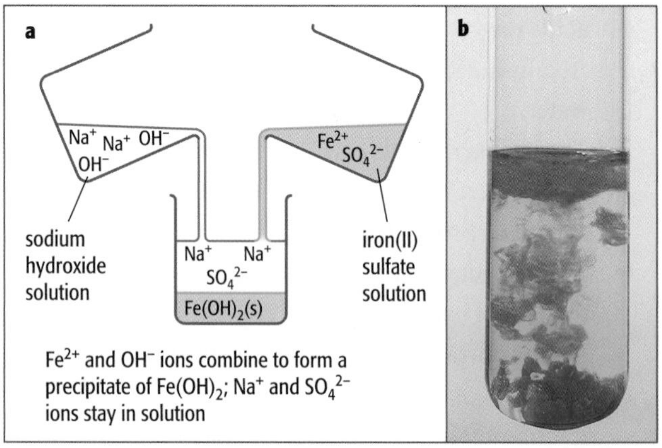

Figure 5.18 **a** The precipitation of iron(II) hydroxide. **b** The precipitation of iron(III) hydroxide. Note the different colour of the precipitates.

White hydroxide precipitates

Certain hydroxide precipitates are white. They are the hydroxides of calcium, zinc and aluminium. The addition of sodium hydroxide to a solution of a salt of these metals produces a white precipitate in each case. For example:

zinc sulfate + sodium hydroxide
→ zinc hydroxide + sodium sulfate

$$ZnSO_4(aq) + 2NaOH(aq) \rightarrow Zn(OH)_2(s) + Na_2SO_4(aq)$$

Even though the precipitates are all white the test is still useful. When an excess of sodium hydroxide is added, the zinc and aluminium hydroxide precipitates re-dissolve to give colourless solutions. The calcium hydroxide precipitate does not re-dissolve.

To identify a zinc or aluminium salt, the test needs to be repeated with ammonia solution. The same white precipitates of zinc or aluminium hydroxide are produced. However, with excess ammonia solution it is only the zinc hydroxide precipitate that re-dissolves, not the aluminium hydroxide. Therefore we can tell the two apart using ammonia solution.

The test for ammonium salts using alkali

Ammonium salts are important as fertilisers, for example ammonium nitrate and ammonium sulfate are used extensively as fertilisers. These are industrially important chemicals made by reacting ammonia with nitric acid or sulfuric acid, respectively. They are salts containing ammonium ions, NH_4^+ ions. These salts react with alkali solutions to produce ammonia gas, which can be detected because it turns damp red litmus paper blue:

ammonium nitrate + sodium hydroxide
→ sodium nitrate + water + ammonia

$$NH_4NO_3(s) + NaOH(aq) \rightarrow NaNO_3(aq) + H_2O(l) + NH_3(g)$$

This reaction occurs because ammonia is a more **volatile** base than sodium hydroxide. Ammonia is therefore easily displaced from its salts by sodium hydroxide. The reaction can be used to test an unknown substance for ammonium ions. It can also be used to prepare ammonia in the laboratory.

Key ideas so far

- Acids and alkalis are useful in the analysis of unknown salts to see which ions are present.
- Hydrochloric acid is useful to test for carbonates.
- Sodium hydroxide solution is useful when testing for metal ions present in salt solutions.
- Sodium hydroxide solution is also useful in testing for ammonium salts.

? Quick-check questions

1. Write the word equation for the reaction between a carbonate and hydrochloric acid.
2. What colour precipitate is produced when testing for copper ions with sodium hydroxide solution? What is the name of this precipitate?
3. Which alkali solution must be used to distinguish between zinc ions and aluminium ions in solution? What is the observation that distinguishes between the two?

5.8 Salts

E

The importance of salts – an introduction

A salt is a compound formed from an acid by the replacement of the hydrogen in the acid by a metal. Salts are ionic compounds. There is a wide range of types of salt. A great number of them play an important part in our everyday life (Table **5.10**, overleaf).

Many important minerals are single salts, for example fluorite (calcium fluoride) and gypsum (calcium sulfate). Common salt (sodium chloride) is mined from underground in many parts of the world including Britain and Ireland. The Detroit Salt Company in the USA has a mining complex directly under the city. It has an area of 10 km^2! The Wieliczka salt mine in Poland is one of the world's oldest mines and is a UNESCO World Heritage site. The mine is noted for the statues and rooms carved underground (Figure **5.19**, overleaf), and is visited by millions of people each year.

Salt	Parent acid	Colour and other characteristics	Uses
ammonium chloride	hydrochloric acid	white crystals	fertilisers; dry cells (batteries)
ammonium nitrate	nitric acid	white crystals	fertilisers; explosives
ammonium sulfate	sulfuric acid	white crystals	fertilisers
calcium carbonate (marble, limestone, chalk)	carbonic acid	white	decorative stones; making lime and cement and extracting iron
calcium sulfate (gypsum, plaster of Paris)	sulfuric acid	white crystals	wall plaster; plaster casts
sodium carbonate (washing soda)	carbonic acid	white crystals or powder	in cleaning; water softening; making glass
magnesium sulfate (Epsom salts)	sulfuric acid	white crystals	health salts (laxative)
copper(II) sulfate	sulfuric acid	blue crystals	fungicides
calcium phosphate	phosphoric acid	white	making fertilisers

Table 5.10 Salts in common use.

Figure 5.19 A statue carved out of salt in the Wieliczka salt mine, Poland.

These salt deposits were formed by the evaporation of ancient seas millions of years ago. Solid 'rock salt' is mined directly in some of these, including the Winsford mine in the UK. In other mines a technique known as solution mining is used. In these cases, the salt is dissolved underground and the solution, known as 'brine', is pumped up to the surface.

Figure 5.20 Salt flats beside the ocean in Lanzarote. Seawater is allowed to evaporate and then the salt is harvested. Piles of collected salt can be seen on the far right.

In hotter regions where the land is flat, for example the west coast of France, Lanzarote and the coast near Adelaide in Australia, the sea can be fed into shallow inland pools. Here the water slowly evaporates in the sun and crystals of 'sea salt' form (Figure 5.20). These crystals are then scraped up from the surface. 'Sea salt' is not just sodium chloride; it also contains magnesium chloride, calcium sulfate, potassium bromide and other salts.

Sodium chloride is essential for life and is an important raw material for industries. Biologically, it has a number of functions: it is involved in muscle contraction; it enables the conduction of nerve impulses in the nervous system; it regulates osmosis (the passage of solvent molecules through membranes); and it is converted into the hydrochloric acid that aids digestion in the stomach. When we sweat, we lose both water and sodium chloride. Loss of too much salt during sport and exercise can give us muscle cramp. Isotonic drinks are designed to replace this loss of water and to restore energy and the balance of mineral ions in our body.

While a number of salts can be obtained by mining, others must be made by industry. Therefore, it is worth considering the methods available to make salts. Some of these can be investigated in the laboratory.

Two things are important in working out a method of preparation:

- Is the salt soluble or insoluble in water?
- Do crystals of the salt contain water of crystallisation?

The first point influences the preparation method chosen. The second point affects how the crystals are handled at the end of the experiment.

Salts	Soluble	Insoluble
sodium salts	all are soluble	none
potassium salts	all are soluble	none
ammonium salts	all are soluble	none
nitrates	all are soluble	none
ethanoates	all are soluble	none
chlorides	most are soluble	silver chloride, lead(II) chloride
sulfates	most are soluble	barium sulfate, lead(II) sulfate, calcium sulfate
carbonates	sodium, potassium and ammonium carbonates	most are insoluble

Table 5.11 The patterns of solubility for various types of salts.

The solubility of salts

Soluble salts are made by neutralising an acid. Insoluble salts are made by other methods. Table **5.11** outlines the general patterns of solubility for the more usual salts.

Exam tip

This information may seem complicated to learn – but there are certain key features to understand and then it is easier. The table is organised to help you to remember:

- All the common sodium, potassium and ammonium salts are soluble.
- All nitrates and ethanoates are soluble.
- Most chlorides and sulfates are soluble. The most important exceptions here are silver chloride and barium sulfate, which are important precipitates in chemical analysis.
- Almost all carbonates are insoluble.

We shall look at the preparation of both soluble salts and insoluble salts. But first we consider the second point mentioned above.

Water of crystallisation

The crystals of some salts contain **water of crystallisation**. This water gives the crystals their shape. In some cases it also gives them their colour (copper sulfate crystals, for instance, Figure **5.21**, overleaf). Such salts are known as **hydrated salts** (Table **5.12**).

Hydrated salt	Formula	Colour
copper(II) sulfate	$CuSO_4.5H_2O$	blue
cobalt(II) chloride	$CoCl_2.6H_2O$	pink
iron(II) sulfate	$FeSO_4.6H_2O$	green
magnesium sulfate	$MgSO_4.7H_2O$	white
sodium carbonate	$Na_2CO_3.10H_2O$	white
calcium sulfate	$CaSO_4.2H_2O$	white

Table 5.12 Some hydrated salts.

Figure 5.21 Crystals of hydrated copper(II) sulfate are blue. They contain water of crystallisation in their structure ($CuSO_4.5H_2O$).

When these hydrated salts are heated, their water of crystallisation is driven off as steam. The crystals lose their shape and become a powder. Copper(II) sulfate crystals are blue, but when heated they are dehydrated to form a white powder:

copper(II) sulfate crystals
→ anhydrous copper(II) sulfate + water vapour

$$CuSO_4.5H_2O(s) \rightarrow CuSO_4(s) + 5H_2O(g)$$

Crystals that have lost their water of crystallisation are said to be **anhydrous**. If water is added back to the white anhydrous copper(II) sulfate powder, the powder turns blue again and heat is given out. This can be used as a test for the presence of water.

Exam tip

When preparing crystals of a hydrated salt, we must be careful not to heat them too strongly when drying them; otherwise the product is a dehydrated powder, not crystals.

Be careful, then, when you describe the method of drying crystals in an exam question.

Key ideas so far

- Salts are prepared from acids by neutralisation.
- All the common sodium, potassium and ammonium salts are soluble.
- All nitrates and ethanoates are soluble.
- Almost all carbonates are insoluble.
- When crystallised, many salts are hydrated; the solids contain water of crystallisation.
- When heated, the crystals of hydrated salts lose their water of crystallisation and become powders. This reaction can often be reversed.

Quick-check questions

1 The diagram shows some reactions of dilute sulfuric acid. Use the information in it to answer the questions that follow.

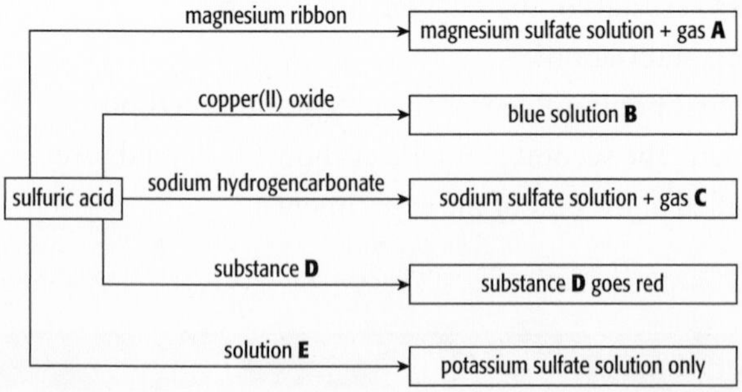

Name or give the formula of each of the following:

a gas A
b solution B
c gas C
d substance D
e solution E

5.9 Preparing soluble salts

Soluble salts can be made from their parent acid using any of the three characteristic reactions of acids we outlined earlier (Section 5.6).

Method A – Acid plus solid metal, base or carbonate

Method A is essentially the same whether starting with a solid metal, a solid base, or a solid carbonate. The method can be divided into four stages (Figure 5.22).

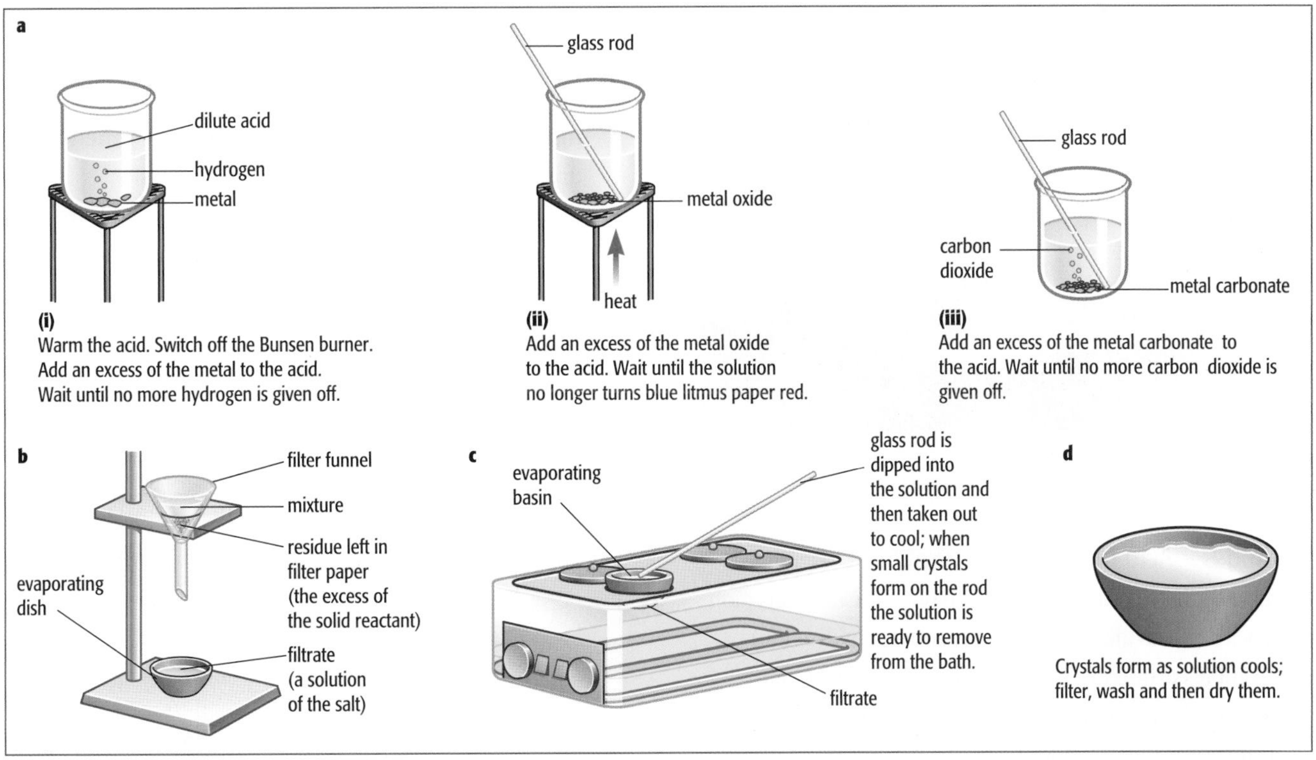

Figure 5.22 Method A for preparing a soluble salt. **a** *Stage 1*: the acid is reacted with either **(i)** a metal, **(ii)** a base or **(iii)** a carbonate. **b** *Stage 2*: the excess solid is filtered out. **c** *Stage 3*: the solution is carefully evaporated. **d** *Stage 4*: the crystals are allowed to form.

- *Stage 1:* An **excess** (more than enough) of the solid is added to the acid and allowed to react. Using an excess of the solid makes sure that all the acid is used up. If it is not used up at this stage, the acid would become more concentrated when the water is evaporated later (stage 3).
- *Stage 2:* The excess solid is filtered out.
- *Stage 3:* The filtrate is gently evaporated to concentrate the salt solution. This can be done on a heated water bath (Figure 5.23).
- *Stage 4:* When crystals can be seen forming (crystallisation point), heating is stopped and the solution is left to crystallise.
- *Stage 5:* The concentrated solution is cooled to let the crystals form. The crystals are filtered off and washed with a little distilled water. Then the crystals are dried carefully between filter papers (Figure 5.24, overleaf).

Exam tip

Always remember to finish your description of a method of preparing salt crystals with at least the words 'filter, wash and carefully dry the crystals' to cover the final stages of the preparation.

Figure 5.23 Evaporating off the water to obtain salt crystals. Here a sand tray is being used to heat the solution carefully.

Figure 5.24 Dried crystals of zinc nitrate.

Method B – Acid plus alkali by titration

Method B (the **titration** method) involves the neutralisation of an acid with an alkali (for example sodium hydroxide) or a soluble carbonate (for example sodium carbonate). Since both the reactants and the products are colourless, an indicator is used to find the neutralisation point or **end-point** (when all the acid has **just** been neutralised). The method is divided into three stages (Figure 5.25).

- *Stage 1:* The acid solution is poured into a burette. The **burette** is used to accurately measure the volume of solution added. A known volume of alkali solution is placed in a conical flask using a pipette. The **pipette** delivers a fixed volume accurately. A few drops of an indicator (for example phenolphthalein or methyl orange, Figure 5.26) are added to the flask.
- *Stage 2:* The acid solution is run into the flask from the burette until the indicator **just** changes colour. Having found the end-point for the reaction,

the volume of acid run into the flask is noted. The experiment is then repeated without using the indicator. The same known volume of alkali is used in the flask.

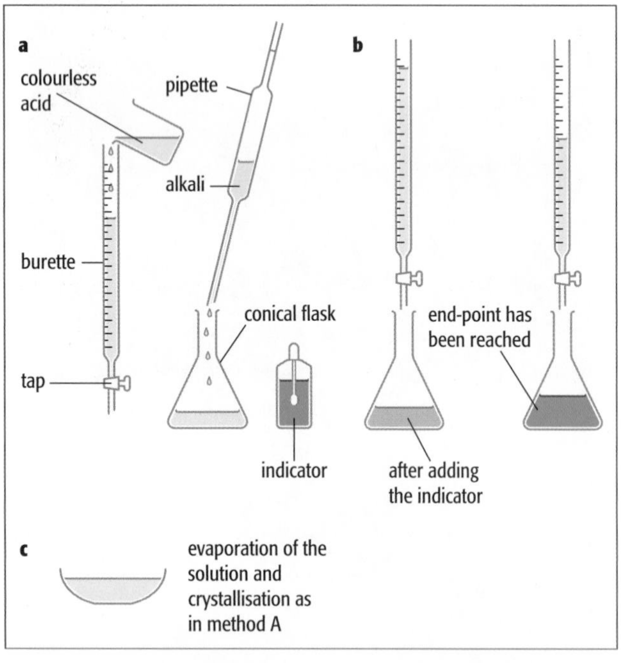

Figure 5.25 Method B (the titration method) for preparing a soluble salt. **a** *Stage 1*: the burette is filled with acid and a known volume of alkali is added to the conical flask. **b** *Stage 2*: the acid is added to the alkali until the end-point is reached. **c** *Stage 3*: the solution is evaporated and crystallised as for method A.

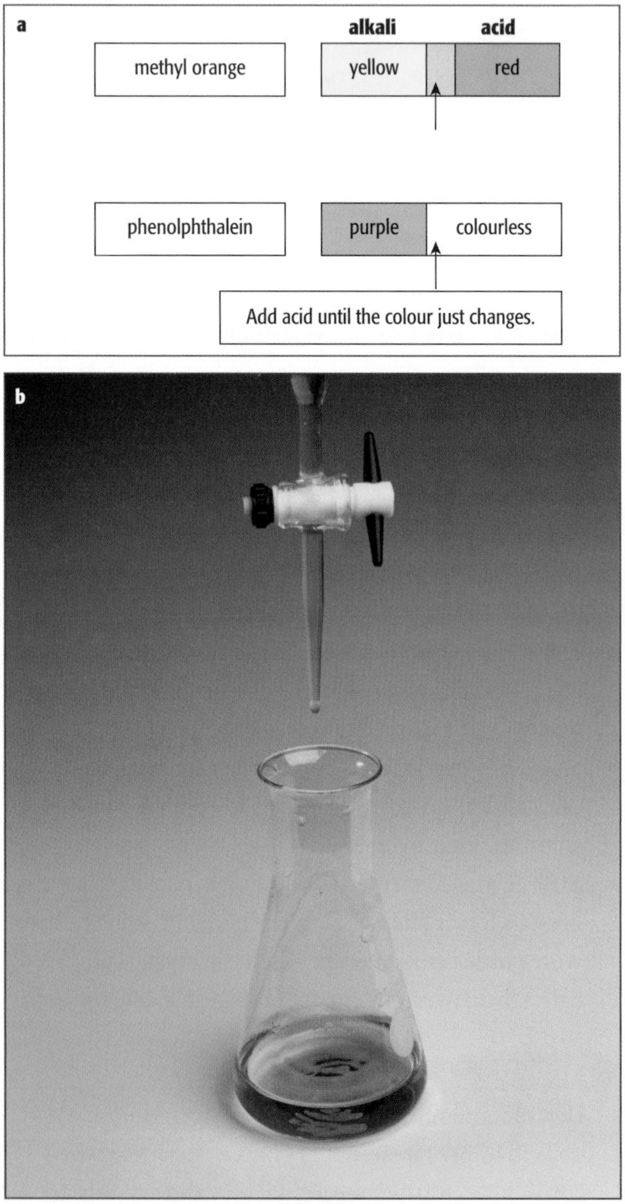

Figure 5.26 **a** The colour changes for the indicators methyl orange and phenolphthalein. **b** The pink colour of phenolphthalein in alkali.

The same volume of acid as noted in the first part is then run into the flask. Alternatively, activated charcoal can be added to remove the coloured indicator. The charcoal can then be filtered off.

- *Stage 3:* The salt solution is evaporated and cooled to form crystals as described in method A.

This titration method is very useful not simply for preparing salts but also for finding the concentration of a particular acid or alkali solution (see page **192**).

Key ideas so far

- Salts are substances produced from acids by reactions in which the hydrogen in the acid is replaced by a metal.
- Salts are widely used in the home and in industry.
- Salts are ionic compounds and many are soluble in water.
- Soluble salts can be made by reaction between
  - an acid and (an excess of) a metal
  - an acid and (an excess of) a metal oxide
  - an acid and (an excess of) a metal carbonate
  - an acid and an alkali (using a titration method).

Quick-check questions

1. What colour is the indicator phenolphthalein in alkali?
2. In the methods of preparing a salt using a solid metal, base or carbonate, why is the solid used in excess?
3. In such methods, what method is used to remove the excess solid once the reaction has finished?
4. Name the two important pieces of graduated glassware used in the titration method of preparing a salt.
5. Why should the crystals prepared at the end of these experiments not be heated too strongly when drying them?

5.10 Preparing insoluble salts

Choosing a method of salt preparation

The choice of method for preparing a soluble salt (see Section **5.9**) depends on two things:

- Is the metal reactive enough to displace the hydrogen in the acid? If it is, is it too reactive and therefore unsafe?
- Is the base or carbonate soluble or insoluble?

Figure **5.27** (overleaf) shows a flow chart summarising the choices.

Making salts by precipitation

The reaction between marble chips (calcium carbonate) and sulfuric acid would be expected to produce a strong reaction, with large amounts of carbon dioxide being given off. However, the reaction quickly stops after a very short time. This is caused by the fact that calcium sulfate is insoluble. It soon forms a layer on the surface of the marble chips, stopping any further reaction (Figure **5.28**, overleaf).

This reaction emphasises that some salts are insoluble in water (for example, silver chloride and barium sulfate – see Table **5.11** on page **155**). Such salts cannot be made by the crystallisation methods we have described earlier. They are generally made by ionic precipitation.

Precipitation is the sudden formation of a solid, either:

- when two solutions are mixed, or
- when a gas is bubbled into a solution.

For example, barium sulfate can be made by taking a solution of a soluble sulfate (such as sodium sulfate). This is added to a solution of a soluble barium salt (for example, barium chloride). The insoluble barium sulfate is formed immediately. This solid 'falls' to the bottom of the tube or beaker as a precipitate (Figure **5.29**, overleaf). The precipitate can be filtered off. It is then washed with distilled water and dried in a warm oven. The equation for this reaction is:

barium chloride + sodium sulfate
→ barium sulfate + sodium chloride

$$BaCl_2(aq) + Na_2SO_4(aq) \rightarrow BaSO_4(s) + 2NaCl(aq)$$

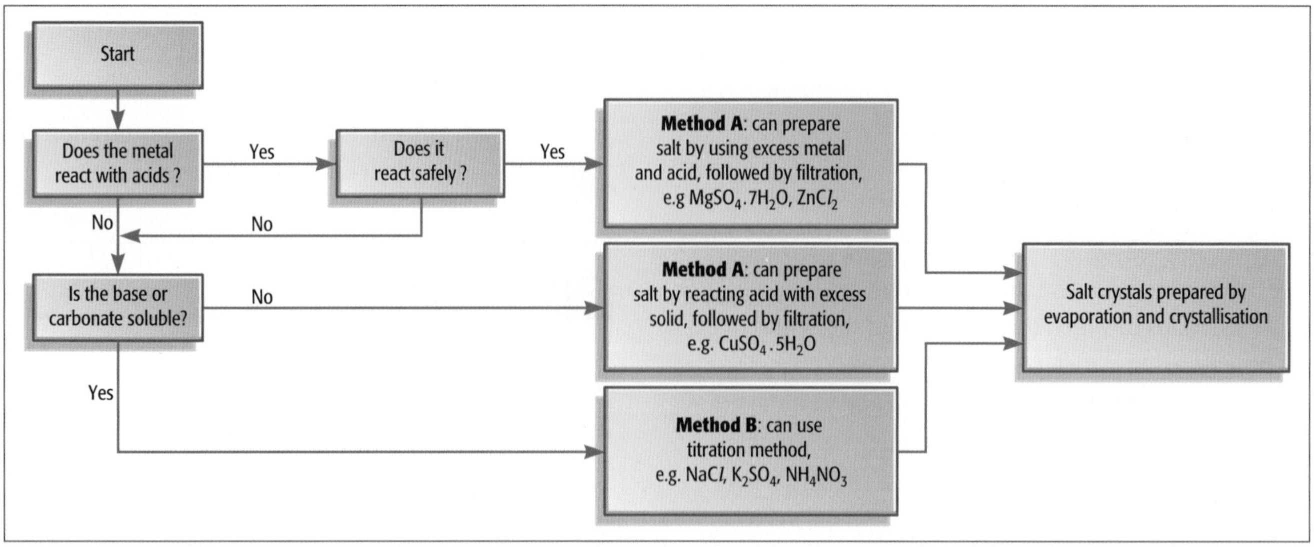

Figure 5.27 Flow chart showing which method to use for preparing soluble salts. The two methods A and B are described in the text and in Figures **5.22** and **5.25**.

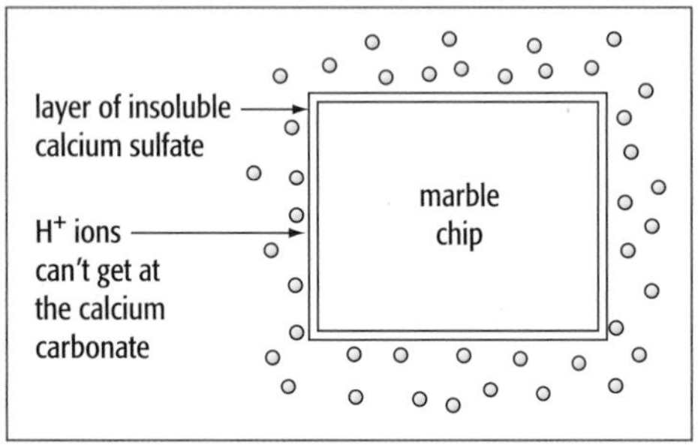

Figure 5.28 The formation of a layer of insoluble calcium sulfate stops the reaction of marble chips with sulfuric acid by forming a protective layer over the surface of the solid.

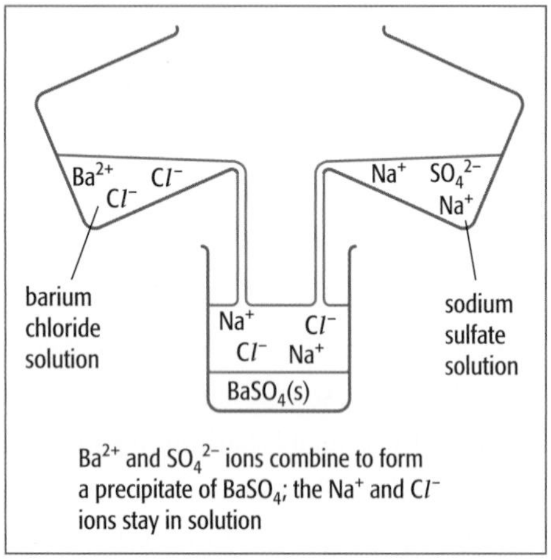

Figure 5.29 The precipitation of barium sulfate. The solid can be collected by filtration or centrifugation.

This equation shows how important state symbols can be – it is the only way we can tell that this equation shows a precipitation.

The equation can be simplified to show **only** those ions that take part in the reaction and their products:

$$Ba^{2+}(aq) + SO_4^{2-}(aq) \rightarrow BaSO_4(s)$$

This type of equation is known as an **ionic equation.** The ions that remain in solution are left out of the equation. They are known as **spectator ions**. The diagram below shows the formation of a precipitate of silver chloride when solutions of silver nitrate and sodium chloride are mixed.

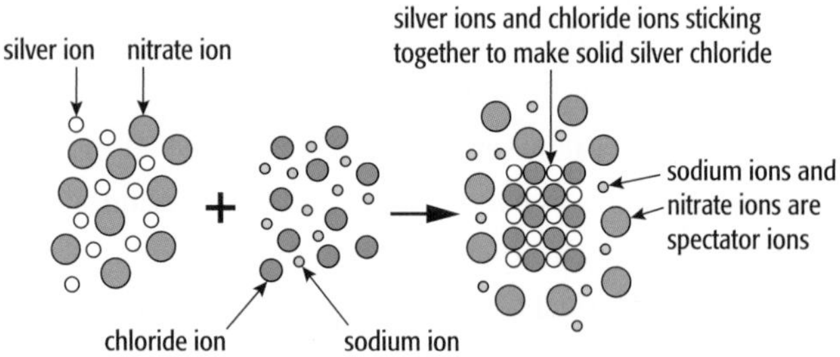

silver nitrate + sodium chloride
→ silver chloride + sodium nitrate

$$AgNO_3(aq) + NaCl(aq) \rightarrow AgCl(s) + NaNO_3(aq)$$
$$Ag^+(aq) + Cl^-(aq) \rightarrow AgCl(s)$$

Precipitation reactions are often used in analysis to identify salts such as chlorides, iodides and sulfates (see page 342). Figure **4.11a** on page **113** shows the precipitation of yellow lead iodide by mixing lead nitrate and potassium iodide solutions.

Exam tip

You should not be put off writing ionic equations for precipitation reactions, as there is a quite straightforward 'trick' to writing them. The approach here is essentially to work backwards. First write down the formula for the solid product on the right-hand side. Then, on the left-hand side, write down the ions that combine together to form the precipitate. Finally, write in the state symbols.

Key ideas so far

- Remind yourself of the three major reactions covered so far that can be used to prepare salts:
  - acid + metal
  - acid + base (or alkali)
  - acid + metal carbonate.
- Remember, too, the major methods of preparing salts from an acid:
  - reacting an acid with an alkali by titration
  - reacting an acid with excess insoluble base
  - reacting an acid with excess insoluble carbonate.
- Remember the solubility rules regarding salts – see Table **5.11**. Certain salts are insoluble in water and this gives us a way of preparing them by precipitation, followed by filtration.

Quick-check questions

1 There are three methods of preparing salts:
Method A – use a burette and an indicator.
Method B – mix two solutions and obtain the salt by precipitation.
Method C – add an excess of base or metal to a dilute acid and remove the excess by filtration.
For each of the following salt preparations, choose one of the methods A, B or C, name any additional reagent needed and then write or complete the equation asked for.

a the soluble salt, zinc sulfate, from the insoluble base, zinc oxide
i method
ii reagent
iii word equation.

b the soluble salt, potassium chloride, from the soluble base, potassium hydroxide
i method
ii reagent
iii copy and complete the following symbol equation

$$\ldots\ldots\ldots\ldots + \ldots\ldots\ldots\ldots \rightarrow KCl + H_2O$$

c the insoluble salt, lead(II) iodide, from the soluble salt, lead(II) nitrate
i method
ii reagent
iii copy and complete the following ionic equation

$$Pb^{2+}(aq) + \ldots\ldots\ldots\ldots \rightarrow \ldots\ldots\ldots\ldots$$

5.11 Strong and weak acids and alkalis

Strong and weak acids

Not all acids are equally strong. The vinegar used in salad dressing and to pickle vegetables is significantly less acidic than a hydrochloric acid solution of the same concentration. If differences in concentration are not the reason for this, then what does cause the difference? After all, we can eat fruit and drink wine or carbonated drinks without damage. Yet our bodies are not as resistant to all acids.

The difference lies in the ionic nature of acid solutions; more precisely, in the concentration of hydrogen ions (H^+ ions) in a solution. In Section **5.2** we stressed the importance of water as the necessary solvent for acid solutions. There is a relationship between H^+ ion concentration, acidity and pH: the higher the H^+ ion concentration, the higher the acidity and the lower the pH. We saw in Section **5.1** that the pH scale goes from 1 to 14. Each pH unit means a ten-fold difference in H^+ ion concentration. An acid of pH 1.0 has ten times the H^+ ion concentration of an acid of pH 2.0.

When hydrochloric acid is formed in water, the hydrogen chloride molecules completely separate into ions:

$$HCl(g) \xrightarrow{H_2O} H^+(aq) + Cl^-(aq)$$

In a similar way, sulfuric acid and nitric acid molecules completely separate into ions when dissolved in water:

$$H_2SO_4(l) \xrightarrow{H_2O} H^+(aq) + HSO_4^-(aq)$$

$$HNO_3(l) \xrightarrow{H_2O} H^+(aq) + NO_3^-(aq)$$

Exam tip

In general, two equivalent terms are used instead of 'separate into ions': we say that the acids 'ionise' or 'dissociate into ions'. Also, for various substances the separation into ions may or may not be complete. In this book, if the separation is complete, we say the substance is 'completely ionised'. If the separation is not complete, we say the substance is 'partially dissociated into ions'.

Complete separation into ions (complete ionisation) produces the maximum possible concentration of H^+ ions, and so the lowest possible pH for that solution.

When pure ethanoic acid is dissolved in water, only a small fraction of the covalently bonded molecules are dissociated into hydrogen ions and ethanoate ions:

$$\underset{\text{most molecules intact}}{CH_3COOH(l)} \xrightarrow{H_2O} \underset{\text{only a small number of molecules are dissociated into ions at any one time}}{H^+(aq) + CH_3COO^-(aq)}$$

Thus an ethanoic acid solution will have far fewer hydrogen ions present in it than a hydrochloric acid solution of the same concentration, and its pH will be higher. In school laboratory ethanoic acid solution, only one molecule in 250 is dissociated into ions.

Carbonic acid (H_2CO_3) is an example of a weak mineral acid. The other organic acids, such as methanoic acid, citric acid, etc. (see Table **5.1** on page **137**), also only partially dissociate into ions when dissolved in water.

Strong acids are **completely ionised** in solution in water. **Weak acids** are **partially dissociated into ions** in solution in water.

Strong and weak alkalis

Alkalis can also differ in the way that they are ionised when dissolved in water. Sodium hydroxide and potassium hydroxide are ionic solids. When they dissolve in water, the crystal lattice is broken down and the ions are spread throughout the solution. These alkalis are completely ionised in water:

$$\underset{\text{ionic crystals}}{Na^+OH^-(s)} \xrightarrow{H_2O} \underset{\text{ions spread through the solution}}{Na^+(aq) + OH^-(aq)}$$

This means that a solution contains the maximum possible concentration of OH^- ions, and therefore has the maximum possible pH. The pH of calcium hydroxide as an alkali is limited by its poor solubility.

Ammonia solution, on the other hand, is a weak alkali because it is only partially dissociated into ions:

$$\underset{\text{most remain as molecules}}{NH_3(g) + H_2O(l)} \rightarrow \underset{\text{only a few ions present}}{NH_4^+(aq) + OH^-(aq)}$$

Such a solution contains only a low concentration of ammonium (NH_4^+) ions and hydroxide (OH^-) ions. Solutions of ammonia only have a moderately high pH value.

Strong alkalis are **completely ionised** in solution in water. **Weak alkalis** are **partially dissociated into ions** in solution in water.

Because of their high concentration of ions, solutions of strong acids and strong alkalis conduct electricity well. Compounds such as nitric acid, sulfuric acid and sodium hydroxide are **strong electrolytes** in solution. Ethanoic acid and ammonia solution are only **weak electrolytes**. The large difference in conductivity between weak and strong acids and alkalis shows clearly the differences in ionisation in these solutions.

E

Dynamic equilibria in solutions of weak acids and weak alkalis

In solutions of weak acids and weak alkalis, only a small number of molecules are dissociated into ions at any given time. For weak acids and weak alkalis, the process of dissociation is **reversible**: it can go in either direction. In an ethanoic acid solution, molecules are constantly dissociating into ions. At the same time, ethanoate ions and hydrogen ions are also re-combining. A **dynamic equilibrium** is reached and the equation can be written:

$$CH_3COOH(aq) \rightleftharpoons H^+(aq) + CH_3COO^-(aq)$$

The double arrow shows that the reaction can go in either direction.

In this case we say that the position of the equilibrium lies well over to the left-hand side, because the concentration of molecules is much greater than the concentration of ions.

The partial dissociation of ammonia solution is also an equilibrium. Again the position of the equilibrium lies over to the left-hand side:

$$NH_3(g) + H_2O(l) \rightleftharpoons NH_4^+(aq) + OH^-(aq)$$

All the dissociation reactions of weak acids and weak alkalis are equilibria.

Exam tip

When comparing two acids (or alkalis) and trying to decide whether they are weak or strong, it is very important to compare two solutions of the **same concentration.**

If the concentrations are the same, then you can use the pH, the conductivity or the rate of a particular reaction to help you make a judgement as to the extent of ionisation.

What happens to the ions in neutralisation?

An acid can be neutralised by an alkali to produce a salt and water only, according to the general equation:

acid + alkali ⟶ salt + water

For example,

hydrochloric acid + sodium hydroxide ⟶ sodium chloride + water

$$HCl(aq) + NaOH(aq) \rightarrow NaCl(aq) + H_2O(l)$$

All these compounds are completely ionised, except for the water produced.

The hydrogen ions from the acid and the hydroxide ions from the alkali have combined to form water molecules:

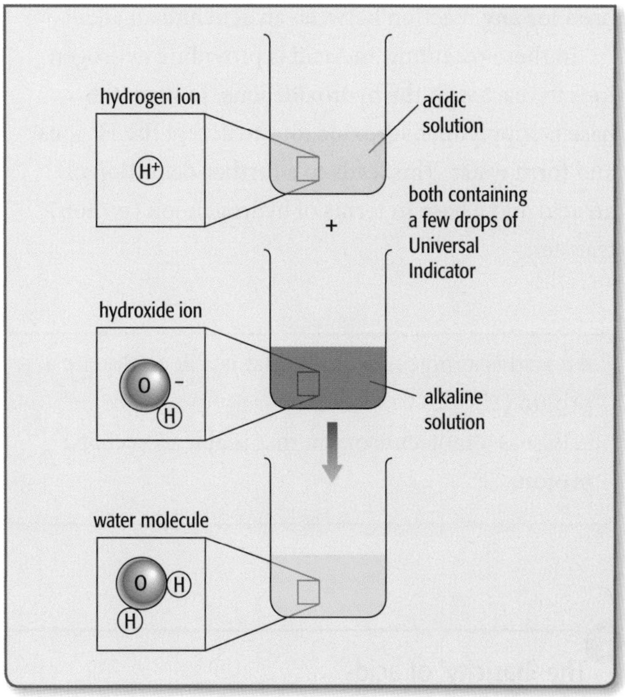

We can show this in the following equation:

$$\underset{\text{hydrogen ions (in water)}}{H^+(aq)} + \underset{\text{hydroxide ions (in water)}}{OH^-(aq)} \rightarrow \underset{\text{water}}{H_2O(1)}$$

This is the ionic equation for this neutralisation reaction. The spectator ions (chloride and sodium ions) remain in solution – which becomes a solution of sodium chloride (Figure 5.30).

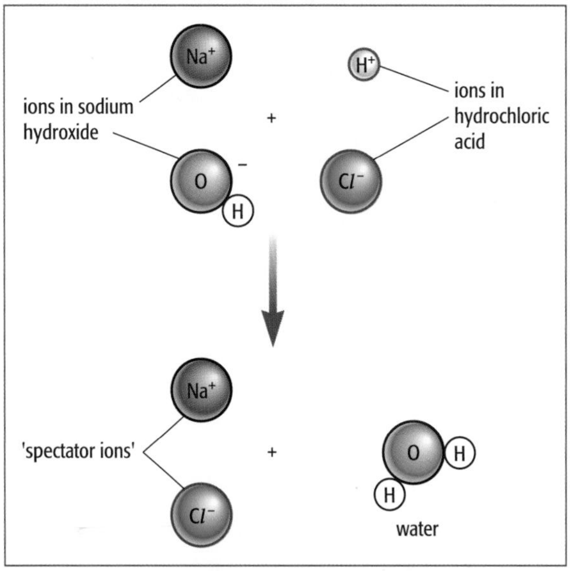

Figure 5.30 The reactions of the ions when hydrochloric acid is mixed with sodium hydroxide.

By evaporating some of the water, the salt can be crystallised out. In fact, the **same** ionic equation can be used for **any** reaction between an acid and an alkali.

In these reactions, the acid is providing hydrogen ions to react with the hydroxide ions. In turn, the base is supplying hydroxide ions to accept the H^+ ions and form water. This leads to a further definition of an acid and a base in terms of hydrogen ion (proton) transfer:

An acid is a molecule or ion that is able to **donate a proton** (H^+ ion) to a base.
A base is a molecule or ion that is able to **accept a proton**.

Exam tip

It is important to realise that a hydrogen ion (H^+) is simply a proton. Once the single electron of a hydrogen atom has been removed to form the positive ion, all that is left is the proton of the nucleus (Figure **5.31**).

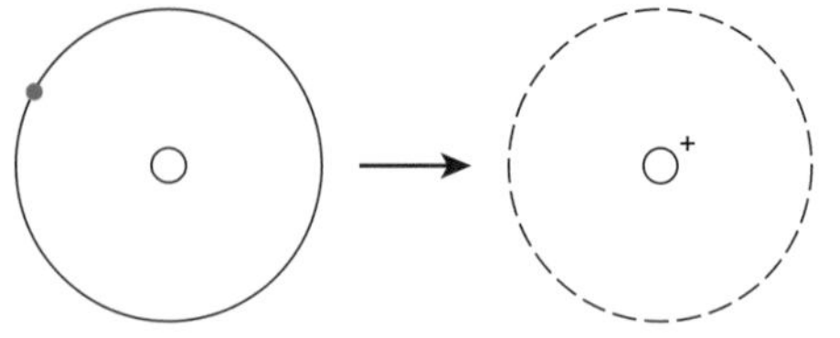

Figure 5.31 A hydrogen ion is simply a proton.

The 'basicity' of acids

Sodium carbonate and sodium hydrogencarbonate are both salts of carbonic acid (H_2CO_3). Two different salts of this acid exist because there are two hydrogen atoms present that can be replaced by a metal. Carbonic acid is said to be a **dibasic acid** because it has **two** replaceable hydrogen atoms per molecule.

Sulfuric acid is the most important dibasic acid in the laboratory. It too forms two different salts, depending on the amount of alkali used to react with the acid:

$$H_2SO_4(aq) + NaOH(aq) \rightarrow \underset{\text{sodium hydrogensulfate}}{NaHSO_4(aq)} + H_2O(l)$$

$$H_2SO_4(aq) + 2NaOH(aq) \rightarrow \underset{\text{sodium sulfate}}{Na_2SO_4(aq)} + 2H_2O(l)$$

Hydrochloric acid, nitric acid and ethanoic acid are all **monobasic acids**. They have **one** replaceable hydrogen atom per molecule and they each produce only one salt. Phosphoric acid (H_3PO_4) is a **tribasic acid**, producing three salts (Table **5.13**). Since the acidity of a solution depends on the number of hydrogen ions (protons) released by each acid molecule, a dibasic acid can also be known as a **diprotic acid** (see Table **5.13**).

Acid type	Name	Formula	Normal salts	Acid salts
Monobasic (monoprotic) acids	hydrochloric acid	HCl	chlorides, e.g. $NaCl$	
	nitric acid	HNO_3	nitrates, e.g. $NaNO_3$	
	ethanoic acid	CH_3COOH	ethanoates, e.g. CH_3COONa	
Dibasic (diprotic) acids	carbonic acid	H_2CO_3	carbonates, e.g. Na_2CO_3	hydrogencarbonates, e.g. $NaHCO_3$
	sulfuric acid	H_2SO_4	sulfates, e.g. Na_2SO_4	hydrogensulfates, e.g. $NaHSO_4$
Tribasic (triprotic) acids	phosphoric acid	H_3PO_4	phosphates, e.g. Na_3PO_4	dihydrogenphosphates, e.g. NaH_2PO_4, and hydrogenphosphates, e.g. Na_2HPO_4

Table 5.13 The basicity of some common acids.

Exam tip

If you are in doubt about the basicity of a particular acid, simply ask yourself how many moles of sodium hydroxide one mole of the acid would react with.

Note that not all the hydrogens in a structure count in this – there are four hydrogens in an ethanoic acid molecule, but only one is replaceable by a metal (the H in the —COOH group). Ethanoic acid is just a monobasic acid.

Key ideas so far

- Acid solutions contain an excess of H^+ ions. Alkali solutions contain an excess of OH^- ions.
- Acids and alkalis can be described as weak or strong, depending on how far they are ionised in solution.
- A strong acid (or alkali) is completely ionised in water.
- A weak acid (or alkali) is only partially ionised in water.
- An acid is an H^+ ion (or proton) donor.
- An alkali is an H^+ ion (or proton) acceptor.
- The basicity of an acid is related to how many H^+ ions can be released for each molecule of acid. So hydrochloric acid (HCl) is monobasic because it releases one H^+ ion per molecule when it dissolves in water, and sulfuric acid (H_2SO_4) is a dibasic acid.

Quick-check questions

1. Write an equation to show what happens when hydrogen chloride dissolves in water.
2. Write an equation to show what happens when ammonia gas dissolves in water.
3. Why does ethanoic acid have a lower conductivity than hydrochloric acid?
4. Explain why an H^+ ion is simply a proton.
5. Define an acid and a base using the ideas of proton (H^+ ion) transfer.
6. What is **a** an ionic equation, **b** a spectator ion?
7. Write the ionic equations that correspond to
   - **a** magnesium oxide reacting with nitric acid
   - **b** sodium carbonate reacting with hydrochloric acid
   - **c** potassium hydroxide reacting with nitric acid.

Summary

You should know that:

- the oxides of non-metals mainly form acidic solutions, and the oxides of metals, if soluble, mainly form alkaline solutions
- all acids contain hydrogen and dissolve in water to give solutions with a pH below 7
- pH is a measure of the acidity or alkalinity of an aqueous solution of a substance
  - solutions with a pH less than 7 are acidic
  - solutions with a pH greater than 7 are alkaline
  - a pH of 7 shows that a solution is neutral
- acid and alkali solutions conduct electricity – they contain ions
- acid solutions contain an excess of hydrogen ions, and alkali solutions contain an excess of hydroxide ions
- acids turn litmus red, and alkalis turn litmus blue – other single indicators have their own specific colour change
- Universal Indicator shows a range of colours depending on the pH of the solution tested
- bases are the 'chemical opposites' of acids and neutralise the effects of acids
- some bases are soluble in water – these bases are called alkalis

- acids react with bases to produce a salt and water only – this is a neutralisation reaction
- acids also show characteristic reactions with
  - some metals, to give a salt and hydrogen gas
  - metal carbonates, to give a salt, water and carbon dioxide gas
- salts are substances produced from acids by reactions in which the hydrogen in the acid is replaced by a metal
- salts are widely used in the home and in industry
- salts are ionic compounds and many are soluble in water
- soluble salts can be made by reaction between
  - an acid and an alkali
  - an acid and (an excess of) a metal
  - an acid and (an excess of) a metal oxide
  - an acid and (an excess of) a metal carbonate

S

- acids and alkalis can be either strong or weak
- strong acids and strong alkalis are completely ionised in water
- weak acids and weak alkalis are only partially dissociated into ions in water
- the dissociations of weak acids and weak alkalis into ions are examples of dynamic equilibria
- water itself is partially dissociated into ions, the concentrations of hydrogen ions and hydroxide ions in water being equal, hence water is neutral
- the pH of a solution depends on the balance of hydrogen ions and hydroxide ions in the solution
- the neutralisation of any acid with any alkali can be represented by the ionic equation

$$H^+(aq) + OH^-(aq) \rightarrow H_2O(l)$$

- acids can be defined as molecules or ions that can donate a proton (H^+ ion)
- bases can be defined as molecules or ions that can accept a proton
- acids may be monobasic, dibasic or tribasic depending on how many hydrogen ions can be released by each acid molecule
- a few non-metal oxides are neutral, but most are acidic
- some metal oxides and hydroxides are amphoteric – they react with both acids and alkalis.

Exam-style questions

1 In Table 5.1 on page **137**, methanoic acid, ethanoic acid and lactic acid all have one group of atoms in common.

a What is the formula of that group? [1]

b The formulae of citric acid and ascorbic acid (vitamin C) can be written:

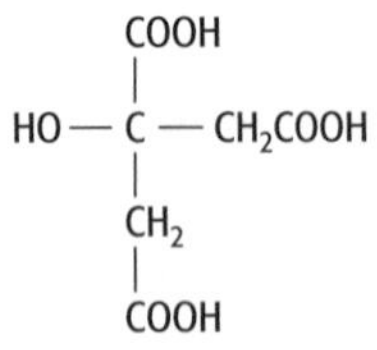

citric acid

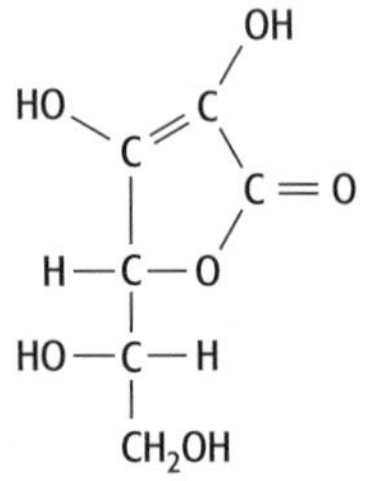

ascorbic acid

Do citric acid and ascorbic acid contain the same group as found in ethanoic acid?

i Citric acid? [1]

ii Ascorbic acid? [1]

c Tartaric acid has the structure:

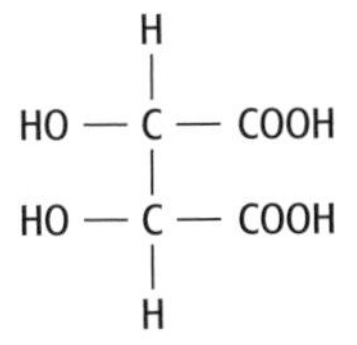

What is its molecular formula? [1]

2 A group of students measured the pH of some substances they found in their homes. The solids were first mixed with water before testing. Their results (to the nearest whole pH unit) are given in the table below.

Substance	**pH**
apples	3.0
baking soda (sodium hydrogencarbonate)	8.0
black coffee	5.0
household ammonia	12.0
lemon juice	3.0
milk	6.0
salt	7.0
sugar	7.0
toothpaste	9.0
vinegar	3.0
washing soda (sodium carbonate)	11.0

a What would the students have used to measure the pH? [1]

b Which solution is

i the most acidic? [1]

ii the most alkaline? [1]

c Which solutions are neutral? [2]

d A first aid manual suggests that vinegar should be used to treat wasp stings and baking soda for bee stings.

i What does this information tell you about the chemical nature of wasp stings? [1]

ii Which chemical substance is present in bee stings? [1]

iii If there was no baking soda in the house, what other household substance could you use to treat bee stings? [1]

3 The descriptions that follow are taken from 'HAZARD CARDS' for two mineral acids.

SULFURIC ACID

VERY CORROSIVE

Causes severe burns.

Solutions of concentration 1.5 mol/dm^3 or greater should be labelled CORROSIVE.
Solutions of concentration between 0.5 and 1.5 mol/dm^3 should be labelled IRRITANT.
Fuming sulfuric acid (oleum) is more hazardous and is not recommended for use in schools.

DANGEROUS WITH:

Water. Vigorous reaction when the concentrated acid is diluted.
Hydrochloric Acid, Chlorides. Hydrogen chloride given off.
Sodium, Potassium and many other metals. Dangerous reactions can take place.
ALWAYS ADD THE CONCENTRATED ACID SLOWLY TO COLD WATER WHEN DILUTING, NEVER THE REVERSE. STIR FREQUENTLY TO ENSURE THOROUGH MIXING.

HYDROCHLORIC ACID

CORROSIVE

May cause burns.

The vapour is very irritating to the respiratory system.
Solutions of concentration 6.5 mol/dm^3 or greater are CORROSIVE.
Solutions of concentration 2 mol/dm^3 or greater are IRRITANT.
It may be sensible to label 1 mol/dm^3 solutions as irritant as well.

a Which of the hazard symbols (**1**–**8**) would you put on bottles of the following solutions?
  i concentrated sulfuric acid [1]
  ii bench dilute sulfuric acid (1 mol/dm^3) [1]
  iii bench dilute hydrochloric acid (2 mol/dm^3) [1]

b What safety equipment should you always wear when using either of these acids? [2]

c Comparing solutions of the two acids with the same concentration, which of the two acids do you think is the more dangerous? Explain your reasons. [3]

4 A garden centre sells a simple soil testing kit. It consists of a tube containing a small amount of an off-white solid and an instruction card. The instructions are as follows:

INSTRUCTION CARD

(1) Take a sample of soil from 10 cm below the surface of the soil.
(2) Quarter fill the tube with the soil sample.
(3) Three-quarters fill the tube with water.
(4) Shake the tube for half a minute and then allow to settle.
(5) Compare the colour of the liquid with the colour guide on the card:

Chart colour	Soil
bright orange	very acid
pale orange	acid
pale green	neutral
dark green	alkaline

a How was the colour produced in the tube? [3]
b What scale do scientists use to measure acidity and alkalinity? [1]
c Give the name of **one** substance that a gardener would use to remove acidity from the soil. [1]
d Gardeners sometimes treat an alkaline soil by adding peat. What does this tell you about the chemical nature of peat? [1]

5 The diagram shows a cross-section of a soil.

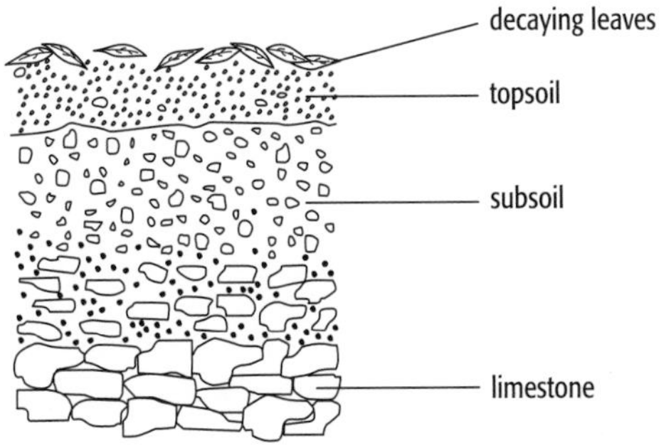

a A student took 10 g of topsoil and shook it with 200 cm^3 of distilled water.
  i How can the student separate the solids in the soil from the solution? [1]
  ii The topsoil had a pH of 6.
  Which of the following gives the best description of this pH?
  strongly acidic **weakly acidic** **neutral** **weakly alkaline** [1]
b The soil contained large amounts of calcium ions and carbonate ions.
  i Use the information in the diagram to suggest where these ions came from. [1]
  ii Copy and complete the word equation for the reaction of calcium carbonate with hydrochloric acid.

  calcium carbonate + hydrochloric acid → calcium chloride + ... + ... [2]

c The table shows the mass of each ion present in 200 cm^3 of soil solution.

Ion	Formula of ion	Mass present (milligrams)
calcium	Ca^{2+}	12
carbonate	CO_3^{2-}	20
iron(III)	Fe^{3+}	4
magnesium	Mg^{2+}	5
nitrate	NO_3^-	2
phosphate	PO_4^{3-}	1
others		6

i Which negative ion has the highest concentration in the soil solution? [1]

ii Calculate the mass of iron(III) ions in one litre (1000 cm^3 or 1 dm^3) of solution. [1]

iii Which ion in the table will release ammonia when heated with aqueous sodium hydroxide and aluminium foil? [1]

iv Describe a test for iron(III) ions. Give the test and the expected result. [3]

d Decaying leaves produce ethanoic acid.
Copy and complete the formula for ethanoic acid, showing all atoms and bonds. [1]

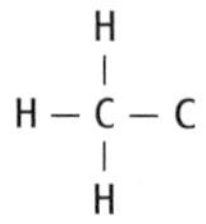

[1]

CIE IGCSE, June 2006, paper 2, q.5 part

6 Sulfuric acid is a typical strong acid.

a Change the equations given into a different format.

i $Mg + H_2SO_4 \rightarrow MgSO_4 + H_2$
Change into a word equation. [1]

ii lithium oxide + sulfuric acid → lithium sulfate + water
Change into a symbol equation. [2]

iii $CuO + 2H^+ \rightarrow Cu^{2+} + H_2O$
Change the ionic equation into a symbol equation. [2]

iv $Na_2CO_3 + H_2SO_4 \rightarrow Na_2SO_4 + CO_2 + H_2O$
Change into a word equation. [1]

b When sulfuric acid dissolves in water, the following reaction occurs.

$H_2SO_4 + H_2O \rightarrow HSO_4^- + H_3O^+$

Explain why water is behaving as a base in this reaction. [2]

c Sulfuric acid is a strong acid, ethanoic acid is a weak acid.
Explain the difference between a strong acid and a weak acid. [2]

CIE IGCSE, June 2008, paper 3, q.4

S

7 **a** Aqueous solutions of acid **X** and acid **Y** were used for the following experiments. The concentration of each solution was 1.0 mol/dm^3.

Experiment	**Acid X**	**Acid Y**
1 Measure the electrical conductivity of the solutions of these acids, i.e. the current which flows under identical conditions	0.020 A	0.3 A
2 Measure the temperature increase when the same volume of aqueous sodium hydroxide is added to equal volumes of these acids	2 °C	3 °C
3 Measure the time for equal volumes of the solutions of these acids to react with identical pieces of magnesium	20 minutes	2 minutes

i Explain the term **acid.** [2]

ii What type of reaction has taken place in experiment **2**? [1]

iii What explanation would you give for the two acids giving different results in these experiments? [2]

iv Describe **two** ways of reducing the time for a solution of acid **X** to react with magnesium. [2]

v For solutions of the two acids **X** and **Y**, each with the same concentration, which solution would have the higher pH value? Explain your answer. [2]

b Methods of preparing salts are:

Method A – add an excess of a chemical to a dilute acid and then filter.

Method B – use a burette and indicator.

Method C – mix two solutions and obtain the salt by precipitation.

For each of the following salt preparations, choose **one** of the methods A, B or C and name any additional reagent needed. Equations are not required.

i Preparation of the soluble salt, cobalt sulfate, from the insoluble compound, cobalt carbonate. [2]

ii Preparation of potassium chloride from potassium hydroxide: both compounds are soluble in water. [2]

c The formula of a compound can be determined by knowing the formulae of the ions that are present in the compound or by experiment.

i State the formula of the compound which contains Ca^{2+} and PO_4^{3-} ions. [1]

ii A 3 cm^3 sample of a solution of the nitrate of metal **Q**, concentration 1.0 mol/dm^3, was added to 2 cm^3 of potassium fluoride, concentration 1.0 mol/dm^3. When the precipitate had settled, its height was measured. The experiment was then repeated using different volumes of potassium fluoride solution. The results are shown in the diagram below.

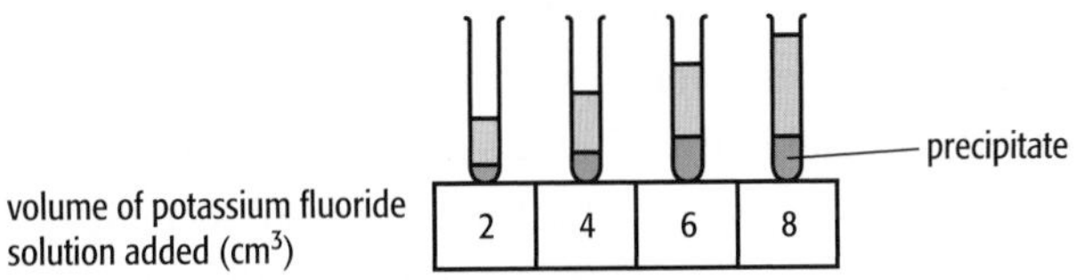

What is the formula of the fluoride of metal **Q**? [2]

8 a Insoluble compounds are made by precipitation.

i Copy and complete the word equation for the preparation of zinc carbonate.

.... + sodium carbonate → zinc carbonate + ... [2]

ii Copy and complete the following symbol equation.

$Pb(NO_3)_2$ + ...NaCl → .... + ... [2]

iii Write an ionic equation for the precipitation of the insoluble salt, silver(I) chloride. [2]

b 2.0 cm^3 portions of aqueous sodium hydroxide were added to 4.0 cm^3 of aqueous iron(III) chloride. Both solutions had a concentration of 1.0 mol/dm^3. After each addition, the mixture was stirred, centrifuged and the height of the precipitate of iron(III) hydroxide was measured.
The results are shown on the following graph.

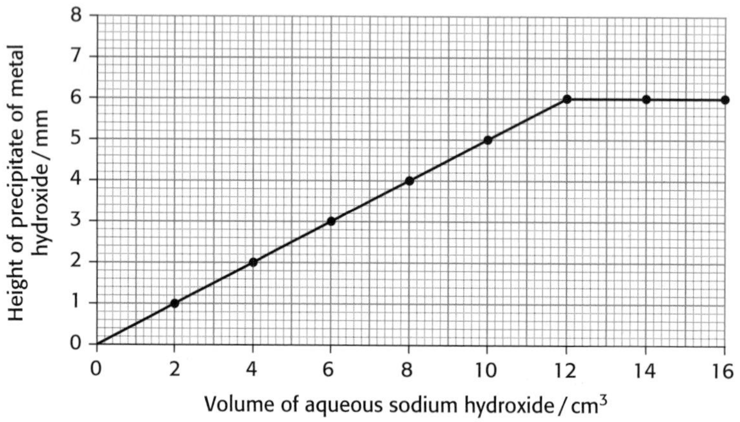

i Copy and complete the ionic equation for the reaction.

Fe^{3+} + ...OH^- → .... [2]

ii On the same grid, sketch the graph that would have been obtained if iron(II) chloride had been used instead of iron(III) chloride. [2]

iii If aluminium chloride had been used instead of iron(III) chloride, the shape of the graph would be different. How are the shapes of these two graphs different, and why? [2]

CIE IGCSE, June 2004, paper 3, q.4

9 A student carried out an experiment to measure the temperature changes during the neutralisation of sodium hydroxide solution with dilute hydrochloric acid. The instructions were as follows.
Step 1. Allow the acid and alkali to stand in the laboratory for about 15 minutes.
Step 2. Pour 25 cm^3 of the alkali into a polystyrene beaker and record its temperature.
Step 3. Add 10 cm^3 of acid to the alkali, stirring all the time. Record the highest temperature reached.
Step 4. Repeat the experiment, using 25 cm^3 of alkali with different volumes of acid.
The results of all the experiments are shown in the table.

Volume of alkali / cm^3	25	25	25	25	25	25
Volume of acid added / cm^3	0	10	20	30	40	50
Highest temperature recorded / °C	28	32	36	37	35	33

a Why were the solutions left standing in the laboratory for about 15 minutes before the experiment? [1]
b Why were the reactions carried out in a polystyrene beaker rather than a glass beaker? [1]
c i Plot the results on graph paper. Plot the highest temperature recorded against the volume of acid added. Draw two straight lines through the points and extend them until they cross. [3]
ii What was the temperature in the laboratory? [1]
iii Circle on the graph where the mixture becomes neutral. [1]
iv What volume of acid was needed to neutralise 25 cm^3 of the alkali? [1]
d Name the salt solution formed in this reaction. [1]
e Why can this reaction be described as 'exothermic'? [1]
f Write a symbol equation for the reaction. [1]

10 a Copy out and complete the passage:
The neutralisation of an acid involves the transfer of protons. Compounds that can accept protons from acids are called .... To make ammonium sulfate, sulfuric acid would need to react with the chemical, ... [2]
b Rock phosphate (calcium phosphate) is obtained by mining. It reacts with concentrated sulfuric acid to form the fertiliser, superphosphate.

$Ca_3(PO_4)_2 + 2H_2SO_4 \rightarrow Ca(H_2PO_4)_2 + 2CaSO_4$

i Use the above equation to deduce the charge on the phosphate ion. [1]
ii Why must the chemicals in fertilisers be soluble in water? [1]
iii The phosphate ion is behaving as a base in this reaction. What is a base? [2]

11 a i Oxides can be classified as acidic, amphoteric or basic. Copy out and classify the following.
Magnesium oxide is ....
Aluminium oxide is ....
Silicon(IV) oxide (silicon dioxide) is .... [3]
ii Name a reagent that reacts with an amphoteric oxide but not with a basic one. [1]
iii Name a reagent that reacts with a basic oxide and with an amphoteric oxide. [1]
b Beryllium hydroxide is amphoteric.
i Describe what would be observed when an excess of aqueous sodium hydroxide is gradually added to aqueous beryllium sulfate. [2]
ii Name another metal, other than beryllium or aluminium, which has an amphoteric hydroxide. [1]
iii Copy out and complete the ionic equation:

Be^{2+} + ... $\rightarrow Be(OH)_2$ [1]

iv Give the balanced chemical equation for the reaction of beryllium hydroxide with hydrochloric acid. [2]

12 **a** Four bottles were known to contain aqueous ammonia, dilute hydrochloric acid, sodium hydroxide solution and vinegar, which is dilute ethanoic acid. The bottles had lost their labels. The pH values of the four solutions were 1, 4, 10 and 13.

Copy and complete the table.

Solution	**pH**
aqueous ammonia	
dilute hydrochloric acid	
sodium hydroxide solution	
vinegar	

[2]

b The following apparatus was set up to investigate the electrical conductivity of dilute acids.

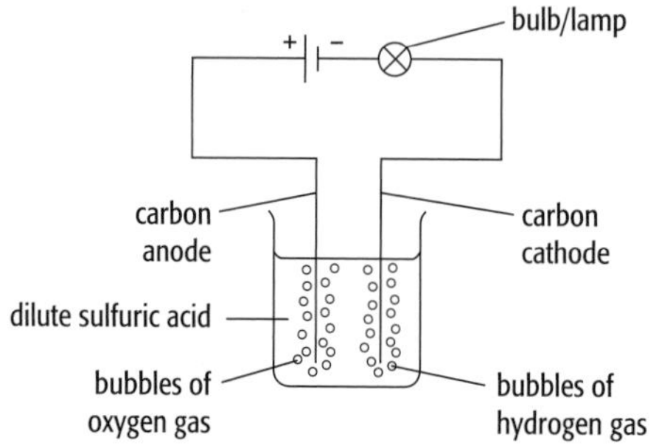

Dilute sulfuric acid is a strong acid. If it was replaced by a weak acid, what two differences in the observations would you expect to make? [2]

c When nitric acid is added to water the following reaction occurs.

$HNO_3 + H_2O \rightarrow NO_3^- + H_3O^+$

Give the name and the formula of the particle which is transferred from nitric acid to water. [2]

d This question is concerned with the following oxides.

aluminium oxide	Al_2O_3	calcium oxide	CaO
carbon dioxide	CO_2	carbon monoxide	CO
magnesium oxide	MgO	sulfur dioxide	SO_2

i Which of the above oxides will react with hydrochloric acid but not with aqueous sodium hydroxide? [1]

ii Which of the above oxides will react with aqueous sodium hydroxide but not with hydrochloric acid? [1]

iii Which of the above oxides will react both with hydrochloric acid and with aqueous sodium hydroxide? [1]

iv Which of the above oxides will react neither with hydrochloric acid nor with aqueous sodium hydroxide? [1]

CIE IGCSE, June 2006, paper 3, q.3

6 Quantitative chemistry

This chapter covers the following ideas:

- the relative atomic mass of elements
- the relative formula mass of compounds
- calculating the percentage by mass of an element in a compound
- that substances react in fixed proportions by mass
- S the mole as the 'accounting unit' in chemistry
- S simple calculations involving the mole
- S the empirical formula of a compound
- S the molecular formula of a compound
- S calculations involving the mole and reacting masses
- S percentage yield and percentage purity
- S calculations involving gases
- S the concentration of solutions
- S the titration of acid and alkali solutions
- S solubility curves

6.1 Chemical analysis and formulae

The fertiliser bags found around a farm often carry three numbers (Figure **6.1**). The numbers tell the farmer the amounts of the three key elements present in the fertiliser: that is, the percentages of nitrogen (N), phosphorus (P) and potassium (K).

It is important to know not only **what** is in a chemical product, but also **how much** of each substance there is. The same idea lies behind the rules controlling the food industry. For instance, European Union regulations mean that all breakfast cereal packets must show the amounts of the various chemical substances (such as protein, fat and vitamins) present in the cereal.

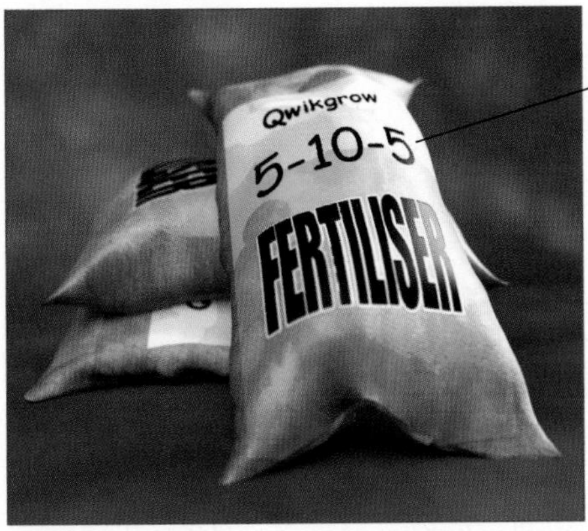

Figure 6.1 NPK fertiliser contains the plant nutrients nitrogen, phosphorus and potassium. The 5-10-5 on the bag refers to the ratio of these nutrients in the fertiliser.

In many areas of chemistry, it is very important to know the amounts of substances used and produced in reactions. An environmental chemist needs to check levels of pollutants in the air, caused by burning a particular fuel. A polymer chemist needs an estimate of how much material a new and different reaction method will yield. He or she needs to check on losses through the purification process. A medical researcher must find out a safe dose for an experimental drug. He or she must consider its possible side-effects by measuring the amounts of its metabolic products in cells. A chemical formula or equation not only tells us what happens but puts 'numbers' to it. This is vital to modern chemistry.

Chemical 'accountancy'

We need to be able to predict the amounts of substances involved in chemical reactions. To do this, we must have a good understanding of the atom. For some time now we have been able to use the mass spectrometer as a way of 'weighing' atoms.

Relative atomic mass

The mass of a single hydrogen atom is incredibly small when measured in grams (g):

$$\text{mass of one hydrogen atom} = 1.7 \times 10^{-24}\,\text{g} = 0.000\,000\,000\,000\,000\,000\,000\,0017\,\text{g}$$

It is much more useful and convenient to measure the masses of atoms **relative** to each other (Table **6.1**). To do this, a standard atom has been chosen, against which all others are then compared. This **standard atom** is an atom of the carbon-12 isotope, the 'mass' of which is given the value of exactly 12 (Figure **6.2**).

The use of the mass spectrometer first showed the existence of isotopes. These are atoms of the same element that have different masses because they have different numbers of neutrons in the nucleus (see page 52). The majority of elements have several isotopes (Figure **6.3**).

This must be taken into account. The relative atomic mass (A_r) of an element is the average mass of an atom of the element, taking into account the different natural isotopes of that element (Table **6.2**). So most relative atomic masses are not whole numbers. But in this book,

Atom	Mass in grams	Whole-number ratio
hydrogen	1.7×10^{-24}	1
carbon-12	2.0×10^{-23}	12
fluorine	3.2×10^{-23}	19

Table 6.1 The relative masses of some atoms.

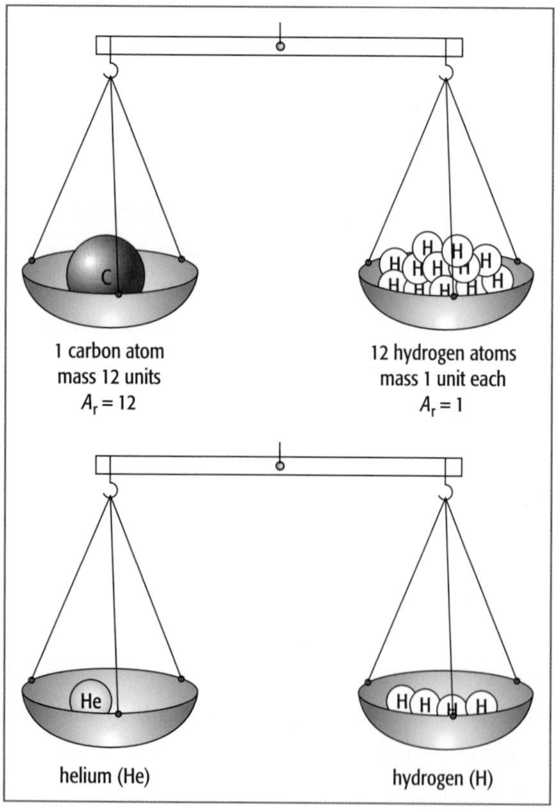

Figure 6.2 The relative mass of atoms. Twelve hydrogen atoms have the same mass as one atom of carbon-12. A helium atom has the same mass as four hydrogens.

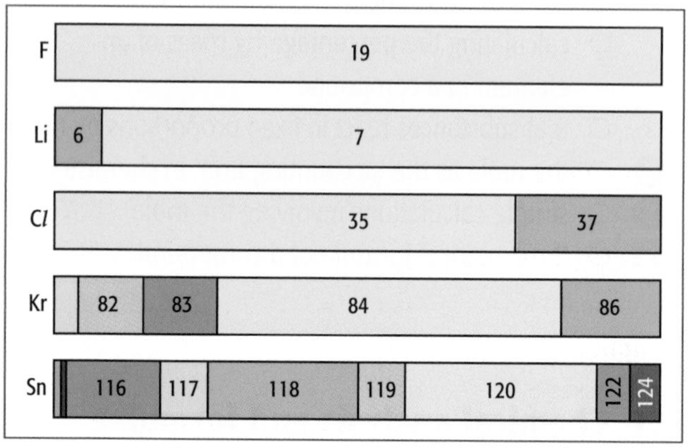

Figure 6.3 Many different elements have more than one isotope. These bars show the proportions of different isotopes for some elements. Fluorine is rare in having just one.

Element	Symbol	Relative atomic mass, A_r
hydrogen	H	1
carbon	C	12
nitrogen	N	14
oxygen	O	16
fluorine	F	19
sodium	Na	23
magnesium	Mg	24
aluminium	Al	27
sulfur	S	32
chlorine	Cl	35.5
copper	Cu	64

[a] *Except for chlorine, all values have been rounded to the nearest whole number.*

Table 6.2 The relative atomic masses of some elements[a].

with the exception of chlorine, they are rounded to the nearest whole number to make our calculations easier.

The **relative atomic mass** (A_r) of an element is the average mass of the naturally occurring atoms of the element, using a scale where an atom of carbon-12 has a mass of exactly 12.

It is important to note that the mass of an ion will be the same as that of the parent atom. The mass of the electron(s) gained or lost in forming the ion can be ignored in comparison to the total mass of the atom.

Relative formula mass

Atoms combine to form molecules or groups of ions. The total masses of these molecules or groups of ions provide useful information on the way the elements have combined with each other. The **formula** of an element or compound is taken as the basic unit (the formula unit). The masses of the atoms or ions in the formula are added together. The mass of a substance found in this way is called the **relative formula mass** (M_r). Here we illustrate the method by calculating the relative formula masses of three simple substances.

- *Hydrogen:* Hydrogen gas is made up of H_2 molecules (H—H). Each molecule contains two hydrogen atoms. So its relative formula mass is twice the relative atomic mass of hydrogen:

  $M_r(H_2) = 2 \times 1 = 2$

- *Water:* Water is a liquid made up of H_2O molecules (H—O—H). Each molecule contains two hydrogen atoms and one oxygen atom. So its relative formula mass is twice the relative atomic mass of hydrogen plus the relative atomic mass of oxygen:

  $M_r(H_2O) = (2 \times 1) + 16 = 18$

- *Sodium chloride:* Sodium chloride is an ionic solid. It contains one chloride ion for each sodium ion present. The formula unit of sodium chloride is therefore Na^+Cl^-. So its relative formula mass is the relative atomic mass of sodium plus the relative atomic mass of chlorine:

  $M_r(NaCl) = 23 + 35.5 = 58.5$

- The relative formula mass (M_r) of a substance is the sum of the relative atomic masses of the elements present in a formula unit.
- If the substance is made of simple molecules, this mass may also be called the **relative molecular mass** (M_r).

The practical result of these definitions can be seen by looking at further examples (Table **6.3**, overleaf).

The **percentage by mass of a particular element** in a compound can be found from calculations of relative formula mass. Figure **6.4** shows how this works for the simple case of sulfur dioxide (SO_2), whose mass is made up of 50% each of the two elements.

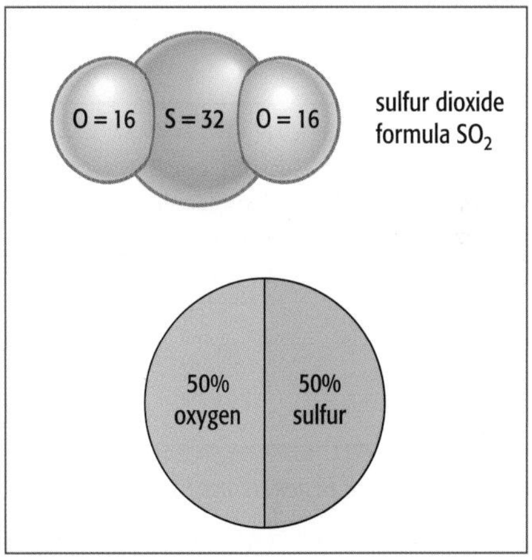

Figure 6.4 The percentage composition by mass of sulfur dioxide.

This type of calculation is useful, for instance, in estimating the efficiency of one fertiliser compared with another. Ammonium nitrate is a commonly used fertiliser. It is an important source of nitrogen. What percentage of the mass of the compound is nitrogen?

The formula of ammonium nitrate is NH_4NO_3 (it contains the ions NH_4^+ and NO_3^-). Using the A_r values for N, H and O we get

$$M_r = (2 \times 14) + (4 \times 1) + (3 \times 16) = 28 + 4 + 48 = 80$$

Then

mass of nitrogen in the formula = 28

mass of nitrogen as a fraction of the total = $\frac{28}{80}$

mass of nitrogen as percentage of total mass

$$= \frac{28}{80} \times 100 = 35\%$$

Substance	Formula	Atoms in formula	Relative atomic masses			Relative formula mass, M_r		
hydrogen	H_2	2H	H	=	1	2×1	=	**2**
carbon dioxide	CO_2	1C	C	=	12	1×12	=	12
		2O	O	=	16	2×16	=	32
								44
calcium carbonate	$CaCO_3$ (one Ca^{2+} ion, one CO_3^{2-} ion)	1Ca	Ca	=	40	1×40	=	40
		1C	C	=	12	1×12	=	12
		3O	O	=	16	3×16	=	48
								100
ammonium sulfate[(a)]	$(NH_4)_2SO_4$ (two NH_4^+ ions, one SO_4^{2-} ion)	2N	N	=	14	2×14	=	28
		8H	H	=	1	8×1	=	8
		1S	S	=	32	1×32	=	32
		4O	O	=	16	4×16	=	64
								132
hydrated magnesium sulfate[(b)]	$MgSO_4.7H_2O$ (one Mg^{2+} ion, one SO_4^{2-} ion, seven H_2O molecules)	1Mg	Mg	=	24	1×24	=	24
		1S	S	=	32	1×32	=	32
		4O	O	=	16	4×16	=	64
		14H	H	=	1	14×1	=	14
		7O	O	=	16	7×16	=	112
								246

[(a)] *The Figure 2 outside the brackets multiplies everything in the brackets; there are two ammonium ions in this formula.*

[(b)] *The 7 means there are seven H_2O molecules per $MgSO_4$ formula unit.*

Table 6.3 The relative formula masses of some compounds.

Similar calculations can be used to work out the **percentage by mass of water of crystallisation** in crystals of a hydrated salt, for example magnesium sulfate (Epsom salts).

The formula of magnesium sulfate is $MgSO_4.7H_2O$. Using the A_r values for Mg, S, O and H we get

$$M_r = 24 + 32 + (4 \times 16) + (7 \times 18) = 246$$

Then

mass of water in formula = 126

mass of water as a fraction of the total = $\frac{126}{246}$

percentage mass of water in the crystals

$$= \frac{126}{246} \times 100 = 51.2\%$$

Exam tip

Pay particular attention to the example of ammonium sulfate in Table **6.3**. This is an example of a formula that has brackets. Remember to take into account the number outside the bracket when counting up all the atoms of a particular type.

Compound formation and chemical formulae

The idea that compounds are made up of elements combined in fixed amounts can be shown experimentally. Samples of the **same compound** made in different ways always contain the **same elements**. Also, the masses of the elements present are always in the **same ratio**.

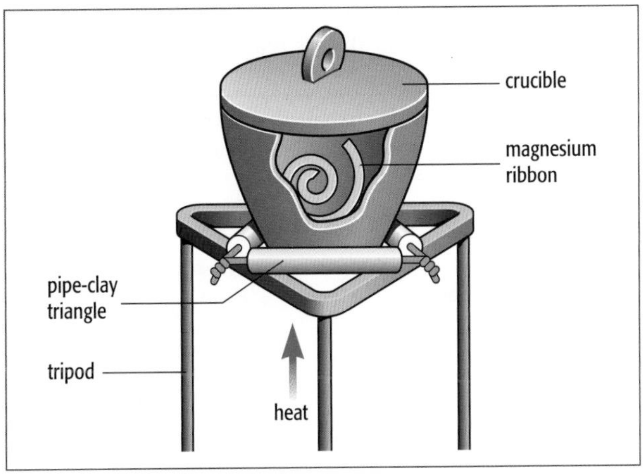

Figure 6.5 Heating magnesium in a crucible.

Several different groups in a class can prepare magnesium oxide by heating a coil of magnesium in a crucible (Figure **6.5**). The crucible must first be weighed empty, and then re-weighed with the magnesium in it. The crucible is then heated strongly. Air is allowed in by occasionally lifting the lid very carefully. Solid must not be allowed to escape as a white smoke. After a while the lid may be taken off and the open crucible heated strongly. The crucible and products are then allowed to cool before re-weighing.

Exam tip

Make sure you are familar with this type of quantitative experiment, particularly the need to re-weigh until there is no further change in mass. This 'heating to constant mass' is a way of making sure the reaction has completely finished.

The increase in mass is due to the oxygen that has now combined with the magnesium. The mass of magnesium used and the mass of magnesium oxide produced can be found from the results. Here are some results obtained from this experiment:

(a) mass of empty crucible + lid = 8.52 g
(b) mass of crucible + lid + magnesium = 8.88 g
(c) mass of crucible + lid + magnesium oxide = 9.12 g
mass of magnesium ($b - a$) = 0.36 g
mass of magnesium oxide ($c - a$) = 0.60 g
(d) mass of oxygen combined with magnesium
= 0.60 − 0.36 = 0.24 g

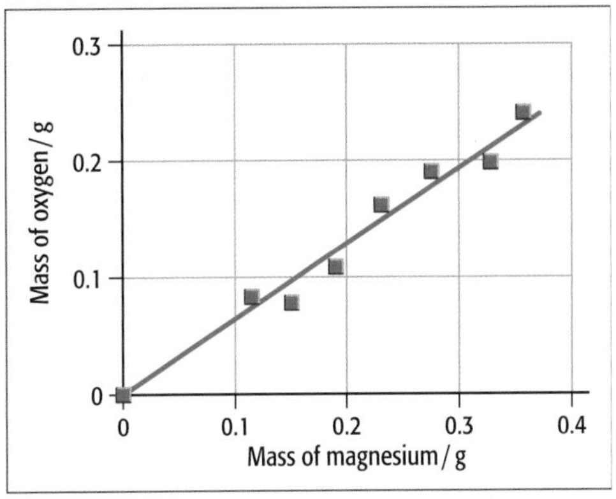

Figure 6.6 A graph of the results obtained from heating magnesium in air. The graph shows the mass of oxygen (from the air) that reacts with various masses of magnesium.

The results of the various experiments in the class can be plotted on a graph. The mass of oxygen combined with the magnesium (y-axis) is plotted against the mass of magnesium used (x-axis). Figure **6.6** shows some results obtained from this experiment.

The results show that:

- the more magnesium used, the more oxygen combines with it from the air and the more magnesium oxide is produced
- the graph is a straight line, showing that the ratio of magnesium to oxygen in magnesium oxide is fixed. A definite compound is formed by a chemical reaction.

- A particular compound always contains the same elements.
- These elements are always present in the same proportions by mass.
- It does not matter where the compound is found or how it is made.
- These proportions cannot be changed.

For example, magnesium oxide always contains 60% magnesium and 40% oxygen by mass; and ammonium nitrate always contains 35% nitrogen, 60% oxygen and 5% hydrogen by mass.

Similar experiments can be done to show that the water of crystallisation present in a particular hydrated salt, for example hydrated copper(II) sulfate ($CuSO_4.5H_2O$), is always the same fraction of the total mass of the salt.

Reacting amounts of substance

Relative formula masses can also be used to calculate the amounts of compounds reacted together or produced in reactions. Here is an example.

If 0.24 g of magnesium react with 0.16 g of oxygen to produce 0.40 g of magnesium oxide (Figure 6.5), how much magnesium oxide (MgO) will be produced by burning 12 g of magnesium?

We have

0.24 g Mg producing 0.40 g MgO

so $1\,\text{g Mg produces } \frac{0.40}{0.24}\,\text{g MgO}$

$= 1.67\,\text{g MgO}$

so $12\,\text{g Mg produces } 12 \times 1.67\,\text{g MgO}$

$= 20\,\text{g MgO}$

Calculations of quantities like these are a very important part of chemistry. These calculations show how there is a great deal of information 'stored' in chemical formulae and equations. The equation for the reaction between magnesium and oxygen defines the proportions in which the two elements **always** react (Figure 6.7).

Magnesium reacts with oxygen to form magnesium oxide. Work out the reacting masses and the product mass.

$2Mg \quad + \quad O_2 \quad \rightarrow \quad 2MgO$

2 magnesium atoms + 2 oxygen atoms → 2 magnesium atoms + 2 oxygen atoms

Mg = 24 O = 16

(2 × 24) + (2 × 16) = [(2 × 24) + (2 × 16)]
48 + 32 = [48 + 32]
48 + 32 = 80

For the product, work out the inner brackets first.

48 + 32 → 80

48 grams of magnesium react with 32 grams of oxygen to form 80 grams of magnesium oxide.

Figure 6.7 The proportions in which magnesium and oxygen react are defined by the chemical equation for the reaction.

Key ideas so far

- The atoms of the elements have an atomic mass which has been found using a mass spectrometer.
- We usually talk about the relative atomic mass of an atom rather than its actual mass in grams.
- The relative atomic mass of an element given on the Periodic Table takes into account the isotopes of that element that exist.
- By adding up the relative atomic masses of the atoms present in the formula of a compound we can find the relative formula mass of the compound.

Quick-check questions

1 The diagrams represent the structure of six different compounds (A–F).

a What type of bonding is present in compounds A, C, D, E and F?

b What type of bonding is present in compound B?

c State the simplest formula for each compound A to F.

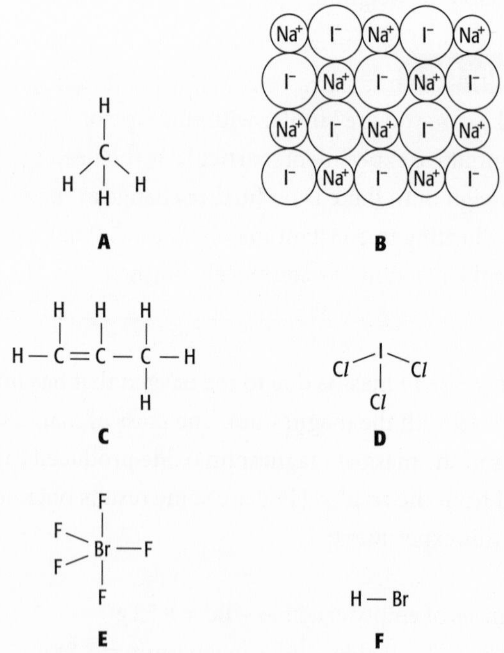

2 Calculate the relative formula masses (M_r) of the following substances:
   a oxygen, O_2
   b ammonia, NH_3
   c sulfur dioxide, SO_2
   d octane, C_8H_{18}
   e sulfuric acid, H_2SO_4
   f potassium bromide, KBr
   g copper nitrate, $Cu(NO_3)_2$
   h aluminium chloride, $AlCl_3$
   (Relative atomic masses: H = 1, C = 12, N = 14, O = 16, Al = 27, S = 32, Cl = 35.5, K = 39, Cu = 64, Br = 80)
3 Calculate the percentage by mass of nitrogen in the following fertilisers and nitrogen-containing compounds:
   a ammonium sulfate, $(NH_4)_2SO_4$
   b ammonium phosphate, $(NH_4)_3PO_4$
   c urea, $CO(NH_2)_2$
   d calcium cyanamide, $CaCN_2$
   e glycine, $CH_2(NH_2)COOH$ (an amino acid)
   (Relative atomic masses: H = 1, C = 12, N = 14, O = 16, P = 31, S = 32, Ca = 40)
4 A class of students carry out an experiment heating magnesium in a crucible (as described on page 179). The table shows the results of the experiments from the different groups in the class.

Experiment	Mass/g		
	Magnesium	Magnesium oxide	Oxygen
1	0.06	0.10	0.04
2	0.15	0.25	0.10
3	0.22	0.36	0.14
4	0.24	0.40	0.16
5	0.30	0.50	
6	0.28	0.46	
7	0.10	0.16	
8	0.20	0.32	

   a Write down the correct mass of oxygen that reacts with the magnesium in the last four experiments.
   b Plot a graph of the mass of oxygen reacted against the mass of magnesium used. Draw in the line of best fit for these points.
   c Comment on what this graph line shows about the composition of magnesium oxide.

6.2 The mole and chemical formulae

A particular compound always contains the same elements. They are always present in a fixed ratio by mass (Figure **6.8**, overleaf). These two experimental results were of great historical importance in developing the ideas of chemical formulae and the bonding of atoms. How can we make the link between mass ratios and the chemical formula of a compound? To do this, we need to use the idea of the **mole**.

The mole – the chemical counting unit

When carrying out an experiment, a chemist cannot weigh out a single atom or molecule and then react it with another one. Atoms and molecules are simply too small. A 'counting unit' must be found that is useful in practical chemistry. This idea is not unusual when dealing with large numbers of small objects. For example, banks weigh coins rather than count them – they know that a fixed number of a particular coin will always have the same mass. The number of sweets in a jar can be estimated from their mass. Assuming that you know the mass of one sweet, you could calculate how many sweets were in the jar from their total mass. How can we estimate the number of iron atoms in an iron block? Again, we can try to link mass to the number of items present.

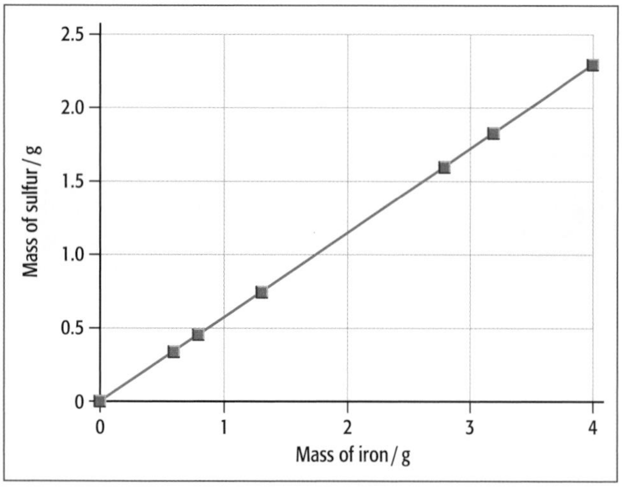

Figure 6.8 Experiments on heating iron with sulfur show that the two elements react in a fixed ratio by mass to produce iron sulfide.

Chemists count atoms and molecules by weighing them. The standard 'unit' of the 'amount' of a substance is taken as the relative formula mass of the substance in grams. This 'unit' is called one mole (1 mol) of the substance (mol is the symbol or shortened form of mole or moles). The unit 'moles' is used to measure amounts of elements and compounds. The idea becomes clearer if we consider some examples (Table **6.4**).

One mole of each of these different substances contains the **same** number of atoms, molecules or formula units. That number per mole has been worked out by several different experimental methods. It is named after the nineteenth-century Italian chemist, Amedeo Avogadro, and is 6.02×10^{23} per mole (this is called the **Avogadro constant**, and is given the symbol *L*). The vast size of this constant shows just how small atoms are! For instance, it has been estimated that 6.02×10^{23} soft-drink cans stacked together would cover the surface of the Earth to a depth of 200 miles.

- One mole of a substance has a mass equal to its relative formula mass in grams.
- One mole of a substance contains 6.02×10^{23} (the Avogadro constant) atoms, molecules or formula units, depending on the substance considered.

Calculations involving the mole

You can find the **molar mass** (mass of one mole) of any substance by following these steps.

1. Write down the formula of the substance; for example, ethanol is C_2H_5OH.
2. Work out its relative formula mass; for example, ethanol contains two carbon atoms ($A_r = 12$), six hydrogen atoms ($A_r = 1$) and one oxygen atom ($A_r = 16$). So for ethanol $M_r = (2 \times 12) + (6 \times 1) + 16 = 46$.
3. Express this in grams per mole; for example, the molar mass of ethanol is 46 g/mol.

For any given mass of a substance:

$$\text{number of moles} = \frac{\text{mass}}{\text{molar mass}}$$

where the mass is in grams and the molar mass is in grams per mole. The triangle shown can be a useful

Substance	Formula	Relative formula mass, M_r	Mass of one mole (molar mass)	This mass (1 mol) contains
carbon	C	12	12 g	6.02×10^{23} carbon atoms
iron	Fe	56	56 g	6.02×10^{23} iron atoms
hydrogen	H_2	$2 \times 1 = 2$	2 g	6.02×10^{23} H_2 molecules
oxygen	O_2	$2 \times 16 = 32$	32 g	6.02×10^{23} O_2 molecules
water	H_2O	$(2 \times 1) + 16 = 18$	18 g	6.02×10^{23} H_2O molecules
magnesium oxide	MgO	$24 + 16 = 40$	40 g	6.02×10^{23} MgO 'formula units'
calcium carbonate	$CaCO_3$	$40 + 12 + (3 \times 16) = 100$	100 g	6.02×10^{23} $CaCO_3$ 'formula units'
silicon(IV) oxide	SiO_2	$28 + (2 \times 16) = 60$	60 g	6.02×10^{23} SiO_2 'formula units'

Table 6.4 Calculating the mass of one mole of various substances.

aid to memory: cover the quantity to be found and you are left with how to work it out.

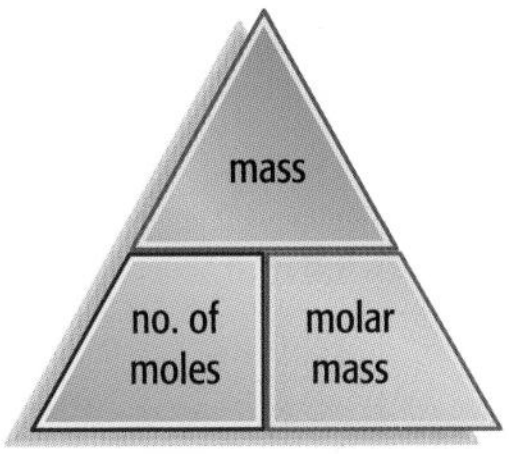

This shows that if we need to calculate the mass of one mole of some substance, the straightforward way is to work out the relative formula mass of the substance and write the word 'grams' after it. Using the above equation it is possible to convert any mass of a particular substance into moles, or vice versa. We shall look at two examples.

1 How many moles are there in 60 g of sodium hydroxide?
We have: the relative formula mass of sodium hydroxide is

$M_r(NaOH) = 23 + 16 + 1 = 40$
molar mass of NaOH = 40 g/mol

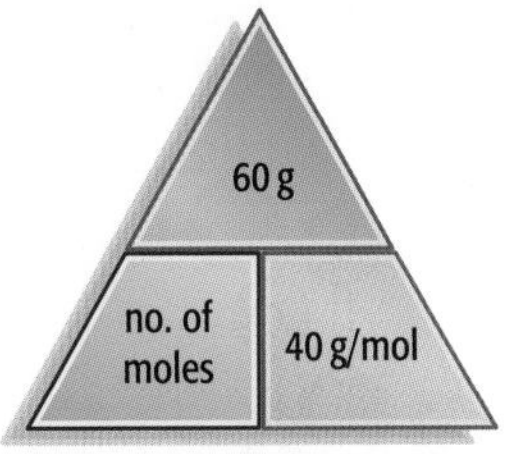

$$\text{number of moles} = \frac{\text{mass}}{\text{molar mass}}$$

$$= \frac{60\ \text{g}}{40\ \text{g/mol}}$$

number of moles = 1.5

2 What is the mass of 0.5 mol of copper(II) sulfate crystals?
We have: the relative formula mass of hydrated copper(II) sulfate is

$M_r(CuSO_4.5H_2O) = 64 + 32 + (4 \times 16) + (5 \times 18) = 250$
molar mass of $CuSO_4.5H_2O$ = 250 g/mol

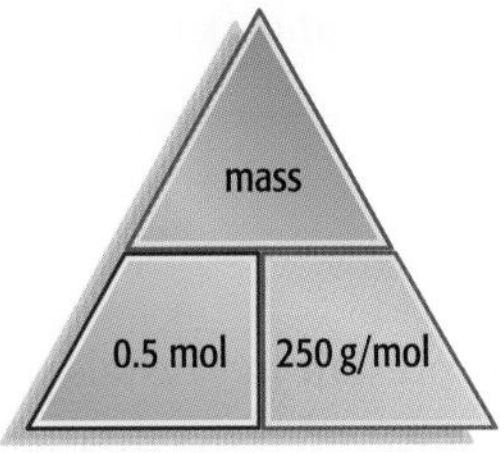

$$\text{number of moles} = \frac{\text{mass}}{\text{molar mass}}$$

Therefore,

$$0.5\ \text{mol} = \frac{\text{mass}}{250\ \text{g/mol}}$$

$$\text{mass} = 0.5 \times 250 = 125\ \text{g}$$

Working out chemical formulae

The idea of the mole means that we can now work out chemical formulae from experimental data on combining masses. It provides the link between the mass of an element in a compound and the number of its atoms present.

In the experiment to make magnesium oxide (see Section **6.1**), a constant ratio was found between the reacting amounts of magnesium and oxygen. If 0.24 g of magnesium is burnt, then 0.40 g of magnesium oxide is formed. This means that 0.24 g of magnesium combines with 0.16 g of oxygen (0.40 – 0.24 = 0.16 g). We can now use these results to find the formula of magnesium oxide (Figure **6.9**).

The formula of magnesium oxide tells us that 1 mol of magnesium atoms combine with 1 mol of oxygen atoms. The atoms react in a 1 : 1 ratio to form a giant ionic lattice of Mg^{2+} and O^{2-} ions.

For giant structures, the formula of the compound is the simplest whole-number formula – in this example, MgO. A formula found by this method is also known as an **empirical formula**.

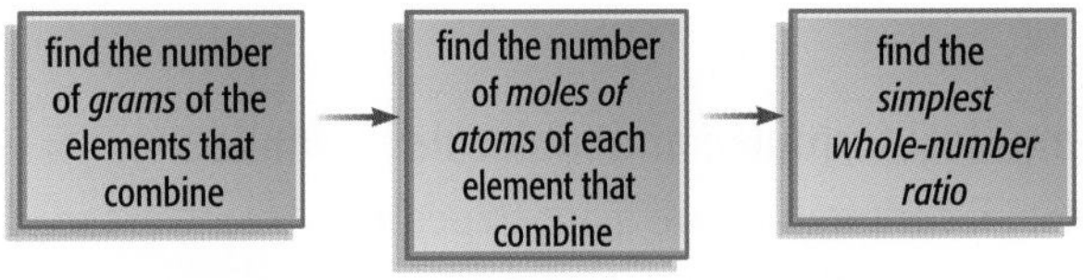

	Mg	O
mass combined	0.24 g	0.16 g
molar mass	24 g/mol	16 g/mol
number of moles	0.01 mol	0.01 mol
simplest ratio	1	1
Formula	MgO	

Figure 6.9 Calculating the empirical formula of magnesium oxide from experimental data on the masses of magnesium and oxygen that react together.

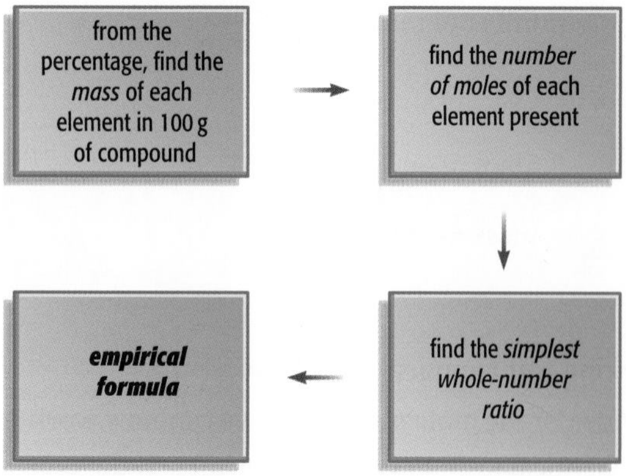

	Si	O
percentage by mass	47%	100 − 47 = 53%
mass in 100 g	47 g	53 g
molar mass	28 g/mol	16 g/mol
number of moles	1.68 mol	3.31 mol
simplest ratio	1	2
Formula	SiO_2	

Figure 6.10 Finding the empirical formula of silicon(IV) oxide from percentage mass data.

Silicon(IV) oxide is a giant covalent structure. A sample of silicon oxide is found to contain 47% by mass of silicon. How can we find its empirical formula? This is done in Figure **6.10**. The empirical formula of silicon(IV) oxide is SiO_2. It consists of a giant molecular lattice of covalently bonded silicon and oxygen atoms in a ratio 1 : 2. Since it is a giant structure, the formula we use for this compound is SiO_2.

Empirical formulae and molecular formulae

Not all compounds are giant structures – some are made up of simple molecules. Here we sometimes have to make a distinction between the empirical formula and the actual formula of the molecule, the **molecular formula**.

Phosphorus burns in air to produce white clouds of phosphorus oxide. From experiments it is found that the oxide contains 44% phosphorus. The empirical formula of phosphorus oxide is P_2O_5 (Table **6.5**). However, it is found experimentally that its relative molecular mass (M_r) is 284. The sum of the relative atomic masses in

	P	O
percentage by mass	44%	100 − 44 = 56%
mass in 100 g	44 g	56 g
molar mass	31 g/mol	16 g/mol
number of moles	1.4 mol	3.5 mol
simplest ratio	1	2.5
or	2	5
Formula	P_2O_5	

Table 6.5 Calculating the empirical formula of phosphorus oxide.

the empirical formula (P_2O_5) is $(2 \times 31) + (5 \times 16) = 142$. The actual relative molecular mass is twice this value. Therefore the molecular formula of phosphorus oxide is $(P_2O_5)_2$ or P_4O_{10}. The empirical formula is **not** the actual molecular formula of phosphorus oxide. A molecule of phosphorus oxide contains four P atoms and ten O atoms (Figure **6.11**).

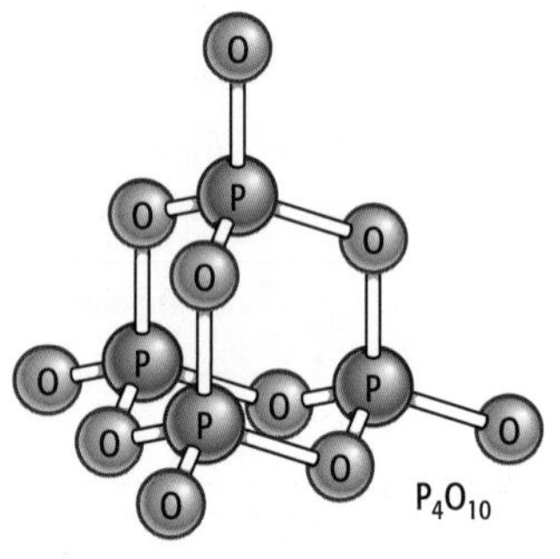

Figure 6.11 Phosphorus oxide, P_4O_{10}.

- The empirical formula of a compound is the simplest whole-number formula.
- For simple molecular compounds, the empirical formula may not be the actual molecular formula. The molecular formula must be calculated using the relative molecular mass (M_r) of the compound as found by experiment.

Hydrated salts

The mass of water present in crystals of hydrated salts is always a fixed proportion of the total mass. The formula of such a salt can be worked out by a method similar to that used to calculate the empirical formula of a compound.

If 5.0 g of hydrated copper(II) sulfate crystals are heated to drive off the water of crystallisation, the remaining solid has a mass of 3.2 g. The ratio of the salt and water in the crystal can be calculated. This gives the formula of the crystals (Table **6.6**).

	$CuSO_4$	H_2O
mass	3.2 g	5.0 − 3.2 = 1.8 g
molar mass	160 g/mol	18 g/mol
number of moles	0.02 mol	0.10 mol
simplest ratio	1	5
Formula	$CuSO_4.5H_2O$	

Table 6.6 Calculating the formula of hydrated copper(II) sulfate.

Key ideas so far

- The mole is the measure of 'amount of substance' in chemistry.
- One mole of a substance contains the Avogadro constant of characteristic particles (atoms, molecules, etc.) of that substance.
- In practical terms, one mole of a substance is the formula mass in grams of that substance.
- Using the concept of the mole it is possible to work out the empirical formula of a substance from data on the mass of the elements in a compound.
- If the relative formula mass of the compound is known then it is possible to work out the actual molecular formula of the compound from the empirical formula.

Quick-check questions

1 One of the ores of copper is the mineral chalcopyrite. A laboratory analysis of a sample showed that 15.15 g of chalcopyrite had the following composition by mass: copper 5.27 g and iron 4.61 g. Sulfur is the only other element present. Use these figures to find the empirical formula of chalcopyrite.
(Relative atomic masses: S = 32, Fe = 56, Cu = 64)

2 A sample of antifreeze has the composition by mass: 38.7% carbon, 9.7% hydrogen, 51.6% oxygen.
(Relative atomic masses: H = 1, C = 12, O = 16)

a Calculate its empirical formula.

b The relative molecular mass of the compound is 62. What is its molecular formula?

c This compound is a diol. The molecule contains two alcohol groups attached to different carbon atoms. Suggest a structure for the compound.

6.3 The mole and chemical equations

We can now see that the chemical equation for a reaction is more than simply a record of what is produced. In addition to telling us **what** the reactants and products are, it tells us **how much** product we can expect from particular amounts of reactants. When iron reacts with sulfur, the equation is:

$$Fe + S \rightarrow FeS$$

This indicates that we need equal numbers of atoms of iron and sulfur to react. We know that 1 mol of iron (56 g) and 1 mol of sulfur (32 g) contain the same numbers of atoms. Reacting these amounts should give us 1 mol of iron(II) sulfide (88 g). The equation is showing us that

Fe	+	S	→	FeS
1 mol		1 mol		1 mol
56 g		32 g		88 g

The mass of the product is equal to the total mass of the reactants. This is the law of conservation of mass, which we met in Chapter 4. Although the atoms have rearranged themselves, their total mass remains the same. A chemical equation must be balanced. In practice, we may not want to react such large amounts. We could scale down the quantities (that is, use **smaller** amounts). However, the mass of iron and the mass of sulfur must always be in the ratio 56 : 32.

We could use:

Fe	+	S	→	FeS
5.6 g		3.2 g		8.8 g

If we tried to react 5 g of sulfur with 5.6 g of iron, the excess sulfur would remain unreacted. Only 3.2 g of sulfur could react with 5.6 g of iron: 1.8 g of sulfur (5.0 − 3.2 = 1.8 g) would remain unreacted.

- When we write a chemical equation, we are indicating the **number of moles** of reactants and products involved in the reaction.

The reacting amounts given by an equation can also be scaled up (that is, use **larger** amounts). In industry, tonnes of chemical reactants may be used, but the ratios given by the equation still apply. The manufacture of lime is important for the cement industry and agriculture. Lime is made by heating limestone in lime kilns. The reaction is an example of thermal decomposition:

calcium carbonate	→	calcium oxide	+	carbon dioxide
$CaCO_3$	→	CaO	+	CO_2
1 mol		1 mol		1 mol
$40 + 12 + (3 \times 16)$ $= 100\,g$		$40 + 16$ $= 56\,g$		$12 + (2 \times 16)$ $= 44\,g$

This can be scaled up to work in tonnes:

100 tonnes	56 tonnes	44 tonnes

Similarly, if 10 tonnes of calcium carbonate were heated, we should expect to produce 5.6 tonnes of lime (calcium oxide).

Calculating reacting amounts – a chemical 'footbridge'

We can use the idea of the mole to find reactant or product masses from the equation for a reaction. There are various ways of doing these calculations. The balanced equation itself can be used as a numerical 'footbridge' between the two sides of the reaction (Figure **6.12**).

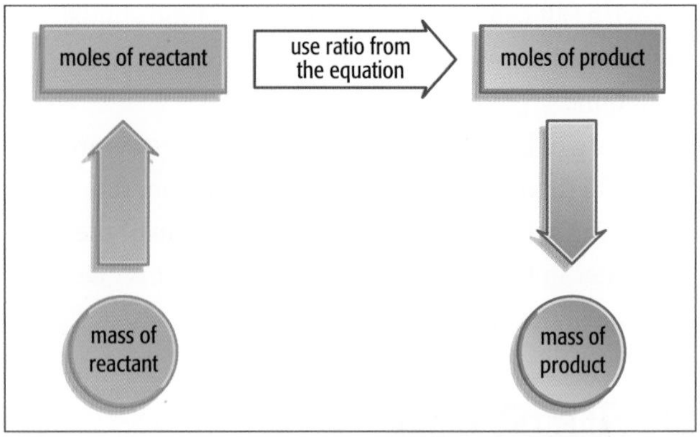

Figure 6.12 A chemical 'footbridge'. Following the sequence 'up–across–down' helps to relate the mass of product made to the mass of reactant used. The 'bridge' can, of course, be used in the reverse direction.

We shall consider an example. What mass of aluminium oxide is produced when 9.2 g of aluminium metal reacts completely with oxygen gas?

To answer this question, we first work out the balanced equation:

$$4Al \quad + \quad 3O_2 \quad \rightarrow \quad 2Al_2O_3$$

↑ ratio = 4 mol : 2 mol ↓

9.2 g mass = ?

Then we work through the steps of the 'footbridge'.

- *Step 1* (the 'up' stage): Convert 9.2 g of Al into moles:

  $$\text{number of moles} = \frac{9.2\,g}{27\,g/mol} = 0.34\,mol$$

- *Step 2* (the 'across' stage): Use the ratio from the equation to work out how many moles of Al_2O_3 are produced:

  4 mol of Al produce 2 mol of Al_2O_3

  so

  0.34 mol of Al produce 0.17 mol of Al_2O_3

- *Step 3* (the 'down' stage): Work out the mass of this amount of aluminium oxide (the relative formula mass of Al_2O_3 is 102):

  $$0.17\,mol = \frac{\text{mass}}{102\,g/mol}$$

  so

  $$\text{mass of } Al_2O_3 \text{ produced} = 0.17 \times 102\,g = 17.3\,g$$

Exam tip

Remember to read questions on reacting masses carefully. If you set out the calculation carefully, using the equation as we have done here, you will be able to see which substances are relevant to your calculation.

Remember, too, to take the balancing numbers into account in making your calculation (this is called the **stoichiometry** of the equation).

Exam tip

In carrying out a reaction, one of the reactants may be present in excess. Some of this reactant will be left over at the end of the reaction.

The **limiting reactant** is the one that is not in excess – there will be a smaller number of moles of this reactant present, taking into account the reacting ratio from the equation.

Percentage yield and percentage purity of product

A reaction may not always yield the total amount of product predicted by the equation. The loss may be due to several factors.

- The reaction may not be totally complete.
- Errors may be made in weighing the reactants or the products.
- Material may be lost in carrying out the reaction, or in transferring and separating the product.

The equation gives us an ideal figure for the yield of a reaction; reality often produces less. This can be expressed as the **percentage yield** for a particular experiment.

Consider an example. Heating 12.4 g of copper(II) carbonate in a crucible produced only 7.0 g of copper(II) oxide. What was the percentage yield of copper(II) oxide?

$CuCO_3$	$\rightarrow$	CuO	+	CO_2
1 mol		1 mol		1 mol
$64+12+48$		$64+16$		
$= 124\,g$		$= 80\,g$		

Therefore heating 12.4 g of copper(II) carbonate should have produced 8.0 g of copper(II) oxide. So

expected yield = 8.0 g
actual yield = 7.0 g
and percentage yield = $\frac{7.0}{8.0} \times 100 = 87.5\%$

In other, more complex, reactions, a particular product may be contaminated by other products or unreacted material. The 'crude' product may prove to contain less than 100% of the required substance.

The **percentage purity** of a chemical product can be calculated in a similar way to the percentage yield. The purity of a chemical for use in the laboratory is usually displayed on the container (Figure **6.13**), for instance.

Information on the purity of a particular chemical is important in many situations. This is particularly true for compounds that are to be used medically. Preparations of such compounds undergo rigorous testing and repeated purifications, by methods such as recrystallisation or re-distillation, before they are marketed.

In Chapter **4** we saw that the copper used for electrical circuits had to be exceptionally pure (page **130**). The following calculation uses this example to show how percentage purity is calculated.

An initial crude sample of copper is prepared industrially and then tested for purity. A sample of 10.15 g of the crude copper is analysed by various methods and shown to contain 9.95 g of copper, with the remaining mass being made up of other metals.

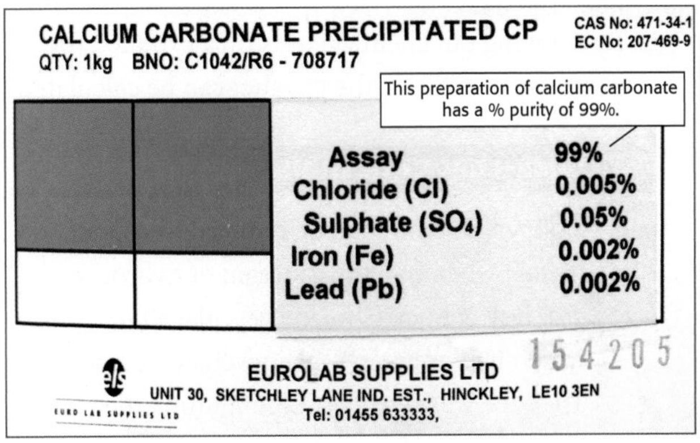

Figure 6.13 The percentage purity of a chemical product is displayed on the label. 'Sulphate' is an alternative spelling of 'sulfate'.

Generally,

$$\% \text{ purity} = \frac{\text{mass of pure product}}{\text{mass of impure product}} \times 100$$

Therefore

% purity of the copper sample

$$= \frac{\text{mass of copper in sample}}{\text{mass of impure copper}} \times 100$$

$$= \frac{9.95}{10.15} \times 100$$

$$= 98.03\%$$

This result shows that this batch of copper would need to be refined electrolytically before it could be used for electrical circuits such as those inside TVs, MP3 players and computers (Figure **6.14**).

The percentage yield of a chemical reaction and the percentage purity of a chemical product are calculated in a similar way.

$$\text{percentage yield} = \frac{\text{actual yield}}{\text{predicted yield}} \times 100$$

$$\text{percentage purity} = \frac{\text{mass of pure product}}{\text{mass of impure product}} \times 100$$

Figure 6.14 Very pure copper is required for printed circuit boards as the conductivity falls greatly with even a small amount of impurity.

Key ideas so far

- A chemical equation does not simply tell us the reactants and products of a chemical reaction. Using the idea of the mole, an equation can also give us information on the amounts of substances reacting, and being produced.
- Knowing the theoretical maximum yield from the equation enables us to calculate the percentage yield of a practical experiment or procedure.
- By carrying out chemical tests on a product, the percentage purity of the product can be calculated.

? Quick-check questions

1 Copper(II) oxide can be reduced to copper metal by heating it in a stream of hydrogen gas. Dry copper(II) oxide was placed in a tube which had previously been weighed empty. The tube was re-weighed containing the copper(II) oxide and then set up as in the diagram.

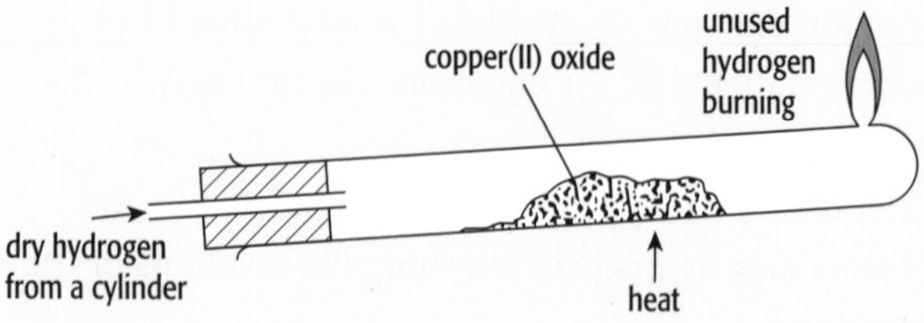

Hydrogen was passed through the tube for 15 seconds before the escaping gas was lit.
The tube was heated for a few minutes.
The apparatus was then allowed to cool with hydrogen still passing through.
The tube was re-weighed.
The process was repeated until there was no further change in mass.

a **i** Where is the most suitable place to clamp the tube?

ii Why was the hydrogen passed through for 15 seconds before the gas was lit?

iii Why was it necessary to repeat the process until there was no further change in mass?

b The results for the experiment are given below.

A	Mass of empty tube	= 46.12 g
B	Mass of tube + copper(II) oxide	= 47.72 g
C	Mass of copper(II) oxide (*B* – *A*)	= .... g
D	Mass of tube + copper	= 47.40 g
E	Mass of copper produced (*D* – *A*)	= .... g
F	Mass of oxygen in the copper(II) oxide	= .... g

i Copy out and complete the results table above.

ii How many moles of copper atoms are involved in the reaction? (Relative atomic mass: Cu = 64)

iii How many moles of oxygen atoms are involved in the reaction? (Relative atomic mass: O = 16)

iv From the results of the experiment, how many moles of oxygen atoms have combined with one mole of copper atoms?

v From the results of the experiment, what is the formula of copper(II) oxide?

vi Write a word equation for the reaction and then, using the calculated formula for copper(II) oxide, write a full balanced equation for the reaction with hydrogen.

6.4 Calculations involving gases

The volume of one mole of a gas

Many reactions, including some of those we have just considered, involve gases. Weighing solids or liquids is relatively straightforward. In contrast, weighing a gas is quite difficult. It is much easier to measure the volume of a gas. But how does gas volume relate to the number of atoms or molecules present?

In a gas, the particles are relatively far apart. Indeed, any gas can be regarded as largely empty space. Equal volumes of gases are found to contain the same number of particles (Table **6.7**); this is **Avogadro's law**. This leads to a simple rule about the volume of one mole of a gas.

Substance	Molar mass / g/mol	Molar volume / dm^3/mol	Number of particles
hydrogen (H_2)	2	24	6.02×10^{23} hydrogen molecules
oxygen (O_2)	32	24	6.02×10^{23} oxygen molecules
carbon dioxide (CO_2)	44	24	6.02×10^{23} carbon dioxide molecules
ethane (C_2H_6)	30	24	6.02×10^{23} ethane molecules

Table 6.7 The molar mass and molar volume of various gases.

- One mole of any gas occupies a volume of approximately 24 dm^3 (24 litres) at room temperature and pressure (r.t.p.).
- The **molar volume** of any gas therefore has the value 24 dm^3/mol at r.t.p.
- Remember that 1 dm^3 (1 litre) = 1000 cm^3.

Exam tip

Remember that the molar gas volume is given at the bottom of the Periodic Table you are given in the exam. The value is given as 24 dm^3 at r.t.p. Do not forget that 1 dm^3 = 1000 cm^3.

This rule applies to all gases. This makes it easy to convert the volume of any gas into moles, or moles into volume:

$$\text{number of moles} = \frac{\text{volume}}{\text{molar volume}}$$

where the volume is in cubic decimetres (dm^3) and the molar volume is 24 dm^3/mol.

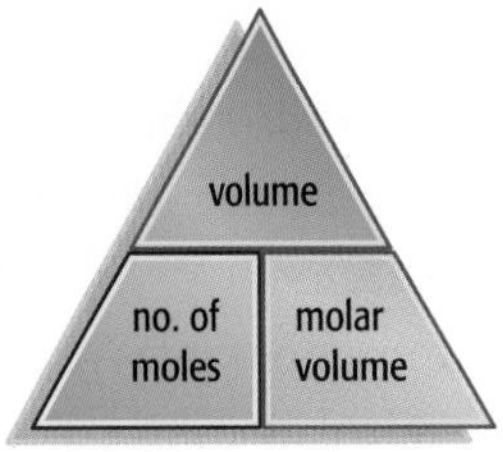

Reactions involving gases

For reactions in which gases are produced, the calculation of product volume is similar to those we have seen already.

For example, consider the reaction of sulfur burning in oxygen:

sulfur	+	oxygen	→	sulfur dioxide
$S(s)$	+	$O_2(g)$	→	$SO_2(g)$
1 mol		1 mol		1 mol
32 g		24 dm^3		24 dm^3

If 8 g of sulfur are burnt, what volume of SO_2 is produced?

We have

$$\text{number of moles of sulfur burnt} = \frac{8\,\text{g}}{32\,\text{g/mol}} = 0.25\,\text{mol}$$

From the equation

1 mol of sulfur → 1 mol of SO_2

Therefore

0.25 mol of sulfur → 0.25 mol of SO_2

So from the above rule,

$$\text{number of moles} = \frac{\text{volume}}{\text{molar volume}}$$

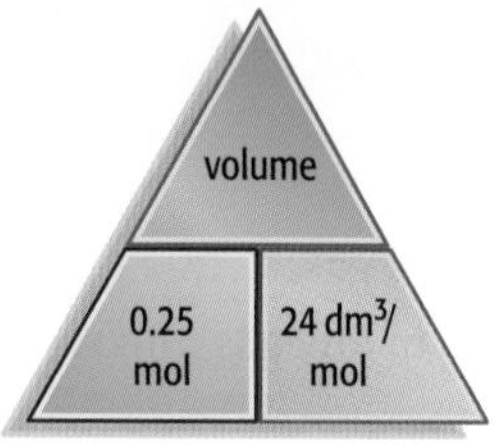

$$0.25\,\text{mol} = \frac{\text{volume}}{24\,\text{dm}^3/\text{mol}}$$

$$\text{volume of sulfur dioxide} = 0.25 \times 24\,\text{dm}^3 = 6\,\text{dm}^3 \text{ at r.t.p.}$$

The approach used is an adaptation of the 'bridge' method used earlier for calculations involving solids. It is shown in Figure **6.15**.

Some important reactions involve only gases. For such reactions, the calculations of expected yield are simplified by the fact that the value for molar volume applies to any gas.

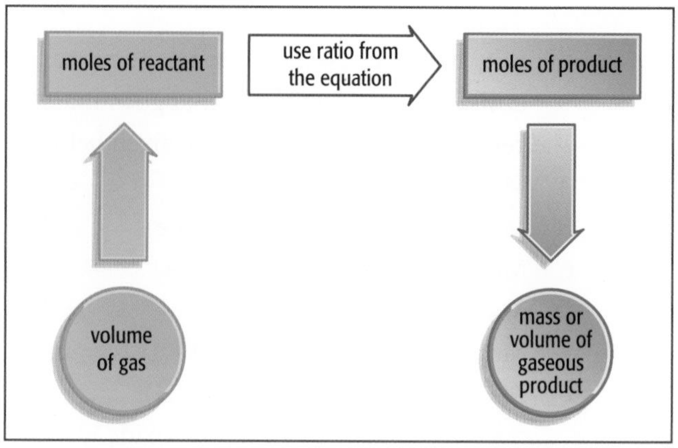

Figure 6.15 An outline of the 'footbridge' method for calculations involving gases.

For example:

hydrogen	+	chlorine	→	hydrogen chloride
$H_2(g)$	+	$Cl_2(g)$	→	$2HCl(g)$
1 mol		1 mol		2 mol
24 dm^3		24 dm^3		48 dm^3

The volumes of the gases involved are in the same ratio as the number of moles given by the equation:

$H_2(g)$	+	$Cl_2(g)$	→	$2HCl(g)$
1 volume		1 volume		2 volumes

If we react 20 cm^3 of hydrogen with sufficient chlorine, it will produce 40 cm^3 of hydrogen chloride gas.

Key ideas so far

- One mole of any gas has the same volume under the same conditions. This is known as the molar gas volume.
- At room temperature and pressure the molar gas volume is 24 dm^3.

Quick-check questions

1 Calculate the number of moles of gas there are in the following:

a 480 cm^3 of argon

b 48 dm^3 of carbon dioxide

c 1689 cm^3 of oxygen.

2 Calculate the volume in cm^3 of the following at r.t.p.
- **a** 1.5 moles of nitrogen
- **b** 0.06 moles of ammonia
- **c** 0.5 moles of chlorine.

6.5 Moles and solution chemistry

Colourful tricks can be played with chemical substances. A simple reaction can produce a 'water into wine' colour change – when two colourless solutions mixed together produce a wine-coloured mixture. These reactions all take place in solution, as do many others. The usual solvent is water. When setting up such reactions, we normally measure out the solutions by volume. To know how much of the reactants we are actually mixing, we need to know the **concentrations** of the solutions.

The concentration of solutions

When a chemical substance (the **solute**) is dissolved in a volume of **solvent**, we can measure the 'quantity' of solute in two ways. We can measure either its **mass** (in grams) or its **amount** (in moles). The final volume of the **solution** is normally measured in cubic decimetres, dm^3 ($1\,dm^3 = 1$ litre or $1000\,cm^3$). When we measure the mass of the solute in grams, it is the **mass concentration** that we obtain, in grams per cubic decimetre of solution (g/dm^3).

But it is more useful to measure the amount in moles, in which case we get the **molar concentration** in moles per cubic decimetre of solution (mol/dm^3):

$$\text{concentration} = \frac{\text{amount of solute}}{\text{volume of solution}}$$

- The mass concentration of a solution is measured in grams per cubic decimetre (g/dm^3).
- The molar concentration of a solution is measured in moles per cubic decimetre (mol/dm^3).
- When 1 mol of a substance is dissolved in water and the solution is made up to $1\,dm^3$ ($1000\,cm^3$), a solution with a concentration of $1\,mol/dm^3$ is produced.

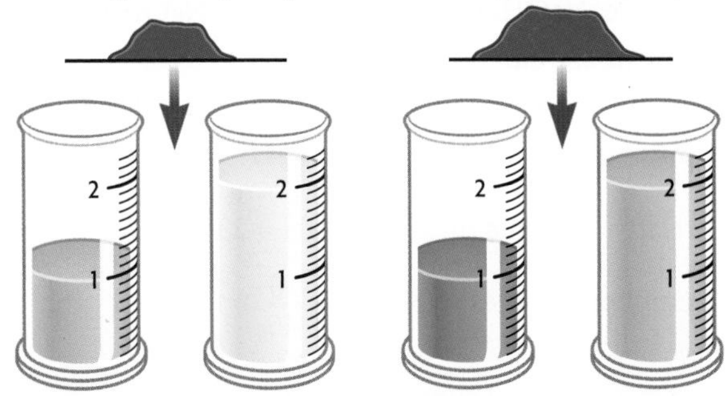

Figure 6.16 Making copper(II) sulfate solutions of different concentrations.

For example, a $1\,mol/dm^3$ solution of sodium chloride contains 58.5 g of NaCl (1 mol) dissolved in water and made up to a final volume of $1000\,cm^3$. Figure **6.16** shows how the units are expressed for solutions of differing concentrations. It also shows how solutions of the same final concentration can be made up in different ways.

Calculations using solution concentrations

The following equation is useful when working out the number of moles of a substance present in a particular solution:

$$\text{number of moles in solution} = \frac{\text{concentration}}{1000} \times \text{volume of solution (in cm}^3\text{)}$$

where concentration is in moles per cubic decimetre, but volume of solution is in cubic centimetres.

For example, how many moles of sugar are there in $500\,cm^3$ of a $3.0\,mol/dm^3$ sugar solution?

We get

$$\text{number of moles} = \frac{3.0}{1000} \times 500 = 1.5\,\text{mol}$$

In practice, a chemist still has to weigh out a substance in grams. So questions and experiments may also involve converting between moles and grams. We shall look at an example.

Calculate the concentration of a solution of sodium hydroxide, NaOH, that contains 10 g of NaOH in a final volume of 250 cm^3.

- *Step 1:* Find out how many moles of NaOH are present:

relative formula mass of NaOH = 23 + 16 + 1 = 40

$$\text{number of moles of NaOH} = \frac{10}{40} = 0.25\,\text{mol}$$

- *Step 2:* Find the concentration:

$$\text{number of moles} = \frac{\text{concentration}}{1000} \times \text{volume (in cm}^3)$$

$$0.25 = \frac{\text{concentration}}{1000} \times 250$$

$$\text{concentration} = \frac{0.25 \times 1000}{250} = 1\,\text{mol/dm}^3$$

Acid–base titrations

The concentration of an unknown acid solution can be found if it is reacted with a standard solution of an alkali. A **standard solution** is one that has been carefully made up so that its concentration is known precisely. The reaction is carried out in a carefully controlled way. The volumes are measured accurately using a pipette and a burette. Just sufficient acid is added to the alkali to neutralise the alkali. This end-point is found using an indicator. The method is known as **titration**, and can be adapted to prepare a soluble salt. It is summarised in Figure **6.17**.

We shall now look at an example of the type of calculation that can be carried out. A solution of hydrochloric acid is titrated against a standard sodium hydroxide solution. It is found that 20.0 cm^3 of acid neutralise 25.0 cm^3 of 0.10 mol/dm^3 NaOH solution. What is the concentration of the hydrochloric acid solution?

The calculation goes like this.

- *Step 1:* Use information about the standard solution. How many moles of alkali are in the flask?
  We have

number of moles of NaOH

$$= \frac{\text{concentration}}{1000} \times \text{volume (in cm}^3)$$

$$= \frac{0.10}{1000} \times 2.5 = 2.5 \times 10^{-3}\,\text{mol}$$

- *Step 2:* Use the chemical equation. How many moles of acid are used?
  The equation is

$$HCl + NaOH \rightarrow NaCl + H_2O$$

1 mol   1 mol

1 mol of NaOH neutralises 1 mol of HCl and so:

2.5×10^{-3} mol of NaOH neutralise 2.5×10^{-3} mol of HCl

- *Step 3:* Use the titration value. What is the concentration of the acid?
  The acid solution contains 2.5×10^{-3} mol in 20.0 cm^3.

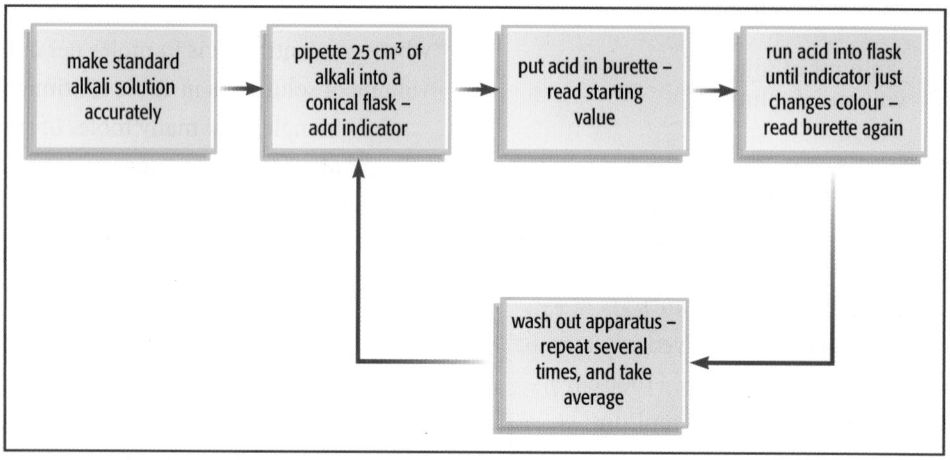

Figure 6.17 Summary of the titration method.

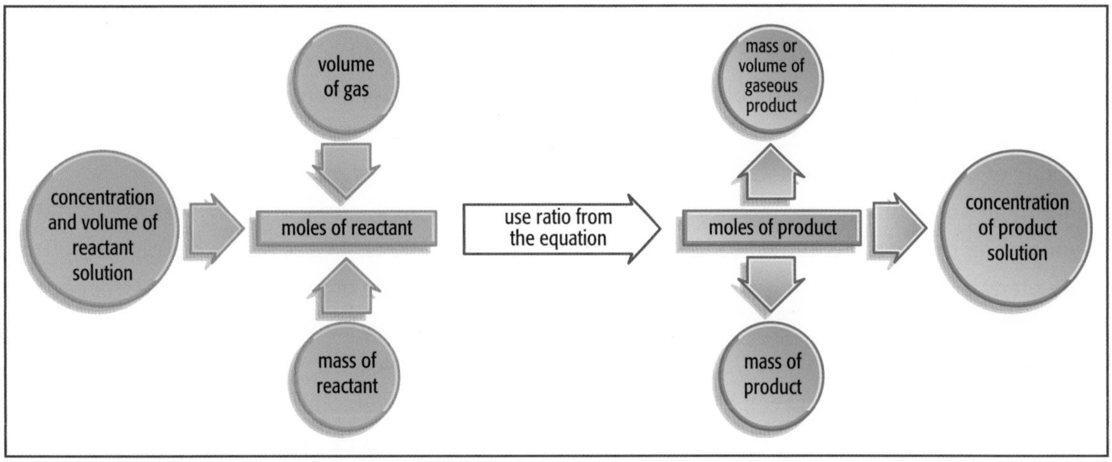

Figure 6.18 A summary of the different ways in which a balanced equation acts as a 'footbridge' in calculations.

So

$$\text{number of moles} = \frac{\text{concentration}}{1000} \times \text{volume (in cm}^3\text{)}$$

$$2.5 \times 10^{-3} = \frac{\text{concentration}}{1000} \times 20.0$$

$$\text{concentration of acid} = \frac{2.5 \times 10^{-3} \times 1000}{20}$$

$$= 0.125\,\text{mol/dm}^3$$

The method uses a further variation of the 'footbridge' approach to link the reactants and products (Figure **6.18**).

Exam tip

In any of the types of calculation in this chapter, the exam question will normally structure the calculation for you. Make sure you work your way through the question as far as you can go, so that you get as many marks as you can.

Make sure you show your working, particularly if there is more than 1 mark for a calculation, as you may well gain some marks for the working even if you made a mistake in the final stage.

Solubility curves

In general, water-soluble solids dissolve more with increasing temperature. The **solubility** of a particular solid in water can be measured over a range of temperatures up to 100 °C. The **maximum** mass of solid that will dissolve in 100 g of water is found at each temperature. Such a solution is said to be **saturated** at that temperature. The values at each temperature can then be plotted to give a **solubility curve**. The idea of solubility curves was introduced in Chapter **2** (see page **41**). Figure **6.19** shows the solubility curves for potassium nitrate and potassium chloride.

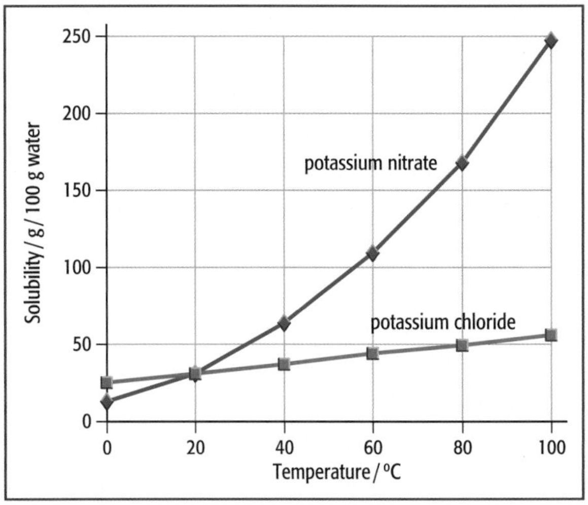

Figure 6.19 Solubility curves for potassium chloride and potassium nitrate. The solubility is measured in grams of solute per 100 g of solvent. The solute is potassium chloride or potassium nitrate and the solvent is water.

The curves in Figure **6.19** show that:

- at room temperature (20 °C), the solubility of the two salts is equal
- the solubility of both salts increases with temperature
- the solubility of potassium nitrate increases much more than that of potassium chloride with increasing temperature.

Using solubility curves

There are various ways in which data can be obtained from solubility curves.

For example, look at the curves in Figure **6.19**.

1 What mass of potassium nitrate dissolves in 100 g of water at **a** 90 °C and **b** 30 °C?

From the graph:

a at 90 °C, 205 g of KNO_3 dissolve in 100 g of water

b at 30 °C, 45 g of KNO_3 dissolve in 100 g of water.

2 What mass of potassium nitrate will crystallise out when a saturated solution in 100 g of water is cooled from 90 °C to 30 °C?

From the graph:

mass of KNO_3 crystallising = 205 – 45 = 160 g

Key ideas so far

- The concentration of a solution is the amount of solute in a given volume of solution, and is most usually expressed in mol/dm³. A 1 mol/dm³ solution contains 1 mole of solute per 1 cubic decimetre of solution.
- By using solutions of known concentration it is possible to carry out quantitative experiments on solutions. Such experiments are useful in helping us determine the concentration of unknown solutions.
- Solubility curves show how the solubility of a substance varies with temperature and can help us to predict the yield of crystals when a solution cools.

Quick-check questions

1 Calculate the concentration (in mol/dm³) of the following solutions.

a 1.0 mol of sodium hydroxide is dissolved in distilled water to make 500 cm³ of solution.

b 0.2 mol of sodium chloride is dissolved in distilled water to make 1000 cm³ of solution.

c 0.1 mol of sodium nitrate is dissolved in distilled water to make 100 cm³ of solution.

d 0.8 g of solid sodium hydroxide is dissolved in distilled water to a final volume of 1 dm³.

(Relative atomic masses: H = 1, O = 16, Na = 23, N = 14, Cl = 35.5)

2 In this question you must select from the graph a letter A, B, C, D or E, that represents the solid described in the questions. (Each letter may be used once, more than once or not at all.)

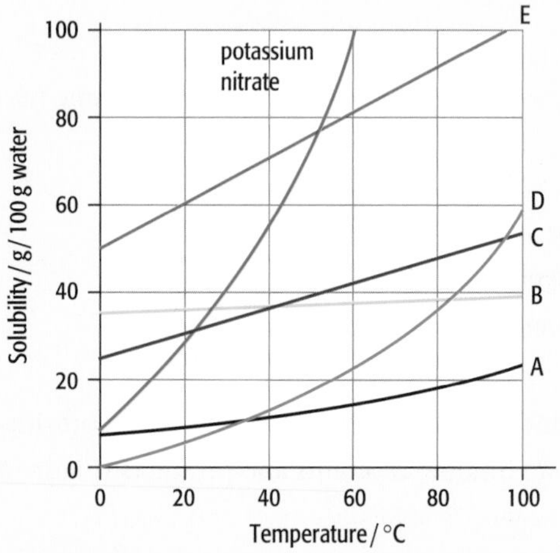

The solubility curves for potassium nitrate and five solids, A, B, C, D and E, are shown for the temperature range 0 °C to 100 °C. The solubility is given in grams of the solid that will dissolve in 100 grams of water.

Which solid:

a has the lowest solubility at 60 °C?

b has the same solubility as potassium nitrate at 52 °C?

c has a solubility that changes least with temperature?

d would give a deposit of 20 g if a saturated solution in 100 grams of water at 60 °C was cooled to 20 °C?

e would be deposited in the greatest mass if a saturated solution in 100 grams of water at 100 °C was cooled to 80 °C?

Summary

You should know that:

- the atomic masses of atoms have been found using a mass spectrometer
- many elements are made up of different isotopes – atoms of the same element with different mass numbers
- the masses of atoms are measured relative to a standard – a carbon-12 atom is fixed as having a mass of 12 exactly
- calculation of the average mass of an atom of an element must take into account the different isotopes present
- this average mass is known as the relative atomic mass
- the relative formula mass of a compound can be calculated by adding up the masses of the atoms or ions in the formula
- relative formula masses are useful for calculating the percentage by mass of an element in a compound
- experiments show that compounds are made from elements combining in fixed ratios by mass
- the mole is the unit used in chemistry to express the amount of a substance taking part in a reaction
- one mole of any substance contains the same number of constituent particles per mole (the Avogadro constant) whether they are atoms, molecules or formula units
- the idea of the mole can be used to calculate empirical formulae and molecular formulae from data on the masses of elements in a compound
- the formulae of hydrated salts can be worked out in a similar way
- the balanced chemical equation can be used to calculate the reacting masses of substances and the amount of product formed
- one mole of any gas has a volume of approximately 24 dm^3 at room temperature and pressure
- for reactions involving only gases, the ratio of the reactant volume and product volume is the same as the ratio of the number of moles in the balanced equation
- the 'concentration' of a solution can be expressed in terms of the mass of solute dissolved (in grams) – this gives the mass concentration in grams per cubic decimetre (g/dm^3)
- the 'concentration' of a solution can be more usefully expressed in terms of the amount of solute dissolved (in moles) – this gives the concentration in moles per cubic decimetre (mol/dm^3)
- the concentration values (mol/dm^3) are important in calculating the results of titration experiments
- calculations using solubilities can be used to predict the mass of crystals formed by cooling a solution.

S

Exam-style questions

S

1 Chemists use the concept of the mole to calculate the amounts of chemicals involved in a reaction.

a Define **mole**. [1]

b 3.0 g of magnesium was added to 12.0 g of ethanoic acid.

$Mg + 2CH_3COOH \rightarrow (CH_3COO)_2Mg + H_2$

The mass of one mole of Mg is 24 g.
The mass of one mole of CH_3COOH is 60 g.

i Which one, magnesium or ethanoic acid, is in excess? You must show your reasoning. [3]

ii How many moles of hydrogen were formed? [1]

iii Calculate the volume of hydrogen formed, measured at r.t.p. [2]

c In an experiment, 25.0 cm^3 of aqueous sodium hydroxide, 0.4 mol/dm^3, was neutralised by 20.0 cm^3 of aqueous oxalic acid, $H_2C_2O_4$.

$2NaOH + H_2C_2O_4 \rightarrow Na_2C_2O_4 + 2H_2O$

Calculate the concentration of the oxalic acid in mol/dm^3.

i Calculate the number of moles of NaOH in 25.0 cm^3 of 0.4 mol/dm^3 solution. [1]

ii Use your answer to part **i** and the mole ratio in the equation to find out the number of moles of $H_2C_2O_4$ in 20 cm^3 of solution. [1]

iii Calculate the concentration, mol/dm^3, of the aqueous oxalic acid. [2]

CIE IGCSE, June 2004, paper 3, q.7

2 The following method is used to make crystals of hydrated nickel sulfate.
An excess of nickel carbonate, 12.0 g, was added to 40 cm^3 of sulfuric acid, 2.0 mol/dm^3.
The unreacted nickel carbonate was filtered off and the filtrate evaporated to obtain the crystals.

$NiCO_3 + H_2SO_4 \rightarrow NiSO_4 + CO_2 + H_2O$
$NiSO_4 + 7H_2O \rightarrow NiSO_4.7H_2O$

mass of one mole of $NiSO_4.7H_2O$ = 281 g
mass of one mole of $NiCO_3$ = 119 g

a Copy the following and calculate the mass of unreacted nickel carbonate.
Number of moles of H_2SO_4 in 40 cm^3 of 2.0 mol/dm^3 acid = 0.08
Number of moles of $NiCO_3$ reacted = ...
Mass of nickel carbonate reacted = ... g
Mass of unreacted nickel carbonate = ... g [3]

b The experiment produced 10.4 g of hydrated nickel sulfate. Calculate the percentage yield.
The maximum number of moles of $NiSO_4$.$7H_2O$ that could be formed = ...
The maximum mass of $NiSO_4.7H_2O$ that could be formed = ... g
The percentage yield = ... % [3]

CIE IGCSE, November 2005, paper 3, q.6 part

3 Calcium and other minerals are essential for healthy teeth and bones.
Tablets can be taken to provide these minerals.

Healthy Bones
Each tablet contains
calcium
magnesium
zinc
copper
boron

Each tablet contains the same number of moles of $CaCO_3$ and $MgCO_3$.
One tablet reacted with excess hydrochloric acid to produce 0.24 dm^3 of carbon dioxide at r.t.p.

$$CaCO_3 + 2HCl \rightarrow CaCl_2 + CO_2 + H_2O$$
$$MgCO_3 + 2HCl \rightarrow MgCl_2 + CO_2 + H_2O$$

a Copy the sequence below and calculate how many moles of $CaCO_3$ there are in one tablet.
number of moles CO_2 = ...
number of moles of $CaCO_3$ and $MgCO_3$ = ...
number of moles of $CaCO_3$ = ... [3]

b Calculate the volume of hydrochloric acid, 1.0 mol/dm^3, needed to react with one tablet.
number of moles of $CaCO_3$ and $MgCO_3$ in one tablet = ...
Use the answer you gave in **a**.
number of moles of HCl needed to react with one tablet = ...
volume of hydrochloric acid, 1.0 mol /dm^3, needed to react with one tablet = ... [2]

CIE IGCSE, June 2003, paper 3, q.2 part

4 Experiments show that volumes of gases react together in a ratio that can be predicted from the chemical equation for the reaction.

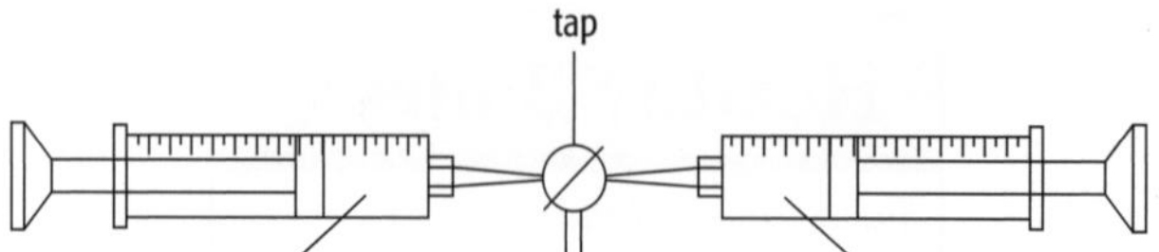

Nitrogen monoxide (NO) reacts with oxygen (O_2) to form one product, which is a brown gas.
In an experiment, 5.0 cm³ portions of oxygen were pushed from syringe **B** into syringe **A**.
After each addition, the tap was closed, the gases cooled, and then the total volume of gases remaining was measured. The results are shown in the graph.

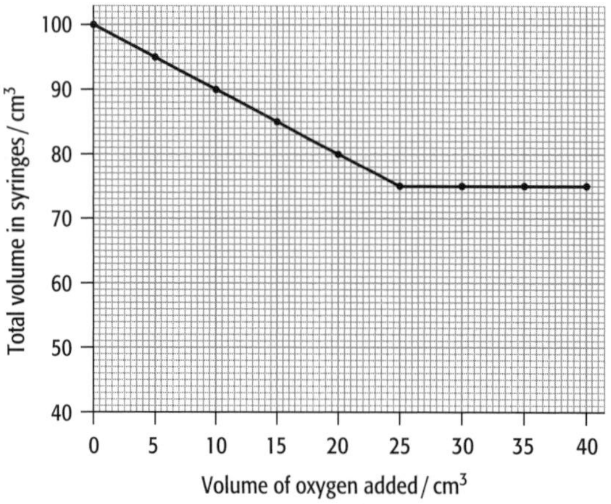

a What is the total volume of gases when the reaction is complete? [1]

b What volume of oxygen reacts with 50 cm³ of nitrogen monoxide? [1]

c What is the volume of the brown gas formed? [1]

d Copy and complete the following to work out the formula of the brown gas:

.... NO + O_2 → ....

5 cm³ ..... cm³ ..... cm³ [2]

7 How far? How fast?

This chapter covers the following ideas:

- exothermic and endothermic reactions
- experiments on heat of reaction
- (S) breaking bonds in a reaction as an endothermic process
- (S) making bonds as an exothermic process
- heat of reaction for burning fuels
- factors affecting the rate of reaction
  - surface area of reactants
  - reactant concentration
  - temperature
- the role of catalysts in a reaction
- experiments on rates of reaction
- enzymes as biological catalysts
- (S) collision theory and activation energy
- (S) photochemical reactions
  - photosynthesis
  - (S) photography using silver salts
- some reactions are reversible
- (S) chemical equilibrium
- (S) the Haber process as an industrially important reversible reaction
  - the effect of changing conditions

7.1 Energy changes in chemical reactions

Some chemical reactions are capable of releasing vast amounts of energy. For example, at the end of the Gulf War in 1991, oil and gas fires in the oil-fields were left burning out of control. The heat given out was sufficient to turn the sand around the burning wells into glass. Forest fires can rage impressively, producing overpowering waves of heat (Figure 7.1). Bringing such fires under control requires great expertise, and a great deal of courage!

Figure 7.1 A forest fire.

Yet we use similar reactions, under control, to provide heat for the home and for industry. Natural gas, which is mainly methane, is burnt under controlled conditions to produce heat for cooking in millions of homes (Figure 7.2).

Figure 7.2 A lighted gas ring on a cooker.

The reaction between methane and oxygen

Hydrocarbon molecules contain only the elements carbon and hydrogen (see page **287**). Methane is the simplest hydrocarbon molecule. When it burns, it reacts with oxygen. The products are carbon dioxide and water vapour:

methane + oxygen → carbon dioxide + water

$$CH_4(g) + 2O_2(g) \rightarrow CO_2(g) + 2H_2O(g)$$

During this reaction, as with all others, bonds are first broken and then new bonds are made (Figure 7.3). In methane molecules, carbon atoms are covalently bonded to hydrogen atoms. In oxygen gas, the atoms are held together in diatomic molecules. During the reaction, all these bonds must be broken. Chemical bonds are forces of attraction between atoms or ions. To break these bonds requires energy; energy must be taken in to pull the atoms apart.

> **Breaking** chemical bonds takes in energy from the surroundings. This is an **endothermic process.**

New bonds are then formed: between carbon and oxygen to make carbon dioxide, and between hydrogen and oxygen to form water. Forming these bonds gives out energy.

> **Making** chemical bonds gives out energy to the surroundings. This is an **exothermic process.**

When methane reacts with oxygen, the total energy given out is greater than the total energy taken in.

So, overall, this reaction gives out energy – it is an exothermic reaction. The energy is released as heat.

The overall change in energy for this exothermic reaction can be shown in an **energy level diagram** (or energy profile) (Figure 7.4). In this reaction, energy is given out because the bonds in the products (CO_2 and H_2O) are stronger than those in the reactants (CH_4 and O_2). This means that the products are more stable than the reactants.

> Some bonds are stronger than others. They require more energy to break them, but they give out more energy when they are formed.

Generally, the combustion reactions of fossil fuels such as oil and gas are exothermic. Indeed, the major characteristics that make these fuels so useful are that:

- they are easy to ignite and burn
- they are capable of releasing large amounts of energy as heat.

Other reactions are less obviously exothermic, but may have new and unusual uses. For example, the rusting reaction of iron generates heat for several hours and is used in pocket hand-warmers for expeditions to cold regions. Similar hand-warmers can be made using the heat given out by crystallisation of a solid from a super-saturated solution (Figure 7.5).

The reaction between nitrogen and oxygen

Endothermic reactions are far less common than exothermic ones. Here, energy is absorbed from the

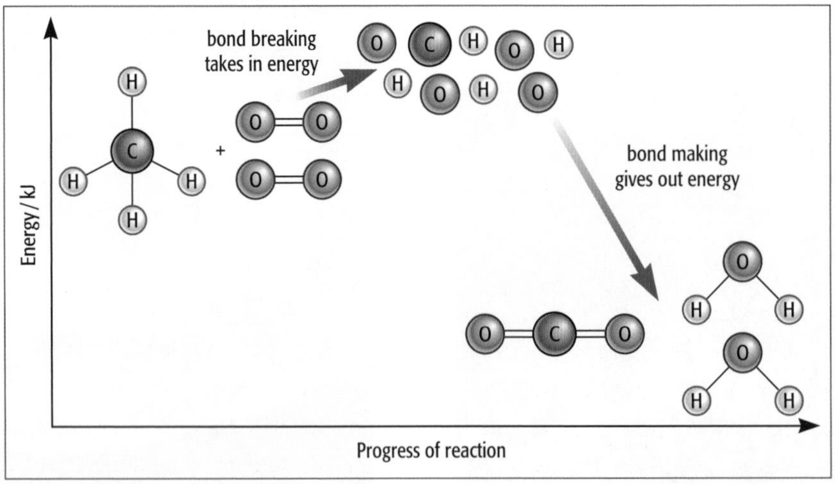

Figure 7.3 The burning of methane first involves the breaking of bonds in the reactants. This is followed by the formation of the new bonds of the products.

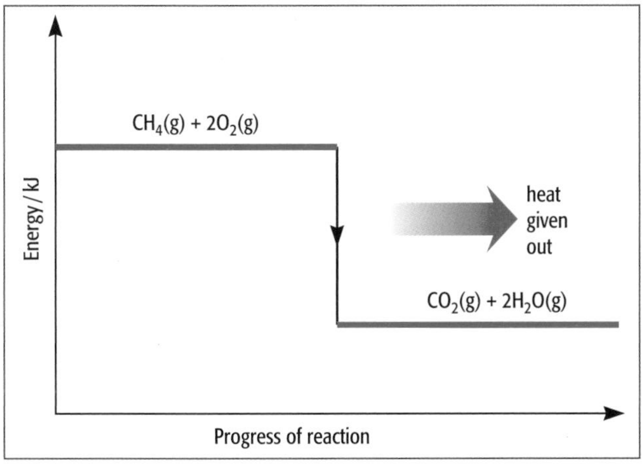

Figure 7.4 An energy profile for the burning of methane. The products are more stable than the reactants. Energy is given out to the surroundings. This is an exothermic reaction.

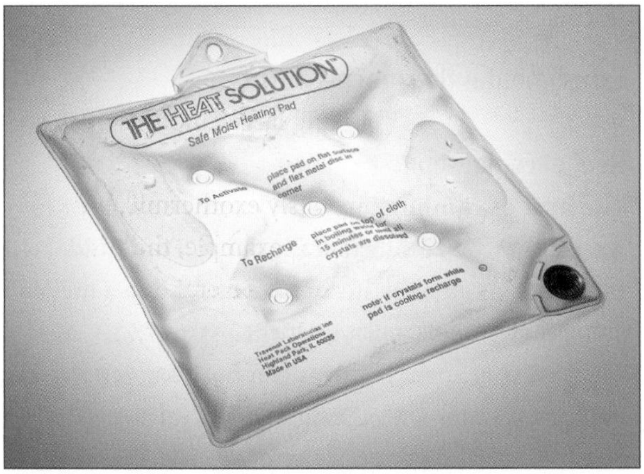

Figure 7.5 This hand-warmer depends on the heat given out when the solid crystallises out from the super-saturated solution in the warmer.

surroundings. The reaction between nitrogen and oxygen is endothermic. It is one of the reactions that take place when fuel is burnt in car engines. The equation for this reaction is:

$$\text{nitrogen} + \text{oxygen} \rightarrow \text{nitrogen monoxide}$$
$$N_2(g) + O_2(g) \rightarrow 2NO(g)$$

Here the bonding in the products is weaker than in the reactants. Overall, energy is taken in by the reaction (Figure **7.6**, overleaf).

Photosynthesis in green plants and the thermal decomposition of limestone are other important examples of endothermic reactions. They will be studied later in this chapter on pages **216** and **223**.

Heat of reaction

The energy change in going from reactants to products in a chemical reaction is known as the **heat of reaction** (Figures **7.4** and **7.6**). It is given the symbol ΔH (pronounced 'delta aitch' – the symbol Δ means 'change in'). The energy given out or taken in is measured in kilojoules (kJ); 1 kilojoule (1 kJ) = 1000 joules (1000 J). It is usually calculated per mole of a specific reactant or product (kJ/mol).

The starting point for the calculation is the reacting mixture. If a reaction gives out heat to the surroundings, the mixture has lost energy. It is an exothermic reaction. In an **EX**othermic reaction, heat **EX**its the reaction mixture. An exothermic reaction has a negative value of ΔH.

If a reaction takes in heat from the surroundings, the mixture has gained energy. It is an endothermic reaction. In an **EN**dothermic reaction, heat **EN**ters the reaction mixture. An endothermic reaction has a positive value of ΔH.

This is what we know about heat of reaction:

- for exothermic reactions, heat energy is given out (exits) and ΔH is **negative**
- for endothermic reactions, heat energy is taken in (enters) and ΔH is **positive**.

Exam tip

When trying to remember these particular terms concentrate on the first letters of the words involved: **EX**othermic means that heat **EX**its the reaction; **EN**dothermic means that heat **EN**ters the reaction.

These ideas fit with the direction of the arrows shown in the energy diagrams (Figures **7.4** and **7.6**). The heat of reaction for the burning of methane is high. This makes it a useful fuel:

$$CH_4(g) + 2O_2(g) \rightarrow CO_2(g) + 2H_2O(g) \qquad \Delta H = -728\,\text{kJ/mol}$$

Making and breaking bonds

Experiments have been carried out to find out how much energy is needed to break various covalent bonds in compounds. The average value obtained for a particular bond is known as the **bond energy** (Table **7.1**, overleaf). It is a measure of the strength of the bond.

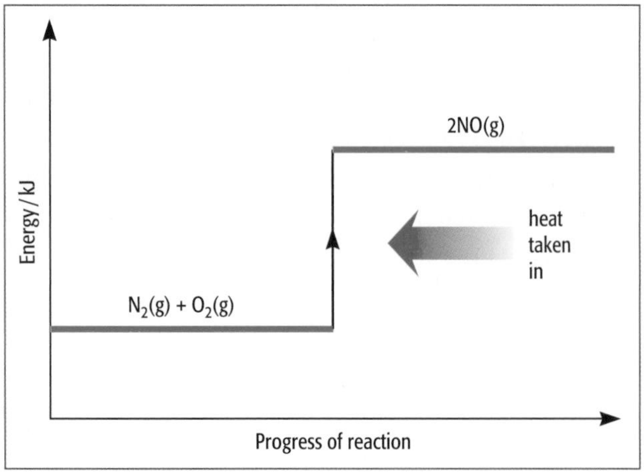

Figure 7.6 An energy profile for the reaction between nitrogen and oxygen. The products are less stable than the reactants. Energy is taken in from the surroundings. This is an endothermic reaction.

Bond	Bond energy (kJ/mol)	Comment
H—H	436	in hydrogen
C—H	435	average of four bonds in 6methane
O—H	464	in water
C—C	347	average of many compounds
O═O	498	in oxygen
C═O	803	in carbon dioxide
N≡N	945	in nitrogen

Table 7.1 The bond energies for some covalent bonds.

We can use these values to find the heat of reaction for the burning of methane. The equation is

$$CH_4(g) + 2O_2(g) \rightarrow CO_2(g) + 2H_2O(g)$$

The left-hand side involves **bond breaking** and needs energy:

four C—H bonds	$4 \times 435 = 1740$ kJ/mol	
two O═O bonds	$2 \times 498 = 996$ kJ/mol	
total energy needed	$= 2736$ kJ/mol	

The right-hand side involves **bond making** and gives out energy:

two C═O bonds	$2 \times 803 = 1606$ kJ/mol	
four O—H bonds	$4 \times 464 = 1856$ kJ/mol	
total energy given out	$= 3462$ kJ/mol	

The heat of reaction, ΔH, is the energy change on going from reactants to products. So for the burning of methane,

heat of reaction = energy difference

ΔH = (energy needed to break bonds) – (energy given out when bonds form)

$\Delta H = 2736 - 3462$

$\Delta H = -726$ kJ/mol

Exam tip

It is useful to remember that combustion reactions are always exothermic.

Experimental thermochemistry

Heat of combustion

The **heat of combustion** is the energy change of a reaction when a substance is burnt. For liquid fuels such as ethanol, it can be found using a metal **calorimeter** and a spirit burner (Figure 7.7).

The experiment involves heating a known volume of water with the flame from burning ethanol. The temperature rise of the water is measured. From this, the heat energy given to the

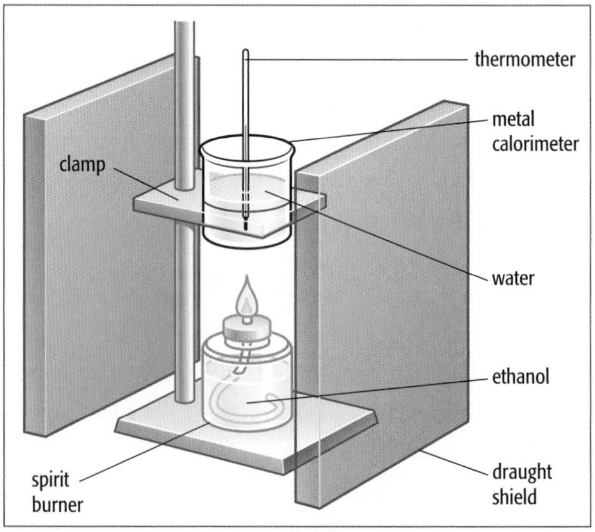

Figure 7.7 Apparatus for finding the heat of combustion of ethanol.

water by burning a known amount of ethanol can be worked out. There is a method for working out a precise value for the heat of combustion of a fuel from this type of experiment. However, that is currently beyond the requirements of the syllabus.

This type of experiment can be useful, though, for comparing different fuels to see which would give the most heat to warm a known amount of water. The amount of liquid fuel put into the spirit burner would need to be controlled. The method could also be adapted to compare the heat produced by the same mass of different solid fuels.

Heat of neutralisation

Polystyrene is a good heat insulator and is used to make disposable cups for warm drinks. These cups can be used as simple calorimeters to measure the temperature rise of exothermic reactions between solutions (Figure 7.8). The solutions are mixed in a polystyrene cup and the initial temperature is measured quickly. The mixture is then stirred well with the thermometer. The temperature is checked frequently during the reaction, and the maximum temperature is recorded.

This equipment can be used to measure the heat energy given out during the neutralisation reactions between acids and alkalis. This energy change is known as the **heat of neutralisation**. By using solutions whose concentrations are known, it can be calculated for a particular combination of acid and alkali. For a strong acid reacting with a strong alkali, this value is 57 kilojoules of heat given out per mole of water produced; that is −57 kJ/mol.

The method can also be adapted for reactions involving

- a solid base and an acid
- a solid carbonate and an acid, and
- displacement reactions between a metal and a solution of a salt of a less reactive metal.

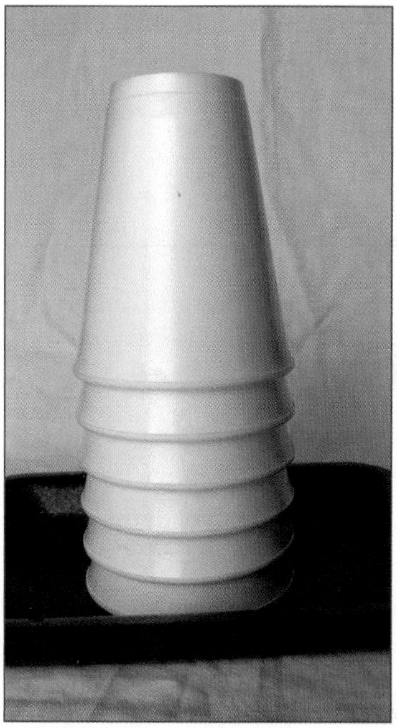

Figure 7.8 Polystyrene cups can be used as 'calorimeters' because of their good heat insulation properties.

Activation energy

Although the vast majority of reactions are exothermic, only a few are totally spontaneous and begin without help at normal temperatures; for example, sodium or potassium reacting with water. More usually, energy is required to start the reaction. When fuels are burnt, for example, energy is needed to ignite them (Figure 7.9). This energy may come from a spark, a match or sunlight. It is called the **activation energy** (given the symbol E_A). It is required because initially some bonds must be broken before any reaction can take place.

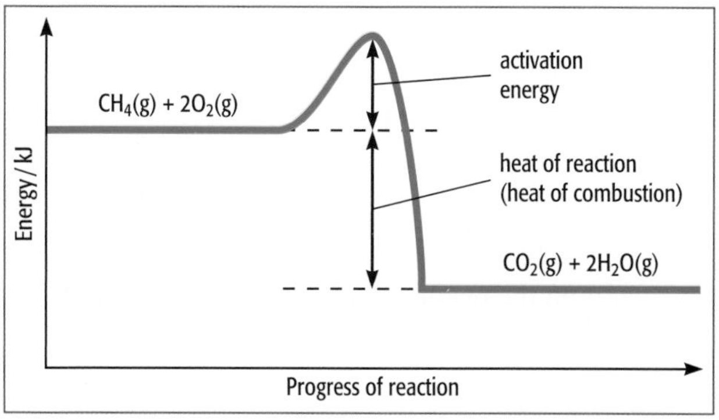

Figure 7.9 An energy profile for the burning of methane, showing the need for activation energy to start the reaction.

Sufficient atoms or fragments of molecules must be freed for the new bonds to begin forming. Once started, the energy released as new bonds are formed causes the reaction to continue.

Exam tip

For a chemical reaction to happen, some bonds in the reactants must first break before any new bonds can be formed. That is why all reactions have an activation energy.

All reactions require some activation energy. For the reaction of sodium or potassium with water the activation energy is low, and there is enough energy available from the surroundings at room temperature for the reaction to begin spontaneously. Other exothermic reactions have a higher activation energy; for example, the burning of magnesium can be started with heat from a Bunsen burner. Reactions can be thought of as the result of collisions between atoms, molecules or ions. In many of these collisions, the colliding particles do not have enough energy to react, and just bounce apart, rather like 'dodgem cars'. A chemical reaction will only happen if the total energy of the colliding particles is greater than the required activation energy of the reaction.

Key ideas so far

- Chemical reactions that give out heat are said to be exothermic.
- Reactions that take in heat are said to be endothermic.
- The breaking of bonds in the reactants in a chemical reaction is an endothermic process – it requires energy.
- The making of bonds to form the products of a chemical reaction gives out energy – it releases energy.
- If the energy released in making the products is greater than the energy needed to break the bonds in the reactants, then the reaction is exothermic.
- The combustion of methane gives out a considerable amount of energy, which is why methane is such a good fuel.
- All reactions involve a change in heat energy. This change in heat energy is given the symbol ΔH (pronounced 'delta aitch' – the symbol Δ means 'change in').
- All reactions need an input of energy in order to start off the reaction. This energy is known as the activation energy for the reaction.

Quick-check questions

1 Which type of reaction takes in heat from its surroundings?

2 Is bond breaking an endothermic or an exothermic process?

3 Why is a polystyrene cup useful for carrying out thermochemistry experiments with solutions?

4 Hydrogen peroxide decomposes to produce water and oxygen. The equation is

$$2H_2O_2(g) \rightarrow 2H_2O(g) + O_2(g)$$

Using the following values, calculate the heat change for the reaction and say whether it is exothermic or endothermic.

Bond energies:
H—H = 436 kJ/mol;
O—O = 144 kJ/mol;
O=O = 498 kJ/mol;
O—H = 464 kJ/mol.

5 Draw a reaction profile for the following reaction, which is exothermic.

$$Zn(s) + CuSO_4(aq) \rightarrow ZnSO_4(aq) + Cu(s)$$

7.2 Rates of reaction

On 7 May 1915, the British liner *Lusitania* was sunk off the south-west coast of Ireland (Figure 7.10). The liner was torpedoed by a German submarine and 1198 passengers lost their lives. The sinking was accompanied by a second explosion. This explosion gave possible support to the idea that the ship was carrying explosives to Britain for use in the war. The wreck of the *Lusitania* has now been investigated by divers. Evidence suggests that the second explosion was caused by coal dust exploding in the hold. If so, this is a dramatic example of explosive combustion.

This type of explosion can also occur with fine powders in flour mills (Figure 7.11), in mines when dangerous gases collect, and with dust. Dust particles have a large surface area in contact with the air. A simple spark can set off an explosive reaction. For example, *Lycopodium* powder piled in a dish does not burn easily – but if it is sprayed across a Bunsen flame, it produces a spectacular reaction. Even metal powders can produce quite spectacular effects (Figure 7.12).

The same idea does have a more positive use. In some modern coal-fired power stations, powdered coal is burnt instead of the usual lumps of coal because it burns very efficiently.

Figure 7.11 A fireball produced by dropping powdered flour into a flame.

Factors affecting the rate of reaction

Explosive reactions represent one end of the 'spectrum' of reaction rates. Other reactions, such as rusting, take place over much longer time periods. What factors influence the speed of a reaction? Experiments have

Figure 7.10 The sinking of the *Lusitania*.

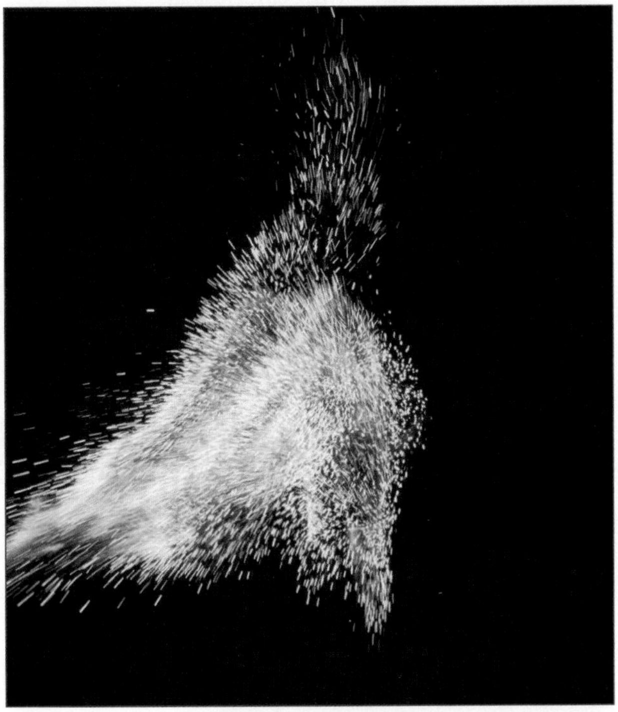

Figure 7.12 Iron dust ignited in a Bunsen flame.

been carried out to study a wide range of reactions, and there seem to be five major influences on **reaction rate**:

- the **surface area** of any solid reactants
- the **concentration** of the reactants
- the **temperature** at which the reaction is carried out
- the use of a **catalyst**
- the influence of **light** on some reactions.

The surface area of solid reactants

Where one or more of the reactants is a solid, the more finely powdered (or finely divided) the solid(s) are, the greater is the rate of reaction. This is because reactions involving solids take place on the surface of the solids. A solid has a much larger surface area when it is powdered than when it is in larger pieces.

For reactions involving two solids, grinding the reactants means that they can be better mixed. The mixed powders are then in greater contact with each other and are more likely to react.

If a solid is being reacted with a liquid (or solution), the greater the surface area, the more the solid is exposed to the liquid. A good demonstration of this is the reaction between limestone or marble chips (two forms of calcium carbonate) and dilute hydrochloric acid:

calcium carbonate + hydrochloric acid
→ calcium chloride + water + carbon dioxide

$$CaCO_3(s) + 2HCl(aq) \rightarrow CaCl_2(aq) + H_2O(l) + CO_2(g)$$

The experiment can be done as shown in Figure **7.13**. Using this arrangement, we can compare two samples of marble chips, one sample (B) being in smaller pieces than the other (A). The experiment is carried out twice, once with sample A and once with sample B. In each experiment the mass of sample used is the same, and the same volume and concentration of hydrochloric acid is used. The flask sits on the balance during the reaction. A loose cotton wool plug prevents liquid spraying out of the flask but allows the carbon dioxide gas to escape into the air. This means that the flask will lose mass during the reaction. Balance readings are taken at regular time intervals and the loss in mass can be worked out. When the loss in mass is plotted against time, curves such as those in Figure **7.14** are obtained.

There are several important points about the graph.

1 The reaction is fastest at the start. This is shown by the steepness of the curves over the first few minutes. Curve B is steeper than curve A. This means that gas (CO_2) is being produced faster with sample B. The sample with smaller chips, with a greater surface area, reacts faster. Beyond this part of the graph, both reactions slow down as the reactants are used up (Figure 7.15).

2 The total volume of gas released is the same in both experiments. The mass of $CaCO_3$ and the amount of acid are the same in both cases. Both curves flatten out at the same final volume. Sample B reaches the horizontal part of the curve (the plateau) first.

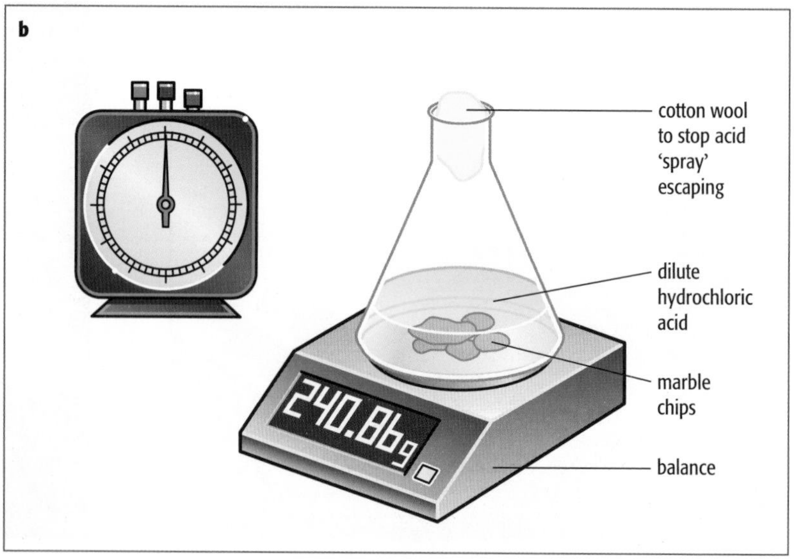

Figure 7.13 Apparatus for experiments A and B: the reaction of marble chips with dilute hydrochloric acid. The loss of carbon dioxide from the flask produces a loss in mass. This is detected by the balance.

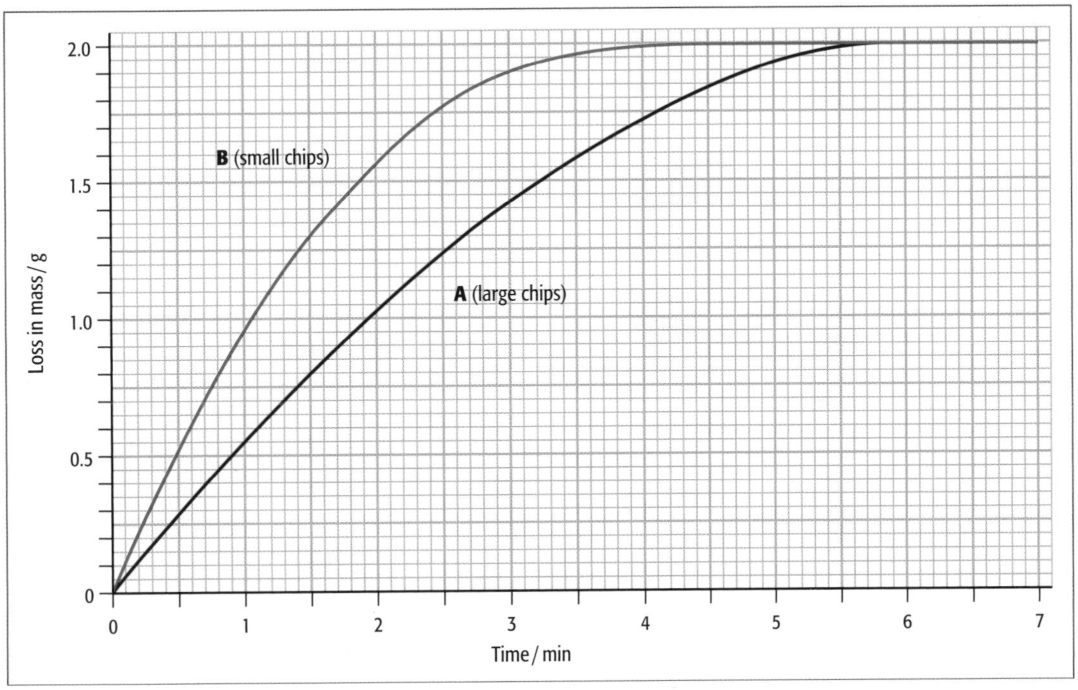

Figure 7.14 The graph shows the loss in mass against time for experiments A and B. The reaction is faster if the marble chips are broken into smaller pieces (curve B).

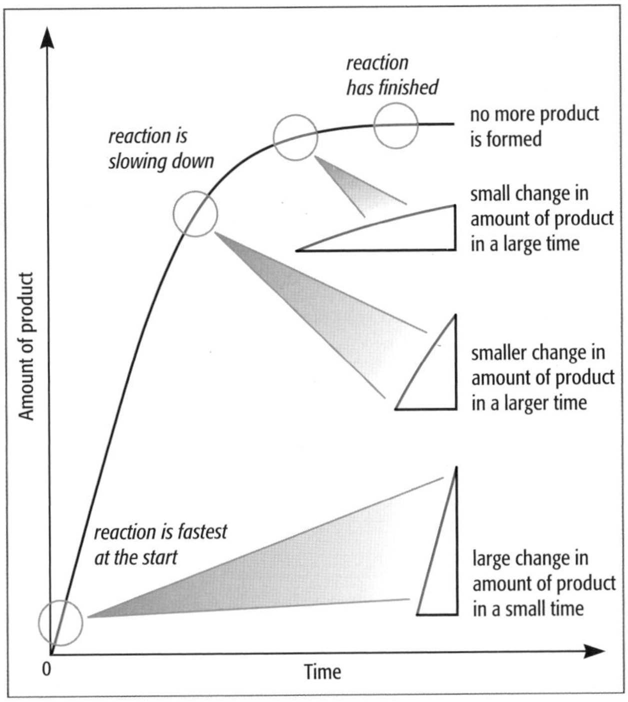

Figure 7.15 A chemical reaction is fastest at the start. It slows down as the reactants are used up.

These results show that:
the rate of a reaction increases when the **surface area** of a solid reactant is **increased**.

Exam tip

It is important that you understand how to interpret the different regions of the graphs obtained in this area of study.

For the extended paper you should also be able to work out a value for the rate of reaction from these graphs.

The concentration of reactants

Reactions that produce gases are also very useful in studying the effect of solution concentration on the reaction rate. The reaction between marble chips and acid could be adapted for this. Another reaction that can be used to study this is the reaction between magnesium and excess dilute hydrochloric acid:

magnesium + hydrochloric acid
$\rightarrow$ magnesium chloride + hydrogen

$Mg(s) + 2HCl(aq) \rightarrow MgCl_2(aq) + H_2(g)$

The apparatus is shown in Figure **7.16**, overleaf. As in the previous experiment, we will compare two different experiments, which we will call C and D. The acid in experiment C is twice as concentrated as in experiment D.

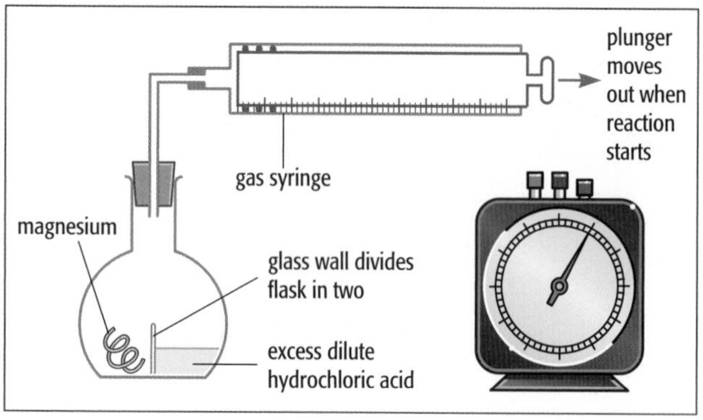

Figure 7.16 Apparatus for experiments C and D: the reaction of magnesium with dilute hydrochloric acid. The hydrogen given off can be collected and measured in a gas syringe.

doubling the concentration of the acid doubles the rate of reaction.

3 The total volume of hydrogen produced is the same in both experiments. Both reactions produce the same volume of hydrogen, though experiment C produces it faster.

These results show that:
the rate of a reaction increases when the **concentration** of a reactant in solution is **increased.**

Apart from changing the concentration of the acid, everything else must stay the same. So the volume of acid, the temperature and the mass of magnesium used must be the same in both experiments. The gas produced in this reaction is hydrogen and is collected in a gas syringe. The volume of gas produced is measured at frequent time intervals. We can then plot a graph of volume of gas collected against time, like that in Figure 7.17.

Again the graph shows some important points.

1 The curve for experiment C is steeper than for D. This shows clearly that reaction C, using more concentrated acid, is faster than reaction D.

2 The curve for experiment C starts off twice as steeply as for D. This means that the reaction in C is twice as fast as in experiment D initially. So

E We most often use the term 'concentration' in chemistry when talking about solutions. But we can also change the concentration of a gas mixture by compressing it into a smaller volume. A gas at high pressure is more concentrated than it is at low pressure.

This is used in the petrol engine. During the compression stroke in the engine, the piston moves up and compresses the mixture of petrol vapour and air. The concentrated mixture reacts explosively when ignited by the spark plug. The piston is forced downwards by the explosion. This movement of the piston turns the crankshaft, which then turns the road wheels of the car.

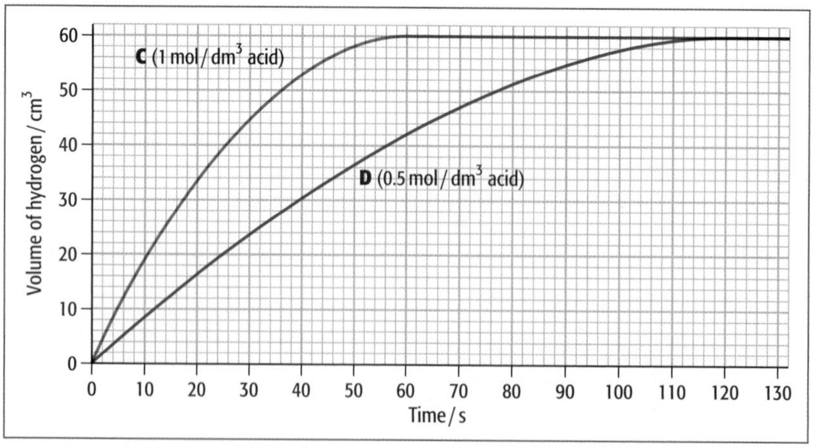

Figure 7.17 The graph shows the volume of hydrogen against time for experiments C and D. The reaction is faster if the acid solution is more concentrated (curve C).

Temperature

A reaction can be made to go faster or slower by changing the temperature of the reactants. Some food is stored in a refrigerator, because the food 'keeps better'. The rate of decay and oxidation is slower at lower temperatures.

The previously described experiments (A/B or C/D) could be altered to study the effect of temperature on the rate of production of gas.

An alternative approach is to use the reaction between sodium thiosulfate and hydrochloric acid. In this case (which we shall call experiment E), the formation of a precipitate is used to measure the rate of reaction.

sodium thiosulfate + hydrochloric acid
→ sodium chloride + sulfur + sulfur dioxide + water

$$Na_2S_2O_3(aq) + 2HCl(aq) \rightarrow 2NaCl(aq) + S(s) + SO_2(g) + H_2O(l)$$

The experiment is shown in Figure 7.18. A cross is marked on a piece of paper. A flask containing sodium thiosulfate solution is placed on top of the paper. Hydrochloric acid is added quickly. The yellow precipitate of sulfur produced is very fine and stays suspended in the liquid. With time, as more and more sulfur is formed, the liquid becomes cloudier and more difficult to see through. The time taken for the cross to 'disappear' is measured. The faster the reaction, the shorter the length of time during which the cross is visible. The experiment is carried out several times with solutions pre-warmed to different temperatures. The solutions and conditions of the experiment must remain the same; only the temperature is altered. A graph can then be plotted of the time taken for the cross to disappear against temperature, like that shown in Figure 7.19.

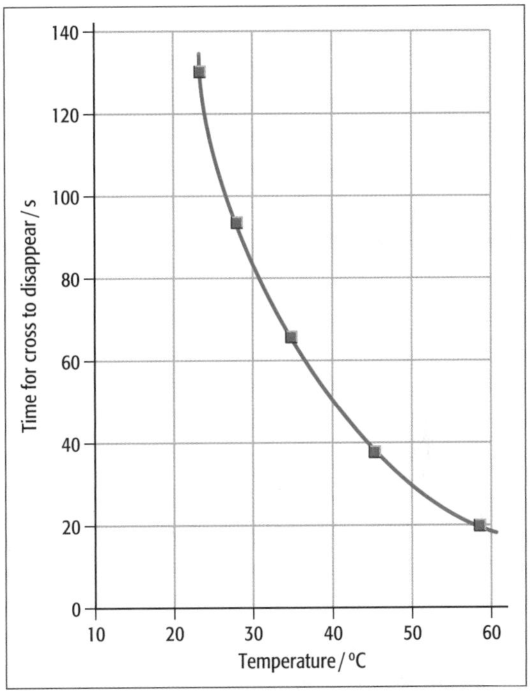

Figure 7.19 The graph for experiment E. As the temperature is increased, the time taken for the cross to disappear is shortened. The reaction speeds up at higher temperature.

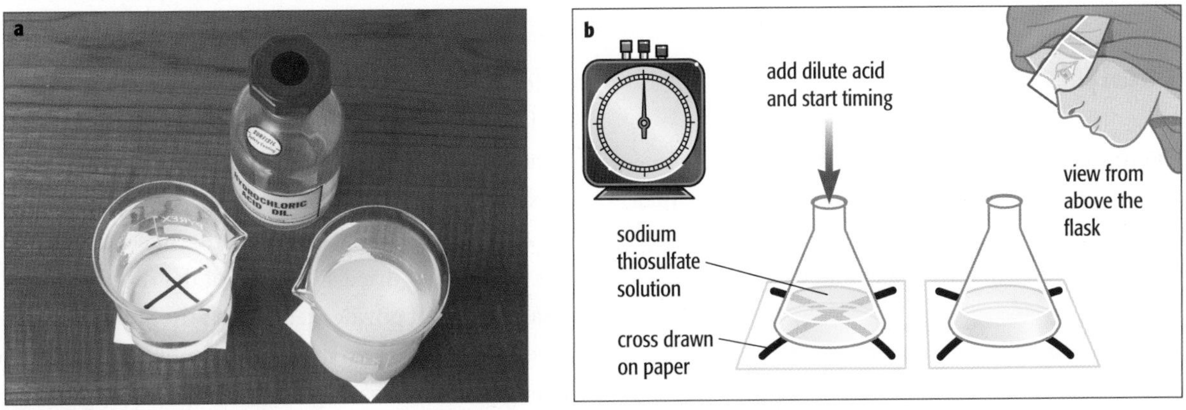

Figure 7.18 Apparatus for experiment E: the reaction between hydrochloric acid and sodium thiosulfate. This can be studied by following the appearance of the precipitate. The cross drawn on the paper appears fainter with time. Time how long it takes for the cross to disappear.

The graph shows two important points.

1 The cross disappears more quickly at higher temperatures. The shorter the time needed for the cross to disappear, the faster the reaction.

2 The curve is not a straight line.

These results show that:
the rate of a reaction increases when the **temperature** of the reaction mixture is **increased**.

To be more precise, the speed of the reaction is **inversely proportional** to the time taken for the reaction to finish:

$$\text{rate of reaction} \propto \frac{1}{\text{time}}$$

A graph of 1/time against temperature would show how the rate increases with a rise in temperature.

Exam tip

It is important to realise in this experiment that the shorter the time taken for the cross to disappear, the faster the reaction has taken place.

Key ideas so far

- Different chemical reactions take place at different rates.
- The rate of a reaction is dependent on various factors, which include
  - temperature
  - the concentration of any solutions involved
  - the particle size of any solid used.
- The rate of reaction increases when smaller pieces of solid (with larger surface area) are used.
- The rate of a reaction increases with increased concentration of reactants.
- The rate of a reaction increases with increasing temperature.
- There are various practical methods for following a chemical reaction to study its rate of reaction.
- A chemical reaction is fastest at the start of the reaction. It then slows down and eventually stops when one or all of the reactants are used up.

? Quick-check questions

1 What do we observe happen to the rate of a chemical reaction in response to the following?
  a an increase in temperature
  b an increase in the surface area of a solid reactant
  c an increased concentration of a reacting solution

2 Why is perishable food kept in a refrigerator?

3 When is a chemical reaction at its fastest?

4 Why does the rate of a chemical reaction slow down at the end?

7.3 Catalysts

The decomposition of hydrogen peroxide

Hydrogen peroxide is a colourless liquid with the formula H_2O_2. It is a very reactive oxidising agent. Hydrogen peroxide decomposes to form water and oxygen:

$$\text{hydrogen peroxide} \rightarrow \text{water} + \text{oxygen}$$
$$2H_2O_2(l) \rightarrow 2H_2O(l) + O_2(g)$$

We can follow the rate of this reaction by collecting the oxygen in a gas syringe. The formation of oxygen is very slow at room temperature. However, the addition of 0.5 g of powdered manganese(IV) oxide (MnO_2) makes the reaction go much faster (we shall call this experiment F). The black powder does not disappear during the reaction (Figure **7.20**). Indeed, if the solid is filtered and dried at the end of the reaction, the same mass of powder remains. If the amount of MnO_2 powder added is doubled (experiment G), the rate of reaction increases (Figure **7.21**). If the powder is more finely divided (powdered), the reaction also speeds up. Both these results suggest that it is the surface of the manganese(IV) oxide powder that is important here.

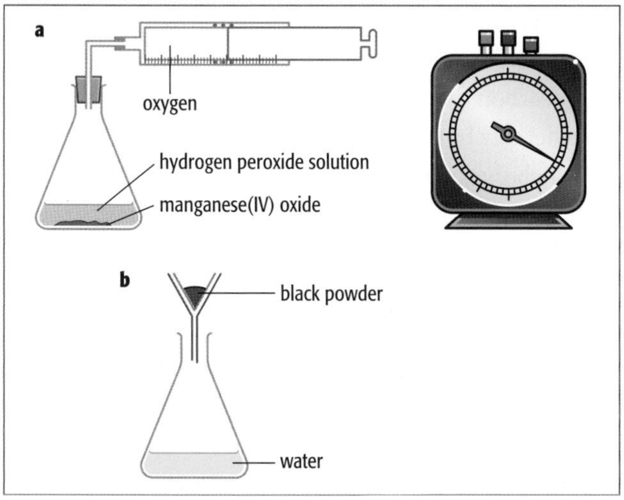

Figure 7.20 Apparatus for experiments F and G: the decomposition of hydrogen peroxide to water and oxygen. The decomposition is very slow at room temperature. **a** It can be speeded up by adding a catalyst, manganese(IV) oxide. **b** The catalyst is unchanged at the end, and can be separated from the water by filtration.

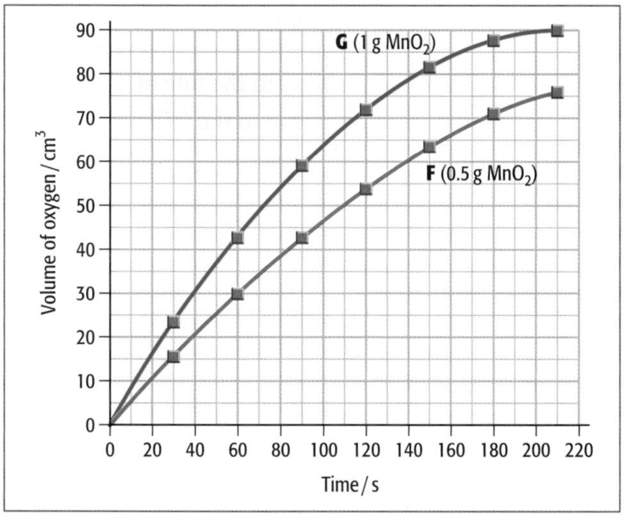

Figure 7.21 Increasing the amount of catalyst increases the rate of reaction. Here the amount of manganese(IV) oxide has been doubled in experiment G compared to F.

By increasing the surface area, the rate of reaction is increased. We say that manganese(IV) oxide is a **catalyst** for this reaction.

A **catalyst** is a substance that **increases** the rate of a chemical reaction. The catalyst remains **chemically unchanged** at the end of the reaction.

Many catalysts work by providing a surface on which other molecules or atoms can react. However, others work in more complex ways. Thus it is wrong to say that catalysts do not take part in the reaction: some do. But at the end of the reaction, there is the same amount of catalyst as at the beginning, and it is chemically unchanged.

Exam tip

Remember to give a full definition of a catalyst in an exam. Include in your answer the fact that the catalyst itself remains unchanged at the end of the reaction.

Other examples of catalysts

S

Catalysts have been found for a wide range of reactions. They are useful because a **small** amount of catalyst can produce a **large** change in the rate of a reaction. Also, since they are unchanged at the end of a reaction, they can be re-used. Industrially, they are very important. Industrial chemists use catalysts to make everything from polythene and painkillers, to fertilisers and fabrics. If catalysts did not exist, many chemical processes would go very slowly and some reactions would need much higher temperatures and pressures to proceed at a reasonable rate. All these factors would make these processes more expensive, so that the product would cost much more. If it cost more than people wanted to pay for it, it would be uneconomic.

Table 7.2, (overleaf) shows some examples of industrial catalysts. You should notice that transition elements (see Chapter **8**) or their compounds make particularly good catalysts.

Catalytic converters

One way to reduce the polluting effects of car exhaust fumes is to fit the car with a catalytic converter (Figure 7.22, overleaf). In many countries these converters are a legal requirement. Car exhaust fumes contain gases such as carbon monoxide (CO), nitrogen monoxide (nitrogen(II) oxide, NO) and unburnt hydrocarbons (HC) from the fuel which cause pollution in the air. The catalytic converter converts these to less harmful products such as carbon dioxide (CO_2),

Industrial process	Catalyst
ammonia manufacture (Haber process)	iron
sulfuric acid manufacture (Contact process)	vanadium(V) oxide
margarine production (hydrogenation of fats)	nickel
nitric acid manufacture (oxidation of ammonia)	platinum–rhodium
fermentation of sugars (alcoholic drinks industry)	enzymes (in yeast)
conversion of methanol to hydrocarbons	zeolite ZSM-5

Table 7.2 Some examples of industrial catalysts.

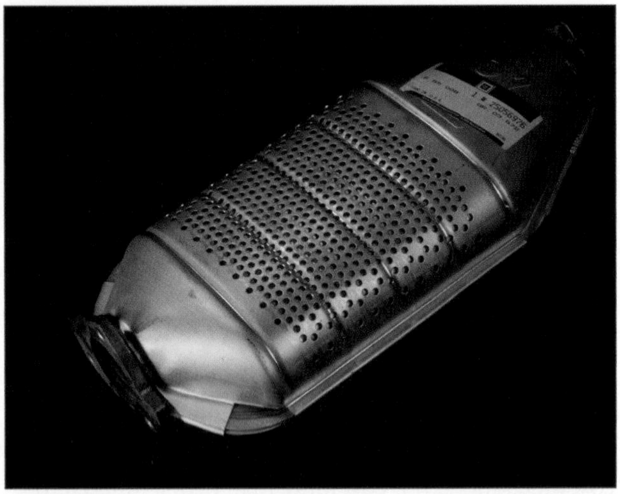

Figure 7.22 A catalytic converter can be fitted to a car exhaust system.

nitrogen (N_2) and water (H_2O). Some of the reactions that occur are:

carbon monoxide + oxygen → carbon dioxide

$$2CO(g) + O_2(g) \rightarrow 2CO_2(g)$$

nitrogen monoxide + carbon monoxide → nitrogen + carbon dioxide

$$2NO(g) + 2CO(g) \rightarrow N_2(g) + 2CO_2(g)$$

nitrogen monoxide → nitrogen + oxygen

$$2NO(g) \rightarrow N_2(g) + O_2(g)$$

hydrocarbons + oxygen → carbon dioxide + water

The catalytic converter therefore 'removes' polluting oxides and completes the oxidation of unburnt hydrocarbon fuel. It speeds up these reactions considerably by providing a 'honeycombed' surface on which the gases can react. The converter contains a thin coating of rhodium and platinum catalysts on a solid honeycomb surface. These catalysts have many tiny pores which provide a large surface area for the reactions.

Catalytic converters can only be used with unleaded petrol. The presence of lead would 'poison' the catalyst and stop it working. Other impurities do get deposited on the catalyst surface, so the converter eventually needs replacing after a number of years.

Exam tip

The equations for the reactions taking place in the catalytic converter are quite difficult to remember so do remember that the reactions finish back at components that are present in normal air, that is, carbon dioxide and nitrogen.

Biological catalysts (enzymes)

Living cells also produce catalysts. They are protein molecules called **enzymes** (Figure 7.23). Many thousands of reactions happen in every kind of organism. Enzymes speed up these reactions. Each enzyme works only for a particular reaction. We say that it is **specific** for that reaction.

The general features of enzymes are:

- enzymes are **proteins**
- they are very **specific** – each enzyme controls one reaction
- they are generally **temperature-sensitive** – they are inactivated (denatured) by heat (most stop working above 45 °C),
- they are sensitive to pH – most enzymes work best in neutral conditions around pH 7.

Enzymes are being used increasingly as catalysts in industry. Biological washing powders use enzymes

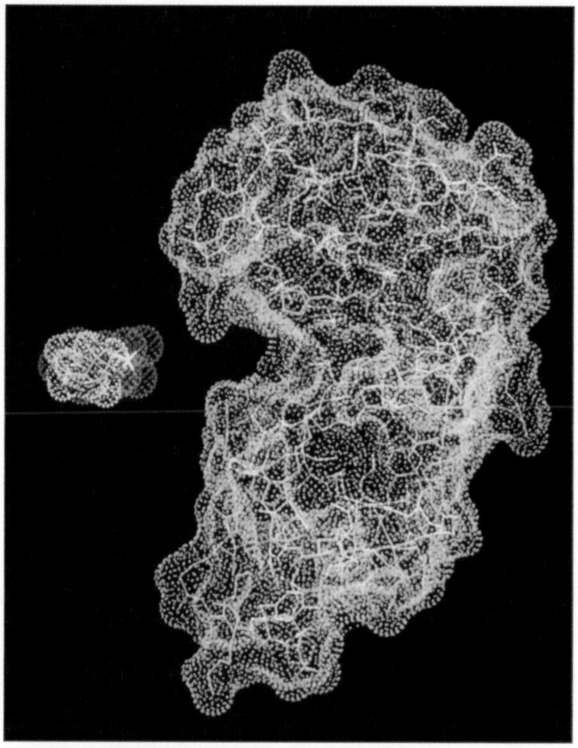

Figure 7.23 A computer image of an enzyme and the smaller molecule it is about to carry out a reaction with (the substrate).

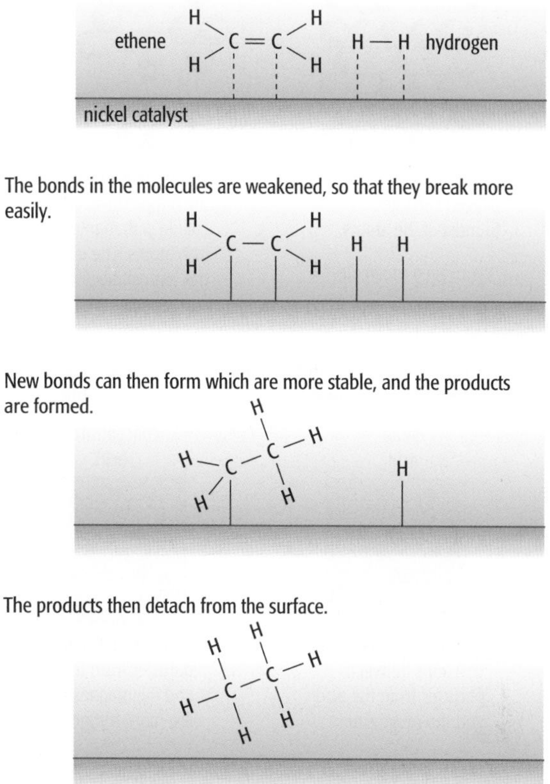

Figure 7.24 The reaction between ethene (C_2H_4) and hydrogen (H_2) on the surface of a nickel catalyst. The catalyst speeds up the reaction.

to remove biological stains such as sweat, blood and food. The enzymes in these powders are those which break down proteins and fats. Because the enzymes are temperature-sensitive, these powders are used at a wash temperature of around 40 °C.

Surface catalysts and collision theory

E

Solid catalysts

Different chemical reactions need different catalysts. One broad group of catalysts works by adsorbing molecules onto a solid surface. This process of **adsorption** brings the molecules of reactants closer together. Some of the most important examples of industrial catalysts work in this way, for example iron in the **Haber process**, vanadium(V) oxide in the **Contact process**, and finely divided nickel where hydrogen is added to unsaturated hydrocarbons (Figure 7.24).

Collision theory

S

The importance of surface area in reactions involving solids helps us understand how reactions take place. In these cases, reactions can only occur when particles collide with the surface of a solid. If a solid is broken into smaller pieces, there is more surface exposed. This means there are more places where collisions can take place, and so there is more chance of a reaction taking place. Iron reacts more readily with oxygen if it is powdered (Figure 7.25a, overleaf).

We can see how these ideas – sometimes referred to as the **collision theory** – apply in other situations. When solutions are more concentrated, the speed of a reaction is faster. A more concentrated solution means that there are more reactant particles in a given volume. Collisions will occur more often. The more often they collide, the more chance the particles have of

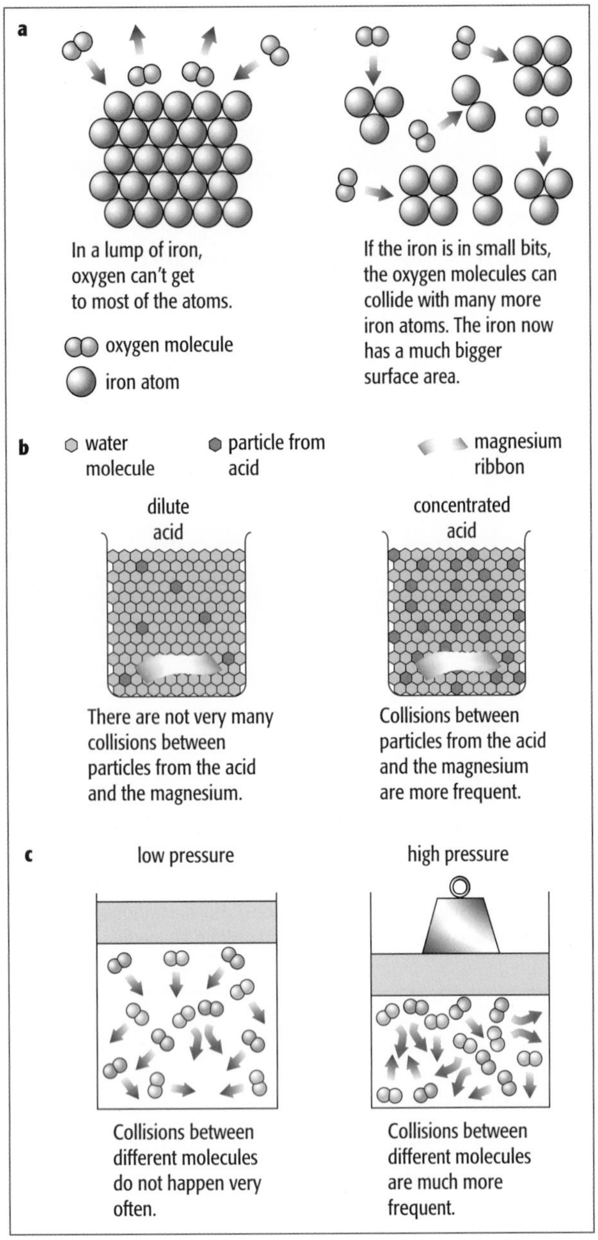

Figure 7.25 The effect of changing conditions on the frequency of collisions.

reacting. This means that the rate of a chemical reaction will increase if the concentration of the reactants is increased. A more concentrated acid reacts more vigorously with a piece of magnesium ribbon than a dilute one (Figure **7.25b**).

For reactions involving gases, increasing the pressure has the same effect as increasing the concentration, so the rate of a reaction between gases increases with pressure (Figure **7.25c**).

When the temperature is raised, a reaction takes place faster. At higher temperatures, the particles are moving faster. Again, this means that collisions will occur more often, giving more chance of reaction. Also, the particles have more energy at the higher temperature. This increases the chances that a collision will result in bonds in the reactants breaking and new bonds forming to make the products. If we look at the reaction between zinc and hydrochloric acid, we can see how the rate of reaction changes with changes in collision frequency (Figure 7.**26**).

When solutions are more concentrated, the speed of a reaction is faster. A more concentrated solution means that there are more reactant particles in a given volume. Collisions will occur more often. The more often they collide, the more chance the particles have of reacting. This means that the rate of a chemical reaction will increase if the concentration of the reactants is increased (Figure 7.**26b**). When the temperature is raised, a reaction takes place faster. At higher temperatures, the particles are moving faster. Again, this means that collisions will occur more often, giving more chance of reaction. Also, the particles have more energy at the higher temperature. This increases the chances that a collision will result in bonds in the reactants breaking and new bonds forming to make the products (Figure 7.**26c**).

Exam tip

When explaining the effects of concentration and temperature using the collision theory, remember that it is 'collision frequency' that is the key factor – don't talk vaguely about 'more collisions': it is the fact that there are **more frequent** collisions of the particles that is important.

A closer look at activation energy

Not every collision between particles in a reaction mixture produces a reaction. We have seen earlier that a certain amount of energy is needed to begin to break bonds. This minimum amount of energy is known as the **activation energy** of the reaction.

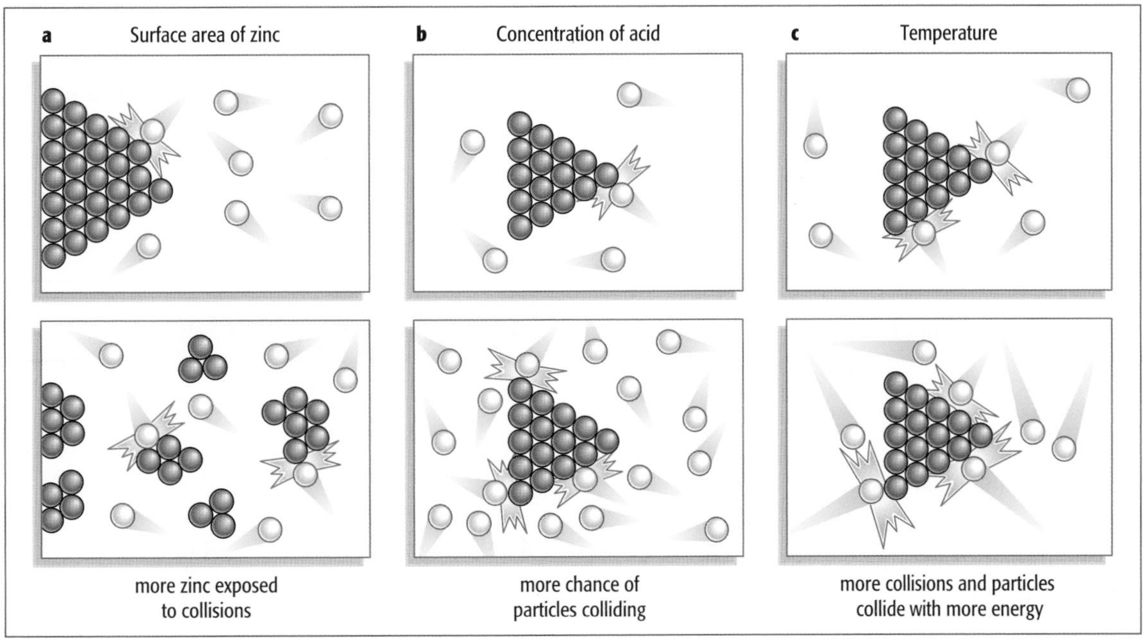

Figure 7.26 The collision theory can be used to explain how various factors affect the rate of the reaction. Here we use the reaction between zinc and hydrochloric acid as an example.

- Each reaction has its own different value of activation energy.
- When particles collide, they must have a combined energy greater than this activation energy, otherwise they will not react.
- Chemical reactions occur when the reactant particles collide with each other.

A catalyst increases the rate of reaction by reducing the amount of energy that is needed to break the bonds. This reduces the activation energy of the reaction and makes sure that more collisions are likely to give products. The rate of the reaction is therefore increased.

We can think of an 'analogy' for this. Suppose we are hiking in the Alps (Figure 7.27). We start on one

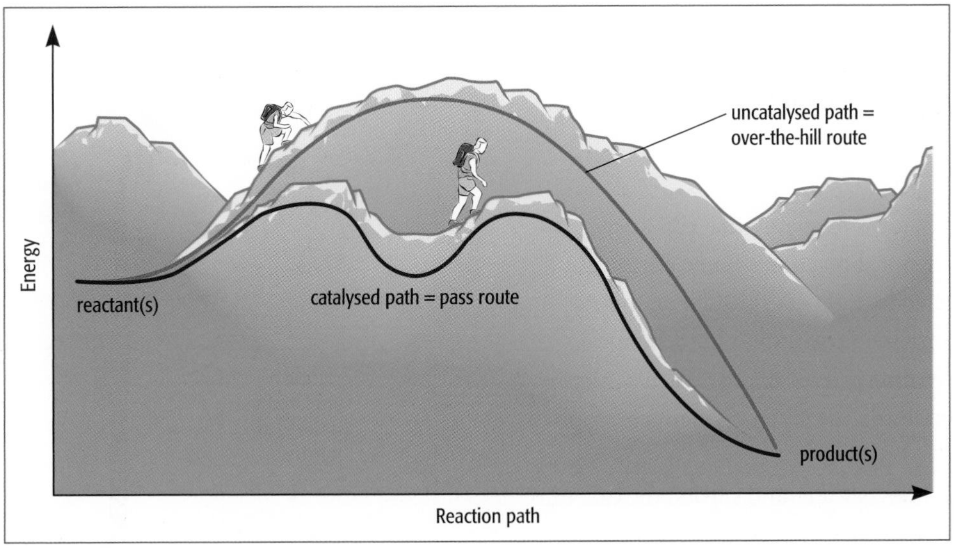

Figure 7.27 The barrier between reactant(s) and product(s) may be so high that it defeats all but the most energetic. The catalyst's route is an easy pass through the mountains.

side of a mountain and want to get to the other side. We **could** go right over the summit of the mountain. This would require us to be very energetic. What we might prefer to do would be to find an alternative route along a pass through the mountains. This would be less energetic. In our analogy, the starting point corresponds to the reactants and the finishing point to the products. The route over the top of the mountain would be the uncatalysed path. The easier route through the pass would be a catalysed path.

Key ideas so far

- A catalyst is a substance that speeds up a chemical reaction.
- A catalyst is not itself used up in the course of a reaction.
- Enzymes are biological catalysts.
- The collision theory is a useful idea which helps us understand the various effects relating to the rate of chemical reactions.
- The more frequently the reactant molecules collide, the faster the rate of reaction.
- Transition metals and their compounds are often good catalysts.
- A catalyst lowers the activation energy of the reaction.
- A catalytic converter (catalyser) is a device fitted into the exhaust system of cars to help reduce the level of polluting gases leaving in the exhaust fumes. They help convert nitrogen oxides back to nitrogen, and carbon monoxide to carbon dioxide.

Quick-check questions

1 What is a catalyst?
2 What is an enzyme?
3 What is a solid catalyst that will speed up the decomposition of hydrogen peroxide?
4 What are the catalysts used in
  a the Haber process, and
  b the Contact process?
5 What changes in physical conditions are enzymes particularly sensitive to?
6 Does the presence of a catalyst increase or decrease the activation energy for a reaction?
7 In terms of the collision theory, explain why the rate of a reaction increases with
  a an increase in temperature
  b an increase in the surface area of a solid reactant
  c an increased concentration of a reacting solution.

7.4 Photochemical reactions

Photosynthesis

Heat is not the only form of energy that can break bonds and start chemical reactions. Some chemical reactions are affected by light energy. Life on this planet would be impossible without photochemical reactions. **Photosynthesis** traps energy when sunlight falls on leaves containing the green pigment chlorophyll (Figure 7.28).

The reaction converts water and carbon dioxide into glucose and oxygen:

$$\text{carbon dioxide} + \text{water} \xrightarrow[\text{chlorophyll}]{\text{sunlight}} \text{glucose} + \text{oxygen}$$

$$6CO_2 + 6H_2O \longrightarrow C_6H_{12}O_6 + 6O_2$$

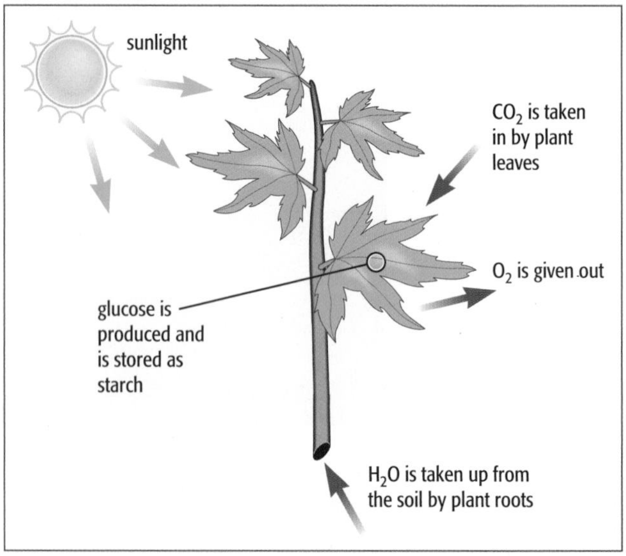

Figure 7.28 Green plants contain chlorophyll and take part in photosynthesis. This is a process that is crucial to the existence of life on Earth.

The glucose produced is used to make other sugars and starch. These are **carbohydrates**. It is estimated that the mass of carbon 'fixed' as carbohydrates is 2×10^{11} tonnes per year. Algae, some bacteria and marine micro-organisms can also get their energy directly from sunlight by photosynthesis.

Photosynthesis is part of a global cycle of carbon atoms (page 4). It is counter-balanced in the natural world by the reaction known as **respiration**. Respiration is the reaction that takes place in biological cells when they use glucose molecules as a source of energy:

$$C_6H_{12}O_6 + 6O_2 \rightarrow 6CO_2 + 6H_2O$$

It has been estimated that, on average, all the carbon dioxide on Earth passes through the process of photosynthesis once every 300 years, and all the oxygen once every 2000 years. Every carbon atom in your body has been through the photosynthetic cycle many times. The energy stored directly by plant life through photosynthesis is called **biomass energy** and it provides us with important sources of food and warmth. As a result of heat and pressure over millions of years, biomass can be changed into fossil fuels. The energy stored in biomass and fossil fuels can be used to generate electricity, to manufacture clothing, to run cars and to pursue many other activities (Table 7.3).

Biomass	Fossil fuels
food	coal
biogas	oil
peat	natural gas
wood	
vegetable oils	
alcohols	

Table 7.3 Some of the end-products of photosynthesis.

Exam tip

Remember that there are relatively few photochemical reactions. Those you need to be familiar with are listed in the 'Key ideas' at the end of this section.

Photography

People were aware that silver salts darken on exposure to light as long ago as the sixteenth century. The darkening is caused by the production of specks of silver metal. Precipitates of silver chloride (white) or silver bromide (cream) will darken if left to stand in sunlight for a few hours. For example:

$$2AgBr \xrightarrow{\text{sunlight}} 2Ag + Br_2$$

The reaction is a redox reaction; bromide ions lose electrons (they are oxidised), and silver ions gain electrons (they are reduced):

$$2Br^- \rightarrow Br_2 + 2e^-$$
$$Ag^+ + e^- \rightarrow Ag$$

This photochemical reaction, in which silver ions are converted to silver atoms, is used as the basis of both black-and-white and colour photography. The photographic film itself is simply a flexible plastic support for the light-sensitive 'emulsion'. An 'emulsion' in photography is not a true emulsion but a layer of gelatine with millions of microcrystals of silver bromide spread through it. Black-and-white film has a single layer of 'emulsion'. Colour film has three layers, each layer containing a different dye (Figure 7.29).

Figure 7.29 Photographic film produces a negative image.

The basis of producing a photographic print is as follows.

1 Light falls on the silver halide crystals in the photographic film. The silver ions in the exposed part of the film are converted to silver atoms. The more light that falls on a part of the film, the more silver atoms are deposited.
2 The film is immersed in a developer. The partly exposed crystals are completely converted to silver.
3 The film is immersed in a fixer. Unchanged (that is unexposed) silver halide crystals dissolve. This leaves black metallic silver where the film was exposed to light. This is the 'negative'.
4 To produce a photographic print, the negative image is then transferred to photographic paper using an enlarger.

Print-paper 'emulsion' usually contains silver chloride. This reacts more slowly than silver bromide, giving the photographer greater control of the image. High-speed films use silver iodide, the most light-sensitive of the three salts.

Another important photochemical reaction, the chlorination of methane, is discussed on page **296**.

Key ideas so far

- There are some reactions that are promoted by light – they are photochemical reactions.
- Three photochemical reactions are
  - photosynthesis
  - the decomposition of silver bromide to produce a deposit of silver (the reaction used in photography)
  - the substitution reactions of methane with chlorine.
- Photosynthesis takes place in the green leaves of plants and relies on the involvement of chlorophyll in the leaves. It converts carbon dioxide and water to glucose and oxygen.
- In the natural world, photosynthesis is balanced by respiration – a reaction which takes place in cells, using glucose to produce energy.

Quick-check questions

1 What are the essential conditions for photosynthesis to take place?
2 Write the word and balanced symbol equations for photosynthesis.
3 What type of reaction are photosynthesis and the decomposition of silver bromide in a photographic emulsion?
4 Write the word equation for the respiration reaction.
5 Why does the use of photographic film produce a negative at first?

7.5 Reversible reactions and chemical equilibria

The physical and biological world is the product of a complex set of chemical interactions and reactions. Some reactions can even be reversed if we change the conditions.

Our life depends on the reversible attachment of oxygen to a protein called **haemoglobin**. This protein is found in our red blood cells (Figure 7.30). Oxygen is picked up as these cells pass through the blood vessels of the lungs. It is then carried to tissues in other parts of the body. As the conditions change in other regions of our body, for example the muscles and brain, the oxygen is detached and used by the cells of these organs.

Simpler reactions that can be reversed by changing the conditions include the re-formation of hydrated salts by adding back the water to the dehydrated powder.

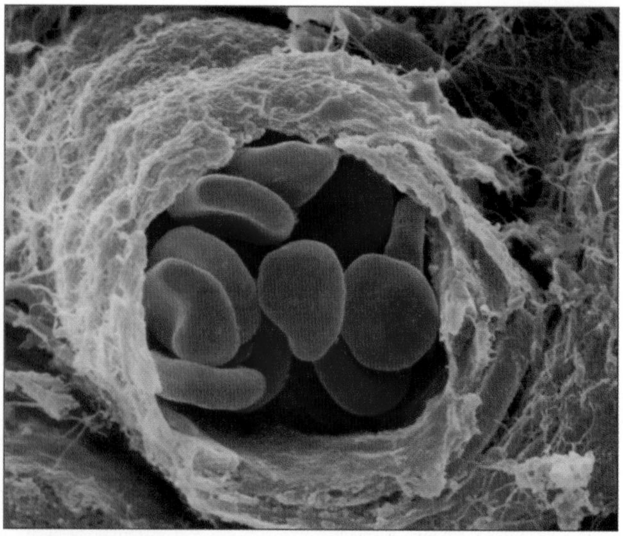

Figure 7.30 A false-colour scanning electron micrograph of red blood cells in a small branch off an artery.

However, there are **reversible reactions** that are more complex than this. In these reactions, under the same conditions in a **closed system**, the products can interact to reverse the reaction. No sooner are the products formed than some molecules of the product react to give back the original reactants. One industrially important example of this is the reaction between nitrogen and hydrogen to produce ammonia:

$$N_2(g) + 3H_2(g) \rightleftharpoons 2NH_3(g)$$

A German chemist, Fritz Haber, was the first to show how this reaction could be controlled to make useful amounts of ammonia. The first industrial plant making ammonia by the **Haber process** opened in Germany in 1913. Now, over 100 million tonnes of ammonia are produced each year by this process.

The reversible hydration of salts

Thermal decomposition of salts such as hydrated copper(II) sulfate ($CuSO_4.5H_2O$) results in the dehydration of the salt:

$$\underset{\text{light blue crystals}}{CuSO_4.5H_2O(s)} \xrightarrow{\text{heat}} \underset{\text{white powder}}{CuSO_4(s)} + 5H_2O(g)$$

In this case, the reaction results in a colour change from blue to white. The physical structure of the crystals is also destroyed. The water driven off can be condensed separately (Figure 7.31).

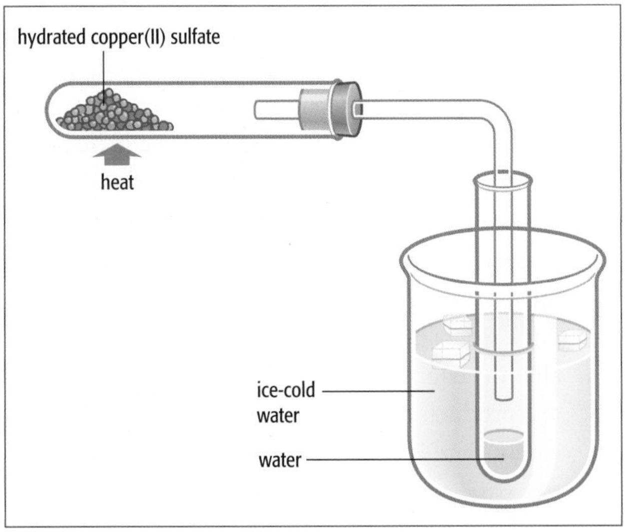

Figure 7.31 Apparatus for condensing the water vapour driven off from blue crystals of hydrated copper(II) sulfate by heating. The change can be reversed by adding the liquid water back to the white anhydrous copper(II) sulfate.

The white anhydrous copper(II) sulfate and the water are cooled down. Then the dehydration reaction can be reversed by slowly adding the water back to the powder (Figure 7.32). This reaction is strongly exothermic and the colour of the powder returns to blue.

Some reactions, for example the dehydration of hydrated salts, can be reversed if the conditions are changed.

The decomposition of ammonium chloride is a further example of this type of change (Figure 7.33). When

Figure 7.32 Adding water back to dehydrated copper(II) sulfate.

Figure 7.33 The reversible reaction involving ammonium chloride.

warmed in a test tube, the white solid decomposes to ammonia and hydrogen chloride:

$$NH_4Cl(s) \rightarrow NH_3(g) + HCl(g)$$

However, on the cooler surface of the upper part of the tube, the white solid is re-formed:

$$NH_3(g) + HCl(g) \rightarrow NH_4Cl(s)$$

Chemical equilibria and Le Chatelier's principle

Imagine a hotel swimming pool on a hot, sunny day. Some people are by the pool sunbathing; others are swimming in the pool. Over the most popular part of the day, the number of people swimming remains approximately the same. However, it is not the same people all the time. Some stop swimming to sunbathe, while other sunbathers take a swim. The balance between the numbers of people entering and leaving the pool keeps the overall number swimming the same. This is a **dynamic equilibrium**. The pool and the sunbathing area are the system, and the system is in equilibrium. This example is an analogy to help you to understand dynamic equilibria in chemical reactions.

One other analogy that has been used to illustrate this idea is that of a fish swimming upstream (Figure 7.34).

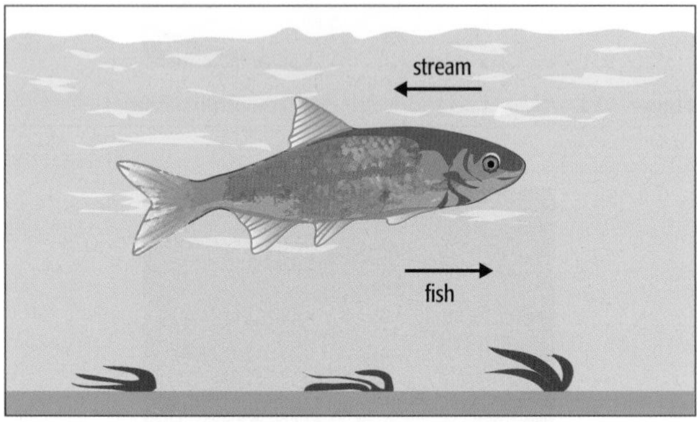

Figure 7.34 Dynamic equilibrium: the fish appears to be still. However, it is swimming upstream at the same velocity as the stream is flowing in the opposite direction.

The Haber process – making ammonia

The reaction to produce ammonia from nitrogen and hydrogen is a reversible reaction. That is why the symbol $\rightleftharpoons$ is used in the equation:

$$N_2(g) + 3H_2(g) \rightleftharpoons 2NH_3(g)$$

When nitrogen and hydrogen are mixed, they react to form ammonia – this is the **forward reaction:**

$$N_2(g) + 3H_2(g) \rightarrow 2NH_3(g)$$

However, this reaction never goes to completion – the reactants are not all used up. This is because ammonia molecules collide and break down under the same conditions – this is the **reverse reaction:**

$$2NH_3(g) \rightarrow N_2(g) + 3H_2(g)$$

In the reaction mixture, these two competing reactions are going on at the same time.

As the reactions proceed, a dynamic equilibrium is reached. Ammonia molecules are breaking down as fast as they are being formed. The rate of the forward reaction is the same as the rate of the reverse reaction. The concentrations of N_2, H_2 and NH_3 do not change even though molecules are reacting.

This reaction is a difficult one to get to work at a reasonable rate. A catalyst can be added. Chemists have tried more than 2500 different combinations of metals and metal oxides as catalysts for this reaction. Finely divided iron has been found to be the best. However, the presence of a catalyst does not alter the equilibrium concentrations of N_2, H_2 and NH_3. The catalyst shortens the time taken to reach equilibrium by increasing the rates of both the forward and reverse reactions.

- A reversible reaction is in equilibrium when the rates of the forward and reverse reactions are equal.
- At equilibrium, the concentrations of reactants and products do not change.
- The equilibrium concentrations (the equilibrium position) for a particular reaction depend on the conditions used. Changing the temperature alters the equilibrium position. Changing the working pressure can also alter the equilibrium position for some reactions involving gases.
- For a reversible reaction, a catalyst does not alter the equilibrium concentrations of reactants and products. It does increase the rate at which equilibrium is reached.

Because of its importance, the Haber process for making ammonia has been studied under a wide range of conditions of temperature and pressure (Figure 7.35).

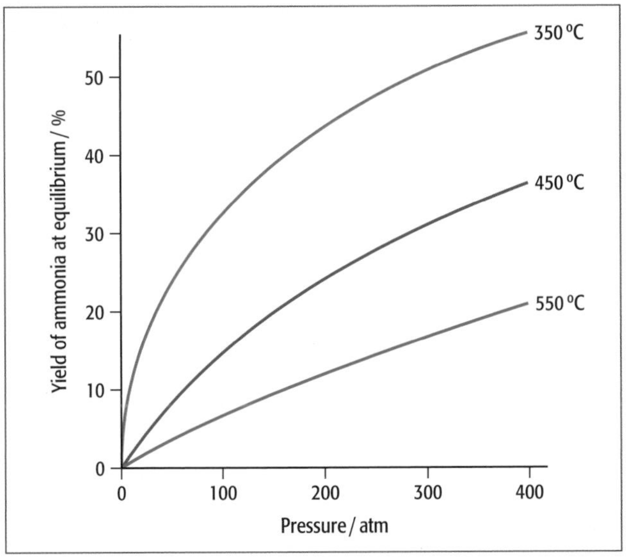

Figure 7.35 A wide range of conditions of temperature and pressure have been tried for the Haber process. The curves show the yields that would be obtained for some of them.

The percentage amount of ammonia in the equilibrium mixture depends on both the temperature and the pressure. Under the conditions Haber first used, only 8% of the equilibrium mixture was ammonia. Modern plants now use a temperature of about 450 °C, a pressure of 200 atmospheres and an iron catalyst.

How could conditions be changed to improve this yield? The French chemist Le Chatelier put forward a generalisation that gives clues to chemists as to how this can be done.

Le Chatelier's principle states that:
when a change is made to the conditions of a system in dynamic equilibrium, the system moves so as to **oppose** that change.

So how can this reaction system be changed to produce more ammonia at equilibrium – to shift the equilibrium to the right (Figure 7.36)?

- *Changing the pressure:* How will increasing the pressure affect the amount of ammonia made? The pressure of a gas is caused by collisions of the gas particles with the walls of the container – the fewer molecules present, the lower the pressure. If we apply more pressure to the equilibrium, the system will

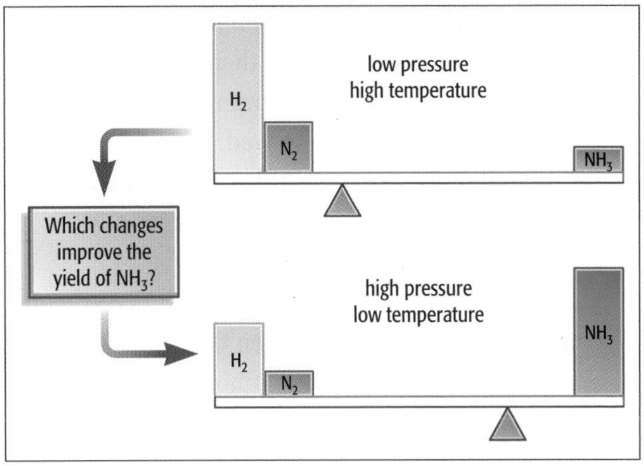

Figure 7.36 What shifts in the conditions will favour ammonia production in the Haber process? Increasing the pressure and lowering the temperature both move the equilibrium to the right to give more ammonia in the mixture.

shift to favour the side of the equation that has fewer molecules:

$$\underbrace{N_2(g) + 3H_2(g)}_{\text{four molecules}} \rightleftharpoons \underbrace{2NH_3(g)}_{\text{two molecules}}$$

So there will be a shift to the right. More ammonia will form to reduce the number of molecules in the mixture. High pressures will increase the yield of ammonia (Figure 7.35). Modern industrial plants use a pressure of 200 atmospheres.

Higher pressures could be used, but high-pressure reaction vessels are expensive to build.

- *Changing the temperature:* The forward reaction producing ammonia is exothermic, and the reverse reaction is therefore endothermic:

$N_2(g) + 3H_2(g) \rightarrow 2NH_3(g)$
exothermic – heat given out

$2NH_3(g) \rightarrow N_2(g) + 3H_2(g)$
endothermic – heat taken in

If we raise the temperature of the system, more ammonia will break down to take in the heat supplied. Less ammonia will be produced at high temperatures. Lowering the temperature will favour ammonia production (Figure 7.35). However, the rate at which the ammonia is produced will be so slow as to be uneconomic. In practice, a compromise or **optimum temperature** is used to produce enough ammonia at an acceptable rate. Modern plants use temperatures of about 450 °C.

- *Reducing the concentration of ammonia:* If the system was at equilibrium and then some of the ammonia was removed, more ammonia would be produced to replace that removed. Industrially, it is easy to remove ammonia. It has a much higher boiling point than nitrogen or hydrogen (Table 7.4) and condenses easily, leaving the others still as gases. In modern plants, the gas mixture is removed from the reaction chamber when the percentage of ammonia is about 15%. The ammonia is condensed by cooling, and the remaining nitrogen and hydrogen are recycled.

Compound	Boiling point / °C
nitrogen (N_2)	−196
hydrogen (H_2)	−253
ammonia (NH_3)	−33

Table 7.4 The boiling points of nitrogen, hydrogen and ammonia.

The conditions used in the **Haber process** are as follows.

- N_2 and H_2 are mixed in a ratio of 3 : 1.
- An optimum temperature of 450 °C is chosen.
- A pressure of 200 atmospheres is applied.
- A catalyst of finely divided iron is used.
- The ammonia is condensed out of the reaction mixture and the remaining N_2 and H_2 recycled.

Conditions affecting a chemical equilibrium

The general ideas resulting from our discussion of the effects of changing the conditions of a reaction in equilibrium are summarised in Table 7.5. The effects are consistent with Le Chatelier's principle.

Condition	Effect on equilibrium position
catalyst	Using a catalyst does **not** affect the position of equilibrium, but the reaction reaches equilibrium faster.
temperature	**Increasing** the temperature makes the reaction move in the direction that takes in heat (the endothermic direction).[a]
concentration	**Increasing** the concentration of one substance in the mixture makes the equilibrium move in the direction that produces less of that substance.[a]
pressure	This **only** affects reactions involving gases – **increasing** the pressure shifts the equilibrium in the direction that produces fewer gas molecules.[a]

[a] *The reverse of these statements is true when these factors are decreased.*

Table 7.5 The effect of changing conditions on a chemical equilibrium.

The Contact process – making sulfuric acid

In the manufacture of sulfuric acid, the main reaction that converts sulfur dioxide (SO_2) to sulfur trioxide (SO_3) is reversible:

$$2SO_2(g) + O_2(g) \rightleftharpoons 2SO_3(g) \qquad \Delta H = -197\,\text{kJ/mol}$$

The ideas of Le Chatelier can be applied to this equilibrium too. The reaction to produce sulfur trioxide is exothermic. This means that sulfur trioxide production would be favoured by low temperatures. The reaction would be too slow to be economic if the temperature were too low. An optimum temperature of 450 °C is used. This gives sufficient sulfur trioxide at an economical rate. A catalyst of vanadium(V) oxide is also used to increase the rate. There are fewer gas molecules on the right of the equation. Therefore, increasing the pressure would favour the production of sulfur trioxide. In fact the process is run at only slightly above atmospheric pressure because the conversion of sulfur dioxide to sulfur trioxide is about 96% complete under these conditions.

The conditions used in the **Contact process** are as follows.

- An optimum temperature of about 450 °C is chosen.
- A catalyst of vanadium(V) oxide is used.
- An operating pressure of about 1 atmosphere is applied.

Exam tip

Remember that when the equilibrium conditions are changed, the reaction always tends to oppose the change and act in the opposite direction.

The manufacture of lime

Limestone (calcium carbonate) can be decomposed by heat in a lime kiln to produce lime (calcium oxide):

$$CaCO_3(s) \rightarrow CaO(s) + CO_2(g)$$

If this reaction is carried out in a **closed** container, it is actually a reversible reaction:

$$CaCO_3(s) \rightleftharpoons CaO(s) + CO_2(g)$$

Not all the calcium carbonate decomposes. An equilibrium is set up with a limiting pressure of carbon dioxide in the container.

However, a lime kiln is **open** and the carbon dioxide can escape from the furnace (Figure 7.37). This means that the reaction never reaches equilibrium. More and more calcium carbonate decomposes in an 'attempt' to reach an equilibrium that can never be achieved. Eventually, all the calcium carbonate decomposes.

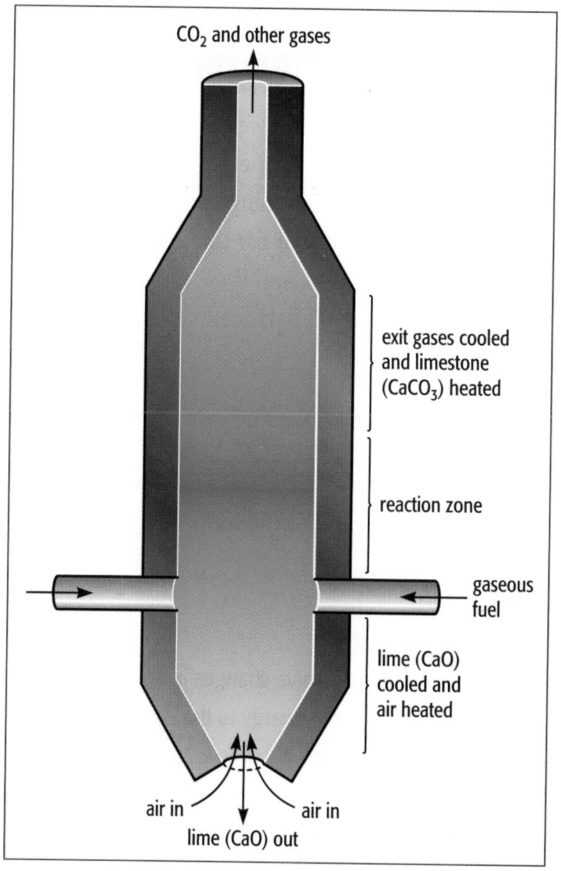

Figure 7.37 In the industrial manufacture of lime, limestone (calcium carbonate) is decomposed in a lime kiln. This is an open system where the carbon dioxide can escape. No equilibrium is possible, and all the limestone decomposes.

Weak acids and alkalis

Dynamic equilibria are set up in solutions of weak acids such as ethanoic acid:

$$CH_3COOH(aq) \rightleftharpoons CH_3COO^-(aq)$$

and in solutions of weak alkalis such as ammonia solution:

$$NH_3(g) + H_2O(l) \rightleftharpoons NH_4^+(aq) + OH^-(aq)$$

Because these molecules are only partially dissociated into ions in water, the pH values of the solutions are not as low as those of solutions of strong acids or as high as those of strong alkalis of the same concentration (see page **162**).

Key ideas so far

- Some chemical reactions are reversible under appropriate conditions.
- The dehydration of a hydrated salt such as copper sulfate can be reversed if water is added back to the dehydrated solid.
- In certain chemical reactions the reverse reaction can take place at the same time as the forward reaction.
- In a closed system these reactions will reach an equilibrium position, where the rate of the reverse reaction is equal to the rate of the forward reaction. A dynamic equilibrium is set up.
- The equilibrium set up depends on various conditions of temperature, and pressure (if a gas is involved).
- The Haber process for the industrial manufacture of ammonia is an important example of a reversible reaction.

Quick-check questions

1 What colour change do we see when water is added to anhydrous copper(II) sulfate powder?
2 What can this colour change be used as a test for?
3 What are the equations for the major reactions of the Haber process and the Contact process? Give both word and balanced symbol equations.
4 What are the conditions used for the Haber process?
5 Will increasing the pressure in the Haber process produce more or less ammonia?
6 What would be the effect of increasing the temperature in the Haber process on the level of ammonia produced?

Summary

You should know that:

- chemical reactions involve changes in energy
- most reactions release energy to their surroundings and this is usually in the form of heat – these are exothermic reactions
- some reactions take in energy from the surroundings – these are endothermic reactions
- chemical reactions can occur at vastly different rates, from the explosively rapid to those taking place over a timescale of years
- the rate of a particular reaction can be changed by altering several factors concerning the reactants, including
  - the surface area of any solids present
  - the concentration of any solutions involved
  - the temperature at which the reaction is carried out
- some reactions can be speeded up by the presence of a catalyst
- catalysts increase the rate of a reaction but remain chemically unchanged at the end of the reaction
- transition elements or their compounds are particularly useful as catalysts
- catalysts are important for a wide range of industrial processes
- enzymes are biological catalysts
- these enzyme proteins are highly specific and sensitive to conditions of temperature and pH
- certain reactions can be reversed if the conditions are changed – the dehydration of hydrated salts, for example
- some of these reactions can be vital to life, for example the transport of oxygen by haemoglobin
- chemical bonds must first be broken during a reaction so that new, different, bonds can be formed
- the breaking of bonds is an endothermic process requiring energy, while the making of bonds is an exothermic process with energy being released
- the heat change taking place during a reaction can be measured using a simple calorimeter
- very few reactions are spontaneous, and even strongly exothermic reactions require an initial input of energy to start them
- the 'energy barrier' that must be overcome at the start of a reaction is known as the activation energy of a particular reaction
- the activation energy is needed because bonds must first be broken before new 'attachments' can be made
- the energy released by the forming of new bonds causes the reaction to continue
- the factors controlling the rate of a reaction can be explained on the basis of collision theory
- changes that increase the frequency of collisions between reactant particles (for example an increase in temperature) will increase the rate of a reaction

- not all collisions produce reactions – the colliding particles must possess a certain minimum energy to react
- this minimum energy is the activation energy of the reaction
- certain reactions respond to light energy – these reactions are known as photochemical reactions
- reversible reactions in a closed system reach a position of dynamic equilibrium
- at equilibrium, the rate of the reverse reaction equals that of the forward reaction
- at equilibrium, the overall concentrations of the reactants and products do not change
- the position of an equilibrium can be altered by changing the temperature of the system
- for reversible reactions involving gases, the position of equilibrium can be altered by changing the pressure
- several important industrial reactions, for example the Haber process, are based on reversible reactions
- the conditions used industrially for these reactions are optimised to produce enough product at an economic rate
- a catalyst is often involved in these processes, but its presence does not alter the equilibrium position
- solutions of weak acids, for example ethanoic acid, which are only partially dissociated into ions, are also examples of dynamic equilibria.

Exam-style questions

1 A student investigates the reaction between zinc and hydrochloric acid. The hydrochloric acid is in excess. The student uses the apparatus shown in the diagram.

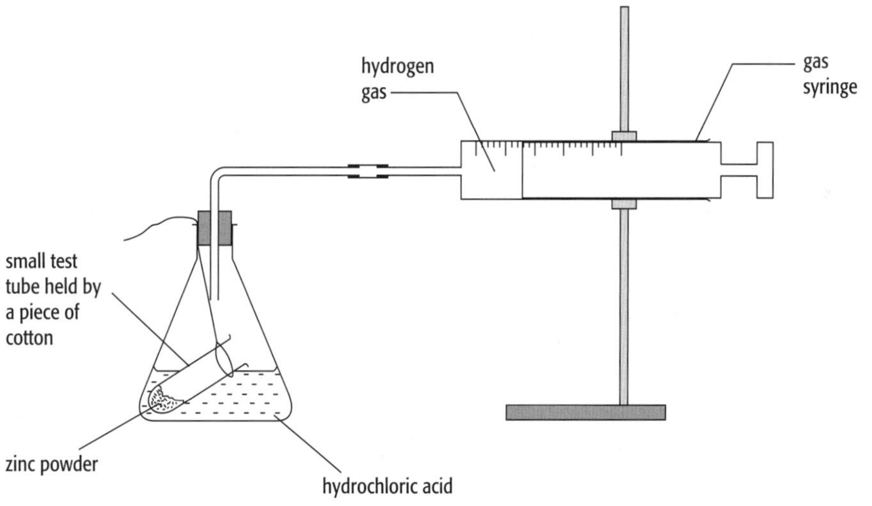

a What should the student do to start the reaction? [1]

b The student reads the volume of gas in the syringe every minute. The results are shown in the table.

Time in minutes	0	1	2	3	4	5	6	7
Volume of gas in cm^3	0	23	35	45	50	53	55	55

i Copy the grid and plot the results.

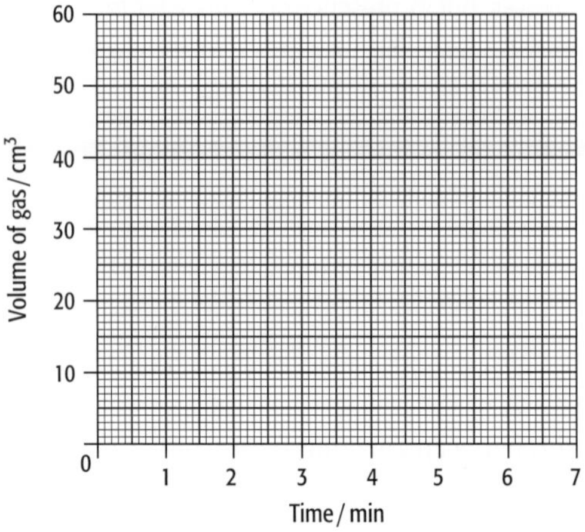

ii Draw the best curve through the points.

iii Explain why the volume of gas stays the same after 6 minutes. [5]

c The student does the experiment again. The only difference is that the student uses warm, rather than cold, hydrochloric acid. On your graph, draw the shape of the graph you would expect for the experiment with the warm hydrochloric acid. [2]

CIE IGCSE, June 2003, paper 2, q.2 part

2 The diagram shows the apparatus used for oxidising ammonia in the laboratory.

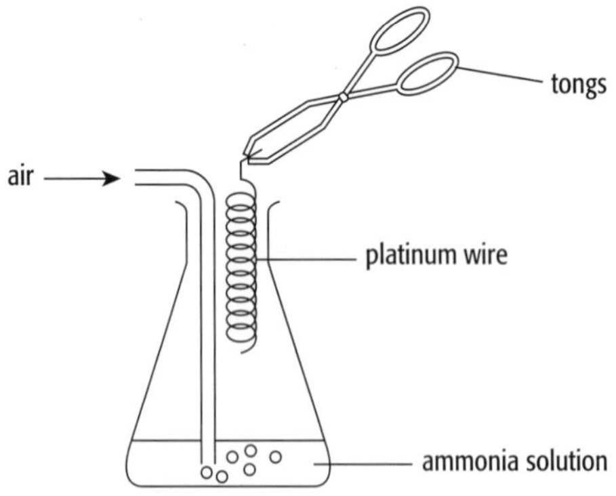

First, nitrogen(II) oxide, NO, is produced. This then reacts with oxygen to form nitrogen(IV) oxide, NO_2.

a Where does the oxygen come from in this reaction? [1]

b Balance the equation for the reaction of nitrogen(II) oxide with oxygen.

$2NO + O_2 \rightleftharpoons .....NO_2$ [1]

c What is the meaning of the symbol $\rightleftharpoons$? [1]

d The platinum wire acts as a catalyst in the reaction. As the reaction takes place, the wire begins to glow red hot. What does this show about the reaction? [1]

CIE IGCSE, June 2005, paper 2, q.3 part

3 A student used the apparatus shown below for investigating the speed of the reaction between iron and sulfuric acid.

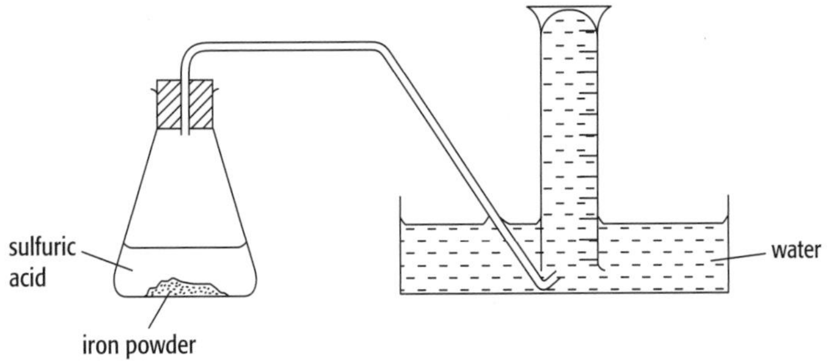

a Describe how this apparatus can be used to investigate the speed of this reaction. [3]

b The student repeated the experiment with different concentrations of sulfuric acid. In each experiment the mass of iron powder was the same, and the temperature was kept at 30 °C. The results are shown in the table.

Concentration of sulfuric acid (moles per dm^3)	Speed of reaction (cm^3 hydrogen per second)
0.4	4.2
0.8	8.5
1.6	17.0

i Use the information in the table to help you work out how the speed of the reaction is affected by the concentration of sulfuric acid. [2]

ii What will happen to the speed of the reaction if lumps of iron are used instead of iron powder? [1]

iii What will happen to the speed of the reaction if it is carried out at 20 °C rather than at 30 °C? [1]

CIE IGCSE, November 2006, paper 2, q.7 part

4 An organic compound decomposes to form nitrogen.

$C_6H_5N_2Cl(aq) \rightarrow C_6H_5Cl(l) + N_2(g)$

The rate of this reaction can be measured using the following apparatus.

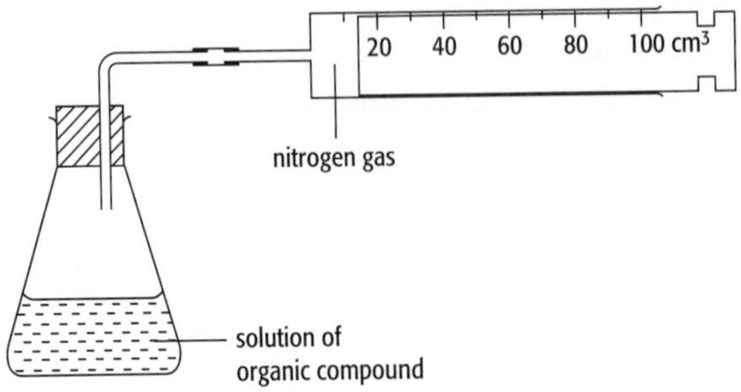

The results of this experiment are shown on the graph below.

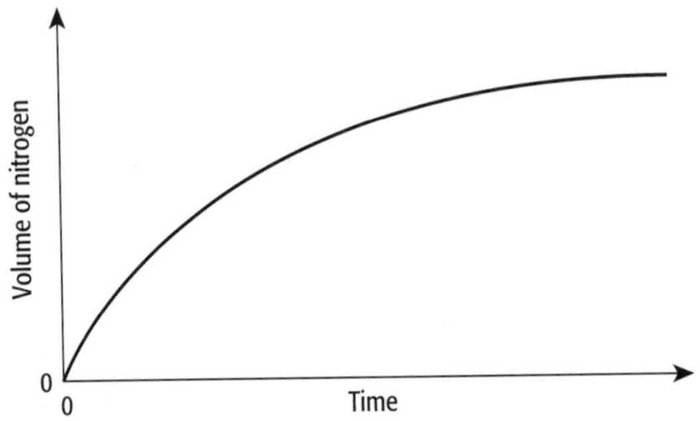

a How does the rate of this reaction vary with time? [1]

b Why does the rate vary? [2]

c The reaction is catalysed by copper powder. Sketch the graph for the catalysed reaction on the same grid. [2]

d Why is copper powder more effective as a catalyst than a single piece of copper? [1]

CIE IGCSE, June 2004, paper 3, q.3 part

5 Exothermic reactions produce heat energy.
An important fuel is methane, natural gas. The equation for its combustion is as follows.

$CH_4 + 2O_2 \rightarrow CO_2 + 2H_2O$

a In chemical reactions bonds are broken and new bonds are formed. Using this reaction, give an example of

i a bond that is broken

ii a bond that is formed. [2]

b Explain, using the idea of bonds forming and breaking, why this reaction is exothermic, that is, it produces heat energy. [2]

CIE IGCSE, June 2006, paper 3, q.6 part

6 Hydrogen and iodine react to form hydrogen iodide:

$$H_2 + I_2 \rightarrow 2HI$$

When a reaction takes place, chemical bonds are broken and new chemical bonds are formed.
To break a chemical bond, energy has to be supplied; this is represented by +.
When a chemical bond forms, energy is given out; this is represented by –.

a Copy out and insert the missing signs and the missing value in the table below. [3]

energy to break H—H	=	+ 436 kJ
energy to break I—I	=	...151 kJ
energy to make H—I	=	...299 kJ
energy to make H—Br	=	.... kJ

b Calculate the overall energy change for this reaction. [1]

c Is the overall reaction exothermic or endothermic? [1]

7 Ammonia contains the elements nitrogen and hydrogen. It is manufactured from these elements in the Haber process.

$$N_2(g) + 3H_2(g) \rightleftharpoons 2NH_3(g)$$

The forward reaction is exothermic. The table shows how the percentage of ammonia in the equilibrium mixture varies with pressure at 600 °C.

Percentage ammonia	8	12	15	20
Pressure / atm	200	300	400	500

a Explain why the percentage of ammonia increases as the pressure increases. [2]

b How would the percentage of ammonia change if the measurements had been made at a lower temperature? Explain your answer. [2]

c State **two** of the reaction conditions used in the Haber process. [2]

CIE IGCSE, November 2003, paper 3, q.1 part

8 Patterns and properties of metals

This chapter covers the following ideas:

- the alkali metals – trends in properties
- S aluminium and its protective oxide layer
- the transition elements – distinctive properties of these metals
- the reactivity series
- methods of extraction in relation to reactivity
- S metal displacement reactions
- S electrochemical cells – link to reactivity

8.1 The alkali metals

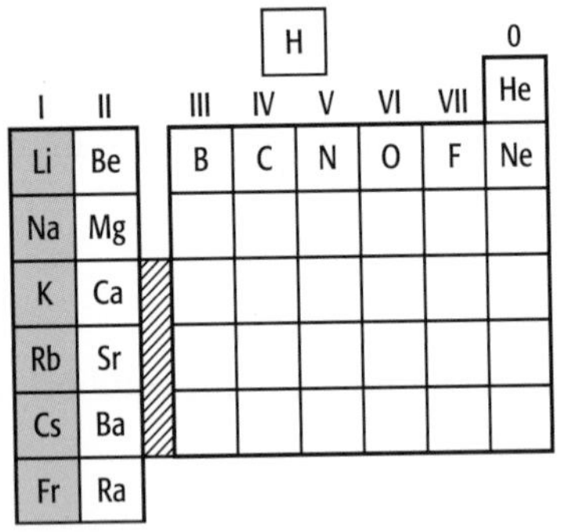

The distinctive metals of Group I are called the **alkali metals**. The most memorable thing about them is their spectacular reaction with cold water (Figure **8.1**). These metals do not have many uses because they are so reactive and tarnish easily. They have to be stored under oil. The one familiar use of sodium is in sodium vapour lamps. These are the yellow street and motorway lights seen throughout towns and cities.

The melting points of the alkali metals decrease gradually as you go down the group. There is a similar trend in the hardness of the metals. They are all soft, low-density metals. Lithium is the hardest, but it can still be cut with a knife. The metals get easier to cut going down the group. The **density** of the metals tends to increase down the group, though potassium is an exception, being slightly less dense than sodium.

Figure 8.1 The reaction of sodium with water. Note that the hydrogen released burns with the metal's characteristic flame colour.

There are many ways in which the different elements of Group I show similar properties. Some of these common characteristics are given in the box that follows.

> The common properties of the alkali metals are as follows.
> - They are all reactive metals. They have to be stored under oil to stop them reacting with the oxygen and water vapour in the air (Table **8.1**).
> - They are soft and can be cut with a knife.
> - Like all metals they form positive ions. The metals of Group I form ions with a single positive charge (for example Li^+, Na^+, K^+).

- As a result they form compounds that have similar formulae; for example, their carbonates are lithium carbonate (Li_2CO_3), sodium carbonate (Na_2CO_3) and potassium carbonate (K_2CO_3).
- They all react strongly and directly with non-metals to form salts. These salts are all white, crystalline, ionic solids that dissolve in water.

Exam tip

Make sure of the wording of your answers in exams. The alkali metals have 'similar' properties to each other, they are not the same. There is a gradual change in properties as you go down the group.

Remember that you can be asked to 'predict' properties of these elements by comparison with others in the group, so practise that type of question.

The reaction of the alkali metals with water

All the alkali metals react spontaneously with water to produce hydrogen gas and the metal hydroxide (Table **8.1**). The reactions are exothermic. The heat produced is sufficient to melt sodium and potassium as they skid over the surface of the water. Lithium does not melt as it reacts. This begins to show the gradual differences in reactivity between the metals as you go down the group. Lithium (at the top) is the least reactive and caesium (at the bottom) is the most reactive.

Element	Reaction with water	Reaction with air	
lithium	reacts steadily $2Li + 2H_2O \rightarrow 2LiOH + H_2$	tarnishes slowly to give a layer of oxide	increasing reactivity ↓
sodium	reacts strongly $2Na + 2H_2O \rightarrow 2NaOH + H_2$	tarnishes quickly to give a layer of oxide	
potassium	reacts violently $2K + 2H_2O \rightarrow 2KOH + H_2$	tarnishes very quickly to give a layer of oxide	

Table 8.1 Reactions of lithium, sodium and potassium with air and water.

The reaction with water is the same in each case:

metal + water → metal hydroxide + hydrogen

For example,

$$\text{sodium} + \text{water} \rightarrow \text{sodium hydroxide} + \text{hydrogen}$$
$$2Na(s) + 2H_2O(l) \rightarrow 2NaOH(aq) + H_2(g)$$

The reaction gets more vigorous as you move down the group. The reaction of lithium with water is quite steady: the metal does not melt and the hydrogen does not ignite. Sodium reacts more strongly: the metal melts but, if the sodium is free to move, the hydrogen does not usually ignite. Restricting the movement of the sodium, by placing it on a piece of filter paper on the water surface, results in the hydrogen gas igniting. The flame is coloured yellow by the sodium. Potassium reacts so strongly with water that the hydrogen gas ignites spontaneously. The potassium may even explode dangerously. The flame is coloured lilac. Rubidium and caesium explode as soon as they are put into water. The metal hydroxide produced in each case makes the water become alkaline.

Exam tip

Remember to read exam questions carefully. When asked, 'What would you observe?', make sure that you give your observations carefully – talk about what you see, hear and smell. If there is a gas given off then state its colour, for instance. Make sure you give detail.

E

Flame tests for the alkali metals

Compounds of the alkali metals can be detected by a **flame test**. All alkali-metal ions give characteristic colours in a Bunsen flame. Table **8.2** lists the colours obtained. The intensity (brightness) of the flame colour can be measured using a flame photometer. This

Metal ion	Formula	Flame colour
lithium	Li^+	red
sodium	Na^+	yellow
potassium	K^+	lilac

Table 8.2 Flame colours of Group I metal ions.

instrument is used in hospitals to measure the levels of sodium ions and potassium ions in body fluids. Sodium and potassium are essential to good health. The cells in our body are surrounded by a solution that usually contains more sodium ions, while the fluid inside the cells contains more potassium ions. The balance between the two ions is very important. The nerve impulses in our bodies are controlled by the movement of these two ions.

Our bodies can store excess sodium ions but not potassium ions. This means that the body levels of potassium ions, which come from fresh fruit and vegetables, may fall in some people. An imbalance between sodium and potassium is set up, which can lead to high blood pressure. A low-sodium alternative to ordinary table salt can be purchased that contains two-thirds potassium chloride and only one-third sodium chloride. This can be used instead of common table salt in cooking and for flavouring food. This salt alternative must be used carefully by people who have other medical conditions.

Compounds of the alkali metals

The alkali metals themselves do not have many general uses. But the compounds of the alkali metals are very important. Sodium chloride (common salt) has a very wide range of uses, both domestic and industrial. Its importance stretches back in history. Salt is a major food preservative, which was even more significant before the development of refrigeration. The word 'salary' derives from a time when workers were paid with salt. In 1930, when Britain still ruled over India, Mahatma Gandhi led a protest march to the sea to collect salt. This was to demonstrate the Indians' wish to be free of the British monopoly of salt and the taxes they imposed on it.

Sodium nitrate and potassium nitrate deposits in South America, particularly in Chile, were of great importance as fertilisers and explosives. These salts were so important that masses of 'guano', nitrate-rich droppings deposited by sea birds, were transported from South America to Europe. Potassium nitrate is used as the oxidiser in black gunpowder – a mixture of nitrate, charcoal and sulfur. When ignited, the reactions produce large quantities of gases. This causes a sudden expansion in volume. In the home, sodium carbonate (washing soda), sodium hydrogencarbonate (bicarbonate of soda, baking soda) and sodium hydroxide (oven cleaner) all have their uses. Sodium hydroxide is important in the laboratory in testing for metal and ammonium ions.

Group II metals

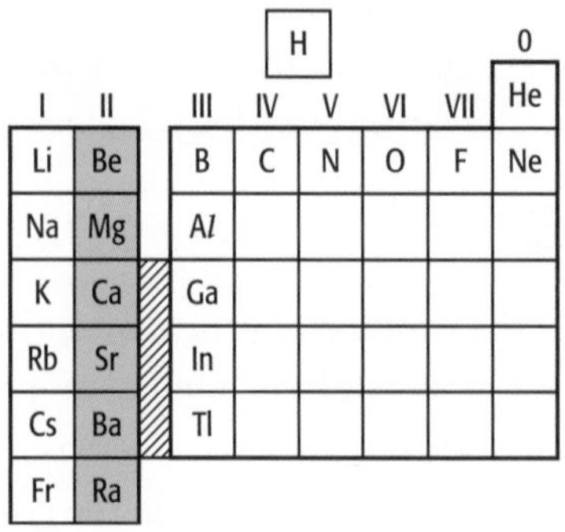

The Group II metals are called the **alkaline earth metals**. The Group shows similar trends in reactivity to Group I. They are less reactive than the metals in Group I, but still take part in a wide range of reactions. Like the alkali metals, compounds of these metals produce characteristic flame colours (Figure **8.2**). The colours obtained are listed in Table **8.3**. Compounds of the Group II metals are often used in fireworks, because of these colours.

Metal ion	Ion	Flame colour
magnesium	Mg^{2+}	no colour
calcium	Ca^{2+}	brick red
strontium	Sr^{2+}	scarlet
barium	Ba^{2+}	apple green

Table 8.3 Flame colours of Group II metal ions.

Magnesium ions do not give a characteristic flame colour. Magnesium metal burns fiercely with a brilliant (very bright) white light. For this reason it is used in distress flares, in flashbulbs and in fireworks that give a white light.

Trends in reactivity

As in Group I, the reactivity of the alkaline earth metals increases going down the group. Beryllium (at the top) is the least reactive and barium (at the bottom) is the most reactive. Again the change in reactivity is best shown by using their reactions with water.

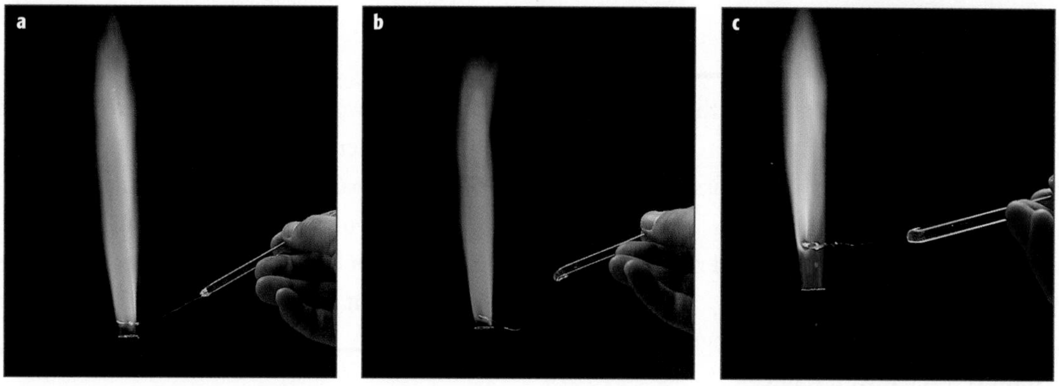

Figure 8.2 Some Group II metals give characteristic colours in the flame test: **a** calcium, **b** strontium, and **c** barium.

Magnesium reacts **very slowly** when placed in **cold** water. If left for some time, hydrogen can be collected and the solution becomes slightly alkaline:

magnesium + water
→ magnesium hydroxide + hydrogen

$$Mg(s) + 2H_2O(l) \rightarrow Mg(OH)_2(s) + H_2(g)$$

Magnesium hydroxide is not very soluble in water. The reaction is speeded up if **warm** water is used.

A much **more vigorous** reaction is obtained if **steam** is passed over heated magnesium. The magnesium glows brightly to form hydrogen and magnesium oxide:

magnesium + steam
→ magnesium oxide + hydrogen

$$Mg(s) + H_2O(g) \rightarrow MgO(s) + H_2(g)$$

Calcium, however, **reacts strongly** with **cold** water, giving off hydrogen rapidly:

calcium + water → calcium hydroxide + hydrogen

$$Ca(s) + 2H_2O(l) \rightarrow Ca(OH)_2(aq) + H_2(g)$$

Calcium hydroxide is more soluble than magnesium hydroxide, so an alkaline solution is produced (limewater). As the reaction proceeds, a white suspension is obtained because not all the calcium hydroxide dissolves.

The reactions of burning magnesium

Magnesium burns readily in air with a brilliant white flame. It burns even brighter in pure oxygen, producing a white ash, magnesium oxide:

magnesium + oxygen → magnesium oxide

$$2Mg(s) + O_2(g) \rightarrow 2MgO(s)$$

Exam tip

To extend your knowledge, remember that magnesium is so reactive that when it burns it can react with nitrogen in the air as well as with oxygen.

Burning magnesium can also reduce carbon dioxide to carbon if it is lowered into a gas jar of the gas.

Key ideas so far

- The alkali metals are the most reactive metals in the Periodic Table.
- The reactivity of these metals increases as you go down the group.
- The alkali metals have similar properties to each other.
- They all have the same number of electrons in their outer shell.
- These metals give characteristic colours in the flame test.
- The alkali metals react strongly with water to give hydrogen gas and an alkaline solution.
- The Group II metals show similar trends in properties to Group I. They are less reactive than the alkali metals.

Quick-check questions

1. State **two** physical characteristics of the alkali metals.
2. Give the colours of sodium and potassium if their salts are tested in the flame test.
3. What gas is given off when the alkali metals are reacted with water?
4. Name the product, other than hydrogen, when potassium is reacted with water.
5. Write a word equation for the reaction of sodium with water.
6. Write a balanced chemical equation for the reaction of potassium with water.
7. Which of the alkali metals does not melt when a piece of it is placed on the surface of water?

8.2 Aluminium

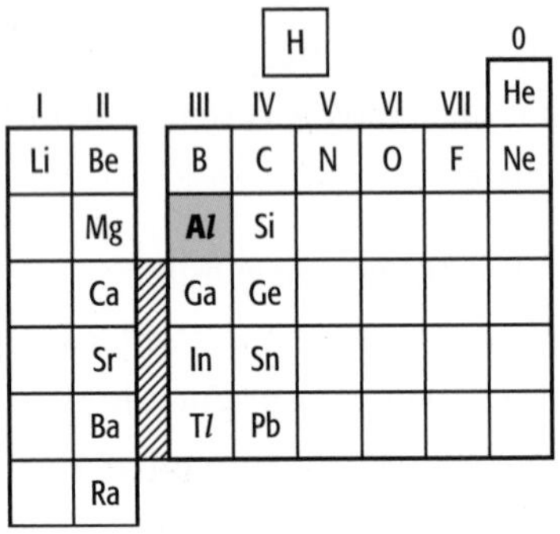

Aluminium was, for a long time, an expensive and little used metal. In France, around the 1860s, at the Court of Napoleon III (the nephew of the better-known Napoleon Bonaparte), honoured guests used cutlery made of aluminium rather than gold. At that time the metal was expensively extracted from aluminium chloride using sodium:

aluminium chloride + sodium
→ sodium chloride + aluminium

$$AlCl_3(s) + 3Na(s) \rightarrow 3NaCl(s) + Al(s)$$

The breakthrough came in 1886 when Charles Hall and Paul Héroult independently found a way to obtain the metal by electrolysis.

Aluminium is the most common metal in the Earth's crust. The one major ore of aluminium is **bauxite**, and aluminium oxide is purified from this. Electrolysis of molten aluminium oxide produces aluminium at the cathode.

Aluminium's usefulness

Aluminium is a light, strong metal and has good electrical conductivity. Increasingly it is being used for construction purposes. The Lunar Rover 'moon-buggy' was built out of aluminium, and so too are some modern cars. For use in aeroplanes, it is usually alloyed with other metals such as copper (Figure **8.3**). Its low density and good conductivity have led to its use in overhead power lines.

Figure 8.3 The supersonic passenger jet *Concorde* was built out of an aluminium alloy.

Aluminium is particularly useful because it is protected from corrosion by the stable layer of aluminium oxide that forms on its surface. This protective layer stops the aluminium (a reactive metal) from reacting. This makes aluminium foil containers ideal for food packaging as they resist corrosion by natural acids. Aluminium is also used for external structures such as window frames as they resist weathering. Figure **8.4** shows the uses made of aluminium produced in the USA.

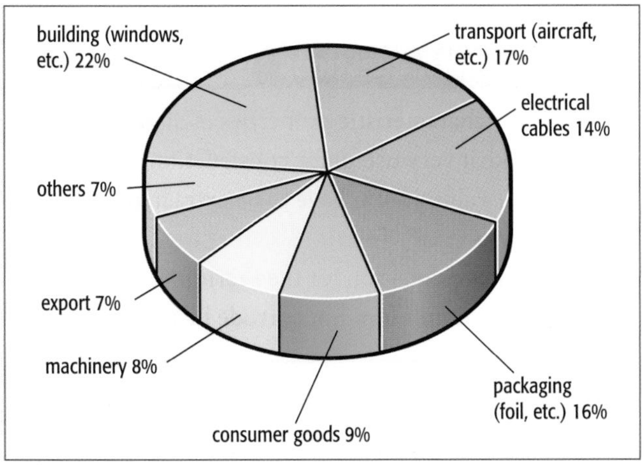

Figure 8.4 The widespread and increasing uses of the aluminium produced in the USA.

The thermit reaction

The high reactivity of aluminium is used to extract some metals from their oxides in small quantities. Thus aluminium can be used to produce iron from iron(III) oxide:

iron(III) oxide + aluminium
→ aluminium oxide + iron

$$Fe_2O_3(s) + 2Al(s) \rightarrow Al_2O_3(s) + 2Fe(l)$$

The aluminium and iron(III) oxide are powdered and well mixed to help them react (Figure **8.5a**). The reaction is powerful, exothermic and produces iron in the molten state. Because of this, the reaction is used to weld together damaged railway lines (Figure **8.5b**). The reaction is an example of reduction–oxidation (**redox**) and is known as the **thermit reaction**. Other metals such as chromium can be prepared from their oxides by such redox reactions.

chromium(III) oxide + aluminium
→ aluminium oxide + chromium

$$Cr_2O_3(s) + 2Al(s) \rightarrow Al_2O_3(s) + 2Cr(s)$$

The analytical test for aluminium ions

Aluminium ions do not give a characteristic colour in the flame test. The presence of aluminium ions (Al^{3+}) in a compound must be detected by some other method. If an aluminium salt is dissolved in water and sodium hydroxide solution is added, a white precipitate is formed. For example:

aluminium chloride + sodium hydroxide
→ aluminium hydroxide + sodium chloride

$$AlCl_3(aq) + 3NaOH(aq) \rightarrow \underset{\text{white precipitate}}{Al(OH)_3(s)} + 3NaCl(aq)$$

Other metal ions such as calcium and magnesium also give a white precipitate in this test, so the test is not conclusive. However, the aluminium hydroxide precipitate will re-dissolve if **excess** sodium hydroxide is added. The precipitates of calcium hydroxide or magnesium hydroxide will not do this; they are basic hydroxides, whereas aluminium hydroxide is **amphoteric**. Aluminium hydroxide reacts with sodium hydroxide to produce the soluble salt, sodium aluminate:

aluminium hydroxide + sodium hydroxide
→ sodium aluminate

$$\underset{\text{white precipitate}}{Al(OH)_3(s)} + 3NaOH(aq) \rightarrow \underset{\text{colourless solution}}{Na_3Al(OH)_6(aq)}$$

A strong alkali such as sodium hydroxide is needed to produce this reaction. Ammonia solution, which is only a weak alkali, will not re-dissolve the aluminium hydroxide precipitate.

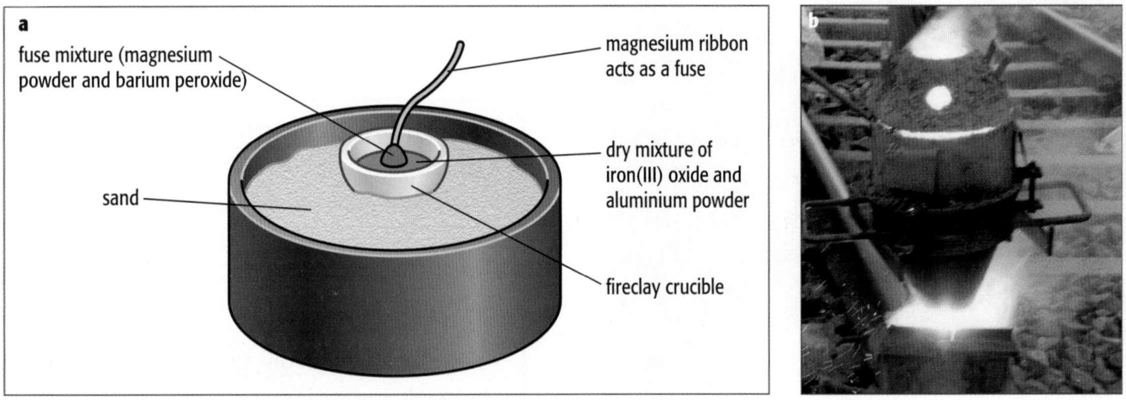

Figure 8.5 **a** The thermit reaction. **b** Using the thermit reaction to weld fractured railway lines.

Key ideas so far

- Aluminium is an abundant metal in the Earth's crust.
- Aluminium is extracted from alumina by electrolysis.
- Aluminium is a light and strong metal, which makes it useful for building aircraft.
- Aluminium does not corrode, which makes it useful for food containers and external structures.
- Aluminium reduces iron(III) oxide to iron in the thermit reaction. The reaction is very exothermic.

Quick-check questions

1 Give **two** characteristic properties of aluminium that make it very useful for construction.
2 Why does aluminium have to be extracted by electrolysis?
3 Write a word equation for the thermit reaction.
4 Why does aluminium not corrode like iron?

8.3 The transition elements

II											III
Be											B
Mg											Al
Ca	Sc	Ti	V	Cr	Mn	Fe	Co	Ni	Cu	Zn	Ga
Sr	Y	Zr	Nb	Mo	Tc	Ru	Rh	Pd	Ag	Cd	In
Ba		Hf	Ta	W	Re	Os	Ir	Pt	Au	Hg	Tl
Ra											

The famous bridge at Ironbridge in Shropshire, England (Figure **8.6**) marks a historic industrial revolution in Europe. Made from cast iron and opened in 1781, it was the first iron bridge in the world. The metal iron is a **transition element**. We use about nine times more iron than all the other metals put together. Modern bridges (such as the Forth road bridge, in Scotland) are now made of steel, where iron is alloyed with other transition elements and carbon to make it stronger.

Figure 8.6 The bridge at Ironbridge was the first ever built of iron.

The general features of transition elements (also called transition metals) make them the most useful metallic elements available to us. They are much less reactive than the metals in Groups I and II. Many have excellent corrosion resistance, for example chromium. The very high melting point of tungsten (3410 °C) has led to its use in the filaments of light bulbs.

The transition metals have all the major properties we think of as being characteristic of metals. They
- are hard and strong
- have high melting points
- have high densities
- are good conductors of heat and electricity
- are malleable and ductile.

These **general** properties mean that the transition elements are useful in a number of different ways. In addition there are **particular** properties that make these metals distinctive and useful for more specific purposes.

The distinctive properties of the transition elements:
- Many of their compounds are coloured.
- These metals often show more than one valency – they form more than one type of ion.
- The metals or their compounds often make useful catalysts.
- A few of the metals are strongly magnetic (iron, cobalt and nickel).

Coloured compounds

The salts of the metals in Groups I, II and III are generally white solids. They give colourless solutions if they dissolve in water. In contrast, the salts of the transition elements are often coloured and produce coloured solutions when dissolved. For example, vanadium compounds in solution can be yellow, blue, green or purple. Some other examples of the colours produced by transition-element ions are given in Table **8.4**. The presence of such metals in negative ions also gives rise to colour.

The transition elements are one of the major contributors to colour in our lives. The impressive colours of stained glass windows are produced by the presence of these metal ions in the glass (Figure **8.7**). Similar trace amounts (very small amounts) of metals produce the colours of gemstones such as sapphire and ruby. These stones are corundum, the naturally occurring crystalline form of aluminium oxide (Al_2O_3). Pure corundum is colourless but trace amounts of titanium and iron ions together produce the blue colour of sapphires, while chromium ions (Cr^{3+}) produce the red colour of rubies.

The colours associated with transition elements also help in chemical analysis. When testing a salt solution by adding sodium hydroxide, the transition elements give hydroxide precipitates with a characteristic colour. For example, iron(II) hydroxide is grey-green whereas iron(III) hydroxide is red-brown.

Metal ion in solution	Formula	Colour
copper(II)	Cu^{2+}	blue
iron(II)	Fe^{2+}	green
iron(III)	Fe^{3+}	red-brown
chromium(III)	Cr^{3+}	green
cobalt(II)	Co^{2+}	pink
manganate(VII)	MnO_4^-	purple
chromate(VI)	CrO_4^{2-}	yellow
dichromate(VI)	$Cr_2O_7^{2-}$	orange

[a] *Including some negative ions that contain these metals.*

Table 8.4 The colours of some transition-element ions in solution[a].

Figure 8.7 Meherangarah Fort stained glass windows, Jodhpur, India. The colours of the stained glass are due to the presence of transition metal ions in the glass.

Variable valency

The metals in Group I always show a valency of 1. When reacting to form ionic compounds, their atoms **lose** their one outer electron to form ions with a single positive charge (Na^+, K^+, etc.). The metals in Group II all show a valency of 2; they form ions with two positive charges (Mg^{2+}, Ca^{2+}, etc.). Aluminium in Group III has a valency of 3 and always forms the Al^{3+} ion.

Transition-element atoms, however, are not so straightforward. For example, iron atoms can lose either two electrons, to form the Fe^{2+} ion, or three electrons, to give Fe^{3+}. Compounds containing these ions have different colours and different properties. A distinction is made in their name: iron(II) oxide has the formula FeO, iron(III) oxide the formula Fe_2O_3. Other transition elements also have more than one valency.

Catalytic properties

Catalysts are substances that speed up a chemical reaction without themselves being used up or changed at the end of the reaction. Many of the important industrial catalysts are either transition elements or their compounds, for example iron in the Haber process.

Magnetic properties

Three of the first row of transition elements are strongly magnetic. They are iron, cobalt and nickel. The Earth's magnetic field is produced by the liquid and solid iron and nickel in the outer and inner core of the planet.

It is important to realise that most metals, aluminium for instance, are not magnetic.

The reactions of certain transition elements

Iron

Iron is only a moderately reactive metal, but it will still react with steam or acids to displace hydrogen gas. For example:

iron + hydrochloric acid → iron(II) chloride + hydrogen

$$Fe(s) + 2HCl(aq) \rightarrow FeCl_2(aq) + H_2(g)$$

The fact that iron can form two different positive ions means that an analytical test is needed to distinguish between the two. The salt being tested is dissolved in water and then alkali is added.

With solutions of iron(II) salts, a grey-green gelatinous (jelly-like) precipitate of iron(II) hydroxide is formed on adding the alkali:

iron(II) chloride + sodium hydroxide → iron(II) hydroxide + sodium chloride

$$FeCl_2(aq) + 2NaOH(aq) \rightarrow \underset{\text{grey-green precipitate}}{Fe(OH)_2(s)} + 2NaCl(aq)$$

The precipitate is not affected by adding excess alkali. The same precipitate is formed if ammonia solution is used instead of sodium hydroxide. With solutions of iron(III) salts, a red-brown gelatinous precipitate of iron(III) hydroxide is formed when alkali is added:

iron(III) chloride + sodium hydroxide → iron(III) hydroxide + sodium chloride

$$FeCl_3(aq) + 3NaOH(aq) \rightarrow \underset{\text{red-brown precipitate}}{Fe(OH)_3(s)} + 3NaCl(aq)$$

Copper

Copper has a distinctive colour. It is one of the least reactive metals in common use. It does **not** react with dilute acids to produce hydrogen. If the metal is heated in air, then a black layer of copper(II) oxide is formed on the metal:

copper + oxygen $\xrightarrow{\text{heat}}$ copper(II) oxide

$$2Cu(s) + O_2(g) \rightarrow 2CuO(s)$$

Copper statues and roofs become coated in a green layer of basic copper(II) carbonate (Figure **8.8**) when exposed to the atmosphere for a long time.

Figure 8.8 The copper sheets of this roof have become coated in a layer of green copper carbonate.

Copper(II) carbonate is also found in the Earth's crust as the mineral malachite. Like most other carbonates, copper(II) carbonate will decompose on heating to release carbon dioxide:

copper(II) carbonate $\xrightarrow{\text{heat}}$ copper(II) oxide + carbon dioxide

$$\underset{\text{green}}{CuCO_3(s)} \xrightarrow{\text{heat}} \underset{\text{black}}{CuO(s)} + CO_2(g)$$

The presence of copper ions in compounds can be detected using the flame test. Copper gives a characteristic blue-green colour. Solutions of copper salts also give a blue gelatinous precipitate of copper(II) hydroxide if sodium hydroxide is added:

copper(II) sulfate + sodium hydroxide → copper(II) hydroxide + sodium sulfate

$$CuSO_4(aq) + 2NaOH(aq) \rightarrow \underset{\text{blue precipitate}}{Cu(OH)_2(s)} + Na_2SO_4(aq)$$

If the precipitate formed is heated carefully, it will turn black. Copper(II) hydroxide is unstable when heated and is converted to copper(II) oxide.

Ammonia solution will also produce the same blue precipitate of copper(II) hydroxide when added to copper(II) sulfate solution. However, if excess ammonia is added, the precipitate re-dissolves to give a deep-blue solution.

Zinc

Zinc is a moderately reactive metal that will displace hydrogen from steam or dilute acids:

$$\text{zinc} + \text{steam} \xrightarrow{\text{heat}} \text{zinc oxide} + \text{hydrogen}$$
$$Zn(s) + H_2O(g) \xrightarrow{\text{heat}} ZnO + H_2(g)$$

$$\text{zinc} + \text{hydrochloric acid} \rightarrow \text{zinc chloride} + \text{hydrogen}$$
$$Zn(s) + 2HCl(aq) \rightarrow ZnCl_2(aq) + H_2(g)$$

Zinc carbonate decomposes on heating to give off carbon dioxide:

$$\text{zinc carbonate} \xrightarrow{\text{heat}} \text{zinc oxide} + \text{carbon dioxide}$$
$$\underset{\text{white}}{ZnCO_3(s)} \xrightarrow{\text{heat}} \underset{\text{white}}{ZnO(s)} + CO_2(g)$$

Interestingly, when hot, the zinc oxide produced is yellow. However, when it cools down it turns white again. This is simply a physical change that occurs on heating, not a chemical reaction.

Solutions of zinc salts produce a white precipitate of zinc hydroxide when sodium hydroxide solution is added:

$$\text{zinc sulfate} + \text{sodium hydroxide} \rightarrow \text{zinc hydroxide} + \text{sodium sulfate}$$
$$ZnSO_4(aq) + 2NaOH(aq) \rightarrow \underset{\text{white precipitate}}{Zn(OH)_2(s)} + Na_2SO_4(aq)$$

Zinc hydroxide, like aluminium hydroxide, is an amphoteric hydroxide and it re-dissolves if excess sodium hydroxide is added. Zinc hydroxide reacts with excess sodium hydroxide to form sodium zincate:

$$\text{zinc hydroxide} + \text{sodium hydroxide} \rightarrow \text{sodium zincate}$$
$$\underset{\text{white precipitate}}{Zn(OH)_2(s)} + 2NaOH(aq) \rightarrow \underset{\text{colourless solution}}{Na_2Zn(OH)_4(aq)}$$

These reactions with sodium hydroxide do not help us to distinguish between zinc salts and aluminium salts. Both give white precipitates that re-dissolve in excess alkali. The two **can** be distinguished, however, if ammonia solution is used, not sodium hydroxide. In both cases, the hydroxide precipitate forms; but zinc hydroxide re-dissolves in excess ammonia solution, whereas aluminium hydroxide does not.

Key ideas so far

- The transition metals lie in a block in the centre of the Periodic Table.
- They are relatively unreactive as metals and so are useful for construction.
- Iron is by far the most used metal for construction purposes.
- The transition metals have several characteristic properties:
  - they are hard, dense metals
  - they generally form coloured compounds
  - they can show more than one valency in their compounds
  - they, or their compounds, are often good catalysts.

? Quick-check questions

1. Give **three** distinctive properties of the transition metals.
2. What are the two valencies of iron in its compounds?
3. What colour do you associate with copper compounds?
4. Iron corrodes to form rust. What is the chemical name and formula for 'rust'?
5. Name an important industrial process for which iron is the catalyst.

8.4 The reactivity of metals

Most of the elements in the Periodic Table are metals. Many of them are useful for a wide variety of purposes; some, such as iron, have an enormous number of uses.

The early history of human life is marked by the metals used in making jewellery, ornaments and tools. Early civilisations used metals that could be found 'native' (for example gold) for decorative items, and then alloys such as bronze. Later, iron was used for tools. Even after the Bronze and Iron Ages, only a few metals continued to be used widely. Other more reactive metals could not be obtained until the nineteenth century. Even among the metals that were available, there were obvious differences in resistance to corrosion. The Viking sword in Figure **8.9** emphasises the different reactivities of the gold and silver of the hilt and the iron of the blade.

Figure 8.9 This Viking sword had a handle made from gold and silver and an iron blade. The blade has corroded badly but the handle is untouched.

We have seen how reactivity changes in a particular group. But the more important metals we use come from more than one group. Is there a broader picture in which we can compare these?

An overview of reactivity

We can get information on reactivity by investigating the following aspects of metal chemistry:

- ease of extraction
- reactions with air or oxygen
- reactions with water
- reactions with dilute acids
- metal displacement reactions and redox reactions
- heat stability of metal compounds.

The overall picture that emerges is summarised in Figure **8.10**. This is known as the **reactivity series** of metals.

The extraction of metals

A few metals are so **unreactive** that they occur in an uncombined (**native**) state. These unreactive metals include copper (Figure **8.11**), gold and silver. The metals that occur native form the first broad group of metals. They are found as metals in the Earth's crust.

However, most metals are **too reactive** to exist on their own in the ground. They exist combined with other elements as compounds called **ores** (Table **8.5**). These are the raw materials for making metals. The metals that

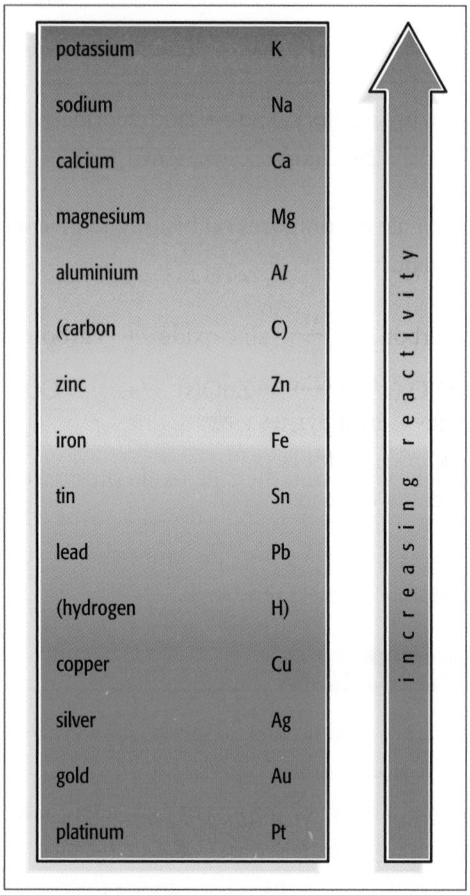

Figure 8.10 The reactivity series for metals.

Figure 8.11 A piece of copper found 'native'.

Metal	Name of ore	Compound present
aluminium	bauxite	aluminium oxide, Al_2O_3
copper	copper pyrites	copper iron sulfide, $CuFeS_2$
iron	hematite	iron(III) oxide, Fe_2O_3
sodium	rock salt	sodium chloride, NaCl
tin	cassiterite	tin(IV) oxide, SnO_2
zinc	zinc-blende	zinc sulfide, ZnS
lead	galena	lead(II) sulfide, PbS

Table 8.5 Some metals and their ores.

must be mined as ores can be subdivided into two other broad groups.

The moderately reactive metals such as iron, zinc, tin and lead occur either as oxide or as sulfide ores (Figure **8.12**). One sulfide ore that is quite noteworthy is iron pyrites which, because of its colour, became known as 'fool's gold' (Figure **8.13**). The sulfide ores can easily be converted to the oxide by heating in air. For example:

$$\text{zinc sulfide} + \text{oxygen} \rightarrow \text{zinc oxide} + \text{sulfur dioxide}$$
$$2ZnS(s) + 3O_2(g) \rightarrow 2ZnO(s) + 2SO_2(g)$$

The oxide must then be reduced to give the metal. Carbon, in the form of coke, is used for this. Coke can be made cheaply from coal. At high temperatures, carbon has a strong tendency to react with oxygen. It is a good reducing agent and will remove oxygen from these metal ores:

$$\text{zinc oxide} + \text{carbon} \rightarrow \text{zinc} + \text{carbon dioxide}$$
$$2ZnO(s) + C(s) \rightarrow 2Zn(s) + CO_2(g)$$

So this group of moderately reactive metals can be extracted by reduction with carbon using essentially the blast furnace method (page **252**).

Figure 8.12 The major ores of iron: limonite, hematite and magnetite.

Figure 8.13 'Fool's gold' – a notorious ore of iron called iron pyrites (FeS_2).

However, some metals are too reactive to be extracted by this method. The very reactive metals such as aluminium, magnesium and sodium have to be extracted by electrolysis of their molten ores. The three broad groups are summarised in Table **8.6**.

	Metal	Method of extraction
	potassium	**electrolysis** of molten ores
	sodium	
	calcium	
	magnesium	
	aluminium	
decreasing reactivity	zinc	**reduction** of oxides with carbon (sulfide ores heated to give oxide)
	iron	
	tin	
	lead	
	copper	**occur native** in the ground
	silver	
	gold	

Table 8.6 Methods of extraction in relation to the reactivity series.

Reactions of metals with air, water and dilute acids

Considering the methods of extraction of the metals gives a broad pattern of reactivity. More detail can be found by looking at certain basic reactions of metals. The results are summarised in Table **8.7** (overleaf).

Reactivity series	Reaction with ...		
	Air	Water	Dilute HCl
sodium	burn very strongly in air to form oxide	react with cold water to give hydrogen	react very strongly to give hydrogen
calcium			
magnesium			
aluminium[a]	burn less strongly in air to form oxide	react with steam, when heated, to give hydrogen	react less strongly to give hydrogen
zinc			
iron			
lead	react slowly to form oxide layer when heated	do not react	do not react
copper			
silver	do not react	do not react	do not react
gold			

[a] *These reactions only occur if the protective oxide layer is removed from the aluminium.*

Table 8.7 The reaction of metals with air, water and dilute hydrochloric acid.

Metal displacement reactions

This type of reaction can help us to place particular metals more precisely in the reactivity series. We can use it to compare directly the reactivity of two metals. In a displacement reaction, a more reactive metal displaces a less reactive metal from solutions of salts of the less reactive metal.

In this type of reaction, the two metals are in direct 'competition'. If a piece of zinc is left to stand in a solution of copper(II) sulfate, a reaction occurs:

zinc + copper(II) sulfate → zinc sulfate + copper

$Zn(s) + CuSO_4(aq) \rightarrow ZnSO_4(aq) + Cu(s)$

grey — blue — colourless — red-brown

The observed effect of the reaction is that the zinc metal becomes coated with a red-brown layer of copper. The blue colour of the solution fades. The solution will eventually become colourless zinc sulfate (Figure **8.14**).

> Zinc displaces copper from solution, so zinc is more reactive than copper.

The reverse reaction does not happen. A piece of copper does not react with zinc sulfate solution.

Figure 8.14 Zinc is more reactive than copper and displaces copper from copper(II) sulfate solution. Note the brown deposit of copper, and the fact that the blue colour of the solution has faded.

It is possible to confirm the reactivity series using displacement reactions of this type. For example, if copper metal is put into colourless silver nitrate solution, the copper will become coated with silver, and the solution becomes blue, owing to the formation of copper nitrate solution:

$$2AgNO_3(aq) + Cu(s) \rightarrow Cu(NO_3)_2(aq) + 2Ag(s)$$

Copper displaces silver from solution, so copper is more reactive than silver.

Other redox competition reactions

Reactive metals are good reducing agents. The thermit reaction discussed earlier is an example of a competition reaction in the solid state. Aluminium, the more reactive metal, removes oxygen from the less reactive iron in iron(III) oxide:

$$\text{iron(III) oxide} + \text{aluminium} \xrightarrow{\text{heat}} \text{aluminium oxide} + \text{iron}$$

$$Fe_2O_3(s) + 2Al(s) \xrightarrow{\text{heat}} Al_2O_3(s) + 2Fe(s)$$

This is a redox reaction.

The nature of the reaction taking place between zinc and copper sulfate can be explored in more detail by looking at the ionic equation:

$$\text{zinc} + \text{copper(II) ions} \rightarrow \text{zinc ions} + \text{copper}$$

$$Zn(s) + Cu^{2+}(aq) \rightarrow Zn^{2+}(aq) + Cu(s)$$

This shows that the reaction is a redox reaction involving the transfer of two electrons from zinc atoms to copper(II) ions. Zinc atoms are oxidised to zinc ions, while copper(II) ions are reduced (Figure **8.15**). In general, the atoms of the more reactive metal lose electrons to become positive ions.

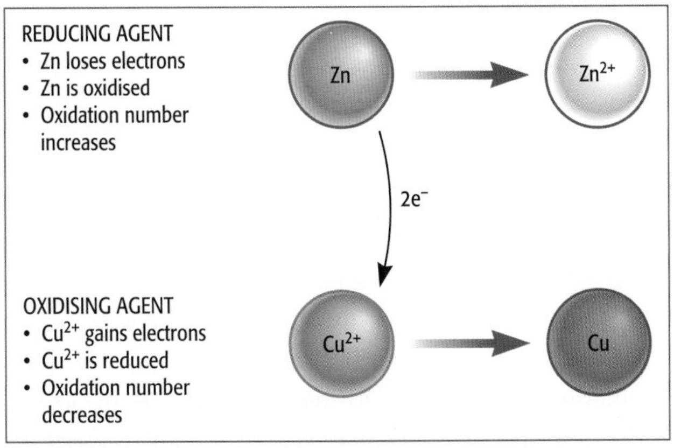

Figure 8.15 The displacement reaction between zinc and copper(II) sulfate is a redox reaction. A summary of the redox change in terms of oxidation number and electron exchange is shown.

Similar redox reactions can be used to extract metals other than iron. As we noted on page **234**, before the electrolytic method for extracting aluminium was devised, the metal was prepared from aluminium chloride using sodium as a reducing agent:

$$\text{aluminium chloride} + \text{sodium} \xrightarrow{\text{heat}} \text{sodium chloride} + \text{aluminium}$$

$$AlCl_3 + 3Na(s) \xrightarrow{\text{heat}} 3NaCl(s) + Al(s)$$

Like displacement reactions in solution, this type of reaction helps us to compare directly the reactivity of two metals and to establish the order of the reactivity series.

Thermal decomposition of metal compounds

The stability of certain metal compounds is related to the reactivity of the metal. For instance, most metal carbonates are decomposed on heating:

$$\text{magnesium carbonate} \xrightarrow{\text{heat}} \text{magnesium oxide} + \text{carbon dioxide}$$

$$MgCO_3(s) \xrightarrow{\text{heat}} MgO(s) + CO_2(g)$$

However, sodium carbonate is stable to heat. So also are the carbonates of metals below sodium in Group I, as they are more reactive than sodium.

Metal hydroxides and nitrates are also unstable to heat. Most decompose to give the metal oxide:

$$\text{magnesium hydroxide} \xrightarrow{\text{heat}} \text{magnesium oxide} + \text{water}$$

$$Mg(OH)_2(s) \xrightarrow{\text{heat}} MgO(s) + H_2O(g)$$

$$\text{lead(II) nitrate} \xrightarrow{\text{heat}} \text{lead(II) oxide} + \text{nitrogen dioxide} + \text{oxygen}$$

$$2Pb(NO_3)_2(s) \xrightarrow{\text{heat}} 2PbO(s) + 4NO_2(g) + O_2(g)$$

However, sodium and potassium hydroxides are stable to heat: they do not decompose. The nitrates of sodium and potassium do not decompose in the same way as those of less reactive metals. They lose oxygen to form sodium or potassium nitrite:

$$\text{potassium nitrate} \xrightarrow{\text{heat}} \text{potassium nitrite} + \text{oxygen}$$

$$2KNO_3(s) \xrightarrow{\text{heat}} 2KNO_2(s) + O_2(g)$$

Key ideas so far

- Some metals are more reactive than others and this is shown in the method we use to extract them from their ores.
- The most reactive metals must be extracted by electrolysis; less reactive metals can be extracted by reduction of the oxide with carbon.
- The differences in the reactivity of metals can be seen in their reactions with water and acids.
- A more reactive metal will displace a less reactive metal from a solution of one of its salts.
- The displacement reactions of metals are examples of redox reactions. They involve the transfer of electrons from the more reactive metal to the less reactive.

Quick-check questions

1. Write a word equation for the reaction of zinc and dilute hydrochloric acid.
2. Select from this list a metal that will not react with hydrochloric acid to produce hydrogen: magnesium, iron, copper.
3. Write a word equation for the reaction between magnesium and copper(II) sulfate solution.
4. State **two** observations you would see when a piece of magnesium ribbon is placed in copper(II) sulfate solution.
5. Write a balanced chemical equation and an ionic equation for the reaction between magnesium and copper(II) sulfate solution.

8.5 Electrical cells and energy

Electrochemical cells

An unusual way to power a simple digital clock is with an electrical cell made using a potato. The current is produced by pushing two different metals (for example, copper and zinc) into the potato. The metals make contact with the solution inside the potato. Connecting up these electrodes to the clock produces a small current in the circuit which powers the clock. You could even use the apple you were going to have for lunch, or a water melon, to power the clock!

This cell works because the two metals have different reactivities. Zinc is more reactive and so forms ions more easily. The zinc releases electrons as its atoms become ions, and these electrons give the zinc electrode a negative charge. The electrons move around the circuit to the copper electrode.

A simple **electrochemical cell** works best if the metals used as the electrodes are far apart in the reactivity series. The voltage of a cell made using zinc and copper electrodes is about 1.1 V. If a magnesium strip is used instead of zinc, then the voltage increases to about 2.7 V because magnesium is more reactive than zinc (Figure **8.16**). The further apart the metals are in the reactivity series, the greater the cell voltage becomes.

This explains the use of lithium, the very reactive metal at the top of Group I, as one of the electrodes in modern lithium batteries. The aim is to make the difference in reactivity as large as is safely possible.

Oxidation and reduction in power cells

In electrical power cells, the electrode made from the more reactive metal is the one at which electrons are released. The first electrochemical cell, for example, consisted of zinc and copper electrodes in a copper(II) sulfate solution. Zinc is more reactive than copper. At this electrode, zinc atoms become zinc ions:

$$Zn(s) \rightarrow Zn^{2+}(aq) + 2e^- \qquad \text{oxidation}$$

while at the other terminal, copper ions become copper atoms:

$$Cu^{2+}(aq) + 2e^- \rightarrow Cu(s) \qquad \text{reduction}$$

The zinc electrode becomes the negative terminal as electrons are released (oxidation takes place). The copper electrode becomes the positive terminal where electrons are removed, and gained by the copper(II) ions (reduction takes place). The overall reaction of the cell is the same as the ionic equation for the displacement reaction that can be done in a test tube:

$$Zn(s) + Cu^{2+}(aq) \rightarrow Zn^{2+}(aq) + Cu(s)$$

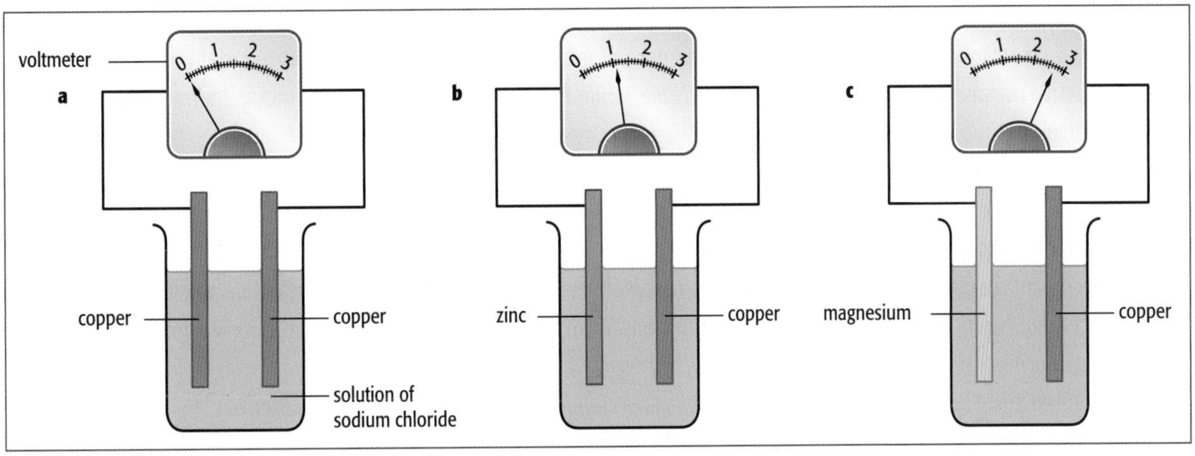

Figure 8.16 Setting up a simple cell with strips of different metals. **a** Although the solution is an electrolyte, with two copper strips nothing happens. **b** With one zinc and one copper electrode, there is a voltage. **c** With magnesium and copper electrodes, the voltage is even bigger.

Key ideas so far

- Electrical energy is released when two different metal electrodes are placed in a salt solution.
- The voltage set up in this case depends on the difference in reactivity between the two metals.
- The more reactive metal of the two loses electrons to become metal ions in solution.

Quick-check questions

1 Which of these metals will give the biggest voltage when combined with a copper electrode in an electrochemical cell: zinc, tin or magnesium?

2 Write the half-equation for the reaction at the magnesium electrode when it is combined with a copper electrode in a cell.

Summary

You should know that:

- the alkali metals (Group I) are soft metals with low densities
- they are very reactive – they displace hydrogen from cold water and must be stored under oil
- their reactivity increases as you move down the group
- their compounds give characteristic flame test colours
- as with the Group I metals, the reactivity of the alkaline earth metals (Group II) increases down the group
- aluminium is used to extract small quantities of some metals from their oxides (for example, iron from iron(III) oxide)
- its properties as a strong metal with low density combined with its resistance to corrosion make it a useful construction metal
- the transition elements are less reactive than the metals in Groups I and II
- they have certain distinctive properties, which include
  - their variable valency
  - the formation of coloured compounds
  - the metals or their compounds often make good catalysts

- the metals can be arranged into a series based on their ease of extraction and reactivity in a number of different situations
- the most reactive metals lie to the left of the Periodic Table, while the least reactive are found among the transition elements
- within a particular group of metals in the Periodic Table, reactivity increases down the group
- aluminium is a reactive metal, but its reactivity is masked by a protective oxide layer
- the salts of iron, copper and zinc have characteristic reactions with sodium hydroxide and ammonia solutions that help to distinguish them in analysis
- metal displacement reactions can take place in which a reactive metal displaces a less reactive metal from a solution of one of its salts
- such displacement reactions are examples of redox reactions – the more reactive metals act as reducing agents as their atoms lose electrons during the reaction
- differences in reactivity between metals can be used to generate electrical energy in cells and batteries
- the further apart the metals are in the reactivity series, the greater the voltage of the cell
- the reactions taking place in cells are redox reactions.

Exam-style questions

1 This question is about different metals.

The list below shows part of the metal reactivity series.

potassium **more reactive**
magnesium
aluminium
zinc
iron
copper **less reactive**

a From this list, choose a metal which is extracted using electrolysis. [1]

b Two thousand years ago, people were able to extract iron and copper from their ores.
They were not able to extract aluminium.
Suggest why they were not able to extract aluminium from its ore. [1]

c Uranium is between magnesium and zinc in the reactivity series. Equal sized strips of magnesium, uranium and zinc were placed in hydrochloric acid. The hydrochloric acid was the same concentration. The results are shown in the table.

Metal	Observations on adding to hydrochloric acid
magnesium	many bubbles of gas produced very rapidly and magnesium dissolves quickly
uranium	
zinc	a few bubbles produced at a steady rate and zinc dissolves slowly

i Copy the table and complete the result for uranium and hydrochloric acid.

ii Uranium has several isotopes which are radioactive. One of these isotopes is uranium-235 (^{235}U).
What do you understand by the term **isotopes**?

iii State **one** use of uranium-235. [3]

d Metals high in the reactivity series react readily with oxygen.
Name the compound formed when magnesium reacts with oxygen. [1]

e Copper is alloyed with tin to make bronze.

i State what is meant by the term **alloy**.

ii Suggest why metals are often used in the form of alloys. [2]

f Zinc can be extracted by heating zinc oxide with carbon.

$$ZnO + C \rightarrow Zn + CO$$

Explain why carbon is a reducing agent (reductant) in this reaction. [1]

CIE IGCSE, June 2003, paper 2, q.6 part

2 A group of students looked at the reactions of metal sulfate solutions with different metals. They used the same concentration and always added an excess of the metal. Their observations are given in the table below.

Metal sulfate	Colour of sulfate solution	Metals			
		Chromium	Cobalt	Copper	Magnesium
chromium	green	—	no reaction	no reaction	colourless solution, grey solid
cobalt	pink	green solution, grey solid	—	no reaction	colourless solution, grey solid
copper	blue	green solution, grey solid	pink solution, grey solid	—	colourless solution, grey solid
magnesium	colourless	no reaction	no reaction	no reaction	—

a Which metal reacted with all the other metal sulfate solutions? [1]

b Which metal did not react with any of the other metal sulfate solutions? [1]

c Put the metals in their order of reactivity, with the most reactive first. [2]

d Iron is slightly more reactive than cobalt. With which other metal sulfate solution will it react? [1]

3 The table below gives some information about the elements in Group I of the Periodic Table.

Element	Boiling point / °C	Density/g/cm³	Radius of atom in the metal / nm	Reactivity with water
lithium	1342	0.53	0.157	
sodium	883	0.97	0.191	rapid
potassium	760	0.86	0.235	very rapid
rubidium		1.53	0.250	extremely rapid
caesium	669	1.88		explosive

a How does the density of the Group I elements change down the Group? [2]

b Suggest a value for the boiling point of rubidium. [1]

c Suggest a value for the radius of a caesium atom. [1]

d Use the information in the table to suggest how fast lithium reacts with water compared with the other Group I metals. [1]

e State **three** properties shown by **all** metals. [3]

f When sodium reacts with water, hydrogen is given off.

$2Na(s) + 2H_2O(l) \rightarrow 2NaOH(aq) + H_2(g)$

i State the name of the other product formed in this reaction. [1]

ii Describe a test for hydrogen. [2]

CIE IGCSE, November 2004, paper 2, q.1 part

S

4 Some reactions of metals W, X, Y and Z are given below.

Metal	Reaction with water	Reaction with dilute hydrochloric acid
W	A few bubbles form slowly in cold water.	vigorous reaction gas given off
X	vigorous reaction metal melts gas given off	explosive reaction Should not be attempted.
Y	no reaction	no reaction
Z	Does not react with cold water. Hot metal reacts with steam.	steady fizzing

a Arrange these metals in order of reactivity. [2]

b Which of these metals could be

i magnesium, [1]

ii copper? [1]

c The equation for the reaction of X with cold water is given below.

$2X(s) + 2H_2O \rightarrow 2XOH(aq) + H_2(g)$

i Describe the test you would use to show that the gas evolved is hydrogen. [1]

ii How could you show that the water contained a compound of the type XOH? [2]

iii In which Group of the Periodic Table does metal X belong? [1]

iv The ore of X is its chloride. Suggest how metal X could be extracted from its chloride. [2]

CIE IGCSE, June 2006, paper 3, q.2

5 **a** Cell reactions are both exothermic and redox. They produce electrical energy as well as heat energy.

i The diagram shows a simple cell.

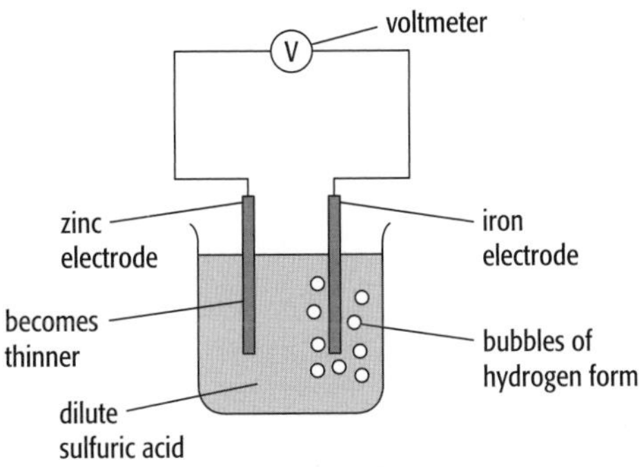

Which substance in this cell is the reductant and which ion is the oxidant? [2]

ii How could the voltage of this cell be increased? [1]

iii What is the important large-scale use, relating to iron and steel, of this type of cell reaction? [1]

b Cells can be set up with inert electrodes and the electrolytes as oxidant and reductant.

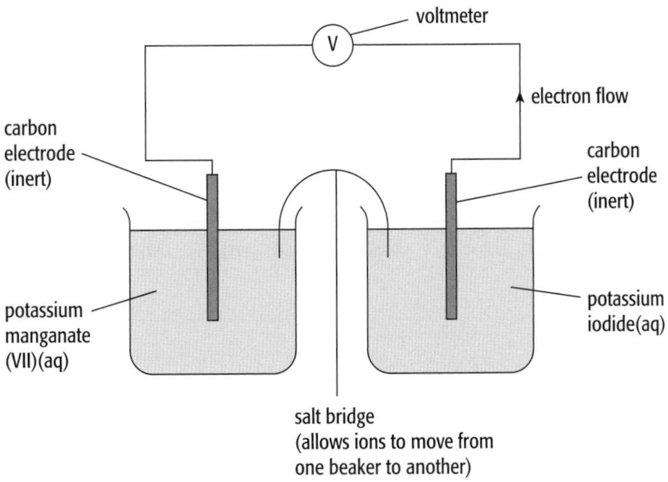

The potassium manganate(VII) is the oxidant and the potassium iodide is the reductant.

i Describe the colour change that would be observed in the left-hand beaker. [2]

ii Write an ionic equation for the reaction in the right-hand beaker. [2]

CIE IGCSE, June 2006, paper 3, q.6 part

6 The reactivity series lists metals in order of reactivity.

a To find out which is the more reactive metal, zinc or tin, the following experiment could be carried out.

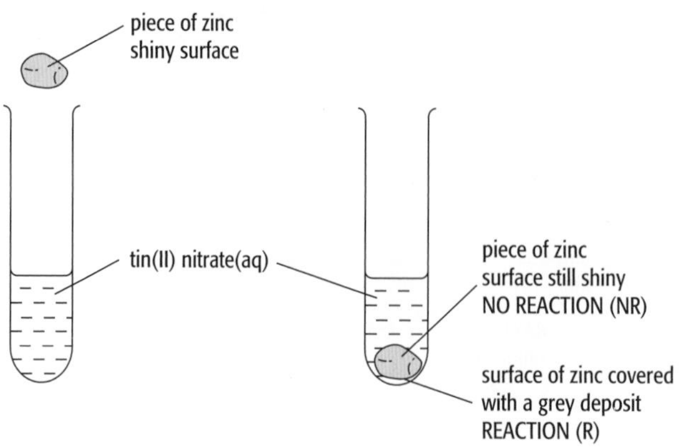

This experiment could be carried out with other metals and the results recorded in a table. Then the order of reactivity can be deduced.

i The order was found to be:

manganese **most reactive**

zinc

tin

silver **least reactive**

Copy and complete the table of results from which this order was determined.

Aqueous solution	Tin, Sn	Manganese, Mn	Silver, Ag	Zinc, Zn
tin(II) nitrate		R	NR	R
manganese(II) nitrate				
silver(I) nitrate				
zinc nitrate				

[3]

ii Write the ionic equation for the reaction between tin atoms and silver(I) ions. [2]

iii The following is a redox reaction.

$Mn + Sn^{2+} \rightarrow Mn^{2+} + Sn$

Indicate on a copy of the equation the change which is oxidation. Give a reason for your choice. [2]

iv Explain why experiments of this type cannot be used to find the position of aluminium in the reactivity series. [2]

b Potassium and calcium are very reactive metals at the top of the series. Because their ions have different charges, K^+ and Ca^{2+}, their compounds behave differently when heated.

i Explain why the ions have different charges. [2]

ii Their hydroxides are heated.
If the compound decomposes, copy and complete the word equation. If it does not decompose, write 'no reaction'.

potassium hydroxide →

calcium hydroxide → [2]

iii Copy and complete the equations for the decomposition of their nitrates.

$2KNO_3 \rightarrow$ .... + ...

$2Ca(NO_3)_2 \rightarrow$ .... + ... [4]

CIE IGCSE, November 2008, paper 3, q.6

9 Industrial inorganic chemistry

This chapter covers the following ideas:

- the production of iron in the blast furnace
- steel making
- rusting of iron and its prevention
- (S) the extraction of zinc
- (S) the extraction of copper
- (S) the extraction of aluminium
- (S) the Haber–Bosch process for the manufacture of ammonia
- the manufacture and use of fertilisers
- (S) the manufacture of sulfuric acid
- (S) the uses of sulfur compounds
- (S) the commercial electrolysis of brine
- the uses of chlorine
- limestone and its uses
- the production of lime and its uses
- the economics of the chemical industry
- the siting of chemical plants
- the environmental cost of industry
- recycling

9.1 The extraction of metals by carbon reduction

Iron and steel

In our modern world, we have invented and shaped many machines and clever devices. These are often made of **steel.** It is the most widely used of all metals. The durability, tensile strength and low cost of steel make it the basis of countless industries, from ship-building to watch-making. Iron and steel making are at the centre of our heavy industries.

Steel is mainly iron with between 0.2 and 1.5% carbon. The carbon makes the iron harder and stronger. Small quantities of other transition metals can also be added to make special steels. Steels are alloys in which the main metal is iron. The magnetic properties of iron make it easy to separate steel products from other waste. This means that the metal can be easily recycled.

Figure 9.1 A worker in protective clothing takes a sample from a blast furnace in a steel works.

The production of iron in the blast furnace

The main ore of iron is hematite (Fe_2O_3). The iron is obtained by reduction with carbon in a **blast furnace** (Figures **9.1** and **9.2**). The furnace is a steel tower about 30 metres high. It is lined with refractory (heat-resistant) bricks of magnesium oxide which are cooled by water. The furnace is loaded with the 'charge', which consists of iron ore, coke (a form of carbon made from coal) and limestone (calcium carbonate). The charge is **sintered** (the ore is heated with coke and limestone) to make sure the solids mix well, and is mixed with more coke. Blasts of hot air are sent in through holes near the bottom of

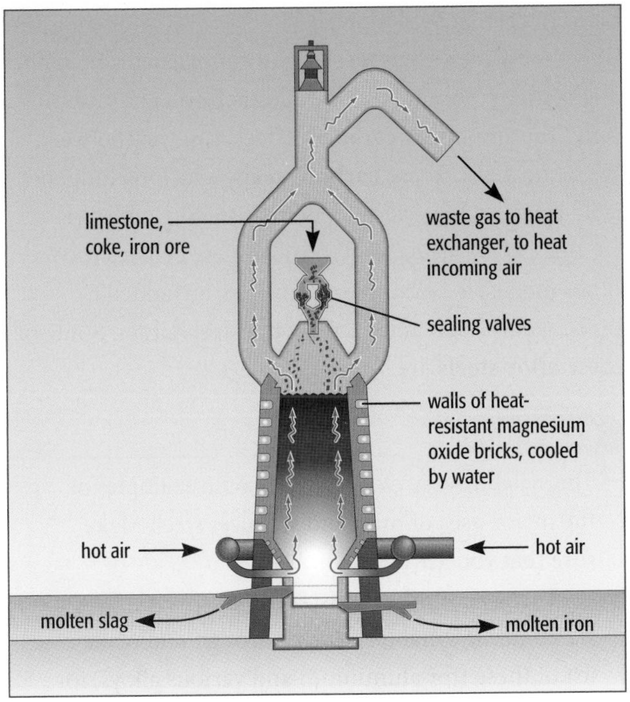

Figure 9.2 The blast furnace reduction of iron ore to iron.

the furnace. The carbon burns in the air blast and the furnace gets very hot.

A series of chemical reactions takes place to produce molten iron (Figure 9.3). The most important reaction that occurs is the reduction of the ore by carbon monoxide:

$$Fe_2O_3(s) + 3CO(g) \rightarrow 2Fe(s) + 3CO_2(g)$$

The iron produced flows to the bottom of the furnace where it can be 'tapped off' because the temperature at the bottom of the furnace is higher than the melting point of iron.

One of the major impurities in iron ore is sand (silica, SiO_2). The limestone added to the furnace helps to remove this impurity. The limestone decomposes to lime in the furnace. This then reacts with the silica:

$$\text{limestone} \xrightarrow{\text{heat}} \text{lime} + \text{carbon dioxide}$$
$$CaCO_3(s) \xrightarrow{\text{heat}} CaO(s) + CO_2(g)$$

$$\text{lime} + \text{silica} \rightarrow \text{calcium silicate}$$
$$CaO(s) + SiO_2(s) \rightarrow CaSiO_3(l)$$

The calcium silicate formed is also molten. It flows down the furnace and forms a molten layer of **slag** on top of the iron. It does not mix with the iron, and is less dense. The

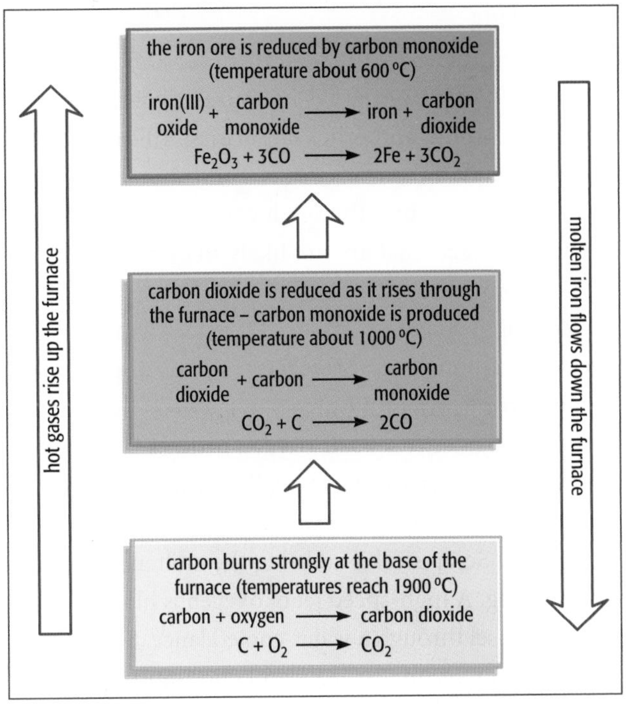

Figure 9.3 Iron is produced in the blast furnace by a series of reactions. Carbon monoxide is thought to be the main reducing agent.

molten slag is 'tapped off' separately. When solidified, the slag is used by builders and road-makers. The hot waste gases escape from the top of the furnace. They are used in heat exchangers to heat the incoming air. This helps to reduce the energy costs of the process. The extraction of iron is a continuous process. It is much cheaper than the electrolytic processes used to extract other metals.

The **blast furnace** extraction of iron:

- uses iron ore, coke, limestone and hot air
- involves the reduction of iron(III) oxide by carbon monoxide
- uses limestone to remove the main impurity (sand) as slag (calcium silicate).

Exam tip

You will not be asked to draw a diagram of the blast furnace in an exam but you should be able to label a diagram of it and know what is fed into it.

Importantly, you should also know the key reactions of the furnace, including the formation of slag.

Steel-making

The iron produced by the blast furnace is known as 'pig iron' or 'cast iron' and is not pure. It contains about 4% carbon, and other impurities. This amount of carbon makes the iron brittle. This limits the usefulness of the iron, though it can be cast (moulded) into large objects that are not likely to be subjected to deforming forces.

Most of the pig iron produced is taken to make steel. The carbon content is reduced by burning it off as carbon dioxide. Any sulfur contamination is oxidised to sulfur dioxide. This **basic oxygen process** is carried out in a tilting furnace (Figure **9.4**). The method is fast: 350 tonnes of molten iron can be converted in 40 minutes. Scrap steel is added to the molten pig iron for recycling. A high-speed jet of oxygen is blown into the vessel through a water-cooled lance. Some impurities, for example silicon and phosphorus, do not produce gaseous oxides, so lime (CaO) is added to the furnace. The impurities form a 'slag', which floats on top of the molten iron. The molten iron is poured off by tilting the furnace. Controlled amounts of other elements such as chromium, manganese, tungsten or other transition metals are added to make different types of steel (see Tables **9.1** and **9.2**).

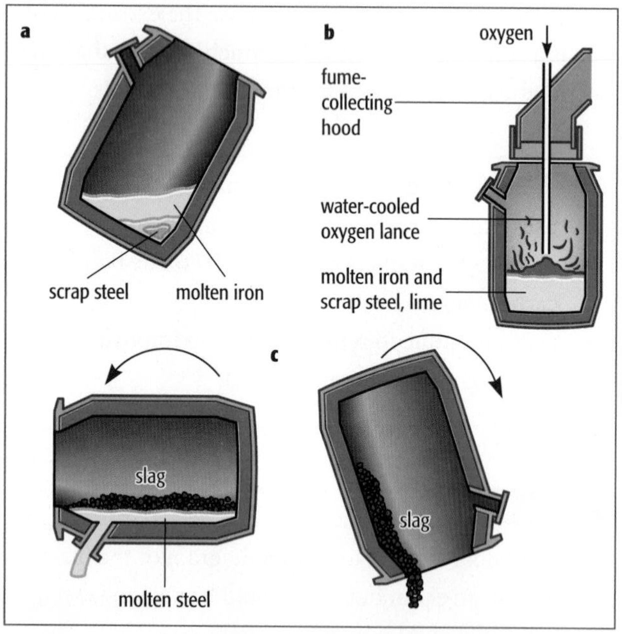

Figure 9.4 The different stages of the steel-making process (the basic oxygen process). **a** The furnace is charged with scrap steel and molten iron. **b** Oxygen is blown in through an 'oxygen lance'. **c** The molten steel, and then the slag, are poured from the furnace by tilting it in different directions.

Carbon steels and alloy steels

There is a wide variety of steels to suit particular applications. Some steels are alloys of iron and carbon only. The amount of carbon in steels can vary between 0.2% and 1.5%. These **carbon steels**, which include the mild steel used for car bodies, are listed in Table **9.1**.

But carbon steels tend to rust unless protected. So other metals, for example chromium, are added to prevent corrosion and to make the steel harder. Some of these **alloy steels** are listed in Table **9.2**.

Exam tip

The syllabus very clearly states some examples of the major uses of mild and stainless steel. Make sure that you are aware of these.

The uses of other substances are also explicitly stated in the syllabus – so go through and make a list of these (for aluminium and various alloys, for example) and specifically learn them.

The rusting of iron and its prevention

When a metal is attacked by air, water or other surrounding substances, it is said to **corrode**. In the case of iron and steel, the corrosion process is also known as **rusting**. Rusting is a serious economic problem. Large sums of money are spent each year replacing damaged iron and steel structures, or protecting structures from such damage. Rust is a red-brown powder consisting mainly of hydrated iron(III) oxide ($Fe_2O_3.xH_2O$). Water and oxygen are essential for iron to rust (Figure **9.5**). The problem is made worse by the presence of salt; seawater increases the rate of corrosion. Pictures from the seabed of the wreck of the *Titanic* show that it has a huge amount of rust (Figure **9.6**). Acid rain also increases the rate at which iron objects rust.

Aluminium is **more** reactive than iron, but it does not corrode in the damaging way that iron does. Both metals react with air. In the case of aluminium, a very thin single layer of aluminium oxide forms, which sticks strongly to the surface of the metal. This micro-layer seals the metal surface and protects it from further attack. Aluminium is a useful construction material because it is protected by this layer. The protective layer can be made thicker by electrolysis (**anodising**, see page **259**).

Metal	Carbon content (%)	Properties	Uses
mild steel	< 0.25	easily worked; not brittle	car bodies, chains, pylons
medium steel	0.25–0.45	tougher than mild steel	car springs, axles, bridges
high-carbon steel	0.45–1.5	hard and brittle	chisels, cutting tools, razor blades
cast iron	2.5–4.5	cheaper than steel; easily moulded	gear boxes, engine blocks, brake discs

Table 9.1 Cast iron and carbon steels.

Steel[a]	Typical composition		Properties	Uses
stainless steel	iron	74%	tough; does not corrode	cutlery, surgical instruments, kitchen sinks, chemical plant
	chromium	18%		
	nickel	8%		
tungsten steel	iron	95%	tough; hard, even at high temperatures	edges of high-speed cutting tools
	tungsten	5%		
manganese steel	iron	87%	tough; springy	drill bits, springs
	manganese	13%		

[a] *All these alloys have a low content of carbon (< 0.45%).*

Table 9.2 Some typical alloy steels.

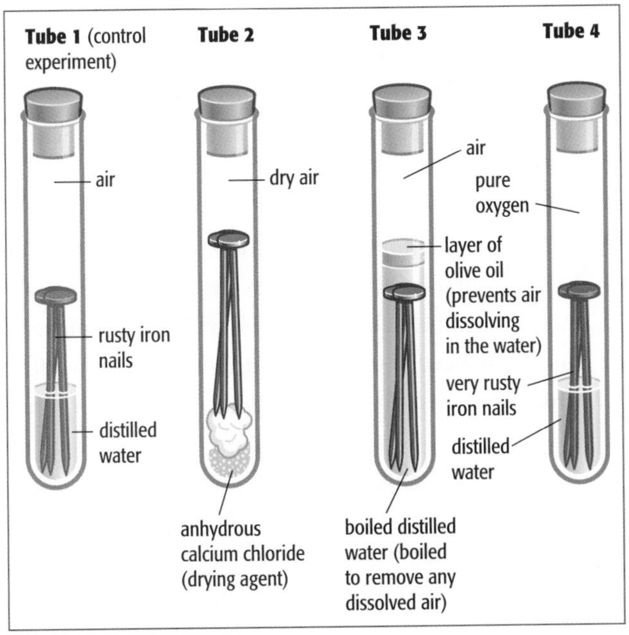

Figure 9.5 The results of an experiment to investigate the factors that are involved in rusting. In tube 2, the air is dry, so the nails do not rust. In tube 3, there is no oxygen in the water, so the nails do not rust. In tube 4, pure oxygen and water are present, so the nails are very rusty.

Figure 9.6 Photograph of the highly-rusted bow of the *Titanic* taken from a submersible.

In contrast, when iron corrodes, the rust forms in flakes. It does not form a single layer. The attack on the metal can continue over time as the rust flakes come off. Indeed, a sheet of iron can be eaten right through by the rusting process.

Chromium is another metal, similar to aluminium, that is protected by an oxide layer. If chromium is alloyed with iron, a 'stainless' steel is produced. However, it would be too expensive to use stainless steel for all the objects built out of iron. Electroplating a layer of chromium on steel is used to protect some objects from rusting, for example car bumpers and bicycle handlebars.

Rust prevention

There is a saying, 'Necessity is the mother of invention!'. The need to protect iron and steel from rusting has led to many methods being devised. Some of these are outlined here.

- *Painting:* This method is widespread, and is used for objects ranging in size from ships and bridges to garden gates. Some paints react with the iron to form a stronger protective layer. However, generally, painting only protects the metal as long as the paint layer is unscratched. Regular re-painting is often necessary to keep this protection intact.
- *Oiling and greasing:* The oiling and/or greasing of the moving parts of machinery forms a protective film, preventing rusting. Again, the treatment must be repeated to continue the protection.
- *Plastic coatings:* These are used to form a protective layer on items such as refrigerators and garden chairs. The plastic poly(vinyl chloride), PVC, is often used for this purpose.
- *Electroplating:* An iron or steel object can be electroplated with a layer of chromium or tin to protect against rusting. A 'tin can' is made of steel coated on both sides with a fine layer of tin. Tin is used because it is unreactive and non-toxic. However, this does raise a problem. With both these metals, if the protective layer is broken, then the steel beneath will begin to rust.
- *Galvanising:* An object may be coated with a layer of the more reactive metal, zinc. This is called **galvanising**. It has the advantage over other plating methods in that the protection still works even if the zinc layer is badly scratched. The zinc layer can be applied by several different methods. These include electroplating or dipping the object into molten zinc. The bodies of cars are dipped into a bath of molten zinc to form a protective layer.
- *Sacrificial protection:* This is a method of rust prevention in which blocks of a reactive metal are attached to the iron surface. Zinc or magnesium blocks are attached to oil-rigs and to the hulls of ships (Figure 9.7). These metals are more reactive than iron and will be corroded in preference to it. Underground gas and water pipes are connected by wire to blocks of magnesium to obtain the same protection. In all cases the metal blocks lose electrons in preference to the iron, and so prevent the iron forming iron(III) oxide.
- *Cathodic protection:* This method involves setting up an electrolytic cell using the iron or steel object as the anode of the cell. An inert electrode and a power supply are needed to complete this form of protection, which is used to protect oil-rigs, for example.

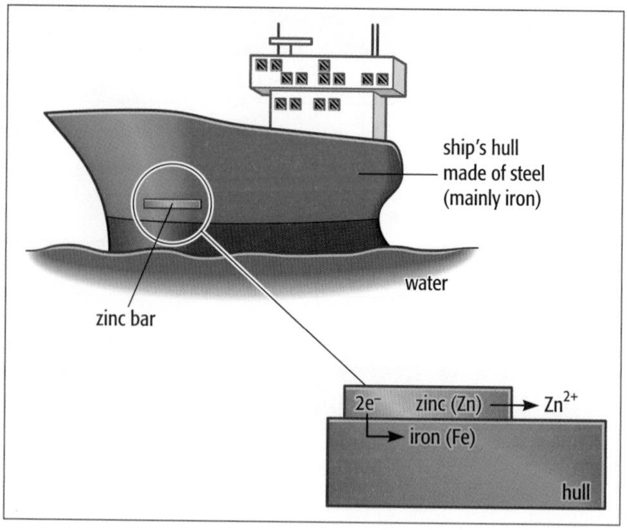

Figure 9.7 Blocks of zinc (or magnesium) are used for the sacrificial protection of the hulls of ships.

The extraction of zinc

The main ore of zinc is its sulfide: zinc blende (ZnS). The sulfide ore is heated very strongly in a current of air. This converts the sulfide to the metal oxide:

$$\text{metal sulfide} + \text{oxygen} \xrightarrow{\text{heat}} \text{metal oxide} + \text{sulfur dioxide}$$

$2ZnS(s) + 3O_2(g) \xrightarrow{heat} 2ZnO(s) + 2SO_2(g)$

The sulfur dioxide produced can be used to make sulfuric acid. The metal oxide is heated in a blast furnace with coke (Figure **9.8**). Carbon reduces the oxide to the metal:

zinc oxide + carbon → zinc + carbon monoxide

$ZnO + C \rightarrow Zn + CO$

Zinc vapour passes out of the furnace and is cooled and condensed (note particularly the condensing tray at the top of the furnace in Figure **9.8**). Zinc is used in alloys such as brass and for galvanising iron.

Exam tip

As with the blast furnace for extracting iron, you will not be expected to draw a diagram of the furnace for zinc extraction. You must be able to label a diagram, including the key feature of the condensing tray to collect the molten zinc. This is quite different from the blast furnace for iron.

The extraction of copper

Copper is less reactive than the other metals we have considered so far. It can be found native in the USA, but most copper is extracted from copper pyrites, $CuFeS_2$.

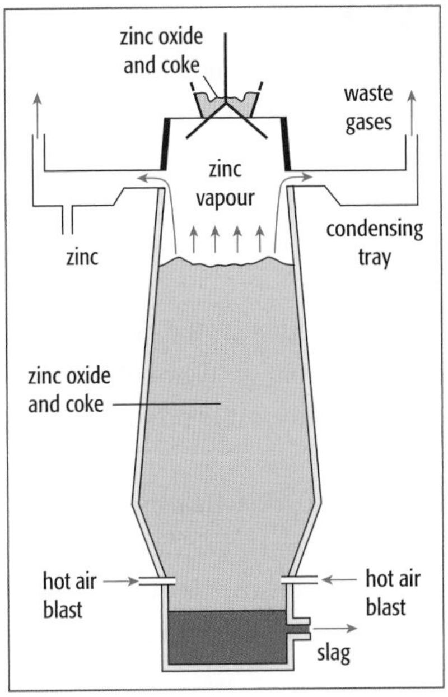

Figure 9.8 A blast furnace for extracting zinc.

The copper produced from this ore is suitable for piping, boilers and cooking utensils. When it is to be used for electrical wiring, it must be refined (purified) by electrolysis (see page **130**).

Figure **9.9** summarises the overall approach to chemically extracting metals such as iron, zinc and copper that sit in the middle to lower range of the reactivity series from their ores.

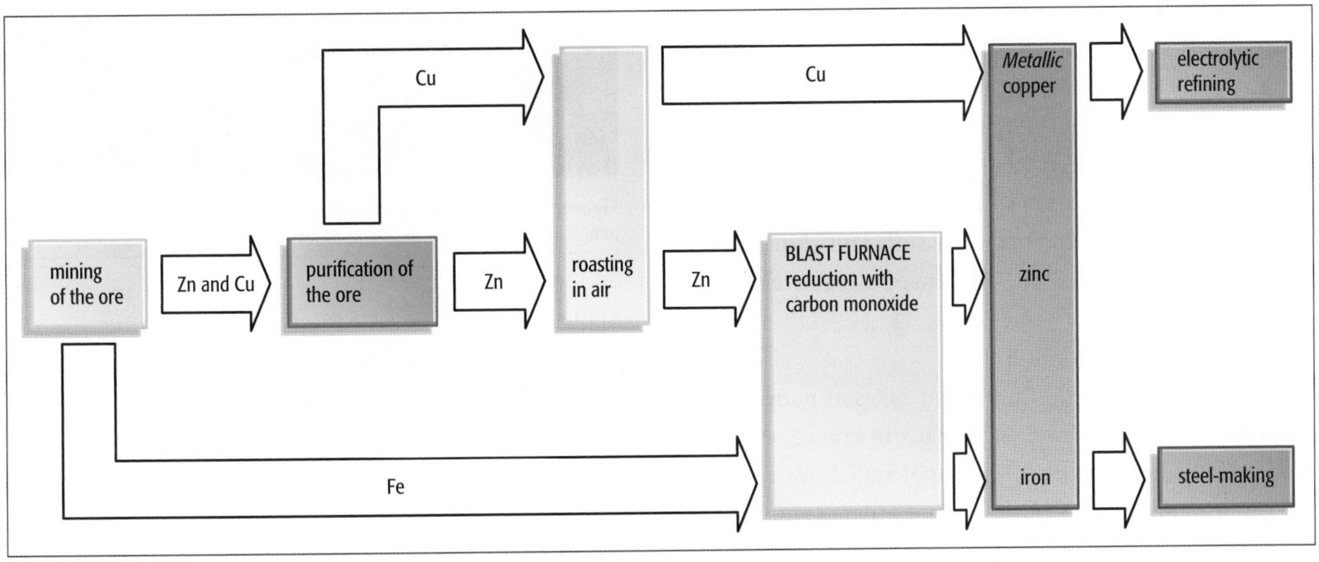

Figure 9.9 A summary of the metal extraction methods using reduction by carbon.

Key ideas so far

- The extraction of iron in the blast furnace is the most important example of chemical reduction.
- The iron produced can be converted into various forms of steel designed to suit a particular purpose.
- Iron and steel, although the major construction metals, suffer from problems of corrosion.
- Various methods exist to protect iron objects from corrosion (rusting).
- Moderately reactive metals may be extracted by chemical reduction using carbon.
- Metals such as zinc can be extracted by methods similar to the blast furnace process for iron.

Quick-check questions

1 Why is limestone added to the blast furnace?
2 Write an equation for the reduction of iron(III) oxide.
3 Which element is used to remove the carbon from cast iron?
4 Why is chromium sometimes added to steel?
5 Which **two** substances are essential for the rusting of iron?
6 Give **two** ways in which zinc can be used to stop the rusting of iron.
7 How is zinc separated from the rest of the substances in the blast furnace?
8 Why is it sometimes necessary to purify copper by electrolysis?

9.2 The extraction of metals by electrolysis

Reduction with carbon does not work for more reactive metals. The metals are held in their compounds (oxides or chlorides) by stronger bonds which need a lot of energy to break them. This energy is best supplied by electricity. Extracting metals in this way is a three-stage process.

1 mining the ore
2 purification of the ore
3 electrolysis of the molten ore.

The extraction of a metal by electrolysis is expensive. Energy costs to keep the ore molten and to separate the ions can be very high. Because of this, many of these metals are extracted in regions where hydroelectric power is available. Aluminium plants are the most important examples. They produce sufficient aluminium to make it the second most widely used metal after iron.

The extraction of aluminium

Bauxite, the major ore of aluminium, takes its name from the mediaeval village of Les Baux in France, where it was first mined (Figure **9.10**). Napoleon III saw its possibilities for military purposes and ordered studies on its commercial production. A method of extraction using sodium to displace aluminium from aluminium chloride existed at that time. However, in 1886, the Hall–Héroult electrolytic method for extracting aluminium was invented by Hall (an American)and Héroult (a Frenchman).

Figure 9.10 The major ore of aluminium is bauxite. It is usually mixed with iron(III) oxide, which gives the ore its brown colour.

The Hall–Héroult process

Bauxite (Figure **9.10**) is an impure form of aluminium oxide. Up to 25% of bauxite consists of the impurities iron(III) oxide and sand. The iron(III) oxide gives it a red-brown colour.

The Hall–Héroult process involves the following stages.

1 The bauxite is treated with sodium hydroxide to obtain pure aluminium oxide (alumina). The alumina produced is shipped to the electrolysis plant.
2 The purified aluminium oxide (Al_2O_3) is dissolved in molten cryolite (sodium aluminium fluoride, Na_3AlF_6). Cryolite is a mineral found naturally in Greenland. It is no longer mined commercially there, and all the cryolite now used is made synthetically. Cryolite is used to lower the working temperature of the electrolytic cell. The melting point of aluminium oxide is 2030 °C. This is reduced to 900–1000 °C by dissolving it in cryolite. The cryolite thus provides a considerable saving in energy costs.
3 The molten mixture of aluminium oxide and cryolite is electrolysed in a cell fitted with graphite electrodes (Figure **9.11**).

    Aluminium ions are attracted to the cathode where they are discharged to form liquid aluminium metal:

$$Al^{3+} + 3e^- \rightarrow Al$$

Oxide ions are attracted to the anode where they are discharged to form oxygen gas. At the high temperature of the cell this reacts with the carbon of the anode to form carbon dioxide:

$$\text{carbon} + \text{oxygen} \xrightarrow{\text{heat}} \text{carbon dioxide}$$

$$C(s) + O_2(g) \xrightarrow{\text{heat}} CO_2(g)$$

The anodes burn away and have to be replaced regularly. The Hall–Héroult process uses a great deal of energy. It is also costly to replace the anodes, which are burned away during the process. It is **much** cheaper to recycle the metal than to manufacture it. The energy requirement for recycling is about 5% of that needed to manufacture the same amount of 'new' metal (see page **273**).

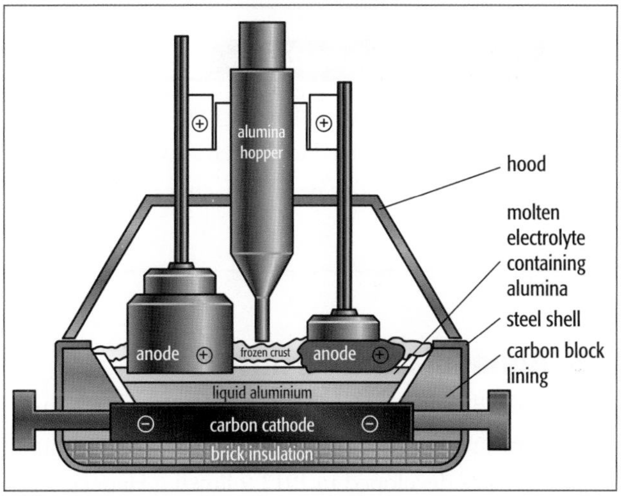

Figure 9.11 A cross-section of the electrolytic cell for extracting aluminium. At the cathode: $Al^{3+} + 3e^- \rightarrow Al$. At the anode: $2O^{2-} \rightarrow O_2 + 4e^-$.

Other industrial electrolytic processes

Anodising aluminium

The protective layer of oxide that covers the surface of aluminium can be artificially thickened by anodising. The aluminium is used as the anode in an electrolytic cell which contains dilute sulfuric acid and has a carbon cathode. The oxygen produced at the anode reacts with the aluminium, thickening the oxide film. A coloured dye can be included during electrolysis; the oxide layer formed traps the dye to give a coloured surface to the metal.

Electroplating and copper refining

When electrolytic cells are set up with appropriate metal electrodes, metal can be effectively transferred from the anode to the cathode. Such methods can be used to plate objects with metals such as chromium or tin, or to refine copper to a very high degree of purity (see page **130**).

Key ideas so far

- Metals can be extracted from their ores by methods that depend on the reactivity of the metal concerned.
- The most reactive metals must be extracted from their molten ores by electrolysis.
- Aluminium is the major example of a metal extracted from its ore (bauxite) by electrolysis.
- Aluminium is a useful construction metal because it is protected from corrosion by an oxide layer.
- Production of aluminium by electrolysis is costly.
- Methods of recycling aluminium and steel are becoming increasingly important.
- Highly purified copper can be produced by electrolytic refining.

Quick-check questions

1 Why is aluminium expensive to extract?
2 Why is cryolite added to the cell as well as alumina?
3 Why do the anodes need replacing regularly?
4 Write an equation for the reaction at the cathode.
5 Aluminium is a reactive metal. Why, then, is it useful for window frames and aircraft?

9.3 Ammonia and fertilisers

The Haber–Bosch process for the synthesis of ammonia was one of the most significant new ideas of the twentieth century. It was developed in 1913 following Haber's earlier experiment (Figure **9.12**), and it allowed industrial chemists to make ammonia cheaply and on a huge scale.

Ammonia has the following general properties as a gas:

- colourless
- distinctive smell
- less dense than air
- very soluble in water to give an alkaline solution.

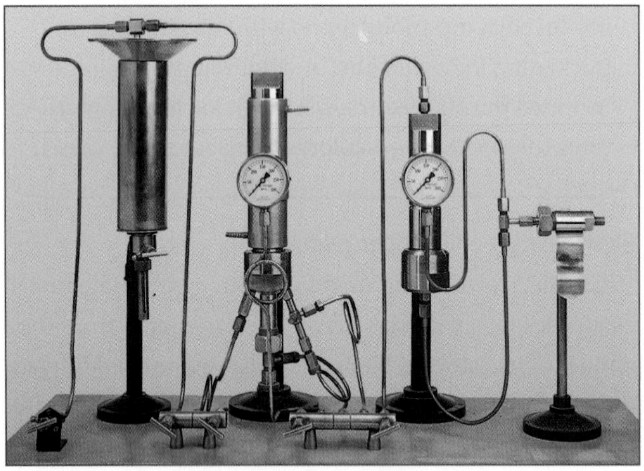

Figure 9.12 Haber's original experimental apparatus, designed for adjusting the pressure of the reacting mixture.

As a raw material for both fertilisers and explosives, ammonia played a large part in human history. It helped to feed a growing population in peace-time, and it was used to manufacture explosives in wartime.

Nitrogen is an unreactive gas, and changing it into compounds useful for plant growth (**nitrogen fixation**) is important for agriculture. Most plants cannot directly use (or **fix**) nitrogen from the air. The purpose of the factory (and of the whole industry) is to manufacture ammonia to make agricultural fertilisers. In the Haber process (Figure **9.13**), nitrogen and hydrogen are directly combined to form ammonia:

$$\text{nitrogen} + \text{hydrogen} \rightleftharpoons \text{ammonia}$$
$$N_2(g) + 3H_2(g) \rightleftharpoons 2NH_3(g)$$

Nitrogen is obtained from air, and hydrogen from natural gas by reaction with steam. The two gases are mixed in a 1 : 3 ratio and compressed to 200 atmospheres. They are then passed over a series of catalyst beds containing finely divided iron. The temperature of the converter is about 450 °C. The reaction is reversible and does not go to completion. A mixture of nitrogen, hydrogen and ammonia leaves the converter. The proportion of ammonia in the mixture is about 15%. This is separated from the other gases by cooling the mixture. Ammonia has a much higher boiling point than nitrogen or hydrogen, so it condenses easily. The unchanged nitrogen and hydrogen gases are re-circulated over the catalyst. By re-circulating in this way, an eventual yield of 98% can be achieved. The ammonia produced is stored as a liquid under pressure.

Exam tip

For the Haber process, and the Contact process for making sulfuric acid, it is important that you know the conditions used and how these are chosen. Remember these are both reversible reactions that reach an equilibrium under the conditions used (see Section 7.5).

Most of the ammonia produced is used to manufacture **fertilisers**. Liquid ammonia itself can in fact be used directly as a fertiliser, but it is an unpleasant liquid to handle and to transport. The majority is converted

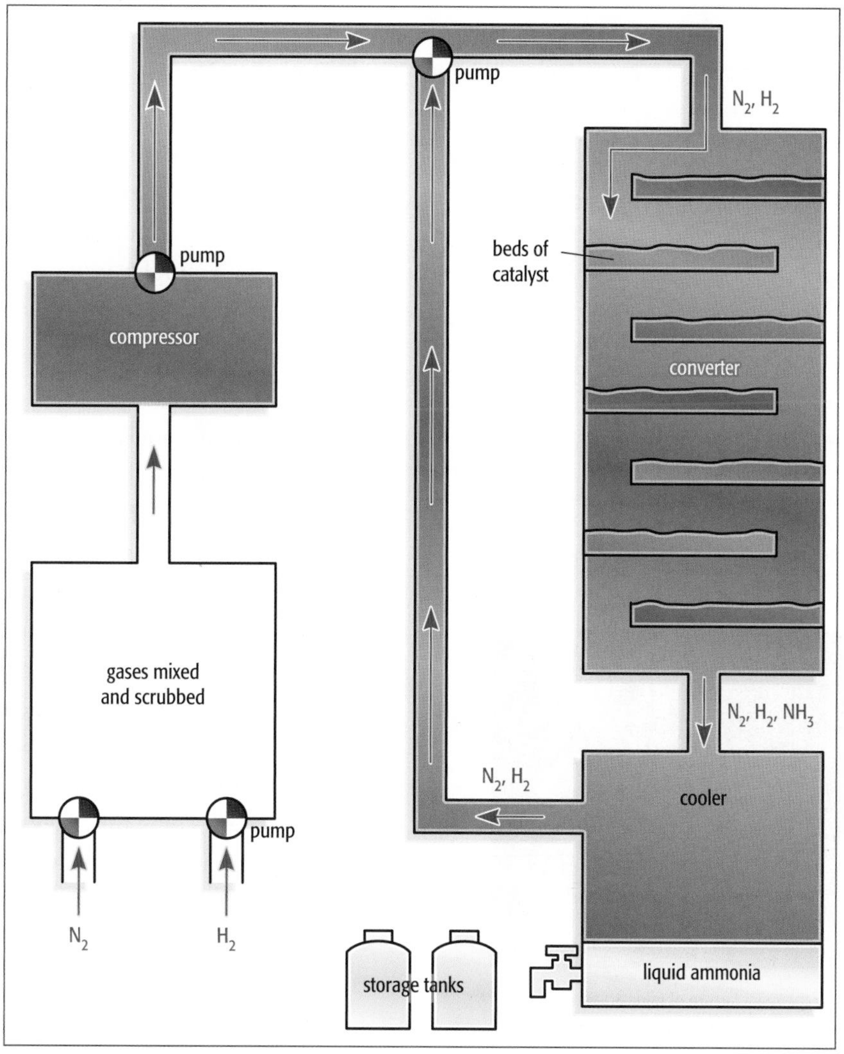

Figure 9.13 A schematic drawing of the different stages of the Haber process. Nitrogen and hydrogen are mixed in a ratio of 1 : 3 at the start of the process.

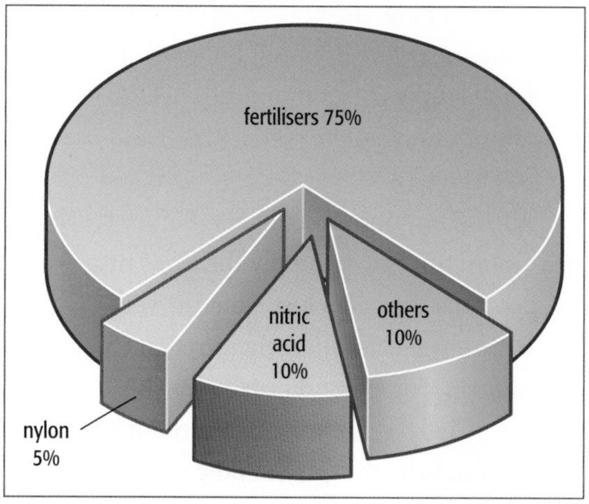

Figure 9.14 The uses of ammonia produced by the Haber process.

into a variety of **solid** fertilisers. A substantial amount of ammonia is converted into nitric acid by oxidation (Figure **9.14**).

Nitric acid

Some ammonia is used to make nitric acid (Figure **9.15**, overleaf).

Ammonia is reacted with oxygen from the air in the presence of a catalyst. The catalyst is a series of layers of platinum–rhodium gauze (Figure **9.16**).

$$\underset{\text{ammonia}}{4NH_3} + \underset{\text{air}}{7O_2} \rightleftharpoons \underset{\text{nitrogen dioxide}}{4NO_2} + \underset{\text{water}}{6H_2O}$$

The nitrogen dioxide formed is dissolved in water in the presence of more air.

$$\underset{\text{nitrogen dioxide}}{4NO_2} + \underset{\text{water}}{2H_2O} + \underset{\text{air}}{O_2} \rightarrow \underset{\text{nitric acid}}{4HNO_3}$$

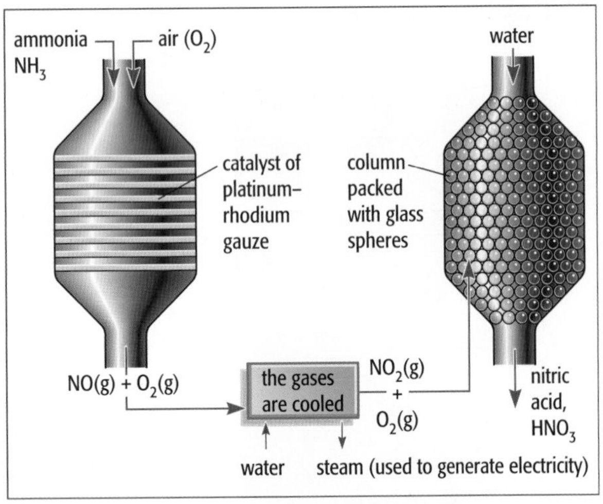

Figure 9.15 Producing nitric acid by the oxidation of ammonia.

Figure 9.16 The catalyst for the manufacture of nitric acid takes the form of a fine gauze of platinum and rhodium, seen here being fitted into a reaction vessel.

This acid can then be reacted with more ammonia to make ammonium nitrate, an important fertiliser.

Ammonium nitrate and other fertilisers

Ammonium nitrate ('Nitram') is the most important of the **nitrogenous fertilisers**. It is produced when ammonia solution reacts with nitric acid:

ammonia + nitric acid → ammonium nitrate

$NH_3(aq) + HNO_3(aq) \rightarrow NH_4NO_3(aq)$

The ammonium nitrate can be crystallised into pellet form suitable for spreading on the land.

Exam tip

Writing equations for neutralisation reactions involving ammonia solution is the one time when a neutralisation equation does not involve water as one of the products. The equation is simply: ammonia plus the acid gives the salt.

Ammonium nitrate is soluble in water, as are all other ammonium salts, for example ammonium sulfate, $(NH_4)_2SO_4$. This solubility is important because plants need soluble nitrogen compounds that they can take up through their roots. There are two types of nitrogen compounds that plants can use – ammonium compounds (which contain the NH_4^+ ion) and nitrates (which contain the NO_3^- ion). Ammonium nitrate provides both these ions.

Ammonium salts tend to make the soil slightly acidic. To overcome this, they can be mixed with chalk (calcium carbonate), which will neutralise this effect. 'Nitro-chalk' is an example of a **compound fertiliser**.

A modern fertiliser factory will produce two main types of product:

- **straight N fertilisers** are solid nitrogen-containing fertilisers sold in pellet form, for example ammonium nitrate (NH_4NO_3), ammonium sulfate ($(NH_4)_2SO_4$) and urea ($CO(NH_2)_2$)
- **NPK compound fertilisers** (Figure **9.17b**) are mixtures that supply the three most essential elements lost from the soil by extensive use, namely nitrogen (N), phosphorus (P) and potassium (K). They are usually a mixture of ammonium nitrate, ammonium phosphate and potassium chloride, in different proportions to suit different conditions.

The production process for an NPK fertiliser is complex. It involves the production not only of ammonia, but also of sulfuric acid and phosphoric acid. A fertiliser factory is not just a single unit but six separate plants built close together on the same site (Figure **9.17a**; see also the aerial view of the factory complex on Burrup Peninsula, Western Australia, Figure **9.33**, page **273**).

Environmental aspects of fertiliser use

Ammonium nitrate is a particularly good fertiliser. It contains 35% by mass of nitrogen, all of which is available to plants because the compound dissolves easily. However, this solubility poses problems. Some nitrate ions will be washed from the soil into nearby streams and rivers. This 'run-off' from the soil encourages rapid growth in the number of algae. The algae multiply swiftly to produce what is called an **algal bloom** (Figure **9.18**, overleaf). When the algae die, they are decomposed by bacteria. The increased bacterial activity uses up the oxygen dissolved in the water. Eventually there is little or no oxygen left, and fish die from lack of oxygen. This process is known as **eutrophication**.

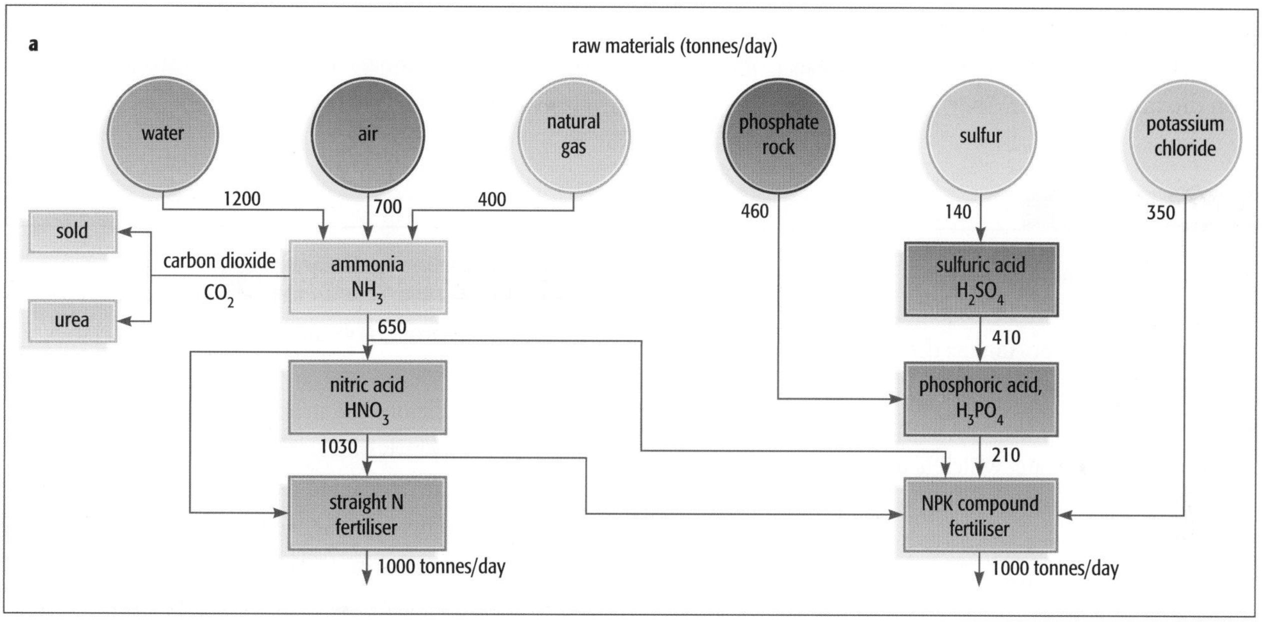

Figure 9.17 **a** The production of fertiliser requires the coordination of various industrial plants. The figures (in tonnes per day) show the raw materials needed to produce 1000 tonnes of straight and compound fertiliser per day. **b** Some fertiliser products; note the three key numbers (N : P : K) on the fertiliser bags.

Figure 9.18 Algal bloom on a small stream.

Why fertilisers are important for plants

Plants make their own food by photosynthesis from carbon dioxide and water. They also need other chemicals for producing healthy leaves, roots, flowers and fruit. They get these chemicals from minerals in the soil. When many crops are grown on the same piece of land, these minerals get used up and have to be replaced by **artificial fertilisers**. The three most important additional elements which plants need are:

- nitrogen (N), which is specially important for healthy leaves
- phosphorus (P), specially important for healthy roots
- potassium (K), which is important for the production of flowers and fruit.

Different plants need different combinations of these elements which is why NPK fertilisers are produced. The NPK value (Figure **9.17b**) informs the farmer how much of each element is present. Fruits like apples and tomatoes need a lot of potassium, whereas leafy vegetables like cabbage need a lot of nitrogen and root crops like carrots need a lot of phosphorus.

Key ideas so far

- Ammonia is manufactured by the Haber process from nitrogen and hydrogen.
- Ammonia is important as the basis of the fertiliser and other industries.
- Nitric acid can react with ammonia to produce ammonium nitrate, which is used extensively as a fertiliser and explosive.
- There is a range of fertilisers based on ammonia, but the most important elements added to the soil by these fertilisers are nitrogen, phosphorus and potassium (NPK).

? Quick-check questions

1. How is hydrogen obtained for use in the Haber process?
2. What conditions are needed to ensure the process works efficiently?
3. Why are the unreacted gases re-circulated?
4. Why do many fertilisers contain N, P and K?
5. How can fertilisers cause pollution?

S 9.4 Sulfur and sulfuric acid

Sulfuric acid is a major product of the chemical industry. It is made from sulfur by the Contact process.

Sulfur is produced as a by-product of the petrochemical industry, as it is removed from fuels such as gasoline before they are sold for use. It can also be obtained from the craters of volcanoes (Figure **9.19**) and is mined by pumping steam into sulfur beds underground. The sulfur is then forced to the surface by compressed air. This method of mining is called the **Frasch process** (Figure **9.20**).

Sulfur is then burned in air to form sulfur dioxide. The main reaction in the Contact process (Figure **9.21**, overleaf) is the one in which sulfur dioxide and oxygen combine to form sulfur trioxide. This reaction is reversible. The conditions needed to give the best equilibrium position are carefully considered.

Figure 9.19 A man carrying baskets of sulfur deposits from around the crater lake in Ijen volcano, Java.

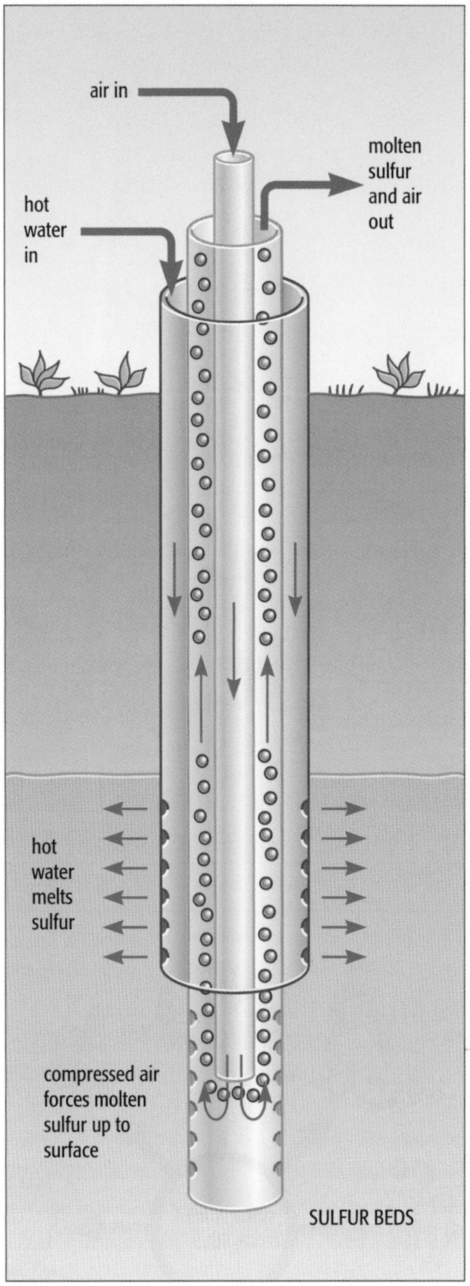

Figure 9.20 Sulfur is mined from underground deposits using super-heated water and compressed air.

A temperature of 450 °C and 1–2 atmospheres pressure are used. The gases are passed over a catalyst of vanadium(V) oxide. A yield of 98% sulfur trioxide is achieved. The overall process is summarised in the flow chart shown in Figure **9.21b**.

The sulfur trioxide produced is dissolved in 98% sulfuric acid, and not water, in order to prevent environmental problems of an acid mist which is formed if sulfur trioxide is reacted directly with water. The reaction between sulfur trioxide and water is extremely exothermic. The solution formed means that the acid can be transported in concentrated form (98.5% acid, sometimes known as **oleum**) and then diluted on-site.

Sulfuric acid is important for the fertiliser industry because it is needed to make ammonium sulfate and phosphoric acid. Figure **9.22** (overleaf) summarises the various uses of sulfuric acid.

The uses of sulfur compounds

Sulfur dioxide is an important compound in its own right. It is used in the manufacture of paper. When made from wood pulp or from other materials, paper is usually pale yellow in colour. Sulfur dioxide is used to bleach it to the white colour which is needed. Sulfur dioxide is used in preference to chlorine as it is less harmful to the environment.

Sulfur dioxide is also used in the food industry. It is used to kill bacteria in foods to prevent them from 'going bad'. Examples of foods where it is used include dried apricots and wine.

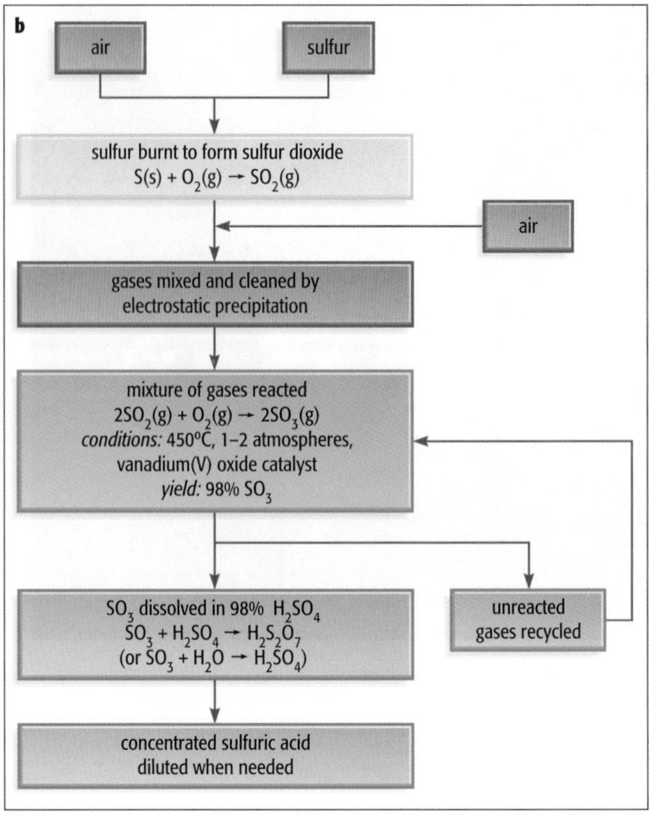

Figure 9.21 **a** The Contact process plant at Billingham, Teesside, in the UK . **b** A flow chart for making sulfuric acid by this process.

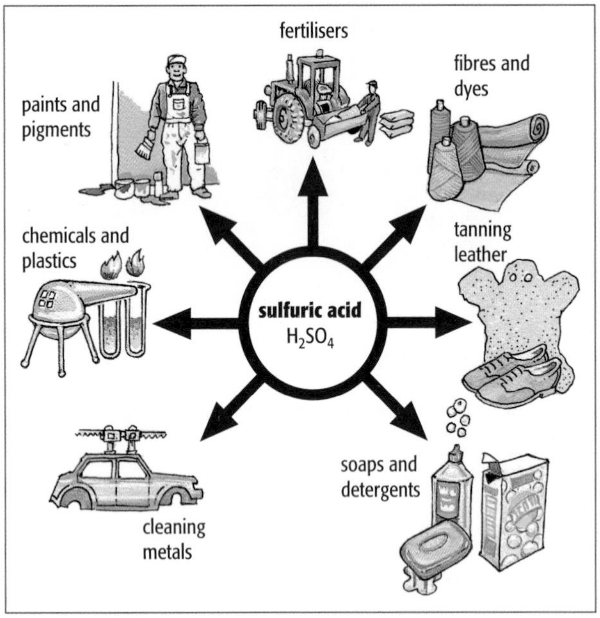

Figure 9.22 The uses of sulfuric acid.

When concentrated, sulfuric acid is very dangerous. It is a powerful dehydrating agent and oxidising agent and can cause very severe burns.

> Concentrated sulfuric acid is:
> - a powerful dehydrating agent
> - a powerful oxidising agent
> - very corrosive.

> **Dehydration** is the removal of water, or the elements of water, from a substance.

The dehydrating properties of the concentrated acid can be demonstrated in the laboratory by its reaction with sugar (sucrose) as shown in Figure **9.23**. Sugar is a carbohydrate – it contains carbon, hydrogen and oxygen. The concentrated acid removes the hydrogen and oxygen as water, leaving carbon behind:

$$\text{sugar (sucrose)} \xrightarrow[\text{(– water)}]{\text{conc.}H_2SO_4} \text{carbon}$$

$$C_{12}H_{22}O \xrightarrow[(-\,11H_2O)]{\text{conc.}H_2SO_4} 12C$$

The acid will dehydrate other carbohydrate materials, for example paper, clothing and wood, in a similar way.

When dilute, sulfuric acid is safer, but it is still a strong acid with normal acid properties (see page **141**).

Figure 9.23 Concentrated sulfuric acid will dehydrate sugar: **a** the start of the reaction, and **b** when it is completed.

Key ideas so far

- Sulfur is found as an element in the ground and can be obtained by mining and quarrying.
- Sulfur is also produced during the refining of petroleum.
- When sulfur is burned in air sulfur dioxide is produced.
- Sulfur dioxide can be used as a bleach and to kill bacteria.
- Sulfur dioxide can be changed into sulfur trioxide by reacting it with more oxygen (air) using a catalyst.
- Sulfur trioxide reacts with water to produce sulfuric acid, a very useful acid.

? Quick-check questions

1. Write an equation for the burning of sulfur.
2. What conditions are needed to convert sulfur dioxide into sulfur trioxide?
3. Why is sulfur trioxide not reacted with water to make sulfuric acid?
4. Give **two** uses of sulfur dioxide and **two** uses of sulfuric acid.

S 9.5 The chlor–alkali industry

The chlor–alkali industry is a major branch of the chemical industry that has been built up around a single electrolysis reaction. The industry is centred around the electrolysis of concentrated sodium chloride solution (**brine**). Three different types of electrolytic cell have been used for this process.

- *Mercury cathode cell:* In this, sodium (Na) is produced at, and dissolves in, the flowing mercury (Hg) cathode. Sodium hydroxide is

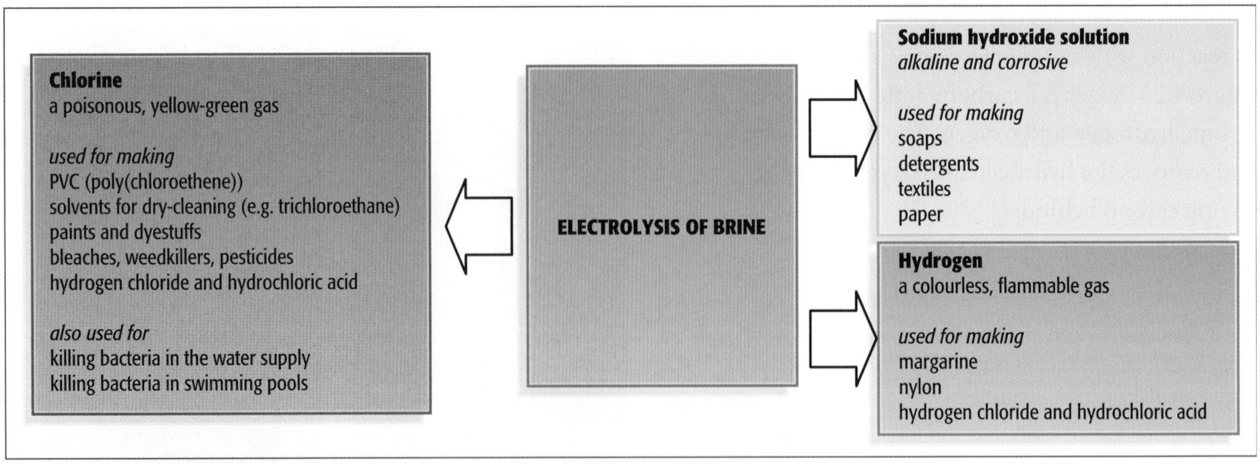

Figure 9.24 The chlor–alkali industry.

produced by treating the Na–Hg cathode material with water.

- *Diaphragm cell:* Here the products of electrolysis are kept separate by an asbestos diaphragm.
- *Membrane cell:* This is the most modern system, and it uses a selective ion-exchange membrane (see page **126**) to keep the products apart.

All three systems are currently in use, but the membrane cell is likely to replace the others.

In all three processes chlorine is produced at the anode (positive electrode) and hydrogen is produced at the cathode (negative electrode). Sodium ions from the sodium chloride and hydroxide ions from the water are left behind as sodium hydroxide. All three products are useful; their uses are summarised in Figure **9.24**.

In Britain, the industry has developed around the Cheshire salt deposits (see page **271**). In this region, salt is brought to the surface by both underground mining and solution mining. One factory in Cheshire uses 1% of the entire UK electricity output just to electrolyse brine.

The uses of chlorine

One use of chlorine we tend to be aware of is its use in water treatment, both for the domestic water supply (see page **13**) and for swimming pools (Figure **9.25**). Chlorine is also used in the manufacture of bleach and to make the plastic PVC.

Taken together, the halogens are a very important group of elements. Because of their reactivity, they form a wide range of useful compounds, including polymers, solvents, bleaches and disinfectants. Their uses are summed up in Table **9.3**.

Figure 9.25 The water of our swimming pools is chlorine-treated to kill harmful bacteria.

Halogen	Product and/or use
fluorine	fluoride in toothpaste and drinking water PTFE – non-stick coating for pans, etc.
chlorine	water treatment bleach PVC – plastic pipes, windows, clothing fabric, etc. solvents for dry-cleaning and degreasing disinfectants and antiseptics pesticides
bromine	flame retardants pesticides petrol additives photographic film
iodine	antiseptics photographic film and paper

Table 9.3 The halogens are involved in the making of a wide range of useful products.

Key ideas so far

- A concentrated solution of sodium chloride can be split by electrolysis.
- Hydrogen is produced at the cathode.
- Chlorine is produced at the anode.
- A solution of sodium hydroxide remains in the cell.
- All three products are important to industry.

Quick-check questions

1 Give **two** important uses of chlorine.
2 What is brine?
3 Why is the electrolysis of brine such an important process?
4 What is the most efficient method of electrolysing brine?

9.6 Limestone

Limestone is quarried (Figure **9.26**) in large amounts world-wide. It has a wide range of uses (see page **16**). In some of these, the limestone is used directly; in others, it acts as a raw material for making other compounds.

Direct uses

Powdered limestone is often used to neutralise acid soils and lakes acidified by acid rain. It is cheaper than using lime (calcium oxide), which has to be produced by heating limestone. In the blast furnace for the extraction of iron, limestone is used to remove impurities found in the iron ore as slag (calcium silicate).

Cement is made by heating powdered limestone with clay in a rotary kiln (Figure **9.27**). This material is then powdered and mixed with gypsum (calcium sulfate, $CaSO_4.2H_2O$). When water is added to this mixture, complex chemical changes take place, giving a hard interlocked mass of crystals of hydrated calcium aluminate ($Ca(AlO_2)_2$) and calcium silicate ($CaSiO_3$).

Figure 9.26 A limestone quarry in Maizeret, Belgium.

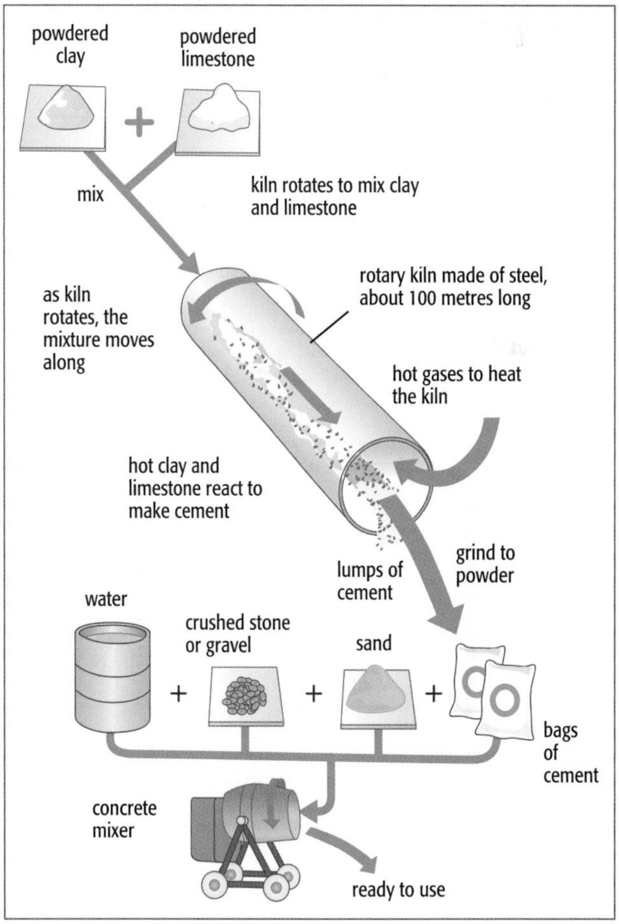

Figure 9.27 Limestone is used to make cement.

Concrete is a mixture of cement and aggregate (stone chippings and gravel), which give it body. The mixture is mixed with water and can be poured into wooden moulds. It is then allowed to harden. Reinforced concrete is made by allowing the concrete to set around steel rods or mesh (Figure **9.28**).

Figure 9.28 Construction workers using a pump to lay concrete around a mesh of metal rods. The rods will strengthen this reinforced concrete.

Sodium carbonate (Na_2CO_3) is an important industrial chemical, which is manufactured from limestone. It is used in the manufacture of glass (Figure **9.29**), soaps, detergents, paper, dyes and other chemicals.

The manufacture of lime (calcium oxide)

Lime (quicklime) is calcium oxide and is produced by roasting limestone in a lime kiln (Figure **9.30**). The limestone is decomposed by heat:

$$\text{calcium carbonate} \xrightarrow{\text{heat}} \text{calcium oxide} + \text{carbon dioxide}$$

$$CaCO_3(s) \xrightarrow{\text{heat}} CaO(s) + CO_2(g)$$

Lime is used in agriculture to neutralise acid soils and to improve drainage in soils that contain a large amount of clay. It is used with sodium carbonate and sand in making glass. Large amounts of lime are converted into slaked lime (hydrated lime), which is calcium hydroxide ($Ca(OH)_2$). Equal amounts of lime and water are mixed to produce this material. It is used to make bleaching powder, in making glass and for water purification. It is mixed with sand to give mortar. When mixed with water and then allowed to dry, mortar sets into a strongly bonded material to hold bricks together: the calcium hydroxide reacts with carbon dioxide in the air to form calcium carbonate.

Exam tip

Remember that the reaction involved in the production of lime is an example of thermal decomposition. The calcium carbonate is not reacting with anything else. It is breaking up into simpler substances because of the high temperature. When writing the equation do not try to include anything else on the left-hand side of the equation.

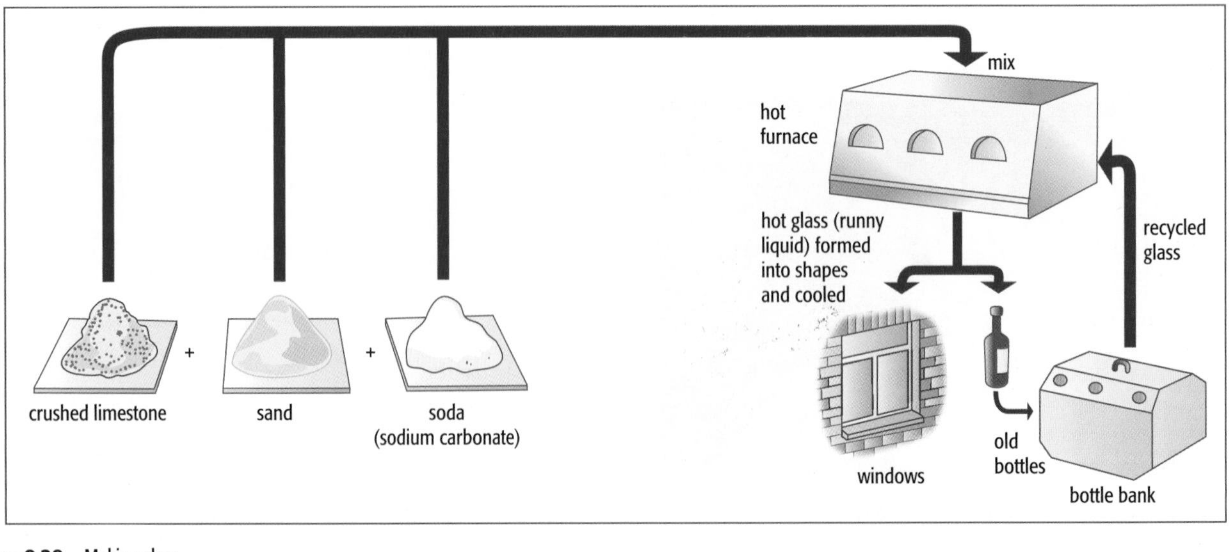

Figure 9.29 Making glass.

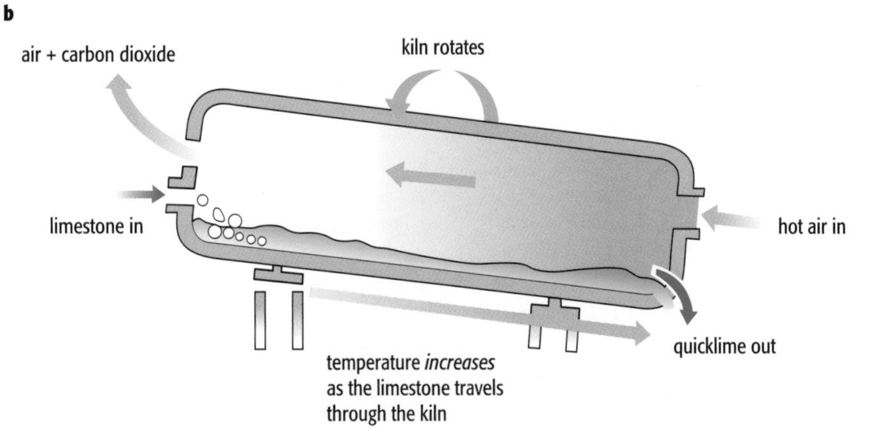

Figure 9.30 **a** A functioning rotary lime kiln in Belgium. Note the heated glow at the far end of the kiln. **b** A diagram of a rotary kiln.

Key ideas so far

- Limestone (calcium carbonate) is a plentiful resource with many uses.
- Strongly heating limestone decomposes it to lime (calcium oxide).
- Adding water to lime forms slaked lime (calcium hydroxide).
- Lime and slaked lime also have many uses, mostly due to the fact that they are bases.

? Quick-check questions

1. Why is limestone sometimes added to lakes?
2. How is it used in iron production?
3. Write an equation for the thermal decomposition of limestone.
4. Write the chemical formula of slaked lime.
5. Give **two** important uses of lime.

9.7 The economics of the chemical industry

Siting a chemical plant

When building a chemical processing plant, many things need to be taken into consideration. Some of the most important are:

- availability of the raw materials needed by the process
- transport links for importing raw materials and export of products
- availability of a work force
- nearness of customers for the products
- environmental considerations.

The chlor-alkali industry in the UK

The map (Figure **9.31**, overleaf) shows the location of the industry.

- The only raw material is salt, which is obtained from the rock salt deposits in Cheshire. The major salt mine here is the Winsford mine.
- Transport links are plentiful, with motorways, railways and seaports all close at hand.
- Greater Manchester with its large population provides the work force.
- There are many other chemical industries in the area which use the hydrogen, chlorine and sodium hydroxide produced in their own processes.
- The process itself causes few environmental problems. The salt is extracted by solution mining. Water is pumped down into the salt deposits, where it dissolves salt to become brine as it rises back to the surface.

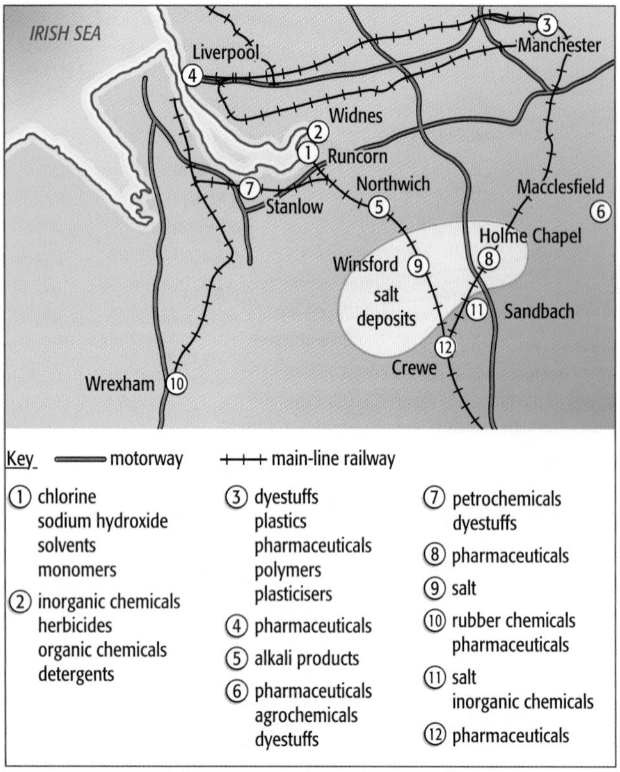

Figure 9.31 The location of the chlor–alkali industry in Cheshire, England.

The fertiliser industry in Burrup, Western Australia

This is the largest ammonia plant of its type in the world. It can produce 760 000 tonnes of liquid ammonia a year.

- The raw materials for the production of ammonium nitrate fertiliser are air and natural gas (Figure **9.32**). This factory is situated next to the onshore base for an offshore gas field (Figure **9.33**).
- The products are transported to customers from the deep-water port by ship. They are transported directly to the port by pipeline.
- The process is largely automated and the work force needed is not large.
- Australian and worldwide customers are supplied by sea.
- The Burrup peninsula is an area well known for its aboriginal art. The companies involved in the development contribute to its preservation.

The environmental costs of industry

Any factory has an effect on its surroundings. In the case of a chemical plant the effects can be serious. There have been a number of accidents in different parts of the world, where something has gone wrong with disastrous results. Most chemical plants, however, run successfully without causing any great harm. The ways in which the environment could be affected are as follows.

- *Air pollution:* Acidic or poisonous gases are often produced in chemical processes. At one time these gases were released into the atmosphere, causing health problems nearby and acid rain further afield. Nowadays gases have to be treated before they are released into the atmosphere to make sure anything harmful is removed. For example, acidic gases are removed by 'scrubbing' – passing them over an alkaline material with which they react. This removes them from the waste gases before they are released.
- *Water pollution:* Liquid waste and cooling water from chemical plants were, at one time, released into rivers. Now this waste must be treated first. Water boards and river authorities test the water leaving chemical plants to ensure it is clean, and chemical companies receive large fines if they fail to stick to the rules. For example, poisonous metal compounds are removed by adding sodium hydroxide, which removes the metals as a precipitate that can be filtered out.

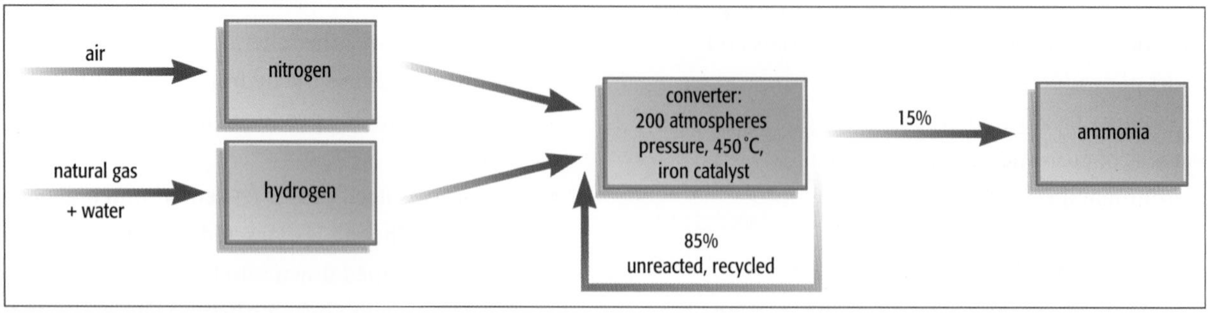

Figure 9.32 A summary of the steps involved in the Haber process.

Figure 9.33 An aerial view of the ammonia and fertiliser plants on the Burrup Peninsula, Western Australia.

- *Land pollution:* Chemical processes often produce solid waste which used to be left in large 'spoil heaps'. These often contained poisonous substances. Most countries in the world still have areas of land where it is not safe to live because of poisons in the ground. Solid waste products now have to be treated to make them harmless, and then have to be disposed of safely.
- *Appearance of the surroundings:* Quarrying and mining can leave the land surrounding a chemical plant looking very much the worse for wear. Chemical companies now have a responsibility, when they have finished using land, to restore it to the sort of environment it used to be (Figure **9.34**).

All of these responsibilities placed on chemical companies increase the cost of producing the chemicals which they make, but they decrease the cost to the environment and make the world a more pleasant place to live in.

Figure 9.34 Orchids growing on a reclaimed quarry site.

Recycling

Recycling used substances is good for three reasons:

- It conserves the raw materials which the substances were made from.
- It often uses less energy to recycle something than would be needed to re-make it from raw materials.
- It avoids the need to bury the substances in landfill sites, possibly causing pollution.

Many substances can be recycled. Some of those most commonly recycled are aluminium, steel, glass, plastic and paper.

- *Aluminium:* This metal is the ideal candidate for recycling as it costs so much to extract it from its ore. Using recycled aluminium saves 95% of the energy needed to make new aluminium. Recycling one aluminium can saves enough energy to run a television for 3 hours. 60% of the aluminium used in the UK and 50% worldwide is recycled.

(aluminium)

- *Steel:* Steel, too, is cheaper to recycle than to make from scratch but the difference in cost is not as great as for aluminium. However, steel is easy to recycle because it is magnetic and so can easily be separated from other rubbish. For this reason quite a lot of steel is recycled.

(steel)

- *Glass:* If glass is left in landfill it never decomposes. Recycling it again saves energy. Recycling one glass bottle saves enough energy to run a light bulb for 4 hours. It is important to separate different colours of glass. In the UK clear glass is needed most, whereas in Europe green glass is in greater demand.

(glass)

- *Plastics:* PET and HDPE are the commonest plastics used, and both can be recycled. In 2006, 2700 million plastic bottles were recycled but 13 000 million were thrown away. A plastic bottle takes around 700 years to decompose in landfill, and recycling one bottle saves enough energy to keep a light bulb lit for 6 hours. When recycling plastic, the different types of plastic need to be kept separate.

1 PET or PETE (plastics)

2 HDPE (plastics)

- *Paper:* Paper has been recycled for many years. Recycling uses over 60% less energy than making new paper from trees. In Europe around 54.6% of paper is recycled and in the USA around 53.4%.

RESY (paper)

Recycling not only saves energy and raw materials: it avoids the need for huge piles of rubbish in landfill sites. The highest point in the state of Ohio, USA, is Mount Rumpke at a height of 1000 ft. It is made of rubbish.

Key ideas so far

- The siting of a modern chemical plant involves a wide range of considerations, including important aspects of environmental planning.
- Recycling is an important aspect of managing the Earth's finite resources.
- Recycling is particularly important for aluminium, as the high energy demands of the extraction process make it particularly expensive.

Quick-check questions

1. Why is the recycling of aluminium the most profitable type of recycling?
2. Saving energy is one reason for recycling. What other reasons are there?
3. Why can recycling plastics be difficult?

Summary

You should know that:

- the extraction of iron in the blast furnace is the most important example of chemical reduction
- the iron produced can be converted into various forms of steel designed to suit a particular purpose
- iron and steel, although the major construction metals, suffer from problems of corrosion
- various methods exist to protect iron objects from corrosion (rusting)
- metals can be extracted from their ores by methods that depend on the reactivity of the metal concerned
- the most reactive metals must be extracted from their molten ores by electrolysis
- aluminium is the major example of a metal extracted from its ore (bauxite) by electrolysis
- aluminium is a useful construction metal because it is protected from corrosion by an oxide layer
- the production of aluminium by electrolysis is expensive
- methods of recycling aluminium and steel are becoming increasingly important
- important chemical products such as ammonia and sulfuric acid can be manufactured using conditions which ensure that reversible reactions still give economic amounts of the product
- the conversion of nitrogen into compounds such as nitrates, which plants can use for making proteins, is known as 'nitrogen fixing'
- ammonia (NH_3) is a strong-smelling alkaline gas
- ammonia and sulfuric acid are important as the basis of the fertiliser and other industries
- nitric acid can react with ammonia to produce ammonium nitrate, which is used extensively as a fertiliser and explosive
- there is a range of fertilisers based on ammonia, but the most important elements added to the soil by these fertilisers are nitrogen, phosphorus and potassium (NPK)
- the halogens and their compounds are used in a wide range of situations – from plastics, antiseptics and pesticides, to photographic films
- limestone is a very important raw material from which lime and cement, as well as other important materials, are made
- the siting of a modern chemical plant involves a wide range of considerations, including important aspects of environmental planning
- recycling is an important aspect of managing the Earth's finite resources
- recycling is particularly important for aluminium, as the high energy demands of the extraction process make it particularly expensive

S

- moderately reactive metals may be extracted by chemical reduction using carbon
- metals such as zinc, lead and copper can be extracted by methods similar to the blast furnace process for iron
- reactive metals such as sodium and magnesium are produced by very similar methods in which their molten chlorides are electrolysed
- zinc can be extracted by an electrolytic process and highly purified copper can be produced by electrolytic refining
- ammonia is manufactured by the Haber process from nitrogen and hydrogen
- nitric acid can be manufactured from ammonia by oxidation
- chlorine is produced by the electrolysis of brine and is the basis of the chlor-alkali industries
- sulfur is a yellow, non-metallic solid
- sulfur can form two acidic oxides – sulfur dioxide (SO_2) and sulfur trioxide (SO_3)
- sulfuric acid is manufactured by the Contact process from sulfur dioxide
- sulfuric acid is a strong acid and is used as either a dilute or concentrated solution
- concentrated sulfuric acid is a powerful dehydrating agent.

Exam-style questions

1 **a** Choose from the list of compounds to answer questions **i** to **v**.

calcium carbonate **carbon dioxide** **hydrogen chloride**
iron(III) oxide **lead(II) bromide** **methane** **sodium hydroxide**

Each compound can be used once, more than once or not at all.

Name the compound which

i is a transition metal compound
ii produces brown fumes at the anode when electrolysed
iii is used to manufacture lime
iv dissolves in water to form an alkaline solution
v is the main constituent of natural gas. [5]

b At a high temperature iron(III) oxide is reduced by carbon.

$$Fe_2O_3 + 3C \rightarrow 2Fe + 3CO$$

i Explain how the equation shows that iron(III) oxide is reduced by carbon. [1]
ii Copy and complete these sentences about the extraction of iron, using words from the list.

bauxite **blast** **converter** **hematite** **lime**
limestone **sand** **slag**

Iron is extracted from .... by mixing the ore, coke and .... in a .... furnace.
The iron ore is reduced to iron, and impurities in the ore react with calcium oxide to form .... [4]

CIE IGCSE, June 2009, paper 2, q.1

2 Iron is extracted from its ore in a blast furnace.

a State the name of the ore from which iron is extracted. [1]
b The diagram shows a blast furnace.

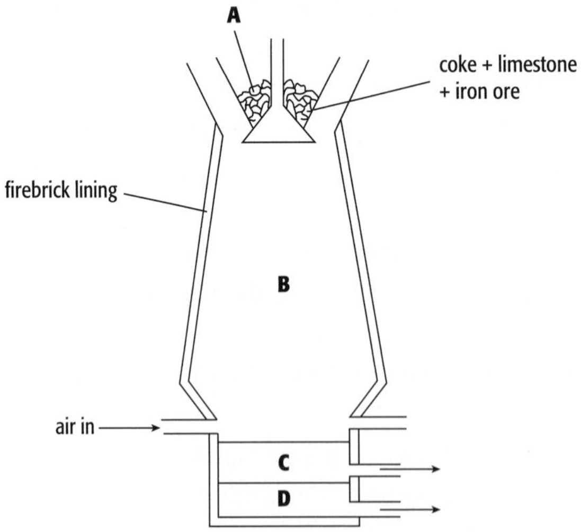

i Which **one** of the raw materials is added to the blast furnace to help remove the impurities from the iron ore? [1]
ii The impurities are removed as a slag. Which letter on the diagram shows the slag? [1]

c Carbon monoxide is formed in the blast furnace by reaction of coke with oxygen.

i Copy and complete the equation for this reaction.

......C + ... → ......CO [2]

ii State the adverse effect of carbon monoxide on human health. [1]

d In the hottest regions of the blast furnace, the following reaction takes place.

$Fe_2O_3 + 3C \rightarrow 2Fe + 3CO$

Which **two** of these sentences correctly describe this reaction?

i The iron oxide gets reduced.

ii The reaction is a thermal decomposition.

iii The carbon gets oxidised.

iv The carbon gets reduced.

v Carbon neutralises the iron oxide. [2]

e Aluminium cannot be extracted from aluminium oxide in a blast furnace. Explain why aluminium cannot be extracted in this way. [1]

f i State the name of the method used to extract aluminium from its oxide ore. [1]

ii State **one** use of aluminium. [1]

CIE IGCSE, November 2008, paper 2, q.4

3 An experiment was set up to investigate the rusting of iron.

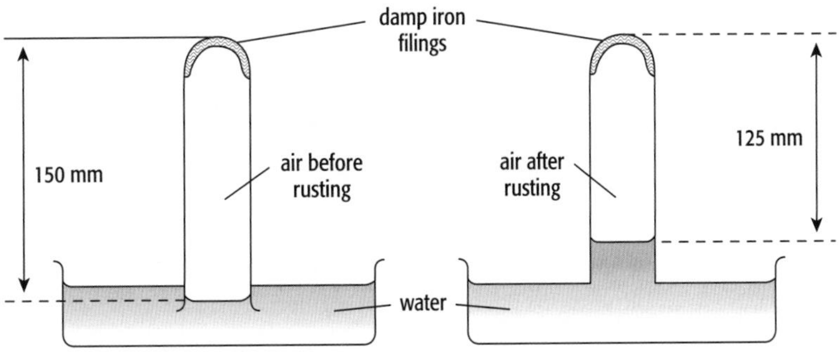

a Describe the appearance of the iron after rusting. [1]

b i Why does the water rise up the tube? [1]

ii Calculate the percentage change in the volume of air in the tube. [1]

c What difference would be observed if

i an iron nail was suspended in the tube instead of using iron filings? [1]

ii the water contained salt? [1]

CIE IGCSE, November 2007, paper 6, q.2

4 Iron is extracted from its ore in a blast furnace using carbon (coke) as a reducing agent and as a source of heat.

a The coke burns in hot air. The equation for this reaction is

$$2C(s) + O_2(g) \rightarrow 2CO(g)$$

State the name of the gas produced in this reaction. [1]

b Near the top of the blast furnace, the iron(III) oxide in the iron ore gets reduced to iron.

$$Fe_2O_3(s) + 3CO(g) \rightarrow 2Fe(l) + 3CO_2(g)$$

Use the equation to explain why the change of iron(III) oxide to iron is a reduction reaction. [1]

c In the hottest regions of the furnace, iron(III) oxide is reduced by carbon. Complete the equation for this reaction.

$$Fe_2O_3(s) + \ldots .C(s) \rightarrow \ldots .Fe(l) + 3CO(g)$$ [2]

d The iron from the blast furnace contains up to 10% by mass of impurities. The main impurities are carbon, silicon and phosphorus. The diagram below shows one method of making steel from iron.

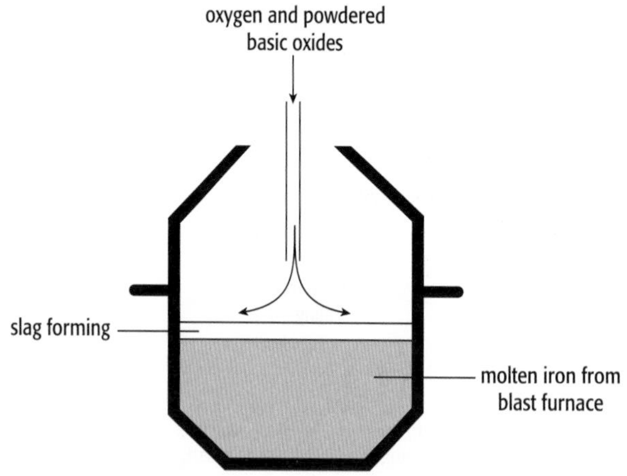

A mixture of oxygen and basic oxides is blown onto the surface of the molten iron.

i What is the purpose of blowing oxygen onto the molten iron? [1]

ii A large amount of energy is released in the process of steelmaking. What name is given to chemical reactions which release energy? [1]

iii The basic oxides react with the impurities in the iron and form a slag. What information in the diagram suggests that the slag is less dense than the molten iron? [1]

iv Which one of the following is a basic oxide? [1]

calcium oxide **carbon dioxide** **sulfur dioxide** **water**

v Why is steel rather than iron used for constructing buildings and bridges? [1]

e Special steels contain added elements such as vanadium, chromium, cobalt or nickel. These are all transition metals.
State **three** properties of transition metals which are **not** shown by non-transition metals. [3]

f What is the name given to metals which are mixtures of more than one metal? [1]

CIE IGCSE, June 2004, paper 2, q.6

5 Aluminium is extracted by the electrolysis of aluminium oxide dissolved in cryolite.

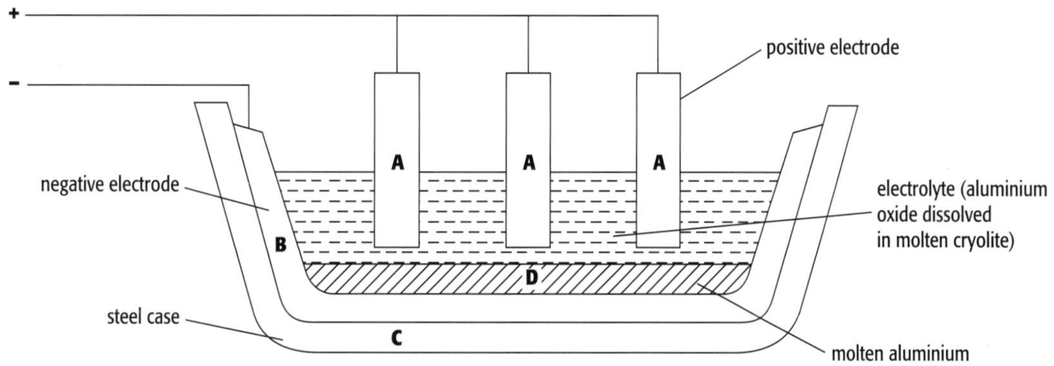

a What information in the diagram shows that aluminium is more dense than the electrolyte? [1]

b What form of carbon is used for the electrodes in this electrolysis? [1]

c Which letter in the diagram, **A**, **B**, **C** or **D**, represents the anode? [1]

d Suggest why electrolysis is used to extract aluminium rather than reduction using carbon. [1]

e Oxygen gas is released at the anode.

i Where does this oxygen come from? [1]

ii The oxygen reacts with the carbon anode to form carbon dioxide. What is the formula of carbon dioxide? [1]

iii Why does the anode decrease in size during electrolysis? [1]

f Each electrolysis cell makes 212 kg of aluminium per day from 400 kg of aluminium oxide. Calculate how much aluminium can be made from 1 tonne (1000 kg) of aluminium oxide. [1]

g Copy and complete the following sentence about the electrolysis of aluminium oxide using words from the following list.

atoms **gaseous** **molten** **solid** **ions** **molecules**

Aluminium oxide conducts electricity when it is .... because it contains .... which are free to move. [2]

CIE IGCSE, June 2007, paper 2, q.7

6 Zinc is extracted from zinc blende, ZnS.

a Zinc blende is heated in air to give zinc oxide and sulfur dioxide. Most of the sulfur dioxide is used to make sulfur trioxide. This is used to manufacture sulfuric acid. Some of the acid is used in the plant, but most of it is used to make fertilisers.

i Give another use of sulfur dioxide. [1]

ii Describe how sulfur dioxide is converted into sulfur trioxide. [3]

iii Name a fertiliser made from sulfuric acid. [1]

b Some of the zinc oxide was mixed with an excess of carbon and heated to 1000 °C. Zinc distils out of the furnace.

$$2ZnO + C \rightleftharpoons 2Zn + CO_2$$
$$C + CO_2 \rightarrow 2CO$$

i Name the **two** changes of state involved in the process of distillation. [2]

ii Why is it necessary to use an excess of carbon? [2]

S

- **c** The remaining zinc oxide reacts with sulfuric acid to give aqueous zinc sulfate. This is electrolysed with inert electrodes (the electrolysis is the same as that of copper(II) sulfate with inert electrodes).

  ions present: $Zn^{2+}(aq)$ $SO_4^{2-}(aq)$ $H^+(aq)$ $OH^-(aq)$

  - **i** Zinc forms at the negative electrode (cathode). Write the equation for this reaction. [1]
  - **ii** Write the equation for the reaction at the positive electrode (anode). [2]
  - **iii** The electrolyte changes from aqueous zinc sulfate to …………………… . [1]
- **d** Give **two** uses of zinc. [2]

CIE IGCSE, November 2007, paper 3, q.4

7 Steel is an alloy made from impure iron.

- **a** Both iron and steel rust.
  The formula for rust is $Fe_2O_3.2H_2O$. It is hydrated iron(III) oxide.
  - **i** Name the **two** substances that must be present for rusting to occur. [2]
  - **ii** Painting and coating with grease are two methods of preventing iron or steel from rusting. Give **two** other methods. [2]
- **b**
  - **i** Name a reagent that can reduce iron(III) oxide to iron. [1]
  - **ii** Write a symbol equation for the reduction of iron(III) oxide, Fe_2O_3, to iron. [2]
- **c**
  - **i** Calculate the mass of one mole of $Fe_2O_3.2H_2O$. [1]
  - **ii** Use your answer to part **i** to calculate the percentage of iron in rust. [2]
- **d** Iron from the blast furnace is impure. Two of the impurities are carbon and silicon.
  These are removed by blowing oxygen through the molten iron and adding calcium oxide.
  - **i** Explain how the addition of oxygen removes carbon. [1]
  - **ii** Explain how the addition of oxygen and calcium oxide removes silicon. [2]

CIE IGCSE, November 2008, paper 3, q.3

8 Aluminium is extracted by the electrolysis of a molten mixture that contains alumina, which is aluminium oxide, Al_2O_3.

- **a** The ore of aluminium is bauxite. This contains alumina, which is amphoteric, and iron(III) oxide, which is basic. The ore is heated with aqueous sodium hydroxide. Copy and complete the following sentences.
  The ………………… dissolves to give a solution of ………………… .
  The ………………………… does not dissolve and can be removed by ………………………… . [4]
- **b** Copy the diagram and complete the labelling.

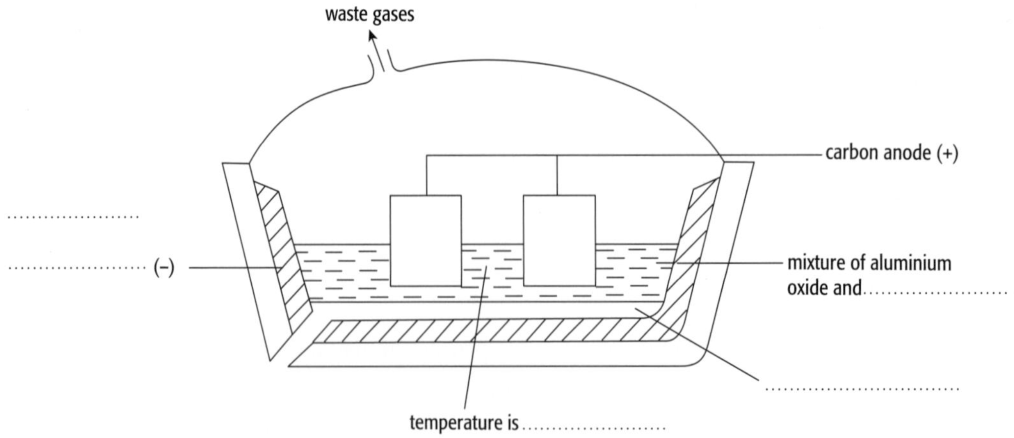

[4]

c The ions that are involved in the electrolysis are Al^{3+} and O^{2-}.

i Write an equation for the reaction at the cathode. [2]

ii Explain how carbon dioxide is formed at the anode. [2]

d Give an explanation for each of the following.

i Aluminium is used extensively in the manufacture of aircraft. [1]

ii Aluminium is used to make food containers. [2]

iii Aluminium electricity cables have a steel core. [1]

CIE IGCSE, June 2007, paper 3, q.6

9 Ammonia is manufactured by the Haber process.

$N_2(g) + 3H_2(g) \rightleftharpoons 2NH_3(g)$ the forward reaction is exothermic

a i Name the raw materials from which nitrogen and hydrogen are obtained. [2]

ii Name the catalyst used in this process. [1]

iii What is the most important use of ammonia? [1]

b The following graph shows how the percentage of ammonia in the equilibrium mixture changes with temperature.

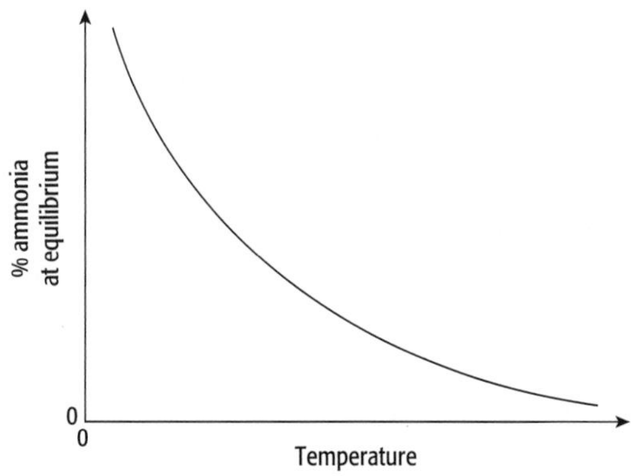

i Explain the term **equilibrium**. [2]

ii How does the percentage of ammonia vary with temperature? [1]

c i Sketch a graph which shows how the percentage of ammonia in the equilibrium mixture varies with pressure. [1]

ii Explain why the graph has the shape shown. [2]

CIE IGCSE, June 2009, paper 3, q.6

10 No one knows where iron was first isolated. It appeared in China, the Middle East and in Africa. It was obtained by reducing iron ore with charcoal.

a Copy and complete the following equation.

Fe_2O_3 (iron ore) + ...C (charcoal) → .... + ... [2]

b In 1705 Abraham Darby showed that iron ore could be reduced using coke in a blast furnace.

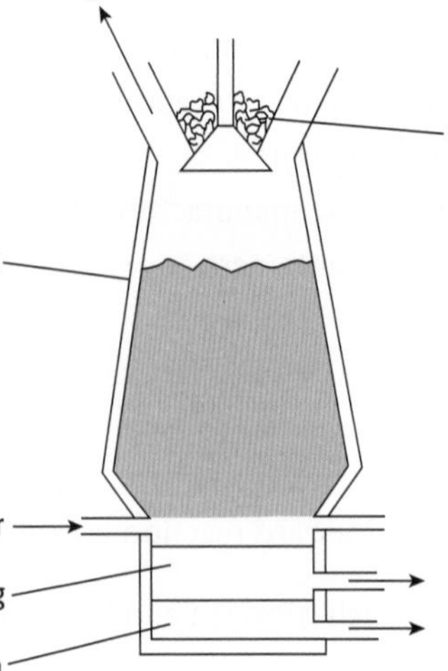

- **i** The temperature in the furnace rises to 2000 °C. Write an equation for the exothermic reaction that causes this high temperature.
- **ii** In the furnace, the ore is reduced by carbon monoxide. Explain how this is formed. [3]

c The formation of slag removes an impurity in the ore. Write a word equation for the formation of the slag. [2]

d Stainless steel is an alloy of iron. It contains iron, other metals and about 0.5% of carbon.

- **i** State a use of stainless steel.
- **ii** Name a metal, other than iron, in stainless steel.
- **iii** The iron from the blast furnace is impure. It contains about 5% of carbon and other impurities, such as silicon and phosphorus. Describe how the percentage of carbon is reduced and the other impurities are removed. [6]

e One of the methods used to prevent iron or steel from rusting is to electroplate it with another metal, such as tin. Copy and complete the following.

The anode is made of ....

The cathode is made of ....

The electrolyte is a solution of .... [3]

CIE IGCSE, June 2003, paper 3, q.1

11 Ammonia is manufactured by the Haber process.

$$N_2(g) + 3H_2(g) \underset{\substack{200\ \text{atmospheres} \\ 450\,°\text{C}}}{\rightleftharpoons} 2NH_3(g)$$

The forward reaction is exothermic.

a **i** What is the catalyst for this reaction? [1]

- **ii** Newer catalysts have been discovered for this process.
Using these catalysts, the operating temperature is lowered from 450 °C to 400 °C.
What is the advantage of using a lower temperature? Explain your answer. [2]

b After passing over the catalyst, the mixture contains 15% of ammonia. It is cooled and the ammonia liquefies and is separated from the unreacted nitrogen and hydrogen. They are recycled.

- **i** How are the gases recycled? [1]
- **ii** Only ammonia gas liquefies. Suggest an explanation for this. [1]

c Urea, $CO(NH_2)_2$, is one of the fertilisers manufactured from ammonia. Ammonia is heated with carbon dioxide.

i Write an equation for the manufacture of urea. [2]

ii Explain why urea on its own might not be very effective in promoting crop growth. [1]

d Give a diagram showing the arrangement of the valency electrons in one molecule of the covalent compound urea. Its structural formula is given below.

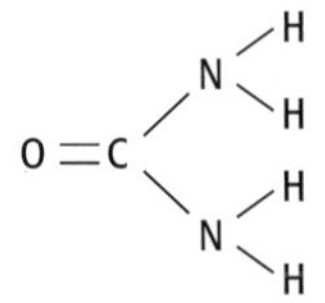

Use o to represent an electron from a carbon atom. Use × to represent an electron from a hydrogen atom. Use • to represent an electron from a nitrogen atom. [3]

CIE IGCSE, November 2006, paper 3, q.5

12 The electrolysis of concentrated aqueous sodium chloride produces three commercially important chemicals: hydrogen, chlorine and sodium hydroxide.

a The ions present are $Na^+(aq)$, $H^+(aq)$, $Cl^-(aq)$ and $OH^-(aq)$.

i Copy and complete the ionic equation for the reaction at the negative electrode (cathode).

.... + ... → H_2 [1]

ii Copy and complete the ionic equation for the reaction at the positive electrode (anode).

.... − .... → Cl_2 [1]

iii Explain why the solution changes from sodium chloride to sodium hydroxide. [1]

b i Why does the water supply industry use chlorine? [1]

ii Name an important chemical that is made from hydrogen. [1]

iii How is sodium hydroxide used to make soap? [2]

CIE IGCSE, November 2008, paper 3, q.5

13 Calcium carbonate is an important raw material.

a Name a rock which is made up of calcium carbonate. [1]

b When calcium carbonate is heated strongly, it decomposes.

$CaCO_3 \rightarrow CaO + CO_2$

i Calculate the relative formula mass of $CaCO_3$ and CaO. [2]

ii 7.00 kg of calcium oxide was formed. What mass of calcium carbonate was heated? [2]

c Calcium carbonate is used to control soil acidity.

i Why is it important to control soil acidity? [1]

ii Both calcium carbonate, insoluble in water, and calcium oxide, slightly soluble, are used to increase soil pH. Suggest **two** advantages of using calcium carbonate. [2]

iii Give **one** use of calcium carbonate other than for making calcium oxide and controlling soil pH. [1]

CIE IGCSE, November 2006, paper 3, q.3

14 Sulfuric acid is made by the Contact process in the following sequence of reactions.

sulfur → sulfur dioxide → sulfur trioxide → sulfuric acid

a **i** How is sulfur dioxide made from sulfur? [1]

ii Sulfur dioxide has other uses. Why is it used in the manufacture of paper? [1]

iii How does it preserve food? [1]

b The equation for a stage of the Contact process is

$2SO_2 + O_2 \rightleftharpoons 2SO_3$

The percentage of sulfur trioxide in the equilibrium mixture varies with temperature.

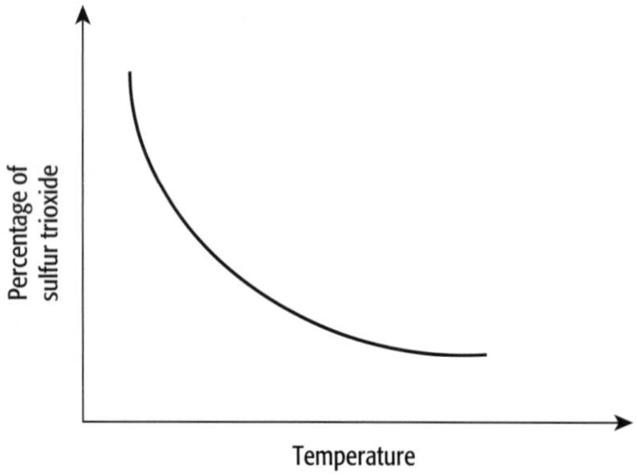

i How does the percentage of sulfur trioxide in the equilibrium mixture vary as the temperature increases? Does it increase, stay the same, or decrease? [1]

ii Is the forward reaction in the equilibrium $2SO_2 + O_2 \rightleftharpoons 2SO_3$ exothermic or endothermic? Give a reason for your choice. [2]

iii Explain, mentioning both rate and percentage yield, why the temperature used in the Contact process is 450 °C. [2]

iv Describe how the sulfur trioxide is changed into concentrated sulfuric acid. [2]

CIE IGCSE, June 2006, paper 3, q.5

10 Organic chemistry

This chapter covers the following ideas:

- the unique properties of carbon
- hydrocarbons as compounds of carbon and hydrogen only
- the alkanes and their properties
- S isomerism
- the halogen compounds of the alkanes
- the alkenes
- the reactivity of the C=C double bond in alkenes
- S addition reactions
- the alcohols as a homologous series
- fermentation as a source of ethanol
- comparing the methods of ethanol production
- the reactions of ethanol
- S carboxylic acids as a homologous series
- S ethanoic acid as a weak acid
- S esterification
- soap-making (saponification)

10.1 The unique properties of carbon

Amino acids, simple sugar molecules and even fats may be relatively simple molecules but the construction of complex molecules, such as long-chain carbohydrates and proteins, shows the versatility of carbon-containing compounds. The peak of this complexity must be DNA (deoxyribonucleic acid), the molecule that makes life possible (Figure **10.1**, overleaf).

Carbon is unique in the variety of molecules it can form. The chemistry of these molecules is a separate branch of the subject known as **organic chemistry**. Organic chemistry is the chemistry of carbon-containing compounds.

There are three special features of covalent bonding involving carbon:

- Carbon atoms can join to each other to form long chains. Atoms of other elements can then attach to the chain.
- The carbon atoms in a chain can be linked by single, double or triple covalent bonds.
- Carbon atoms can also arrange themselves in rings.

Only carbon can achieve all these different bonding arrangements to the extent that we see. Indeed, there are more compounds of carbon than of all the other elements put together. Figure **10.2** (overleaf) gives some idea of how these bonding arrangements can produce different types of molecules.

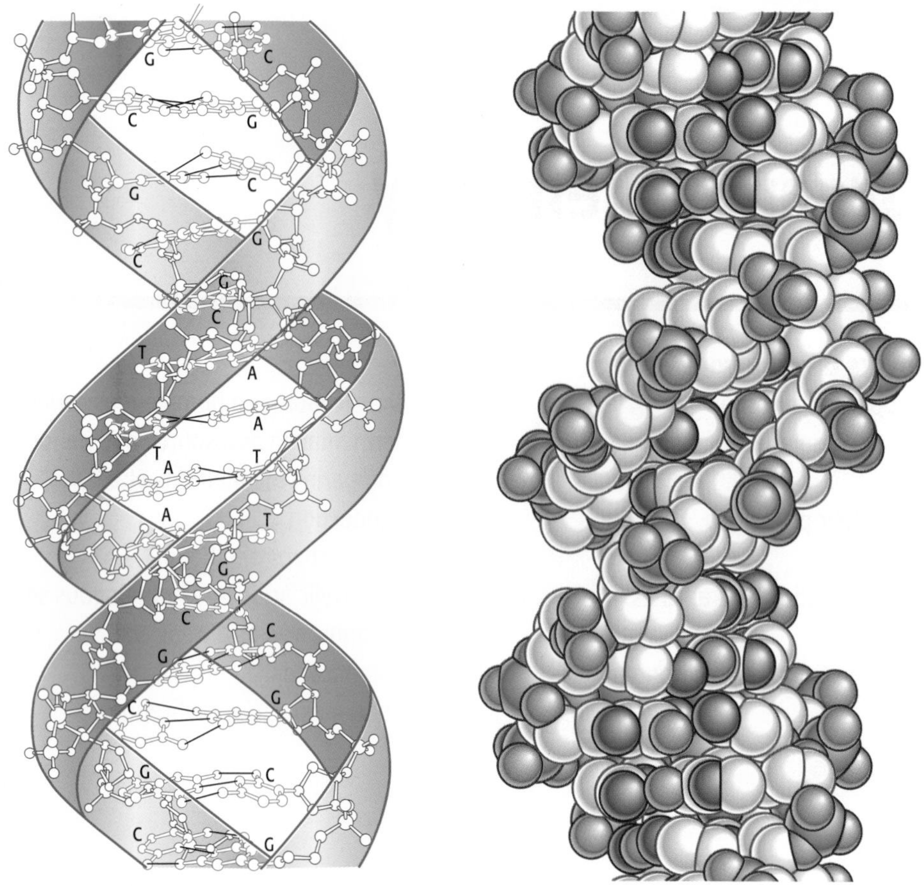

Figure 10.1 Two ways of showing a section of the complex molecule DNA.

a Carbon can form four bonds, and carbon atoms can join to one another to form long chains.

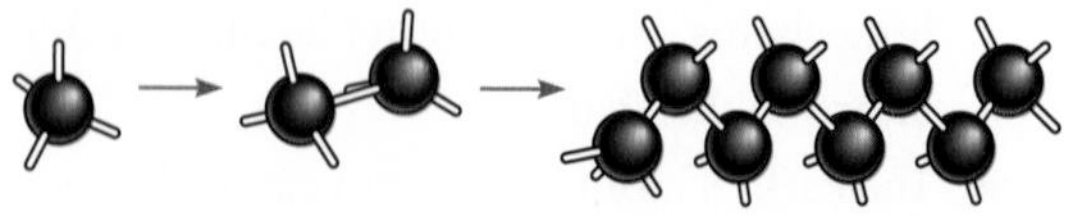

b In alkanes, only hydrogen atoms are joined to the side positions on the chains. Other atoms can be attached instead, forming other families of organic compounds.

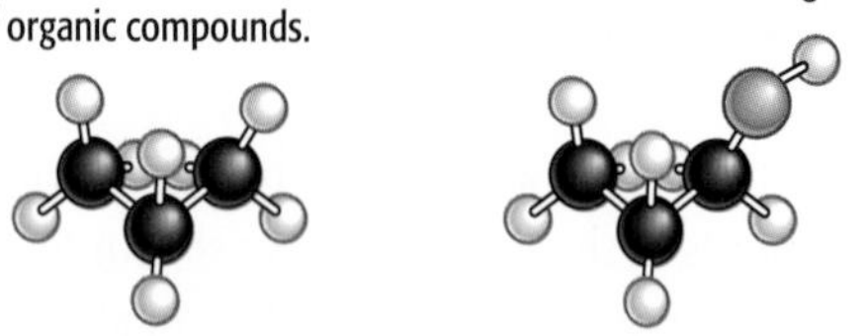

c Double bonds can occur in simple molecules and in the long chains.

d Carbon atoms can also join to form ring molecules, for example glucose, as shown here.

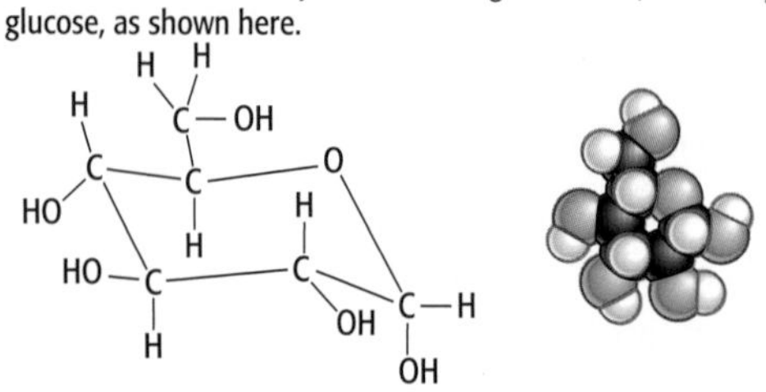

e Long-chain fat molecules can be formed, as well as numerous other molecules.

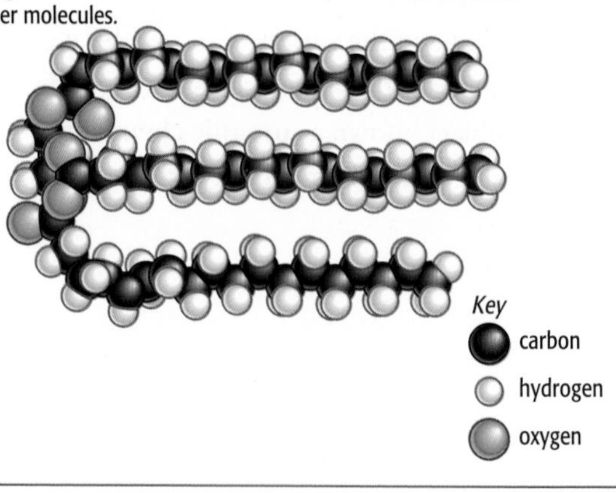

Figure 10.2 Carbon is very versatile.

Carbon is a non-metal in Group IV of the Periodic Table. It forms covalent compounds. The uniqueness of carbon lies in the different ways in which it can form bonds. The element carbon exists in several different forms. Two of the forms we have met earlier (see page **91**): diamond and graphite. A third form, the fullerenes and carbon nanotubes (Figure **10.3**), have been discovered relatively recently and their exploitation is one of the major features of the exciting new area of research referred to as **nanotechnology**.

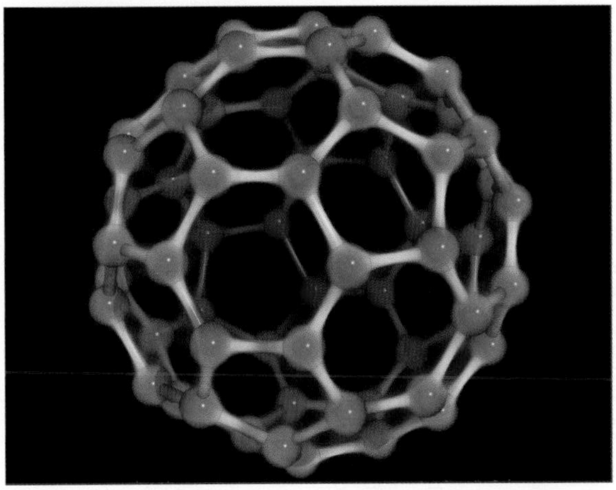

Figure 10.3 A computer image of the structure of carbon-60 (C_{60}) – the first fullerene to be discovered. The structure resembles the panelled structure of a modern soccer ball.

Key ideas so far

- Carbon is a non-metallic element in Group IV of the Periodic Table.
- Carbon exists in two different structural forms – diamond and graphite (see page **91**) – and also as the fullerenes.
- The versatility that carbon begins to show as an element is also shown in its bonding in compounds.
- As a non-metal, carbon forms covalent bonds in its compounds.
- The versatility of its bonding is shown by the fact that atoms of carbon can
  - form long covalent chains with themselves
  - form multiple bonds between atoms, and
  - form ring structures.
- Life on Earth evolved using carbon-containing molecules such as nucleic acids, proteins and carbohydrates.

Quick-check questions

1. What type of bonding do carbon atoms normally participate in?
2. What is the valency of carbon?
3. What are the **two** different structural forms of carbon? What is the name of the new form of carbon, discovered relatively recently?
4. What are the names of **two** different carbon-containing molecules that are important for living organisms?

10.2 Alkanes

What is a hydrocarbon?

Around **six million** compounds of carbon are already known! Because there are so many, it is helpful to pick out those compounds which have similar structures. One of the simplest types of organic compound is the **hydrocarbons**.

A **hydrocarbon** is a compound that contains carbon and hydrogen only.

The hydrocarbons that we study at this level can be subdivided into two 'families'. Some hydrocarbons are **saturated**. These molecules contain **only** single covalent bonds between carbon atoms. Since carbon has a valency of 4, the bonds not used in making the chain are linked to hydrogen atoms (see Figure **10.2**). No further atoms can be added to molecules of these compounds. This family of saturated hydrocarbons is known as the **alkanes**.

The **alkanes** are **saturated** hydrocarbons. Molecules of these compounds contain only **single bonds** between the carbon atoms in the chain.

Table **10.1** gives the names and formulae of the first six members of the series of alkanes. The simplest alkane contains one carbon atom and is called methane. Note that the names of this series of hydrocarbons all end in *-ane*. The first part of the name (the **prefix**) tells you the number of carbon atoms in the chain. These prefixes are used consistently in naming organic compounds.

The formulae given in Table **10.1** are the **molecular formulae** of the compounds. Each molecule increases by a $—CH_2—$ group as the chain gets longer (see Figure **10.2**). Indeed, the formulae of long-chain alkanes can be written showing the number of $— CH_2—$ groups in the chain. For example, octane (C_8H_{18}) can be written as $CH_3— (CH_2)_6— CH_3$. The formulae of these molecules all fit the general formula C_nH_{2n+2} (where *n* is the number of carbon atoms present).

In organic chemistry, the **structure** of a molecule is also very important. Figure **10.4** shows the structural formulae of the first six alkanes in the series. A **structural formula** shows the bonds between the atoms. As the length of the hydrocarbon chain increases, the strength of the weak forces between the molecules (**intermolecular forces** or **van der Waals' forces**) is increased. This shows itself in the increasing boiling points of the members of the series (Table **10.1**). The melting points and boiling points of the alkanes increase gradually. Under normal conditions, the first four members of the family are gases, and those between C_5H_{12} and $C_{16}H_{34}$ (which in short are called C_5 to C_{16} alkanes) are liquids. The compounds in the alkane family with 17 or more carbon atoms are waxy solids.

Every organic compound has three different formulae. The first of these is the **empirical formula** (see page **183**). This formula is the simplest possible whole-number ratio of the atoms in a compound; thus for methane it is CH_4, but for ethane it is CH_3.

The second formula for any compound, and the most crucial, is the **molecular formula.** This represents the actual number of atoms present in the molecule; thus for methane it is CH_4, for ethane it is C_2H_6, and so on.

The final formula for any compound, and a highly important one, is the **structural formula** of the molecule of the compound. This formula shows all the atoms in the molecule and how they are bonded together. The structural formulae of the first six alkanes are shown in Figure **10.4**.

Exam tip

It is important to read an exam question carefully when you are asked to give the formula of a compound. Make sure you realise whether you are being asked for the molecular formula or the structural formula, and give the correct type.

Alkane	Molecular formula C_nH_{2n+2}	Number of carbon atoms	Boiling point/°C		Physical state at room temperature
methane	CH_4	1	−164		gas
ethane	C_2H_6	2	−87		gas
propane	C_3H_8	3	−42		gas
butane	C_4H_{10}	4	0		gas
pentane	C_5H_{12}	5	+36		liquid
hexane	C_6H_{14}	6	+69	b.p. increasing	liquid

Table 10.1 Some details of the early members of the alkane series.

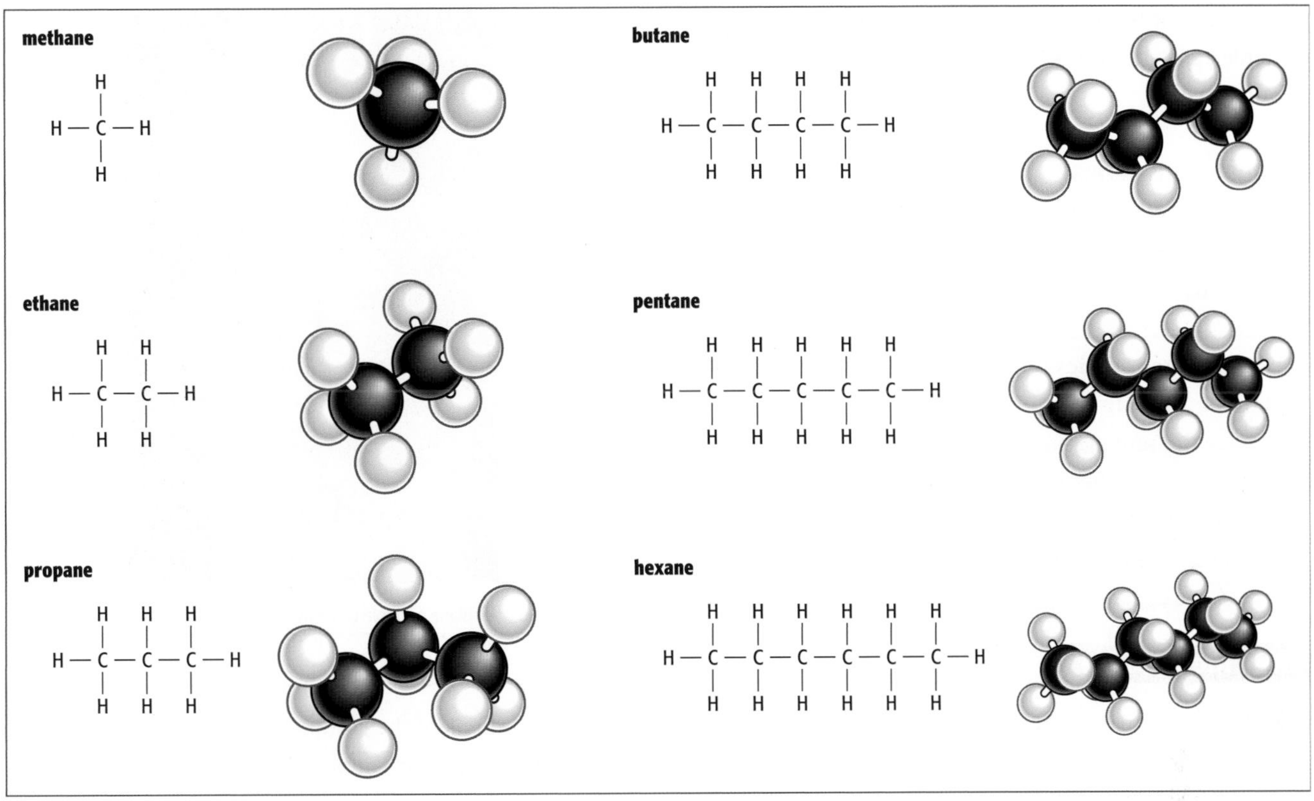

Figure 10.4 The structures of the first six alkanes.

> When giving the structural formula of a compound, make sure you show all the atoms and all the bonds.
>
> Remember, too, to count the bonds around each carbon atom you draw; there can only be four. It is worth practising drawing some of the regular molecules that are asked about.

Burning alkanes

One chemical property that all these alkanes have in common is that they burn very exothermically (Figure 10.5). They make good fuels. Controlling their availability and cost can have great political consequences. When they burn in a good supply of air, the products are carbon dioxide and water vapour:

methane + oxygen → carbon dioxide + water

$$CH_4(g) + 2O_2(g) \rightarrow CO_2(g) + 2H_2O(g)$$

ethane + oxygen → carbon dioxide + water

$$2C_2H_6(g) + 7O_2(g) \rightarrow 4CO_2(g) + 6H_2O(g)$$

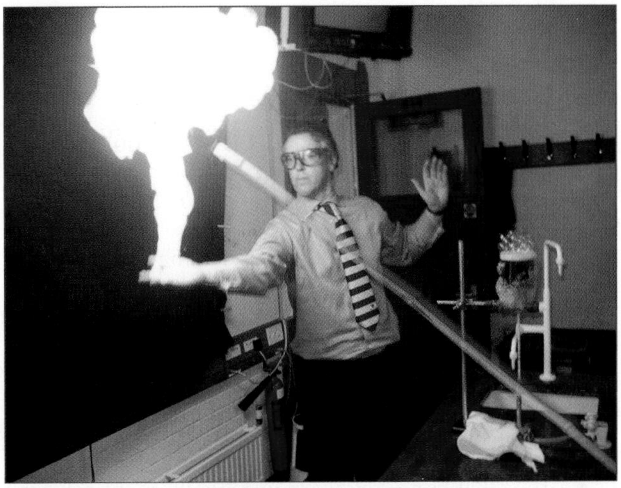

Figure 10.5 A spectacular demonstration of methane burning on the hand.

Methane forms the major part of natural gas. Propane and butane burn with very hot flames and are sold as liquefied petroleum gas (LPG). They are kept as liquids under pressure, but they vaporise easily when that pressure is released. In areas where there is no mains supply of natural gas, you may have seen propane tanks in gardens, which supply the fuel for heating systems. Cylinders of butane (Calor gas) are used in portable gas fires in the home. Butane is also used in portable camping stoves, blow-torches and gas-lighters (Figure 10.6).

Figure 10.6 A butane portable camping stove.

A homologous series

The family of alkanes has similar chemical properties. Together they are an example of a homologous series of compounds.

> A **homologous series** is a family of organic compounds that:
> - have the same general formula
> - have similar chemical properties
> - show a gradual increase in physical properties such as melting point and boiling point.

Key ideas so far

- Hydrocarbons are compounds that contain carbon and hydrogen only.
- The first series of hydrocarbons are known as the alkanes.
- The alkanes are saturated hydrocarbons because the carbon atoms in the chain are joined together with carbon-carbon single bonds.
- The alkanes form a homologous series of compounds. The chain lengths of the molecules in the series increase progressively by the addition of a $—CH_2—$ group.
- The molecules in the alkane series have the same general formula, C_nH_{2n+2}.
- The alkanes have similar chemical properties and there is a regular increase in certain physical properties (boiling point, for example) as chain length increases.
- The alkanes are relatively unreactive chemically but they do burn well, giving out a significant amount of heat. They are used as fuels.
- The products of the complete combustion of any alkane are carbon dioxide and water.

Quick-check questions

1 Write down the names and formulae of the first **six** alkanes.
2 Draw the structural formulae of methane and butane.
3 Plot a graph of the boiling points of the first six alkanes against the number of carbon atoms in the molecule. Comment on the shape of the graph.
4 What is the formula of the first alkane that is
 a a liquid at room temperature and pressure?
 b a solid at room temperature?
5 Write a word equation for the complete combustion of ethane.
6 What is the major natural source of methane?
7 Draw a diagram of the arrangement of the electrons in the bonding of methane, showing just the outer (valency) electrons.

10.3 Alkenes

Unsaturated hydrocarbons

The ability of carbon atoms to form double bonds gives rise to the **alkenes**. The alkenes are another family of hydrocarbons or homologous series.

> The **alkenes** are **unsaturated** hydrocarbons. Molecules of these compounds contain a C=C **double bond** somewhere in the chain.

Alkenes have the general formula C_nH_{2n} (where n is the number of carbon atoms). Such molecules are unsaturated because it is possible to break this double bond and add extra atoms to the molecule.

The simplest alkene must contain **two** carbon atoms (needed for one C=C double bond) and is called ethene (Figure **10.7**). Table **10.2** shows the molecular formulae of the first alkenes. The boiling points of these compounds again show a gradual increase as the molecules get larger. Figure **10.7** also shows the structures of the first three alkenes.

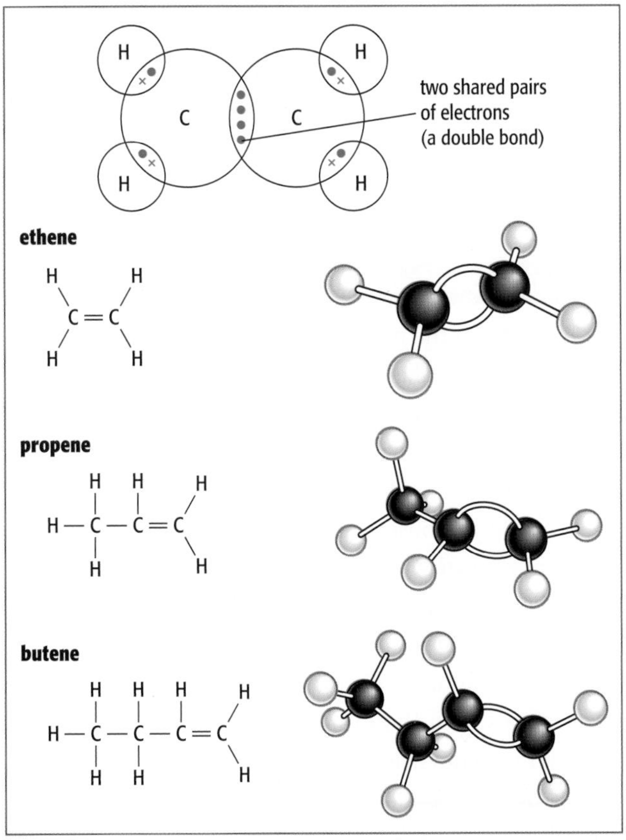

Figure 10.7 The structures of the first three alkenes, and the bonding in ethene.

Alkenes are similar to other hydrocarbons when burnt. They give carbon dioxide and water vapour as long as the air supply is sufficient:

$$\text{ethene} + \text{oxygen} \rightarrow \text{carbon dioxide} + \text{water}$$
$$C_2H_4(g) + 3O_2(g) \rightarrow 2CO_2(g) + 2H_2O(g)$$

The presence of the C=C double bond in an alkene molecule makes alkenes much more reactive than alkanes (alkanes contain only C—C single bonds). Other atoms can add on to alkene molecules when the double bond breaks open. This difference produces a simple test for unsaturation.

It is the presence of the C=C double bond in an alkene molecule that gives the homologous series its characteristic properties. For this reason the C=C double bond is known as the **functional group** of the alkenes. We will meet other functional groups, such as that for the alcohols (—OH) later in the chapter. All the members of a particular homologous series contain the same functional group.

Chemical tests for unsaturation

If an alkene, such as ethene, is shaken with a solution of bromine in water, the bromine loses its colour. Bromine has reacted with ethene, producing a colourless compound:

$$\text{ethene} + \text{bromine} \rightarrow \text{1,2-dibromoethane}$$
$$C_2H_4(g) + \underset{\text{orange-brown solution}}{Br_2(aq)} \rightarrow \underset{\text{colourless}}{C_2H_4Br_2(l)}$$

The double bond in ethene breaks open and forms new bonds to the bromine atoms (Figure **10.8**, overleaf). This type of reaction, where a double bond breaks and adds two new atoms, is known as an **addition reaction**. An alkane would give no reaction with bromine water; the

Alkene	Molecular formula C_nH_{2n}	Number of carbon atoms	Boiling point / °C		Physical state at room temperature
ethene	C_2H_4	2	−104		gas
propene	C_3H_6	3	−47		gas
butene	C_4H_8	4	−6		gas
pentene	C_5H_{10}	5	+30	b.p. increasing	liquid

Table 10.2 Details of the first four alkenes.

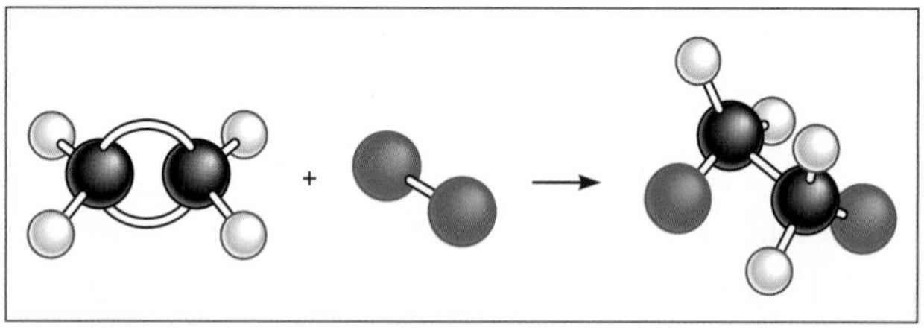

Figure 10.8 The addition of bromine to ethene.

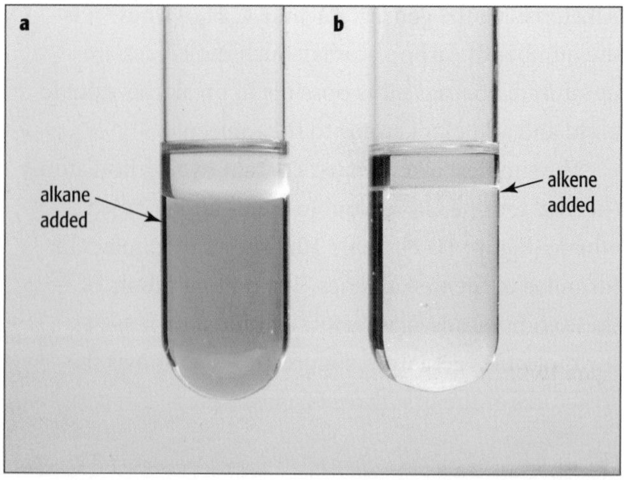

Figure 10.9 The test for unsaturation: bromine water with **a** an alkane and **b** an alkene added and then shaken. The bromine water is decolorised by the alkene. There is no reaction with the alkane.

solution would stay orange-brown (Figure **10.9**). In an addition reaction, two substances add together to form a single product.

A similar colour reaction occurs between alkenes and an acidified dilute solution of potassium manganate(VII). This solution is purple, and it turns colourless when shaken with an unsaturated compound. Again, an alkane would produce no change.

Key ideas so far

- The alkenes are a second homologous series of hydrocarbons. The molecules have the general formula C_nH_{2n}.
- An alkene molecule contains a carbon–carbon double bond somewhere in the chain.
- The alkenes are unsaturated hydrocarbons.
- The first member of the alkene series is ethene, C_2H_4.
- The alkenes, like other hydrocarbons, burn to give carbon dioxide and water as the products.
- The chemical test for an alkene is that it will decolorise bromine water.
- The functional group of the alkenes is the C=C double bond.

? Quick-check questions

1 Write down the names and molecular formulae of the first **four** alkenes.
2 Draw the structures of ethene and propene.
3 What is the common empirical formula of the first **four** alkenes?
4 What do you observe if ethene is bubbled though bromine water?
5 Write a word equation for the reaction between ethene and bromine water.
6 Draw a diagram showing the arrangement of electrons in the bonding of ethene. Show just the outer (valency) electrons.

10.4 Hydrocarbon structure and isomerism

Naming organic compounds

The alkanes are a 'family' (or homologous series) of saturated hydrocarbons. Their names all end in *-ane*; so Figure **10.10** shows a model of tetradecane ($C_{14}H_{30}$). The names of the first six alkanes were given in Figure **10.4** (page **289**).

The prefixes to the names of the alkanes are standard and indicate the number of carbon atoms in the chain (see Table **10.1**, page **288**). So a compound in any homologous series with just one carbon atom will always have a name beginning with *meth-*, one with two carbon atoms *eth-*, and so on. Hence the names of the alcohols and carboxylic acids are as shown in Tables **10.4** and **10.6** (pages **299** and **304**). When a halogen atom is introduced into a chain the name of the compound contains a prefix indicating which halogen is present.

The different homologous series all have particular endings to their names (Table **10.3**).

Figure 10.10 A model of a straight chain alkane ($C_{14}H_{30}$).

Homologous series	Name ending	Example
alkane	-ane	propane
alkene	-ene	propene
alcohol	-ol	propanol
carboxylic acid	-oic acid	propanoic acid

Table 10.3 The naming of the different homologous series.

Many different organic compounds are formed when a hydrogen in the original alkane 'backbone' is replaced by another group. The product formed when ethene reacts with bromine in solution (Figure **10.8**) illustrates the system of naming organic compounds.

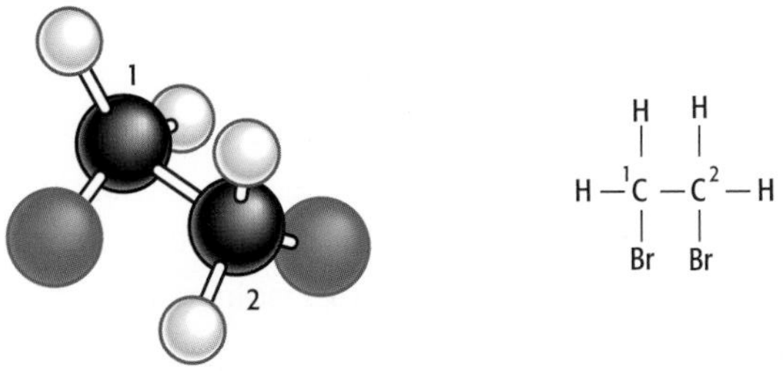

- The product has **two** carbon atoms joined by a **single** bond. So it is named after **ethane**.
- The molecule contains **two bromine** atoms. It is called **dibromoethane**.
- The bromine atoms are not both attached to the same carbon atom. One bromine atom is bonded to each carbon atom. The carbon atoms are numbered 1 and 2.

The full name of the compound is **1,2-dibromoethane**.

Branched-chain alkanes exist where a hydrocarbon side-chain has replaced a hydrogen to produce a more complex molecule. In order to show where this side-chain is attached, we number the carbon atoms in the chain. This means that we can indicate where the side-chain is, in the name. The numbering always starts at one end of the chain. The counting starts at the end which keeps the number of the side-chain position as low as possible. You will see some examples of this numbering in the next section.

Isomerism

The system of naming compounds emphasises the importance of structure. Molecules with the same molecular formula can have different structures. The same number of atoms can be connected together in different ways. This is known as **isomerism**.

There are two **different** compounds with the molecular formula C_4H_{10}:

- butane

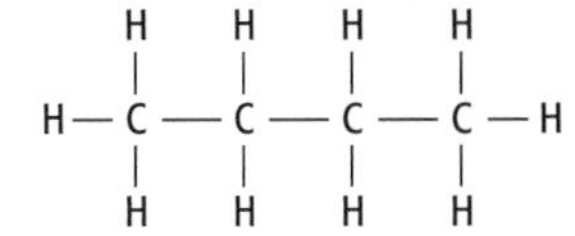

burns in air to form CO_2 and H_2O
liquefies at 0 °C

- 2-methylpropane

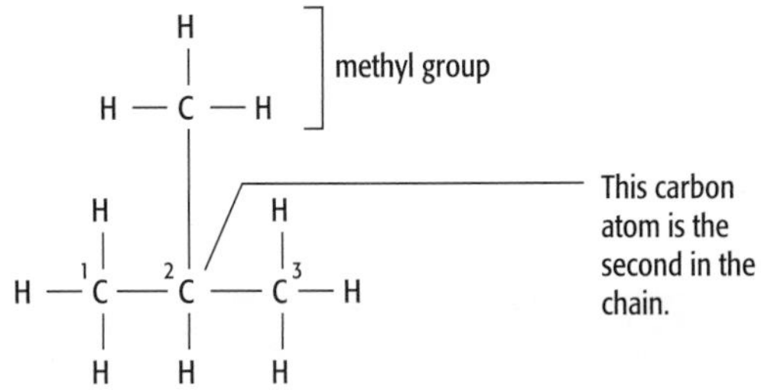

colourless gas
burns in air to form CO_2 and H_2O
liquefies at −12 °C

In butane, all four carbon atoms are arranged in one 'straight' main chain. However, the atoms do not have to be arranged in this way. The fourth carbon atom can go off from the main chain to give the 'Y-shaped' or branched structure of 2-methylpropane. Compounds such as these are known as **isomers**. The properties of these particular isomers are quite similar; the difference shows itself mainly in their melting points and boiling points. Hydrocarbons containing branched chains have lower melting points and lower boiling points than straight-chain compounds with the same number of carbon atoms.

All the **alkane** molecules with four or more carbon atoms possess isomers. For example, there are three isomers with the formula C_5H_{12}. The **alkenes** with four or more carbon atoms can show a different kind of isomerism. In this, the **position** of the C=C double bond is moved along the chain. There are two molecules with a 'straight' chain of four carbon atoms and the molecular formula C_4H_8:

- but-1-ene

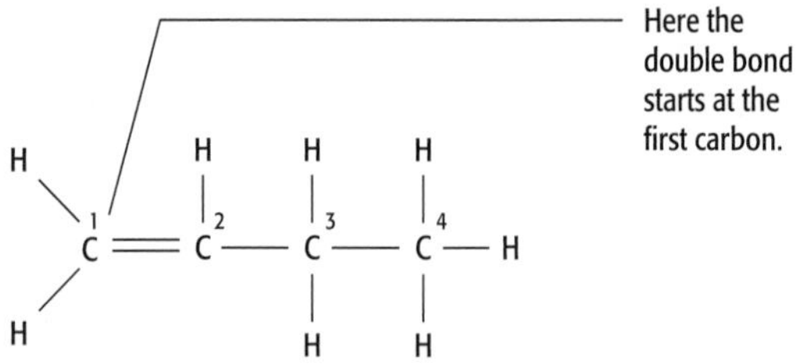

- but-2-ene

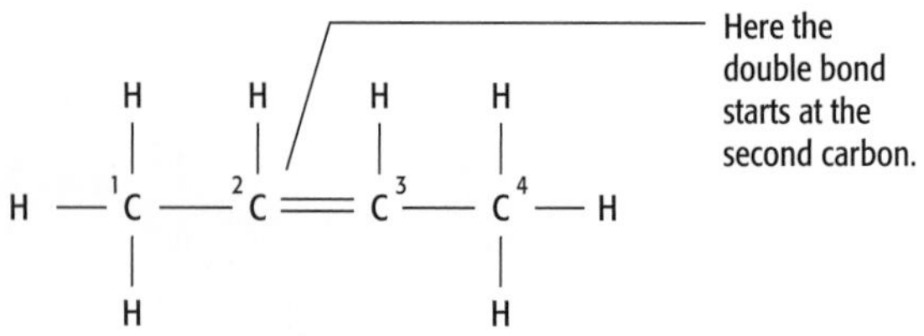

The structures are different. Again, the carbon atoms are numbered. The number added to the formula indicates the position of the double bond. In but-1-ene the double bond is between carbon atoms 1 and 2, whereas in but-2-ene it is between carbon atoms 2 and 3.

Isomers are compounds that have the same molecular formula but different structural formulae.

Alkynes are a third family of hydrocarbons. In alkynes, the molecules contain a C≡C triple bond. The simplest member is ethyne (C_2H_2). This highly reactive gas used to be known as acetylene. It is used in oxy-acetylene welding torches. We do not study the alkynes any further at this level.

Key ideas so far

- There is a systematic method of naming organic molecules.
- Hydrocarbon chains can be either straight or branched in their structure.
- It is possible for two or more molecules to have the same molecular formula, but different structures. This is known as isomerism.
- Isomers are molecules with the same molecular formula but different structural formulae.

Quick-check questions

1 Give the names of the first member of each of these homologous series:
   a the alkenes **b** the alcohols
   c the carboxylic acids.

2 Define the term **isomer**.

3 Draw the structures of but-1-ene and but-2-ene.

4 Draw the structures of the **two** isomers having the formula C_4H_{10}.

5 Draw **two** isomers of an alkane with five carbon atoms.

6 Draw the structure of 1,2-dibromoethane.

7 Structures **A** to **H** are the structural formulae of some organic compounds.
   a Give the letters that represent:
      i two alkanes
      ii two compounds which are not hydrocarbons
      iii the molecule that is ethene.
   b What is the name of H?

A

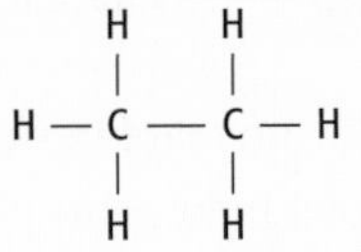

B

C

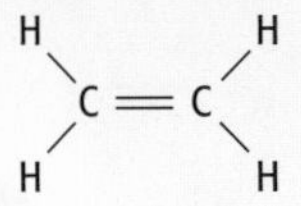

D

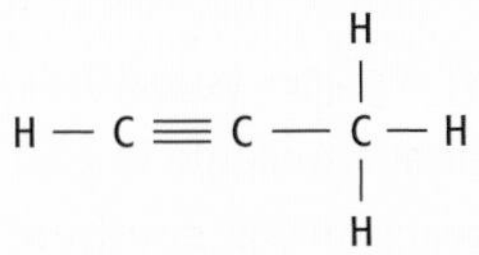

E

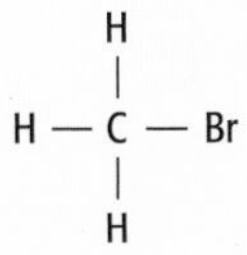

F

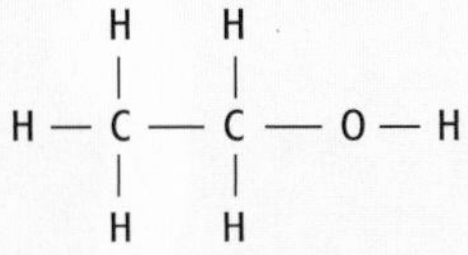

G

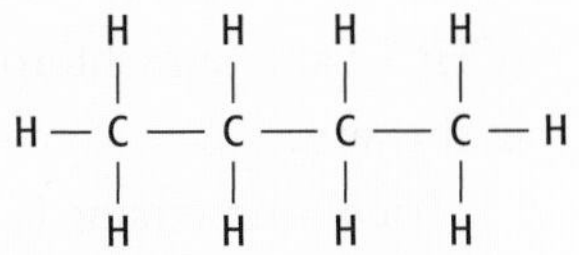

H

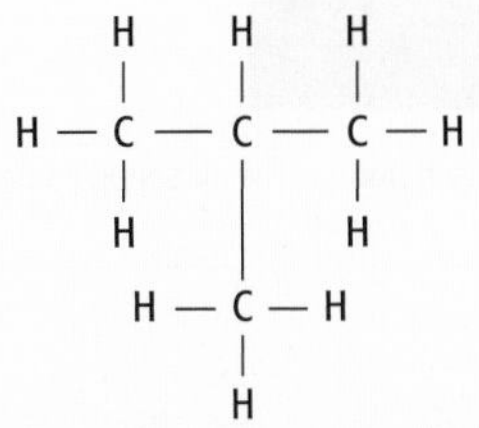

10.5 Chemical reactions of the alkanes

The alkanes are rather unreactive compounds. They are saturated, so they cannot take part in addition reactions. They are unaffected by acids or alkalis. However, they can take part in substitution reactions, particularly with the halogens.

Combustion

We have seen earlier that when a hydrocarbon burns in a good supply of air or oxygen then the two products are carbon dioxide and water. The word equation for the burning of butane, for instance, is

butane + oxygen → carbon dioxide + water

$$2C_4H_{10}(g) + 13O_2(g) \rightarrow 8CO_2(g) + 10H_2O(g)$$

The same products are obtained whichever alkane is burnt, so long as there is a sufficient oxygen supply.

However, if the air supply is limited, then the poisonous gas carbon monoxide can also be formed. Carbon monoxide is the product of incomplete combustion of a hydrocarbon. For example:

methane + oxygen → carbon monoxide + water

$$2CH_4(g) + 3O_2(g) \rightarrow 2CO(g) + 4H_2O(g)$$

Carbon monoxide (CO) is toxic because it interferes with the transport of oxygen around our bodies by our red blood cells. Every year a number of people die accidentally of carbon monoxide poisoning because of poorly serviced gas fires in their homes. If the flues to the fire are blocked then insufficient air is supplied to the fire and carbon monoxide is produced. Simple carbon monoxide detectors can be bought in supermarkets, or electronic detectors fitted in homes (Figure **10.11**).

Figure 10.11 An electronic carbon monoxide detector.

Incomplete combustion can also produce fine particles of carbon itself. These have not even reacted to produce carbon monoxide. It is these fine carbon particles (or soot) which can glow yellow in the heat of a flame. They give a candle flame or the 'safety' flame of a Bunsen burner their characteristic yellow colour (Figure **10.12**, overleaf).

Figure 10.12 The 'safety' flame of the Bunsen burner. The air supply to the flame is restricted.

Exam tip

You can very frequently be asked about the combustion products of organic fuels and hydrocarbons, both in the presence of sufficient, and insufficient, air. It is useful to make sure you know the word equations.

Questions on the combustion of hydrocarbons are also quite often asked in the form of equations that you have to complete by balancing them.

Substitution reactions with the halogens

The **substitution reaction** with chlorine is interesting because it is a **photochemical reaction**:

$$\text{methane} + \text{chlorine} \xrightarrow{\text{sunlight}} \text{chloromethane} + \text{hydrogen chloride}$$

$$CH_4(g) + Cl_2(g) \xrightarrow{\text{sunlight}} CH_3Cl(g) + HCl(g)$$

Methane and chlorine react in the presence of sunlight. Ultraviolet light splits chlorine molecules into separate energised atoms. These atoms then react with methane. So the overall result is that a chlorine atom replaces (substitutes for) a hydrogen atom in a methane molecule to give chloromethane (CH_3Cl). The reaction can continue further as more hydrogen atoms are substituted. Compounds such as dichloromethane (CH_2Cl_2), trichloromethane ($CHCl_3$) and tetrachloromethane (CCl_4) are formed in this way.

Trichloromethane ($CHCl_3$), or **chloroform**, was an early anaesthetic. However, the dose which can kill a patient is not much higher than the amount needed to anaesthetise a patient! So it was very easy to make mistakes. Something else was needed. Investigations were carried out on the anaesthetic effect of other substituted alkanes. In 1956, **halothane** was discovered. It is a more useful anaesthetic. Its formula is $CF_3CHBrCl$, and its structure is:

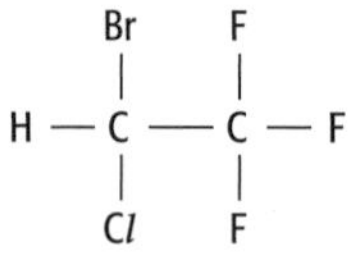

halothane

Substituted alkanes are also good organic solvents. 1,1,1-trichloroethane is one solvent that is used a lot, in dry cleaning, for example.

Key ideas so far

- The alkanes are a relatively unreactive series of compounds.
- The alkanes burn completely in an excess of air to give carbon dioxide and water.
- If the air supply is limited then the toxic gas carbon monoxide can be formed by the incomplete combustion of the hydrocarbon.
- Carbon monoxide is toxic because it interferes with the transport of oxygen around the body by red blood cells.
- The alkanes can take part in substitution reactions with chlorine.
- These substitution reactions are photochemical reactions: they require ultraviolet light to allow them to take place.

Quick-check questions

1 Write a word equation for the incomplete combustion of methane.
2 What is the formula of carbon monoxide?
3 What causes a candle flame to be yellow?
4 Why is carbon monoxide toxic?
5 What are the name and formula of the first substitution product of the reaction between methane and chlorine?
6 The hydrocarbon propane is an important constituent of the fuel liquid petroleum gas (LPG). For the burning of propane in an excess of air, give:
  a a word equation
  b a balanced symbol equation.
7 What source of energy is required for the substitution reaction between methane and chlorine to take place?
8 Bromine reacts with alkanes in a similar way to chlorine. Hydrogen bromide is made in the substitution reaction between propane and bromine:

propane + bromine
→ bromopropane + hydrogen bromide

  a Draw the structure of propane.
  b Draw the structure of a form of bromopropane.
  c The reaction between propane and bromine is a photochemical reaction. Suggest what is meant by **photochemical**.

10.6 Chemical reactions of the alkenes

Alkenes are much more reactive than alkanes. Under suitable conditions, molecules such as bromine, hydrogen and water (steam) will add across the C=C double bond.

Bromination

This reaction is used as the chemical test for an unsaturated hydrocarbon (see Figure **10.9**, page **292**). Bromine water is decolorised when shaken with an alkene. The reaction will also work with the bromine dissolved in an organic solvent such as hexane.

Hydrogenation

The addition of hydrogen across a C=C double bond is known as **hydrogenation**. Ethene reacts with hydrogen if the heated gases are passed together over a catalyst. The unsaturated ethane is the product:

$$\text{ethane} + \text{hydrogen} \xrightarrow[\text{nickel}]{150\text{–}300\,°\text{C}} \text{ethane}$$

$$C_2H_4(g) + H_2(g) \xrightarrow[\text{nickel}]{150\text{–}300\,°\text{C}} C_2H_6(g)$$

Hydrogenation reactions similar to the reaction with ethene are used in the manufacture of margarine from vegetable oils.

The vegetable oils of interest include corn oil and sunflower oil. They are edible oils and contain long-chain organic acids (**fatty acids**). The hydrocarbon chains of these acids contain one or more C=C double bonds; they are unsaturated molecules (Figure **10.13**). Oils such as sunflower oil are rich in **poly-unsaturated** molecules. This means that the melting point is relatively

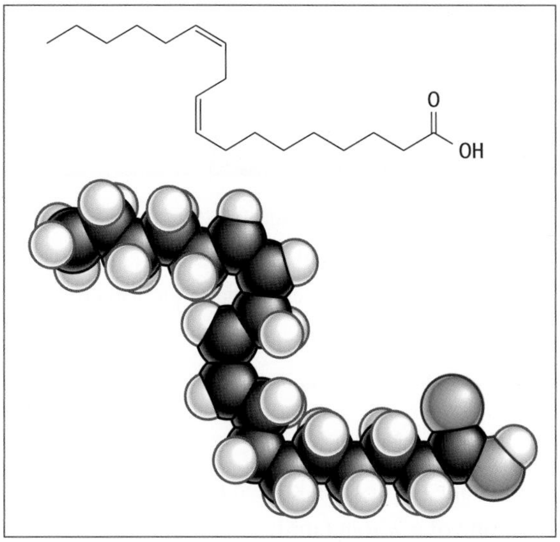

Figure 10.13 Sunflower oil and its products are rich in fats containing unsaturated molecules (note the C=C double bonds in the chain).

low and the oil remains liquid at normal temperatures (and even with refrigeration). By hydrogenating some, but not all, of the C=C double bonds, the liquid vegetable oil can be made into a solid but spreadable fat (margarine).

Animal fats tend to be more saturated than vegetable oils and fats. The animal fats in cream can be made into butter. Many doctors now believe that unsaturated fats are healthier than saturated ones. This is why margarines are left partially unsaturated: not all the C=C double bonds are hydrogenated. Olive oil is distinctive in having a high content of oleic acid, which is a **mono-unsaturated** fatty acid. Margarine can be made from olive oil without any hydrogenation.

Hydration

Another important addition reaction is the one used in the manufacture of ethanol. Ethanol is an important industrial chemical and solvent. It is formed when a mixture of steam and ethene is passed over a catalyst of immobilised phosphoric(V) acid (the acid is adsorbed on silica pellets) at a temperature of 300 °C and a pressure of 60 atmospheres:

$$\text{ethene} + \text{steam} \xrightarrow[\text{phosphoric acid}]{300\,°\text{C, 60 atmospheres}} \text{ethanol}$$

$$C_2H_4(g) + H_2O(g) \rightarrow C_2H_5OH(g)$$

This reaction produces the ethanol of high purity needed in industrial organic chemistry.

Key ideas so far

- Alkenes are much more reactive than alkanes.
- The alkenes can take part in addition reactions where atoms are added across the C=C double bond.
- Unsaturated alkenes can be converted to saturated alkanes by the addition of hydrogen. This is referred to as hydrogenation.
- Hydrogenation is used in the production of margarine.
- Alkenes can be reacted with steam to produce alcohols. This is known as hydration. The elements of water are added across the C=C double bond.
- One of the major ways of making ethanol is to react ethene with steam.

Quick-check questions

1 What are the molecular and structural formulae of 1,2-dibromoethane?

2 Write the word and chemical equations for the hydrogenation of ethene.

3 What is the catalyst used in hydrogenation reactions?

4 Unsaturated hydrocarbons take part in addition reactions.

  a Write a word equation for the reaction between propene and hydrogen.

  b Write a symbol equation for the reaction between butene and steam.

5 a Chloroethane is one of the chemicals manufactured from ethene.

  i Name the compound that reacts with ethene in an addition reaction to give chloroethane.

  ii Draw the structural formula of chloroethane.

  b Chloroethane can also be made by a substitution reaction. What are the reagents and reaction conditions for this reaction?

10.7 Alcohols

Ethanol is one of the best-known organic compounds. It is just one of a whole family of compounds – the **alcohols**. The alcohols are a homologous series of compounds that contain —OH as the functional group (Figure **10.14**). A functional group is a group of atoms in a structure that determines the characteristic reactions of a compound.

Table **10.4** shows the molecular formulae of the early members of the series. The simplest alcohol contains one carbon atom and is called methanol. Note that

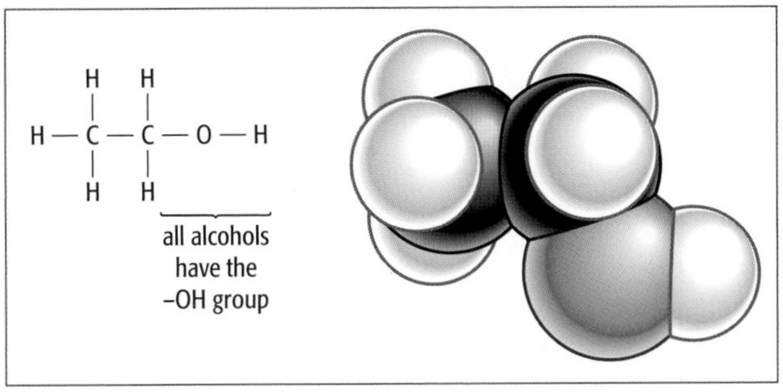

Figure 10.14 The structure of ethanol.

Alcohol	Molecular formula $C_nH_{2n+1}OH$	Boiling point / °C	
methanol	CH_3OH	65	
ethanol	C_2H_5OH	78	
propan-1-ol	C_3H_7OH	97	
butan-1-ol	C_4H_9OH	117	
pentan-1-ol	$C_5H_{11}OH$	137	b.p. increasing

Table 10.4 Some alcohols.

the names all have the same ending (*-ol*). The general formula of the alcohols is $C_nH_{2n+1}OH$, and they can be referred to as the **alkanols**. The structural formulae of the first four alcohols are as shown in Figure **10.15**. The early alcohols are all neutral, colourless liquids that do not conduct electricity.

Making ethanol

Hydration of ethene

The industrial method of making ethanol involves the addition reaction that we saw at the end of Section **10.6**. In this, ethene and steam are compressed to 60 atmospheres and passed over a catalyst (immobilised phosphoric(V) acid) at 300 °C:

$$\text{ethene} + \text{steam} \xrightarrow[\text{phosphoric acid}]{300\,°\text{C, 60 atmospheres}} \text{ethanol}$$

$$C_2H_4(g) + H_2O(g) \rightarrow C_2H_5OH(g)$$

Ethanol is an important solvent and a raw material for making other organic chemicals. Many everyday items use ethanol as a solvent. These include paints, glues, perfumes, aftershave, etc.

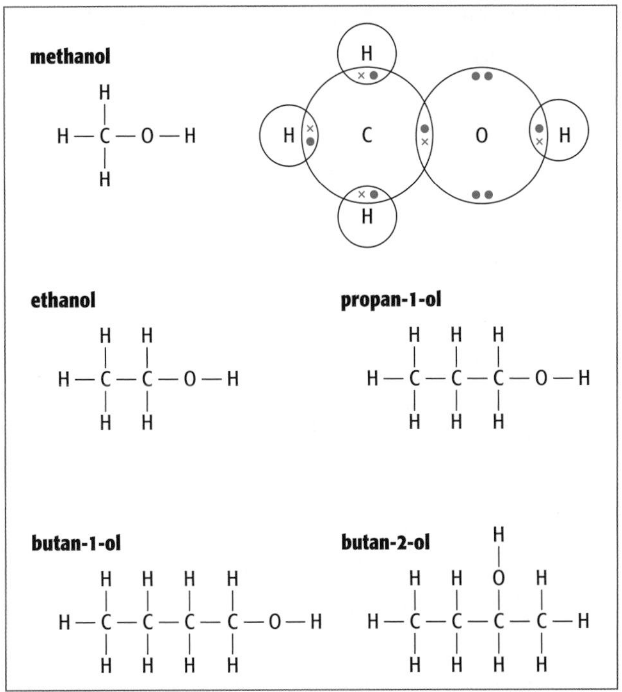

Figure 10.15 Alcohols are a homologous series – these are the structures of the first four members. Two isomers of butanol are shown.

Fermentation

Ethanol and carbon dioxide are the natural waste products of yeasts when they ferment sugar. Sugar is present in all fruit and grains, and in the sap and nectar of all plants. Yeasts are found everywhere. The ancient Babylonians and Egyptians found that, if they crushed grapes or germinated grain, the paste would bubble and produce an intoxicating drink. Pasteur discovered that yeasts are single-cell, living fungi. They ferment sugar to gain energy – by **anaerobic respiration**. As ethanol is toxic to yeast, fermentation is self-limiting. Once the ethanol concentration has reached about 14%, or the sugar runs out, the multiplying yeast die and fermentation ends. The best temperature for carrying out the process is 37 °C. The reaction is catalysed by enzymes in the yeast:

$$\text{glucose} \xrightarrow{\text{yeast}} \text{ethanol} + \text{carbon dioxide}$$

$$C_6H_{12}O_6(aq) \xrightarrow{\text{enzymes}} 2C_2H_5OH(aq) + 2CO_2(g)$$

Alcoholic drinks such as beer and wine are made on a large scale in vast quantities in copper or steel fermentation vats. Beer is made from barley, with hops and other ingredients added to produce distinctive flavours. Wine is made by fermenting grape juice. Beer contains about 4% by volume of ethanol, whereas wine contains between 8 and 14%.

Stronger, more alcoholic, drinks are made in one of two ways. Fortified wines, such as sherry and port, have pure ethanol added to them. Spirits, such as whisky, brandy and vodka, are made by distillation (see page **38**).

Fermentation can be carried out in the laboratory using the apparatus in Figure **10.16**. The air-lock allows gas to escape from the vessel but prevents airborne bacteria entering.

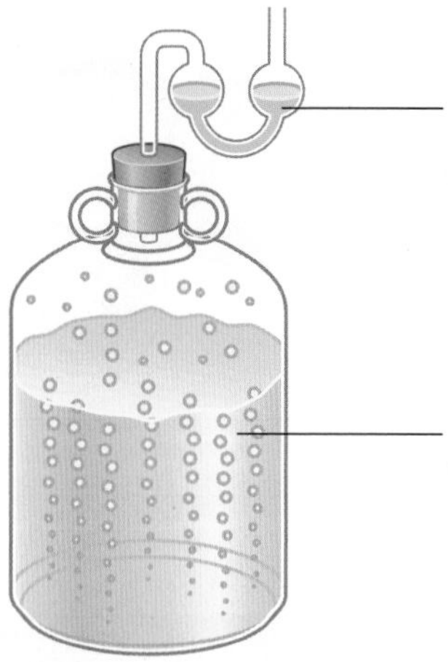

Figure 10.16 A laboratory fermentation vessel.

Exam tip

Fermentation is an anaerobic process. It takes place under conditions where there is no air or oxygen available.

Therefore, there is no oxygen (O_2) present in the equation for the reaction taking place.

Carbon dioxide is the gas produced in the reaction.

Comparing the methods of ethanol production

The two different methods of producing ethanol have their respective advantages and disadvantages. The method chosen will depend on the availability of resources and the main purpose for producing the ethanol. A comparison of the methods is summarised in Table **10.5**.

The ethanol produced by fermentation comes from a renewable resource. When used as a fuel, the ethanol produced in this way is potentially 'carbon neutral'. The carbon dioxide released during fermentation and by burning the fuel is balanced by that absorbed from the atmosphere by the crop, usually sugar cane, as it grows.

Ethanol by the hydration of ethene	Ethanol by fermentation
originates from a non-renewable resource – crude oil	made from readily renewable resources
small-scale equipment capable of withstanding pressure	relatively simple, large vessels
a continuous process	a batch process – need to start process again each time
a fast reaction rate	a relatively slow process
yields highly pure ethanol	ethanol must be purified by subsequent distillation – though fermented product can be used as it is for some purposes
a sophisticated, complex method	a simple, straightforward method

Table 10.5 A comparison of the methods of ethanol production.

Key ideas so far

- The alcohols are a homologous series that contain the functional group —OH.
- The alcohols burn to give carbon dioxide and water.
- The alcohols are useful solvents and fuels.
- Ethanol can be manufactured by two different methods. One is the hydration of ethene obtained from cracking. The other is by fermentation using carbohydrate material and yeast.
- S Alcohols from propanol onwards have isomers that differ in the position of the —OH group in the chain.

Quick-check questions

1 Name the first **three** members of the alcohol homologous series.
2 Write the word and chemical equations for the hydration of ethene by steam.
3 What are the essentials needed for the production of ethanol by fermentation?

4 Ethanol can be made by the addition of water to ethene. Ethanol can also be made by the fermentation of sugars using the apparatus shown here.

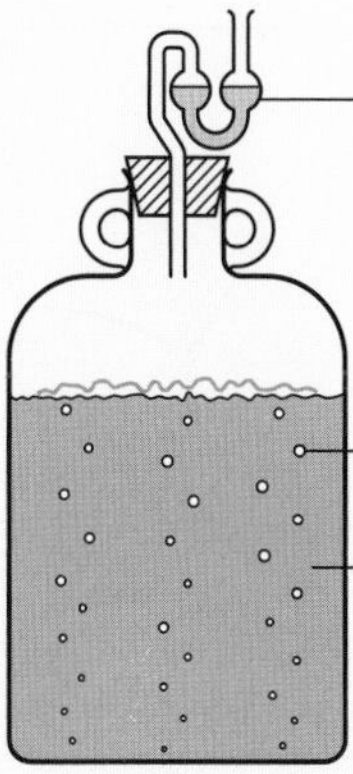

a Name the gas produced during the fermentation shown above.

b This gas escapes through the piece of apparatus labelled A. What is the main purpose of this piece of apparatus?

c What must be added to a sugar solution to make it ferment?

d At about what temperature does fermentation take place at its fastest rate?

e Explain your choice of temperature given in **d**.

5 Methanol and ethanol are members of a homologous series.

a Draw the molecular structures of methanol and ethanol.

b Explain what the term **homologous series** means.

6 What are the names and structures of the two isomers of propanol? S

10.8 The reactions of ethanol

Ethanol as a fuel

Ethanol burns with a clear flame, giving out quite a lot of heat:

$$\text{ethanol} + \text{oxygen} \rightarrow \text{carbon dioxide} + \text{water}$$

$$C_2H_5OH(l) + 3O_2(g) \rightarrow 2CO_2(g) + 3H_2O(g)$$

On a small scale, ethanol can be used as methylated spirit (ethanol mixed with methanol or other compounds) in spirit lamps and stoves. However, ethanol is such a useful fuel that some countries have developed it as a fuel for cars.

E

Brazil, whose climate is suitable for growing sugar cane, started producing ethanol fuel in 1973. It has one of the largest ethanol fuel programmes in the world (Figure **10.17**). The ethanol is produced by fermenting crop residues, and as such is considered a **biofuel**. Ethanol and other biofuels are used in motor vehicles as an alternative to fuel obtained from oil deposits. Ethanol produced by fermentation of sugar from sugar cane has been used as an alternative fuel to gasoline (petrol), or mixed with gasoline to produce 'gasohol'. It is a renewable resource and has the potential to reduce petroleum imports. 'Gasohol' now accounts for 10% of the gasoline sales in the USA. 'Gasohol' and other 'oxygenated fuels' have the advantage of **reducing** the emissions of carbon monoxide from cars. It is thought that biofuels can reduce environmental damage if developed and controlled properly, but overuse of biofuels could be harmful if it leads to more deforestation to grow biofuel crops.

Figure 10.17 An ethanol and petrol station in Sao Paulo, Brazil.

Exam tip

Exam questions often ask you to balance the equations for the combustion reactions of either hydrocarbons or alcohols.

Make sure you balance the oxygen (O) atoms in the equation. Remember, with alcohols, that there is an oxygen atom in the alcohol molecule itself.

Oxidation

Vinegar is a weak solution of ethanoic acid (previously called acetic acid). It is produced commercially from wine by biochemical oxidation using bacteria (*Acetobacter*). Wine can also become 'vinegary' if it is left open to the air. The same oxidation can be achieved quickly by powerful oxidising agents such as warm acidified potassium manganate(VII):

ethanol + oxygen (from oxidising agent) → ethanoic acid + water

$$C_2H_5OH + 2[O] \rightarrow CH_3COOH + H_2O$$

The colour of the potassium manganate(VII) solution turns from purple to colourless.

Dehydration

Ethanol can be dehydrated to produce ethene. This is one way of preparing ethene in the laboratory. Ethanol vapour is passed over a heated catalyst. The catalyst can be aluminium oxide or broken pieces of porous pot. Ethene is not soluble in water, so it can be collected as shown in Figure **10.18**.

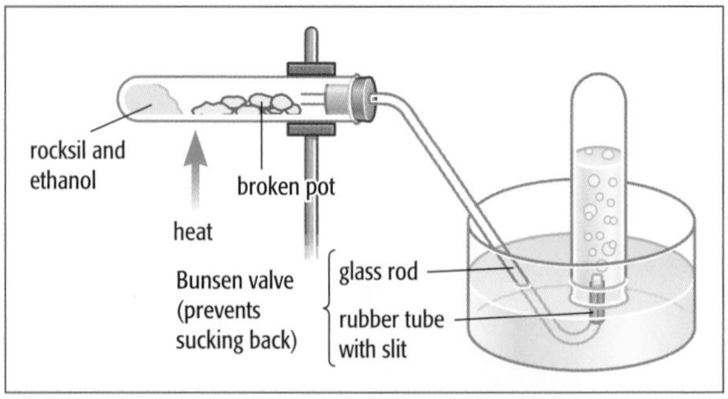

Figure 10.18 The dehydration of ethanol in the laboratory.

Esterification

Alcohols react with organic acids (see Section **10.9**) to form sweet-smelling oily liquids known as **esters**. For example:

ethanoic acid + ethanol → ethyl ethanoate + water

$$CH_3COOH(l) + C_2H_5OH(l) \rightarrow CH_3COOC_2H_5(l) + H_2O(l)$$

Concentrated sulfuric acid is added as a catalyst for this esterification reaction.

Alcohol and health

Ethanol is the only alcohol that is safe to drink. It must only be drunk in moderation, if at all. Methanol is very toxic and even in small amounts can cause blindness and death.

Ethanol mixes totally with water, which takes it everywhere in the body that water goes. The amount of alcohol that a person may drink varies with age, sex, weight and drinking history. The route taken by alcohol through the human body is shown in Figure **10.19**. First, it goes into the mouth and throat (1), and then on to the stomach (2). Some alcohol is absorbed in the stomach, but most moves into the small intestine (3). From here it passes rapidly into the bloodstream (4). The presence of food can delay absorption – for up to six hours

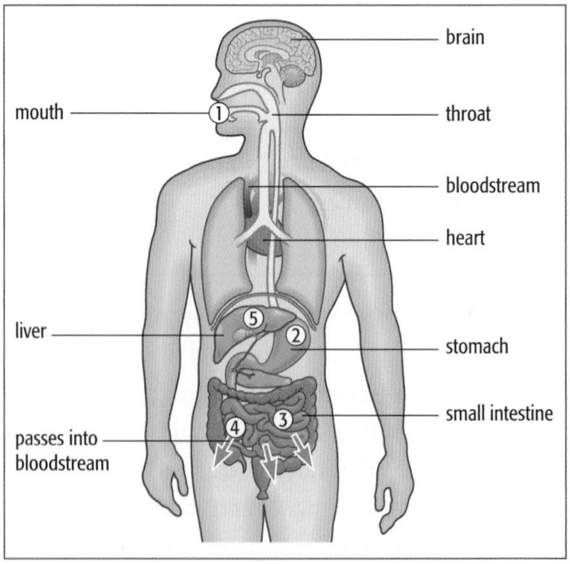

Figure 10.19 The normal route of metabolism for ethanol in the human body.

for one drink on a full stomach. Alcohol is spread throughout the body by the blood. It is broken down mainly in the liver (5), where it is converted into carbon dioxide and water.

Moderate amounts of alcohol seem to reduce coronary heart disease. Heavy drinking, however, eventually damages the muscle tissue of the heart. Heavy drinking can cause a healthy liver to become fatty and enlarged. Eventually scarring (**cirrhosis**) can cause liver failure and death. There may well be some long-term damage to the brain with prolonged heavy drinking. Alcohol is a depressive drug and can be addictive. Drinking heavily on a particular occasion produces drunkenness, during which speech becomes slurred, vision is blurred and reaction times are slowed. Some cultures forbid its use.

Key ideas so far

- The alcohols burn to give carbon dioxide and water. Their combustion is highly exothermic.
- They are used as fuels, and ethanol and other alcohols represent possible alternative fuels for cars.
- Alcohols can be oxidised to form the corresponding carboxylic acid. Thus ethanol is oxidised to ethanoic acid.
- Alcohols can also be dehydrated to form an alkene.
- Alcohols react with carboxylic acids to form esters. Ethanol reacts with ethanoic acid to produce ethyl ethanoate.

Quick-check questions

1 Sugar cane grows quickly in tropical areas. Sugar can be fermented to make ethanol. Either ethanol or mixtures of petrol and ethanol (gasohol) can be used as the fuel for cars.

a Ethanol consists of organic molecules.

i What type of compound is ethanol?

ii Ethanol has the formula C_2H_5OH. Draw its structure.

b Gasohol boils over a temperature range of 40–150 °C in the laboratory. Ethanol has a boiling point of 78 °C. Draw a labelled diagram to show how a sample of ethanol may be obtained from gasohol.

2 Ethanol is a fuel. In laboratories that do not have a gas supply, it may be used in a spirit burner.

a The diagram shows a spirit burner being used to heat a beaker of water. A black solid is formed on the bottom of the beaker.

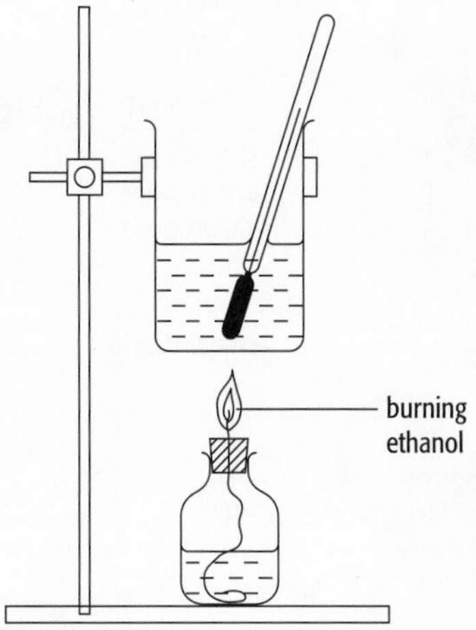

i Name the black substance formed on the beaker.

ii Suggest why the black substance is formed when the ethanol is burnt.

b Both methanol and ethanol burn in an excess of air to form the same products.

i Name these products.

ii Suggest why it is not possible to set fire to the contents of a bottle of wine.

3 Write the word and chemical equations for the oxidation of ethanol to ethanoic acid (use [O] for the oxidising agent).

4 What alkene is produced when propan-1-ol is dehydrated?

5 Name the ester produced when ethanol reacts with ethanoic acid. Write the word equation for the reaction. What is the catalyst for the reaction?

10.9 Organic acids and esters

Carboxylic acids

The **carboxylic acids** are another homologous series of organic compounds. All these acids have the functional group —COOH attached to a hydrocarbon chain. Table **10.6** shows the molecular formulae of the first two members of the series. The compounds have the general formula $C_nH_{2n+1}COOH$ (or $C_nH_{2n+1}CO_2H$). Figure **10.20** shows the structural formulae of the first four acids in the series.

The first two acids in the series are liquids at room temperature, though ethanoic acid will solidify if the temperature falls only slightly. The acids dissolve in water to produce solutions that are weakly acidic. Methanoic acid is present in nettle stings and ant stings, while ethanoic acid (once called acetic acid) is well known as the acid in vinegar.

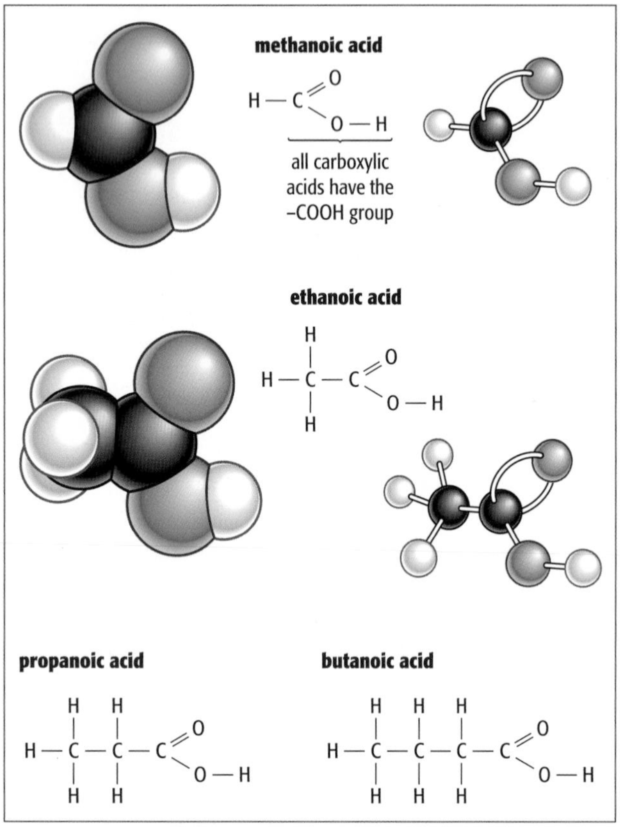

Figure 10.20 The structures of methanoic, ethanoic, propanoic and butanoic acids.

Exam tip

When naming a carboxylic acid, remember that the carbon atom of the acid group is part of the chain. It is counted as the first carbon in the chain.

That is why CH_3COOH is the formula of ethanoic acid: there are two carbon atoms in the molecule.

E

Ethanoic acid as a weak acid

Whereas a strong acid such as hydrochloric acid is completely split into ions, ethanoic acid only partially dissociates into ions in water. A dynamic equilibrium is set up in the solution. The solution does contain an excess of hydrogen ions (H^+) over hydroxide ions (OH^-), so the solution is weakly acidic (see page **162**):

ethanoic acid ⇌ ethanoate ions + hydrogen ions

$$CH_3COOH(aq) \rightleftharpoons CH_3COO^-(aq) + H^+(aq)$$

A solution of the acid will show the characteristic reactions of an acid. For example, it will react with bases to form salts:

ethanoic acid + sodium hydroxide → sodium ethanoate + water

$$CH_3COOH(aq) + NaOH(aq) \rightarrow CH_3COONa(aq) + H_2O(l)$$

Carboxylic acid	Molecular formula $C_nH_{2n+1}COOH$	Melting point / °C	Boiling point / °C	
methanoic acid	HCOOH	9	101	
ethanoic acid	CH_3COOH	17	118	m.p. and b.p. increasing

Table 10.6 The first two carboxylic acids.

Vinegar can be used as a 'descaler' in hard water areas. The ethanoic acid in vinegar reacts with limescale (calcium carbonate), producing carbon dioxide and dissolving the scale:

calcium carbonate + ethanoic acid
→ calcium ethanoate + water + carbon dioxide

$$CaCO_3(s) + 2CH_3COOH(aq) \rightarrow (CH_3COO)_2Ca(aq) + H_2O(l) + CO_2(g)$$

Commercial descalers are often based on weak acids, methanoic acid for instance, or on moderately strong acids such as sulfamic acid.

Esterification

Ethanoic acid will react with ethanol, in the presence of a few drops of concentrated sulfuric acid, to produce ethyl ethanoate. The concentrated sulfuric acid is a catalyst for the reaction:

$$\text{ethanoic acid} + \text{ethanol} \xrightarrow{\text{conc. } H_2SO_4} \text{ethyl ethanoate} + \text{water}$$

$$CH_3COOH(l) + C_2H_5OH(l) \rightarrow CH_3COOC_2H_5(l) + H_2O(l)$$

This type of reaction is known as **esterification**. The structure of ethyl ethanoate is shown below:

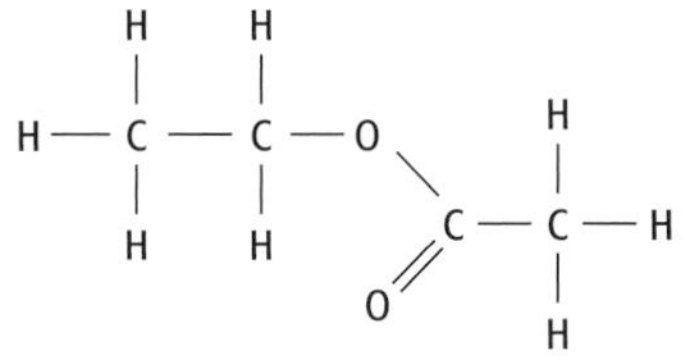

Ethyl ethanoate is just one example of an **ester**. This family of compounds have strong and pleasant smells. Many of these compounds occur naturally. They are responsible for the flavours in fruits and for the scents of flowers (Table **10.7**). We use them as food flavourings and in perfumes. The ester group or linkage is also found in complex molecules such as natural fats and oils (see below), and in man-made fibres such as Terylene (see page **329**).

Fats and vegetable oils as esters

Animal fats and vegetable oils (Figure **10.21**) are esters. They are liquids or solids, depending on the size and shape of the molecules present. They are all esters of **glycerol**, an alcohol with three hydroxyl (—OH) groups (Figure **10.22**). Fats and oils are an essential part of our diet (see page **332**) and, although they are quite complex molecules, they are not polymers.

Ester	Smell or flavour
ethyl 2-methylbutanoate	apple
3-methylbutyl ethanoate	pear
1-methylbutyl ethanoate	banana
butyl butanoate	pineapple
octyl ethanoate	orange
methylpropyl methanoate	raspberry
pentyl butanoate	strawberry

Table 10.7 The smells of esters.

Figure 10.21 A field of sunflowers growing in France. It is an important oil-seed crop, with the seed being eaten by humans and fed to livestock, poultry and cage birds. The oil is used in cooking and in the manufacture of margarine.

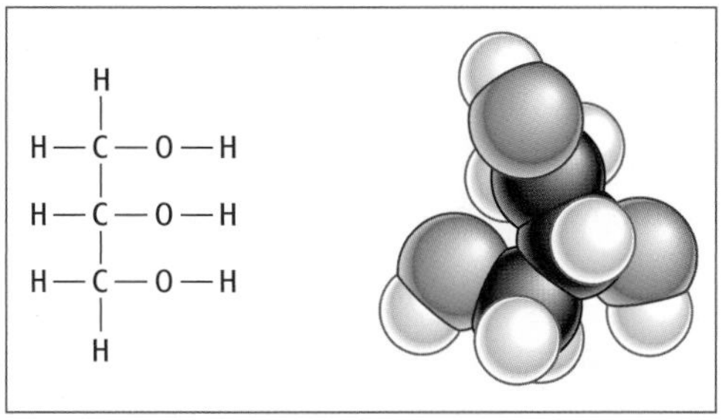

Figure 10.22 Glycerol (propane-1,2,3-triol) is an alcohol with three —OH groups.

Each —OH group forms an ester with a molecule of a carboxylic acid. These acids tend to have long chains (they are sometimes called fatty acids). Stearic acid ($C_{17}H_{35}COOH$) (Figure **10.23**) is one such acid that occurs in animal fats.

A complex molecule can be formed from glycerol and three molecules of stearic acid (Figure **10.24**). This is the type of molecule present in fats and oils. Vegetable oils tend to have long-chain acids that are more unsaturated than those in animal fats.

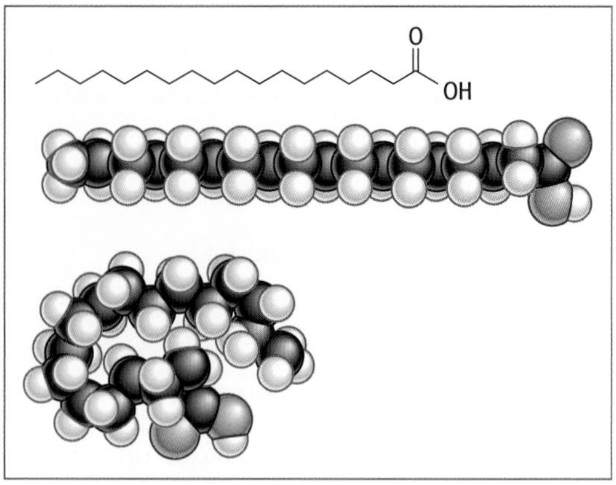

Figure 10.23 Stearic acid is a saturated fatty acid.

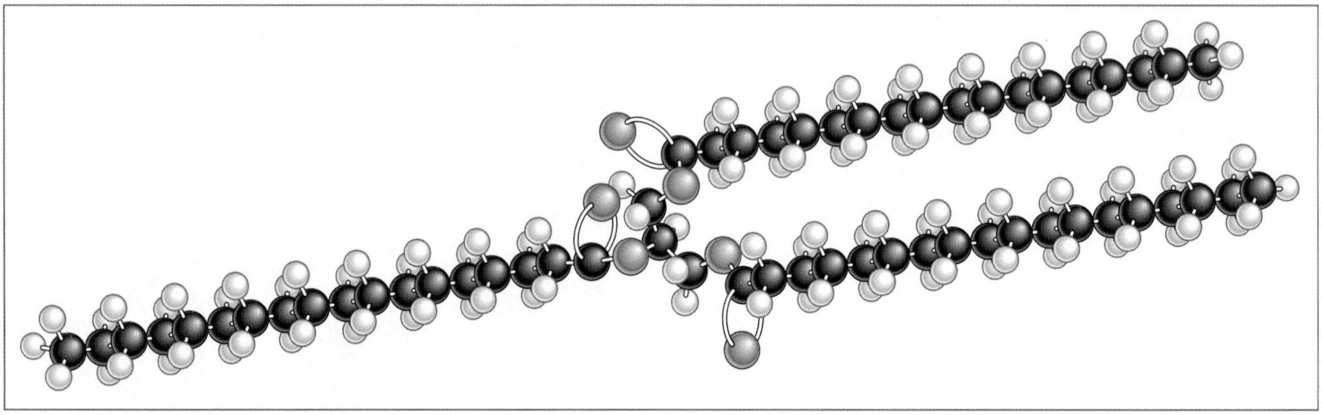

Figure 10.24 Glycerol and three molecules of stearic acid join together to form an ester present in animal fats.

Making soap

Many millions of tonnes of **soaps** and **detergents** are made worldwide each year. Soap is made by heating animal fats or vegetable oils with sodium hydroxide solution. The reaction involves the **hydrolysis** of the ester links in the fats or oils. The esters present are broken down to glycerol and the sodium salts of the acids:

fat + sodium hydroxide → soap + glycerol
(sodium salts of long-chain fatty acids)

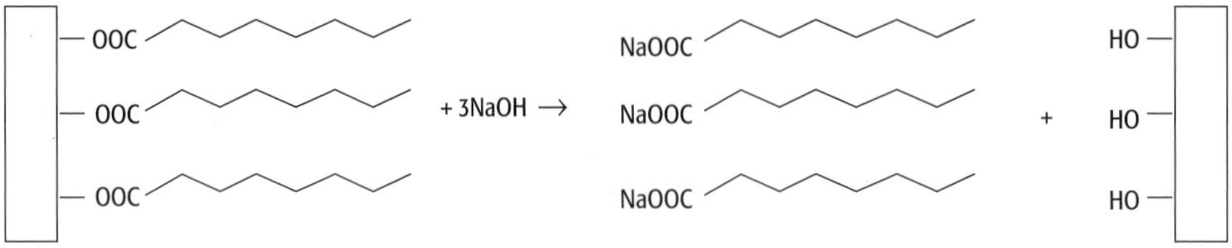

This process is known as **saponification**.

The action of soap and detergent

Water has a high surface tension and therefore does not necessarily wet things very well! In addition, it does not dissolve grease. To clean clothes with water, we need to add compounds to the water that will:

- wet and soak in between the fibres of the cloth
- separate the grease, dirt and dust from the fibres
- suspend the grease in the water so that it can be washed away.

Similar needs apply when cleaning food from dishes. Anything that will do these things is known as a **detergent**.

There are two types of detergent:

- **soap detergents** (generally called 'soaps') are made from animal fats or vegetable oils
- **soapless detergents** (usually just called 'detergents') are made using chemicals from oil.

Soapless detergents work in a similar way to soap but their structure and use are beyond the scope of the IGCSE syllabus.

The cleaning properties of **soap** depend on its structure. Sodium stearate, for instance, consists of a long hydrocarbon chain, which is hydrophobic ('water-hating'), attached to an ionic head, which is hydrophilic ('water-loving') (Figure **10.25**). These molecules dissolve in water because of the ionic end to the molecule.

When added to water, the soap molecules lower the surface tension of the water, so that it wets objects more easily. The molecules also interact with the grease present (Figure **10.26**, overleaf). The hydrophobic hydrocarbon chain is attracted to the grease and becomes embedded in it.

The hydrophilic ionic head of the molecule sits outside the grease, in contact with water. When the water is agitated, the grease is released from the cloth fibre or dish and is completely surrounded by soap molecules. Rinsing with fresh water removes these grease–detergent droplets.

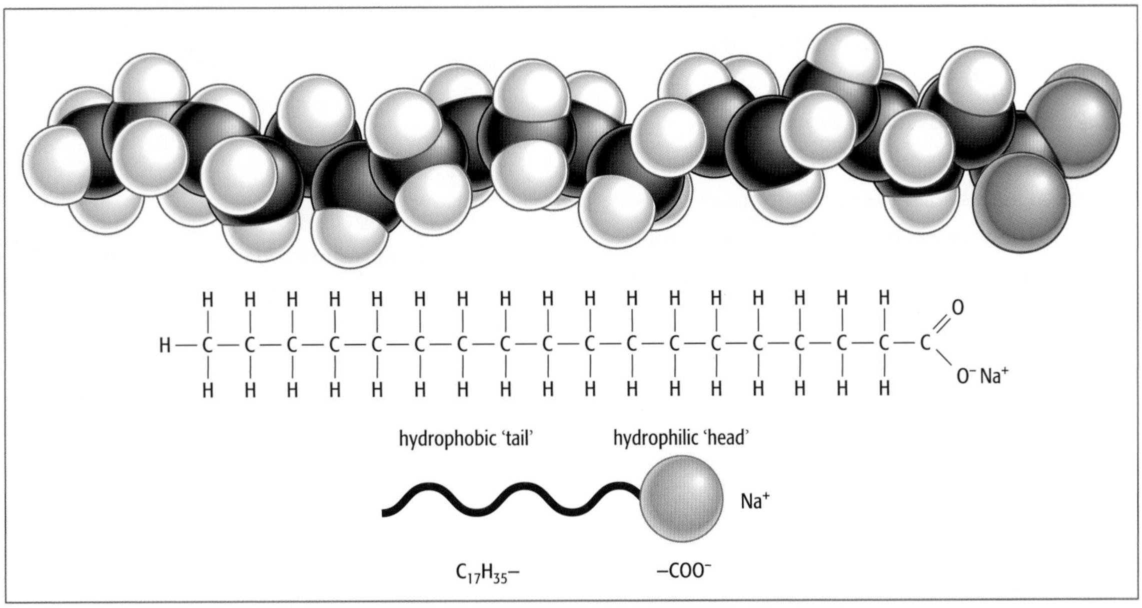

Figure 10.25 Sodium stearate in soap is a molecule with 'water-loving' (hydrophilic) and 'water-hating' (hydrophobic) regions.

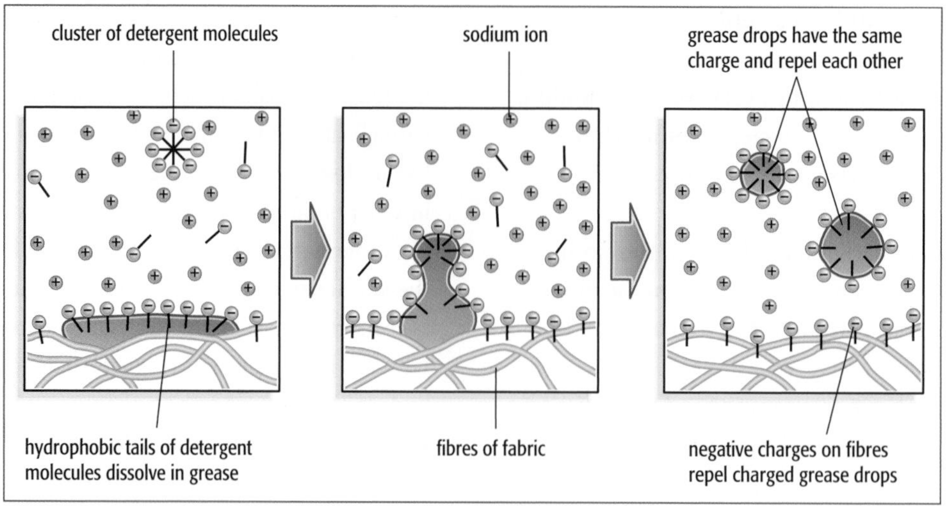

Figure 10.26 Soap molecules arrange themselves in such a way that grease droplets are lifted from fabrics.

S

Key ideas so far

- The carboxylic acids are a homologous series of weak organic acids.
- Methanoic acid and ethanoic acid are the first two members of the series.
- These acids will take part in the normal characteristic reactions of acids.
- They will also react with alcohols to produce esters. Ethanoic acid reacts with ethanol to produce ethyl ethanoate.
- Esters are important as food flavourings.
- Fats and vegetable oils are esters of long-chain carboxylic acids; as such they are important parts of our diet. They are esters formed from glycerol (propane-1,2,3-triol) and long-chain acids such as stearic acid.
- Fats and vegetable oils can be hydrolysed by heating with concentrated sodium hydroxide solution. The product from this is soap. This process is known as saponification.

S

? Quick-check questions

1 Fats and vegetable oils can be saturated or unsaturated. A simple experiment can be carried out to measure the degree of unsaturation in these compounds.

Five drops of a liquid, or a similar volume of a solid, are dissolved in $4\,cm^3$ of ethanol. Dilute bromine water is added a drop at a time. At first, the brown colour disappears. When enough bromine has been added to react with all the double bonds in the sample, the brown colour remains. The number of drops of bromine water needed to produce a permanent brown colour is recorded. This test was carried out on a variety of cooking products. The results are shown in the table opposite.

a Why was ethanol, not water, used as a solvent in this experiment?

b Suggest a value to complete the table.

c One medical theory is that using unsaturated fats in the diet, instead of saturated fats, will reduce the number of cases of heart disease. Which of the cooking products in the table is the least likely to cause heart disease?

Cooking product	Mass of saturated fat in 100 g of cooking product / g	Mass of unsaturated fat in 100 g of cooking product / g	Number of drops of bromine water
olive oil	11	84	14
peanut oil	20	72	12
butter	45	30	5
soft margarine	35	40	7
poly-unsaturated margarine	11	66	

2 Ethanol is a product of many a fermentation reaction. The molecular formula of ethanol is C_2H_5OH.

a Draw the structural formula for ethanol.

b When ethanol is heated with an excess of acidified potassium dichromate, it is converted to ethanoic acid:

$$\underset{\text{ethanol}}{C_2H_5OH} \rightarrow \underset{\text{ethanoic acid}}{CH_3COOH}$$

What type of chemical reaction is this?

c Some synthetic flavourings are made by reacting an alcohol with a carboxylic acid:

alcohol + carboxylic acid → ester + water

What other substance and conditions are needed to carry out this reaction?

d The structure of the ester propyl butanoate is shown here.

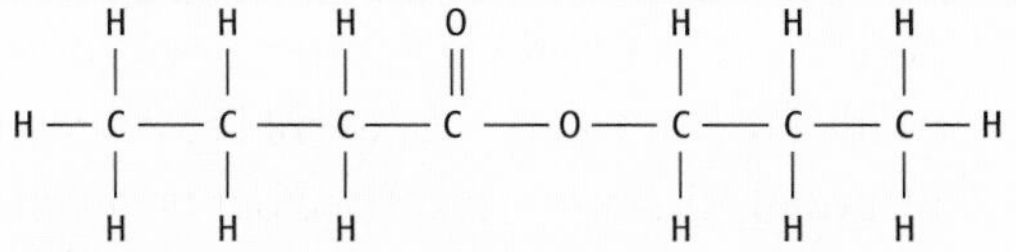

Draw the structural formula of the carboxylic acid from which this ester is made.

3 The flavour and smell of foods are partly due to esters. An ester can be made from ethanol and ethanoic acid.

a Name this ester.

b Write a word equation for the reaction between ethanol and ethanoic acid.

4 The diagram below shows a method used in France to change wine into vinegar. Living organisms (*Acetobacter*) bringing about a chemical change and producing a marketable product is an example of traditional biotechnology.

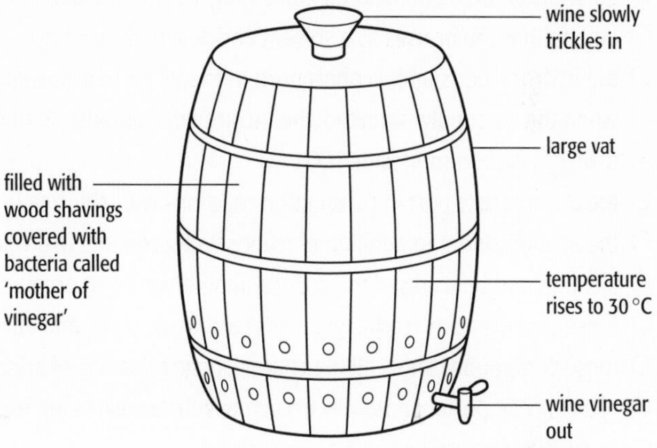

a What type of reaction has occurred in the vat?

b Name a chemical reagent, other than oxygen, that can change ethanol into ethanoic acid.

c Name a technique that could be used to separate ethanoic acid from the other liquids in vinegar.

d Describe a chemical test that would distinguish between wine and vinegar.

5 Olive oil, an example of a vegetable oil, contains esters.

a What type of compound is produced by the alkaline hydrolysis of olive oil?

b What other class of compound contains the ester linkage?

Summary

You should know that:

- there is a vast range of carbon compounds, and the study of their properties is known as organic chemistry
- the simplest organic compounds are the hydrocarbons
- because of the versatility of carbon atoms in their bonding, there are whole 'families' (homologous series) of hydrocarbons
- the alkanes are a series of saturated hydrocarbons, the simplest member of which is methane (CH_4), the main component of natural gas
- the alkenes are a second homologous series of hydrocarbons
- the alkenes contain a C=C double bond in the chain and their molecules have the general formula C_nH_{2n}
- the alkanes are important as fuels but are fairly unreactive, though they can take part in substitution reactions, particularly with the halogens, whereas the alkenes are considerably more reactive because they contain a C=C double bond
- the alkenes take part in addition reactions
- the test for unsaturation (the presence of a C=C double bond in a molecule) is to use bromine water, which is decolorised
- separate series of organic compounds exist with different functional groups attached to the hydrocarbon 'backbone'
- one important homologous series is the alcohols, the most significant of which is ethanol
- ethanol can be manufactured chemically and also obtained by fermentation
- ethanol can be manufactured industrially by the hydration of ethene with steam or by large-scale fermentation
- ethanol has major uses as a solvent and as a fuel
- the hydrocarbons and alcohols burn in excess air to give carbon dioxide and water
- when the air supply is limited, the incomplete combustion of these hydrocarbons and alcohols can result in the production of the toxic gas carbon monoxide (CO)

S

- the alkanes take part in substitution reactions with chlorine in the presence of ultraviolet light
- the alkenes undergo addition reactions with bromine, hydrogen and steam
- alcohols can be oxidised to produce another series of organic compounds that are acidic
- these organic acids (carboxylic acids) are weak acids, and ethanoic acid is the one most commonly used in the laboratory
- these compounds show all the characteristic reactions of acids but also react with alcohols to produce esters
- esters are important naturally occurring substances, being present in animal fats and vegetable oils
- as such, esters are important in our diet
- treatment of the esters of long-chain acids with sodium hydroxide produces soap.

Exam-style questions

1 The table below shows the composition of the mixture of gases coming from a typical car exhaust.

Gas	% of the gas in the exhaust fumes
carbon dioxide	9
carbon monoxide	5
oxygen	4
hydrogen	2
hydrocarbons	0.2
nitrogen oxides	0.2
sulfur dioxide	less than 0.003
gas X	79.6

a State the name of the gas **X**. [1]

b The carbon dioxide comes from the burning of hydrocarbons, such as octane, in the petrol.

i Copy and complete the word equation for the complete combustion of octane.

octane + ... → carbon dioxide + ... [2]

ii Which **two** chemical elements are present in hydrocarbons? [1]

iii To which homologous series of hydrocarbons does octane belong? [1]

c Suggest a reason for the presence of carbon monoxide in the exhaust fumes. [1]

CIE IGCSE, November 2004, paper 2, q.4 part

2 Hydrogen obtained by electrolysis of brine can be used in the manufacture of margarine.

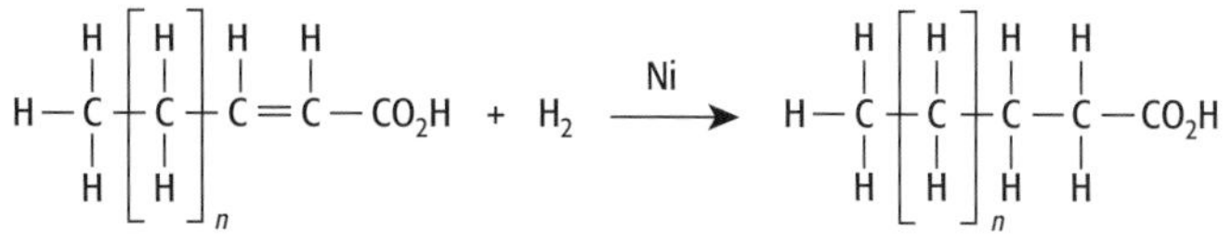

Copy and complete the following sentences about this reaction using words from the list.

catalyst **inhibitor** **monomeric** **saturated** **unsaturated**

Hydrogen gas is bubbled through .... carbon compounds using a nickel .... which speeds up the reaction.

The margarines produced are .... compounds. [3]

CIE IGCSE, November 2004, paper 2, q.6 part

3 Some organic compounds found in ripe fruits are shown below.

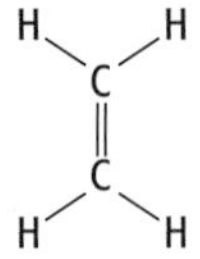

A

CH_3CO_2H

B

$CH_3CH_2CH_2CO_2H$

C

CH_3CH_2OH

D

CH_3CH_2CHO

E

a What do you understand by the term **organic compound**? [1]

b Which **two** of the compounds belong to the same homologous series? [1]

c Which **one** of these compounds is an unsaturated hydrocarbon? [1]

d Which **one** of these compounds is an alcohol? [1]

e Which **one** of these compounds can be formed directly by cracking the paraffin fraction from petroleum? [1]

f Compound **D** burns readily.

i Burning is an exothermic reaction. Explain the meaning of the term **exothermic**. [1]

ii State the products formed when **D** burns in excess air. [2]

iii Name the carbon compound formed when **D** undergoes incomplete combustion. [1]

g Write down the molecular formula of compound **C**. [1]

h Calculate the relative molecular mass of compound **C**. [1]

i Many fruits contain a variety of different coloured compounds. What separation technique can you use to separate these different coloured compounds? [1]

CIE IGCSE, November 2002, paper 2, q.4

4 The diagram shows a modern landfill site for the disposal of waste materials.

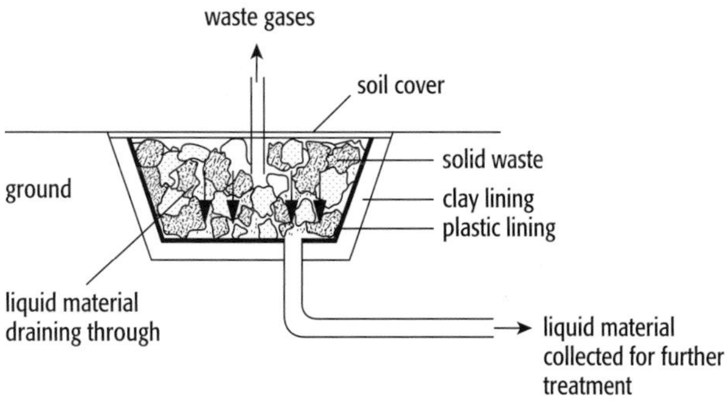

The waste materials are broken down naturally in several stages.

a In the first stage, micro-organisms (mainly bacteria) break down some of the organic material in the waste to carbon dioxide. What is the name given to the process by which organisms use food to produce carbon dioxide? [1]

b In the third stage, ethanoic acid is produced. Draw the structure of ethanoic acid showing all atoms and bonds. [1]

c In the fourth stage, carbon dioxide reacts with hydrogen to form methane and oxygen.

i Copy and complete the equation for this reaction.

CO_2 + ……… → CH_4 + O_2

ii State **one** use of methane.

iii Methane is a gas. Which **two** of the following statements about gas molecules are true?

- The molecules are far apart.
- The molecules are not moving.
- The molecules are randomly arranged.
- The molecules are arranged in a regular manner. [4]

d Ethane is a compound related to methane. Bromine water can be used to distinguish between ethane and ethene.

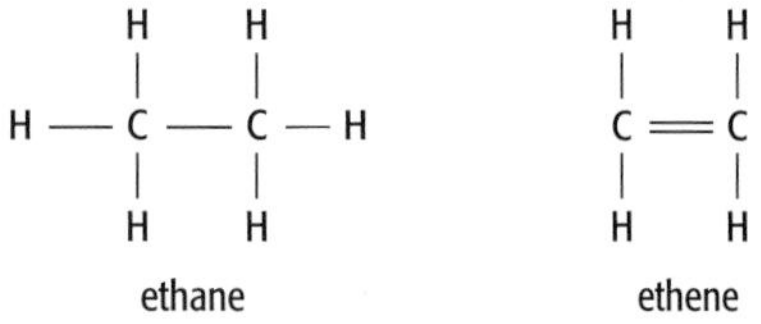

Describe what you would observe when bromine water is added to ethene. [1]

CIE IGCSE, November 2003, paper 2, q. 2 & 4 part

S

5 The alcohols form a homologous series.

The first four members are methanol, ethanol, propan-1-ol and butan-1-ol.

a One characteristic of a homologous series is that the physical properties vary in a predictable way. The table below gives the heats of combustion of the first three alcohols.

Alcohol	**Formula**	**Heat of combustion in kJ/mol**
methanol	CH_3OH	−730
ethanol	$CH_3—CH_2—OH$	−1370
propan-1-ol	$CH_3—CH_2—CH_2—OH$	−2020
butan-1-ol	$CH_3—CH_2—CH_2—CH_2—OH$	

i The minus sign indicates that there is less chemical energy in the products than in the reactants. What form of energy is given out by the reaction? [1]

ii Is the reaction exothermic or endothermic? [1]

iii Copy and complete the equation for the complete combustion of ethanol.

C_2H_5OH + ...O_2 → .... + ... [2]

iv Determine the heat of combustion of butan-1-ol by plotting the heats of combustion of the first three alcohols as a bar chart against the number of carbon atoms per molecule. Use a graph paper grid set up similar to the one shown opposite.

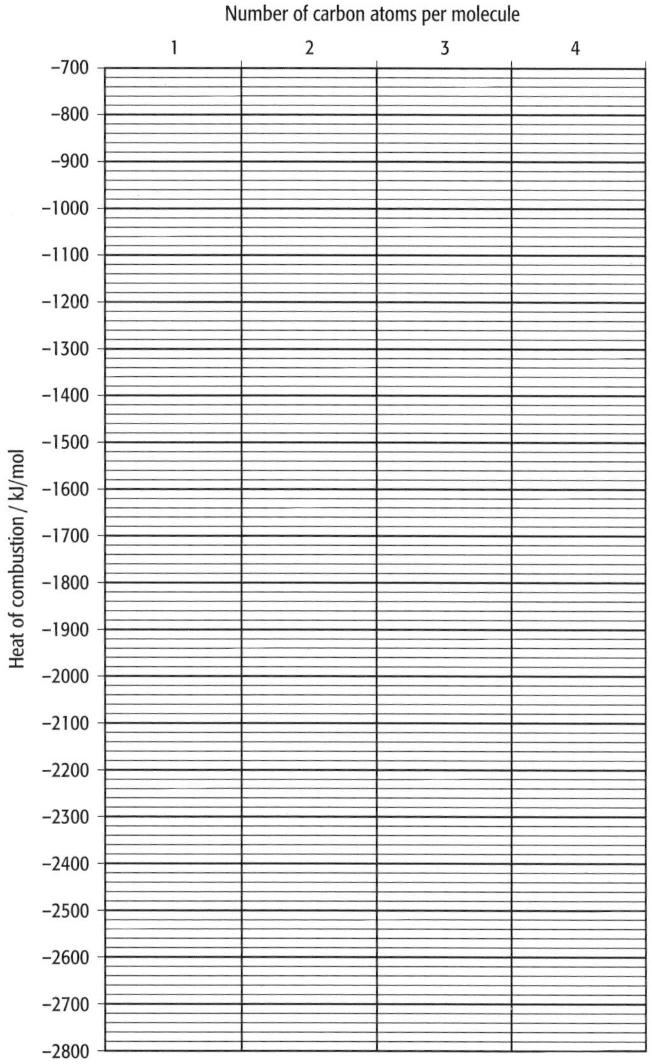

The heat of combustion of butan-1-ol = ...kJ/mol [3]

v Describe **two** other characteristics of homologous series. [2]

b Give the name and structural formula of an isomer of propan-1-ol. [2]

c Methanol is made from carbon monoxide.

$CO(g) + 2H_2(g) \rightleftharpoons CH_3OH(g)$ the forward reaction is exothermic

i Describe how hydrogen is obtained from alkanes. [2]

ii Suggest a method of making carbon monoxide from methane. [2]

iii Which condition, high or low pressure, would give the maximum yield of methanol? Give a reason for your choice. [2]

d For each of the following predict the name of the organic product.

i reaction between methanol and ethanoic acid [1]

ii oxidation of propan-1-ol by potassium dichromate(VI) [1]

iii removal of H_2O from ethanol (dehydration) [1]

CIE IGCSE, November 2007, paper 3, q.6

S

6 **a** **i** Give the essential condition for the reaction between chlorine and butane. [1]

ii What type of reaction is this? [1]

iii This reaction produces a mixture of products.

Give the names of **two** products that contain four carbon atoms per molecule. [2]

b There are two isomers of the hydrocarbon with the molecular formula C_4H_8.

Draw the structural formulae of **two** of these isomers. [2]

c Alkenes are more reactive than alkanes and are used to make a range of organic chemicals.

Propene, $CH_3—CH=CH_2$, is made by cracking.

Give the structural formula of the addition product when propene reacts with the following.

i water [1]

ii bromine [1]

d Propene reacts with hydrogen iodide to form 2-iodopropane.

$$CH_3—CH=CH_2 + HI \rightarrow CH_3—CHI—CH_3$$

1.4 g of propene produced 4.0 g of 2-iodopropane.

Calculate the percentage yield.

moles of $CH_3—CH=CH_2$ reacted = ... moles

maximum moles of $CH_3—CHI—CH_3$ that could be formed = ... moles

mass of one mole of $CH_3—CHI—CH_3$ = 170 g

maximum mass of 2-iodopropane that could be formed = ... g

percentage yield = ... % [4]

CIE IGCSE, June 2006, paper 3, q.7 part

11 Petrochemicals and polymers

This chapter covers the following ideas:

- fossil fuels
- the formation and fractional distillation of petroleum (crude oil)
- catalytic cracking
- alternative transport fuels
- biogas
- addition polymerisation
- (S) condensation polymerisation
- (S) the disposal and recycling of plastic waste
- (S) biological condensation polymers
  - proteins
  - carbohydrates
  - food

11.1 Petroleum

Fossil fuels were formed in the Earth's crust from material that was once living. Coal comes from fossil plant material. Petroleum (or crude oil) and natural gas are formed from the bodies of marine micro-organisms. The formation of these fuels took place over **geological periods of time** (many millions of years). These fuels are therefore a **non-renewable** and **finite resource**.

There are three major fossil fuels:

- coal
- petroleum (crude oil)
- natural gas.

E

The formation of petroleum

Petroleum is one of the Earth's major natural resources. The oil is the result of a process that began up to 400 million years ago. Prehistoric marine creatures died and sank to the seabed and were covered and surrounded by mud. The change into petroleum and natural gas was brought about by high pressure, high temperature and bacteria acting over millions of years. The original organic material broke down into hydrocarbons. Compression of the mud above the hydrocarbon mixture transformed it into shale. Then geological movements and pressure changed this shale into harder rocks, squeezing out the oil and gas. The oil and gas moved upwards through the porous rocks, moving from high-pressure to low-pressure conditions. Sometimes they reached the surface (Figure 11.1), but often they became trapped by a layer of non-porous rock.

Figure 11.1 The Athabasca Oil Sands, Alberta, Canada. These oil sands supply over 10% of Canada's oil needs, using technology that upgrades bitumen to petroleum.

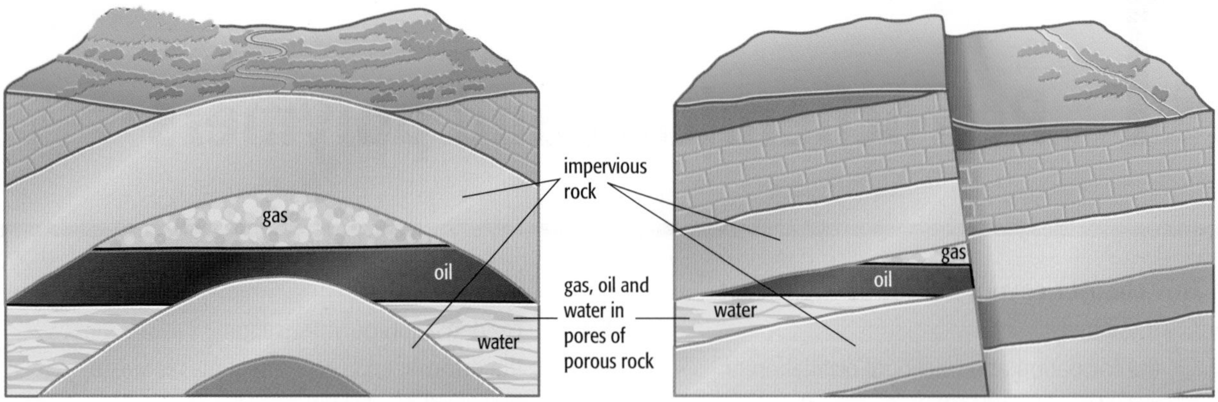

Figure 11.2 Certain rock formations favour the accumulation of oil and natural gas.

Reservoirs of oil and gas were created. These occur where the rock layers form an anticline or at the junction of a fault (Figure **11.2**). These reservoirs are **not** lakes of oil or pockets of gas. Instead, the oil or gas is spread throughout the pores in coarse rocks such as sandstone or limestone, rather as water is held in a sponge.

Oil-fields and gas-fields are detected by a series of geological searches. Surveys from aeroplanes and satellites can provide detailed pictures of surface features. These give clues about the underlying rocks. Variations in gravity and magnetic field can also give clues. Finally, a seismic survey is carried out. These can be carried out both at sea and on land. Shock waves in the ground are produced by setting off small explosions. At sea, compressed air guns are used. Detailed information on the rock formations in an area can be found by tracking and timing the shock waves. Promising areas are then drilled. These drillings can be carried out simply to gain more geological information. But if oil or gas is found, they can be used to see how extensive the oil-field or gas-field is. Once a field is established, production oil-rigs can be set up, whether on land or at sea (Figure **11.3**).

Figure 11.3 An oil-rig in the Caspian Sea.

Fractional distillation

Petroleum is a mixture of many different hydrocarbon molecules. Most of the petroleum that is extracted from the ground is used to make fuel, but around 10% is used as a **feedstock**, or raw material, in the chemical industry. Before it can be used, the various hydrocarbon molecules are separated by refining. This is done by fractional distillation at an **oil refinery**.

At a refinery, petroleum is separated into different fractions – groups of hydrocarbons that have different boiling points. These different boiling points are roughly related to the number of carbon atoms in the hydrocarbons (Table **11.1**).

Separation of the hydrocarbons takes place in a fractional distillation column, or fractionating tower. At the start of the refining process, petroleum is preheated to a temperature of 350–400 °C and pumped in at the base of the tower. As it boils, the vapour passes up the tower. It passes through a series of bubble caps, and cools as it rises further up the column. The different fractions

Fraction	Approximate number of carbon atoms in hydrocarbons		Approximate boiling range / °C	
refinery gas	1–4	C_1–C_4	below 25	↓
gasoline/petrol[(a)]	4–12	C_4–C_{12}	40–100	
naphtha	7–14	C_7–C_{14}	90–150	
kerosene/paraffin[(a)]	12–16	C_9–C_{16}	150–240	b.p. and viscosity increasing
diesel oil/gas oil	14–18	C_{14}–C_{18}	220–300	
fuel oil	19–25	C_{19}–C_{25}	250–320	
lubricating oil	20–40	C_{20}–C_{40}	300–350	
bitumen residue	over 70	> C_{70}	above 350	

[(a)]*Different terms are used in the UK and the USA. Note that 'crude oil' (UK) is the same as 'petroleum' (USA), 'petrol' (UK) is the same as 'gasoline' (USA), and 'paraffin' (UK) is the same as 'kerosene' (USA).*

Table 11.1 Various petroleum[(a)] fractions.

cool and condense at different temperatures, and therefore at different heights in the column. The fractions condensing at the different levels are collected on trays. Fractions from the top of the tower are called 'light' and those from the bottom 'heavy'. Each fraction contains a number of different hydrocarbons. The individual single hydrocarbons can then be obtained by further distillation. Figure **11.4** (overleaf) shows the separation into different fractions and some of their uses.

Exam tip

Take care over names for the different fractions in different parts of the world. Note that the syllabus uses 'petroleum' as the name of the crude oil drilled from the ground.

Exam tip

Make sure you know the order of the fractions as they are produced from the fractionating tower, and a use for each of the fractions.

Catalytic cracking

The demand for the various fractions from the refinery does not necessarily match with their supply from the oil (Figure **11.5**, overleaf). For lighter fractions such as gasoline (petrol), the demand is greater than the supply. The opposite is true for heavier fractions such as kerosene (paraffin) and diesel. Larger molecules from these heavier fractions can be broken into smaller, more valuable, molecules. This process is called **catalytic cracking** ('cat cracking').

Cracking takes place in a huge reactor (Figure **11.6**, overleaf). In this reactor, particles of catalyst (made of powdered minerals such as silica, alumina and zeolites) are mixed with the hydrocarbon fraction at a temperature around 500 °C. The cracked vapours containing smaller molecules are separated by distillation.

The shortened hydrocarbon molecules are produced by the following type of reaction:

$$\text{decane} \xrightarrow[\text{catalyst}]{\text{heat}} \text{octane} + \text{ethene}$$

$$C_{10}H_{22} \rightarrow C_8H_{18} + C_2H_4$$

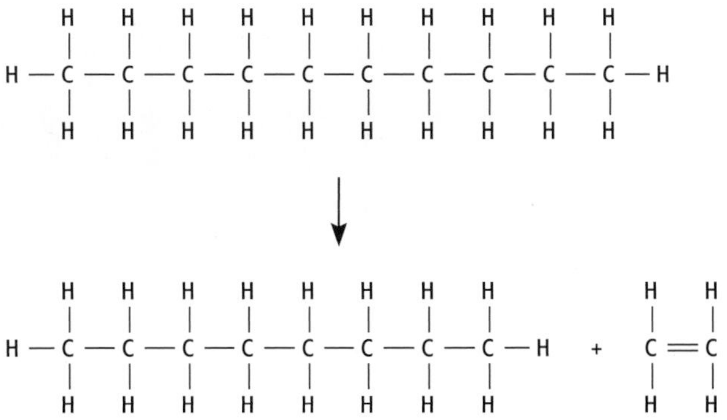

This is just one of the possible reactions when decane is cracked. The molecules may not all break in the same place. The alkene fragment is not always ethene: propene and but-1-ene may also be produced.

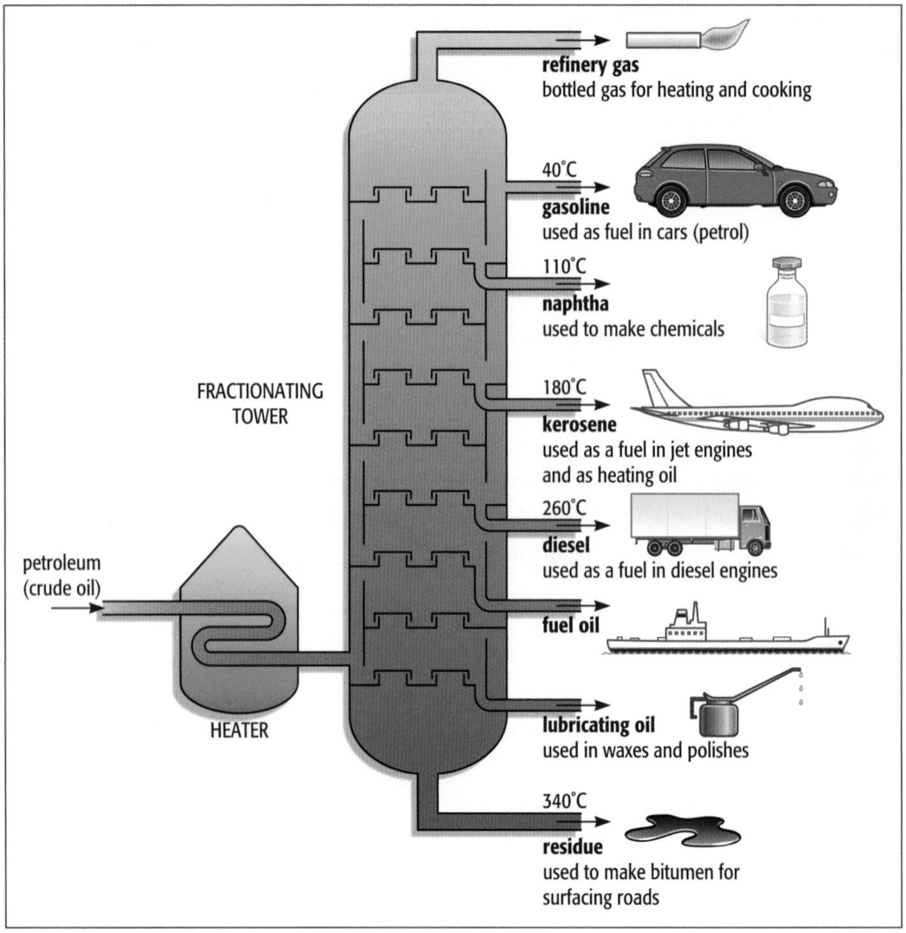

Figure 11.4 Fractional distillation of petroleum in a refinery.

Figure 11.5 There is not the same economic demand for all the fractions from petroleum.

Figure 11.6 A cracking plant in an oil refinery.

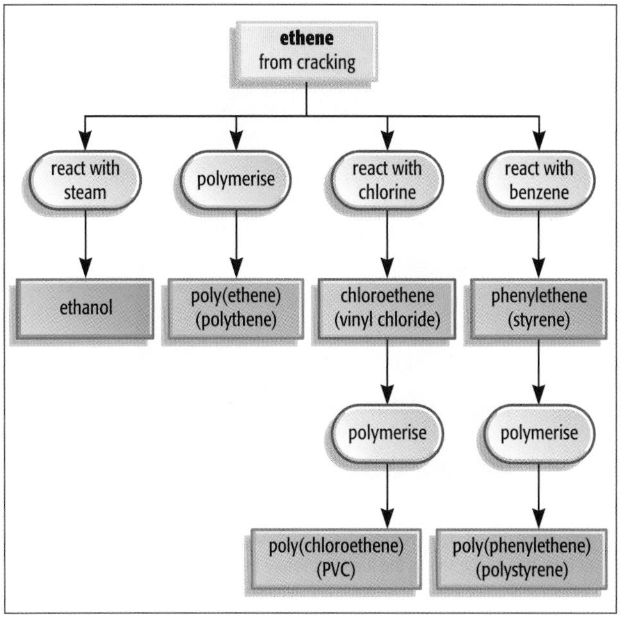

Figure 11.7 Important products can be made from the ethene produced by catalytic cracking.

All cracking reactions give:

- an **alkane** with a shorter chain than the original, and a short-chain **alkene**
- or two or more **alkenes** and **hydrogen**.

Both reactions are useful. The shortened alkanes can be blended with the gasoline fraction to enrich the petrol. The alkenes are useful as raw materials for making several important products. Figure **11.7** shows the various uses for the ethene produced.

Propene polymerises to poly(propene) (trade name 'polypropylene'), while butene polymerises to produce synthetic rubber. The cracking reaction can be carried out in the laboratory using paraffin oil (Figure **11.8**).

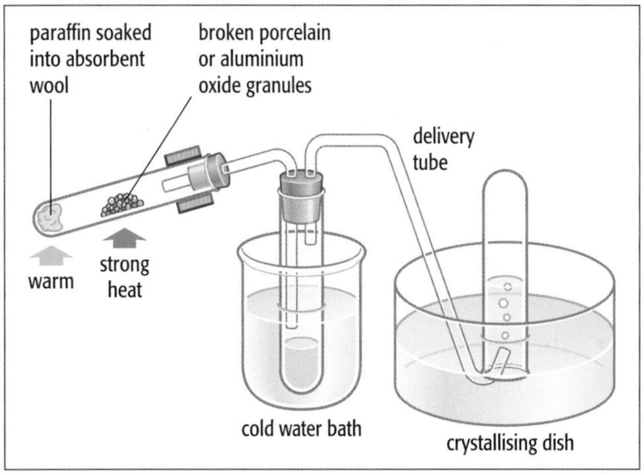

Figure 11.8 The cracking of a long-chain alkane in the laboratory.

E

Blending gasoline

Some of the products from cracking are added to the gasoline fraction to improve the quality of the petrol. As many as 12 different components (containing over 300 different hydrocarbons and additives) may be used in a blend of petrol for the motorist. Different blends are made for winter and summer use. An important consideration is how easily the fuel vapour ignites. If the fuel ignites too easily, then the engine will not run smoothly – 'knocking' will occur. However, if the fuel is too difficult to ignite, then the engine will be difficult to start, especially on cold mornings. High-quality petrol contains many branched-chain hydrocarbons, made in a process known as re-forming, so that the fuel does not ignite too soon (Figure **11.9**, overleaf).

'Lead' (actually tetraethyl-lead) was added to gasoline to prevent 'knocking'. But this caused high

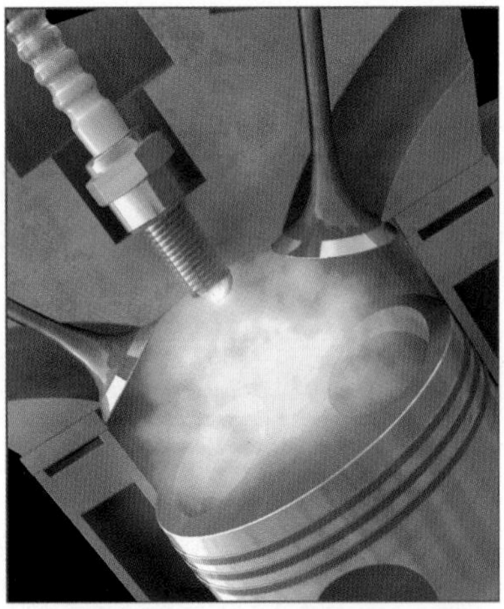

Figure 11.9 Computer image of an internal combustion engine cylinder. The piston (lower right) is moved up and down by the combustion (burning) of fuel. This image shows the fuel/air mixture being ignited by the spark plug.

levels of lead in the air, particularly in large cities. This led to concern over the link with brain damage in young children. Unleaded fuel is now widely available and **has** to be used in modern cars fitted with catalytic converters (the lead would poison the catalyst and so prevent it working).

The removal of sulfur from gasoline fractions is now very efficient. Car exhaust emissions contain very little sulfur dioxide. The carbon monoxide (CO), unburnt hydrocarbons (HC) and oxides of nitrogen (NO_x) in exhaust fumes do continue to cause concern. The levels of emission of these compounds are reduced by fitting a catalytic converter to the exhaust.

Gasoline vapour also escapes into the air at petrol stations. Modern pumps now have hoods on the nozzles to cut down the escape of fumes. When handling liquid fuels generally, you need to consider the flash point and ignition temperature of the fuel. These are not the same. The **flash point** is the temperature at which the vapour will ignite in air in the presence of a flame. This temperature is usually low for a fuel (Table **11.2**). The **ignition temperature** is the temperature at which a fuel : air mixture ignites without a flame – for petrol it is 550 °C.

Liquid	Flash point / °C
methanol	+11
ethanol	+13
hexane	−21
octane	+13

Table 11.2 Flash points of some common flammable liquids.

Key ideas so far

- There are three major fossil fuels: petroleum, coal and natural gas.
- The fossil fuels were formed by high pressure and temperature underground from organic matter over geological periods of time.
- Petroleum is a complex mixture of hydrocarbons. It can be separated into several useful 'fractions' by fractional distillation in an oil refinery. The fractions have different boiling points.
- Each of the fractions from the distillation has its uses.
- Cracking is a process by which long-chain alkanes can be shortened to more economically useful hydrocarbons. Cracking also produces alkenes such as ethene.
- The shorter alkanes can be used to produce better blends of petrol. The alkenes can be used for polymerisation and to produce alcohols.

Quick-check questions

1. Put the following fractions in order of increasing boiling point: kerosene, diesel, petrol, refinery gas, bitumen, naphtha.
2. Name **three** fossil fuels.
3. Explain what is meant by 'cracking', and write word and balanced symbol equations to show how ethene can be formed from decane by this method.
4. State a use for the following fractions from the distillation of petroleum (crude oil): bitumen, fuel oil, diesel, kerosene.

E

11.2 Alternative fuels and energy sources

Alternative transport fuels

There is growing interest and a great deal of development work taking place on alternative transport fuels in order to reduce dependence on fossil fuels and find 'greener' forms of transport.

Diesel

High-speed diesel engines in cars, buses and trucks use a fuel (DERV – diesel engine road vehicle) that contains hydrocarbon molecules consisting of between 6 and 20 carbon atoms (in short this is written as C_6–C_{20} molecules). Slower-speed diesel engines for ships, etc., use a slightly heavier fuel. Diesel engines are compression ignition engines (the fuel ignites spontaneously **without** a spark). Diesel engines are more efficient than petrol engines and produce much less carbon monoxide. However, because their working temperature is higher, they produce more oxides of nitrogen. The major problems are smoke, and the particulates it contains, and odour.

Gasoline from methanol

New Zealand has large reserves of natural gas (mainly methane) but very little crude oil. The problem of producing petrol has been transformed by a catalyst known as zeolite ZSM-5. (A zeolite is one of a large group of alumino-silicates of sodium, potassium, calcium and barium.) Methane is first converted into methanol. The methanol produced is then turned into hydrocarbons using the ZSM-5 catalyst:

$$\text{methanol} \rightarrow \text{hydrocarbons} + \text{water}$$
$$n\mathrm{CH_3OH} \rightarrow (\mathrm{CH_2})_n + n\mathrm{H_2O}$$

ZSM-5 is an artificial zeolite composed of aluminium, silicon and oxygen. It was first made by two chemists working for the US Mobil Oil company.

LPG and CNG

Liquid petroleum gas (LPG or 'autogas') is composed of propane and butane. Compressed natural gas (CNG) is 90% methane. These products already have a significant market in some countries. For example, all the taxis in Japan use LPG. In India, many of the motorised rickshaws in the major cities run on CNG (Figure **11.10**).

Figure 11.10 In India many of the motorised rickshaws ('tuk-tuks') run on CNG.

Biofuels

There have been significant developments in the use of fuels based on ethanol (see page **301**) and vegetable oils such as rapeseed or sunflower oil. The potential for adding plant oils to diesel fuel is being investigated worldwide. The future use of these fuels will depend on economic factors. Some countries grow oil-producing crops but do not have their own reserves of crude oil. Recently there has been controversy about the use of land to grow crops for these fuels and the fact that this diverts farmland from food production. The consequent decrease in food availability and increase in prices have been sources of concern. These have led to other sources of ethanol being explored, including, for instance, using sawdust from sawmills as a starting point for production (Figure **11.11**, overleaf).

Vegetable oils from crops such as rape and sunflowers are also being developed as fuels. Recycled cooking oil is being used as a component of biodiesel. Biodiesel contains esters, which are made from vegetable oils such as rapeseed or animal fats. The continual growth of new oil-producing

Figure 11.11 The sawdust from sawmills can be used as a starting point in making ethanol for biofuels.

plants, which absorb carbon dioxide from the air through photosynthesis, means that biodiesel contributes less to global warming than fossil fuels do. Motor manufacturers have all developed cars with engines adapted to run on these new fuels.

Others

We discussed the use of ethanol- and hydrogen-powered cars on pages **18** and **301**. Electric and solar-powered cars are also being investigated as alternatives to gasoline, and many manufacturers now have hybrid cars that run on a combination of power systems (Figure **11.12**).

Alternative energy sources

Alternative energy sources are very much under discussion. Nuclear energy, wind farms and solar energy are some of the areas being explored. In terms of chemical systems, those based around our use of waste offer an opportunity for development, particularly at local level.

Biogas

Methane gas is formed naturally under a number of different circumstances. Anaerobic bacteria helped to decompose organic matter under geological conditions to produce natural gas. Methane accumulates in coalmines, where it can cause explosions. Marsh gas, which bubbles up through the stagnant water of marshes, swamps and rice paddy fields, is also methane. Methane produced in this way contributes to the 'greenhouse effect'.

Figure 11.12 The Toyota Prius is a hybrid gas/electric car with low emissions. The battery charges while running on petrol and an on-board computer switches when petrol is low.

Figure 11.13 A small-scale biogas generator uses animal waste to produce methane for a village's needs.

Methane is produced from organic waste (**biomass**) when it decays in the absence of air. This can be exploited as a source of energy. In countries such as India and China, biomass digesters are important sources of fuel for rural villages (Figure **11.13**). The methane is useful for heating and cooking, and the solid residue is used as a fertiliser.

Industrialised countries produce large amounts of waste, which is deposited in landfill sites. Biogas forms as the rubbish decays (Figure **11.14**). This gas can be used as a fuel for local industry. On Merseyside in the UK, biogas is used to heat the ovens in a Cadbury's biscuit factory.

Figure 11.14 **a** Deep in the waste of landfill sites, methane gas accumulates and must be burnt off or it could become dangerous – a landfill flare-off. **b** Alternatively, a power generating plant can be set up at a landfill site to generate power for the local area.

Exam tip

Exam questions do come up on biogas and landfill sites so make sure that you know the background to this area.

Key ideas so far

- Alternative fuels are being experimented with and developed for cars.
- Ethanol and vegetable oils are being exploited for combination with petrol to produce biofuels.
- Hydrogen fuel cells are being used to power cars.
- Methane from biogas generators or landfill sites can supply local needs for energy.

11.3 Addition polymerisation

All living things contain **polymers**. Proteins, carbohydrates, wood and natural rubber are all polymers. What nature first invented, chemists have learned to copy, alter and use successfully. Synthetic polymers, often called **plastics**, are to be found everywhere in modern technological societies, made into bulky objects, films and fibres. They have properties to suit particular needs, ranging from car and aircraft components, to packaging and clothing.

Polymers are large organic **macromolecules**. They are made up of small repeating units known as **monomers** (Figure **11.15**) joined together by polymerisation. These units are repeated any number of times from about a hundred to more than a million. Some are **homopolymers**, containing just one monomer. Poly(ethene), poly(propene) and poly(chloroethene) are three examples of homopolymers. Other macromolecules are **copolymers**, made of two or more different types of monomer. For example, nylon is made from two monomers, and biological proteins are made from 20 different monomers, the **amino acids**.

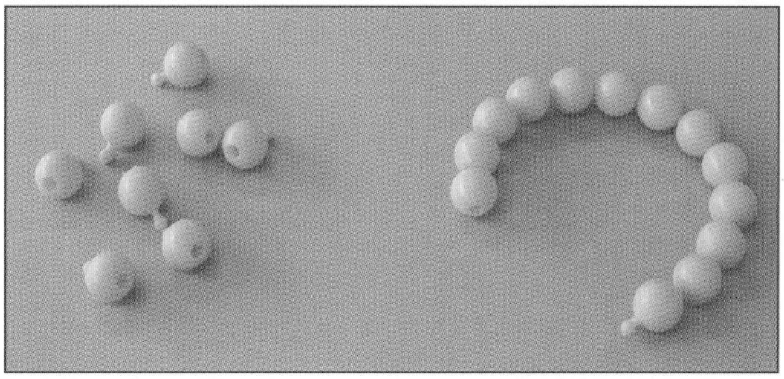

Figure 11.15 Making a chain of beads is similar to joining the monomers together to make a polymer.

The alkene fragments from the catalytic cracking of crude oil fractions produced the starting monomers for the first plastics. Alkenes such as ethene contain a C=C double bond. These molecules can take part in **addition reactions** (see pages **292** and **297**) where the double bond is broken and other atoms attach to the carbons. The double bond in ethene enables many molecules of ethene to join to each other to form a large molecule, poly(ethene) (Figure **11.16**). This is an **addition polymer**. When first made by ICI, it was a revolutionary new material called 'Alkathene'. It is now commonly called by the trade name 'polythene'.

Various conditions can be used to produce different types of poly(ethene). Generally a high pressure, a temperature at or above room temperature and a catalyst are needed. The reaction can be summarised by the equation:

$$\text{ethene} \xrightarrow[\text{heat, catalyst}]{\text{high pressure}} \text{poly(ethene)}$$

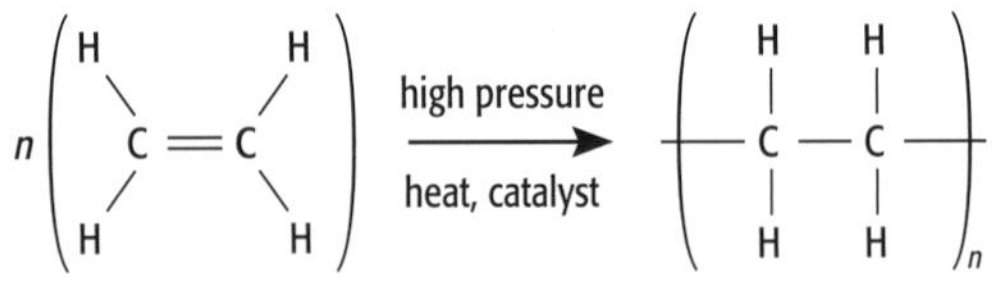

where n is a very large number.

Exam tip

When drawing the structure of poly(ethene), and other polymers, do not forget to put in the n outside the bracket.

Poly(ethene) was found to be a chemically resistant material that was very tough and durable, and a very good electrical insulator.

Other alkene molecules can also produce addition polymers. Propene will polymerise to produce poly(propene):

$$\text{propene} \rightarrow \text{poly(propene)}$$

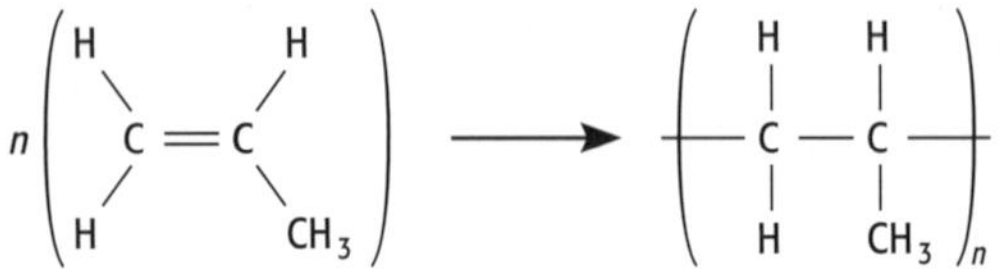

This long-chain molecule is similar in structure to poly(ethene) but with a methyl (—CH_3) group attached to every other carbon atom in the chain (Figure **11.17a**). It is commonly referred to by its trade name 'polypropylene'.

Chemists also experimented with other substituted alkenes to produce plastics with particular properties in

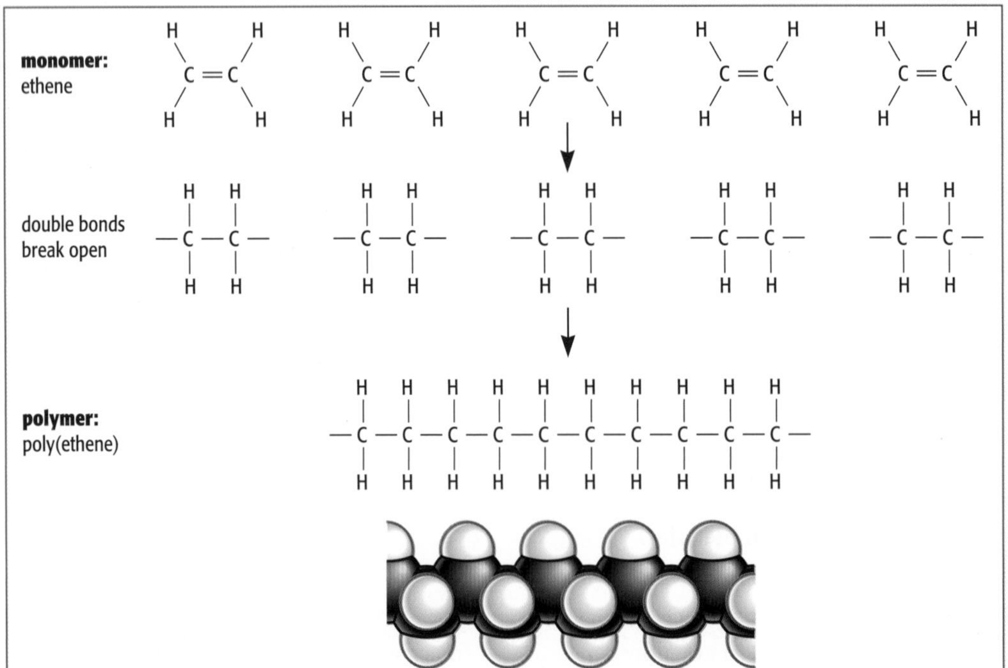

Figure 11.16 The polymerisation of ethene produces poly(ethene), whose structure is shown.

Exam tip

The diagram of the structure of poly(propene) is quite easy to get wrong. It is important to realise that the $—CH_3$ group is a side-group here – it does not become part of the chain. The chain is formed by the carbon atoms that are joined by the C=C bond in the monomer.

mind. Poly(chloroethene) (known by the trade name of polyvinyl chloride or PVC) and poly(tetrafluoroethene) (known by the trade name of polytetrafluoroethylene, 'Teflon' or PTFE) are two such polymers:

chloroethene (vinyl chloride) → poly(chloroethene) (PVC)

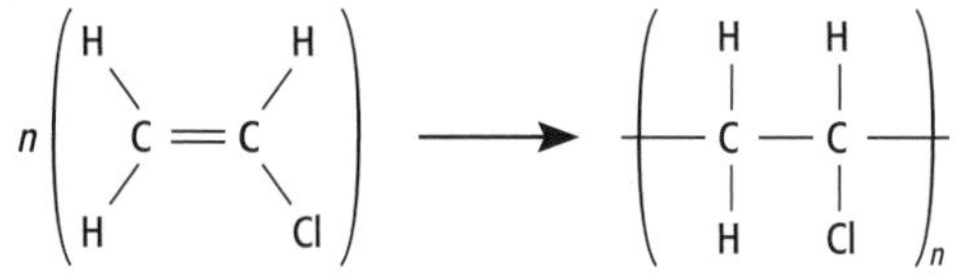

tetrafluoroethene → poly(tetrafluoroethene) (PTFE)

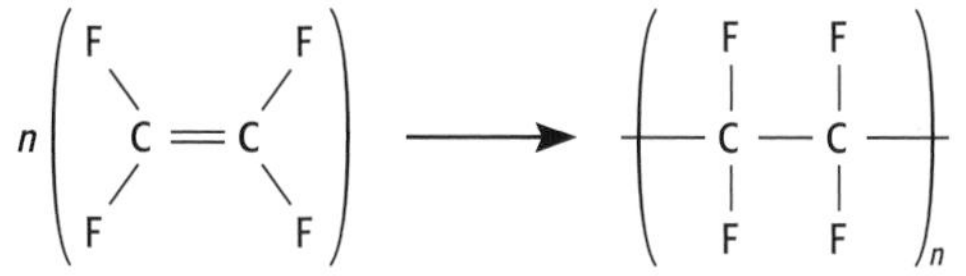

Their structures are shown in Figures **11.17b** and **c**.

Poly(chloroethene) (PVC) was found to be stronger and harder than poly(ethene) and therefore good for making pipes for plumbing. PTFE proved to have some unusual properties. It was very stable at high temperatures and formed a very slippery surface. The properties of some addition polymers are given in Table **11.3**. Such synthetic polymers have proved to be very versatile. Many, for example poly(propene), are easy to shape by melting and moulding. Thus poly(propene) is used to make sturdy

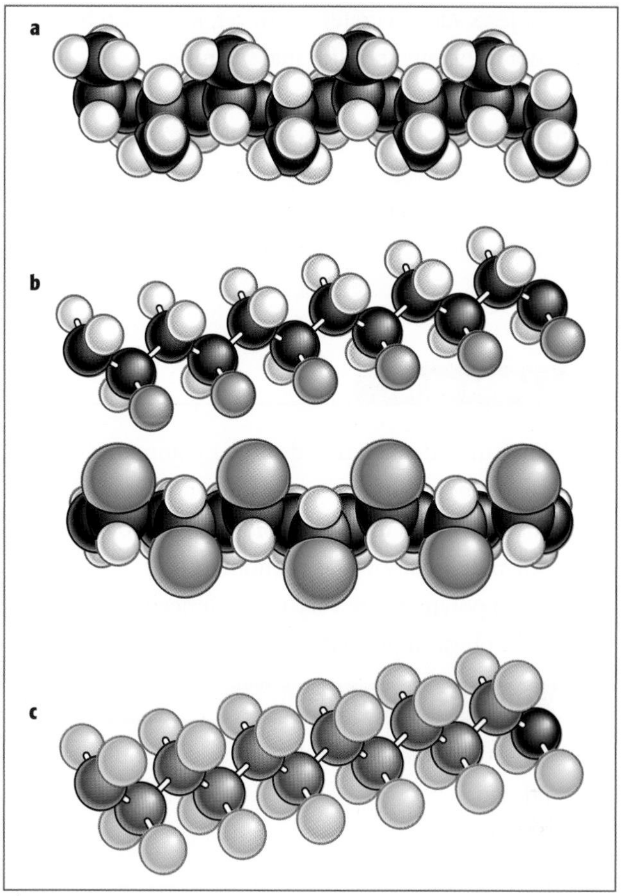

Figure 11.17 The structures of **a** poly(propene), PP, **b** poly(chloroethene), PVC, and **c** poly(tetrafluoroethene), PTFE.

Polymer (and trade name(s))	Monomer	Properties	Examples of use
poly(ethene) (polyethylene, polythene, PE)	ethene $CH_2{=}CH_2$	tough, durable	plastic bags, bowls, bottles, packaging
poly(propene) (polypropylene, PP)	propene $CH_3CH{=}CH_2$	tough, durable	crates and boxes, plastic rope
poly(chloroethene) (polyvinyl chloride, PVC)	chloroethene $CH_2{=}CHCl$	strong, hard (not as flexible as polythene)	insulation, pipes and guttering
poly(tetrafluoroethene) (polytetrafluoroethylene, Teflon, PTFE)	tetrafluoroethene $CF_2{=}CF_2$	non-stick surface, withstands high temperatures	non-stick frying pans, non-stick taps and joints
poly(phenylethene) (polystyrene, PS)	phenylethene (styrene) $C_6H_5CH{=}CH_2$	light, poor conductor of heat	insulation, packaging (foam)

Table 11.3 Examples of some widely used addition polymers.

plastic objects such as crates. However, it can also be drawn out into long fibres for making ropes.

Some of the properties of **addition polymers**:
- All polymers are long-chain molecules made by joining together a large number of monomer molecules.
- Addition polymerisation involves monomer molecules that contain a C=C double bond.
- Addition polymers are homopolymers, made from a single monomer.
- During addition, the double bonds open up and the molecules join to themselves to make a molecule with a very long chain.

Key ideas so far

- Unsaturated alkenes and similar compounds can form long-chain molecules known as polymers.
- The individual units that join together to make a polymer are known as monomers.
- These polymers are very useful indeed because of their physical properties and chemical stability.

Quick-check questions

1 Give the molecular and structural formulae of ethene.

2 State what is meant by addition polymerisation and give an equation for the formation of poly(ethene) from ethene.

3 Draw the structure of the repeating unit in the following polymers:
  a poly(propene) **b** poly(chloroethene) (PVC).

4 What is the monomer used for making Teflon?

5 Give a use for the following polymers:
  a poly(propene), **b** poly(vinyl chloride)
  c poly(tetrafluoroethene).

11.4 Condensation polymerisation

Nylon

In the early 1930s, DuPont were conducting research into artificial fibres. Knowledge of silk and wool gave clues as to how protein molecules are built. Wallace Carothers imitated the linkage in proteins and produced the first **synthetic fibre**, 'nylon'. **Nylon** is a solid when first formed, but it can then be melted and forced through small holes. The long filaments cool, and the fibres produced are stretched to align the polymer molecules and then dried. The fibres can be woven into fabric to make shirts, ties, sheets, etc., or turned into ropes or racquet strings. However, nylon is not just made into fibres. It has proved to be a very versatile material and can be moulded into strong plastic items such as gear-wheels.

Nylon is a copolymer of two different monomers, a diamine and a dicarboxylic acid. Each monomer consists of a chain of carbon atoms (which are shown in the following diagrams simplified as boxes). At both ends of the monomers are functional groups. An amine group ($-NH_2$) on the first monomer reacts with a carboxylic acid group ($-COOH$) on the second monomer to make a link between the two molecules. Each time a link is made, a water molecule is lost:

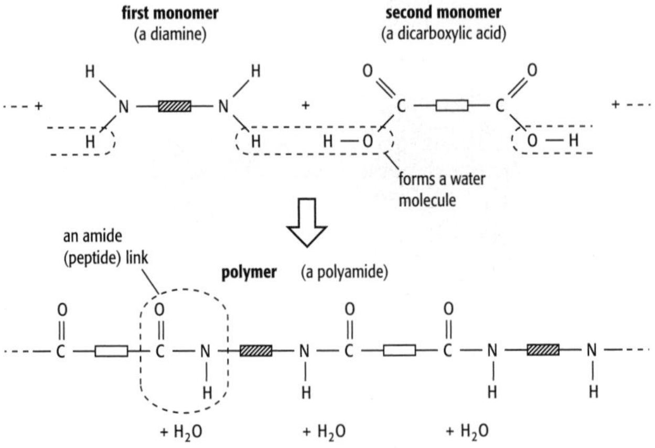

As a result, this type of polymer is known as a **condensation polymer**. Because an **amide link** (or peptide link) is formed during polymerisation, nylon is known as a **polyamide**. A version of nylon polymerisation can be carried out in the laboratory (Figure **11.18**).

Exam tip

Questions on the structure of nylon, and other condensation polymers, are difficult. You will not be asked the detailed structure of the monomers. You can represent the central structure of each monomer as a block, as shown in the diagrams here. You should know the structure (and name) of the links between the monomers in the chain, though – in this case the peptide link.

It is worth practising these diagrams to make sure you are very familiar with them and can recall them readily.

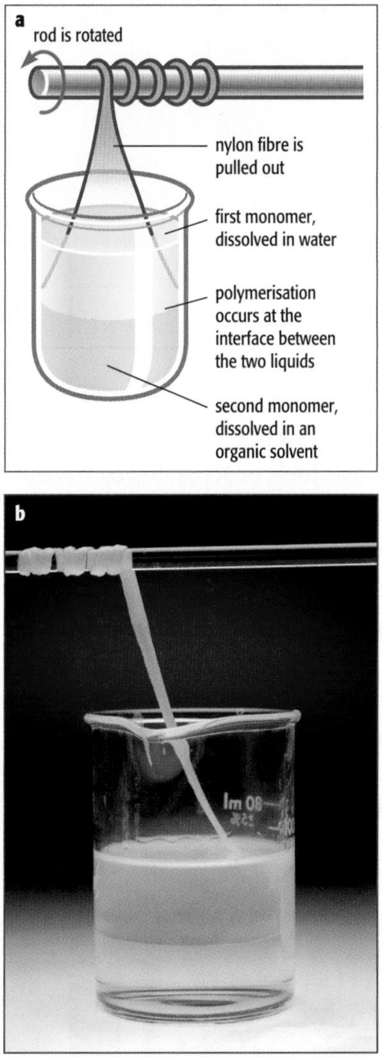

Figure 11.18 Nylon is a polyamide and can be made in the laboratory.

Polyesters

Condensation polymerisation can also be used to make other polymers with properties different from those of nylon. **Polyesters** are condensation copolymers made from two monomers. One monomer has an alcohol group (—OH) at each end. The other monomer has a carboxylic acid group —COOH) at each end. When the monomers react, an **ester link** is formed, with water being lost each time:

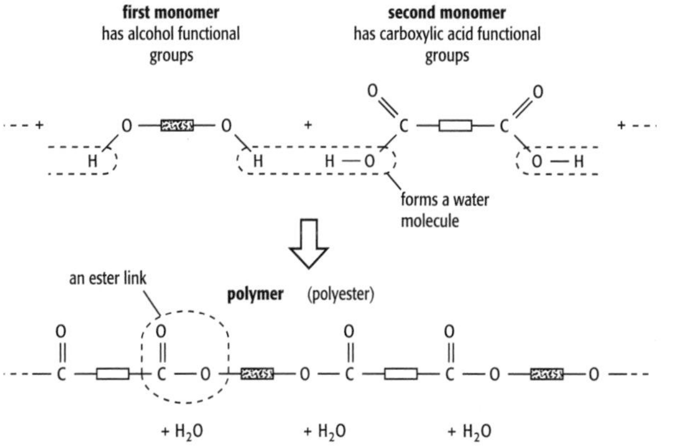

One such polyester has the trade name 'Terylene'. Like nylon, Terylene can be turned into fibres and woven into clothing. Terylene clothing is generally softer than that made from nylon (Figure **11.19**).

The ester linkage that joins the monomer units in the man-made fibre Terylene also occurs naturally in animal fats and vegetable oils, only with different linking units. Fat molecules are quite complex, though not strictly polymers. The ester linkages in such molecules join together the central glycerol molecule to the long chain carboxylic acid molecules (see Figure **10.24**, page **306**). Just as the ester links in natural fats and oils can be broken by alkaline hydrolysis, so Terylene can be broken down by hydrolysis. So it is not good news if spots of alkali fall on your shirts or sweaters!

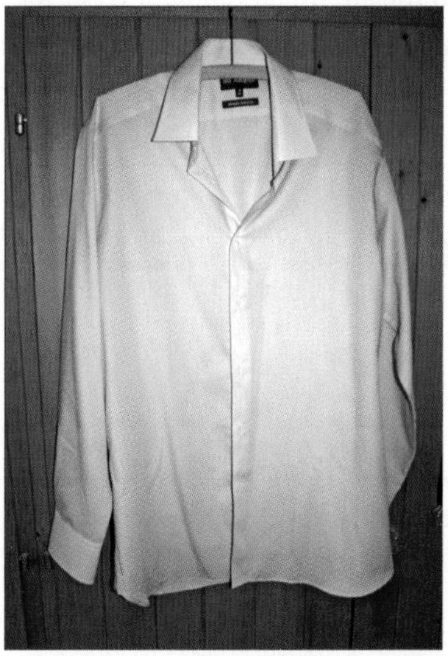

Figure 11.19 Shirts are often made out of a fabric made of Terylene and cotton.

The re-use, recycling and disposal of plastic waste

Plastic rubbish is a common but unwelcome sight around the world. Over the past 30 years, plastics have taken over as replacement materials in many applications. This is not surprising because they are light, cheap and corrosion-resistant, and they can be easily moulded and dyed bright colours. The problem arises because most plastics are not **biodegradable** – there are no natural micro-organisms that can break them down.

Some modern plastics are suitable for re-use. Soft-drinks bottles can be made from a plastic with the trade name 'polyethylene terephthalate' (PET) (Figure **11.20**). These bottles are sturdy and have several advantages for this particular use. In some countries, schemes for the re-use of these bottles are operated. However, such a re-use policy is not suitable for most plastics. So what **do** we do with our waste plastic? We must either recycle it or dispose of it. Recycling is more economical and satisfactory than the alternative, of depositing plastic waste in landfill sites. But there are problems with recycling because most plastic waste is a mixture of different types.

Figure 11.20 Soft-drinks bottles are often made from polyethylene terephthalate, PET.

Identification numbers and symbols (Figure **11.21**) are in use to identify different plastics for recycling. Methods of sorting plastic waste by optical scanners, or manually, are being introduced. Once sorted, alternative treatments are available for recycling the different types of plastic waste.

Incineration can be used to burn plastic waste, though care must be taken not to release toxic fumes into the air. Incineration of PVC, for instance, can release acidic fumes of hydrogen chloride. **Pyrolysis** – the burning of the plastic waste at around 600 °C in the absence of air – is an alternative to incineration. Most of the products from pyrolysis can be used as fuels or separated by fractional distillation (Figure **11.22**). They can then be made into monomers for making more plastics. Research is also being carried out to produce plastics that are biodegradable or **photodegradable** (can be broken down by the action of light). A poly(ethenol) plastic has been developed that is soluble in hot water.

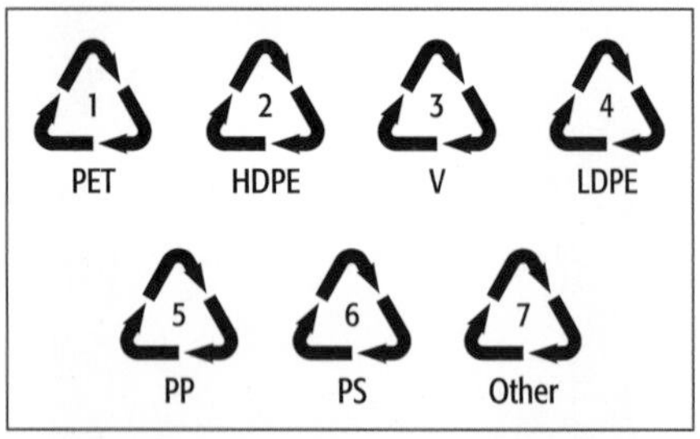

Figure 11.21 Different identification symbols help with the sorting of plastics for recycling. The symbols stand for the following plastics: 1 = polyethylene terephthalate(PET); 2 = high-density poly(ethene); 3 = vinyl polymers such as PVC; 4 = low-density poly(ethene); 5 = poly(propene); 6 = poly(styrene); 7 = others, such as multi-layer plastics.

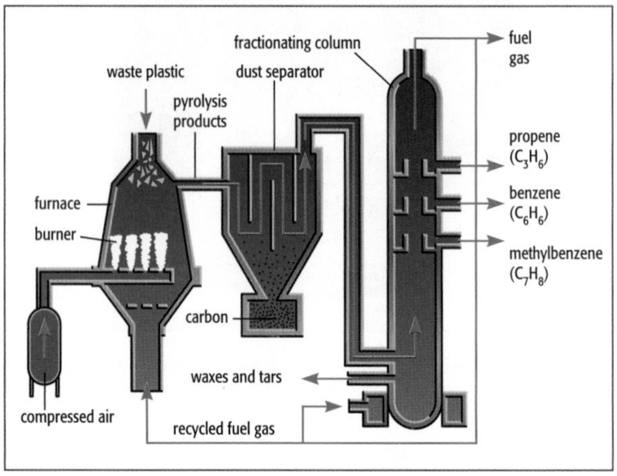

Figure 11.22 Pyrolysis of plastic waste can yield useful fuels and other products.

Biological polymers

All living organisms rely on polymers for their existence. These polymers range from the very complex DNA which makes life itself possible to the more straightforward proteins and carbohydrates that keep living things 'running'.

Proteins

Proteins are what cells are made of. All the tissues and organs of our bodies are made up of protein. In addition, enzymes, which are responsible for controlling the body's chemical reactions, are proteins. DNA makes life possible and allows living things to reproduce, but without proteins there would be no structure or chemistry to keep the living things going.

Proteins are built from **amino acid** monomers. There are 20 different amino acids used, and they each contain two functional groups —NH_2 and —COOH. Glycine and alanine are two of the simplest amino acids. When they react together, an amide linkage (or peptide linkage) is formed to produce a **dipeptide** (two amino acids joined together):

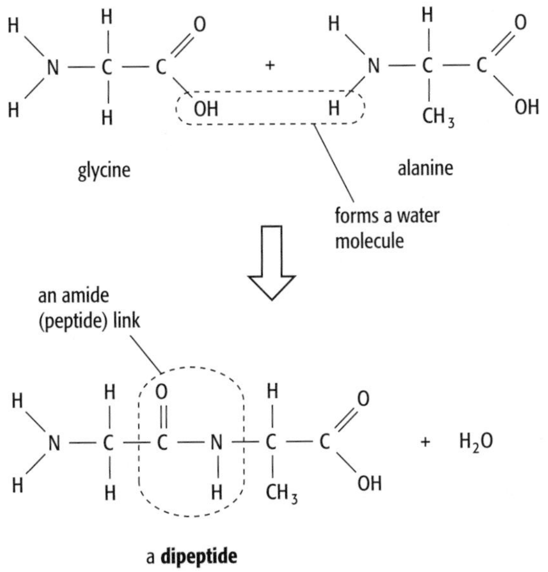

When this is repeated many times using the different amino acids, a polymer is formed. Short polymers (up to 15 amino acids) are known as **peptides**. Chains with between 15 and 100 amino acids are known as **polypeptides**. Chains involving more than 100 amino acids are called **proteins**.

Protein analysis

Proteins can be hydrolysed (broken down) to amino acids by heating in concentrated hydrochloric acid. This is the reverse of the condensation process that formed them:

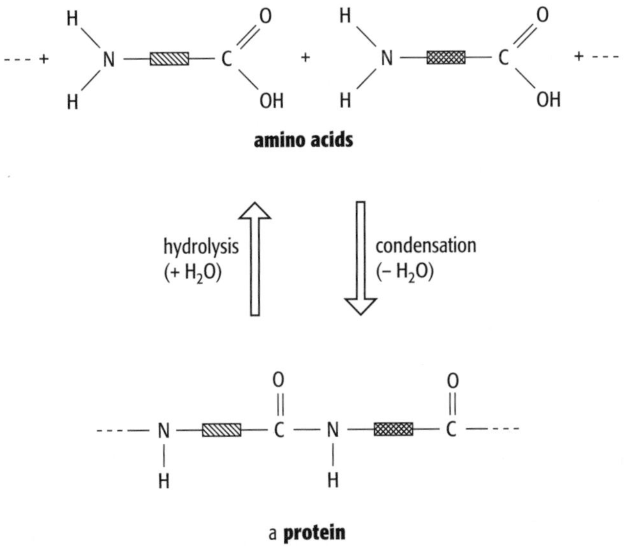

The mixture of amino acids can then be separated by chromatography (see page **347**). Amino acids are colourless substances, so a locating agent is used. The locating agent reacts with the amino acids to produce coloured spots.

Carbohydrates

The sugar we use to sweeten our tea or coffee is sucrose ($C_{12}H_{22}O_{11}$). This is just one example of a carbohydrate; glucose ($C_6H_{12}O_6$) is another.

Carbohydrates are an important source of energy in our bodies, and in all living organisms. A carbohydrate is a compound containing carbon, hydrogen and oxygen only. The ratio of hydrogen to oxygen is always 2 : 1 (as in water).

All long-chain carbohydrates (**polysaccharides**) are long-chain condensation polymers of sugar molecules (monosaccharides). **Starch**, for example, is a polysaccharide found in plants. Condensation polymerisation of sugar monomers produces such long-chain carbohydrates.

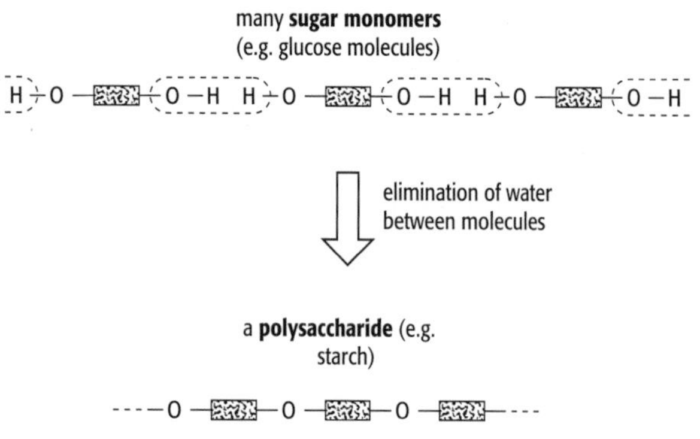

Starch and glycogen are two different polysaccharides of glucose, a monosaccharide. They store the glucose in an insoluble form in plants and animals, respectively. When energy is needed, cells break down the starch or glycogen back to glucose. The glucose is then oxidised by respiration. Cellulose is a third polymer of glucose. It forms the fibrous structure of plant cell walls. These three polymers differ in the way in which the glucose monomer units are linked together.

Polysaccharides can be broken down in the laboratory by warming with hydrochloric acid (**acid hydrolysis**). The sugars present in the hydrolysis mixture can then be analysed by chromatography (see page **347**). A locating agent must be used to detect the spots, because sugars are colourless. An interesting comparison is to analyse the products of the acid and enzyme digestions of starch. Acid hydrolysis breaks down starch to give glucose. However, the enzyme amylase present in human saliva only breaks starch down to give maltose. This is a molecule made of two glucose units joined together. The difference can be seen on chromatography of the products.

The presence of starch can be detected by testing with iodine solution: the solution turns a deep blue colour.

Food

Proteins, fats and carbohydrates are the main constituents of food. They are all digested by cells and organisms, and are converted back to their monomers. These monomers are then used as the building blocks for new molecular structures or as sources of energy. Our bodies can make a whole range of molecules necessary for our cells to function properly. However, some of these building blocks must come from our diet. For instance, there are some amino acids that we must obtain from our food. These are known as the **essential amino acids**.

Fats and oils are mixtures of large molecules that are the esters of long-chain acid molecules and glycerol. Fats that contain unsaturated acids are called unsaturated or poly-unsaturated fats, depending on the number of C=C double bonds in the chain. Fats that contain saturated chains are known as saturated fats. There is evidence that eating a lot of animal fat, which is higher in saturated fats, may increase the risk of heart disease.

Fats and oils (**lipids**) are an essential part of our diet.

- They are an energy source; lipids provide about twice as much energy per gram as do carbohydrates.
- They provide thermal insulation for the body.
- Some vitamins, for example A, D and E, are insoluble in water but soluble in lipids; foods containing lipids provide these vitamins.
- Lipids are an essential part of cell membranes.

Key ideas so far

- Condensation polymerisation is a second way in which monomers can join together to make a polymer.
- In condensation polymerisation, each time a link is made between the monomers a water molecule, or similar small molecule, is formed.
- Nylon is an artificial condensation polymer. The monomers are joined by an amide (or peptide) link.
- Polyesters are a further example of condensation polymers. Terylene is an example of a polyester. The monomers are joined by an ester link.
- Certain natural biological polymers are condensation polymers.
- Proteins are made from amino acids. There are 20 different amino acids that go to make up proteins. The amino acids are joined together by the amide (peptide) link.
- Long-chain carbohydrates are also condensation polymers in which sugar molecules, such as glucose, are joined together.
- Starch is a polymer of glucose in plants.
- Proteins and carbohydrates can be hydrolysed back to their monomers.

Quick-check questions

1 Name **two** natural condensation polymers.

2 What are the essential features of condensation polymerisation?

3 Name **two** artificial condensation polymers, and specify the type of linkage present in each.

4 Draw schematic diagrams representing the formation of

   a Terylene and

   b starch, showing the linkage between the monomers (the structure of the monomer is not required and can be represented as a block).

5 Nylon is a synthetic macromolecule which is held together by the same linkage as protein molecules.

   a What is the name of this linkage?

   b Draw a diagram of the structure of nylon (again, the structure of the monomer is not required and can be represented as a block).

   c Give a major difference between the structure of nylon and of a protein.

   d How can proteins be chemically broken back down to amino acids?

Summary

You should know that:

- there are three major fossil fuels – coal, petroleum (crude oil) and natural gas
- these fuels were created by the action of heat and pressure on buried organic material acting over geological periods of time
- these resources are a source of energy and also of a wide variety of chemicals
- the fractional distillation of crude oil produces a series of different hydrocarbon fractions, each with its own uses
- these hydrocarbons can be further changed by processes such as catalytic cracking – producing shorter-chain alkane molecules and alkenes from the original longer chains
- alkene molecules (containing a C=C double bond) can be polymerised into very useful products
- other unsaturated molecules can be polymerised to extend the range of useful addition polymers
- there are natural and synthetic polymers that are made by a process other than addition polymerisation
- these polymers are produced by condensation polymerisation, and include nylons and polyesters
- plastic materials are usually non-biodegradable and pose problems for waste disposal
- very important biological polymers are also produced by condensation polymerisation, for example DNA, proteins and carbohydrates
- a variety of different protein molecules occur naturally, but one important group is the enzymes – the biological catalysts that control metabolism
- proteins, carbohydrates and fats are the main types of food substances – vitamins, though needed only in small quantities, are important for good health.

Exam-style questions

1 a Distillation can be modified to separate petroleum into useful fractions.

The diagram below shows some of the different fractions obtained from a fractionating column.

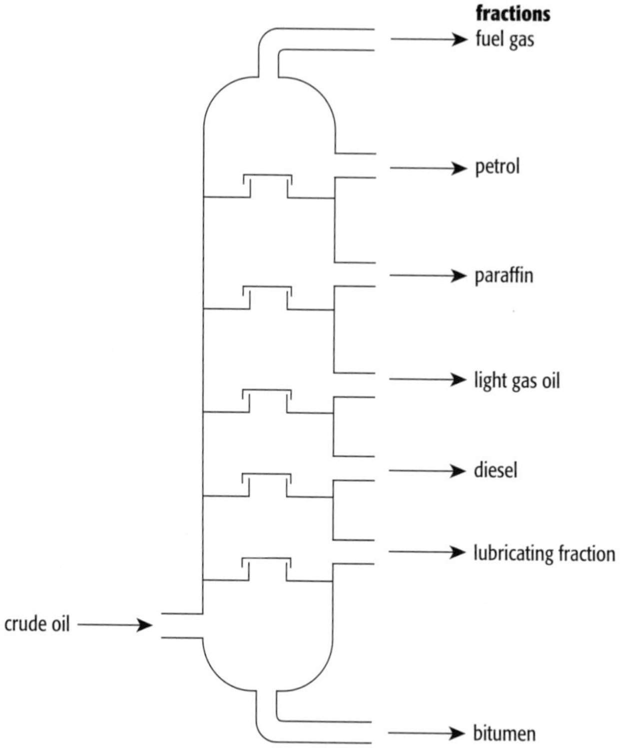

i Which of these fractions has the lowest boiling point?

ii State **one** use for each of the following fractions: paraffin and bitumen. [3]

b Petroleum is a mixture of organic compounds.

Which **one** of the following best describes the compounds found in petroleum?

acids **alcohols** **carbohydrates** **hydrocarbons** [1]

c Before petroleum is fractionated, it is often heated to remove dissolved natural gas. Most of this natural gas is methane, CH_4. Draw a diagram to show how the electrons are arranged in methane. Show hydrogen electrons as •, and carbon electrons as ×. [2]

d Methane, ethane and propane belong to a particular homologous series of compound.

State the name of the homologous series to which these three compounds belong. [1]

CIE IGCSE, November 2003, paper 2, q.1 part

2 Ethene can be made by cracking certain hydrocarbon fractions.

a Explain what is meant by the term **cracking**. [1]

b Copy and complete the equation for the cracking of tetradecane, $C_{14}H_{30}$.

$C_{14}H_{30} \rightarrow$ .... + C_2H_4 [1]

c Ethanol is formed when steam reacts with ethene at high pressure and temperature.

A catalyst of phosphoric acid is used.

ethane + steam $\rightleftharpoons$ ethanol

i What is the function of the catalyst? [1]

ii What is the meaning of the symbol $\rightleftharpoons$? [1]

iii Ethanol is also formed when yeast grows in sugar solution. What is this process called? Choose from the following types of reaction.

addition **combustion** **fermentation** **neutralisation** [1]

CIE IGCSE, June 2008, paper 2, q.6 part

3 The diagram shows a biogas digester. Animal and vegetable waste is fermented by bacteria. The gas produced is a mixture of mainly carbon dioxide and methane.

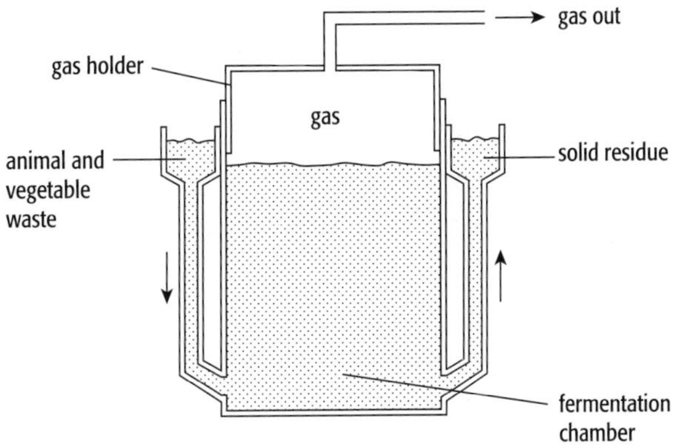

a State the name given to the energy-releasing process in which organisms use food and produce carbon dioxide. [1]

b Hydrogen is also produced during the fermentation.
The hydrogen reacts with the carbon dioxide to form methane and oxygen.

i Copy and complete the equation for this reaction.

$CO_2 + 2H_2 \rightarrow$ .... + ... [2]

ii Suggest a use for the methane produced in this reaction. [1]

iii Describe the arrangement and motion of the molecules in methane gas. [2]

iv State the name of the homologous series to which methane belongs. [1]

v Which one of the following compounds is in the same homologous series as methane?

C_2H_4 C_2H_6 CH_3OH CH_3CO_2H [1]

c Which **one** of the following equations **A**, **B**, **C** or **D** describes fermentation?

A $CH_4 + H_2O \rightarrow CO + 3H_2$

B $C_6H_{12}O_6 + 6O_2 \rightarrow 6H_2O + 6CO_2$

C $C_6H_{12}O_6 \rightarrow 2C_2H_5OH + 2CO_2$

D $C_6H_{14} \rightarrow C_4H_{10} + C_2H_4$ [1]

d Many of the reactions occurring in the biogas digester are catalysed by enzymes.

i Suggest where the enzymes come from. [1]

ii Define the term **catalysis.** [1]

e The solid residue from the biogas digester can be used as a fertiliser.
State the names of **two** non-metallic elements found in fertilisers which are needed for plant growth. [2]

CIE IGCSE, June 2006, paper 2, q.2

4 Poly(ethene) is a plastic which is made by polymerising ethene, C_2H_4.

a Which one of the following best describes the ethene molecules in this reaction?

alcohols alkanes monomers polymers products [1]

b The structure of ethane is shown below.

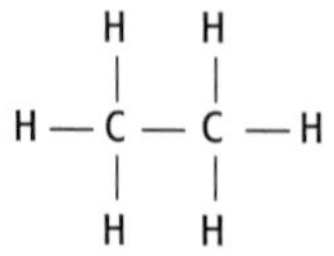

Explain, by referring to its bonding, why ethane cannot be polymerised. [1]

c Draw the structure of ethene, showing all atoms and bonds. [1]

d Ethene is obtained by cracking alkanes.

i Explain the meaning of the term **cracking**. [1]

ii What condition is needed to crack alkanes? [1]

iii Copy and complete the equation for cracking decane, $C_{10}H_{22}$. [1]

$C_{10}H_{22} \rightarrow C_2H_4 + \ldots\ldots\ldots\ldots\ldots .$

e Some oil companies 'crack' the ethane produced when petroleum is distilled.

i Copy and complete the equation for this reaction. [1]

$C_2H_6 \rightarrow C_2H_4 + \ldots\ldots\ldots\ldots\ldots$

ii Describe the process of fractional distillation which is used to separate the different fractions in petroleum. [2]

iii State a use for the following petroleum fractions: the petrol fraction and the lubricating fraction. [2]

CIE IGCSE, June 2005, paper 2, q.4

S

5 Alkenes are unsaturated hydrocarbons. They undergo addition reactions.

a Two of the methods of making alkenes are cracking and the thermal decomposition of chloroalkanes.

i Write an equation for the cracking of the alkane, decane ($C_{10}H_{22}$).

ii Propene can be made by the thermal decomposition of chloropropane.

Describe how chloropropane can be made from propane, giving the reagents and conditions. [4]

b The following alkenes are isomers.

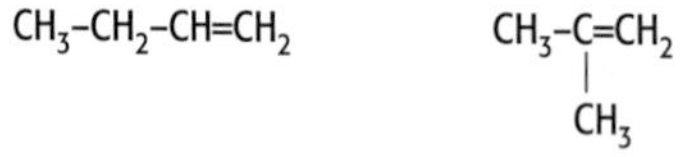

i Explain why they are isomers.

ii Give the name and structural formula of another hydrocarbon that is isomeric with the above. [4]

c Give the name of the product when but-1-ene reacts with each of the following: steam, hydrogen and bromine. [3]

d Alkenes can polymerise.

i Deduce the name and structural formula of the monomer from the structure of the polymer.

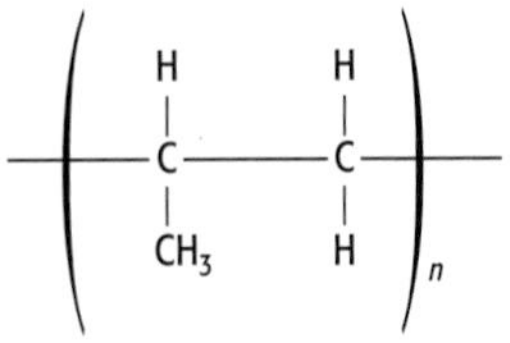

ii Draw the structure of the polymer formed from the following monomer.

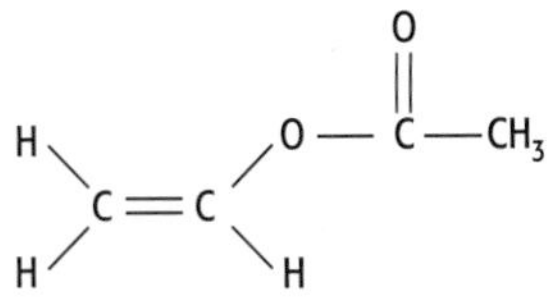

[4]

iii Describe the pollution problems caused by the disposal of polymers in landfill sites and by burning. [3]

CIE IGCSE, June 2003, paper 3, q.3

6 In 2002, Swedish scientists found high levels of acrylamide in starchy foods that had been cooked above 120 °C. Acrylamide, which is thought to be a risk to human health, has the following structure.

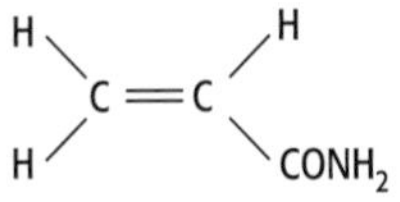

a **i** It readily polymerises to polyacrylamide. Draw the structure of this polymer. [2]

ii Starch is formed by polymerisation. It has a structure of the type shown below. Name the monomer. [1]

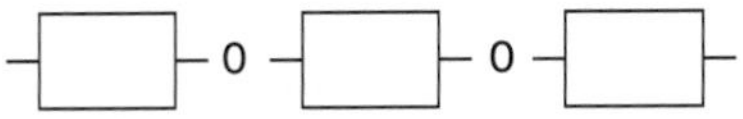

iii What are the differences between these two polymerisation reactions, one forming polyacrylamide and the other starch? [2]

b Acrylamide hydrolyses to form acrylic acid and ammonium ions.

i Describe the test for the ammonium ion. [3]

ii Given an aqueous solution, concentration 0.1 mol/dm^3, how could you show that acrylic acid is a weak acid? [2]

c The structural formula of acrylic acid is shown below. It forms compounds called acrylates.

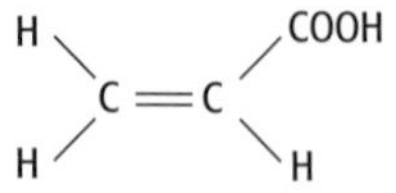

i Acrylic acid reacts with ethanol to form the following compound.

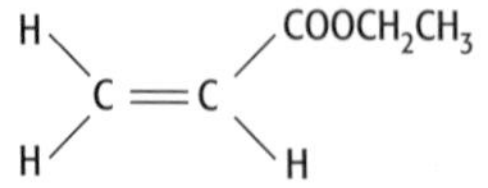

Deduce the name of this compound. What type of organic compound is it? [2]

ii Acrylic acid is an unsaturated compound. It will react with bromine.
Describe the colour change, [2]
and draw the structural formula of the product of this addition reaction. [2]

CIE IGCSE, June 2004, paper 3, q.6

7 Esters, fats and polyesters all contain the ester linkage.

a The structural formula of an ester is given below.

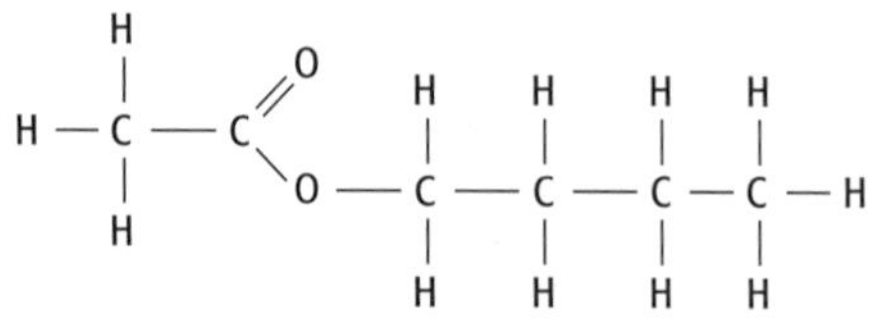

Name **two** chemicals that could be used to make this ester [2]
and draw their structural formulae showing all bonds. [2]

b i Draw the structural formula of a polyester such as Terylene. [2]

ii Suggest a use for this polymer. [1]

c Cooking products, fats and vegetable oils, are mixtures of saturated and unsaturated esters.
One way of measuring the degree of unsaturation of a fat or oil is to find the iodine number of the unsaturated compound. This is the mass of iodine that reacts with all the double bonds in 100 g of the fat.
Use the following information to calculate the number of double bonds in one molecule of a fat.
Mass of one mole of the fat is 884 g.
One mole of I_2 reacts with one mole of C=C double bonds
The iodine number of the fat is 86.2 g.
Complete the following calculation.
100 g of fat reacts with 86.2 g of iodine.
884 g of fat reacts with .... g of iodine.
One mole of fat reacts with .... moles of iodine molecules.
Number of double bonds in one molecule of fat is .... [3]

CIE IGCSE, June 2007, paper 3, q.7 part

8 The three types of food are carbohydrates, proteins and fats.

a Aqueous starch is hydrolysed to maltose by the enzyme amylase. The formula of maltose is:

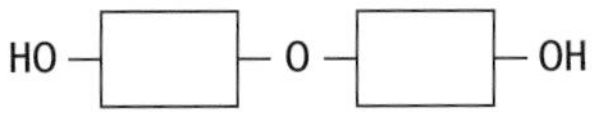

Starch is hydrolysed by dilute sulfuric acid to glucose:

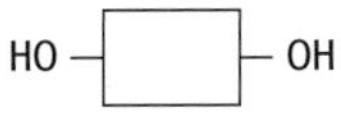

i What is an enzyme? [1]

ii Draw the structure of starch. [1]

iii Name the technique that would show that the products of these two hydrolyses are different. [1]

b Proteins have the same linkage as nylon but there is more than one monomer in the macromolecule.

i Draw the structure of a protein. [2]

ii What class of compound is formed by the hydrolysis of proteins? [1]

c Fats are esters. Some fats are saturated, others are unsaturated.

i Write the word equation for the preparation of the ester, propyl ethanoate. [2]

ii Deduce the structural formula of this ester, showing each individual bond. [2]

iii How could you distinguish between these two fats? Describe the test and the results for the two fats.

Fat 1 has the formula

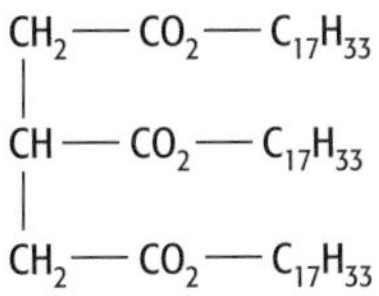

Fat 2 has the formula

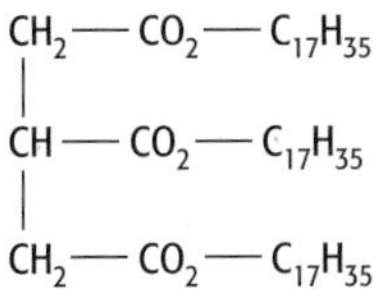

[3]

iv Both of these fats are hydrolysed by boiling with aqueous sodium hydroxide.
What two types of compounds are formed? [2]

CIE IGCSE, November 2006, paper 3, q.8

9 Esters occur naturally in plants and animals. They are manufactured from petroleum.
Ethyl ethanoate and butyl ethanoate are industrially important as solvents.

a **i** Explain the term **solvent**. [1]

ii Give the formula of ethyl ethanoate. [1]

iii Ethyl ethanoate can be made from ethanol and ethanoic acid. Describe how these chemicals can be made.

ethanol from ethene [2]

ethanoic acid from ethanol [2]

iv Name **two** chemicals from which butyl ethanoate can be made. [1]

b The following equation represents the alkaline hydrolysis of a naturally occurring ester.

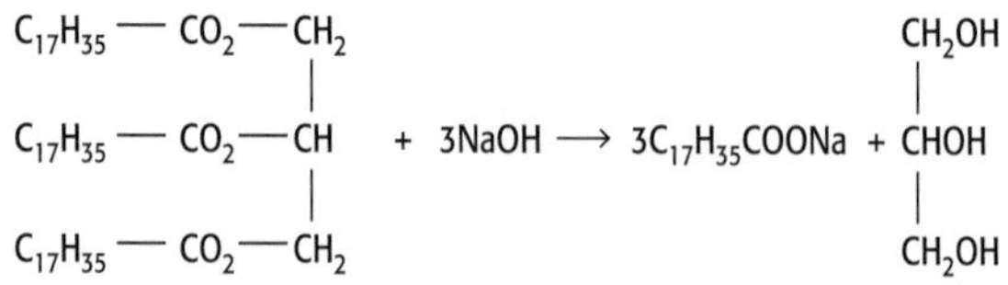

i Which substance in the above equation is an alcohol? [1]

ii What is the major use for compounds of the type $C_{17}H_{35}COONa$? [1]

c A polymer has the structure shown below.

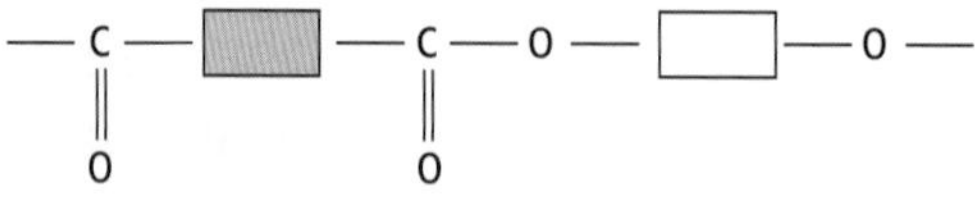

i What type of polymer is this? [1]

ii Using the rectangles coding for the central parts of the monomers, give the structures from which the above polymer could be made.

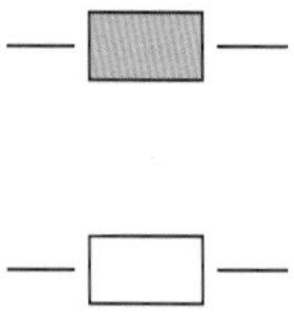

[2]

d Esters are frequently used as solvents in chromatography. A natural macromolecule was hydrolysed to give a mixture of amino acids. These could be identified by chromatography.

i What type of macromolecule was hydrolysed? [1]

ii What type of linkage was broken by hydrolysis? [1]

iii Explain why the chromatogram must be sprayed with a locating agent before the amino acids can be identified. [1]

iv Explain how it is possible to identify the amino acids from the chromatogram. [2]

CIE IGCSE, November 2003, paper 3, q.4

12 Chemical analysis and investigation

This chapter covers the following ideas:

- testing for anions
- testing for cations
- testing for gases
- collecting and drying gases
- testing pH
- testing for water
- test for unsaturated hydrocarbons
- ethanol and ethanoic acid
- chromatography

The following areas are assessed in the 'practical assessment' part of the examination:

- the nature of the scientific method
- planning experimental investigations
- controlling variables
- sources of error and the display of results
- interpreting observations and data

Chemistry can be used in industry, medicine, agriculture and environmental science. Many of the uses in these areas depend on our ability to identify chemical substances. We need to know what chemicals we are dealing with. Analytical techniques, from the simple to the complex, help us to do just that. A drug company might need to analyse the drug paracetamol.
A steel-making company must check if the content of a batch of steel matched the customer's requested composition. An environmental analyst might have to check river water for contamination with small amounts of metal ions. Analytical methods are crucial to all of this, and more.

12.1 Inorganic analysis

There are certain important tests that we can use to identify gases and substances in solution. Testing for inorganic compounds is important in itself, but also because it introduces some of the methods behind this type of analysis. In the first instance, we simply want to know *which* compound is present. This type of analysis is known as **qualitative analysis**. We need to find a reaction that clearly indicates that a particular ion is present. It must be a reaction which only works for that ion. The most useful reactions are precipitation reactions – where two solutions are mixed and an insoluble product is formed. The alternative to forming a characteristic precipitate is to produce a gas that can be tested.

Testing for anions

The tests for the common **anions** (negative ions) are listed in Table **12.1** (overleaf). For example, silver nitrate solution can be used to identify halide ions in solution. All chlorides will react with silver nitrate solution to give a white precipitate of silver chloride, AgCl, all bromides give a cream precipitate of silver bromide, AgBr, and all iodides a yellow precipitate of silver iodide, AgI (Figure **12.1**, overleaf).

Testing for cations

Once we have identified the anion present, the remaining part of the puzzle is to see which **cation** (positive ion) is present in the compound. The situation

Negative ion	Test	Test result[a]
carbonate (CO_3^{2-})	add dilute hydrochloric acid to solid	effervescence (fizzes), carbon dioxide produced (test with limewater)
chloride (Cl^-) (in solution)	acidify solution with dilute nitric acid, then add aqueous silver nitrate	white ppt. of silver chloride formed: ppt. soluble in ammonia solution
bromide (Br^-) (in solution)	acidify solution with dilute nitric acid, then add aqueous silver nitrate	cream ppt. of silver bromide formed: only slightly soluble in ammonia solution
iodide (I^-) (in solution)	acidify solution with dilute nitric acid, then add aqueous silver nitrate	yellow ppt. of silver iodide formed: insoluble in ammonia solution
sulfate (SO_4^{2-}) (in solution)	acidify solution with dilute hydrochloric acid, then add barium chloride solution OR acidify solution with dilute nitric acid, then add barium nitrate solution	white ppt. of barium sulfate formed white ppt. of barium sulfate formed
nitrate (NO_3^-) (in solution)	make solution alkaline with sodium hydroxide solution, then add aluminium foil (or Devarda's alloy) and warm carefully	ammonia gas given off (test with moist red litmus)

[a]*Note: ppt. = precipitate.*

Table 12.1 Tests for negative ions (anions).

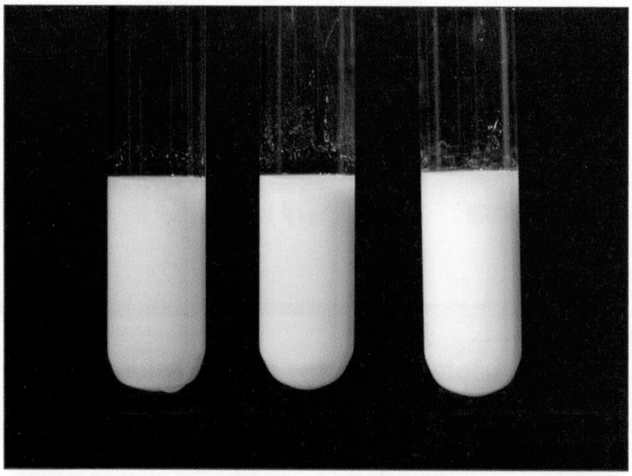

Figure 12.1 The precipitates produced in the tests for halide ions using silver nitrate. The precipitates are silver chloride (white), silver bromide (cream) and silver iodide (yellow).

Metal ion	Formula	Colour of flame
sodium	Na^+	yellow
potassium	K^+	lilac
calcium	Ca^{2+}	brick red (orange-red)
lithium	Li^+	crimson
copper	Cu^{2+}	blue-green
barium	Ba^{2+}	apple green

Table 12.2 Some flame test colours.

is more complicated, as there are more common alternatives, but the basic approach is the same.

We are helped in testing for positive ions by the fact that certain metal ions will give a characteristic colour in the flame test. If a clean nichrome wire is dipped in a metal compound and then held in the hot part of a Bunsen flame, the flame may become coloured (see Figure 8.2, page 233, and Table 12.2).

The precipitation tests for metal ions are based on the fact that most metal hydroxides are insoluble. Some are also coloured and are therefore easily identified. Together these precipitation tests form the basis of a strategy for identifying the common metal ions in solutions of various salts (Figure 12.2). Table 12.3 lists the different tests used to identify positive ions using sodium hydroxide (a strong alkali) and ammonia solution (a weak alkali).

When adding the alkali, add it slowly at first (one drop at a time). If it is added too quickly, it is easy to miss a precipitate that re-dissolves in excess.

When carrying out an analysis using these tests, try not to forget the background chemistry involved. The hydroxides of aluminium and zinc re-dissolve in excess sodium hydroxide because they are amphoteric hydroxides – they react with both acids and bases (see page 143). The hydroxides of the other metals in the table do not re-dissolve in excess sodium hydroxide because they are basic hydroxides – reacting only with acids in neutralisation reactions.

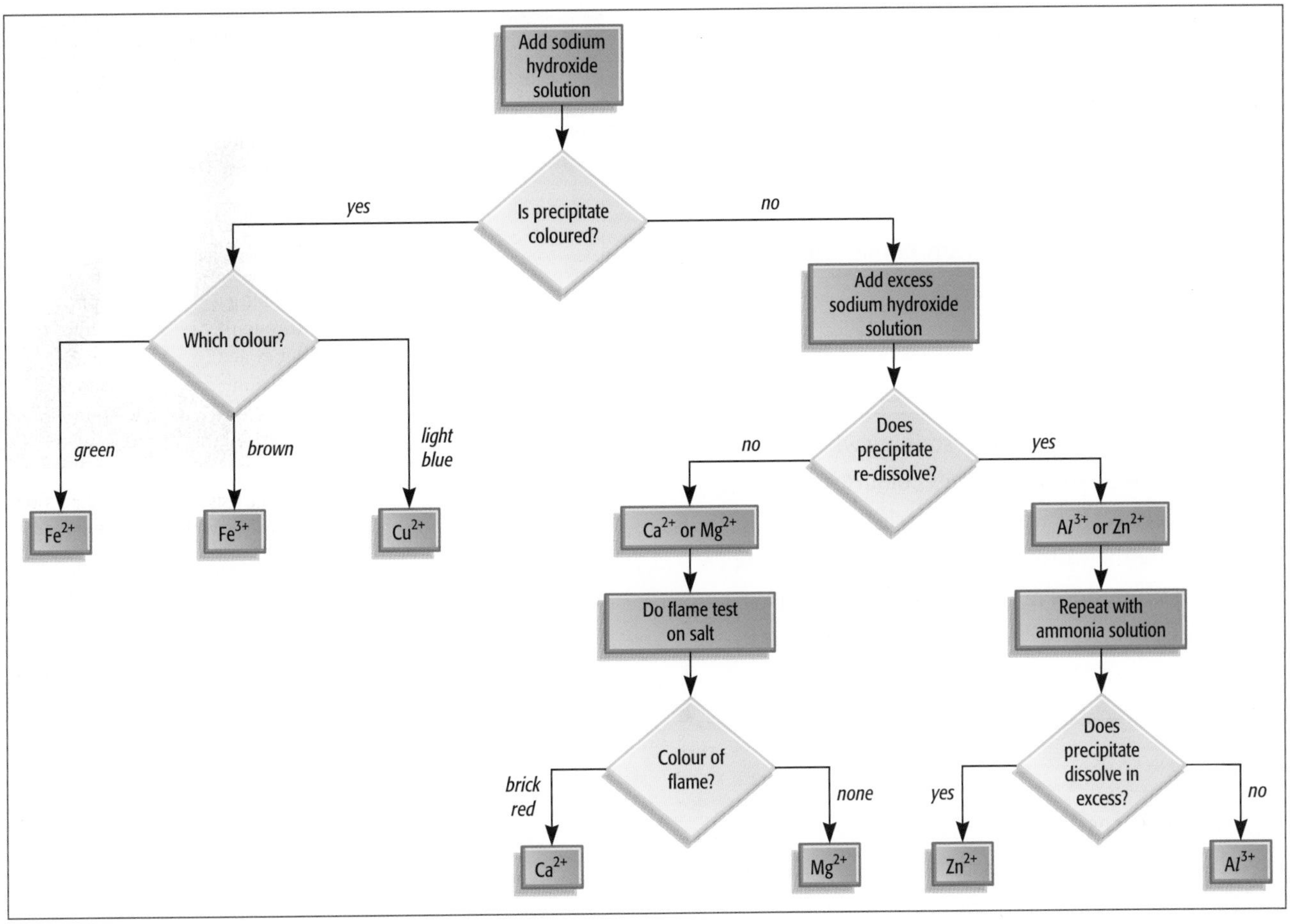

Figure 12.2 The strategy behind testing for metal ions in salts.

Positive ion (in solution)	Effect of adding sodium hydroxide[a]	Effect of adding ammonia solution[a]
ammonium (NH_4^+)	ammonia produced on warming (test with damp red litmus paper)	—
copper(II) (Cu^{2+})	light blue gelatinous ppt. of copper hydroxide; insoluble in excess sodium hydroxide	light blue gelatinous ppt.; dissolves in excess ammonia, giving a deep blue solution
iron(II) (Fe^{2+})	green gelatinous ppt. of iron(II) hydroxide; insoluble in excess	green gelatinous ppt.; insoluble in excess
iron(III) (Fe^{3+})	rust-brown gelatinous ppt. of iron(III) hydroxide; insoluble in excess	rust-brown gelatinous ppt.; insoluble in excess
calcium (Ca^{2+})	white ppt. of calcium hydroxide; insoluble in excess	no ppt. (or only a very slight ppt.)
magnesium (Mg^{2+})	white ppt. of magnesium hydroxide; insoluble in excess	white ppt.; insoluble in excess
zinc (Zn^{2+})	white ppt. of zinc hydroxide; soluble in excess, giving a colourless solution	white ppt.; soluble in excess
aluminium (Al^{3+})	white ppt. of aluminium hydroxide; soluble in excess, giving a colourless solution	white ppt.; insoluble in excess

[a]*Note: ppt. = precipitate.*

Table 12.3 Tests for positive ions (cations).

Exam tip

It is important to learn the tests in Tables **12.1** and **12.3** because you will not have a copy of them in the written examinations, where questions often need knowledge of these tests.

Indeed these tests, and those for gases, are regularly asked for as part of any of the exam papers you will take.

Exam tip

You must be careful, when describing when a precipitate re-dissolves to give a colourless solution, to use precisely that word – 'colourless'. Many students use the word 'clear' here and this is wrong; the word 'clear' does not mean the same thing as colourless, and you will not gain the mark for it in an exam.

The tests for gases

Several of the tests for anions and cations involve detecting gases produced by the test reactions. The gas tests are another important set of general analytical tests (Table **12.4**). The test for carbon dioxide is shown in Figure **12.3**.

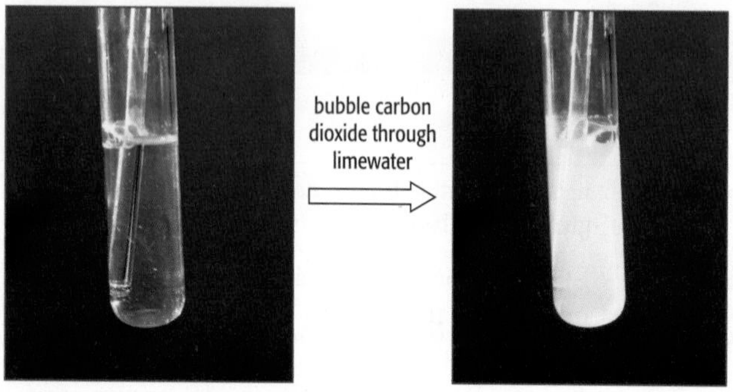

Figure 12.3 The limewater test for carbon dioxide.

Gas	Colour and smell	Test	Test result
ammonia (NH_3)	colourless, pungent smell	hold damp red litmus paper (or Universal Indicator paper) in gas	indicator paper turns blue
carbon dioxide (CO_2)	colourless, odourless	bubble gas through limewater (calcium hydroxide solution)	white ppt. of calcium carbonate formed (solution turns milky) (Figure **12.3**)
chlorine[a] (Cl_2)	pale green, choking smell	hold damp litmus paper (or Universal Indicator paper) in gas	indicator paper is bleached white (blue litmus will turn red first)
hydrogen (H_2)	colourless, odourless	hold a lighted splint in gas	hydrogen burns with a squeaky 'pop'
oxygen (O_2)	colourless, odourless	hold a 'glowing' wooden splint in gas	the splint re-lights

[a] *This gas is poisonous, so test with care and use a fume cupboard.*

Table 12.4 Tests for gases.

To study gases further, samples can be collected in a variety of ways, depending on their density and solubility in water.

Methods of collecting gases

There are four general methods of collecting gases – the apparatus used in each case is shown in Figure **12.4**.

- **Downward delivery** is used for gases that are denser than air (Figure **12.4a**).
- **Upward delivery** is used for gases that are less dense than air (Figure **12.4b**).
- Collection over water is used for gases that are not very soluble in water (Figure **12.4c**).
- Collection in a gas syringe is useful when the volume of gas needs to be measured (Figure **12.4d**).

Sometimes it is necessary to produce a gas by a reaction that requires heating. In such cases, there is a danger of 'sucking back' if the gas is collected over water. The problem arises if heating is stopped **before** the delivery tube is removed from the water. The reduced pressure in the reaction tube as it cools results in water rising up the delivery tube. In the worst case, the cold water can

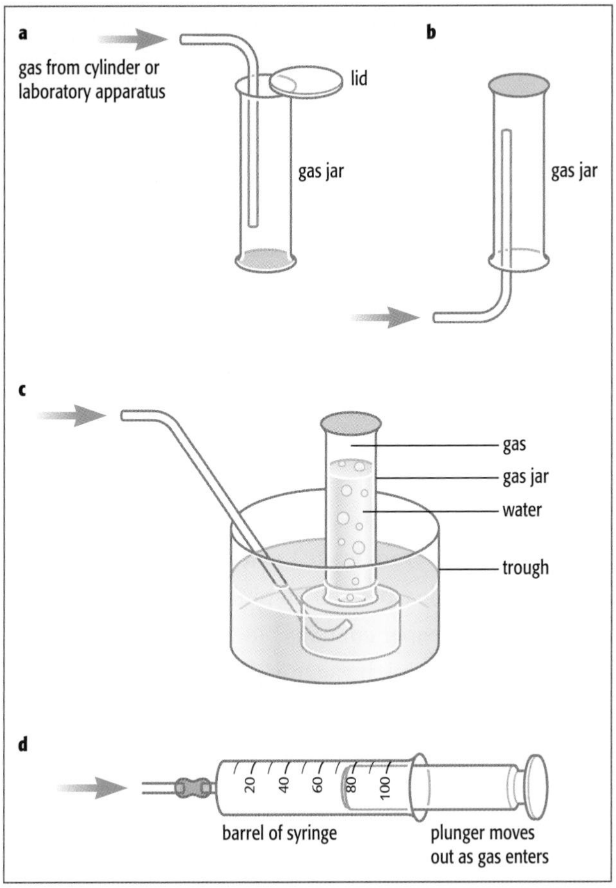

Figure 12.4 The different methods for collecting gases: **a** downward delivery, **b** upward delivery, **c** collection over water, and **d** collection in a gas syringe.

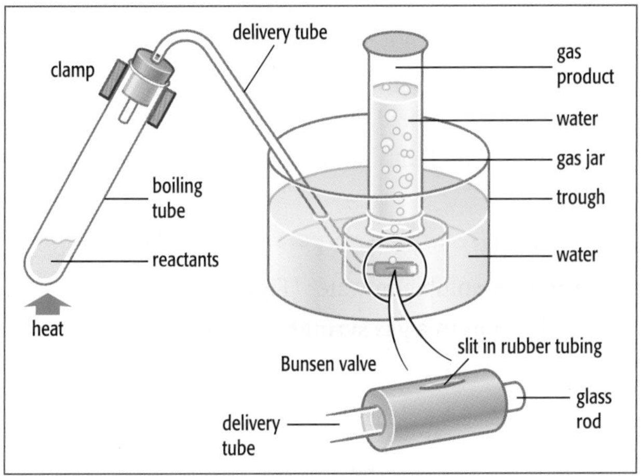

Figure 12.5 Using a Bunsen valve to prevent 'sucking back'.

be sucked back into the hot boiling tube. The tube will crack and an explosion may occur. 'Sucking back' can be prevented by making sure that the delivery tube is removed first, before heating is stopped. Alternatively, a **Bunsen valve** (Figure 12.5) can be fitted to the end of the tube.

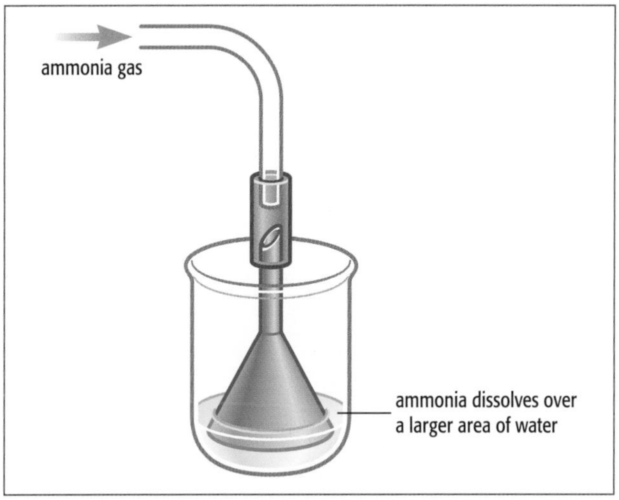

Figure 12.6 Making a solution of a very soluble gas.

One other useful adaptation for the delivery of gases is used for making a solution of a gas that is very soluble in water, for example ammonia or hydrogen chloride. The adaptation is shown in Figure 12.6. The filter funnel increases the area over which the gas can dissolve, and prevents water rising up the delivery tube into the reaction vessel.

Methods of drying gases

Quite often we need to produce a **dry** sample of gas. This is done by passing the gas through a **drying agent**. Figure 12.7 (overleaf) gives the appropriate method for the three commonest drying agents. The different drying agents are suitable for particular gases.

- Concentrated sulfuric acid is used to dry all gases except ammonia.
- Anhydrous calcium chloride is used for all gases except ammonia, which forms a complex with calcium chloride.
- Calcium oxide is used to dry ammonia and neutral gases.

Other tests

There are the two other useful general tests that we need to consider. Then our discussion of qualitative inorganic analysis is complete.

pH testing

The acidity or alkalinity of a solution can be tested using indicator papers (usually litmus or Universal Indicator,

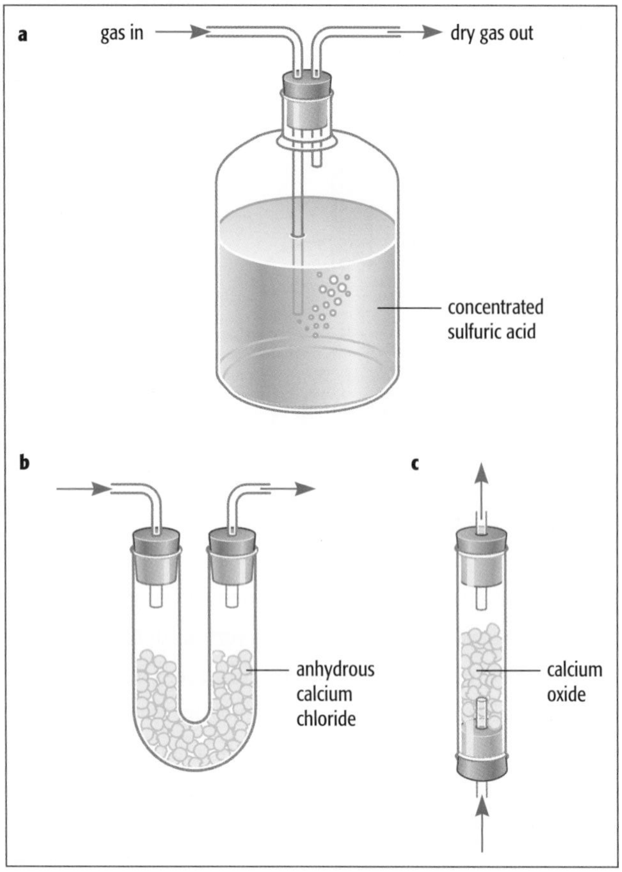

Figure 12.7 The different methods of drying gases with **a** sulfuric acid, **b** anhydrous calcium chloride, and **c** calcium oxide.

see page 138). It is not very good chemical practice to dip the paper directly into the solution. Instead, a glass rod should be used to place a drop of the solution on the paper. Measurements of pH and other analyses are often carried out on soil samples. Soil is stirred with distilled water. The insoluble material settles out and the remaining solution can be tested with Universal Indicator paper. The pH of soil can be important, as different plants 'prefer' to grow at different pH.

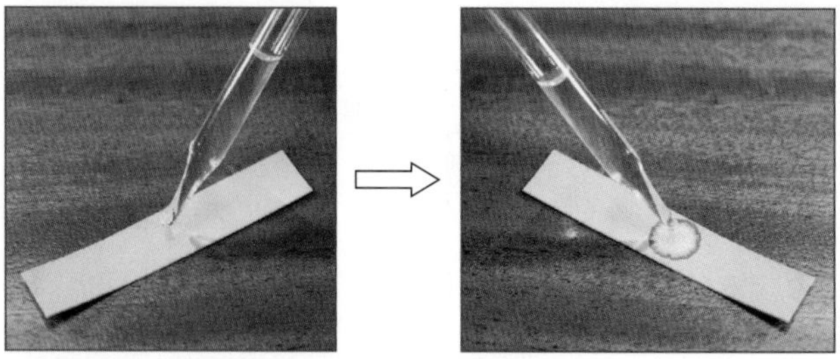

Figure 12.8 The test for the presence of water using cobalt chloride paper. The paper turns from blue to pink.

Testing for the presence of water

Not all neutral colourless liquids are water. The **presence** of water can be detected using anhydrous copper(II) sulfate or cobalt(II) chloride. Water will turn anhydrous copper(II) sulfate from white to blue, and anhydrous cobalt(II) chloride from blue to pink (Figure **12.8**). Cobalt chloride paper contains blue anhydrous cobalt chloride. It turns pink if water is present. To decide whether a liquid is **pure** water, you would need to test to show that its boiling point is exactly 100 °C.

The purity of a solid substance can be checked by finding its melting point. A pure substance has a sharp melting point which agrees with known values.

Exam tip

If you are asked for a chemical test for water, the boiling point will not do, as no chemical change takes place.

The cobalt chloride test is a correct answer but it will not tell you that the water is pure, only that it is there.

A test to see if water is pure must be the boiling point.

Key ideas so far

- There is a series of tests that help us to analyse substances.
- In inorganic chemistry these tests help us to find which cations (positive ions) and anions (negative ions) are present in an ionic compound.
- There is also a series of tests for gases such as hydrogen, oxygen, etc.

Quick-check questions

1 Why can many metal ions be identified by using sodium hydroxide solution?

2 Which metal hydroxides will dissolve in excess sodium hydroxide solution?

Substance	Action on Universal Indicator solution	Action on hydrochloric acid	Action on silver nitrate solution
A	goes red then bleaches	no reaction	no reaction
B	goes blue	fizzes	white precipitate
C	goes red	no reaction	white precipitate
D	stays green	no reaction	no reaction
E	stays green	no reaction	white precipitate

3 Why can iron ions give two different coloured precipitates with sodium hydroxide?

4 What gas is produced when acid is added to a solution of carbonate ions?

5 What solution will give a precipitate with halide ions?

6 What must be added before barium chloride when testing for sulfate ions?

7 Which gas is tested with a glowing splint?

8 Name a cation which is not a metal ion.

9 The table above shows the results of practical tests on substances **A** to **E**.

Choose, from **A** to **E**, the substance that is likely to be:

- **a** distilled water
- **b** sodium chloride solution
- **c** chlorine gas
- **d** hydrochloric acid.

12.2 Organic analysis

There are also tests to characterise certain organic compounds. You should be familiar with a few simple ones at this stage.

The test for unsaturated hydrocarbons

The simplest test for an unsaturated compound such as an alkene (for example, ethene) is to use bromine water (see page **292**). If the unknown compound is a liquid, then a small amount is mixed with bromine water and shaken. If the unknown compound is a gas, the gas should be bubbled through bromine water. The bromine water is initially an orange-brown colour. If the gas or liquid being tested turns it colourless, then that compound is unsaturated – it contains at least one double bond. Alkanes are saturated and would not react.

Exam tip

When describing a test, always give the colour before and after the change. For example, 'Ethene changes bromine water from brown to colourless'.

The test for ethanol and ethanoic acid

These two substances provide a simple test reaction for each other. They react with each other, with the addition of a few drops of concentrated sulfuric acid, to produce a sweet-smelling ester. The mixture is warmed gently, and the fruity smell of the ester can best be detected by pouring the reaction mixture into a beaker of water. This spreads the ester and disperses the distinctive 'pear-drop' smell (Figure **12.9**, overleaf).

Chromatography

Chromatography was originally used as a method of separating coloured substances (Figure **12.10**, overleaf). However, the usefulness of the technique has been extended by the use of locating agents to detect the presence of colourless compounds once the **chromatogram** has been produced.

The individual monomers from proteins and carbohydrates (amino acids and sugars) can be separated by chromatography. In both cases, the spots must be detected using locating agents because the compounds themselves are colourless. If a sample gives only a single

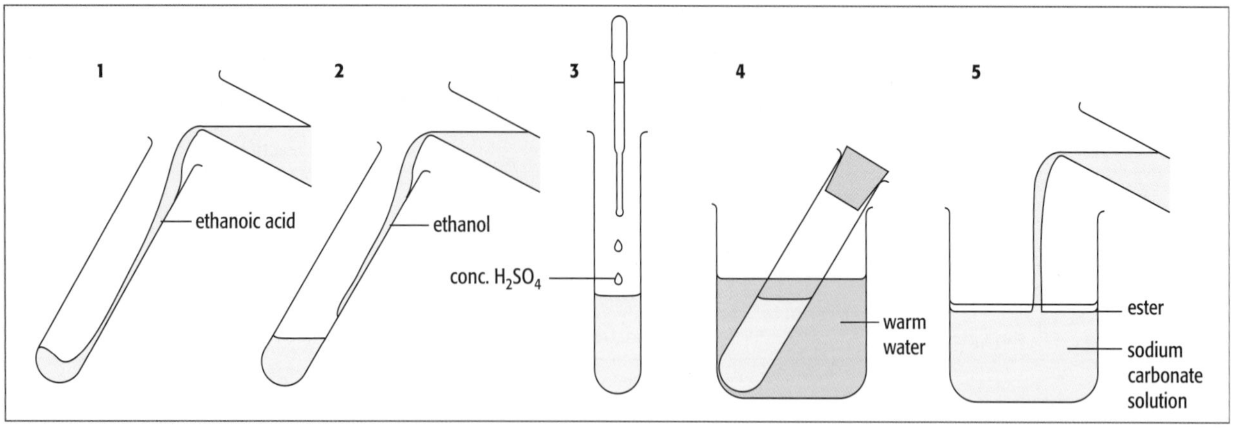

Figure 12.9 The making of an ester.

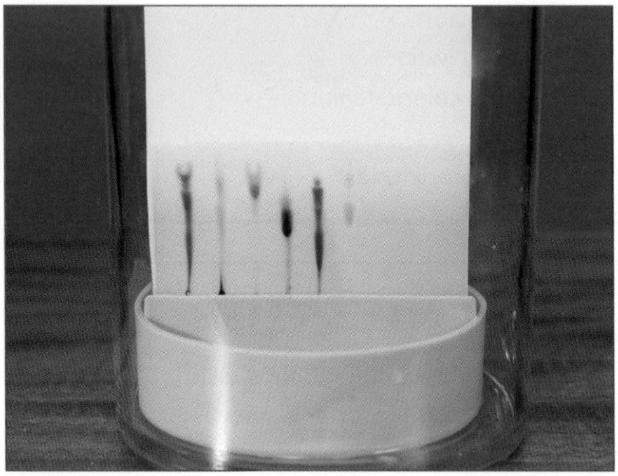

Figure 12.10 Chromatography can be used to separate coloured inks. The solvent front can be seen rising up the paper.

spot, then this is an indication that it might be pure. It would be better to check, using different solvents, for confirmation.

The identity of the compound can be confirmed by measuring its R_f value in the solvent being used. For more detail of this technique see page **39**.

The analyses described in this section are concerned with **which** compounds are present. That is, they are focused on detection and identification. They are **qualitative** tests. However, precipitation reactions can also be carried out to answer questions of **how much** of a substance is present. Titrations can also be carried out to answer such questions in solutions. This type of analysis is known as **quantitative analysis**. More detail of these techniques can be found in Section **6.5**.

Key ideas so far

- Analytical ideas can be applied in organic chemistry as well as in inorganic chemistry.
- Bromine water provides a test for unsaturated compounds.
- Ethanol and ethanoic acid provide a simple test for each other. They react to produce a sweet-smelling ester.
- Chromatography can be used to examine the complexity of mixtures of organic compounds and to tell whether a substance may be pure.
- By using a locating agent, chromatography can be applied to the analysis of colourless substances.
- Quantitative experiments, such as titrations, tell us how much of a substance we have.

Quick-check questions

1 Outline the test for an alkene, giving the reagent used and the colour change observed.
2 How would you test to distinguish between ethanol and a solution of ethanoic acid?
3 Why is a locating agent needed to identify sugars and amino acids on a chromatogram?

12.3 Experimental design and investigation

The scientific method

Science is concerned with providing evidence to explain the world we experience and how it works. **Ideas** of how it may work are a good start, but it is the job of the scientist to provide **evidence** to support those ideas or to prove them wrong. Over many hundreds of years, the ways in which scientists fulfil this role have developed into what we now call 'the scientific method'. Below is a simplified version of what it involves.

1. We start with an **idea** about how something works or how something may be accomplished.
2. We do some **research** to discover if anyone has already done any useful work on this topic. This may be done using books or the internet, or may involve some initial practical investigation.
3. We then develop a **hypothesis.** This is a statement based on our idea and the results of our research which can be tested by means of an experiment.
4. We plan and carry out our **experiment**, or series of experiments, which will tell us whether our hypothesis was correct.
5. We then **analyse** our results and conclude whether or not our hypothesis was correct.
6. Next, a **report** is written, giving the results and the conclusion reached. If the hypothesis was not confirmed we have still learned something and must start again with a new hypothesis.

Planning investigations and controlling variables

Figure **12.11** (overleaf) outlines a basic strategy for planning an investigation in chemistry and making sure you have thought of the issues involved.

The hypothesis

The hypothesis is a statement of the 'If…then…' type; for example, 'If I heat this reaction then it will get faster'. The statement should be one which can be tested with an experiment. Some statements are difficult or impossible to test: 'If the Earth is hit by an asteroid then most living things will die', for instance.

The variables

When marble chips react with hydrochloric acid, a number of factors affect the speed of the reaction (the temperature, the concentration of the acid, the size of the marble chips and the pressure of the air). These are referred to as **variables**. If we wish to investigate the effect of temperature on the speed, the other variables must all be kept constant. Then we can be sure that the effect which we observe is due to the change in temperature.

When we plan our investigation we must decide which variable we are going to vary/control (the **controlled** variable) and which one will change as a result (the **dependent** variable). These will be the two variables in our hypothesis. All the other variables must be kept constant.

Selecting the apparatus

When selecting suitable apparatus for an experiment it is important to consider scale and accuracy. Containers should be of a suitable size and shape. Apparatus for measuring should be capable of giving sufficiently accurate results. In particular, the apparatus used for measuring the controlled and dependent variables should be able to produce precise results.

Measuring time, mass and temperature: A stopclock or stopwatch is often a useful piece of apparatus, particularly when studying rates of reaction. Many are now digital and capable of giving readings in seconds to two decimal places. Be careful of a false sense of accuracy and consider how to report your results. It is unlikely that other parts of your experiment will be set up to this degree of precision.

Digital balances are now available which routinely give readings to two decimal places. Such balances are convenient and straightforward to use provided you remember to set the balance to zero with the empty container in place (called 'taring' the balance).

Temperatures in practical work are measured in 'degrees Celsius' (°C) and thermometers are usually straightforward to read to the nearest degree. This is usually accurate enough, although it is possible with some thermometers to measure to the nearest half degree. Digital thermometers are becoming more available for practical work.

Measuring volumes: When measuring volumes of liquids it is important to be aware of the level of accuracy needed for a particular experiment. Often a measuring cylinder is sufficiently accurate for routine use and for making up large volumes of solutions. However, do remember that they are not as accurate as either a pipette

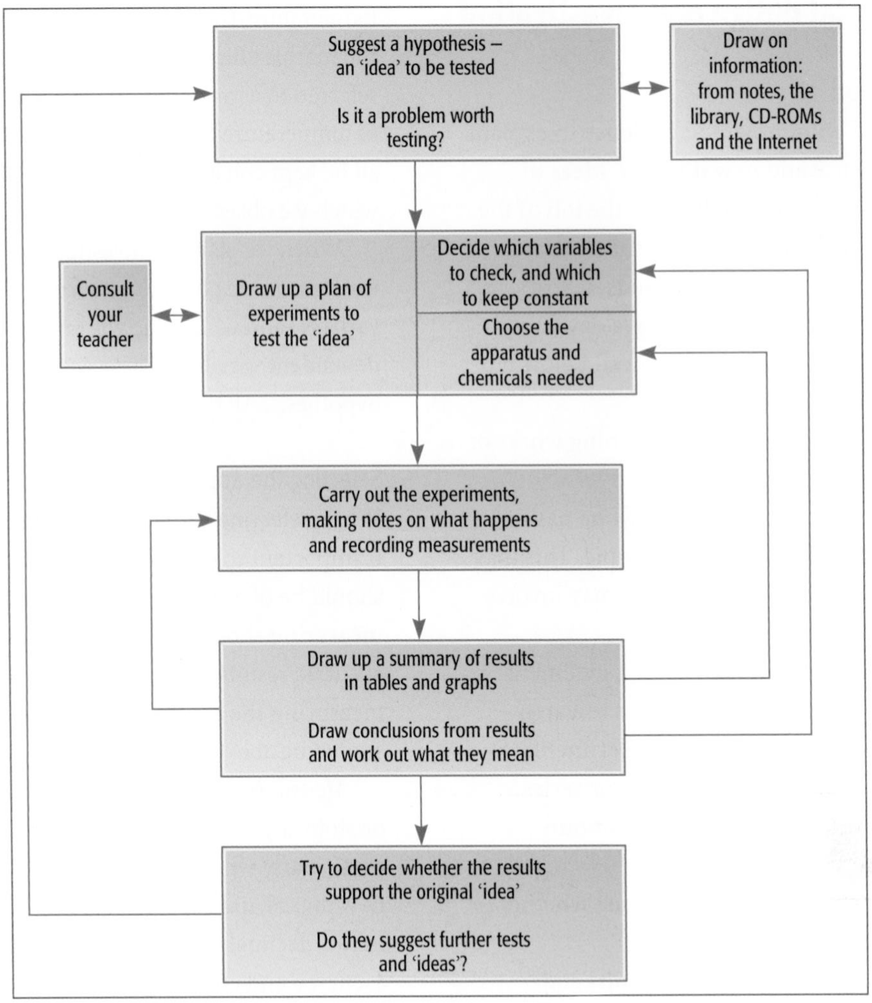

Figure 12.11 The stages involved in an experimental investigation.

or a burette for measuring the volume of a liquid really accurately. Pipettes are the most accurate way of measuring out a fixed volume (usually 10 or 25 cm^3). Burettes are the most accurate way of measuring a variable volume (usually between 0 and 50 cm^3). Burettes and pipettes are the apparatus used in titrations. If we need to make up a solution accurately to a known concentration then a volumetric flask is the container to make it in.

In some rate of reaction experiments, for instance, it is necessary to measure the volume of a gas. In this case a gas syringe is the apparatus of choice. It is possible, however, to use an inverted measuring cylinder for this, and collect the gas over water. Be careful not to use this method for a gas that dissolves in water, though.

You should be aware of the purpose and accuracy of the common pieces of experimental equipment (Figure **12.12**), and make sure you use their correct names when answering questions.

Safety

Safety is of great importance in experiments, and you should be aware of those chemicals that can pose a risk. The meaning of the safety symbols and some chemical examples are shown in Figure **12.13**.

When you plan your investigation, it is important to carry out a **risk assessment** for each part of the experiment. At the end of an experiment, be sure to clean up carefully and wash your hands.

Sources of error and the display of observations

Almost every measurement has some degree of **error** or **uncertainty** in it. Some pieces of apparatus are more accurate than others. An awareness of **accuracy** and sources of error is important in evaluating the results of an experiment. Tables and graphs of results should be checked for results that do not fit the pattern. A typical graph is shown in Figure **12.14** (overleaf). When plotting

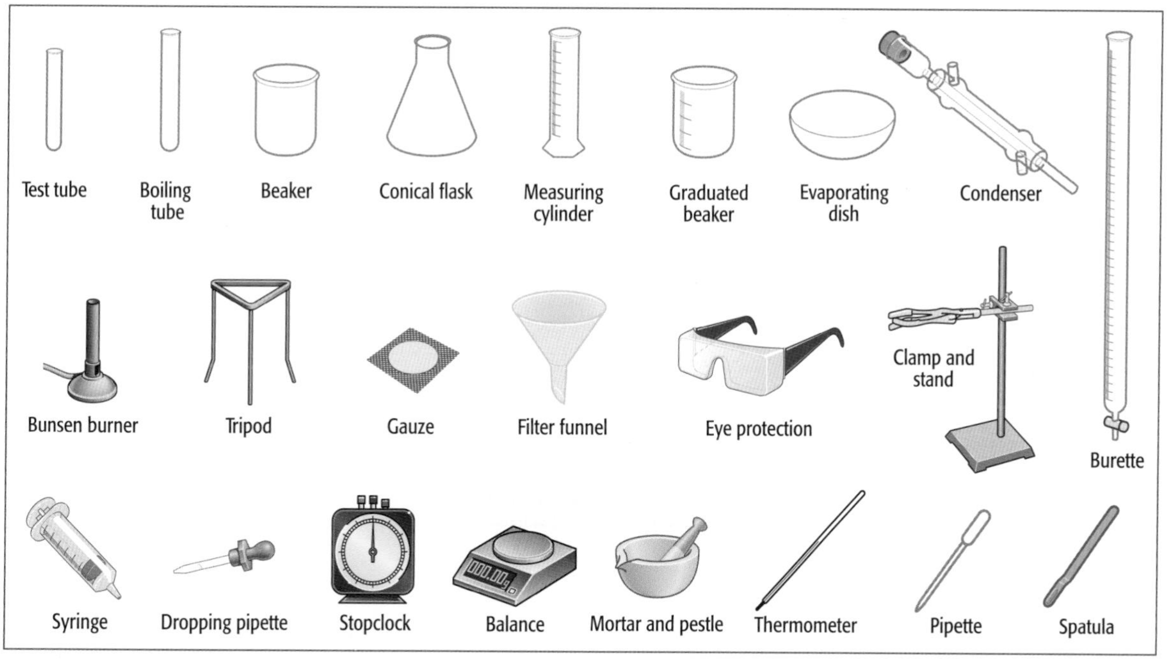

Figure 12.12 Common experimental apparatus.

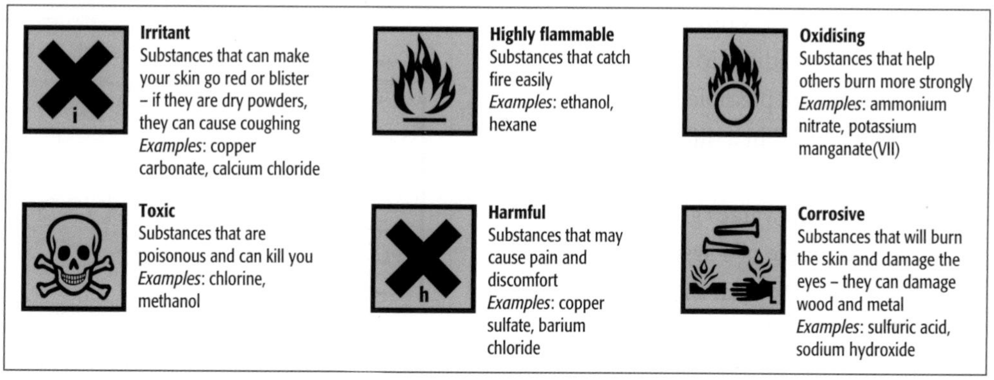

Figure 12.13 Chemical safety symbols.

graphs, the line through the points should be a 'best-fit' line. Do not try to include points that are obviously out of place. The line you draw, after carefully plotting the points, should show up the general pattern of the results. Very often this will be a straight line or a gentle curve. Try to draw the line so that the points are evenly scattered on either side. If a curve seems best, then make it as smooth as possible, avoiding sharp angles.

When plotting graphs:

- Plot the controlled variable ('temperature' in Figure **12.14**) on the horizontal (x) axis, with the scale as large as possible.
- Plot the dependent variable ('time' in Figure **12.14**) on the vertical (y) axis, again with the scale as large as possible.
- Remember that the scales do **not** have to start at zero.
- Label each axis clearly with the name of the variable and its units.
- Give your graph a title.
- Plot the points with a cross (or a dot in a small circle) using a **sharp** pencil.
- Draw the best-fit line, which does not have to pass through **all** the points, and may be a straight line or a curve.

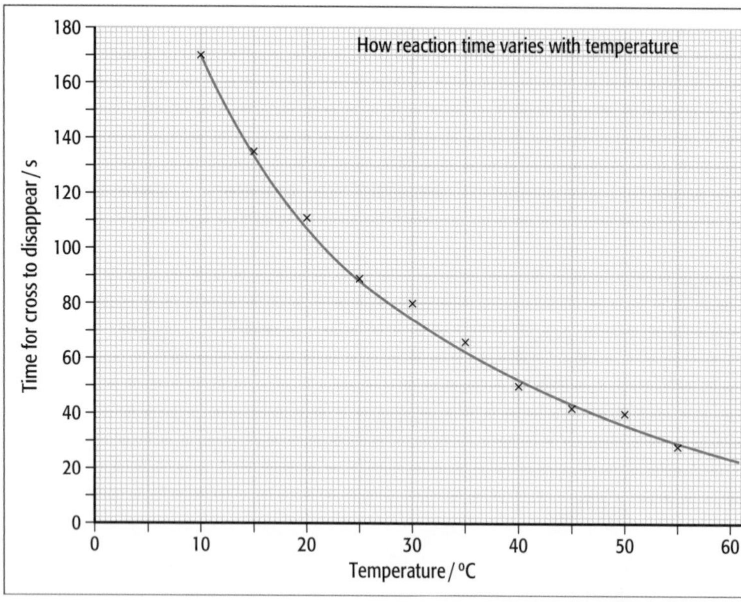

Figure 12.14 Plotting a graph is important to get the most from experimental data. This sample graph is from an experiment like the one in Figure **7.18** (page **210**) and Exam-style question **12** (page **365**).

A point that does not fit the pattern is probably due to a **random error** in a particular reading. Measurements like this should be repeated where possible.

Other errors can be introduced in a different way. For instance, always reading a burette as shown in Figure 12.15 would mean that the values given were always too high. This is an example of a **systematic error**. The presence of such an error can show itself when a graph is drawn. For example, a line that should pass through the origin does not do so.

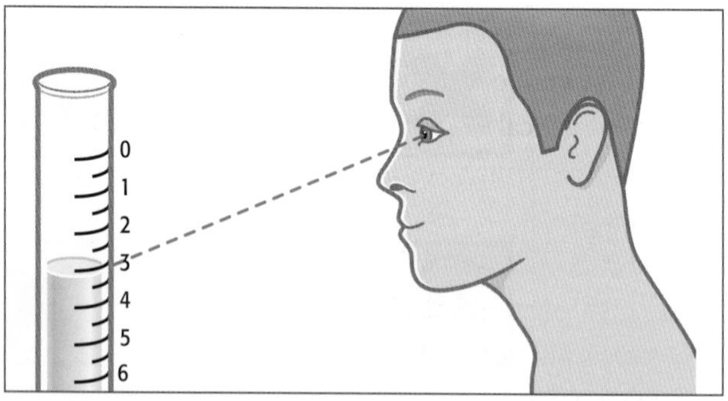

Figure 12.15 Poor experimental technique can result in systematic errors.

- Random errors can be reduced by using apparatus that gives greater accuracy, by making measurements more carefully, or by making multiple measurements and taking an average.
- Systematic errors can be eliminated by using accurate apparatus and improved technique.

Interpreting observations and data

An experiment can produce either observations made directly (usually visually) or numerical data, which is usually obtained via some measuring device. In both cases it is usual to put the results of the experiment into a table with suitably headed columns.

In the case of visual observations, this would normally include the appearance before and after any change, described in as much detail as possible. These observations would be interpreted by linking them with the expected outcomes (from the hypothesis) and by writing an appropriate equation where possible.

Numerical data should be recorded in a table with units and with values shown as accurately as possible. Numerical data are often used to plot a graph, which again should be interpreted by reference to the hypothesis (does it confirm or contradict the hypothesis?). Remember, a straight line often indicates some form of proportional relationship.

Key ideas so far

- In carrying out experiments it is important to control the situation so that only one condition is changing at once.
- This develops into the idea of a fair test, where only one variable is changed at a time.
- The scientific method is based on these ideas, allowing a hypothesis to be tested properly.
- Observations and measurements should be recorded clearly, accurately and as completely as possible.
- The interpretation of the results of the investigation should relate to the hypothesis and should give a scientific explanation.

? Quick-check questions

1 If you were investigating which of three fuels will heat water fastest, what variables would you have to keep constant?

2 If you were investigating the effect of heat on a number of different compounds, what headings would be needed for the columns in the results table?

12.4 How practical work is assessed

In CIE IGCSE Chemistry examinations there are three possible routes for the assessing of practical skills (Papers 4, 5 or 6). Whichever paper is chosen counts for 20% of the total mark for the IGCSE examination.

Coursework (Paper 4)

The coursework option assesses your practical skills through practical work done in your school. Four skills are assessed during your practical sessions, each skill being given a mark out of six each time it is assessed. The skills can be assessed as many times as needed.

You will accumulate a series of marks and the two best marks for each skill are submitted. This gives you a possible total mark of 48 for your practical coursework. The marks given by the school are then moderated by CIE to ensure that they are fair.

The skills assessed are:
C1: Using and organising techniques, apparatus and materials. This assesses your ability to follow instructions for performing practical tasks. More complex instructions successfully followed gain higher marks.
C2: Observing, measuring and recording. This assesses your ability to make accurate measurements and to make complete observations. These must be recorded appropriately to score high marks.
C3: Handling experimental observations and data. For this skill your observations and/or data need to be handled appropriately, for example by drawing a graph, and any patterns in the data must be described and explained.

C4: In this skill you must plan your own investigation, controlling variables as appropriate. You must carry out the investigation and comment on how well it succeeded. You must then suggest any improvements that could be made to your original plan.

Practical examination (Paper 5)

This is a practical test done in school using practical exercises set by the examination board. There are two questions and the test lasts for one hour and fifteen minutes.

The first question is always a quantitative exercise where measurements are taken and a graph is drawn. It may be a titration, an exercise involving measurement of temperature over the course of a reaction or a different exercise involving taking measurements.

The second question is always a qualitative analysis. A number of tests are performed on unknown substances, the observations are recorded and conclusions about the substances are made. The paper is externally marked by the examination board.

The details of this exam paper and the instructions to candidates are as follows:

CIE IGCSE, November 2006, Practical Test, Paper 5
Answer ALL questions
Write in dark blue or black pen in the spaces provided on the Question Paper
You may use a pencil for any diagrams, graphs or rough working
Do not use staples, paper clips, highlighters, glue or correction fluid

1 You are going to investigate the reactions of three different metals.
Magnesium, iron and zinc will be used.
Read all the **instructions** below carefully before starting the experiments.

Instructions

Experiment 1

By using a measuring cylinder, pour 5 cm^3 of the aqueous copper(II) sulphate into the test-tube provided. Measure the initial temperature of the solution and record it in the table below. Add the 1 g sample of zinc powder to the solution in the test-tube and stir the mixture with the thermometer. Record the maximum temperature reached and any observations in the table.
Remove the thermometer and rinse with water.

Experiment 2

Repeat Experiment 1, using 1 g of iron filings instead of zinc. Record the maximum temperature reached and any observations in the table.

Experiment 3

Repeat Experiment 1, using the 0.5 g sample of magnesium. Test the gas given off with a lighted splint.

Table of results

experiment	metal	temperature of solution/°C		observations
		initial	maximum	
1	zinc	24	56	Zinc goes black blue is paler bubbles
2	iron	25	41	Iron goes brown blue goes pale
3	magnesium	23	69	gas goes pop.

[9]

For Examiner's Use

This represents a complete set of answers – the temperatures are filled in accurately and the observations are clearly and simply stated (do not over-elaborate your answers, that is when mistakes creep in).

 0620/05/O/N/06 [Turn over

Again a clear set of precise answers

(a) Use your results and observations to answer the following questions.

(i) Which metal is most reactive with aqueous copper(II) sulphate?

magnesium [1]

(ii) Give two reasons why you chose this metal.

1 biggest temperature rise.

2 lots of bubbles. [2]

(iii) Name the gas given off in Experiment 3.

hydrogen. [1]

You are now going to investigate the reaction between two of the metals and aqueous copper(II) sulphate in more detail.

Experiment 4

Rinse the thermometer with water at room temperature. By using a measuring cylinder pour 10 cm^3 of aqueous copper(II) sulphate into a polystyrene cup. Measure the initial temperature of the solution and record it in the table below.
Add the 1 g sample of magnesium powder to the cup and record the temperature every 10 seconds for 1 minute. Record all of your results in the table.

Experiment 5

Repeat Experiment 4 using the 2 g sample of zinc powder instead of magnesium.

Record all of your results in the table.

Table of results

time/seconds	**temperature/°C**	
	Experiment 4	Experiment 5
0	24	25
10	27	54
20	29	62
30	33	67
40	37	68
50	40	67
60	43	65

[3]

(b) Plot the results of Experiments 4 and 5 on the grid below. Draw two smooth line graphs. Clearly label the graphs.

For Examiner's Use

Points accurately and clearly plotted using sharp pencil – smooth line and curve drawn.

Note that a line of best fit is drawn – you do not have to join up all the points

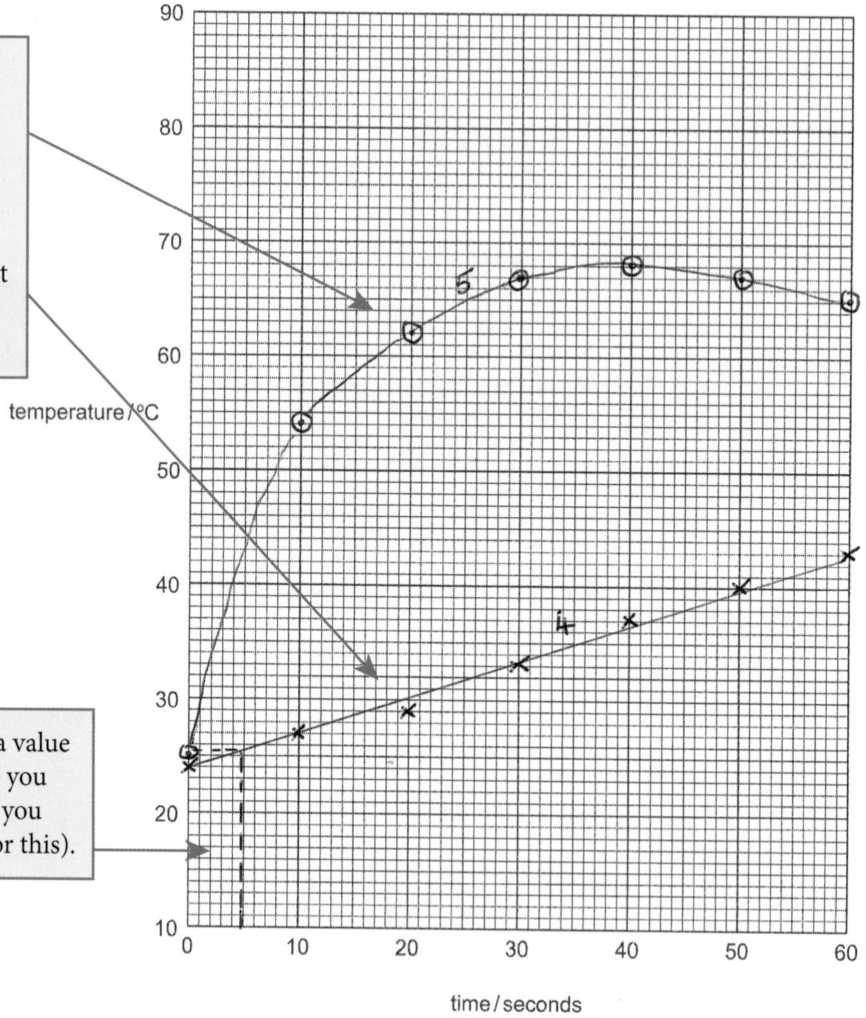

When asked to deduce a value from a graph make sure you show on the graph how you did it (there is a mark for this).

[4]

(c) **Use your graph** to estimate the temperature of the reaction mixture in Experiment 4 after 5 seconds. Indicate **clearly** on the graph how you obtained your answer.

25·5°C .... [2]

 0620/05/O/N/06 **[Turn over**

2 You are provided with two solids, solid **S** and solid **V**.
Carry out the following tests on **S** and **V**.
Record all your observations in the table.
Do not write any conclusions in the table.

For Examiner's Use

tests	observations
<u>tests on solid **S**</u> **(a)** Describe the appearance of solid **S**.	black powder
(b) Place half of solid **S** in a test-tube. Add about 2 cm^3 of hydrogen peroxide and shake the tube. After 1 minute insert a glowing splint into the tube.	slow fizzing splint is brighter [2]
(c) Add the rest of solid **S** to about 5cm^3 of dilute sulfuric acid in a **boiling tube**. Heat the solution **carefully** to boiling point. Place the tube and contents in a test-tube rack. Leave to stand for 1 minute. Decant off the liquid into another test-tube and add an equal volume of distilled water to the tube. Using clean test-tubes, divide the solution into 3 equal portions.	colour of solution blue [1]
(i) Add several drops of aqueous sodium hydroxide to the first portion of the solution and shake the tube. Now add excess sodium hydroxide to the tube.	light blue precipitate no change [2]
Heat the contents of the tube gently.	precipitate turns brown [1]
(ii) To the second portion of the solution add 1 cm^3 of aqueous ammonia solution. Now add excess ammonia solution to the tube.	blue precipitate [2] changes to deep blue solution. [2]
(iii) To the third portion of solution add about 1 cm^3 of dilute hydrochloric acid followed by about 1 cm^3 of barium chloride solution.	white (bluish) precipitate [2]

Observations are clearly and simply stated.

The comments are comprehensive, e.g. 'slow fizzing' and not just 'fizzing' in (b), no change when excess sodium hydroxide is added in (c) (i).

The marks given for each part will help you decide how much detail is needed.

 0620/05/M/J/09

tests	observations
tests on solid **V** (d) Describe the appearance of solid **V**.	dark brown ~~black~~ powder [1]
… of solid **V** in a … Add about 2cm^3 of … peroxide to the … Test the gas with a glowing splint.	fizzes splint relights. [2]

Note that the candidate has not used correcting fluid – if you need to correct something simply cross out the mistake

For Examiner's Use

(f) (i) Compare the reaction of solid **S** and solid **V** with hydrogen peroxide.

V reacts quicker with the hydrogen peroxide [1]

(ii) Identify the gas given off in test **(e)**.

oxygen [1]

(g) What conclusions can you draw about solid **S**?

It contains copper.
It makes copper sulphate with sulfuric acid. [2]

(h) What conclusions can you draw about solid **V**?

It is a catalyst
It might be manganese oxide. [1]

[Total: 20]

Clear, sensible deductions. In the practical paper 5 you are given a table of ion tests at the back of the exam paper. You do not get this in the other exam papers, so it still pays to know the tests.

Alternative to practical examination (Paper 6)

This is an examination lasting one hour in which practical skills are tested. It is important to know about common apparatus and experimental procedures because you will be asked about them. There are usually six or seven questions and these are the sort of things that may be asked:

- labelling diagrams of common apparatus
- taking readings from diagrams of apparatus
- plotting graphs
- interpreting the results of simple experiments
- planning simple investigations.

In addition, modified forms of the two questions from the practical examination (paper 5) are also included.

Summary

You should know that:

- there is a series of tests that help us to analyse substances
- in inorganic chemistry these tests help us to find which positive ions (metals) and negative ions are present in an ionic compound
- there is also a series of tests for gases such as hydrogen, oxygen, etc.
- these analytical ideas can also be applied in organic chemistry
- quantitative experiments, such as titrations, which tell us how much of a substance we have (not just which substance we have), can be carried out
- in carrying out experiments it is important to control the situation so that not too many conditions are changing at once
- when reporting on experiments it is important to be able to present the results clearly, possibly in a table or by plotting a graph
- this develops into the ideas of a fair test and a controlled experiment – ideas central to any experimental investigation
- the scientific method is based in part on these ideas, so that any hypothesis can be properly tested.

Exam-style questions

1 Sulfur dioxide gas is denser than air and soluble in water. A sample of sulfur dioxide can be prepared by adding dilute hydrochloric acid to sodium sulfite and warming the mixture. Study the diagram of the apparatus used.

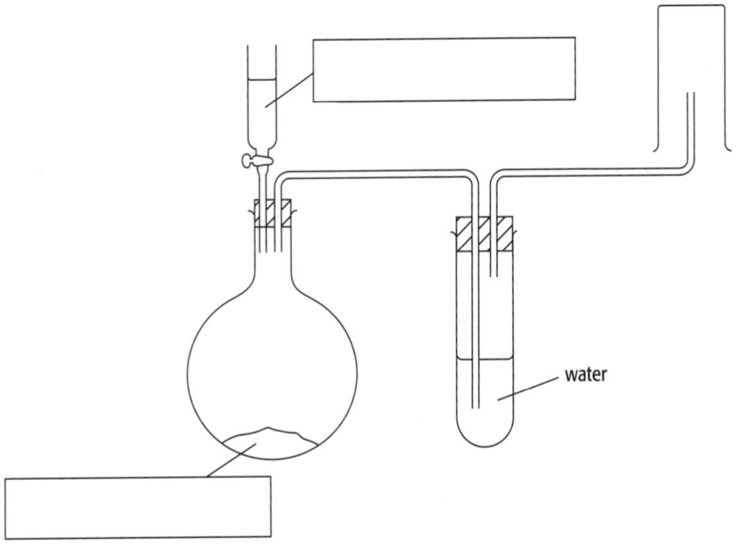

a Copy the diagram and fill in the boxes to show the chemicals used. [2]

b Show, by using an arrow on the diagram, where heat is applied. [1]

c Identify and explain **two** mistakes in the diagram. [2]

CIE IGCSE, June 2008, paper 6, q.3

2 Ethene gas was formed by the cracking of a liquid alkane. The diagram shows the apparatus used.

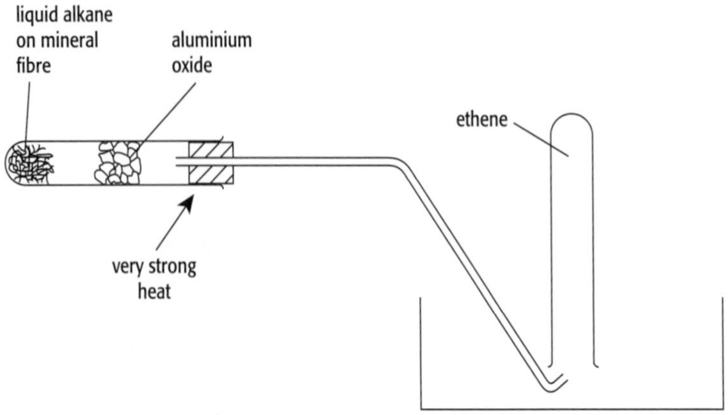

a Identify **two** mistakes in the diagram. [2]

b Describe a test to show the presence of ethene. Give both the test and the expected result. [2]

CIE IGCSE, November 2008, paper 6, q.3

3 The colours present in some blackcurrant sweets can be separated by chromatography.
The colours are water-soluble dyes. The diagrams show how the colours can be extracted from the sweets.

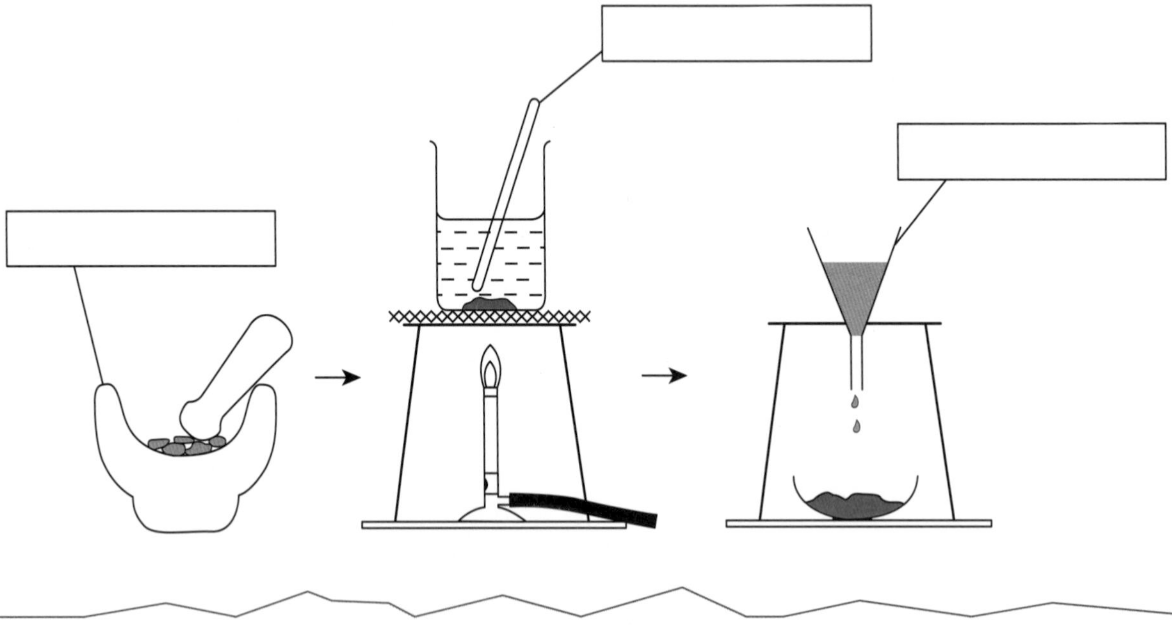

a Copy the diagram and complete the empty boxes to name the pieces of apparatus. [3]

The apparatus below was used to carry out the chromatography.

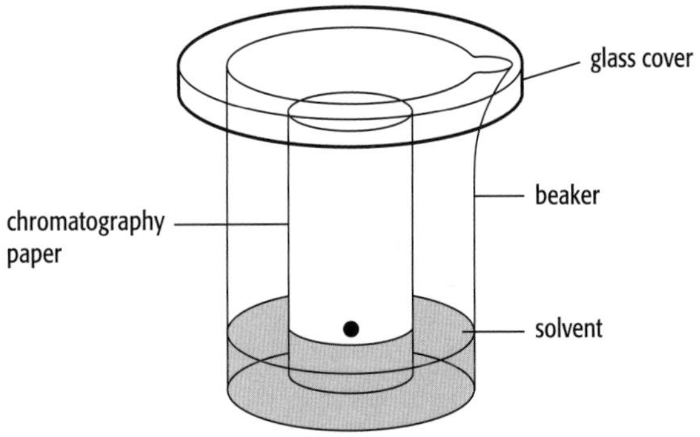

b **i** Name the solvent used. [1]

ii Label, with an arrow, the origin on the diagram. [1]

c Draw a sketch of the chromatogram you would expect if two different colours were present in the sweets. [2]

CIE IGCSE, November 2008, paper 6, q.1

4 This label is from a container of 'Bite Relief' solution.

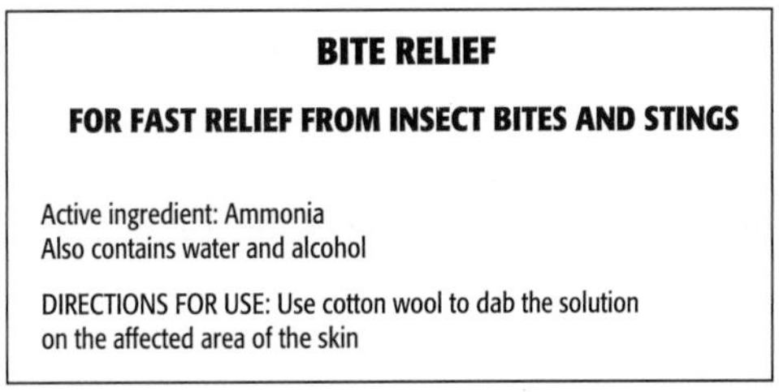

BITE RELIEF

FOR FAST RELIEF FROM INSECT BITES AND STINGS

Active ingredient: Ammonia
Also contains water and alcohol

DIRECTIONS FOR USE: Use cotton wool to dab the solution on the affected area of the skin

a Give a chemical test to show the presence of ammonia in Bite Relief solution. Give both the test and the expected result. [2]

b What practical method could be used to separate the mixture of alcohol (b.p. 78 °C) and water (b.p. 100 °C)? [2]

c Give a chemical test to show the presence of water. Give both the test and the expected result. [2]

d What would be the effect of touching the alcohol with a lighted splint? [1]

CIE IGCSE, June 2008, paper 6, q.7

5 Chromatography can be used to identify amino acids from a sample of protein.
The diagram shows the chromatogram obtained when four samples of amino acids were analysed.
The paper was sprayed with ninhydrin.

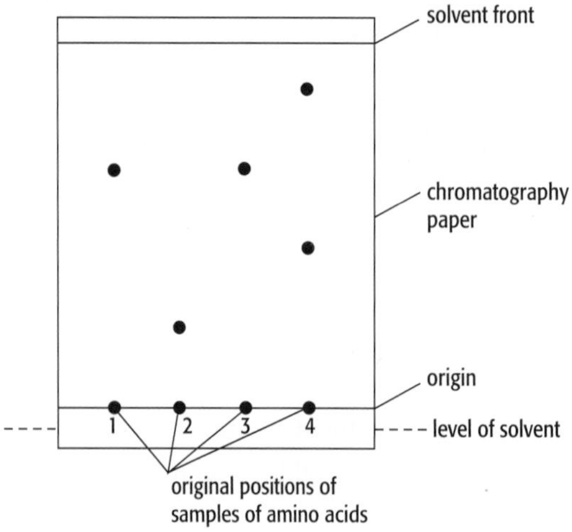

a Why is the origin line drawn in pencil? [1]
b Which amino acids could possibly be the same? [1]
c Which amino acid sample contains more than one amino acid? Explain your answer. [2]
d Suggest why it is necessary to spray the chromatogram with ninhydrin. [1]

CIE IGCSE, June 2007, paper 6, q.3

6 Describe a chemical test to **distinguish** between each of the following pairs of substances. An example is given.

oxygen and carbon dioxide
test: glowing splint
result: re-lights in oxygen, no effect with carbon dioxide

a aqueous chlorine and aqueous sodium chloride
test:
result with chlorine:
result with sodium chloride: [2]

b aqueous iron(II) chloride and aqueous iron(III) chloride
test:
result with iron(II) chloride:
result with iron(III) chloride: [2]

c copper sulfate and copper carbonate
test:
result with copper sulfate:
result with copper carbonate: [2]

CIE IGCSE, November 2004, paper 6, q.6

7 Describe a chemical test to **distinguish** between each of the following pairs of substances. An example is given.

potassium chloride and potassium iodide
test: add aqueous lead(II) nitrate
result: potassium chloride gives a white precipitate, potassium iodide gives a yellow precipitate

a water and ethanol [2]
b sulfuric acid and aqueous sodium sulfate [2]
c hydrochloric acid and nitric acid [2]

CIE IGCSE, June 2004, paper 6, q.7

8 Diesel is a liquid fuel obtained from crude oil.
Biodiesel is a fuel made from oil obtained from the seeds of plants such as sunflowers.
Using the apparatus below, plan an experiment to investigate which of these two fuels produces more energy.

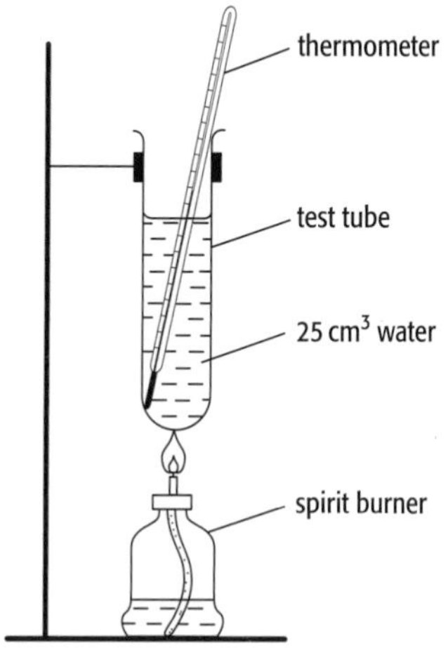

[6]

CIE IGCSE, November 2007, paper 6, q.7

9 The diagram shows two bottles of liquid oven cleaner.

The oven cleaners contain sodium hydroxide solution. Plan an investigation to show which oven cleaner contains the highest concentration of sodium hydroxide. [6]

CIE IGCSE, June 2006, paper 6, q.6

10 A student carried out an experiment to measure the temperature changes during the reaction of two solutions **X** and **Y**. The instructions were as follows.

Leave the solutions to stand in the laboratory for one hour.

Pour 25 cm³ of solution **X** into a polystyrene cup and record its temperature.

Add 10 cm³ of solution **Y** and record the maximum temperature reached.

Repeat the experiment using 25 cm³ of solution **X** with different volumes of solution **Y**.

The results are shown in the table.

a Use the thermometer diagrams to record the maximum temperatures reached.

Volume of solution Y added to 25 cm³ solution X / cm³	Thermometer diagram
0	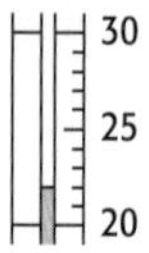
10	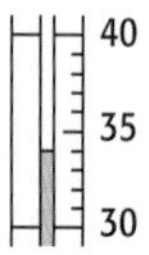
20	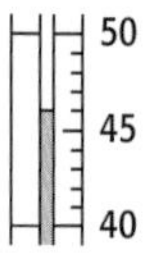
30	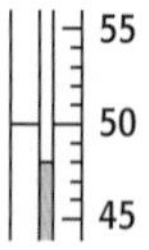
40	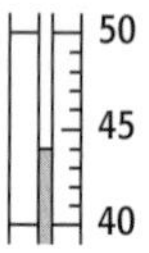
50	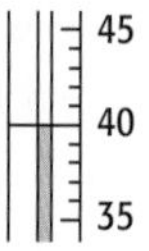

[2]

b Why were the solutions left standing in the laboratory for about one hour before the experiment? [1]

c What was the temperature in the laboratory? [1]

d Why were the reactions carried out in a polystyrene cup rather than a glass container? [1]

e Plot the results on graph paper using a grid such as the one shown here. Draw two **straight** lines through the points, one for the increasing temperatures and one for the decreasing temperatures.

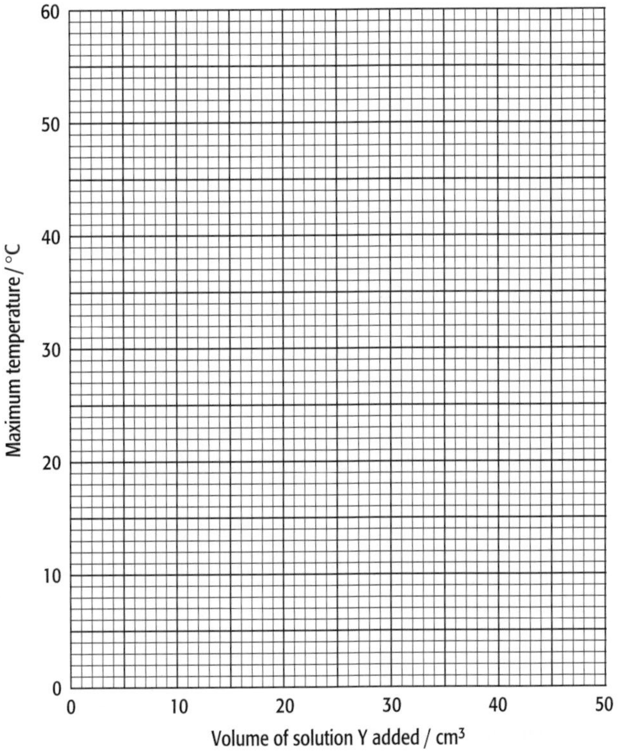

[3]

f i Read from your graph the maximum temperature that could be reached in the reaction. [1]

ii Indicate on the graph where the two solutions completely react with each other. [1]

iii What volume of solution Y exactly reacts with 25 cm^3 of solution **X**? [1]

g Which of these words correctly describes this chemical reaction?

endothermic **reversible** **exothermic** [1]

CIE IGCSE, June 2006, paper 6, q.3

11 A student carried out an experiment to investigate the speed of the reaction between sodium thiosulfate and dilute hydrochloric acid.

$$Na_2S_2O_3 + 2HCl \rightarrow 2NaCl + S + H_2O + SO_2$$

Experiment 1

By using a measuring cylinder, 50 cm^3 of sodium thiosulfate solution was poured into a 100 cm^3 beaker. The beaker was placed on a cross drawn on a piece of paper. 10 cm^3 of hydrochloric acid was added to the beaker and the timer started.

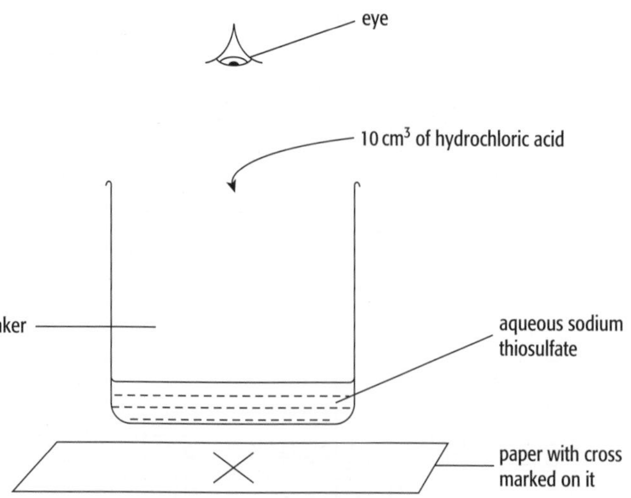

The time was taken until the cross could not be seen. The time was recorded in the table.

Experiments 2, 3, 4 and 5

Experiment 1 was repeated using different volumes of sodium thiosulfate as shown in the table. All experiments were carried out at 25 °C.

Table of results

Experiment	**Volume of sodium thiosulfate / cm^3**	**Volume of water / cm^3**	**Time for cross to disappear / s**
1	50	0	45
2	40	10	60
3	30	20	80
4	20	30	130
5	10	40	255

a Why does the cross on the paper disappear? [2]

b Why was the total volume of solution kept constant? [1]

c In which order should the water, hydrochloric acid and sodium thiosulfate solution be added to the beaker? [1]

d **i** Plot the results on graph paper using a grid similar to the one shown here. Draw a smooth line graph and label it 25 °C.

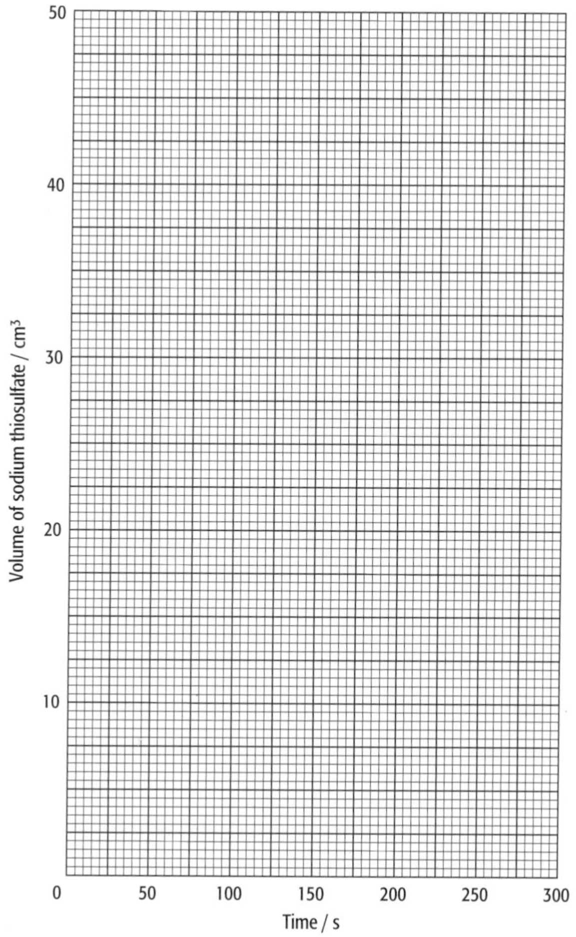

[5]

ii Sketch on the grid the graph you would expect if the experiments were repeated at 50 °C. Label this graph. [2]

e The experiments were repeated using a 250 cm^3 beaker instead of a 100 cm^3 beaker. Suggest how the results would differ. Explain your answer. [2]

CIE IGCSE, June 2003, paper 6, q.2

12 Sulfur dioxide gas is a common pollutant formed when fossil fuels burn in air. Sulfur dioxide can be detected by using an acidic solution of potassium dichromate(VI). The dichromate solution changes colour from orange to green when a certain amount of sulfur dioxide has reacted with it.
Plan an experiment to investigate which of three different samples of coal produces most sulfur dioxide. [6]

CIE IGCSE, November 2003, paper 6, q.6

13 Some plants do not grow well in acidic soil.
A farmer gives you a small sample of soil from a corner of one of his fields.

a Plan an investigation to find out the pH of the soil sample.
You are provided with Universal Indicator solution and common laboratory apparatus. [5]

b Why would further experiments be necessary to inform the farmer which plants should be grown in each of his fields? [2]

CIE IGCSE, November 2005, paper 6, q.7

14 A solid compound **X** was analysed. Solid **X** was an aluminium salt.
The tests on **X** and some of the observations are in the following table.
Complete the observations using a table like the one below.

Tests	Observations
a One spatula measure of **X** was placed into a hard-glass test-tube. The solid was heated gently then strongly. The gas was tested with pH indicator paper.	condensation at top of tube paper went red
Distilled water was added to **X** and shaken to dissolve. The solution was divided into five portions in test-tubes.	
b i To the first portion, drops of aqueous sodium hydroxide were added. Excess aqueous sodium hydroxide was then added.	.... [3]
ii To the second portion, drops of aqueous ammonia were added. Excess ammonia was then added.	.... [3]
iii To the third portion of solution, hydrochloric acid and barium chloride solution were added.	no visible change
iv To the fourth portion of solution, nitric acid and lead nitrate solution were added.	no visible change
v To the fifth portion, aqueous sodium hydroxide and a spatula measure of aluminium granules were added. The mixture was warmed and the gas tested with indicator paper.	pungent gas paper went blue, pH 10

c What does test **a** tell you about the gas given off? [1]
d What conclusions can you draw about **X** from tests **b iii** and **iv**? [2]
e Identify the gas in **b v**. [1]
f What conclusions can you draw about substance **X**? [2]

CIE IGCSE, November 2005, paper 6, q.5

Answers to quick-check questions

Chapter 1

1.1 (page 7)

1 It provides the energy needed to evaporate water from the Earth's surface.
2 It provides the energy needed for photosynthesis, which removes carbon dioxide from the atmosphere.
3 By using solar power to generate electricity, heat water, make solar furnaces, etc.
4 **a** carbon dioxide + water → glucose + oxygen

(chemical equation) $6CO_2 + 6H_2O \rightarrow C_6H_{12}O_6 + 6O_2$

b carbon + oxygen → carbon dioxide

(chemical equation) $C + O_2 \rightarrow CO_2$

c glucose + oxygen → carbon dioxide + water

(chemical equation) $C_6H_{12}O_6 + 6O_2 \rightarrow 6CO_2 + 6H_2O$

1.2 (page 12)

1 sulfur dioxide and nitrogen dioxide
2 the burning of fossil fuels (mainly coal for sulfur dioxide)
3 damage to limestone buildings, death of trees, acidification of lakes leading to death of fish
4 a combination of nitrogen oxides and low-level ozone that causes breathing problems, especially for people with asthma.
5 It combines with the haemoglobin in red blood cells, stopping them from carrying oxygen.
6 Because it does not react with the filament, which would burn in air when it became hot.
7 From rotting vegetable matter and from the intestines of animals such as cows.
8 Heat which would normally escape into space is reflected back to the Earth's surface by gases such as carbon dioxide and methane in the atmosphere.
9 It changes nitrogen oxides and carbon monoxide to nitrogen and carbon dioxide.
10 Because they have different boiling points.

1.3 (page 16)

1 Because solid matter is easiest to remove and would interfere with subsequent processes.
2 To kill bacteria present in the water.
3 Because the energy needed to boil the water is costly.
4 The sewage reacts with oxygen in the water, leaving less for water creatures to breathe.
5 They can cause too many algae to grow and they are not removed by water treatment.

1.4 (page 20)

1 It contains a high concentration of a particular metal compound.
2 Lime is calcium oxide which is reacted with water to make calcium hydroxide (slaked lime).
3 plastics, drugs, paints, detergents, etc.
4 solar power, wind power, wave power, tidal power, geothermal energy (*any four*).
5 It reflects heat back to Earth when present in the atmosphere. Heat is kept in the atmospheric layer.
6 It produces only water when burned.
7 hydrogen + oxygen → water

$2H_2 \quad + \quad O_2 \quad \rightarrow 2H_2O$

Chapter 2

2.1 (page 35)

1 **a** freezing (solidification) **b** boiling
c condensation **d** sublimation
2 The impurity lowers the freezing point of the liquid.

3 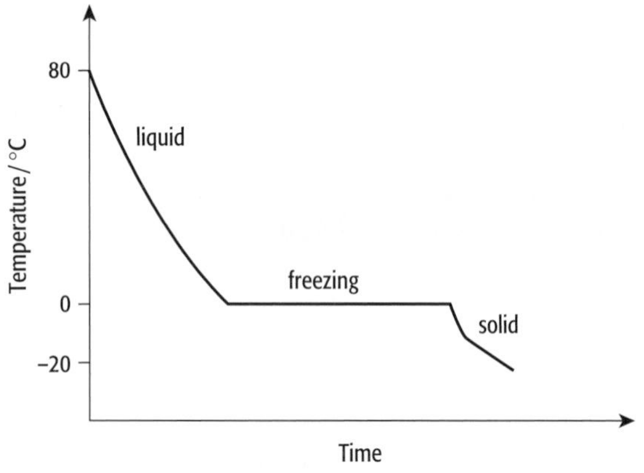

4 A volatile liquid is one that evaporates easily; it has a low boiling point.

5 ethanol > water > ethanoic acid
Ethanol is the most volatile, ethanoic acid the least.

2.2 (page 42)

1 **a** distillation **b** fractional distillation;
c crystallisation (evaporation to concentrate the solution, cooling, crystallisation, filtration and drying)

2 Sublimation is when a solid changes to a gas without passing through the liquid phase (and the reverse).

3 coloured substances (e.g. dyes)

4 By the use of locating agents that react with colourless 'spots' to produce a colour that can be seen.

5 R_f gives a standard measure of how far a sample moves in a chromatography system, as it relates the movement of the sample compound to how far the solvent front has moved. It is equal to the distance moved by the sample divided by the distance moved by the solvent front.

2.3 (page 49)

1 An element is a substance that cannot be broken down into anything simpler by chemical means.

2 A compound is a substance formed from two or more elements chemically bonded together.

3 Solid: particles packed close together in a regular arrangement; each particle only vibrating about a fixed point.
Liquid: particles close together but less regularly arranged; particles able to move about.
Gas: particles far apart and irregularly arranged; particles moving independently.

4 Ammonia, as it has a lower molecular mass.
Place cotton wool plugs soaked in ammonia solution and hydrochloric acid at opposite ends of a tube. Seal the tube at both ends. Allow the gases to diffuse towards each other. A white smoke disc of ammonium chloride will form where the two gases meet. This disc is closer to the hydrochloric acid end of the tube, as ammonia diffuses faster.

5 hydrogen

2.4 (page 56)

1 proton = 1, neutron = 1, electron = 0 (or $\frac{1}{1840}$)

2 15 protons, 16 neutrons, 15 electrons

3 Chlorine-37 has two more neutrons in the nucleus.

4 Medical: radiotherapy treatment of cancer, sterilisation of surgical instruments.
Industrial: detection of leaks in gas pipelines, controlling the thickness of aluminium foil sheets.

2.5 (page 58)

1 First shell, maximum 2: second shell, maximum 8.

2 2,8,8,2

3 8 in both cases

4 6

Chapter 3

3.1 (page 69)

1 fluorine

2 Helium has a full first shell. The others all have eight electrons in the outer energy level (shell/orbit).

3 2

4 the bottom of Group I

5 Metal: can be beaten into sheets, gives a ringing sound when hit, conducts heats, conducts electricity.
Non-metal: is an insulator, has a dull surface.

3.2 (page 73)

1 potassium hydroxide

2 lithium + water → lithium hydroxide + hydrogen

3 chlorine and fluorine

4 It is used in the treatment of drinking water; it will bleach moist litmus paper.

3.3 (page 75)

1 metal to non-metal

2 aluminium

3 sodium
4 Cl_2
5 silicon
6 Because copper is a transition metal.

3.4 (page 84)

1 **a** covalent **b** covalent **c** ionic **d** metallic
2 Because in hydrogen gas two atoms are covalently bonded together.
3 An electrostatic force (attraction between two oppositely charged ions).
4 **a**

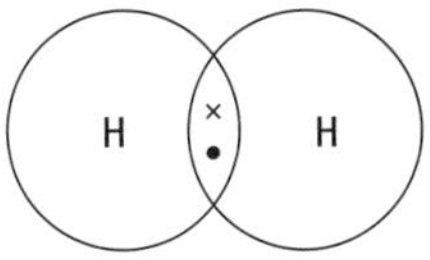

b

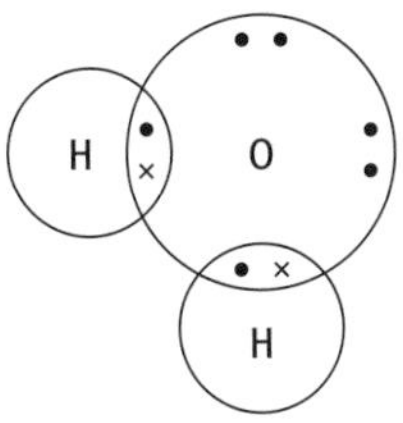

c

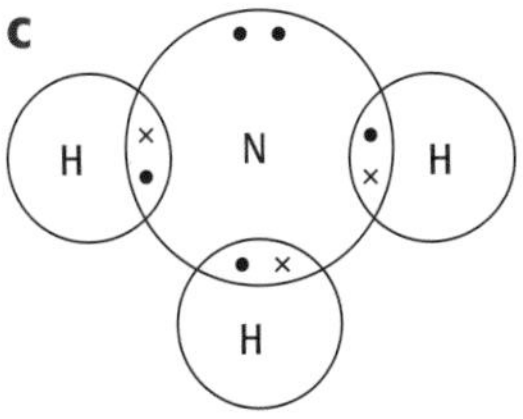

d

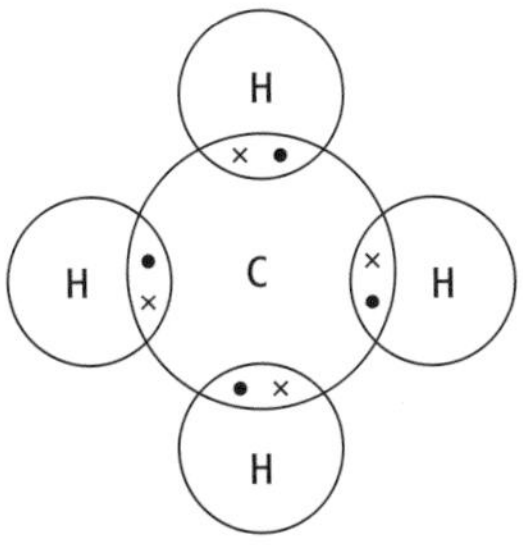

5 **a**

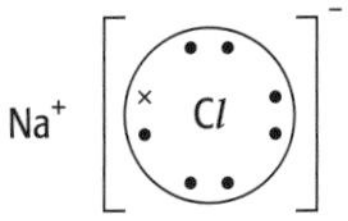

b

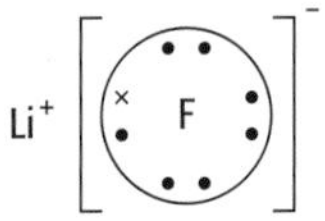

6 The calcium ion is ionically bonded to the carbonate ion but the carbonate ion is held together by covalent bonds.

7 **a**

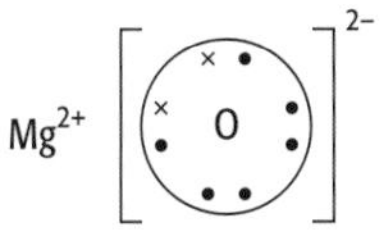

b

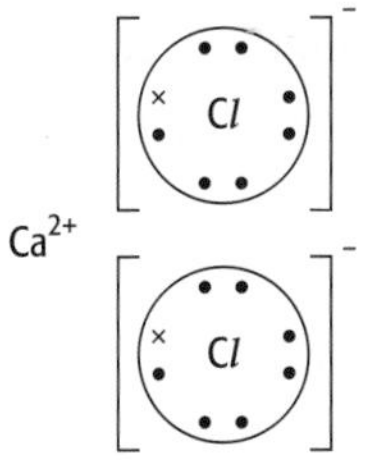

3.5 (page 87)

1 **a** sodium iodide **b** magnesium sulfide **c** potassium oxide **d** lithium nitride **e** calcium hydroxide **f** nitrogen monoxide **g** nitrogen dioxide **h** sulfur trioxide
2 **a** $SiCl_4$ **b** CS_2 **c** PCl_3 (or PCl_5) **d** SiO_2
3 **a i** Na = 1, O = 1, H = 1 **ii** C = 2, H = 6 **iii** H = 2, S = 1, O = 4 **iv** Cu = 1, N = 2, O = 6 **v** C = 12, H = 22, O = 11
b i potassium bromide **ii** aluminium hydroxide **iii** copper carbonate **iv** magnesium nitride **v** phosphorus trichloride **vi** nitric acid **vii** silicon tetrachloride **viii** iron(II) sulfate **ix** methane **x** sulfuric acid
c i K_2SO_4 **ii** AlF_3 **iii** Fe_2O_3 **iv** $Ca(NO_3)_2$ **v** $ZnCl_2$ **vi** NH_3 **vii** HCl **viii** $CuSO_4$ **ix** SO_3
4 **a** carbon, hydrogen and oxygen
b 8
c carbon and oxygen
d 4
e A liquid: it is a small covalent molecule.
f No, it is covalently bonded.

3.6 (page 94)

1 The ions are free to move and they carry the charge.
2 Because the ions are fixed in position and cannot move.
3 **a** Because there are electrons between the flat planes of atoms which are free to move.
b There are only weak forces between the layers in graphite and therefore they can slide over each other.
4 Because, in diamond, each carbon atom is attached to four other carbon atoms, making a strong lattice.
5 Because there are no charged particles to move around.
6 Because there are electrons which are free to move in solid metals.
7 Both substances have a three-dimensional structure in which the atoms are arranged tetrahedrally and all the atoms are joined by covalent bonds.

Chapter 4

4.1 (page 107)

1 **a** physical **b** chemical
c physical **d** physical
2 **a** exothermic **b** exothermic
c exothermic **d** endothermic
3 A new substance(s) has been formed.

4.2 (page 110)

1 a iron + oxygen → iron(III) oxide
 b sodium hydroxide + sulfuric acid → sodium sulfate + water
 c sodium + water → sodium hydroxide + hydrogen
2 a $2Cu + O_2 \rightarrow 2CuO$
 b $N_2 + 3H_2 \rightleftharpoons 2NH_3$
 c $4Na + O_2 \rightarrow 2Na_2O$
 d $2NaOH + H_2SO_4 \rightarrow Na_2SO_4 + 2H_2O$
 e $2Al + 3Cl_2 \rightarrow 2AlCl_3$
 f $3Fe + 4H_2O \rightarrow Fe_3O_4 + 4H_2$

4.3 (page 116)

1 a chlorine + potassium bromide → potassium chloride + bromine
 b Iodine is less reactive than chlorine so it will not displace chlorine from its salts.
2 a combustion
 b decomposition
 c redox
 d neutralisation
3 a sodium + water → sodium hydroxide + hydrogen

$2Na + 2H_2O \rightarrow 2NaOH + H_2$

 b magnesium + steam → magnesium oxide + hydrogen

$Mg + H_2O \rightarrow MgO + H_2$

 c calcium + oxygen → calcium oxide

$2Ca + O_2 \rightarrow 2CaO$

 d bromine + potassium iodide → potassium bromide + iodine

$Br_2 + 2KI \rightarrow 2KBr + I_2$

 e zinc + copper sulfate → zinc sulfate + copper

$Zn + CuSO_4 \rightarrow ZnSO_4 + Cu$

4.4 (page 119)

1 a **Solid** sodium carbonate reacts with hydrochloric acid **solution** to give sodium chloride **solution** and carbon dioxide **gas**. Water, a **liquid**, is also produced.
 b i $Ag^+(aq) + Cl^-(aq) \rightarrow AgCl(s)$
 ii $Ba^{2+}(aq) + SO_4^{2-}(aq) \rightarrow BaSO_4(s)$
 iii $H^+(aq) + OH^-(aq) \rightarrow H_2O(l)$
 iv $2H^+(aq) + CO_3^{2-}(s) \rightarrow H_2O(l) + CO_2(g)$
2 **Reduction** is the gain of electrons; **oxidation** is the loss of electrons. During a redox reaction the oxidising agent **gains** electrons; the oxidising agent is itself **reduced** during the reaction.

4.5 (page 128)

1 a The compound is split into its elements.
 b The ions are not free to move in the solid, so they cannot move to the electrodes to be discharged.
 c The vapour is brown.
 d Because bromine vapour is toxic.
 e the cathode
2 a the cathode
 b copper sulfate solution
3 a $2Br^- \rightarrow Br_2 + 2e^-$
 b Because electrons are gained by the lead ions.
4

Solution (electrolyte)	Gas given off at the anode	Gas given off or metal deposited at the cathode	Substance left in solution at the end of electrolysis
silver sulfate	oxygen	**silver**	**sulfuric acid**
sodium nitrate	**oxygen**	hydrogen	sodium nitrate

4.6 (page 131)

1 a i electrode Y ii a cathode
 b The solution would become acidic.
 c To make the electrode conduct electricity.
2 a the anode b the cathode
 c Oxidation is defined as loss of electrons, which happens at the anode; reduction is defined as gain of electrons, which happens at the cathode.

Chapter 5

5.1 (page 140)

1 A corrosive substance 'eats' things away.
2 citric acid

3 **a** alkaline **b** neutral
c alkaline **d** acidic
4 It changes its colour depending on whether it is in an acidic or alkaline solution.
5 pH 1 is more acidic.
6 green
7 ethanoic acid

5.2 (page 141)

1 hydrogen
2 hydroxide ion, OH^-
3 **a** hydrogen ions and nitrate ions
b calcium ions and hydroxide ions
c ammonium ions and hydroxide ions
4 H_2SO_4, HCl
5 They are equal.

5.3 (page 143)

1 blue
2 white
3 sulfur + oxygen → sulfur dioxide
4 $S + O_2 \rightarrow SO_2$
5 magnesium + oxygen → magnesium oxide
6 carbon monoxide
7 zinc hydroxide *or* aluminium hydroxide

zinc hydroxide + sodium hydroxide
→ sodium zincate + water
$$Zn(OH)_2 + 2NaOH \rightarrow Na_2ZnO_2 + 2H_2O$$

or

aluminium hydroxide + sodium hydroxide
→ sodium aluminate + water
$$Al(OH)_3 + NaOH \rightarrow NaAlO_2 + 2H_2O$$

5.4 (page 146)

1 baking soda
2 hydrochloric acid, to help digest our food
3 calcium carbonate, magnesium hydroxide

5.5 (page 148)

1 insoluble bases: copper oxide, zinc oxide
alkalis: sodium hydroxide, potassium hydroxide
2 **a** sodium hydroxide + hydrochloric acid
→ sodium chloride + water
$$NaOH + HCl \rightarrow NaCl + H_2O$$
b potassium hydroxide + sulfuric acid
→ potassium sulfate + water
$$2KOH + H_2SO_4 \rightarrow K_2SO_4 + 2H_2O$$
c copper oxide + nitric acid
→ copper nitrate + water
$$CuO + 2HNO_3 \rightarrow Cu(NO_3)_2 + H_2O$$
3 sodium hydroxide, potassium hydroxide, calcium hydroxide (limewater), ammonia solution
4 ammonia

5.6 (page 151)

1 hydrochloric acid (HCl), nitric acid (HNO_3), sulfuric acid (H_2SO_4)
2 **a** potassium hydroxide + hydrochloric acid
→ potassium chloride + water
b copper oxide + hydrochloric acid
→ copper chloride + water
c zinc + hydrochloric acid
→ zinc chloride + hydrogen
d sodium carbonate + hydrochloric acid
→ sodium chloride + water + carbon dioxide
3 **a** $KOH + HCl \rightarrow KCl + H_2O$
b $CuO + 2HCl \rightarrow CuCl_2 + H_2O$
c $Zn + 2HCl \rightarrow ZnCl_2 + H_2$
d $Na_2CO_3 + 2HCl \rightarrow 2NaCl + H_2O + CO_2$

5.7 (page 153)

1 a carbonate + hydrochloric acid
→ salt + water + carbon dioxide
2 blue precipitate, copper(II) hydroxide
3 Ammonia solution; get a white precipitate in both cases but the zinc hydroxide precipitate re-dissolves in excess ammonia and the aluminium hydroxide precipitate does not.

5.8 (page 156)

1 **a** hydrogen
b copper(II) sulfate

c carbon dioxide
d litmus
e potassium hydroxide

5.9 (page 159)

1 pink (purple)
2 To make sure all the acid is used up/reacted.
3 filtration
4 pipette, burette
5 If heated too strongly, the salt could dehydrate (lose water of crystallisation) or even decompose.

5.10 (page 161)

1 a i method C **ii** sulfuric acid
iii zinc + sulfuric acid $\rightarrow$ zinc sulfate + water
b i method A **ii** hydrochloric acid
iii $KOH + HCl \rightarrow KCl + H_2O$
c i method B **ii** potassium iodide
iii $Pb^{2+}(aq) + 2I^- \rightarrow PbI_2$

5.11 (page 165)

1 $HCl(aq) + aq \rightarrow H^+(aq) + Cl^-(aq)$
2 $NH_3(aq) + aq \rightarrow NH_4^+(aq) + OH^-(aq)$
3 Ethanoic acid is a weak acid, and so is only partly ionised in solution; hydrochloric acid is a strong acid, so is fully ionised: there are more ions to carry the electric current.
4 The hydrogen atom is just 1 proton and 1 electron; when the electron is lost it is just left with the proton of the nucleus.
5 An acid is a proton donor; a base is a proton acceptor.
6 a An ionic equation includes just those ions and molecules that actually take part in the reaction.
b A spectator ion is present in the reaction mixture but does not actually take part in the reaction.
7 a $2H^+(aq) + O^{2-}(s) \rightarrow H_2O(l)$
b $2H^+(aq) + CO_3^{2-}(s) \rightarrow H_2O(l) + CO_2(g)$
c $H^+(aq) + OH^-(aq) \rightarrow H_2O(l)$

Chapter 6

6.1 (page 180)

1 a covalent **b** ionic
c CH_4, NaI, C_3H_6, ICl_3, BrF_5, HBr

2 a 32 **b** 17 **c** 64 **d** 114 **e** 98 **f** 119
g 188 **h** 133.5
3 a 21.2% **b** 28.2% **c** 46.7% **d** 35.0%
e 18.7%
4 a 0.20 g; 0.18 g; 0.06 g; 0.12 g
b

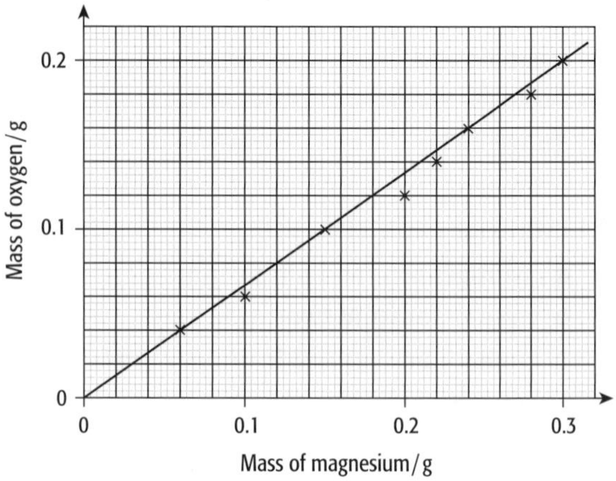

c Graph is a straight line, showing a fixed ratio of oxygen to magnesium; indicates a fixed formula.

6.2 (page 185)

1 molar ratio of Cu : Fe : S is 1 : 1 : 2
empirical formula = $CuFeS_2$
2 a molar ratio of C : H : O is 1 : 3 : 1
empirical formula = CH_3O
b molar mass of CH_3O = 31
so actual formula is $C_2H_6O_2$
c $CH_2(OH)CH_2(OH)$

6.3 (page 188)

1 a i near the neck of the test tube
ii to flush out all of the air from the tube
iii to make sure the reaction was complete
b i $C = 1.60\,g$, $E = 1.28\,g$, $F = 0.32\,g$
ii 0.02 moles
iii 0.02 moles
iv 1 mole
v CuO
vi copper(II) oxide + hydrogen $\rightarrow$ copper + water
$CuO + H_2 \rightarrow Cu + H_2O$

6.4 (page 190)

1 a 0.02 moles **b** 2 moles **c** 0.07 moles
2 a 36 000 cm^3 **b** 1440 cm^3 **c** 12 000 cm^3

6.5 (page 194)

1 **a** 2 mol/dm³ **b** 0.2 mol/dm³ **c** 1 mol/dm³
d 0.8 g of NaOH = 0.2 moles; 0.2 mol/dm³

2 **a** A **b** E **c** B **d** E **e** D

Chapter 7

7.1 (page 204)

1 endothermic
2 endothermic
3 Polystyrene is a good insulator (and absorbs very little heat itself).
4 −210 kJ/mol; exothermic
5

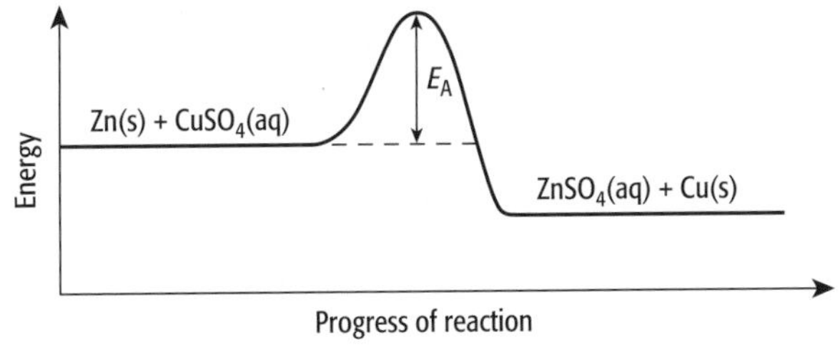

7.2 (page 210)

1 **a** rate increases **b** rate increases
c rate increases
2 The reactions which would spoil the food are slowed down at the lower temperature.
3 at the beginning
4 Because the reactants have all been used up.

7.3 (page 216)

1 A catalyst is a substance that speeds up a chemical reaction, but is not itself used up in the course of the reaction.
2 a biological catalyst
3 manganese(IV) oxide
4 **a** iron **b** vanadium(V) oxide
5 changes in temperature and pH
6 The presence of a catalyst lowers the activation energy of reaction.
7 **a** An increased temperature means that the particles are moving faster and will therefore collide more frequently; when they collide, more particles will have energy greater than the activation energy so there will be more collisions that result in a reaction.
b There will be more surface area of the solid exposed to the reactant and therefore more frequent collisions.
c Greater concentration means there are more reactant molecules present and so there will be a greater frequency of collision.

7.4 (page 218)

1 sunlight (ultraviolet radiation) and the presence of chlorophyll
2 carbon dioxide + water → glucose + oxygen

$$6CO_2 + 6H_2O \rightarrow C_6H_{12}O_6 + 6O_2$$

3 photochemical reactions
4 glucose + oxygen → carbon dioxide + water
5 Where most light falls on the film the most silver is deposited, causing the film to be blackened – so the film is dark where most light hits it.

7.5 (page 224)

1 white to blue
2 the presence of water
3 Haber process: nitrogen + hydrogen ⇌ ammonia

$$N_2 + 3H_2 \rightleftharpoons 2NH_3$$

Contact process: sulfur dioxide + oxygen ⇌ sulfur trioxide

$$2SO_2 + O_2 \rightleftharpoons 2SO_3$$

4 450 °C, 200 atmospheres pressure, iron catalyst
5 Increased pressure will produce more ammonia at equilibrium.
6 Increasing the temperature will produce less ammonia at equilibrium.

Chapter 8

8.1 (page 234)

1 They are soft and have a low density.
2 Sodium gives a yellow flame, potassium a lilac flame.
3 hydrogen
4 potassium hydroxide
5 sodium + water → sodium hydroxide + hydrogen
6 $2K + 2H_2O \rightarrow 2KOH + H_2$
7 lithium

8.2 (page 236)

1. It is strong but light, and does not corrode.
2. It is more reactive than carbon (so its oxide cannot be reduced by carbon).
3. iron(III) oxide + aluminium → iron + aluminium oxide
4. A thin layer of aluminium oxide forms on the surface of the metal and sticks to it, giving it a protective coating; with iron, the oxide forms but flakes off and so does not protect the metal.

8.3 (page 239)

1. They are strong and dense, have high melting points, their compounds are often coloured, they can show more than one valency, they or their compounds often act as catalysts (*any three*).
2. 2 and 3
3. blue
4. (hydrated) iron(III) oxide, Fe_2O_3
5. the Haber process

8.4 (page 244)

1. zinc + hydrochloric acid → zinc chloride + hydrogen
2. copper
3. magnesium + copper(II) sulfate → magnesium sulfate + copper
4. A brown deposit is formed and the blue colour of the solution fades to colourless.
5. $Mg + CuSO_4 \rightarrow MgSO_4 + Cu$
   $Mg(s) + Cu^{2+}(aq) \rightarrow Mg^{2+}(aq) + Cu(s)$

8.5 (page 245)

1. magnesium
2. $Mg(s) \rightarrow Mg^{2+}(aq) + 2e^-$

Chapter 9

9.1 (page 258)

1. To combine with the silicon dioxide (sand) and remove it as slag.
2. $Fe_2O_3 + 3CO \rightarrow 2Fe + 3CO_2$
3. oxygen
4. To make an alloy which doesn't corrode (stainless steel).
5. water and oxygen (air)
6. It can be used to coat iron (galvanisation) or can be attached to iron as blocks (cathodic protection).
7. It distils off as a gas and is condensed back to a liquid.
8. Because very pure copper is needed for electrical conductors.

9.2 (page 260)

1. Because of the high cost of electricity, which is needed in large quantities.
2. Because this makes the temperature needed to melt the aluminium oxide much lower.
3. Because the oxygen produced at the anode causes them to burn away.
4. $Al^{3+} + 3e^- \rightarrow Al$
5. Because it forms an oxide layer which prevents any further reaction with oxygen (corrosion).

9.3 (page 264)

1. By reacting methane gas with steam.
2. An iron catalyst, a moderately high temperature (450 °C) and a high pressure (200 atmospheres).
3. So that they react the second time around (saves producing more raw materials).
4. Because these are the three elements needed by plants which can become used up in soil.
5. They are washed off fields by rain and end up in streams and rivers.

9.4 (page 267)

1. $S + O_2 \rightarrow SO_2$
2. A catalyst (vanadium pentoxide) and a temperature of around 450 °C.
3. Because the reaction is too violent: a mist of sulfuric acid is formed which is very dangerous.
4. SO_2: bleaching paper and sterilising food
   H_2SO_4: making detergents, cleaning metals such as steel, making fertilisers

9.5 (page 269)

1. sterilisation of drinking water, making PVC, use as a bleach (*any two*)
2. a concentrated solution of sodium chloride in water
3. Because it converts a cheap raw material (common salt) into three important chemicals: chlorine, hydrogen and sodium hydroxide. There are no waste products.
4. The membrane cell, followed by the diaphragm cell.

9.6 (page 271)

1 To neutralise acidity in the water.
2 To remove silicon dioxide (sand) from the iron ore.
3 $CaCO_3 \rightarrow CaO + CO_2$
4 $Ca(OH)_2$
5 Treating soil to remove excess acidity; removing impurities from iron during the basic oxygen steel making process.

9.7 (page 274)

1 Because it is quick to recycle, and 'new' aluminium is very expensive to produce.
2 Conserving non-renewable resources such as metal ores; avoiding dumping waste in landfill.
3 It can be difficult to separate the different types of plastic, which ideally need to be recycled separately.

Chapter 10

10.1 (page 287)

1 covalent
2 4
3 diamond and graphite; the fullerenes
4 proteins, carbohydrates, nucleic acids (*any two*)

10.2 (page 290)

1 methane, ethane, propane, butane, pentane, hexane
CH_4, C_2H_6, C_3H_8, C_4H_{10}, C_5H_{12}, C_6H_{14}

2 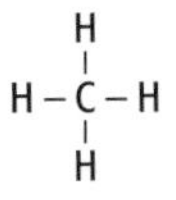
methane

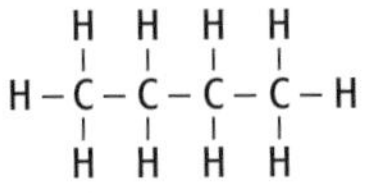
butane

3 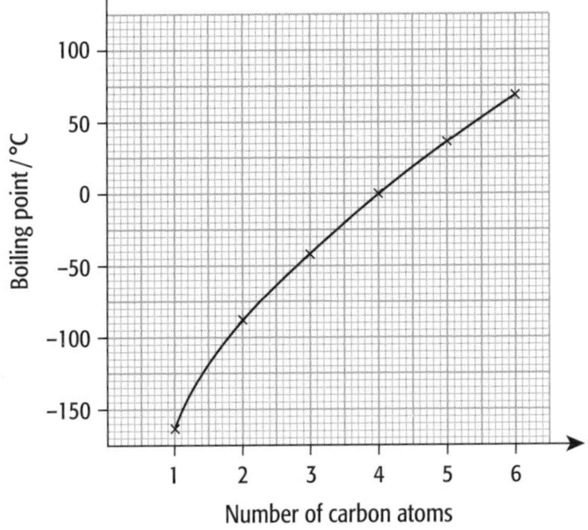

The graph shows a smooth curve with a steady, but decreasing, change in boiling point as the hydrocarbon chain gets longer.

4 **a** C_5H_{12}, pentane **b** $C_{17}H_{36}$
5 ethane + oxygen → carbon dioxide + water
6 natural gas
7 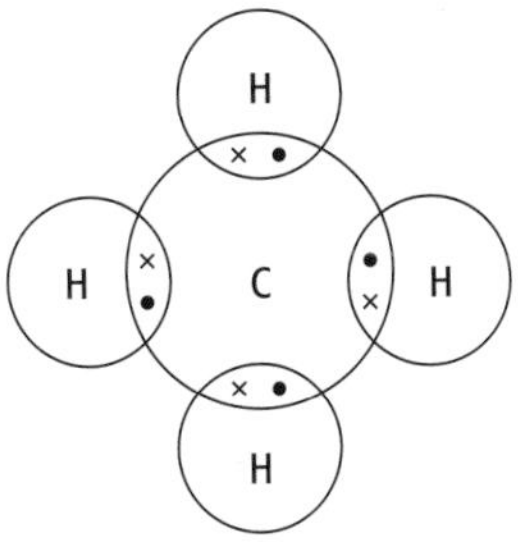

10.3 (page 292)

1 ethene, propene, butene, pentene
C_2H_4, C_3H_6, C_4H_8, C_5H_{10}

2 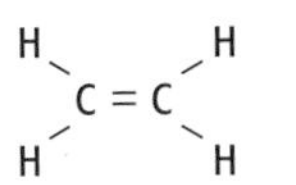
ethene

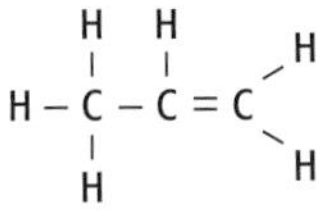
propene

3 CH_2
4 The bromine water is decolorised from brown to colourless.
5 bromine + ethene → 1,2-dibromoethane
6 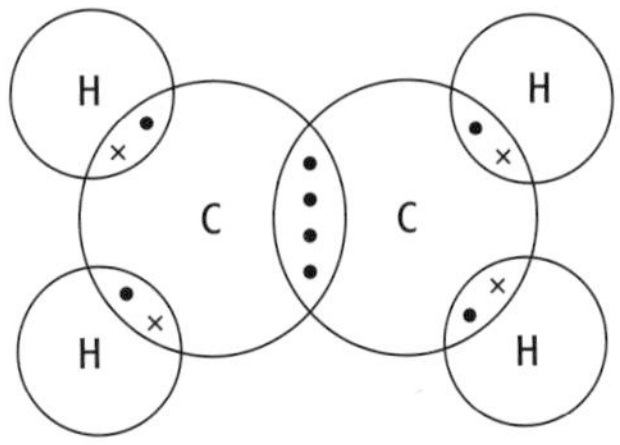

10.4 (page 294)

1 **a** ethene **b** methanol **c** methanoic acid
2 Isomers are compounds with the same molecular formula but different structural formulae.
3 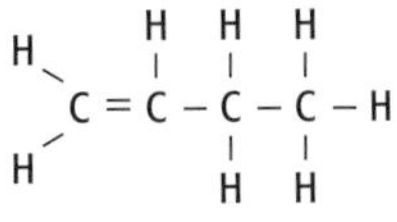
but-1-ene

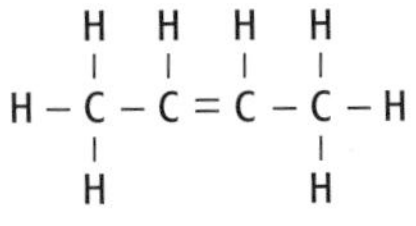
but-2-ene

4

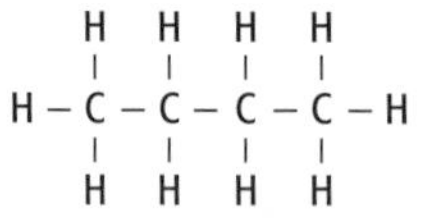

butane

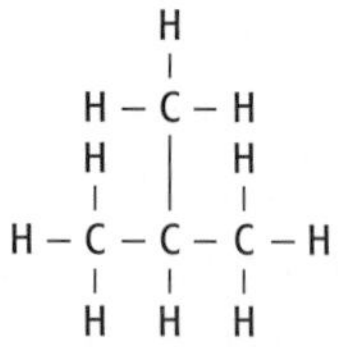

2-methylpropane

5

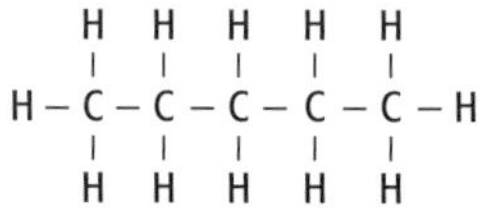

pentane

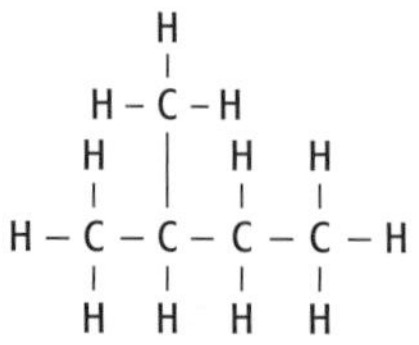

2-methylbutane

or

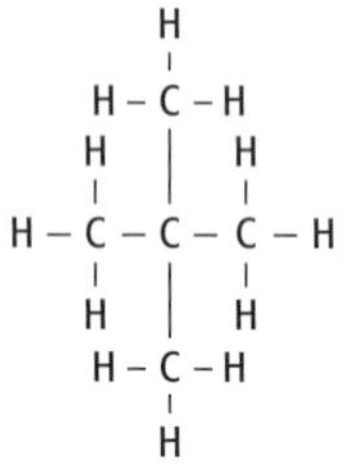

2,2-dimethylpropane

6

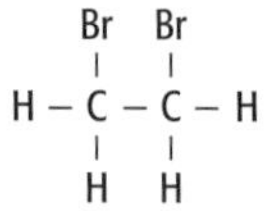

7 a i A, G or H (*any two*) **ii** E and F **iii** C

b (2-)methylpropane

10.5 (page 297)

1 methane + oxygen $\rightarrow$ carbon monoxide + water

2 CO

3 particles of carbon (soot) glowing in the heat

4 It binds to red blood cells (to the haemoglobin) and interferes with the transport of oxygen in the body.

5 chloromethane, CH_3Cl

6 propane + oxygen $\rightarrow$ carbon dioxide + water

$C_3H_8 + 5O_2 \rightarrow 3CO_2 + 4H_2O$

7 sunlight (ultraviolet light)

8 a

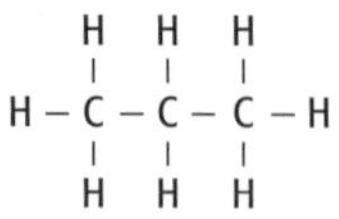

b

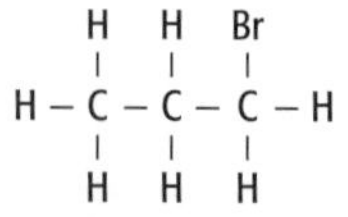

or

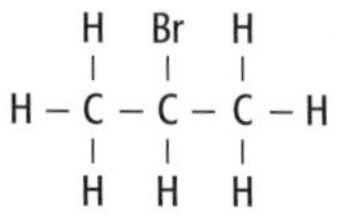

c The reaction requires light for it to take place.

10.6 (page 298)

1 $C_2H_4Br_2$

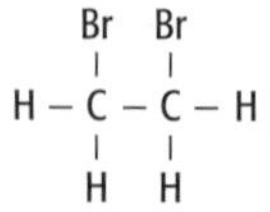

2 ethene + hydrogen $\rightarrow$ ethane

$C_2H_4 + H_2 \rightarrow C_2H_6$

3 finely divided nickel

4 a propene + hydrogen $\rightarrow$ propane

b $C_4H_8 + H_2O \rightarrow C_4H_9OH$

5 a i hydrogen chloride

ii

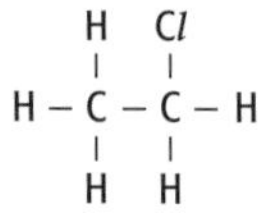

b ethane and chlorine in sunlight (ultraviolet light)

10.7 (page 300)

1 methanol, ethanol, propanol

2 ethene + steam $\rightarrow$ ethanol

$C_2H_4 + H_2O \rightarrow C_2H_5OH$

3 yeast, carbohydrate source, water

4 a carbon dioxide

b It is an airlock – allowing the carbon dioxide to escape, but not allowing air/bacteria in.

c yeast

d at around 37 °C

e This is the temperature favoured by the yeast, which are living organisms.

5 a

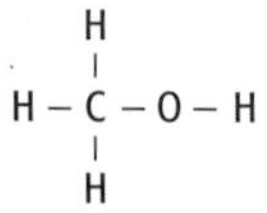

methanol

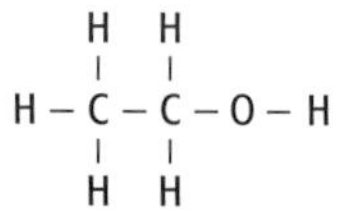

ethanol

b A homologous series of compounds is a family of organic compounds that have the same general formula, similar chemical properties and a gradual trend in their physical properties.

6 propan-1-ol

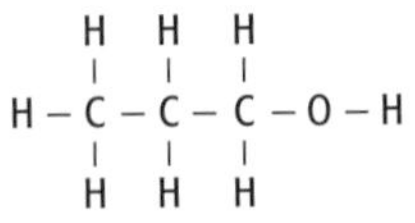

propan-2-ol

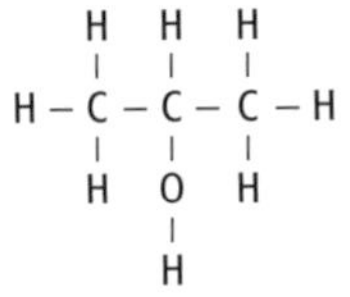

10.8 (page 303)

1 **a i** It is an alcohol.

ii

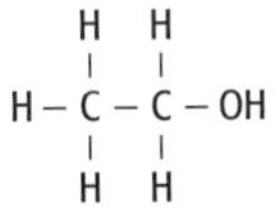

b a diagram showing fractional distillation (see page 38)

2 **a i** carbon (soot)

ii incomplete combustion

b i carbon dioxide and water

ii The alcohol content is not high enough, there is too much water.

3 ethanol + [O] → ethanoic acid + water

$C_2H_5OH + 2[O] \rightarrow CH_3COOH + H_2O$

4 propene

5 ethyl ethanoate

ethanol + ethanoic acid → ethyl ethanoate + water

catalyst: H^+ ions

10.9 (page 308)

1 **a** Ethanol dissolves the oils better; get better mixing with the bromine.

b 11 drops

c olive oil

2 **a**

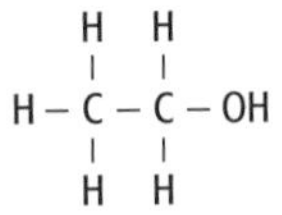

b oxidation

c hydrogen ions as a catalyst (a few drops of concentrated sulfuric acid is added), heat (reflux)

d butanoic acid

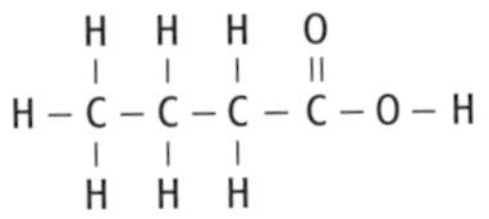

3 **a** ethyl ethanoate

b ethanol + ethanoic acid → ethyl ethanoate + water

4 **a** oxidation

b acidified potassium dichromate

c fractional distillation

d Measure the pH of the two using a pH meter.

5 **a** soap

b polyesters

Chapter 11

11.1 (page 322)

1 refinery gas, petrol (gasoline), naphtha, kerosene (paraffin), diesel, bitumen

2 coal, natural gas, crude oil (petroleum)

3 Cracking is the thermal decomposition of a long-chain alkane to a shorter-chain alkane and an alkene (or hydrogen).

decane → octane + ethene

$C_{10}H_{22} \rightarrow C_8H_{18} + C_2H_4$

4 road surfacing, ships' engines, car engines, aircraft fuel (domestic heating)

11.3 (page 328)

1 C_2H_4

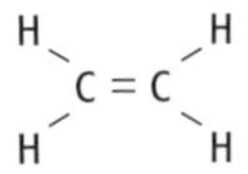

2 Addition polymerisation takes place when many molecules of an unsaturated monomer join together to form a long-chain polymer.

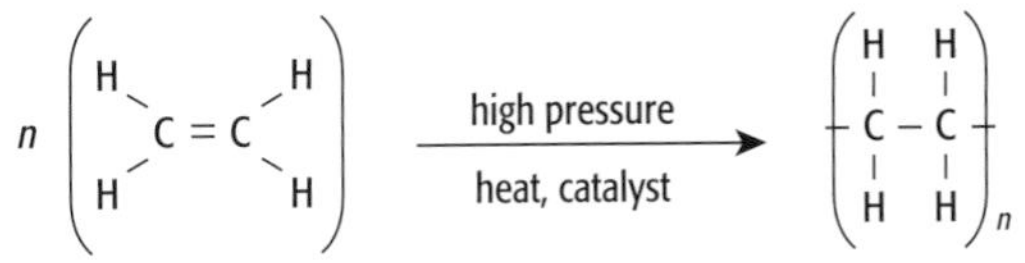

3 **a**

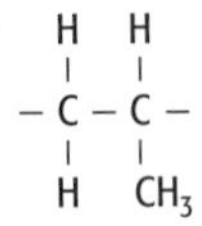

b

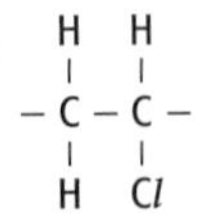

4 tetrafluoroethene

5 **a** crates/plastic rope

b insulation/pipes

c non-stick pans/gear wheels

11.4 (page 333)

1 starch, protein, nucleic acids (*any two*)

2 The monomers join together by a reaction in which a small molecule (usually water) is eliminated each time a link is made.

3 nylon – the amide link (or peptide link)
Terylene (a polyester) – the ester link

4 a

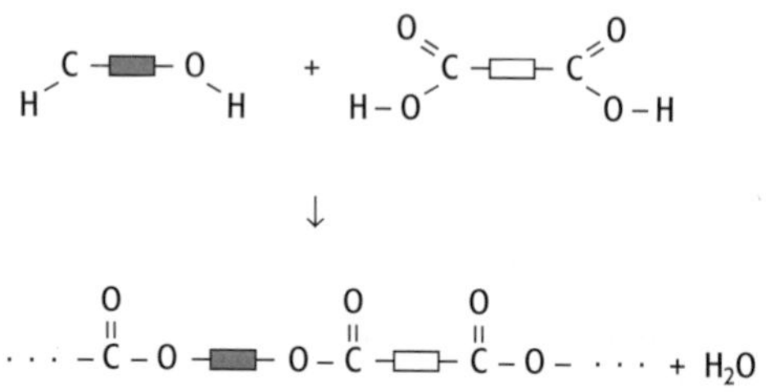

b

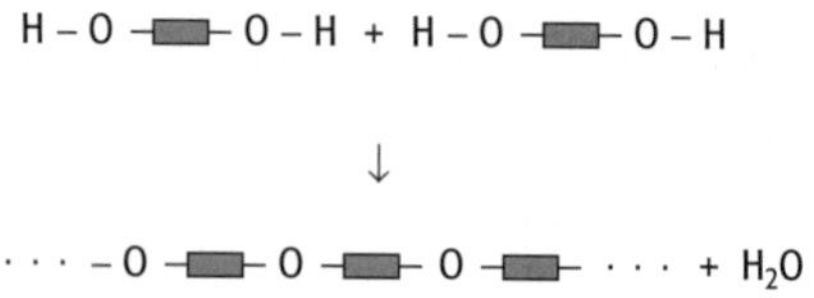

5 a the amide link (or peptide link)

b

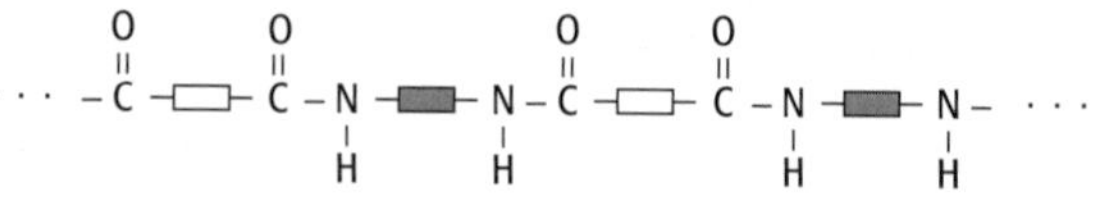

c Proteins are made from 20 different amino acid monomers; nylon is made from just two monomers.

d Proteins can be hydrolysed (broken down) by heating with concentrated hydrochloric acid.

Chapter 12

12.1 (page 346)

1 Because their hydroxides are insoluble and form as precipitates.

2 aluminium and zinc hydroxides

3 Because iron has two different oxidation states (iron(II) and iron(III)).

4 carbon dioxide

5 silver nitrate

6 hydrochloric acid

7 oxygen

8 the ammonium ion

9 **a** D **b** E **c** A **d** C

12.2 (page 348)

1 Add bromine water: it turns from brown to colourless.

2 Add indicator (turns red/orange in the acid), or add sodium carbonate solution (fizzes with the acid).

3 Because they are colourless.

12.3 (page 353)

1 The amount of water, the amount of fuel used, or the time it was used for.

2 substance, appearance before heating, appearance during heating, appearance after cooling

Glossary

absolute temperature a temperature measured with respect to absolute zero on the Kelvin scale – absolute zero is the lowest possible temperature that can be achieved

acid a substance that dissolves in water, producing H^+(aq) ions – a solution of an acid turns litmus red and has a pH below 7; in their reactions acids act as proton donors

acid rain rain which has been made more acidic than normal by the presence of dissolved pollutants such as sulfur dioxide (SO_2) and nitrogen oxides (NO_x)

acidic oxides oxides of non-metals which will react with bases and dissolve in water to produce acid solutions

activation energy (E_A) the energy required to start a chemical reaction – for a reaction to take place the colliding particles must possess at least this amount of energy

addition polymer a polymer formed by an addition reaction – the monomer molecules must contain a C=C double bond

addition reaction a reaction in which a simple molecule adds across the carbon–carbon double bond of an alkene

alcohols (alkanols) a series of organic compounds containing the functional group —OH and the general formula $C_nH_{2n+1}OH$

alkali metals elements in Group I of the Periodic Table; they are the most reactive group of metals

alkaline earth metals elements in Group II of the Periodic Table

alkalis soluble bases which produce OH^-(aq) ions in water – a solution of an alkali turns litmus blue and has a pH above 7

alkanes a series of hydrocarbons with the general formula C_nH_{2n+2}; they are saturated compounds as they have only single bonds between carbon atoms in their structure

alkenes a series of hydrocarbons with the general formula C_nH_{2n}; they are unsaturated molecules as they have a C=C double bond somewhere in the chain

alloy steels steels in which iron is mixed with other transition metals (and a small amount of carbon)

alloys mixtures of elements (usually metals) designed to have the properties useful for a particular purpose; for example, solder (an alloy of tin and lead) has a low melting point

amide link (or peptide link) the link between monomers in a protein or nylon, formed by a condensation reaction between a carboxylic acid group on one monomer and an amine group on the next monomer

amino acids naturally occurring organic compounds which possess both an amino (—NH_2) group and an acid (—COOH) group in the molecule; there are 20 naturally occurring amino acids and they are polymerised in cells to make proteins

amphoteric hydroxides hydroxides which can react with both acids and alkalis to produce salts; for example, zinc hydroxide; certain metal oxides can also be amphoteric

anaerobic decay decay of organic matter which takes place in the absence of air

anion a negative ion which would be attracted to the anode in electrolysis

anode the electrode in any type of cell at which oxidation (the loss of electrons) takes place – in **electrolysis** it is the positive electrode

antacid compound used medically to treat indigestion by neutralising excess stomach acid

artificial fertiliser a substance added to soil to increase the amount of elements such as nitrogen, potassium and phosphorus (**NPK fertilisers**): this enables crops to grow more healthily and produce higher yields

atmospheric pressure the pressure exerted by the atmosphere on the surface of the Earth due to the weight of the atmosphere

atom the smallest particle of an element that can take part in a chemical reaction

atomic number (or proton number) (*Z*) the number of protons in the nucleus of an atom; it is also the number of electrons present in an atom and the position of the element in the Periodic Table

Avogadro constant *see* **mole**

balanced chemical (symbol) equation a summary of a chemical reaction using chemical formulae – the total number of any of the atoms involved is the same on both the reactant and product sides of the equation

base a substance that neutralises an acid, producing a salt and water as the only products; in their reactions bases act as proton acceptors

basic oxide oxide of a metal that will react with acids to neutralise the acid

basic oxygen process the process used to make steel from iron from the blast furnace: oxygen is blown into the molten iron using an 'oxygen lance' and lime is added to remove non-metallic impurities

biodegradable plastics plastics which are designed to be degraded (decomposed) by bacteria

blast furnace a furnace for smelting iron ores such as hematite (Fe_2O_3) with carbon to produce pig (or cast) iron (in a modified form the furnace can be used to extract metals such as zinc)

boiling a condition under which gas bubbles are able to form within a liquid – gas molecules escape from the body of a liquid, not just from its surface

boiling point the temperature at which a liquid boils, when the pressure of the gas created above the liquid equals atmospheric pressure

bond energy the energy required to break a particular type of covalent bond

brine a concentrated solution of sodium chloride in water

carbohydrates a group of naturally occurring organic compounds containing carbon, hydrogen and oxygen; the ratio of hydrogen to oxygen atoms in the molecules is always 2 : 1 and they have the general formula $C_x(H_2O)_y$

carbon cycle the system by which carbon and its compounds in the air, oceans and rocks are interchanged

carbon steel alloys of iron and carbon only; the amount of carbon in steels can vary between 0.2% and 1.5%

carboxylic acids (alkanoic acids) a family of organic compounds containing the functional group —COOH (—CO_2H), with the general formula $C_n H_{2n+1}COOH$

catalyst a substance which increases the rate of a chemical reaction but itself remains unchanged at the end of the reaction

catalytic converter a device for converting polluting exhaust gases from cars into less dangerous emissions

catalytic cracking the decomposition of long-chain alkanes into alkenes and alkanes of lower relative molecular mass; involves passing the larger alkane molecules over a catalyst heated to 500 °C

cathode the electrode in any type of cell at which reduction (the gain of electrons) takes place; in **electrolysis** it is the negative electrode

cation a positive ion which would be attracted to the cathode in electrolysis

centrifugation the separation of an insoluble solid from a liquid by rapid spinning during which the solid collects at the bottom of the sample tubes – the liquid can then be decanted off carefully

ceramics materials such as pottery made from inorganic chemicals by high-temperature processing

chemical bonding the strong forces that hold atoms (or ions) together in the various structures that chemical substances can form – metallic bonding, covalent bonding and ionic (electrovalent bonding)

chemical reaction (change) a change in which a new substance is formed

chromatogram the result of a paper chromatography run, showing where the spots of the samples have moved to

chromatography a technique employed for the separation of mixtures of dissolved substances, which was originally used to separate coloured dyes

coal a black, solid fossil fuel formed underground over geological periods of time by conditions of high pressure and temperature acting on decayed vegetation

collision theory a theory which states that a chemical reaction takes place when particles for the reactants collide with sufficient energy to initiate the reaction

combustion a chemical reaction in which a substance reacts with oxygen – the reaction is exothermic; **burning** is a combustion reaction which produces a flame

compound a substance formed by the chemical combination of two or more elements in fixed proportions

concentration a measure of how much solute is dissolved in a solvent. Solutions can be **dilute** (with a high proportion of the solvent), or **concentrated** (with a high proportion of the solute)

condensation the change of a vapour or a gas into a liquid; during this process heat is given out to the surroundings

condensation polymer a polymer formed by a **condensation reaction**; for example, nylon is produced by the condensation reaction between 1,6-diaminohexane and hexanedioic acid – this is the type of polymerisation used in biological systems to produce proteins, nucleic acids and polysaccharides

Contact process the industrial manufacture of sulfuric acid using the raw materials sulfur and air

core (of Earth) the central, densest part of the Earth, composed mainly of iron and nickel; the outer core is molten and surrounds the solid, inner core which exists at very high temperature and pressure

corrosion the name given to the process that takes place when metals and alloys are chemically attacked by oxygen, water or any other substances found in their immediate environment

corrosive a corrosive substance (an acid, for example) is one that can dissolve or 'eat away' at other materials (wood, metals, or human skin, for instance)

covalent bond a chemical bond formed by the sharing of one or more pairs of electrons between two atoms

crude oil see **petroleum**

crust (of Earth) the solid, outermost, layer of the Earth; it is not continuous, but subdivided into plates of continental or oceanic crust

crystallisation the process of forming crystals from a saturated solution

decanting the process of removing a liquid from a solid which has settled or from an immiscible heavier liquid by careful pouring

decomposition (see also **thermal decomposition**) a type of chemical reaction where a compound breaks down into simpler substances

dehydration a chemical reaction in which water is removed from a compound

density expresses the relationship between the mass of a substance and the volume it occupies: density = mass / volume

detergent soap, or a soap-like substance, which is used with water to remove dirt and grease from clothes, dishes and other objects

diatomic molecule a molecule containing two atoms, for example hydrogen, H_2

dibasic acid (diprotic acid) an acid which contains two replaceable hydrogen atoms per molecule of the acid; for example, sulfuric acid, H_2SO_4

diffusion the process by which different fluids mix as a result of the random motions of their particles

displacement reaction a reaction in which a more reactive element displaces a less reactive element from a solution of its salt

distillate the liquid distilling over during distillation

distillation the process of boiling a liquid and then condensing the vapour produced back into a liquid: used to purify liquids and to separate liquids from solutions

downward delivery a method of collecting a gas which is denser than air by passing it downwards into a gas jar

drug any substance, natural or synthetic, that alters the way in which the body works

drying agent a chemical substance that absorbs water; anhydrous calcium chloride and concentrated sulfuric acid are two examples

ductile a word used to describe the property that metals can be drawn out and stretched into wires

dynamic (chemical) equilibrium two chemical reactions, one the reverse of the other, taking place at the same time, where the concentrations of the reactants and products remain constant because the rate at which the forward reaction occurs is the same as that of the back reaction

electrical conductor a substance that conducts electricity but is not chemically changed in the process

electrochemical cell a system for converting chemical energy to electrical energy, made by connecting two metals of different reactivity via an electrolyte; **fuel cells** are electrolytic cells capable of providing a continuous supply of electricity without recharging

electrode the point where the electric current enters or leaves a battery or **electrolytic cell**

electrolysis a process in which a chemical reaction is caused by the passage of an electric current

electrolyte an ionic compound which will conduct electricity when it is molten or dissolved in water; electrolytes will not conduct electricity when solid

electrolytic cell a cell consisting of an electrolyte and two electrodes (anode and cathode) connected to an external DC power source where positive and negative ions in the electrolyte are separated and discharged

electron a subatomic particle with negligible mass and a charge of −1; electrons are present in all atoms, located in energy levels outside the nucleus

electron (arrangement) configuration a shorthand method of describing the arrangement of electrons within the energy levels of an atom; also referred to as **electronic structure**

electronic structure *see* **electron configuration**

electroplating a process of electrolysis in which a metal object is coated (plated) with a layer of another metal

electrostatic force of attraction a strong force of attraction between particles with opposite charges – such forces are involved in **ionic bonding**

element a substance which cannot be further divided into simpler substances by chemical methods; all the atoms of an element contain the same number of protons

empirical formula a formula for a compound which shows the simplest ratio of atoms present

endothermic change a process or chemical reaction which takes in heat from the surroundings; ΔH has a positive value

energy levels (of electrons) the allowed energies of electrons in atoms – electrons fill these levels (or **shells**) starting with the one closest to the nucleus

enzymes protein molecules that act as biological catalysts

equilibrium *see* **dynamic equilibrium**

ester link the link produced when an ester is formed from a carboxylic acid and an alcohol; also found in polyesters and in the esters present in fats and vegetable oils

esterification the chemical reaction between an alcohol and a carboxylic acid that produces an ester; the other product is water

esters a family of organic compounds formed by esterification, characterised by strong and pleasant tastes and smells

evaporation a process occurring at the surface of a liquid, involving the change of state from a liquid into a vapour at a temperature below the boiling point

exothermic change a process or chemical reaction in which heat energy is produced and released to the surroundings; ΔH has a negative value

filtrate the liquid that passes through the filter paper during filtration

filtration the separation of a solid from a liquid, using a fine filter paper which does not allow the solid to pass through

flue-gas desulfuriser (or 'scrubber') a tower in which the waste gases from a coal- or oil-fired power station are treated to remove acidic gases such as sulfur dioxide

fluid a gas or a liquid, they are able to flow

formula (chemical) a shorthand method of representing chemical elements and compounds using the symbols of the elements

fossil fuels fuels, such as coal, oil and natural gas, formed underground over geological periods of time from the remains of plants and animals

fractional distillation a method of distillation using a fractionating column, used to separate liquids with different boiling points

fractionating column the vertical column which is used to bring about the separation of liquids in **fractional distillation**

fractions (from distillation) the different mixtures that distil over at different temperatures during fractional distillation

Frasch process the process of obtaining sulfur from sulfur beds below the Earth's surface; superheated water is pumped down a shaft to liquefy the sulfur, which is then brought to the surface

fuel a substance that can be used as a source of energy, usually by burning (combustion)

fuel cell a device for continuously converting chemical energy into electrical energy using a combustion reaction; a hydrogen fuel cell uses the reaction between hydrogen and oxygen

functional group the atom or group of atoms responsible for the characteristic reactions of a compound

galvanising the protection of iron and steel objects by coating with a layer of zinc

geological time very long, extended periods of time (over millions of years) during which the Earth was shaped

giant ionic structure a lattice held together by the electrostatic forces of attraction between positive and negative ions

giant metallic lattice a regular arrangement of positive metal ions held together by the mobile 'sea' of electrons moving between the ions

giant molecular structure substance where large numbers of atoms are joined by covalent bonds forming a strong lattice structure

global warming a long-term increase in the average temperature of the Earth's surface, which may be caused in part by human activities

grain boundaries the boundaries between the grains in a metal, along which a piece of metal may fracture

grains the small crystal areas in a metal: controlling the grain size affects the properties of a piece of metal

greenhouse effect the natural phenomenon in which heat from the Sun is 'trapped' at the Earth's surface by certain gases in the atmosphere (greenhouse gases)

group a vertical column of the Periodic Table containing elements with similar properties; atoms of elements in the same group have the same number of electrons in their outer energy levels

Haber process the industrial manufacture of ammonia by the reaction of nitrogen with hydrogen in the presence of an iron catalyst

half-life the time taken for half of the radioactive atoms in a sample of a radio isotope to decay

halides compounds formed between an element and a halogen; for example, sodium iodide

halogens elements in Group VII of the Periodic Table – generally the most reactive group of non-metals

heat of combustion the heat change which takes place when one mole of a substance is completely burnt in oxygen

heat of neutralisation the heat change which takes place when one mole of hydrogen ions is completely neutralised

heat of reaction the heat change during the course of a reaction; can be either **exothermic** or **endothermic**

homologous series a 'family' of organic compounds with the same functional group and similar properties

hydrated salts salts containing water of crystallisation

hydrocarbons compounds which contain carbon and hydrogen only

hydrogenation an addition reaction in which hydrogen is added across the double bond in an alkene

hydrolysis a chemical reaction between a covalent compound and water; covalent bonds are broken during the reaction and the elements of water added to the fragments; can be carried out with acids or alkalis, or by using enzymes

immiscible if two liquids form two layers when they are mixed together, they are said to be immiscible

indicator a substance which changes colour when added to acidic or alkaline solutions; for example, litmus or phenolphthalein

insoluble term that describes a substance that does not dissolve in a particular solvent

insulator substance that does not conduct electricity

intermolecular forces the weak attractive forces which act between molecules

ionic (electrovalent) bond a strong electrostatic force of attraction between oppositely charged ions

ionic equation the simplified equation for a reaction involving ionic substances: only those ions which actually take part in the reaction are shown

ions charged particles made from an atom, or groups of atoms (polyatomic ions), by the loss or gain of electrons

isomerism the property shown by molecules which have the same molecular formula but different structures

isomers compounds which have the same molecular formula but different structural arrangements of the atoms – they have different **structural formulae**

isotopes atoms of the same element which have different numbers of neutrons in their nuclei: they differ in their mass (nucleon) numbers; some isotopes are radioactive because their nuclei are unstable (**radio-isotopes**)

kinetic (particle) theory a theory which accounts for the bulk properties of the different states of matter in terms of the movement of particles (atoms or molecules) – the theory explains what happens during changes in physical state

lattice a regular three-dimensional arrangement of atoms, molecules or ions in a crystalline solid

law of conservation of mass matter cannot be lost or gained in a chemical reaction – the total mass of the reactants equals the total mass of the products

lime a white solid known chemically as calcium oxide (CaO), produced by heating limestone; it can be used to counteract soil acidity, to manufacture calcium hydroxide (slaked lime) and is also used as a drying agent

limestone a form of calcium carbonate ($CaCO_3$)

limewater a solution of calcium hydroxide in water; it is an alkali and is used in the test for carbon dioxide gas

litmus the most common indicator; turns red in acid and blue in alkali

locating agent a compound that reacts with invisible, colourless spots separated by chromatography to produce a coloured product which can be seen

main-group elements the elements in the outer groups of the Periodic Table (Groups I to VII and 0)

malleable a word used to describe the property that metals can be bent and beaten into sheets

mass concentration the measure of the concentration of a solution in terms of the mass of the solute, in grams, dissolved per cubic decimetre of solution (g/dm^3)

mass number (or nucleon number) (*A*) the total number of protons and neutrons present in the nucleus of an atom

mass spectrometer an instrument in which atoms or molecules are ionised and then accelerated; the ions are then separated according to their mass

matter anything which occupies space and has mass

melting point the temperature at which a solid turns into a liquid – it has the same value as the freezing point; a pure substance has a sharp melting point

metallic bond an electrostatic force of attraction between the mobile 'sea' of electrons and the regular array of positive metal ions within a solid metal

metalloid (semi-metal) element which shows some of the properties of metals and some of non-metals; for example, boron and silicon

metals a class of chemical elements (and alloys) which have a characteristic shiny appearance and are good conductors of heat and electricity

miscible if two liquids form a completely uniform mixture when added together, they are said to be miscible

mixture a system of two or more substances that can be separated by physical means

molar concentration the measure of the concentration of a solution in terms of the number of moles of the solute dissolved per cubic decimetre of solution (mol/dm^3)

molar mass the mass, in grams, of one mole of a substance

molar volume of a gas one mole of any gas has the same volume under the same conditions of temperature and pressure ($24\,dm^3$ at one atmosphere and room temperature)

mole the measure of amount of substance in chemistry; one mole of a substance has a mass equal to its relative formula mass in grams – that amount of substance contains 6.02×10^{23} (the **Avogadro constant**) atoms, molecules or formula units depending on the substance considered

molecular formula a formula which shows the actual number of atoms of each element present in a molecule of the compound

molecular mass *see* **relative molecular mass**

molecule a group of atoms held together by covalent bonds

monomer a small molecule, such as ethene, which can be polymerised to make a **polymer**

natural gas a fossil fuel formed underground over geological periods of time by conditions of high pressure and temperature acting on the remains of dead sea creatures; natural gas is more than 90% methane

neutralisation a chemical reaction between an acid and a base to produce a salt and water only; summarised by the ionic equation $H^+(aq) + OH^-(aq) \rightarrow H_2O(l)$

neutron an uncharged subatomic particle present in the nuclei of atoms – a neutron has a mass of 1 relative to a proton

nitrogen cycle the system by which nitrogen and its compounds, both in the air and in the soil, are interchanged

nitrogen fixation the direct use of atmospheric nitrogen in the formation of important compounds of nitrogen; most plants cannot fix nitrogen directly, but bacteria present in the root nodules of certain plants are able to take nitrogen from the atmosphere to form essential protein molecules

noble gases elements in Group 0 – a group of stable, very unreactive gases

non-electrolytes liquids or solutions that do not take part in electrolysis: they do not contain ions

non-metals a class of chemical elements that are typically poor conductors of heat and electricity

non-renewable (finite) resources sources of energy, such as fossil fuels, and other resources formed in the Earth over millions of years, which we are now using up at a rapid rate and cannot replace

nucleon number (or mass number) (*A*) the total number of protons and neutrons present in the nucleus of an atom

nucleus (of an atom) the central region of an atom that is made up of the protons and neutrons of the atom; the electrons orbit around the nucleus in different 'shells' or 'energy levels'

oil refining the industrial plant where the processes of converting petroleum (crude oil) into useful fractions and products are carried out

ore a naturally occurring mineral from which a metal can be extracted

organic chemistry the branch of chemistry concerned with compounds of carbon found originally in living organisms

oxidation there are three definitions of oxidation: (i) a reaction in which oxygen is added to an element or compound; (ii) a reaction involving the loss of electrons from an atom, molecule or ion; (iii) a reaction in which the oxidation state of an element is increased

oxidation state a number given to show whether an element has been oxidised or reduced; the oxidation state of an ion is simply the charge on the ion

oxidising agent a substance which will oxidise another in a redox reaction

percentage purity a measure of the purity of the product from a reaction carried out experimentally:

$$\text{percentage purity} = \frac{\text{mass of pure product}}{\text{mass of impure product}} \times 100$$

percentage yield a measure of the actual yield of a reaction when carried out experimentally compared to the theoretical yield calculated from the equation:

$$\text{percentage yield} = \frac{\text{actual yield}}{\text{predicted yield}} \times 100$$

period a horizontal row of the Periodic Table

Periodic Table a table of elements arranged in order of increasing proton number (atomic number) to show the similarities of the chemical elements with related electron configurations

petroleum (or crude oil) a fossil fuel formed underground over geological periods of time by conditions of high pressure and temperature acting on the remains of dead sea creatures

pH scale a scale running from below 0 to 14, used for expressing the acidity or alkalinity of a solution; a neutral solution has a pH of 7

photochemical reaction a chemical reaction that occurs when light, usually of a particular wavelength, falls on the reactants

photochemical smog a form of local atmospheric pollution found in large cities in which several gases react with each other to produce harmful products

photodegradable plastics plastics designed to degrade under the influence of sunlight

photosynthesis the chemical process by which plants synthesise glucose from atmospheric carbon dioxide and water: the energy required for the process is captured from sunlight by chlorophyll molecules in the green leaves of the plants

physical change a change in the physical state of a substance or the physical nature of a situation that does not involve a change in the chemical substance(s) present

pollution the harmful effects on the air, water and soil of human activity and waste

polyamide a polymer where the monomer units are joined together by amide (peptide) links; for example, nylon and proteins

polyester a polymer where the monomer units are joined together by ester links; for example, Terylene

polymer a substance consisting of very large molecules made by polymerising a large number of repeating units or **monomers**

polymerisation the chemical reaction in which molecules (monomers) join together to form a long-chain polymer

precipitation reaction a reaction in which an insoluble salt is prepared from solutions of two suitable soluble salts

products (in a chemical reaction) the substance(s) produced by a chemical reaction

proteins polymers of amino acids formed by a condensation reaction; they have a wide variety of biological functions

proton a subatomic particle with a relative mass of 1 and a charge +1 found in the nucleus of all atoms

proton number (or atomic number) (*Z*) *see* **atomic number**

pure substance a single chemical element or compound – it melts and boils at definite temperatures

radioactivity the spontaneous decay of unstable radio-isotopes

rancid a term used to describe oxidised organic material (food) – usually involving a bad smell

reactants (in a chemical reaction) the chemical substances that react together in a chemical reaction

reaction rate a measure of how fast a reaction takes place

reactivity series of metals an order of reactivity, giving the most reactive metal first, based on results from a range of experiments involving metals reacting with oxygen, water, dilute hydrochloric acid and metal salt solutions

redox reaction a reaction involving both **reduction** and **oxidation**

reducing agent a substance which will reduce another in a redox reaction

reduction there are three definitions of reduction: (i) a reaction in which oxygen is removed from a compound; (ii) a reaction involving the gain of electrons by an atom, molecule or ion; (iii) a reaction in which the oxidation state of an element is decreased

relative atomic mass (A_r) the average mass of an atom of an element, taking account of the isotopes of the element, on a scale where a carbon-12 atom has a mass of exactly 12

relative formula mass (M_r) the sum of all the relative atomic masses of the atoms present in a 'formula unit' of a substance (see also **relative molecular mass**)

relative molecular mass (M_r) the sum of all the relative atomic masses of the atoms present in a molecule (see also **relative formula mass**)

renewable resources sources of energy and other resources which cannot run out or which can be made at a rate faster than our current rate of use

residue the solid left behind in the filter paper after **filtration** has taken place

resources materials we get from the environment to meet our needs (see also **renewable resources** and **non-renewable resources**)

respiration the chemical reaction (a combustion reaction) by which biological cells release the energy stored in glucose for use by the cell or the body; the reaction is exothermic and produces carbon dioxide and water as the chemical by-products

reversible reaction a chemical reaction which can go either forwards or backwards, depending on the conditions

R_f value in chromatography, the ratio of the distance travelled by the solute to the distance travelled by the solvent front

risk assessment an evaluation of the methods and chemical substances used in a particular experiment to see what safety issues may be involved

rock cycle the natural cycle by which rocks are pushed upwards, then eroded, transported, deposited, and possibly changed into another type of rock by conditions of temperature and pressure – these rocks may then be uplifted to enter a new cycle

rust a loose, orange-brown, flaky layer of hydrated iron(III) oxide, $Fe_2O_3.xH_2O$, found on the surface of iron or steel

salts ionic compounds made by the neutralisation of an acid with a base (or alkali); for example, copper(II) sulfate and potassium nitrate

saponification the name given to the hydrolysis of fats or vegetable oils by hot, concentrated sodium hydroxide solution to produce soap

saturated solution a solution which contains as much dissolved solute as possible at a particular temperature

sewage water released after its use in the home or from factories; contains waste materials that must be removed before the water can be used again domestically or industrially

simple molecular substances substances made up of individual molecules held together by covalent bonds: there are only weak forces between the molecules

soaps substances formed by **saponification**

solubility a measure of how much of a solute dissolves in a solvent at a particular temperature

solubility curve a graph showing how the solubility of a substance in a solvent changes with temperature

soluble term that describes a solute that dissolves in a particular solvent

solute the solid substance that has dissolved in a liquid (the solvent) to form a solution

solution formed when a substance (solute) dissolves into another substance (solvent)

solvent the liquid that dissolves the solid solute to form a solution; water is the most common solvent but liquids in organic chemistry that can act as solvents are called **organic solvents**

solvent front the moving boundary of the liquid solvent that moves up the paper during chromatography

spectator ions ions that are present in a chemical reaction but take no part in it

speed of reaction see **reaction rate**

spontaneous (reaction) a reaction that takes place immediately simply by mixing the reactants

standard atom the atom against which the relative atomic masses of all other atoms are measured using the mass spectrometer; one atom of the carbon-12 isotope is given a mass of exactly 12

standard solution a solution whose concentration is known precisely – this solution is then used to find the concentration of another solution by titration

state symbols symbols used to show the physical state of the reactants and products in a chemical reaction: they are s (solid), l (liquid), g (gas) and aq (in solution in water)

states of matter solid, liquid and gas are the three states of matter in which any substance can exist, depending on the conditions of temperature and pressure

strong acid an acid that is completely ionised when dissolved in water – this produces the highest possible concentration of H^+(aq) ions in solution; for example, hydrochloric acid

strong alkali an alkali that is completely ionised when dissolved in water – this produces the highest possible concentration of OH^-(aq) ions in solution; for example, sodium hydroxide

structural formula the structural formula of an organic molecule shows how the atoms and bonds in a molecule are arranged in space: all the atoms and covalent bonds must be shown

subatomic particles very small particles – **protons, neutrons** and **electrons** – from which all atoms are built

sublimation the direct change of state from solid to gas or gas to solid: the liquid phase is bypassed

substitution reaction a reaction in which an atom (or atoms) of a molecule is (are) replaced by different atom(s), without changing the molecule's general structure

suspension a mixture containing small particles of an insoluble solid, or droplets of an insoluble liquid, spread (suspended) throughout a liquid

symbol (chemical) a simple letter, or group of letters, that represents an element in a chemical formula

synthesis (see also **photosynthesis**) a chemical reaction in which a compound is made from its elements

thermal decomposition the breakdown of a compound due to heating

titration a method of quantitative analysis using solutions: one solution is slowly added to a known volume of another solution using a burette until an end-point is reached

transition elements (or **transition metals**) elements from the central region of the Periodic Table – they are hard, strong, dense metals that form compounds which are often coloured

Universal Indicator a mixture of indicators which has different colours in solutions of different pH

upward delivery a method of collecting a gas that is lighter than air by passing it upwards into an inverted gas jar

valency the combining power of an atom or group of atoms: in ionic compounds the valency of each ion is equal to its charge; in a covalent molecule the valency of an atom is the number of bonds that atom makes

volatile term that describes a liquid that which evaporates easily; it is a liquid with a low boiling point having only weak intermolecular forces between the molecules in the liquid

volatility the property of how easily a liquid evaporates

water cycle the system by which water circulates around the Earth, involving various changes of state in the process; the driving force behind the water cycle is energy from the Sun

water of crystallisation water included in the structure of certain salts as they crystallise; for example, copper(II) sulfate pentahydrate ($CuSO_4.5H_2O$) contains five molecules of water of crystallisation per molecule of copper(II) sulfate

weak acid an acid which is only partially dissociated into ions in water – usually this produces a low concentration of $H^+(aq)$ in the solution; for example, ethanoic acid

weak alkali an alkali which is only partially dissociated into ions in water – usually this produces a low concentration of $OH^-(aq)$ in the solution; for example, ammonia solution

word equation a summary of a chemical reaction using the chemical names of the reactants and products

Index

Appendix: The Periodic Table

Group																	
I	II											III	IV	V	VI	VII	0
							1 **H** Hydrogen 1										4 **He** Helium 2
7 **Li** Lithium 3	9 **Be** Beryllium 4											11 **B** Boron 5	12 **C** Carbon 6	14 **N** Nitrogen 7	16 **O** Oxygen 8	19 **F** Fluorine 9	20 **Ne** Neon 10
23 **Na** Sodium 11	24 **Mg** Magnesium 12											27 **Al** Aluminium 13	28 **Si** Silicon 14	31 **P** Phosphorus 15	32 **S** Sulfur 16	35.5 **Cl** Chlorine 17	40 **Ar** Argon 18
39 **K** Potassium 19	40 **Ca** Calcium 20	45 **Sc** Scandium 21	48 **Ti** Titanium 22	51 **V** Vanadium 23	52 **Cr** Chromium 24	55 **Mn** Manganese 25	56 **Fe** Iron 26	59 **Co** Cobalt 27	59 **Ni** Nickel 28	64 **Cu** Copper 29	65 **Zn** Zinc 30	70 **Ga** Gallium 31	73 **Ge** Germanium 32	75 **As** Arsenic 33	79 **Se** Selenium 34	80 **Br** Bromine 35	84 **Kr** Krypton 36
85 **Rb** Rubidium 37	88 **Sr** Strontium 38	89 **Y** Yttrium 39	91 **Zr** Zirconium 40	93 **Nb** Niobium 41	96 **Mo** Molybdenum 42	– **Tc** Technetium 43	101 **Ru** Ruthenium 44	103 **Rh** Rhodium 45	106 **Pd** Palladium 46	108 **Ag** Silver 47	112 **Cd** Cadmium 48	115 **In** Indium 49	119 **Sn** Tin 50	122 **Sb** Antimony 51	128 **Te** Tellurium 52	127 **I** Iodine 53	131 **Xe** Xenon 54
133 **Cs** Caesium 55	137 **Ba** Barium 56	139 **La** Lanthanum 57 *	179 **Hf** Hafnium 72	181 **Ta** Tantalum 73	184 **W** Tungsten 74	186 **Re** Rhenium 75	190 **Os** Osmium 76	192 **Ir** Iridium 77	195 **Pt** Platinum 78	197 **Au** Gold 79	201 **Hg** Mercury 80	204 **Tl** Thallium 81	207 **Pb** Lead 82	209 **Bi** Bismuth 83	– **Po** Polonium 84	– **At** Astatine 85	– **Rn** Radon 86
– **Fr** Francium 87	226 **Ra** Radium 88	227 **Ac** Actinium 89 †															

*58–71 Lanthanoid series
†90–103 Actinoid series

*	140 **Ce** Cerium 58	141 **Pr** Praseodymium 59	144 **Nd** Neodymium 60	– **Pm** Promethium 61	150 **Sm** Samarium 62	152 **Eu** Europium 63	157 **Gd** Gadolinium 64	159 **Tb** Terbium 65	163 **Dy** Dysprosium 66	165 **Ho** Holmium 67	167 **Er** Erbium 68	169 **Tm** Thulium 69	173 **Yb** Ytterbium 70	175 **Lu** Lutetium 71
†	232 **Th** Thorium 90	– **Pa** Protactinium 91	238 **U** Uranium 92	– **Np** Neptunium 93	– **Pu** Plutonium 94	– **Am** Americium 95	– **Cm** Curium 96	– **Bk** Berkelium 97	– **Cf** Californium 98	– **Es** Einsteinium 99	– **Fm** Fermium 100	– **Md** Mendelevium 101	– **No** Nobelium 102	– **Lr** Lawrencium 103

Key

a **X** b

a = relative atomic mass
X = atomic symbol
b = proton (atomic) number

Acknowledgements

Cover, Martyn F. Chillmaid / SPL

1.1, ESA / Kevin A Horgan/SPL; 1.9, © Leslie Garland Picture Library / Alamy; 1.11, DocStock / www.photolibrary.com; 1.15a, Andy Clarke / SPL; 1.15b, Peter Menzel / SPL; 1.26b, Martin Bond / SPL; 2.1, NASA; 2.4, Charles D. Winters / SPL; 2.5, Andrew Lambert / SPL; 2.6, R. Harwood; 2.12b, Jerry Mason / SPL; 2.16b, 2.17b, Andrew Lambert / SPL; 2.21, Alexis Rosenfeld / SPL; 2.23, 2.24, Andrew Lambert / SPL; 2.25, IBM; 2.29, Andrew Lambert / SPL; 2.30, Andrew Lambert / SPL; 2.36, Pekka Parviainen / SPL; 3.1, Heidas; 3.4, M. C. Talbot; 3.7, 3.9, Andrew Lambert; 3.10, Day Williams / SPL; 3.13, 3.14a, Martyn F. Chillmaid / SPL; 3.14b, Andrew Lambert / SPL; 3.32, Kenneth Libbrecht / SPL; 3.35, M. C. Talbot; 3.37, Lisa Moore / Alamy; 4.2, Andrew Lambert; 4.3, Martyn F. Chillmaid / SPL; 4.4, Charles D. Winters / SPL; 4.5, Trevor Clifford Photography / SPL; 4.7, 4.9, 4.10, 4.11, 4.12, Andrew Lambert; 4.16, Cordelia Molloy / SPL; 4.22, Trevor Clifford Photography / SPL; 4.26, Sam Ogden / SPL; 4.30, Chris R. Sharp; 5.1, David Munns / SPL; 5.2, 5.3a Andrew Lambert / SPL; 5.3b, Trevor Clifford Photography / SPL; 5.5, European Space Agency / SPL; 5.6b, Andrew Lambert Photography / LGPL; 5.8, Gustoimages / SPL; 5.9, Andrew Lambert / SPL; 5.10, Health Protection Agency / SPL; 5.11a, Thierry Berrod, Mona Lisa Production / SPL; 5.11b, Dr Jeremy Burgess / SPL; 5.12, © Jeremy Pardoe / Alamy; 5.13, Martin Bond / SPL; 5.15a, Martyn F. Chillmaid / SPL; 5.15b, Charles D. Winters / SPL; Fig. on p. 150, Arnold Fisher; 5.16, David Taylor / SPL; 5.18b, Andrew Lambert; 5.19, 5.20, 5.21, R. Harwood; 5.23, 5.24, Martyn F. Chillmaid / SPL; 5.26b, Jerry Mason / SPL; 6.1, Christian Darkin / SPL; 6.13, Martyn F. Chillmaid / SPL; 6.14, Andrew Lambert; 7.1, Scott Camazine / K. Visscher / SPL; 7.2, Tek Image / SPL; 7.5, Charles D. Winters / SPL; 7.8, David Talbot; 7.10, Interfoto / Alamy; 7.11, Martyn F. Chillmaid / SPL; 7.12, Charles D. Winters / SPL; 7.13a, Andrew Lambert / SPL; 7.18a, Martyn F. Chillmaid / SPL; 7.22, Astrid & Hanns-Frieder Michler / SPL; 7.23, J.C. Revy, Ism / SPL; 7.29, Christian Darkin / SPL; 7.30, Professors P.M. Motta & S. Correr / SPL; 7.32, Martyn F. Chillmaid / SPL; 7.33, Andrew Lambert / SPL; 8.1, Charles D. Winters / SPL; 8.2, Andrew Lambert; 8.3, James King-Holmes / SPL; 8.5b, photograph courtesy of NT Government; 8.6, David Talbot; 8.7, © Art Directors & TRIP / Alamy; 8.8, J.C.Hurni, Publiphoto Diffusion / SPL; 8.9, © Werner Forman / Corbis; 8.11, R. Harwood; 8.12, M. C. Talbot; 8.13, R. Harwood; 8.14, Charles D. Winters / SPL; 9.1, Rosenfeld Images Ltd / SPL; 9.6, National Oceanic and Atmospheric Administration; 9.10, Ben Johnson; 9.12, courtesy of Deutsches Museum von Meisterwerken der Naurwissenschaft und Technik; 9.16, Malcolm Fielding / SPL; 9.17b, Martyn F. Chillmaid / SPL; 9.18, Robert Brook / SPL; 9.19, Bernhard Edmaier; 9.21a, Martin Bond / SPL; 9.23, Andrew Lambert / SPL; 9.25, M. C. Talbot; 9.26, Dirk Wiersma / SPL; 9.28, Maximillian Stock Ltd / SPL; 9.30a, Dirk Wiersma / SPL; 9.33, Burrups International; 9.34, Bob Gibbons / SPL; 10.1, © Irving Geis; 10.3, Laguna Design / SPL; 10.5, R. Harwood; 10.6, Martyn F. Chillmaid / SPL; 10.9, Andrew Lambert / SPL; 10.10, R. Harwood; 10.11, Martyn F. Chillmaid / SPL; 10.12, David Taylor / SPL; 10.17, David R. Frazier / SPL; 10.21, Adam Jones; 10.23, Adam Jones / SPL; 11.1, David Nunuk / SPL; 11.3, Ria Novosti / SPL; 11.5, 11.6, Paul Rapson / SPL; 11.9, Roger Harris / SPL; 11.10, © Realimage / Alamy; 11.11, Alan Sirulnikoff / SPL; 11.12, Leonard Lessin / SPL; 11.13, Prof. David Hall / SPL; 11.14a, b, Robert Brook / SPL; 11.15, David Talbot; 11.18b, Charles D. Winters / SPL; 11.19, 11.20, 11.24, R. Harwood; 12.1, 12.3, 12.8, 12.10, Andrew Lambert / SPL

SPL = Science Photo Library

Exam-style questions at the end of each Chapter identified as being taken from past CIE IGCSE Chemistry exam papers, as well as the Paper 5 questions with model answers on pages **354–358**, are reproduced by permission of the University of Cambridge Local Examinations Syndicate. The University of Cambridge Local Examinations Syndicate bears no responsibility for the example answers to questions taken from its past question papers which are contained in this publication.

Terms and conditions of use for the CD-ROM

This is a legal agreement between 'You' (which means the individual customer or the Educational Institution and its authorised users) and Cambridge University Press ('the Licensor') for *Cambridge IGCSE Chemistry Coursebook CD-ROM*. By placing this CD in the CD-ROM drive of your computer, You agree to the terms of this licence.

1 Limited licence

a You are purchasing only the right to use the CD-ROM and are acquiring no rights, express or implied, to it, other than those rights granted in this limited licence for not-for-profit educational use only.

b The Licensor grants You the licence to use one copy of this CD-ROM.

c You shall not: **(i)** copy or authorise copying of the CD-ROM, **(ii)** translate the CD-ROM, **(iii)** reverse-engineer, alter, adapt, disassemble or decompile the CD-ROM, **(iv)** transfer, sell, lease, lend, profit from, assign or otherwise convey all or any portion of the CD-ROM or **(v)** operate the CD-ROM from a mainframe system, except as provided in these terms and conditions.

d Permission is explicitly granted for use of the CD-ROM on a data projector, interactive whiteboard or other public display in the context of classroom teaching at a purchasing institution.

e If You are an Educational Institution, once a teacher ceases to be a member of the Educational Institution, all copies of the material on the CD-ROM stored on his/her personal computer must be destroyed and the CD-ROM returned to the Educational Institution.

f You are permitted to print reasonable copies of the printable resources on the CD-ROM. These must be used solely for use within the context of classroom teaching at a purchasing institution.

2 Copyright

a All original content is provided as part of the CD-ROM (including text, images and ancillary material) and is the copyright of the Licensor or has been licensed to the Licensor for use in the CD-ROM, protected by copyright and all other applicable intellectual-property laws and international treaties.

b You may not copy the CD-ROM except for making one copy of the CD-ROM solely for backup or archival purposes. You may not alter, remove or destroy any copyright notice or other material placed on or with this CD-ROM.

3 Liability and Indemnification

a The CD-ROM is supplied 'as is' with no express guarantee as to its suitability. To the extent permitted by applicable law, the Licensor is not liable for costs of procurement of substitute products, damages or losses of any kind whatsoever resulting from the use of this product, or errors or faults in the CD-ROM, and in every case the Licensor's liability shall be limited to the suggested list price or the amount actually paid by You for the product, whichever is lower.

b You accept that the Licensor is not responsible for the availability of any links within or outside the CD-ROM and that the Licensor is not responsible or liable for any content available from sources outside the CD-ROM to which such links are made.

c Where, through use of the original material, You infringe the copyright of the Licensor, You undertake to indemnify and keep indemnified the Licensor from and against any loss, cost, damage or expense (including without limitation damages paid to a third party and any reasonable legal costs) incurred by the Licensor as a result of such infringement.

4 Termination

Without prejudice to any other rights, the Licensor may terminate this licence if You fail to comply with the terms and conditions of the licence. In such an event, You must destroy all copies of the CD-ROM.

5 Governing law

This agreement is governed by the laws of England, without regard to its 'conflict of laws' provision, and each party irrevocably submits to the exclusive jurisdiction of the English courts. The parties disclaim the application of the United Nations Convention on the International Sale of Goods.